BEST PRACTICES SERIES

Enterprise Systems Integration

THE AUERBACH
BEST PRACTICES SERIES

Broadband Networking, James Trulove, Editor,
ISBN: 0-8493-9821-5

Electronic Messaging, Nancy Cox, Editor,
ISBN: 0-8493-9825-8

Healthcare Information Systems, Phillip L. Davidson, Editor,
ISBN: 0-8493-9963-7

Internet Management, Jessica Keyes, Editor,
ISBN: 0-8493-9987-4

Multi-Operating System Networking: Living with UNIX, NetWare, and NT, Raj Rajagopal, Editor,
ISBN: 0-8493-9831-2

Network Manager's Handbook, John Lusa, Editor,
ISBN: 0-8493-9841-X

Project Management, Paul C. Tinnirello, Editor,
ISBN: 0-8493-9998-X

Enterprise Systems Integration, John Wyzalek, Editor,
ISBN: 0-8493-9837-1

AUERBACH PUBLICATIONS

www.auerbach-publications.com
TO Order: Call: 1-800-272-7737 • Fax: 1-800-374-3401
E-mail: orders@crcpress.com

BEST PRACTICES SERIES

Enterprise Systems Integration

Editor
JOHN WYZALEK

AUERBACH

Boca Raton   London   New York   Washington, D.C.

Library of Congress Cataloging-in-Publication Data

Enterprise systems integration / John Wazalek, editor.
     p. cm. — (Best practices series)
     Includes bibliographical references and index.
     ISBN 0-8493-9837-1 (alk. paper)
     1. Information resources management. 2. Management information
systems. I.Wazalek, John. II. Series.
     T58.64.E68 1999
     658.4'038—dc21   99-43598
                                                                  CIP

© 2000 by CRC Press LLC
Auerbach is an imprint of CRC Press LLC

No claim to original U.S. Government works
International Standard Book Number 0-8493-9837-1
Library of Congress Card Number 99-43598
Printed in the United States of America 1 2 3 4 5 6 7 8 9 0
Printed on acid-free paper

Contributors

DAN ADLER, *Chief Technology Officer, Inventure America, New York, NY*

HEDY ALBAN, *Freelance Writer, Cherry Hill, NJ*

MARY AYALA-BUSH, *Principal, Computer Sciences Corporation, Waltham, MA*

CHARLES BANYAY, *Manager, Deloitte & Touche Consulting Group, Toronto, Ontario, Canada*

PETER M. BECK, *Consulting Engineer, SSDS Division, TCI, Fairfax, VA*

PRASAD BINGI, *Department of Management and Marketing, Indiana University, Fort Wayne, IN*

RALPH BOOTH, *Director, HMC International, Montreal, Quebec, Canada*

ANDRE BOUDREAU, *Partner, Boroan Consultation Inc., Montreal, Quebec, Canada*

JANET BUTLER, *Writer and Editor, Managing Systems Development, Rancho de Taos, NM*

KAZEM CHAHARBAGHI, *Faculty Member, Manufacturing Technology and Production Management, Cranfield University, Bedford, England*

BOSCO CHEUNG, *Senior Consultant, Deloitte & Touche Consulting Group, Toronto, Ontario, Canada*

DALE COHEN, *Electronic Messaging Team Project Manager, R.R. Donnelley & Sons Company, Chicago, IL*

GUY COUILLARD, *Director, HMC International, Montreal, Quebec, Canada*

DAVID CURLEY, *Vice President, Worldwide Marketing, Mitel Corporation, Kanata, Ontario, Canada*

JAGDISH R. DALAL, *Vice President of Information Management, Xerox Corporation, Rochester, NY*

JUDY DINN, *Manager, Deloitte & Touche Consulting Group, Toronto, Ontario, Canada*

CHARLES DOW, *Practice Leader, Object-Oriented Technologies, Deloitte & Touche Consulting Group, Toronto, Ontario, Canada*

RAINER FEURER, *Research Student, Cranfield University, Bedford, England*

DAN FOBES, *Software Architect, Yardley, PA*

ELIZABETH N. FONG, *Computer Systems Laboratory, National Institute of Standards and Technology, Gaithersburg, MD*

IDO GILEADI, *Senior Manager, ICS, Deloitte Consulting, Toronto, Ontario, Canada*

JAYANTH K. GODLA, *Pricewaterhouse-Coopers LLP, Bloomfield Hills, MI*

HAL H. GREEN, *Consultant, Setpoint, Inc., Houston, TX*

KATHRYN A. HARVILL, *Computer Systems Laboratory, National Institute of Standards and Technology, Gaithersburg, MD*

DAVID K. HOLTHAUS, *Software Specialist, Nationwide Insurance Enterprise, Columbus, OH*

ASHVIN IYENGAR, *Consultant, Object Technologies, Deloitte & Touche Consulting Group, DRT Systems, Toronto, Ontario, Canada*

JOHN JORDAN, *Principal, Consulting & Systems Integration, Computer Sciences Corporation, Waltham, MA*

MARIE KARAKANIAN, *Senior Manager, Deloitte Consulting, Toronto, Ontario, Canada*

BILL KILLCULLEN, *Principal Consultant, Satellite Group Inc., Bellevue, WA*

KEITH G. KNIGHTSON, *Associate Director, Telecom Architect Program, Canadian Government Telecommunications Agency, Kanata, Ontario, Canada*

WALTER KUKETZ, *Consulting and Systems Integration, Computer Sciences Corporation, Waltham, MA*

POLLY PERRYMAN KUVER, *Consultant, Boston, MA*

CAROL L. LARSON, *Freelance Desktop Publisher, Beaverton, OR*

JAMES A. LARSON, *Senior Software Engineer, Intel Architecture Laboratory, Hillsboro, OR*

RICHARD J. LEWIS, JR., *eCom Connections and Miami University, Oxford, OH*

CONGHUA LI, *MANAGER, Deloitte Consulting, Toronto, Ontario, Canada*

CHANG YANG LIN, *Professor of Computer Information Systems, Department of Information Systems, College of Business, Eastern Kentucky University, Richmond, KY*

DAVID LITWACK, *President, dml Associates, Fairfax, VA*

MICHAEL A. MISCHE, *President, Synergy Consulting Group, Inc., Boalsburg, PA*

NATHAN J. MULLER, *Independent Consultant, Huntsville, AL*

RICHARD J. MURRAY, *Partner-in-Charge, Nolan, Norton & Co., Los Angeles, CA*

ALI H. MURTAZA, *Senior Consultant, Data Warehousing Service Line, Deloitte & Touche Consulting Group, Toronto, Ontario, Canada*

DAVID NELSON, *Director of Marketing, Wingra Technologies, Madison, WI*

RAYMOND J. POSCH, *Manager, Education Services, Covia Technologies, Englewood, CO*

RAJ RAJAGOPAL, *Principal Staff, The MITRE Corporation, McLean, VA*

T.M. RAJKUMAR, *Associate Professor, Department of Decision Sciences and Management Information Systems, Miami University, Oxford, OH*

MARTIN SCHLEIFF, *Technical Lead, Boeing Corp., Seattle, WA*

MANEESH K. SHARMA, *Department of Accounting and Finance, Indiana University, Fort Wayne, IN*

ROSHAN L. SHARMA, *Principal, Telecom Network Science, Dallas, TX*

CHARLES L. SHEPPARD, *Computer Systems Laboratory, National Institute of Standards and Technology, Gaithersburg, MD*

ANTONIO SI, *Assistant Professor, Department of Computing, Hong-Kong Polytechnic University, Hong Kong, China*

MANJIT SIDHU, *Independent Senior Manager, Toronto, Ontario, Canada*

MICHAEL SIMONYI, *Independent Consultant, Entobicoke, Ontario, Canada*

ROBERT L. SLOAN, *Business Information Systems Architect, Nylon Business Unit, E.I. du Pont de Nemours & Co., Charlotte, NC*

DANIEL L. SPAR, *Consultant, Transarc Corp., Falls Church, VA*

NANCY STONELAKE, *Senior Consultant, Deloitte & Touche Consulting Group, Toronto, Ontario, Canada*

BHAVANI THURAISINGHAM, *Lead Engineer, Center for Integrated Intelligence Systems, The MITRE Corporation, Bedford, MA*

DOROTHY E. TREFTS, *Managing Consultant, Transformation Business Practice, IBM, White Plains, NY*

DAVID WADSWORTH, *Java Evangelist, Sun Microsystems, Toronto, Ontario, Canada*

JOHN WARGIN, *Manager, Strategic Consulting and Business Alignment Practice, Hewlett-Packard, Germany*

MICHAEL WEBER, *Project Manager, Redesign and Implementation Processes and IT Support, Hewlett-Packard, Germany*

JASON WEIR, *Technical Writer, DataMirror Corporation, Toronto, Ontario, Canada*

COLIN WYND, *Business Development Manager, NetMetrix Division, Hewlett-Packard Co., Colorado Springs, CO*

Table of Contents

INTRODUCTION xv

SECTION I INTEGRATION DRIVERS
1   Defining Systems Integration 3
       Michael A. Mische
2   The IT Imperative in Business Transformations. 11
       Richard J. Murray and Dorothy E. Trefts
3   Aligning Strategies, Processes, and Information
       Technology: A Case Study 21
       Rainer Feurer, Kazem Chaharbaghi, Michael Weber, and
       John Wargin

SECTION II INTEGRATED ARCHITECTURES
4   Architecture Frameworks for Client/Server and
       Netcentric Computing 43
       Andersen Consulting
5   Information Services 85
       Andersen Consulting
6   Communications Architectures. 111
       Andersen Consulting
7   An Information Architecture for the Global
       Manufacturing Enterprise. 157
       Robert L. Sloan and Hal H. Green
8   Server-Based Computing Architecture. 173
       Bosco Cheung

SECTION III ENABLING TECHNOLOGIES
9   Using Middleware for Interoperable Systems 185
       Raymond J. Posch
10   Evaluating Object Middleware: DCOM and CORBA 197
       T.M. Rajkumar and Richard J. Lewis, Jr.
11   A Technical Primer for Getting Started with JavaBeans
       215
       Charles Dow

12   JavaBeans and Java Enterrpise Server Platform. 225
      David Wadsworth
13   Distributed Objects and Object Wrapping. 237
      Hedy Alban
14   Integrating Package Processes over Multiple
      Application Platforms 253
      Ido Gileadi

SECTION IV DEVELOPMENT IN AN INTEGRATED ENVIRONMENT
15   Developing New Applications in a Heterogeneous
      Environment 265
      Raj Rajagopal
16   Component-Based Development. 299
      Nancy Stonelake
17   Programming Components: COM and CORBA. 309
      T.M. Rajkumar and David K. Holthaus
18   Managing Object Libraries .321
      Polly Perryman Kuver
19   Java Application Development Including Database
      and Network Integration 329
      Nathan J. Muller

SECTION V INTEGRATED DATABASES
20   Distributed Database Design 341
      *Elizabeth N. Fong, Charles L. Sheppard, and
      Kathryn A. Harvill*
21   Component Design for Relational Databases 353
      Ashvin Iyengar
22   Using CORBA to Integrate Database Systems 367
      Bhavani Thuraisingham and Daniel L. Spar
23   Middleware, Universal Data Data Servers, and
      Object-Oriented Data Servers. 377
      James A. Larson and Carol L. Larson
24   Designing an Integrated Data Server 389
      James A. Larson and Carol L. Larson
25   Migrating Data to an Integrated Database. 401
      James A. Larson and Carol L. Larson
26   Mobile Database Interoperability: Architecture and
      Functionality. 411
      Antonio Si
27   Integrating EDMSs and DBMSs 429
      Charles Banyay

28   Interfacing Legacy Applications with RDBMSs and
      Middleware 439
      Dan Fobes

SECTION VI DATA WAREHOUSING
29   Developing a Corporate Data Warehousing
      Strategy 449
      Manjit Sidhu
30   A Framework for Developing an Enterprise Data
      Warehousing Solution 465
      Ali H. Murtaza
31   Web-Enabled Data Warehouses 475
      Mary Ayala-Bush, John Jordan, and Walter Kuketz
32   Distributed Integration: An Alternative to Data
      Warehousing. 485
      Dan Adler

SECTION VII ENTERPRISE RESOURCE PACKAGES
33   Choosing Your ERP Implementation Strategy. 499
      Marie Karakanian
34   Critical Issues Affecting an ERP Implementation 507
      *Prasad Bingi, Maneesh K. Sharma, and
      Jayanth K. Godla*
35   Risk Management Skills Needed in a Packaged
      Environment. 521
      Janet Butler
36   Managing SAP Knowledge Transfer 533
      Guy Couillard, Ralph Booth, and Andre Boudreau
37   Maximizing ROI by Leveraging the Second Wave
      of ERP 545
      Judy Dinn
38   ERP Packages: What's Next?. 551
      Conghua Li

SECTION VIII NETWORKING
39   The Essentials of Enterprise Networking 561
      Keith G. Knightson
40   Planning, Designing, and Optimization of Enterprise
      Networks. 577
      Roshan L. Sharma
41   Enterprise Network Monitoring and Analysis. 595
      Colin Wynd
42   Integrating Voice and LAN Infrastructures
      and Applications 609
      David Curley

SECTION IX ELECTRONIC MESSAGING

43   Introduction to Client/Server Messaging 629
      Bill Killcullen
44   Messaging Gateways 645
      Peter M. Beck
45   Enterprise Directory Services 675
      Martin Schleiff
46   Enterprise Message Migration 689
      David Nelson
47   Preparing Organizations for Lotus Notes/Domino
      Solutions...701
      Michael Simonyi
48   Integrating Electronic Messaging Systems and
      Infrasctructures 717
      Dale Cohen

SECTION X INTERNET AND WORLD WIDE WEB

49   Integrating the Web and Enterprise Business
      Systems...737
      Chang-Yang Lin
50   Business-to-Business Integration to Using
      E-Commerce 747
      Ido Gileadi
51   Developing a Trusted Infrastructure for Electronic
      Commerce..755
      David Litwack
52   Knowledge Management on the Internet: The
      Web/Business Intelligence Solution................769
      Jason Weir

SECTION XI PROJECT AND SYSTEMS MANAGEMENT

53   A Model for Project Management 781
      Michael A. Mische
54   The Systems Integration Life Cycle................815
      Michael A. Mische
55   Symptoms of the Terminally Ill Systems Integration
      Project...831
      Michael A. Mische
56   Contracting for Systems Integration 859
      Jagdish R. Dalal
57   Choosing a Systems Integrator 873
      Michael A. Mische

INDEX 887

Introduction

The wave of recent corporate mergers and growth of business on the Internet have boosted enterprise systems integration's profile in both IT and business. All these factors have contributed to enterprise integration's importance, but the marketplace conditions of today's global and highly competitive economy are still the major reasons why companies choose an integrated solution. Companies that can provide information when it is needed or that can quickly devise and roll out new products and services are today's leading organizations. Integrated enterprise systems can provide information across all points in an organization, and the unique way systems integration blends business practices and information technology enables a company to rapidly meet the demands of a changing market.

Enterprise Systems Integration brings together the perspectives, knowledge, and experience of more than 70 experts in the various areas that involve enterprise integration. Their expertise ranges from hands-on experience with technology and project management to the higher-level issues of business and management strategy. Each chapter examines an issue or technology relevant to today's enterprise. Collectively, these chapters span the range of enterprise computing and systems integration.

As is the case with most information technologies, business is driving the integration of enterprise systems, but translating business strategy and requirements is difficult. The opening section of this book, "Integration Drivers," gives much needed guidance in this area. Its chapters explain how to manage IT in conjunction with business strategy and processes and provide a framework for aligning the enterprise integration strategy with the overall business strategy.

But what does an integrated enterprise mean today? The concept of the enterprise has existed since the heyday of mainframe. At the time, big iron was the enterprise system by default, because no other technology could match its processing capabilities. This notion became outdated by client/server and desktop systems which blurred the notion of a cohesive enterprise. The concept was revived with the advent of Enterprise Resource Packages (ERPs) such as SAP/R3. The notion of the enterprise was also furthered with the discovery of using the Internet as a platform.

Still, ERP software and Internet-based systems do not make up the full picture of today's enterprise. Legacy systems, e-commerce and other web-based systems, client/server applications, networks and communication systems, data warehousing, and integrated databases fill out the picture. The overriding goal of this book is to give a comprehensive picture of the technologies that comprise today's enterprise.

To meet this goal, the book features the following sections:

Enabling Technologies, including middleware, CORBA, COM, and Enterprise Java
Integrated Databases, including legacy, relational, and object databases
Data Warehousing, including web-enabled data warehousing
Enterprise Resource Packages
Networking
Electronic Messaging
Internet and the World Wide Web, including e-commerce

Each section looks at these technologies from an enterprise perspective. An important part of this perspective is how each technology works within the entire organization, and each section covers integration into the overall enterprise.

Section III, "Enabling Technologies," focuses on the growing importance of Java and CORBA as middleware solutions. The section on database technology spans the range from design and architecture to management and integration in the enterprise. The following section on data warehousing provides a strategy and framework for development and application. Section VII, "Enterprise Resource Packages," also looks at strategy, implementation, and management, as well as the next strategic use of ERPs. The section on network features a chapter on enterprise network monitoring and analysis as well as an examination of design and integration issues. A thorough examination of messaging technology is presented in the section on electronic messaging. The book's final section on enterprise technology, "Internet and the World Wide Web," covers such leading edge topics as e-commerce and knowledge management.

Enterprise computing profoundly affects the way in which organizations operate, and this is especially true for the systems development organization. An entire section, "Development in an Integrated Environment," is devoted to carrying out systems development in an enterprise. Development techniques that promote reuse and standardization provide the means for producing enterprise-level software, and this section features chapters on component development and programming as well as managing object libraries of reusable code. The section concludes with a chapter on using Java for integrating databases and networks with application development.

Once armed with the strategy and technologies, IT managers have to successfully deploy them, and the book concludes with a section on managing enterprise integration successfully. Each project has its own unique characteristics, and enterprise systems integration is unlike any other systems development project. The first three chapters in the section "Project and Systems Management" gives practical advice on how to manage integration projects and gives pointers on how to recognize the signs of a project gone awry. The section ends with advice on managing integrated systems and managing IS in an integrated enterprise environment.

Enterprise computing has become a means for leveraging and optimizing individual performance, knowledge, and operational processes. Integration is the construct and infrastructure which provides these ends. It is also central to realizing strategic and financial objectives. This convergence of knowledge, technology, and human performance, which comprises today's enterprise, allows creative business process design. Thus, an organization can create new and innovative ways to service customers or to do business with suppliers and make itself a leader in its field. This capability relies on a successful strategy that integrates the enterprise. *Enterprise Systems Integration* gives the business insight and the technological know-how to ensure a successful systems integration strategy.

Section I
Integration Drivers

Chapter 1
Defining Systems Integration
Michael A. Mische

Major system integration efforts are being performed in most every organization, as the private and public sectors attempt to become more competitive. Some of the motivations to integrate clearly revolve around technological issues, the need to improve the results of technology investments, and cost reductions. Straddled with legacy technologies and systems that are inflexible and expensive to maintain, these organizations have only limited options. They must migrate to newer technologies.

The overwhelming reason to integrate is the need to become more competitive in an environment that is constantly changing and highly competitive. The competitive pressures facing organizations are enormous, and the consequences of failing to integrate and exploit technology to create competitive advantage are indisputable. The competitive landscape has changed dramatically, and companies can no longer depend on the traditional ways of competing to ensure their viability. For example, it is true that:

- A full 70 percent of the largest firms in 1955 no longer exist.
- As much as 10 percent of the 1980 *Fortune 500* have disappeared.
- Only three of the top ten companies in the world in 1972 remain in the top ten today.
- The average life expectancy of a large industrial company is 40 years.
- Employment and security are no longer mainstays of the economy. Companies have downsized and cut employment ranks significantly.
- Investors and Wall Street are demanding that companies take action by rewarding cost cutting and downsizing. For example, the day Sears announced it was discarding 50,000 jobs, its stock climbed nearly 4 percent.

New rules of competition are driving new ways of organizing. Companies can ill afford to continue to compete in the same way that they once did. At the forefront is technology and system integration. Technology and inte-

0-8493-9968-8/99/$0.00+$.50
© 1999 by CRC Press LLC

grated business practices can neutralize the traditional advantages of size and location. Integrated processing solutions can allow a company to compete anywhere, at any time. Electronic commerce, knowledge-based systems, and the Internet know no size or constraints.

The integration of technologies with new organizational designs and business processes also supports the collaboration of workers regardless of where they are located geographically. Integration allows information and knowledge to be simultaneously shared by workers, business partners, and even collaborative competitors. Integration allows for concurrent work on a problem or project regardless of location, time zones, and the location of information. The creation of collaborative work environments also provides opportunities to develop and deploy new organizational designs that exploit technologies and human performance by melding knowledge and business processes. Core knowledge (i.e., knowledge that is essential to the process and the organization) becomes embedded in the process and available to all.

The need to integrate is also driven by new forms of business and partnerships. Groups of companies and workers not only share data and information, but also have exposure to their respective business partners' operations. For example, Toyota, long known as a creative user of technology, provides its suppliers and partners with advanced visibility into parts designs, engineering measures, and inventory levels. Wal-Mart and K-Mart provide suppliers with access and instant information related to item movement. A customer buys a coat at Wal-Mart and a data stream follows that tells the supplier the coat color, size, price, and where it was sold. The supplier, who is responsible for managing the inventory at that Wal-Mart location, immediately begins a replenishment process designed to restock the item in a day or less. The competitive advantage of integrating technology with human performance, knowledge, and organizational designs is powerful.

DEFINING SYSTEMS INTEGRATION

Determining the size and breadth of the integration industry and isolating what exactly is the process for integrating systems are extremely difficult to do with any level of precision. Much rhetoric is produced about system integration, but comparably less authoritative reference material exists on precisely what integration is or is not, and how to perform integration. No uniformly acknowledged definition describes system integration. The term *system integration* enjoys enormous popularity among vendors and consultants, all of whom have an undeniable vested interest in keeping the definition relatively ambiguous. As such, it has also come to mean just about anything, including outsourcing. Some of the largest vendors and consultants define *system integration* rhetorically; that is, integration depends on what the individual calls it and what he or she wants integrated. Undoubtedly, significant marketing advantage can be gained from the ambiguity. Another definition, developed by an industry association of vendors, defines *integrator* as the point of integration for technology solutions delivery. This is hardly an effective definition, especially when considered in a contemporary context of new organizational designs and processes. In contrast, users tend to define *integration process* as a process that concentrates on features and functions. Many information management and technology professionals tend to view integration as more of a technical issue.

In an effort to add some structure to the industry, the Gartner Group has defined integration as a "large [more than $1 million], complex IS project that includes designing and/or building a customized architecture or application, as well as integrating it with new or existing hardware, packaged and custom software, and communications." This definition goes a long way toward creating a credible standard, but it still lacks a tangible quality. There is something limiting to imposing price as a defining component of integration, because too many factors influence the expenditures of an organization. There are too many ways of counting and classifying costs to use price as a differentiating criterion for defining system integration.

The Technological Definition of Systems Integration

Historically, system integration was confined to the technical aspects of hardware and the interconnectivity of computing components. Integration had a mechanical connotation and piecemeal quality: making different pieces of equipment work together. As the industry and knowledge evolved, integration began to include software, data, and communication. Today, system integration encompasses all of these. In a world that places premiums on cyber customers, cyber companies, virtual employees, telecommuting, and speed, integration has come to mean more than just technology. Systems integration involves a complete system of business processes, managerial practices, organizational interactions and structural alignments, and knowledge management. It is an all-inclusive process designed to create relatively seamless and highly agile processes and organizational structures that are aligned with the strategic and financial objectives of the enterprise. A clear economic and competitive value proposition is established between the need and objectives for systems integration and the performance of the enterprise.

Systems integration represents a progressive and iterative cycle of melding technologies, human performance, knowledge, and operational processes together. It is more a journey than a specific set-point project. Some organizations, such as Boeing, Wal-Mart, Merrill Lynch, Federal Express, and Chrysler, are very sophisticated and extremely advanced in their use of integration. For example, Boeing designed and tested the new 777 entirely online before building a prototype or model. Customers of the aircraft, such as United Airlines and Singapore Air, had direct links into the design of the plane. Mechanics, pilots, and engineers were trained on aircraft maintenance, flying characteristics, and design, long before the plane was built, through electronic models and knowledge delivery systems. The result was a super aircraft that employed integrated technologies and business processes; it was built in 40 percent less time than any other plane.

Chrysler has reduced the time it takes to design and build a new car by 40 percent through the integration of technologies, processes, new organizational structures, and human performance. System integration has become the primary vehicle for creating more agile and competitive organizations.

From a technological perspective, system integration is the melding of divergent and often incompatible technologies, applications, data, and communications into a uniform information technology architecture and functional working structure. The reality today is that integration involves many aspects of technology and organizational processes. What may be integration for one company may not be integration for another. For example, what may be defined and practiced as integration for Chrysler probably will be something entirely different for Volvo. Consequently, there may not be one single definition for integration that is appropriate for all situations and projects.

The States of Systems Integration

More appropriately, there are states of system integration. Each state of integration has its own unique definition, properties, aspects, and complexities. Each state also has a unique economic value proposition, and each can be applied to the specific situations of an organization. When considering what is or is not integration, it is important to distinguish what the state of integration is within an organization and what it can realistically achieve. An important dimension of defining integration is the point at which integration is being defined and the status of integration that the organization has achieved.

There are four states of system integration:

1. State 1: Interconnectivity
2. State 2: Interoperability
3. State 3: Semantic consistency
4. State 4: Convergent integration

Three of these are contingent on technology and its status; however, the fourth represents a convergence of technology and human performance, processes, and knowledge. It is the highest and most sophisticated state of integration.

State 1: Interconnectivity. This is the most elementary state of integration. It forms the foundation for all subsequent integration. Interconnectivity involves making various pieces of often disparate equipment and technologies work together. This includes the sharing of peripherals, the simple transferring of files, and the creation of common pathways between different components. The basic applications, functionality, and uses all remain fairly specific with respect to their technologies and users, with little or no integration at the functional levels.

State 2: Interoperability. Interoperability refers to the ability to make one application and technology function with another in a manner that exploits the capabilities of both. Most of the "integrated" vendor software offerings provide this level of integration, which usually updates and feeds other applications and interfaces with other databases. For the majority of organizations, interoperability is the state of their integration.

State 3: Semantic Consistency. Much effort and investment have been directed toward the implementation of database management systems and sophisticated management reporting systems. The trademark for this form of integration is the rationalization of data elements, terms, and meaning. The emphasis is on providing accessibility to data and minimizing the potential for errors in human interpretation through the creation of standard data definitions and formats. In achieving semantic integration, simply implementing database management systems is not enough; data must be rationalized and have significant meaning to the user.

State 4: Convergent Integration. This is the highest and most sophisticated form of the integration states. Systemic integration requires the presence of the first three states but involves much more than the integration of technologies, applications, and the rationalization of shared databases. Convergent integration involves the integration of technology with business processes, knowledge, and human performance. Systems integration is the enabler, the delivery vehicle for new organizational designs and processes. Convergent integration has seven prerequisite components:

1. Technology integration, which requires interconnectivity
2. Applications and software integration, which requires interoperability
3. Data and data repository integration, which requires semantic integration
4. Communications network integration, which requires interconnectivity, interoperability, and semantic integration
5. The design and integration of new business processes with new technical capabilities

6. The embedding of knowledge within new business processes and enabling technologies
7. The integration of human performance with new processes

In its most advanced state and form, convergent integration allows the organization to compete differently by providing the means to reconfigure itself and quickly adapt to changing opportunities.

Operationally, integrated systems have some distinguishing characteristics and share five essential attributes:

1. Functional and technical compatibility is provided.
2. The technologies used to process applications and data are relatively transparent to users. Integration can be achieved at any level and using any technology. The issue is selecting the best technology that optimizes several key criteria: user utility, technology longevity, adaptability and scalability, and speed of solution delivery.
3. Application systems, data, access paths to data, and graphical user interfaces (GUIs) are harmonized and standardized for the user (i.e., they look and work the same and are intuitive to a new user).
4. All enterprisewide data is rationalized; data means the same thing from system to system and application to application, and data is uniformly defined throughout the organization.
5. All enterprisewide applications and computing environments are scalable and portable to a variety of needs. That is, technologies and applications can be rapidly deployed and tailored for specific use in the organization. Essential application code and data structures are replaceable and reproducible, not constantly reinvented.

These five characteristics define the integration process and the integrated system. System integration is achieved when the processing environment, technologies, human performance, and business processes all function in a harmonious and congruent manner.

THE REALITIES AND MYTHS OF SYSTEMS INTEGRATION AND THE MARKETPLACE

With the lack of a clear definition and industry standards for integration, it is little wonder that there are a number of myths and misconceptions about system integration and systems integrators. Some of the more common myths surrounding system integration are discussed in the following sections.

Myth: Systems integration is purely a technical issue. The reality is that systems integration is a progressive process and is situational to the organization attempting to integrate. In some instances, system integration may be predominantly one of technology, but this is not necessarily so in all cases. Systems integration involves many other facets of the enterprise, including applications, data, communications, business processes, and how the organization deploys, manages, and effectively uses information technology to gain competitive advantage. Thus, there are various states of integration that are endemic to the organization, its technology, and its strategic objectives.

Myth: Systems integration drives organizational change and business process reengineering. The reality is that system integration may be an enabler for systemic change in the organization, but the business books are full of cases of integration projects that yielded little, if any, systemic change. Transactions may have been accelerated, but the basic ways in which the business performed, was managed, and was organized did not change. System integration can enable massive process and structural change in the organization. To do so requires the organization to want to change and establish change as a priority.

Depending on the state of integration, system integration may or may not require business process reengineering. Systems integration can be the enabling agent of business process reengineering, but it alone is not reengineering. As the organization moves to a higher state of integration, reengineering and new organizational designs are almost always involved. Organizations that are in the fourth state of integration experience significant change.

Myth: Systems integration projects are driven by application development or the acquisition of third-party software, or both. The reality is that third-party software offerings, such as those provided by SAP-AG, Oracle, and Computer Associates, provide a catalyst for integration and are useful. However, in all cases, achieving a convergent state of integration involves far more than applications and technologies. What is required is systemic change in the way businesses are operated, organized, and managed to best leverage technology and human performance. Software alone can force some changes in the way an organization is managed and structured, but the organization must be led through the journey of change.

Myth: Systems integration projects can be performed without special project management competencies, such as change management or technical skills. The reality is that systems integration projects are large, complex, and risky. They demand a highly skilled and disciplined project team, dedicated leadership, and a formal methodology to provide guidelines for performance and behavior. Because of the size and complexity of these system integration efforts, they demand comprehensive project management techniques not only to track and report on the status of the project, but also to anticipate its needs and challenges.

Myth: Systems integrators and integration firms are unique and different. The reality is that there are a number of differences among systems integrators; however, for the most part they are subtle. Some integrators are very large; others are smaller. Organizations considering the use of an integrator have a large and varied selection from which to choose. The key to selecting an integrator is to understand the state of integration one is in, what state of integration the organization is trying to achieve, and matching the integrator to that state.

SUMMARY

The integration of systems has broad ramifications for the organization. In most situations, system integration involves more than technology; it involves the convergence of technology, processes, knowledge, and human performance. It is a systemic change in the ways organizations operate and are structured. To effectively integrate and optimize their use of technology and competitive performance, organizations attempting integration must transcend the normal boundaries of technology and address their fundamental business and organizational practices.

Integration is a progressive process, a constant evolution of technology, business processes, knowledge, and human capital. As demonstrated by such leaders as Boeing, Chrysler, Federal Express, and Wal-Mart, improved performance and financial returns can be generated through the integration of technologies and the leverage provided. More importantly, the competitive position of the organization can be vastly improved through convergent integration.

This chapter has provided an opening glance into the integration marketplace and some of the key issues regarding system integration. This chapter defined system integration, explored some of the major attributes and qualities of system integration, and discussed some of the more prevalent drivers for system integration. The remaining chapters of this book provide additional insights into the system integration process and a framework to follow to ensure a successful integration effort.

Chapter 2
The IT Imperative in Business Transformation

Richard J. Murray
Dorothy E. Trefts

For business and information systems (IS) management, the information technology (IT) imperative is to construct the organizationwide systems and capabilities needed by businesses to compete. For IS professionals, this means developing a totally new viewpoint regarding the role IT plays in building the business of the future. The new viewpoint embraces the idea that without IS professionals' involvement in and significant understanding of the business — from strategy creation through systems implementation — the business itself will be in jeopardy. IS and business management must act as true partners following this new management process, each supporting the other with goals well aligned toward a common end: creating the optimally performing company.

THE NEW MANAGEMENT PROCESS

To put into practice this notion of partnership and mutually supportive involvement, IS and business managers require a totally new way of working together. This is essential because the restructuring initiatives being undertaken by corporate America require change management on a scale never previously encountered. IT is envisioned as the strategic enabling ingredient in this restructuring. Unless business and IS management agree to partner and work together, the corporation will never accomplish this goal.

Global Demands

Companies are being realigned to address global business opportunities. *Global* is not just another word to describe conducting business as usual, in autonomous, diversified, unintegrated entities around the world. IT is the key to transforming business capabilities from parochial to global.

0-8493-9968-8/99/$0.00+$.50
© 1999 by CRC Press LLC

11

Unless IS and business management can put the pieces together, they will fall short of the global corporation.

Most of corporate America is constrained by information technology islands of automation: solutions that effectively address single, localized, usually departmental issues, but that are disconnected from and unresponsive to the needs of the integrated business. This problem is compounded by different processing platforms, programming languages, software packages, communications protocols, database technologies, and skills — all of which prohibit easy connections between islands of automation. The result is a web of systems that make it impossible to leverage the organization's technology resources to generate true business advantage.

Managing the IT resource to move from these automation islands to organizationwide, global systems requires the development of a new management process — one that is based on a clearly articulated management template. Such a process enables the organization to establish and maintain a focus on those projects that are critical to developing and maintaining a competitive edge.

FUNDAMENTAL MANAGING PRINCIPLES

First, it is important to articulate the principles that govern the new management process. Paradigm shifts always present a challenge and require a more fundamental base of understanding from which to build. The new management process is not a cookbook approach to solving problems. It must be described and understood within the context of a dramatically different role for IT.

Six managing principles govern this new process of management:

- Linkage to strategy
- A focus on business benefits
- The concept of quickstrikes
- Defined roles and responsibilities
- Creeping commitment
- Linkage to architecture

Linkage to Strategy

Organizationwide IT initiatives must be

- Driven by the business vision and strategy
- Tied to specific quantifiable benefits
- Based on the redesign of the business process

This linkage to strategy clarifies what problems must be solved and, more importantly, how success is to be measured. Translation of vague corporate vision statements into specific performance goals permits the organization to grasp how IT can play a leading role in vaulting the corporation ahead. Expectations are clearly understood at the beginning of the transformation process.

There are distinct implications for IS professionals. First, IS management must understand the full business vision (ideally by participating in its development) and be able to communicate it throughout the IS group. Second, business vision and strategy must be translated into conceptual statements of those tasks that the organization must perform exceptionally well to achieve its vision, as well as measurable business objectives (i.e., specific, quantified performance goals, most of which are nonfinancial) that in turn clearly set out the organization's goals. Finally, these new goals trigger a process of reevaluating the organization's strategic business processes. At present, many organizations may have no significant IT component, yet designing a new way of conducting business in the future is fundamental to doing business cheaper, better, and faster.

A Focus on Business Benefits

Executive participation is essential to enable transformation; the ongoing measurement of performance and benefits against strategic objectives drives the transformation process.

Business transformation clearly requires investment. One of the missing ingredients in the management of traditional development efforts has been rigorous financial analysis at all stages of the development process, to revisit initial financial assumptions and to incorporate and test the new information. This process implies incremental funding with go or no-go decision points. Also implied are sunk costs that may or may not be recovered.

The new management process is based on the assumption that program financials will be revisited and challenged at each phase of the process so that the learning acquired at each phase becomes incorporated into the analysis. The corporation is able to continually answer the questions: Is this program accomplishing what it set out to achieve? Is it worth it?

The Concept of Quickstrikes

Quickstrike initiatives — defined as small technical and nontechnical projects of short duration that produce immediate business benefits — can be implemented early on to speed the realization of overall program benefits. The underlying concept of the quickstrike is that benefits should not accrue solely at the end of a program; they should begin to be reaped in the early phases of a program and continue throughout its life. The intention is to move the program in the direction of becoming self-funding as soon as possible, thereby avoiding the traditional model of delayed realization of benefits. Interim benefits must be used to fund the program.

13

Defined Roles and Responsibilities

The new management process defines expectations about behavior that put performance goals on the table and ensure that all players are aware of their roles. This principle is basic; however, it is an element of process design that is often forgotten. Ensuring that each group is aware of its role in the new management process facilitates the success of the program and the organization. The explicit nature of this principle is what is important, so that individuals become aware of and accountable for their contribution to the whole.

Creeping Commitment

Work should be performed according to a standard work process, which produces interim deliverables that permit the continuous management of risk and capital investment. The organization's commitment to a specific transformation program should grow as the program moves through the various phases of the management process. As the strategic vision is defined and clarified, and as ever more detailed pieces of the plan are fleshed out, the organization's commitment level — and financial appetite for the program — grow.

The new management process builds creeping organizational commitment through its rigorous gatekeeping requirements which ensure that the process is managed and monitored. As a transformational program moves forward through the management process, the corporation takes the opportunity to identify and test its assumptions about the program's inherent risk and rewards. Only at the point of maximum information, when the risks have been well calculated, is major capital committed.

Linkage to Architecture

A technological and business architecture is needed to coordinate and integrate individual projects over extended periods of time. New business processes and information systems must be consistent with this architecture.

The new management process embraces the concept of architectural standards for organizationwide IT to guide the development of new systems capabilities. These standards — as they relate to technologies, data, communications, applications, and systems — are analogous to the plumbing, heating, ventilation, air conditioning, and electrical systems standards for a new residential construction project. Without these standards, a house is apt to run on the wrong voltage or be missing drainage pipes. Similarly, without IT architectural standards, organizationwide systems become yet additional islands of automation, akin to existing departmental solutions in that they are useful only to a limited segment of the business.

OBJECTIVES AND DELIVERABLES

The new management process contains six phases, each with a specific set of objectives and deliverables. As shown in Exhibit 1, each phase of the management process generates a series of quickstrike opportunities and benefits analyses. The glue that holds the process together is a tight system of program management activities. Combined, these three factors generate the creeping commitment necessary for the organization to ultimately buy into the program and implement the required systems capabilities. Exhibit 1 embodies the managing principles previously discussed. The six phases, which are usually undertaken in sequential order, are described in the following sections.

Phase 1: Vision and Business Objectives. This phase is used to articulate the corporation's high-level business vision and strategic objectives. It is supported by precise, quantified performance targets. This phase of the management process includes a first pass at the business program, which is a statement of the objectives, scope, and goals of a specific organization-wide initiative and its supporting financial business case.

Phase 2: Business Architecture. This phase entails the identification and definition of the high-impact business processes supporting the business vision. It is the statement of a business model of the organization and serves as the foundation for the IT architecture (phase 3). The business architecture's specific deliverables include a map of the critical business processes as they currently exist and the business process requirements of the future. Another critical deliverable is an initial plan — the improvement action plan — with key steps to achieving the new business architecture.

Phase 3: The IT Architecture. This phase develops the computing structure, beginning with an idealized top-down and bottom-up view of the IS requirements to support the business process. This phase creates a blueprint for technology that enables the organization to conduct business in new ways with strategic potential.

The first step in formulating this architecture is baselining the architecture in place. Other important deliverables for this phase include the risk assessment (an evaluation of the risks inherent in the architectural choices made), a restatement of the business case that incorporates this new information, and the architectural migration strategy and plan. Phase 3 is an important phase for the identification of quickstrike initiatives.

Phase 4: Design and Engineering. This phase covers the translation of business and IT requirements into the guidelines and specifications critical to systems engineering and development efforts at the individual project level. Each broad organizationwide program may consist of several

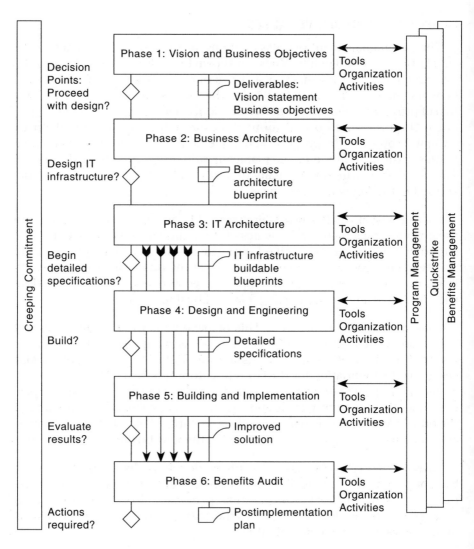

Exhibit 1. The new management process.

systems projects that need to be managed independently. The design phase of the management process includes requirements definition, software evaluation and selection, conceptual design, and detailed design as its key deliverables.

Phase 5: Building and Implementation. This phase includes the coding, testing, documentation, pilot testing, training, installation, maintenance, and system migration activities involved in realizing an information system and propagating it throughout the business. The important deliverables for this phase are the developed system, the first implementation, and subsequent system migrations.

Phase 6: Benefits Audit. This phase entails the ongoing activities to measure performance improvements and program benefits and to ensure that continuous improvement is derived from the effort. Key deliverables for this phase are the benefits evaluation, system evaluation, and an identification of the lessons learned from the project. These lessons need to be consolidated, project by project, to the broader program level to share the learning across projects and other similar transformational programs.

ROLES AND RESPONSIBILITIES

Each phase in the new management process is supported by a group of executives (see Exhibit 2) charged with specific responsibilities to produce a detailed set of deliverables. The matrix in Exhibit 3, which identifies the roles and responsibilities of these key individuals as well as new organization structure implication, highlights how this process differs from the traditional approaches.

Perhaps the most important ingredient in making this process work for the organization is well-orchestrated communication about the process throughout business and IS departments. Exposure to the new management process can be generated through executive awareness sessions, comprehensive documentation, training modules, and educational programs to train the trainers. These efforts support the new ways of accomplishing business, but require time and attention from both business and IT partners.

The ideal way to move forward with the new management process is to educate the organization and then to apply this process at the start of a new organizationwide initiative. Most corporations do not have that luxury, however, because they are already in the midst of undertaking several such initiatives simultaneously.

CONCLUSION

Companies can learn valuable lessons from incorporating this new management process, even in midstream. For example, the process can reveal whether staff members on critical programs understand what their roles are. It can also determine which key phases have been given short shrift or eliminated altogether.

Serious commitment at the highest level of the organization is the key to making the transformation process work, especially when the change

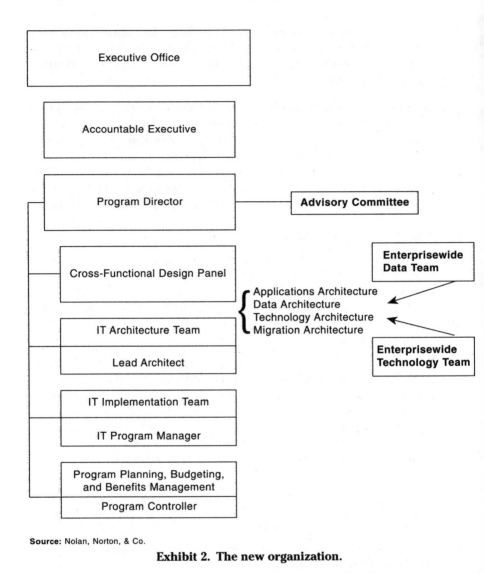

Source: Nolan, Norton, & Co.

Exhibit 2. The new organization.

---

involves reorchestrating the way in which units vital to the corporation work together. Traditional IT management must also accept the challenge and embrace this new management process to truly transform the organization.

Deliverables and Activities

Participants	Vision and Business Objectives	Business Architecture	IT Architecture	Design	Building and Implementation	Benefits Audit
Business Partners						
Executive Office (Content Review)	PR	R	CR	R	R	R
Executive Steering Committee (Process Review)	R	R	R	R	R	R
Accountable Executive	PR	R	R	R	R	R
Program Director	PR	PR	P	R,PR	R,P	PR
Advisory Committee	N	N	N	N	N	P
Cross-Functional Design Panel	P	PR	P	PR	R,PR	P
IT Partners						
IT Program Manager		P	PR	PR	PR	P
IT Architecture Team		P	PR	P	P	P
IT Implementation Team				PR	PR	P
Both		P	P	P	P	R
Program Controller						

Key: PR = primary responsibility for doing the work and leading all aspects of the activity, P = some participation in and responsibility for specific tasks within the activity, N = peripheral (nondirect) involvement in the activity, R = responsibility for reviewing the activity before going on to the next phase, CR = contingent review only if business case changes.

Exhibit 3.   Overview of roles and responsibilities.

Note

1. Murray, R.J. and Hardin, R.C., "The IT Organization of the Future," *Information Systems Management,* 8(4), Fall 1991.

Chapter 3
Aligning Strategies, Processes, and Information Technology: A Case Study

Rainer Feurer
Kazem Chaharbaghi
Michael Weber
John Wargin

Process innovations and process redesigns frequently must employ technology in order to achieve major improvements in performance. Information technology (IT) has become an enabler for newly designed processes by eliminating limitations of time, location, or organizational structure, or by providing a new basis for differentiation. This can only be achieved, however, when processes and IT are carefully aligned with the overall organization's objectives and interfunctional teamwork.

While there is general consensus among practitioners that business/IT alignment is necessary, the way to achieve it is often unclear. This is because business strategies are usually defined first and the operations and supporting strategies, including technologies, are then aligned. Such a sequential approach defines strategies, processes, and actions in light of the technologies available, as opposed to identifying technologies that drive the critical success factors.

A better approach is one in which strategies, processes, technologies, and actions are defined and aligned concurrently. The aim of this chapter

0-8493-9968-8/99/$0.00+$.50
© 1999 by CRC Press LLC

is to present a business alignment approach, one used and developed by Hewlett-Packard Co. (HP) for designing and implementing new business processes that are enabled and supported by new generations of information systems.

This approach has been practiced over several years, both internally and externally, generating a portfolio of best practices. The well-defined activities are closely linked and are applied by multifunctional teams for the purpose of business reengineering as well as redesigning core business processes. The whole approach is complemented by a strong focus on teamwork, specialized and objective-driven business units, and a commitment to quality and customer satisfaction.

FRAMEWORK FOR BUSINESS ALIGNMENT

Strategies are only effective when they are translated into actions readily. This implies that supporting ITs need to be highly responsive. Business processes should be continuously optimized through the application of relevant technologies and carried out by high-performance teams. Strategies must therefore be:

- Formulated by closely examining the role of technology as an enabling source
- Translated into actions through highly interactive processes that consider all current and future business factors

In the past, the design of business processes and IT applications was focused on achieving incremental benefits. Flexibility and ability to react to major changes were largely neglected. The business alignment framework in Exhibit 1 links any given strategy and its corresponding actions.

Linking Strategy and Actions

Strategies determine the critical success factors that in turn define the necessary business processes and their information needs. The availability, cost, and flexibility of different technologies may limit their selection; therefore, business processes must be translated into feasible application models while information requirements are translated into workable data models. In this way, the gap between the ideal and workable solutions can be minimized while ensuring a logical linkage between strategy and optimized actions.

The aim of such a framework is twofold:

- To make process changes without being restricted by or limited to existing technology, applications, and suboptimal data structures
- To make visible the impact of new technologies on processes, and vice versa

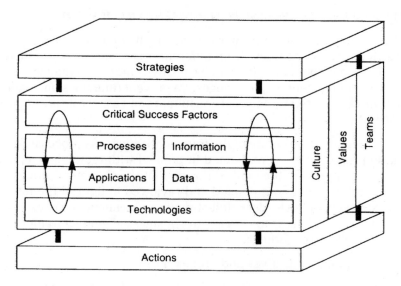

Exhibit 1. Business alignment framework.

The business alignment framework takes into account the necessary process changes resulting from changes in the environment as well as potential advancements in technology. Because any change in strategy and technology potentially results in a change in the value system, culture, and team structures of the organization, it is vital to include these additional factors within the overall framework.

By employing this framework, HP has experienced a number of benefits, including:

- Optimization of all the business processes with the support of integrated technology, as opposed to suboptimization of individual processes and organization units with the support of fragmented technology
- Consistent focus on processes that maximize stakeholder value
- Common understanding of issues and future targets throughout the organization
- High level of transparency and flexibility to act and react to changes stemming from the competitive environment as well as improvements in technology
- High level of commitment from people throughout the organization

In this framework, target processes, technologies, and standards drive the selection of potential solutions. User participation forms an integral part of the framework and helps to ensure fast and effective implementation.

IMPLEMENTING THE BUSINESS ALIGNMENT FRAMEWORK

The business alignment framework is implemented by cross-functional teams that include members from different organizational and functional units. Team members are given a charter by senior-level management to initiate and implement major changes. To prevent tunnel vision, teams are sometimes supported by external consultants and a key role is assigned to management.

According to the structure of the framework, business processes and information requirements are defined in parallel with technology enablers and models, which are then linked throughout the alignment process. Objectives and measures are defined and reviewed in light of the intended overall strategy, which leads to adjustments and refinements of existing results. The approach used to develop the business alignment framework includes the following modules:

- Breakthrough objectives and process links
- Business models
- Technology enablers and models
- Solution mapping and selection
- Functional mapping

Breakthrough Objectives and Processes

The alignment process commences with the existing business strategy or strategic direction of the organization or organizational unit. Based on a strategy review, potential breakthrough objectives are defined. Breakthrough objectives create a distinct competitive differentiation in the eyes of the customer when implemented. This can be achieved through significant improvements in performance in the area of cost, introduction or distribution of new products, outsourcing of noncore activities, consolidation scenarios, or modification of supplier relationships.

After a comprehensive list of potential breakthrough objectives is defined, the most critical (usually two to five) objectives are selected. These objectives form the basis of critical success factors, which in this sense are all those factors that have to go right in order to achieve a breakthrough. In parallel, potential obstacles that prevent the achievement of the breakthroughs are identified. These may fall into different categories, including management practices, technology support, training, and goal conflicts between different stakeholders.

Innovative, Core, and Supportive Processes

The next step is formulating the key processes that have a major effect on achieving the breakthrough objectives. These processes basically support the critical success factors. Processes that support several critical

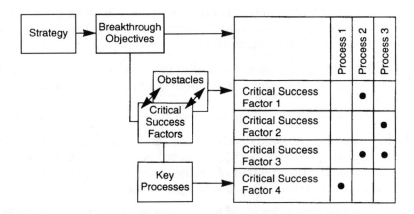

Exhibit 2. Breakthrough objectives, critical success factors, and key processes.

success factors are classed as innovative processes. These usually involve multifunctional activities that directly create stakeholder value. They become the focus of business, process, and information models. Other process categories include supportive and core processes which, although important, do not result in differentiation in the eyes of the stakeholders. This is because these processes usually correlate with only one or two critical success factors. Exhibit 2 shows diagrammatically the way in which breakthrough objectives and innovative processes are identified. Exhibit 3 illustrates the classification process used to determine innovative, core, and supportive processes based on their potential impact on cost, quality, speed, and flexibility.

Business Models

Business models are developed for describing innovative processes and their role within the overall organization. HP designs business models not only for facilitating communications and achieving consensus, but also as

Major Processes	Process Classification	Process Impact			
		Cost	Quality	Speed	Flexibility
Manage Product and Parts Info	Core	X		X	X
Control Production	Innovative		X	X	X
Plan and Procure Material	Innovative	X	X	X	X
Manage Material Flow	Core–Innovative	X		X	X
Manufacturer Products	Core	X	X	X	X
Distribution	Core		X	X	X
Financial	Supportive				X

Exhibit 3. Process classification and potential impact.

a basis for identifying enabling technologies that will allow the organization to achieve major improvements in performance or differentiation. This requires three equally important views:

- The description of business activities or processes (process model)
- The definition of business information requirements (information model)
- The interaction between the business activities and information

Business models can yield highly adapted and flexible IT infrastructures that not only are geared to specific needs but provide benefit to the entire organization. At HP, the creation of business models is performed by several cross-functional teams. The advantages include:

- Users can be closely involved in the modeling process and committed to the definition of their processes from the very early stage.
- Well-defined models can be reused and adapted to other business areas and subsidiaries.
- Work of parallel teams is more efficient if supported by a common structure and hierarchical decomposition.

The business models developed take a tree-shaped form in which each global process can be described as a collection of activities and subprocesses. While global processes are modeled by top-level management or core teams, the more detailed representations are produced by specialist subteams. In developing and linking the models, inconsistencies, omissions, and misunderstandings are observed and corrected. In parallel to developing the process hierarchy, information models are developed.

Information Models

Information models aim to identify and describe business data objects (e.g., assets, orders, locations) together with their interrelationships. For example, an order combined with a location creates the data object called Shipment. Information modeling is therefore concerned with two major questions: What information does the business need? What interrelationship exists with other information?

To support this goal, data objects must be driven by business needs and defined in isolation from existing information systems and applications. This is in contrast to the approach used in the past in which data was designed and created for a specific application system that supported a single function from a limited perspective. This method leads to a high level of data redundancy and inconsistency. Information models, however, regard information as detached from existing or potential applications with the aim of improving the timeliness, completeness, and accuracy of shared information while decreasing redundancy.

There are two levels of information models. At the highest level of abstraction, the global information model identifies the 10 or 20 data objects or clusters that are critical for the implementation of breakthrough objectives. This model is primarily used for communication with senior-level management and setting a framework for detailed modeling performed by dedicated subteams.

The second type of model contains a more detailed explosion with approximately 100 to 200 data objects. This model is also used to validate the appropriate process models in the process hierarchy.

Although the process and information models are developed independent of any application systems, they help to determine where technology can play an enabling role, as discussed next.

Technology Enablers and Models

The impact of IT has several characteristics, the most important of which are:

- *Integrative.* IT supports coordination and integration between different activities and processes.
- *Direct.* IT is used to improve the sequence of activities and processes so that they can be carried out faster and in parallel. Furthermore, unnecessary intermediaries may be eliminated.
- *Information.* IT is used to capture process information for knowledge generation, process analysis, and decision making.

Standards

Technology can be a cost-effective enabler only if certain standards are defined and adhered to. It is therefore necessary to examine and define which technology elements, based on today's technology and standards as well as likely future trends, can be applied in the implementation of the business processes.

The selected standards should be seen not as a limiting factor but rather as a mechanism that improves exchangeability of technology, flexibility, cost effectiveness, and efficiency. The definition of standards, for example, in the area of IT may include such considerations as the design of the physical and logical network concepts including internal and external communications needs, operating systems, and databases, as well as the definition of potential hardware requirements and implementation outlines including outsourcing and multivendor scenarios.

Solution Mapping and Selection

Once the business models and the technology standards are defined, the next step is to select solutions that best support and enable the defined

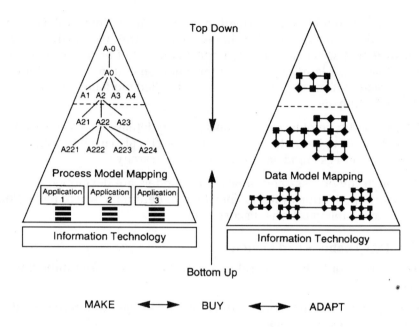

Exhibit 4.   Mapping potential solutions to processes and information requirements.

business processes. This can be achieved by matching the defined process and information models to the process and data models of existing and potential newly developed solutions. This forms a top-down, bottom-up approach, as shown in Exhibit 4.

Using this approach, processes that can be enabled or supported by IT are combined into clusters of potential applications. These could include financial systems, manufacturing resource planning, production control, sales tracking, and customer databases. This clustering is performed at a very high level and, as such, does not yet include detailed functional requirements. In a parallel activity, key objectives for the selection of application solutions, together with importance ratings, are defined.

Based on the solution clusters and the selected objectives and weightings, a market analysis of existing application solutions is performed in which the top two to four candidates within each area are short-listed and then checked for their fit with the process and information models and adherence to agreed-on standards and core concepts. In addition, business fit is evaluated according to such criteria as vendor size, availability of localized application versions, and references.

The selection process is continued by translating the process models into detailed functionality requirements; it may also include prototyping of

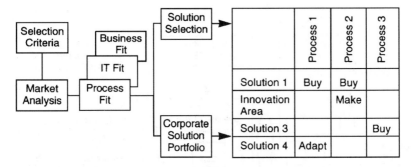

Exhibit 5. Solution mapping and selection.

selected processes or parts of the process. This analysis is used to determine whether:

- The newly defined business processes can be supported or enabled by using standard applications.
- It is possible to modify and adapt existing application solutions.
- It is necessary to develop custom application solutions.

Developing a Corporate Solutions Portfolio

During this step, it is also possible to develop a corporate solutions portfolio of applications that can be shared across different organizational units or used for similar processes. Exhibit 5 illustrates the solution mapping and selection process.

Functional Mapping

Solutions and applications are selected on the basis of process and information models defined by teams of planners and users. Once a specific application is selected, it is possible to go back and really start the process of matching the key functions to the actual selected applications in order to determine the extent of application adaptation or process change required. This process is termed "functional mapping."

Functional mapping (Exhibit 6) is the beginning of the implementation process; however, it must still be regarded as part of the overall business alignment framework because modifications to and changes in business processes and solution adaptation are still possible.

The defined business processes are checked with users in terms of the detailed fit with specific business or process events and compared to the functionality of the selected solutions. In cases where a gap exists, two alternatives are examined:

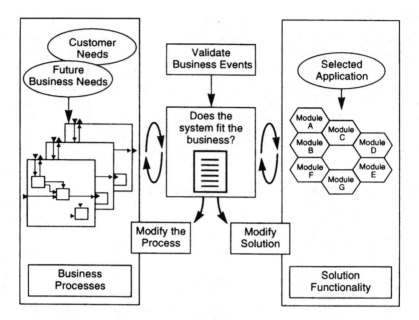

Exhibit 6. Functional mapping.

- Modify the business process.
- Modify the application solution, which may involve minor changes such as report generation or major changes such as recoding specific software modules.

In cases where the implementation of a breakthrough objective depends on the existence of a specific process, the decision will always be the modification of the application rather than sacrificing the process in the defined form. The process of functional mapping operates best if users can test to what extent the selected solution supports the newly defined processes; for this purpose, HP uses piloting centers and laboratories.

INDUSTRIAL APPLICATIONS

Two industrial applications demonstrate the potential of the business alignment framework. The first application reflects work carried out by HP for another organization in support of the construction of a transplant operation. This application illustrates the way in which the framework can be applied to a newly designed business and drive the selection of open-systems-based applications to significantly reduce IT costs. The second application is internal and demonstrates the way in which the framework can be applied to redefine existing operations. It incorporates additional considerations, such as finding a compromise between conflicting goals and objectives of different groups involved in the process of change.

Application to a Greenfield Operation

HP was selected to help a large multinational car manufacturer develop a new transplant operation in the U.S. This transplant was considered to be the first step in the redesign of the organization toward a worldwide network of factories and represented a "greenfield" operation; as such, it was not subject to existing technologies, processes, work methods, and support systems. The only constraints were the short implementation time frame (18 months), certain environmental conditions, and the network of suppliers, customers, and the parent company.

The first step involved the creation of teams, together with the identification and definition of the key project requirements based on strategic considerations of the overall organization, as well as internal and external benchmarks. The most important requirement was defined as achieving a premium on flexibility and adaptability in terms of new products or models, quantity, expandability, and "change of charter" (e.g., serving worldwide versus selected markets).

A balanced approach between using people and technology would allow the organization to adapt the transplant strategy or processes more rapidly with market requirements, while at the same time being more motivational to the transplant personnel. The aim was to commit flexible resources at the latest possible moment in the production process, thus saving additional money. Another requirement was that the factory and infrastructures should be driven by innovative processes, thus allowing the acquisition and transfer of new knowledge and best practices. Finally, the project aimed at establishing new levels and types of partnerships, thus recognizing the role of the transplant as part of a larger network. After identifying these and other key requirements, their significance and the competitive deficit of the organization were determined in the form of a gap analysis. The resulting focus pattern (Exhibit 7) drove the execution of the business alignment and was regularly used for control purposes.

The breakthroughs in the area of process innovation and technology enablers were defined using cross-functional teams from both organizations. The breakthroughs, together with some of the critical success factors for the project, are shown in Exhibit 8. The next step was to identify key processes that would have a major impact on achieving the objectives. High-level business models of the transplant and its environment were developed and subsequently translated into key processes. These key processes were segmented into innovative, core, and supportive processes in order to identify those that would have the strongest impact on overall transplant performance. These subprocesses were subsequently modeled by cross-functional teams in a hierarchical way, as previously described. Exhibit 9 is a simplified representation of the highest level (A0) process model that contains the four subprocesses.

SYSTEMS INTEGRATION SUCCESS STRATEGIES

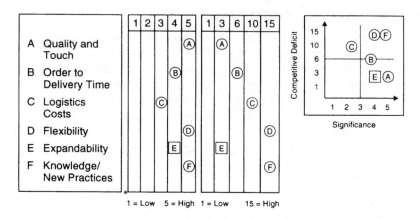

1 = Low   5 = High   1 = Low   15 = High

Exhibit 7. Project goals, significance, and competitive deficit.

Critical Success Factors / Information Technology Breakthroughs	Open systems	Global vendors and suppliers	High level of transparency on process structure and interrelationships with other processes	Multifunctional teamwork	Multiple vendors	Scalability of systems	Standard solutions wherever possible	Incorporation of members of existing plants
Integrated and standardized applications (cost efficiency, flexibility, no vendor dependency)	●	●			●	●	●	
Process, team driven design and execution of approach			●	●				●
IT cost/product at 50% of cost level in existing plants	●	●	●		●	●	●	
Modularity of systems (for flexibility)			●		●	●	●	
Ability to transfer experience to other plants		●			●		●	●

Exhibit 8.   Breakthroughs and critical success factors in the area of technology enablers.

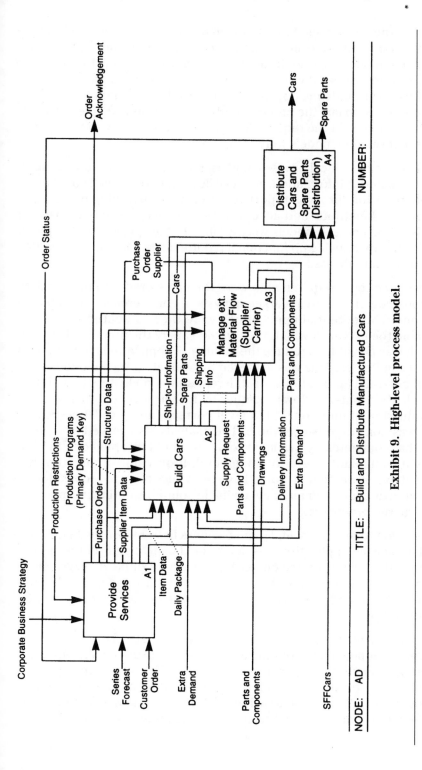

Exhibit 9. High-level process model.

NODE: AD   TITLE: Build and Distribute Manufactured Cars   NUMBER:

Each of the subprocesses was modeled and documented accordingly. While the top levels were modeled by a core team of planners, the subprocesses were modeled by dedicated and specialist subteams that included possible future users as well as experienced users of existing processes. This consistent modeling approach, supported by a computerized tool, made it possible to link the process models, rapidly and completely identify conflicts, and meet the required time frame. In parallel with the process models, information models were generated.

Using the hierarchical process models, structure and resource requirements for material, information, financial flows, and personnel could be defined. In addition, process report requirements, including manual and computerized methods and access to central systems, could easily be identified. The process models were applied in the specification of potential solutions by drawing up functional requirements lists for the activities within a certain process.

These functional requirements were then clustered into potential applications, together with a market analysis of commercially available applications. The potential applications were then evaluated in order to determine the extent to which they would satisfy the functional requirements. It was possible to reduce the number of applications to five potential final candidates. This was achieved by evaluating the functional fit of several potential applications for different solution clusters (e.g., bill-of-material, MRP, material flow) together with their level of integration. In the evaluation of functional fit, a level corresponding to 60 percent or above was considered acceptable. The analysis also served as a cross-check that commercially available solutions could be applied in the running of a transplant operation in general. If only one application had scored above 50 percent, it would have been necessary to reconsider the decision to aim for commercially available solutions in the first place, or to change the processes.

In addition to functional fit, IT and business fit were also evaluated. The overall fit of each application was determined by mapping all the applications with the help of a three-dimensional matrix. Exhibit 10 diagrammatically summarizes the process of application mapping and selection, together with some sample criteria used for the evaluation in each of the three dimensions.

The project resulted in the selection of several standard applications that would support highly optimized processes, ensure effectiveness and efficiency, and maintain a high level of flexibility. The structured approach with which the project was performed, together with the standard solutions used, made it possible to achieve the intended implementation time frame without compromising the quality of the project outcomes.

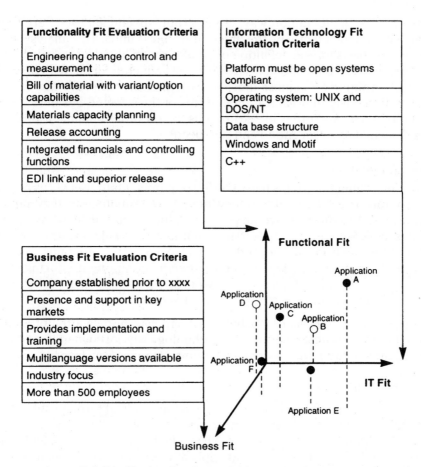

Exhibit 10. Application mapping and selection.

Application to an Existing Business

HP has used the business alignment framework to redesign its order fulfillment process. Although the application of the overall framework remained the same as in the previous example, two additional dimensions had to be addressed:

- Because the business process already existed, it was necessary to evaluate the impact of potential changes.
- Because the process spanned several business units and product groups (some of which had conflicting goals), it was necessary to decide where and how compromises could be achieved.

In this case, the greatest benefits could be achieved by concentrating on improving on-time delivery, speed of new product introduction, and price

35

performance in a common way. Other group-specific factors were then dealt with independently by the different business units. This analysis also formed the basis for the definition of breakthrough objectives, such as 100 percent delivery on customer date and cost reduction of 30 to 40 percent for each group and business unit that would clearly improve the performance of the overall organization in terms of the selected business goals. Based on these and other breakthroughs, a new order fulfillment process was designed using an end-to-end perspective.

Strategy Impact

Because different groups had differing requirements, it was necessary to incorporate a vector called "strategy impact." Determining strategy impact was used to fine-tune the overall process to the requirements of individual groups. It also made it possible to incorporate the changes arising from the competitive environment or product-specific marketing programs, and adjustments of inventory levels due to specific component shortages or trends. Exhibit 11 is a high-level view of the redesigned order fulfillment process together with the strategy impact vectors.

To ensure high levels of flexibility, the process models attempt to balance the use of human support and technology support; wherever no major improvements could be achieved, human support was favored.

Cost Justification

Because order fulfillment processes that had evolved through numerous continuous improvement efforts were already in place, it was necessary to justify the implementation costs of the newly defined processes, including the cost of the new IT systems and applications. The cost of nonalignment that represents the cost of tolerating nonvalue-adding activities had to be determined for comparison purposes. Here, different techniques were employed, including:

- Actually tracking a customer order from the moment of quotation to final delivery
- Measuring the time involved in handling exceptions
- Benchmarking with related and nonrelated industries
- Reexamining core competencies that, for example, resulted in subcontracting the whole postmanufacturing delivery activities
- Establishing common performance measures

When it was determined that the cost of nonalignment outweighed the cost of new process development and implementation, the core processes and relevant subprocesses were modeled and translated into functional requirements so that potential solutions could be selected or developed.

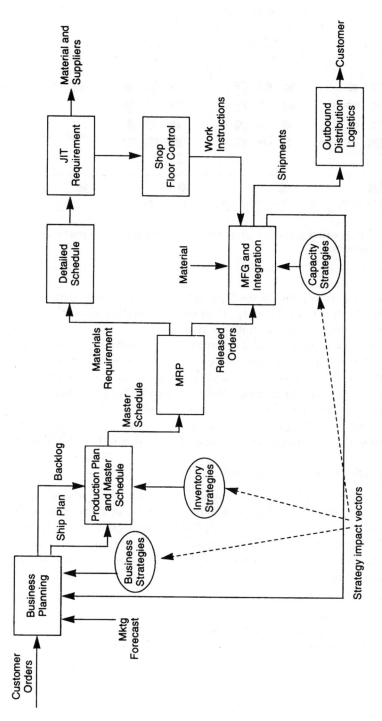

Exhibit 11. High-level order fulfillment process and strategy impact.

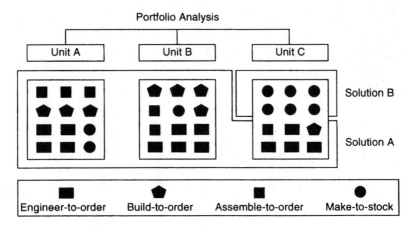

Exhibit 12. Application selection alternatives in multibusiness unit environments.

Because the requirements for each business unit were different, it was impossible to select one uniform application. A portfolio analysis determined the best compromise for limiting the number of application solutions for implementation. Exhibit 12 shows the outcome of the portfolio analysis. For example, business units A and B have similar product portfolios for which application solutions can easily be applied. For business unit C, solution A lends itself to a limited number of products. Therefore, a second application solution was necessary. These solution clusters allowed HP to implement the new processes using a few standard applications while redefining a speedy implementation and minimizing the overall cost.

RECOMMENDED COURSE OF ACTION

Information systems managers recognize the need to align strategies, people, processes, and technologies in dynamic business environments in which speed of implementation is critical. The two examples illustrate step by step how the framework can be applied to define new business models and modify existing ones. This structured framework for alignment allows the user organization to:

- Develop processes that focus on breakthroughs that make a clear difference in the eyes of customers
- Identify and use appropriate enabling technologies
- Achieve a high level of transparency and reduce redundancies

- Use standard applications based on open systems wherever possible in order to reduce cost and implementation time while ensuring integration
- Allow for flexibility so that changes arising from the competitive environment as well as advancements in technology can be rapidly implemented

Section II
Integrated Architectures

Chapter 4

Architecture Frameworks for Client/Server and Netcentric Computing

Andersen Consulting

THE NEED FOR ARCHITECTURES: INSURANCE AGAINST RISK

At the heart of systems development, the use of architectures provides *insurance*: insurance against the complexities of development and maintenance, against the obsolescence of technologies, against the possibility that all the parts of a solution may not work together. Architectures are the master plans that ensure that the solution will work.

This notion implies that risk is involved, and that is so. In client/server and netcentric environments, a number of risks are generally present.

More Complex Development and Maintenance

A number of factors contribute to the complexity of client/server and netcentric solutions:

- Client/server applications incorporate sophisticated graphical user interfaces (GUIs). GUIs are usually event driven rather than hierarchical. They are interactive and require more complex logic than traditional terminal (e.g., 3270) style interfaces.
- Client/server and netcentric applications have to "cooperate" with other applications. Communication code must establish communication connections, ensure that messages are sent and received correctly, manage errors, and handle any required data translation. Care must be taken that programmers and designers have these skill sets.
- The skills required for development, installation, and support of netcentric systems may be difficult to find.

43

More Difficult Operations Support

Operations support for netcentric solutions is more difficult than for traditional systems. The increased complexity of operations support, including hardware and software configuration management, is directly related to the number and location of distributed nodes. If a system has 100 remote nodes, it is more difficult to ensure that they are at the same software and hardware versions than it is with two local nodes.

In addition, data backup/restore must now occur at multiple locations, and support for hardware, software, and communications problems must also be provided locally at multiple sites.

More Complex Data Security

When data are distributed, protecting that data becomes more difficult. Intelligent workstations are inherently less secure than minicomputers and mainframes. The effort required to maintain an equivalent level of data security, therefore, increases.

New Distributed Data Update and Refresh Strategies

Most client/server systems incorporate multiple copies of the same data. This requires logic to ensure that data values in each of those copies are consistent. For example, if a user working off server A wants to change a "balance due" field, how and when will this change be reflected on servers B and C?

Increased Susceptibility to Viruses and Malicious Users

Again, this risk is directly proportional to the number of nodes in a distributed system. Each workstation is a potential point of entry for a virus or a malicious hacker.

Higher Communications Loads

Netcentric applications must communicate with each other and with other applications, typically legacy systems. This is accomplished over communications networks. For a networked system to work well, accurate estimates of the amount of network traffic must be determined. This is often difficult because, as the knowledge and popularity of newly released applications increase, application use (and network traffic) increases. Applications designed with communication speeds in mind may, therefore, end up being "communications bound." In addition, there are not many tools available that model new age computing communication loads.

Missed Opportunities

Because netcentric systems are comprised of hardware and software that are continually being improved, it is often difficult to stop waiting for enhancements. Many development teams become paralyzed, waiting for the next release of some component that promises to facilitate the installation process or enhance the final product.

Lack of a Standard Operating Environment

There are many popular operating system and window manager options that can be used to develop workstation applications. The risk is in choosing a combination that ends up with little or no support in the long run and requires future migrations of applications and data.

Increased Complexity of User ID and Password Strategies

Because netcentric solutions require the use of multiple computers, user ID and password strategies become more complex. For example, a security system on one computer may require password changes more frequently than another, or maximum and minimum password lengths may conflict on different systems. Even if these issues are not present, the maintenance of security information on multiple platforms is difficult.

THE BENEFITS OF ARCHITECTURES

The risks just discussed illustrate the need for architectures as crucial aspects of client/server and netcentric systems development. What is an architecture?

An architecture is a proven mechanism and an approach that can be used to isolate and mitigate the risks of delivering applications now and into the future.

According to the Gartner Group, an architecture is "a formal specification of how a computer solution will be organized." Gartner sets forth seven characteristics of a successful architecture:

1. Delimitation of the problem to be addressed
2. Decomposition of the solution to components with clearly assigned responsibilities
3. Definition of interfaces, formats, and protocols to be used between the components; these should be sufficiently clear and robust to permit asynchronous development and ongoing reimplementation of the components
4. Adequate documentation to permit compliance by implementers.
5. An auditing mechanism that exercises the specified interfaces to verify that specified inputs to components yield specified results.
6. An extendibility mechanism to enable response to changing requirements and technologies
7. Policies, practices, and organizational structures that facilitate adoption of the architecture

45

In the netcentric environment, an architecture is used to define how a system is structured and how the various components of the system interact. In a netcentric computing environment, there are more components and many more interactions that make an architecture even more important.

Organizations that have carefully implemented, delivered, and utilized these architectures have realized some of the following benefits:

1. *Better productivity, and less "reinvention of the wheel."* Architectures can abstract common requirements and approaches from applications and can eliminate having to identify, analyze, and implement them for each application. This improves developer productivity and the quality of the final product.
2. *Consistent, reliable, high-quality applications.* The framework provided by an architecture encourages applications to be built in a consistent fashion or structure, to deliver consistent behavior, and to work with a consistent interface (both to users and other applications), resulting in a system easier to build, use, and maintain.
3. *Rapid delivery of business solutions.* By providing a consistent external interface, an architecture simplifies integration of applications and facilitates rapid delivery of new solutions. This is achieved through the use of standard architecture components, adherence to standards, and the availability of the necessary tools, techniques, and training.
4. *Reduced impact of changes to underlying products and tools.* Because an architecture incorporates "layers of isolation," new products and tools can be more easily integrated into a system. Changes in one element of the architecture are less likely to affect other architecture elements.
5. *Better integration of business applications within and between organization business units.* By providing consistency of architecture components within and across an organization, the opportunity to build applications that have a higher degree of integration is greater. This should facilitate the exchange of critical information across the company.
6. *Isolation of users and applications developers from the complexities of the underlying technologies.* By having a standard architecture that includes a standard set of tools with a consistent interface, users and developers are not required to know the details of the platform technologies (i.e., the operating system, database, and network). Additional technology components could be added in the future with minimal additional training for the users.
7. *A consistent, standard development framework.* An architecture provides a framework for analyzing the requirements of a system or application. It can help business applications developers by providing

a structure from which to work. In a netcentric environment, the requirements of a GUI, distributed data, and distributed processing contribute to the complexity of the solution. Moreover, these requirements have many interdependencies. Without an architecture to help structure the problem, it is easy for applications developers to become overwhelmed by technical issues and spend insufficient time on the business problems they are there to solve.

8. *A common background for IS personnel.* In addition to providing a common approach for building systems, an architecture provides a common means of describing systems and a common language. As a result, IS personnel are more easily interchanged and cross-trained, providing more flexibility in the management of the organization.

This chapter will move from a high-level description of an overall architecture — what is called an Enterprise Information Architecture — to a summary of the primary technical architectures discussed in this book: the execution, development, and operations architectures for client/server and netcentric computing solutions. More detail on each of these architectures — their services and subservices — is provided in subsequent chapters of Section II.

THE ENTERPRISE INFORMATION ARCHITECTURE (EIA)

What are the components of an effective architecture? The Enterprise Information Architecture (EIA) framework provides a starting point for understanding what is meant by the various architectures under consideration. The EIA framework contains seven layers (Exhibit 1).

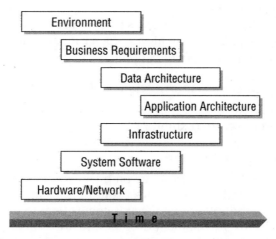

Exhibit 1. Enterprise Information Architecture (EIA).

- The *environment* layer includes those factors that influence the business requirements and technical layers. These factors may be either internal (e.g., profitability) or external (e.g., government regulation and market competition).
- The *business requirements* layer addresses the business needs of the organization. Both the environment layer and the business requirements layer are mainly concerned with business-level processes, strategies, and directions. The layers below are mainly concerned with the information technology to support the business. The business requirements give key input and guidelines on how to define the lower layers. The link from business requirements to the information technology layers is crucial to a successful EIA.
- The *data architecture* layer consists of a high-level data design that describes the structure of an enterprise's data needs in terms of entities and relationships between entities. The structure and relationships of data entities can be used to define the basic relationships of business functions and applications.
- The *applications architecture* layer defines the applications that must exist to support the business functions and their relationships. It also addresses any issues about distributed data processing.
- The *infrastructure* layer deals with those components of an architecture that can be used by multiple applications and that are developed and maintained within the enterprise. Usually, these common technical components help support the applications architecture. This layer also includes the infrastructure of the organization that manages the architecture definition and design and its technical components.
- The *systems software* layer encompasses the software and standards obtained from and maintained by outside vendors (e.g., a database management system.)
- The *hardware/network* layer deals with central processing units, local area network (LAN), wide area networks, and other hardware and physical network components of the environment.

Redefining the Enterprise Information Architecture

For purposes of this volume, these components can be grouped into four categories of architecture (Exhibit 2).

Business Solutions Architecture

Because this chapter does not focus on business specifics, the top three levels can be grouped into a business solutions architecture. It is important to remember, however, that when it comes time to decide what technical architecture to use, many of the answers are found by looking at the business solutions architecture. The decisions made for the application and data architectures drive the requirements of the technical architecture

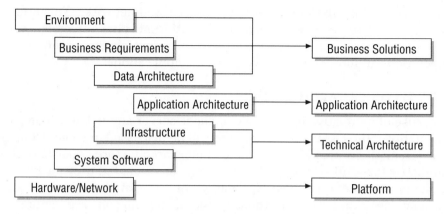

Exhbit 2. EIA Model Redefined.

and platform. At the same time, the constraints of the technical architecture and platform can also shape the application architecture and the business solutions that are possible.

Applications Architecture

The applications architecture layer can be defined here as those services that perform business functions on the computer. It represents the components that provide the automation support for a business function or activity in the business process (but does not include the platform and cross-application architecture). For example, a manufacturer's sales and marketing system application architecture could include sales tracking applications and the distributed data architecture to support both networked sales offices and mobile sales people.

Technical Architecture

The Infrastructure and System Software layers are combined to form the technical architecture. The technical architecture is where the buy decisions of the system software marketplace are combined with the build decisions for the needs of specific applications. We treat these as one architecture by incorporating these two concepts. The technical architecture is comprised of the execution, development, and operations architectures, which are discussed subsequently.

Platform Architecture

The final layer in the EIA model is the platform architecture layer. It is often described as "the things you can see." The netcentric platform architecture provides a framework for selecting the platform components required:

the servers, workstations, operating systems, and networks. This framework represents the overall technology platform for the implementation and deployment of the execution architecture, development architecture, operations architecture, and, of course, the applications.

THE TECHNICAL ARCHITECTURE

Because of its relative importance in client/server and netcentric implementations, the technical architecture will be discussed in some detail in the remainder of this chapter. The technical architecture consists of the infrastructure and systems software layers, as discussed previously. The differentiation between them is primarily a question of "make vs. buy," that is, a key decision for organizations intent on "building an architecture" is how much they want to build vs. how much they can simply buy from pre-existing sources. An organization can choose to build a great deal, thereby making the architecture very close to what it wants. That means that there is a great deal of logic being built by the shop.

Alternatively, the organization can choose to buy most of what it wants. To the extent that business or application demands make it necessary for the tools to be integrated, developers can then do simple assembly, or gluing together, of the pieces. The decision for most organizations depends on balancing demands. On the one hand, the organization has a large front-end commitment to build and an ongoing commitment to maintain an infrastructure architecture; on the other hand, the organization has a tool that is exactly what it wants.

Over the years there has been a tendency to buy rather than make. This is especially the case as the market matures with more technical entrants. It is practical for IS organizations to build technical architecture components only when essential. By purchasing rather than building, they can then more easily apply their strong skills in the applications architecture business.

Components of the Technical Architecture

The technical architecture layer can in turn be broken into three primary components: execution, development, and operations (Exhibit 3).

- An *execution* architecture describes the components required when an application executes.
- A *development* architecture describes the components required to create the execution architecture.
- An *operations* architecture describes the components required to operate and manage the system.

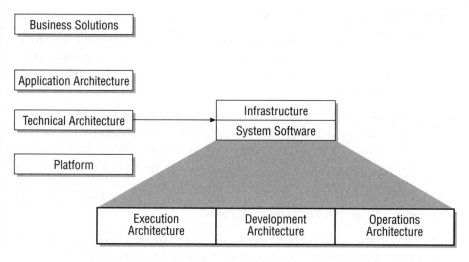

Exhibt 3. Three Components of a Technical Architecture.

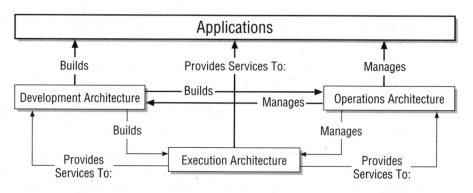

Exhibit 4. Relationships Among the Technical Architectures.

These architectures must be flexible enough to accommodate a wide range of technologies, but they must also be structured enough to provide valuable guidelines and to ensure that interoperability is available where it is required. Exhibit 4 illustrates the relationships among the execution, development, and operations architectures.

The remainder of this chapter will provide an overview of these technical architectures. Because of its relative importance in the design and delivery of netcentric solutions, the execution architecture will be discussed last and in much more detail.

DEVELOPMENT ARCHITECTURE

The development environment is the production environment for one or several systems development projects as well as for the maintenance efforts. Thus, it requires the same attention as a similarly sized end-user execution environment.

The purpose of the development architecture is to support the tasks involved in the analysis, design, construction, and maintenance of business systems as well as the associated management processes. It is important to note that the environment should adequately support *all* the development tasks, not just the code/compile/test/debug cycle. Given this, a comprehensive framework for understanding the requirements of the development environment should be used.

Another reason for the comprehensive framework is that it is important to get the development environment right the first time. Changing the development environment when construction is fully staffed may entail serious disruptions and expensive loss of productivity.

Experience has shown that, within the same medium- to large-size project with the same people, moving from a poor to a good development environment, productivity can be improved by a factor of ten for many tasks. The improvements come in two categories:

- The elimination of redundant and non-value-added tasks
- The streamlining of useful tasks

While it seems intuitive that most tasks can be streamlined, the following list gives a few examples of redundant tasks that must be eliminated:

- Analysis to determine how to merge the uncoordinated changes applied by two programmers to the same module
- Reentry of the source code for and retesting of a module, which was accidentally deleted
- Recurring discussions about "what a design packet should contain" or "what constitutes good programming style in a particular context"
- Repeated design, coding, testing, and maintenance of very similar logic (e.g., error handling, date conversion and manipulation, main structure of a module)
- Searching for the manuals of a particular productivity tool to find information
- Remigration to system test of a cycle because the impact analysis for a change request was incomplete
- Requesting support from another team (e.g., environment support, information management) and waiting unnecessarily for a response

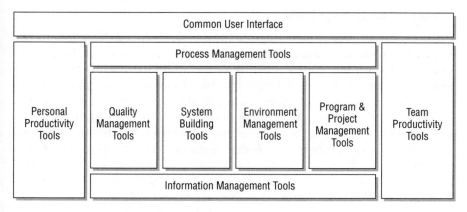

Exhibit 5. Development Architecture.

On a smaller project, these problems can be solved using a brute force approach. This becomes very expensive as the project grows and, finally, impossible. A well-designed development environment becomes important as the project team reaches 20 to 30 people, and is absolutely critical with a project size of more than 50 people.

The investment needed to design, set up, and tune a comprehensive, good development and maintenance environment is typically several hundred man days. Numbers between 400 and 800 days are commonly seen, depending on the platforms, target environment complexity, amount of reuse, and size of the system being developed/maintained. This investment warrants the following considerations:

- *This effort is large enough to justify work that will make it more efficient.* Among the factors that affect the effort, reuse is the most apparent. These guidelines, together with the parallel project to instantiate the model, constitute a step toward greater reuse.
- *The effort is large enough to require a cost/benefit analysis.*

Exhibit 5 is the model used throughout this book to describe the development architecture. The components of the development architecture include the following.

Common User Interface Tools

Common user interface tools provide a common launching place for all the tools in the development environment to make it appear more integrated and consistent. This is the simplest level of integration, in that all the tools are presented to the developer via a single view of the entire environment. Tools that support the common user interface are known as "window managers" (e.g., Microsoft Windows, Presentation Manager, and Motif).

Process Management Tools

Process management tools integrate the development environment by providing tool-to-tool communication and workflow management. Tool-to-tool communication integrates tools by enabling information in the form of short messages to be passed from one tool to another. Workflow management integration builds the development methodology and process into the tool environment. Workflow management enforces the correct sequencing of tasks and tools. Process integration is often implemented through the use of integration frameworks or through custom coding of interfaces.

Personal Productivity Tools

Personal productivity tools are a collection of software applications that enhance the development environment for the individual developer. These applications are typically integrated suites of PC software that allow the developer to work on the workstation independent of the development server or mainframe to complete tasks such as analysis and documentation. These tools are basic office automation software and include spreadsheet software, word processing software, graphics software (e.g., drawing, diagramming, and presentation), and personal calendar software.

Quality Management Tools

Quality management is a management discipline that promotes a customer satisfaction focus and continuous improvement. Quality management tools support the planning and measurement of quality. These tools include quality function deployment tools, measurement and metrics tools, statistical process control tools, and continuous improvement tools.

System Building Tools

System building tools comprise the core of the development architecture and are used to design, build, and test the system. All the system building tools must be integrated and share development objects appropriately. These include:

- Analysis and Design tools
- Reverse Engineering tools
- Construction tools
- Testing tools
- Configuration Management tools

Environment Management Tools

A netcentric development environment is complex and sophisticated. It supports many different functional and technical requirements (illustrated by the Execution Architecture), many different development teams, and tools from many different product vendors, and often must support projects in different stages of the development life cycle. These tools monitor performance, provide help desk support, manage and distribute changes to the development environment, administer the environment, and track and plan development environment capacity.

Environment Management tools include

- Service Management tools
- Systems Management tools
- Managing Change tools
- Service Planning tools

Program and Project Management Tools

Program and project management are usually differentiated by the size of the effort; programs are typically composed of more than one project. Similarly, the program and project management tools are differentiated by the ability to support multiple projects, complex functions, and adequate performance when supporting multiple concurrent projects.

Program and project management tools provide many key features that assist project planners in planning, scheduling, tracking, and reporting on project segments, tasks, and milestones.

These tools include

- Planning tools
- Scheduling tools
- Tracking tools
- Reporting tools

Team Productivity Tools

Team productivity tools are used to make the work cell and project team as a whole more productive. Instead of the software residing on the individual's PC or workstation, these tools typically are LAN based and shared by the project members. These tools are focused on enhancing communication and information sharing.

These tools include:

- E-mail
- Teamware
- Publishing tools
- Group calendars
- Methodology browsing tools

Information Management

Information management of the development architecture is provided through an integrated development repository. At this level of integration, tools share a common repository of development objects, design documents, source code, and test plans and data. Ideally, the repository would be a single database with an all-encompassing information model. Practically, the repository must be built by integrating the repositories of the different development tools through interfaces. Tool vendors may also build part of the integrated repository by integrating specific products.

The repository includes:

- Folder management
- Repository management

OPERATIONS ARCHITECTURE

An operations architecture is a combination of tools, support services, procedures, and controls required to keep a production system up and running well. It differs from an execution architecture in that its primary users are systems administrators and production support personnel. Exhibit 6 shows the framework used throughout this book to illustrate the operations architecture. It depicts a set of tools supporting the execution and development architectures.

The major tool categories of the operations architecture include the following.

Software Distribution

Software distribution is the automated delivery to, and installation of, applications and systems software on servers and end user devices (e.g., workstations, kiosks, etc.). This can be for an organization's internal computing environment as well as for its extended one, i.e., its business partners and customers. The architectural support required to support software distribution is largely driven by the number of workstations, servers, and geographic locations to be served.

Configuration and Asset Management

To manage a netcentric environment successfully, one must have a solid understanding of *what* is *where*, and one must maintain rigor in the change control procedures that govern modifications to the environment. Configuration and asset management information that may need to be tracked includes such details as product licensing information, warranty information, vendor names, logical and physical device information (such as total capacity and current utilization), product configuration tracking, software

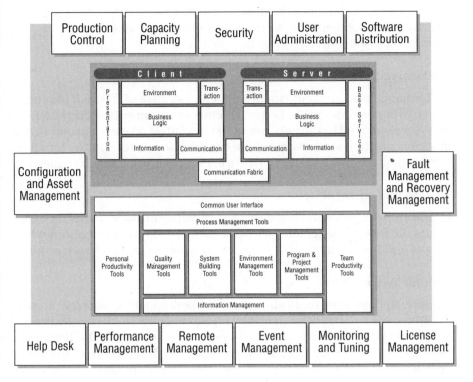

Exhibit 6. Operations Architecture Framework.

and data version levels, network configuration parameters, physical location, and perhaps accounting information.

Fault Management and Recovery Management

The fault management services of an operations architecture assist in the diagnosis and correction of system faults. Faults may include network-, server-, workstation-, or even application-level faults. Fault diagnosis may require services for isolation; viewing of host, server, and workstation error logs; and determining the software and data versions and configurations of affected machines.

Capacity Planning

Capacity planning tools focus on components of an environment such as the network, physical space, and processing power to understand the need to change the capacity of those components based on organizational changes. The tools typically focus on components that are considered to be heavily sensitive to changes in computing resource usage. The tools may use historical management data combined with estimates for growth or changes to configuration to simulate the ability of different system configurations to meet capacity needs.

Performance Management

Performance management is more difficult because of the lack of tools to assist with performance in heterogeneous environments. Performance is no longer confined to the network or to the central processing unit. Performance needs to be viewed in an end-to-end manner, accounting for all the factors that affect the system's performance relative to a user request.

License Management

In addition to guaranteeing compliance with software licensing agreements, license management provides valuable information about which people and how many people are actually using a given software product.

Remote Management

Remote Management tools allow support personnel to "control" a user's desktop over a network so that they do not need to be physically present at a workstation to diagnose problems. Once control of the desktop is established, screen updates for the controlled desktop are displayed at both locations. The support person is then effectively sitting at the workstation he or she controls and can do necessary diagnostics.

Event Management

In addition to hardware devices, applications and systems software also generates events. Common event-handling mechanisms are required to provide information to management in a simple, consistent format, and to forward information on important events for management purposes.

Monitoring and Tuning

The number of devices and the geographic disparity of devices in a netcentric environment increase the effort required to monitor the system. The number of events generated in the system rises due to the increased complexity. Devices such as client machines, network components, and servers generate events on startup or failure to periodically report device status.

Security

The security concerns of netcentric environments have been widely publicized. Although requirements for netcentric security architectures are constantly evolving as new security breaches are discovered, there are many tools categories that can help provide reasonable levels of security.

User Administration

The netcentric environment introduces many new challenges to the task of user administration. The majority of these stem once again from the dramatically increased number of system components. Adding a user to the system may require adding a user to the network, one or more server operating systems, one or more database systems (so that the user can access data), an e-mail system, and an existing host-based system.

Production Control

Scheduling processes across a distributed environment can be quite complex, requiring significant management effort to ensure that the processes run smoothly. Many other day-to-day activities become more difficult in a distributed environment, including print management, file transfer and control, mass storage management, backup and restore, archiving, and system startup and shutdown.

Help Desk

As netcentric computing puts the operations Help Desk closer to the "end user" in terms of visibility and influence, the Help Desk will need to become integrated with the business processes being supported through netcentric. Unless the operations Help Desk is well integrated with the business process, there is risk that the user may be given information that is incorrect, forwarded to the wrong department, or otherwise mishandled. It is also important that the information collected by the Help Desk about a user be properly shared with other stakeholders in the business process.

EXECUTION ARCHITECTURE

The netcentric Execution Architecture Framework identifies those common, run-time services required when an application executes in a netcentric environment. The services can be broken down into logical areas: Presentation Services, Information Services, Communication Services, Communication Fabric Services, Transaction Services, Environment Services, Base Services, and Business Logic (Exhibit 7).

As shown in the figure, the netcentric execution architecture is best represented as an extension to a client/server execution architecture. The figure shows the logical representation of a requester and a provider, designated by the "Client" and the "Server." Although the figure shows only one "Client" and one "Server," a physical implementation of an execution architecture typically has many clients and many servers. Thus, the services described here can be located on one physical machine but most likely will span many physical machines, as shown in Exhibit 8.

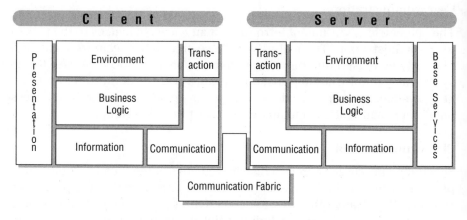

Exhibit 7. Netcentric Execution Architecture.

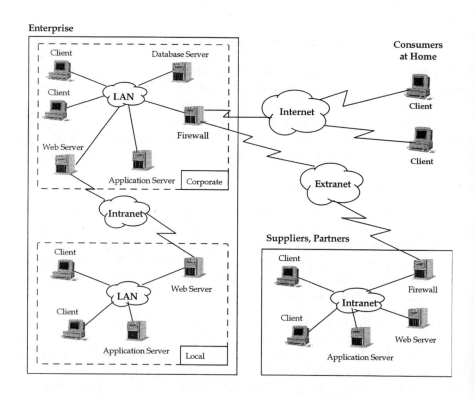

Exhibit 8. Execution Architecture: Physical Picture.

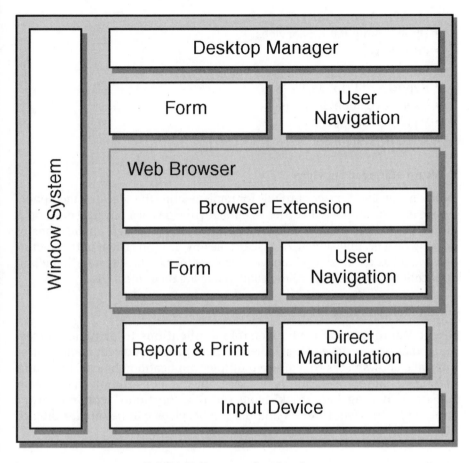

Exhibit 9. Presentation Services.

This section provides an overview of the services and subservices within the execution architecture. More detailed information is provided in the chapters devoted to each of these services in Section II.

PRESENTATION SERVICES

Presentation services (Exhibit 9) enable an application to manage the human–computer interface, including capturing user actions and generating resulting events, presenting data to the user, and assisting in the management of the dialog flow of processing. Typically, presentation services are required only by client workstations.

The major presentation services are:

- Desktop Manager Services
- Direct Manipulation Services
- Form Services
- Input Devices Services
- Report and Print Services
- User Navigation Services
- Web Browser Services
- Window System Services

Desktop Manager Services

Desktop Manager Services provide for implementing the "desktop metaphor," a style of user interface that tries to emulate the idea of a physical desktop. It allows the user to place documents on the desktop, launch applications by clicking on a graphical icon, or discard files by dragging them onto a picture of a wastebasket. Desktop Manager Services include facilities for launching applications and desktop utilities and managing their integration.

Direct Manipulation Services

Direct Manipulation Services enable applications to provide a direct manipulation interface (often called "drag & drop"). A direct manipulation interface allows users to manage multiple "application objects" by manipulating visual representations of those objects. For example, a user may sell stock by dragging "stock" icons out of a "portfolio" icon and onto a "trading floor" icon. Direct Manipulation Services can be further divided into Display and Input/Validation.

Form Services

Form services enable applications to use fields to display and collect data. A field may be a traditional 3270-style field used to display or input textual data, or it may be a graphical field, such as a check box, a list box, or an image. Form services provide support for display, input/validation, mapping support, and field interaction management.

Input Devices

Input devices detect user input from a variety of input technologies, such as pen–based, voice recognition, touchscreen, mouse, and digital camera.

Report and Print Services

Report and Print Services support the creation and on-screen previewing of paper or photographic documents which contain screen data, application data, graphics, or images.

User Navigation Services

User Navigation Services provide a user with a way to access or navigate between functions within or across applications. Historically, this has been the role of a text-based menuing system that provides a list of applications or activities for the user to choose from. However, client/server technologies introduced new navigation metaphors. A common method for allowing a user to navigate within an application is to list available functions or information by means of a menu bar with associated pull-down menus or context-sensitive pop-up menus.

Web Browser Services

Web Browser Services allow users to view and interact with applications and documents made up of varying data types such as text, graphics, and audio. These services also provide support for navigation within and across documents no matter where they are located through the use of links embedded into the document content. Web Browser Services retain the link connection, i.e., document physical location, and mask the complexities of that connection from the user.

Web Browser services can be further subdivided into:

- Browser Extension Services
- Form Services
- User Navigation Services

Browser Extension Services

Browser Extension Services provide support for executing different types of applications from within abrowser. These applications provide functionality that extend browser capabilities. The key browser extensions are plug-ins, helper/application viewers, Java applets, Active/X controls, and JavaBeans.

Form Services

Like Form Services outside the web browser, Form Services within the web browser enable applications to use fields to display and collect data. The only difference is the technology used to develop the forms. The most common type of forms within a browser is Hypertext Markup Language (HTML).

User Navigation Services

Like User Navigation Services outside the web browser, User Navigation Services within the web browser provide a user with a way to access or navigate between functions within or across applications. These User Navigation Services can be subdivided into three categories: Hyperlink, Customized Menu, and Virtual Reality.

Window System

Typically part of the operating systems, Window System Services provide the base functionality for creating and managing a GUI: detecting user actions, manipulating windows on the display, and displaying information through windows and graphical controls.

INFORMATION SERVICES

Information Services (Exhibit 10) manage information assets and enable applications to access and manipulate data stored locally or remotely from documents, databases, or external data sources. They minimize an application's dependence on physical storage and location within the network. Information services may also be used directly by the end user when ad hoc data and document access are integral to the application work task. Information Services are grouped into two primary categories:

- Database Services
- Document Services

Database Services

Database services are responsible for providing access to a local or remote database as well as maintaining integrity of the data within the database. These services also support the ability to store data on either a single physical platform or, in some cases, across multiple platforms. These services are typically provided by database management system (DBMS) vendors and accessed via embedded or call-level SQL variants and supersets. Depending upon the underlying storage model, non-SQL access methods may be used instead.

Database Services include:

- Storage Services
- Indexing Services
- Security Services
- Access Services
- Replication/Synchronization Services

Storage Services

Storage Services manage physical data storage. These services provide a mechanism for saving information so that data will live beyond program execution. Data are often stored in relational format (an RDBMS) but may also be stored in an object-oriented format (OODBMS) or other structures such as IMS and VSAM.

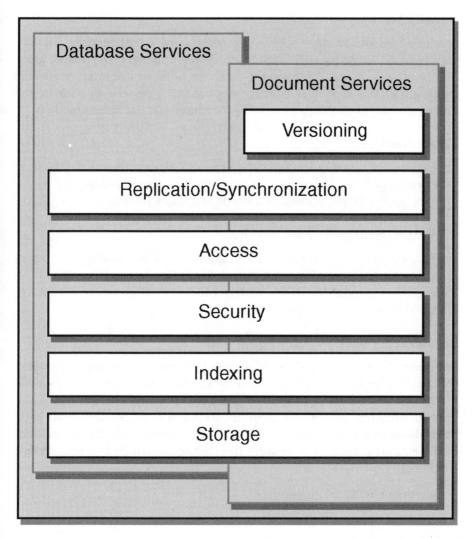

Exhibit 10. Information Services.

Indexing Services

Indexing Services provide a mechanism for speeding up data retrieval. In relational databases one or more fields can be used to construct the index. Therefore, when a user searches for a specific record rather than scanning the whole table sequentially, the index is used to find the location of that record faster.

Security Services

Security Services enforce access control to ensure that records are only visible or editable by authorized people for approved purposes. Most DBMSs provide access control at the database, table, or row levels to specific users and groups as well as concurrency control. They also provide execution control for such things as stored procedures and database functions.

Access Services

Access Services enable an application to retrieve data from a database as well as manipulate (insert, update, or delete) data in a database. SQL is the primary approach for accessing records in today's DBMSs.

Replication/Synchronization Services

Replication Services support an environment in which multiple copies of databases must be maintained. Synchronization Services perform the transactions required to make consistent information sources that are intended to mirror each other.

Document Services

Document Services provide similar structure and control for documents that DBMSs apply to record-oriented data. A document is defined as a collection of objects of potentially different types (e.g., structured data, unstructured text, images, or multimedia) that a business user deals with. Regardless of the software used to create and maintain the component parts, all parts together constitute the document, which is managed as a single entity.

Document Services include:

- Storage Services
- Indexing Services
- Security Services
- Access Services
- Replication/Synchronization Services
- Versioning Services

Storage Services

Storage Services manage the physical storage of documents. Generally, the documents are stored in a repository using one of the following methods: proprietary database, industry standard database, or industry standard database and file system.

Indexing Services

Locating documents and content within documents is a complex problem and involves several alternative methods. Most document management products provide index services that support searching document repositories by the methods of attribute search, full-text search, context search, or Boolean search.

Security Services

Documents should be accessed exclusively through the document management backbone. If a document is checked in, checked out, routed, viewed, annotated, archived, or printed, it should be done only by authorized users. Security services control access at the user, role, and group levels.

Access Services

Access Services support document creation, deletion, maintenance, and retrieval. These services allow users to capture knowledge or content through the creation of unstructured information, such as documents. Access Services also allow users to effectively retrieve documents they created, and documents that were created by others.

Versioning Services

These services maintain a historical record of the changes to a document over time. By maintaining this record, versioning services allow for the recreation of a document as it looked at any given point in time during its evolution.

COMMUNICATION SERVICES

Communication Services enable an application to interact transparently with other applications regardless of whether they reside on the same computer or on a remote computer.

There are five primary communications services categories (Exhibit 11):

- Core Messaging Services
- Specialized Messaging Services
- Communications Security Services
- Virtual Resource Services
- Directory Services

Core Messaging Services

Broadly defined, messaging is sending information or commands between two or more recipients. Recipients may be computers, people, or processes within a computer. To send this message, a protocol (or in some

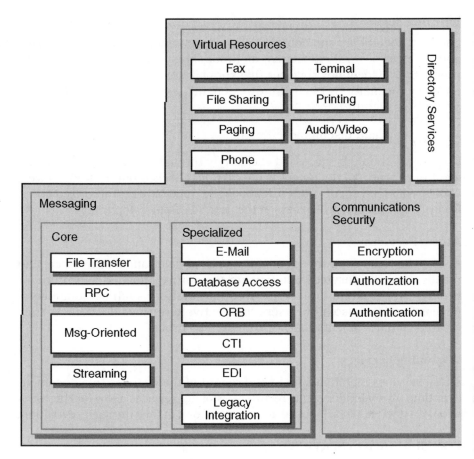

Exhibit 11. Communication Services.

cases, multiple protocols) is used that both the sender and receiver can understand. A protocol is a set of rules describing, in technical terms, how two end points should exchange information. Protocols exist at several levels during the exchange of information. Protocols facilitate transport of the message carrying the information. Both end points must recognize and observe the protocol. As an example, a common protocol in today's networks is the TCP/IP protocol.

Core messaging services can further be divided into the following services:

- *File Transfer Services.* File Transfer Services enable the copying and receiving of files or other large blocks of data between two resources.

- *Remote procedure call (RPC) services.* RPCs are a type of protocol by which an application sends a request to a remote system to execute a designated procedure using supplied arguments and return the result.
- *Message-Oriented Services.* Message-Oriented Services refers to the process of distributing data and control through the exchange of records known as messages. Message-Oriented Services provide the application developer with a set of simple verbs (e.g., connect, send, receive, and disconnect) that are used to exchange information with other distributed applications.
- *Streaming Services.* Streaming is the process of transferring time-sensitive data streams (e.g., video and/or audio) in real time. Streaming differs from the other types of core messaging services in that it delivers a continuous, one-way stream of data rather than the relatively short messages associated with RPC and Message-Oriented messaging, or the large, batch transfers associated with File Transfer. Streaming may be used to deliver video, audio, and other real-time content across the Internet or within enterprise networks.

Specialized Messaging Services

Specialized Messaging Services extend the Core Messaging Services to provide additional functionality. Specialized Messaging Services may extend Core Messaging Services in the following general ways:

- Provide messaging among specialized systems by drawing upon basic messaging capabilities
- Define specialized message layouts
- Define specialized intersystem protocols
- Suggest ways in which messaging draws upon directory and security services to deliver a complete messaging environment

Specialized Messaging Services is comprised of the following subservices:

- *E-Mail Messaging.* E-Mail Messaging services reliably exchange messages using the store-and-forward messaging style. E-Mail message systems traditionally include a rudimentary form of directory services
- *Computer-Telephone Integration (CTI) Messaging.* CTI integrates computer systems and telephone systems to coordinate data and telephony activities. CTI Messaging has two primary functions: device-specific communication and message mapping.
- *EDI (Electronic Data Interchange) Messaging.* EDI supports system-to-system messaging among business partners by defining standard message layouts. Companies typically use EDI to streamline commercial transactions within their supply chains.
- *Object Request Broker (ORB) Messaging.* ORB Messaging enables objects to transparently make requests of and receive responses from

other objects located locally or remotely. Objects communicate through an ORB. An ORB enables client objects to access server objects either locally or remotely over a network and invoke operations (i.e., functions and methods) on them.

- *Database Access Messaging.* Database Messaging services (also known as Database Access Middleware or DBAM) provide connectivity for clients to access databases throughout the enterprise.
- *Legacy Integration Messaging.* Legacy services provide gateways to mainframe legacy systems.

Communications Security Services

Communications Security Services control access to network-attached resources. Combining network Security Services with security services in other parts of the system architecture (e.g., application and database layers) results in robust security.

Communications Security Services are broken down into the following three categories:

- *Encryption Services.* Encryption services encrypt data prior to network transfer to prevent unauthorized interception.
- *Authorization Services.* When a user requests access to network resources, Authorization Services determines if the user has the appropriate permissions and either allows or disallows the access.
- *Authentication Services.* Authentication services verify network access requests by validating that users are who they claim to be. For secure systems, one or more authentication mechanisms can be used to validate authorized users and to verify which functions and data they have access to.

Virtual Resource Services

Virtual Resource Services proxy or mimic the capabilities of specialized, network-connected resources. This allows a generic network node to emulate a specialized physical device. In this way, network users can interface with a variety of specialized resources.

A common example of a Virtual Resource service is the capability to print to a network printer as if it were directly attached to a workstation.

Virtual Resource services include:

- *Terminal Services.* Terminal services allow a client to connect to a nonlocal host via a network and to emulate the profile (e.g., the keyboard and screen characteristics) required by the host application.
- *Print Services.* Print services connect network workstations to shared printers.

- *File Sharing Services.* File Sharing Services allow users to view, manage, read, and write files that may be located on a variety of platforms in a variety of locations.
- *Phone Services.* Phone virtual resource services extend telephony capabilities to computer platforms.
- *Fax Services.* Fax Services provide for the management of both inbound and outbound fax transmissions.
- *Audio/Video Services.* Audio/Video Services allow nodes to interact with multimedia data streams. These services may be implemented as audio only, video only, or combined audio/video.
- *Paging Services.* Paging virtual resource services provide the message formatting and display functionality that allows network nodes to interface with wireless paging systems.

Directory Services

Managing information about network resources involves a variety of processes ranging from simple name/address resolution to the logical integration of heterogeneous systems to create a common view of services, security, etc. This breadth of functionality is discussed as part of Directory Services.

Because of their ability to unify and manage distributed environments, Directory Services play a key role in locating and accessing resources in a network, including Internet/intranet architectures.

COMMUNICATIONS FABRIC SERVICES

As communications networks become increasingly complicated and interconnected, the services provided by the network itself have by necessity increased as well. Clients and servers are rarely directly connected to one another but are commonly separated by a network of routers, servers, and firewalls, providing an ever-increasing number of network services such as address resolution, message routing, and security screening.

The communications fabric extends the client/server computing model by placing intelligence into the physical network, acknowledging the network as a sort of standalone system that provides intelligent shared network services. There is certainly overlap between services typically thought of as part of a client/server architecture and services increasingly provided by the network itself.

Communications Fabric Services is comprised of two subservices: Transport Services and Network Media Services (Exhibit 12).

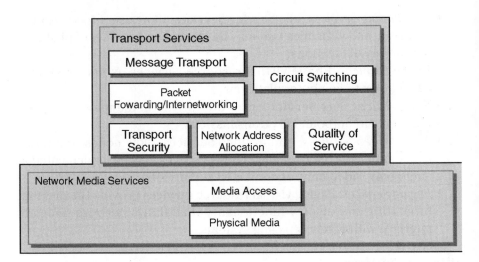

Exhibit 12. Communications Fabric Services.

Transport Services

Transport Services are responsible for establishing, maintaining, and terminating end-to-end communications between users and processes. Connection management provides transfer services that ensure the delivery of data from sender to receiver, which support the transferring of messages from a process running on one machine to a process running on another. In addition, connection management provides services that initiate a connection, gracefully terminate a connection, and handle abrupt termination. These services take place for application before and after the data are formatted for transport over the network.

Transport Services include

- *Message Transport Services.* These are responsible for the end-to-end delivery of messages. They can include functionalities such as end-to-end data transfer, connection control, reliable transfer, flow control, and multiplexing.
- *Packet Forwarding/Internetworking Services.* The Packet Forwarding/Internetworking Service transfers data packets and manages the path that data take through the network. It includes functionalities such as fragmentation/reassembly, addressing, routing, switching, and multicasting.
- *Circuit Switching Services.* Where Message Transport Services and Packet Forwarding/Internetworking Services support the transfer of packetized data, Circuit Switching Services establish physical circuits for the transfer of such things as circuit-switched voice, fax, and video.

- *Transport Security Services.* Transport Security Services (within the Transport Services layer) perform encryption and filtering.
- *Network Address Allocation Services.* Network Address Allocation Services manage the distribution of addresses to network nodes. This provides more flexibility compared to having all nodes assigned static addresses.
- *Quality of Service (QoS) Services.* QoS Services deliver a defined network throughput for designated traffic by allocating dedicated bandwidth, prioritizing data traffic, etc.

Network Media Services

The Network Media layer provides the following capabilities:

- Final framing of data for interfacing with the physical network
- Receiving, interpreting, and acting on signals from the communications fabric
- Transferring data through the physical network

Network Media Services performs two primary service functions:

- *Media Access Services.* Media Access Services manage the low-level transfer of data between network nodes. These services provide functions such as physical addressing, packet transfer, shared access, flow control, error recovery, and encryption.
- *Physical Media Services.* The Physical Media includes both the physical connectors and the physical media (wired or wireless).

ENVIRONMENT SERVICES

Environment Services provide miscellaneous application and system level services that do not deal directly with managing the user interface, communicating to other programs, or accessing data (Exhibit 13).

Runtime Services

Runtime Services convert noncompiled computer languages into machine code during the execution of a program. Two subservices comprise Runtime Services: language interpreter and virtual machine.

- *Language Interpreter Services.* Language Interpreter Services decompose a fourth generation or scripting language into machine code (executable code) at runtime.
- *Virtual Machine Services.* Typically, a Virtual Machine is implemented in software on top of an operating system and is used to run applications. The Virtual Machine provides a layer of abstraction between the applications and the underlying operating system and is often used to support operating system independence.

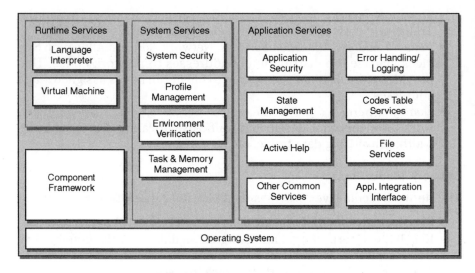

Exhibit 13. Environment Services.

System Services

System Services are services that applications can use to perform system-level functions. These services include:

- *System Security Services* allow applications to interact with the operating system's native security mechanism. The basic services include the ability to login, logoff, authenticate to the operating system, and enforce access control to system resources and executables.
- *Profile Management Services* are used to access and update local or remote system, user, or application profiles. User profiles, for example, can be used to store a variety of information from a user's language and color preferences to basic job function information that may be used by Integrated Performance Support or Workflow Services.
- *Task and Memory Management Services* allow applications and/or other events to control individual computer tasks or processes and manage memory. They provide services for scheduling, starting, stopping, and restarting both client and server tasks (e.g., software agents).
- *Environment Verification Services* ensure functionality by monitoring, identifying, and validating environment integrity prior and during program execution. (e.g., free disk space, monitor resolution, and correct version).

Application Services

Application Services are miscellaneous services that applications can use for common functions. These common functions can apply to one application or can be used across applications. They include:

- *Applications Security Services.* Besides system level security such as logging into the network, there are additional security services associated with specific applications, including user access services, data access services, and function access services.
- *Error Handling/Logging Services.* Error Handling Services support the handling of fatal and nonfatal hardware and software errors for an application. Logging Services support the logging of informational, error, and warning messages.
- *State Management Services.* State Management Services enable information to be passed or shared among windows or web pages or across programs.
- *Codes Table Services.* Codes Table Services enable applications to utilize externally stored parameters and validation rules.
- *Active Help Services.* Active Help Services enable an application to provide assistance to a user for a specific task or set of tasks.
- *File Services.*
- *Application Integration Interface Services.* An Application Integration Interface provides a method or gateway for passing context and control of information to an external application.
- *Other Common Services.* This is a catchall category for additional reusable routines useful across a set of applications (e.g., Date Routines, Time Zone Conversions, and Field Validation Routines).

Component Framework Services

Component Framework Services provide an infrastructure for building components so that they can communicate within an application and across applications, on the same machine or on multiple machines across a network, to work together. COM/DCOM and CORBA are the two leading component industry standards. These standards define how components should be built and how they should communicate.

Operating System Services

Operating System Services are the underlying services such as multitasking, paging, memory allocation, etc., typically provided by today's modern operating systems. Where necessary, an additional layer or APIs may be provided to gain either operating system independence or a higher level of abstraction for application programmers.

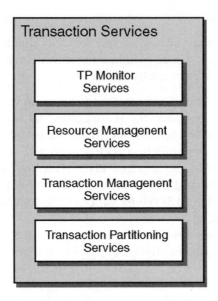

Exhibit 14. Transaction Services.

TRANSACTION SERVICES

Transaction Services provide the transaction integrity mechanism for the application. This allows all data activities within a single business event to be grouped as a single, logical unit of work.

In small- to moderate-scale environments of fewer than 150 simultaneous users on a single server, this service may be provided by the DBMS software with its restart/recovery and integrity capabilities. For larger client/server environments, an emerging class of software, referred to as "distributed online transaction managers," might be more applicable. These transaction managers provide sharing of server processes across a large community of users and can be more efficient than the DBMSs.

Transactions Services include (Exhibit 14):

- TP Monitor Services
- Resource Management Services
- Transaction Management Services
- Transaction Partitioning Services

TP Monitor Services

The TP Services are the primary interface through which applications invoke Transaction Services and receive status and error information. TP Services, in conjunction with Information Access and Communication Services, provide for load balancing across processors or machines and location transparency for distributed transaction processing.

Resource Management Services

A Resource Manager provides for concurrency control and integrity for a singular data resource (e.g., a database or a file system). Integrity is guaranteed by ensuring that an update is completed correctly and entirely or not at all. Resource Management Services use locking, commit, and rollback services and are integrated with Transaction Management Services.

Transaction Management Services

Transaction Management Services coordinate transactions across one or more resource managers either on a single machine or multiple machines within the network. Transaction Management Services ensure that all resources for a transaction are updated or, in the case of an update failure on any one resource, all updates are rolled back. This service allows multiple applications to share data with integrity.

Transaction Partitioning Services

Transaction Partitioning Services provide support for mapping a single logical transaction in an application into the required multiple physical transactions. For example, in a package- or legacy-rich environment, the single logical transaction of changing a customer address may require the partitioning and coordination of several physical transactions to multiple application systems or databases. Transaction Partitioning Services provide the application with a simple, single transaction view.

BASE SERVICES

Base Services provide support for delivering applications to a wide variety of users over the Internet, intranet, and extranet. Base Services include: Web Server Services, Push/Pull Services, Batch Services, Report Services, and Workflow Services (Exhibit 15).

Web Server Services

Web Server Services enable organizations to manage and publish information and deploy netcentric applications over the Internet and intranet environments. These services support:

- Managing documents in most formats such as HTML, Microsoft Word, etc.
- Handling of client requests for HTML pages
- Processing scripts such as Common Gateway Interface (CGI) or Active Server Pages (ASP)
- Caching web pages

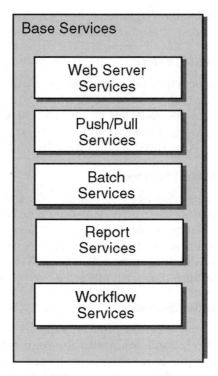

Exhibit 15. Base Services.

Push/Pull Services

Push/Pull Services allow for interest in a particular piece of information to be registered and then changes or new information to be communicated to the subscriber list. Depending upon requirements, synchronous or asynchronous push/pull services may be required. Synchronous push/pull services provide a mechanism for applications to be notified in real time if a subscribed item changes (e.g., a stock ticker). Asynchronous push/pull services do not require that a session-like connection be present between the subscriber and the information.

Batch Services

Batch processing is used to perform large-scale repetitive processing where no user involvement is required, as well as reporting. Areas for design attention include scheduling, recovery/restart, use of job streams, and high availability (e.g., 24-hour running). In addition, close attention must be paid to performance as batch systems usually must be processed within strict batch windows.

Batch Services are comprised of the following subservices:

- *Driver Services.* These services provide the control structure and framework for batch programs. They are also referred to as "Batch Scheduling Services."
- *Restart/Recovery Services.* These services are used to automatically recover and restart batch programs if they should fail during execution.
- *Batch Balancing Services.* These services support the tracking of run-to-run balances and totals for the batch system.
- *Report Services.* Project reporting tools are used to summarize and communicate information, using either printed paper or online reports.

Report Services

Report Services are facilities for simplifying the construction and delivery of reports or generated correspondence. These services help to define reports and to electronically route reports to allow for online review, printing, and/or archiving. Report Services also support the merging of application data with predefined templates to create letters or other printed correspondence. Report Services include:

- Driver Services
- Report Definition Services
- Report Built Services
- Report Distribution Services

Workflow Services

Workflow Services control and coordinate the tasks that must be completed to process a business event. Workflow enables tasks within a business process to be passed to the appropriate participants in the correct sequence, and facilitates their completion within set times and budgets. Task definition includes the actions required as well as work folders containing forms, documents, images, and transactions. It uses business process rules, routing information, role definitions, and queues.

Workflow provides a mechanism to define, monitor, and control the sequence of work electronically. These services are typically provided by the server as they often coordinate activities among multiple users on multiple computers.

Workflow can be further divided into the following components:

- *Role Management Services.* These provide for the assignment of tasks to roles that can then be mapped to individuals.

- *Route Management Services.* These enable the routing of tasks to the next role.
- *Rule Management Services.* Rule Management Services support the routing of workflow activities by providing the intelligence necessary to determine which routes are appropriate given the state of a given process and knowledge of the organization's workflow processing rules.
- *Queue Management Services.* These services provide access to the workflow queues that are used to schedule work.

BUSINESS LOGIC

Business Logic is the core of any application, providing the expression of business rules and procedures (e.g., the steps and rules that govern how a sales order is fulfilled). As such, Business Logic includes the control structure that specifies the flow for processing business events and user requests.

The execution architecture services described thus far are all generalized services designed to support the application's Business Logic. How Business Logic is to be organized is not within the scope of the execution architecture and must be determined based upon the characteristics of the application system to be developed. This section is intended to serve as a reminder of the importance of consciously designing a structure for Business Logic that helps to isolate the impacts of change, and to point out that the underlying netcentric architecture is particularly well suited for enabling the packaging of Business Logic as components.

There are many ways in which to organize Business Logic, including rules-based, object-oriented, components, and structured programming. However, each of these techniques include common concepts, which we can group as Interface, Application Logic, and Data Abstraction (Exhibit 16).

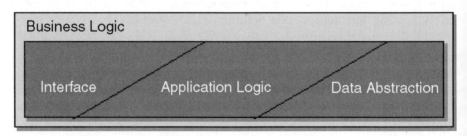

Exhibit 16. Business Logic.

Interface

Interface logic interprets and maps the actions of users into business logic processing activities. With the assistance of Presentation Services, interface logic provides the linkage that allows users to control the flow of processing within the application.

Application Logic

Application Logic is the expression of business rules and procedures (e.g., the steps and rules that govern how a sales order is fulfilled). As such, the Application Logic includes the control structure that specifies the flow for processing for business events and user requests. The isolation of control logic facilitates change and adaptability of the application to changing business processing flows.

Data Abstraction

Information Access Services isolate the Business Logic from the technical specifics of how information is stored (e.g., location transparency, RDBMS syntax, etc.). Data Abstraction provides the application with a more logical view of information, further insulating the application from physical information storage considerations.

The developers of business logic should be shielded from the details and complexity of other architecture services (e.g., information services or component services), and other business logic for that matter.

It is important to decide whether the business logic will be separate from the presentation logic and the database access logic. Today, separation of business logic into its own tier is often done using an application server. In this type of an environment, although some business rules such as field validation might still be tightly coupled with the presentation logic, the majority of business logic is separate, usually residing on the server. It is also important to decide whether the business logic should be packaged as components to maximize software reuse and to streamline software distribution.

Another factor to consider is how the business logic is distributed between the client and the server(s) — where the business logic is stored and where the business logic is located when the application is being executed. There are several ways to distribute business logic:

1. Business logic can be stored on the server(s) and executed on the server(s).
2. Business logic can be stored on the server(s) and executed on the client.

3. Business logic can be stored and executed on the client.
4. Some business logic can be stored and executed on the server(s), and some business logic can be stored and executed on the client.

Having the business logic stored on the server enables developers to centrally maintain application code, thereby eliminating the need to distribute software to client machines when changes to the business logic occur. If all the business logic executes on the server, the application on the client will make requests to the server whenever it needs to execute a business function. This could increase network traffic, which may degrade application performance. On the other hand, having the business logic execute on the client may require longer load times when the application is initially launched. However, once the application is loaded, most processing is done on the client until synchronization with the server is needed. This type of an architecture might introduce complexities into the application that deal with the sharing of and reliance on central data across many users.

If the business logic is stored and executed on the client, software distribution options must be considered. Usually the most expensive option is to have a system administrator or the user physically install new applications and update existing applications on each client machine. Another option is to use a tool that performs automatic software distribution functions. However, this option usually requires the software distribution tool to be loaded first on each client machine. Another option is to package the application into ActiveX controls, utilizing the automatic install/update capabilities available with ActiveX controls — if the application is launched from a web browser.

Currently, Internet applications house the majority of the business processing logic on the server, supporting the thin-client model. However, as technology evolves, this balance is beginning to shift, allowing business logic code bundled into components to be either downloaded at runtime or permanently stored on the client machine. Today, client-side business logic is supported through the use of Java applets, JavaBeans, plug-ins and JavaScript from Sun/Netscape, and ActiveX controls and VBScript from Microsoft.

CONCLUSION

To operate optimally in the world of architectures, it is vital to remember a key point: one should not dwell too long at the abstract level. One can get mired in representations, in logical arguments. Pictures are important, but an architecture must be looked at pragmatically. It lives and breathes. It may evolve as the organization evolves. Yet, without the common understandings, common terminology, and common direction provided by architecture frameworks, project teams are putting their entire organizations at risk.

Chapter 5
Information Services
Andersen Consulting

"Information" in today's client/server and netcentric environment is much broader and diverse in nature than traditional data, that is, data that were understood as characters. Information, or "knowledge," as we characterized it in the introduction to this book, can consist of many things in today's computing solutions, including graphics, image, voice, and full-motion video. This information is extremely complex and difficult to manage, control, and deliver.

The information challenge of the workplace today is the "feast-or-famine" syndrome: workers often cannot find information when they need it, or they may be confronted by too much information at any given time. Information is of no use unless we know where it is and how to get at it. Information Services are where that access is achieved. (Note that although there are many useful distinctions to be made among the words "data," "information," and "knowledge," this chapter will use both the words data and information to refer to the knowledge or content being managed in a netcentric environment.)

In a traditional computing environment, an organization's information is usually centralized in a particular location, or it may be fragmented across multiple locations. In a netcentric environment, however, information is most often distributed because distribution of processors and data is an inherent part of the new styles of netcentric computing.

Exhibit 1 presents an example of how information may be distributed in a netcentric computing environment. In this example from an airline information system, the reservations are centralized in Dallas. Each region has a server to maintain its own flights and maintenance information (horizontally segmented by region), and each workstation at each region maintains replicated airport and plane data. In general, the following may be said about the information within this system:

- Information that is stable or static is often found on all clients.
- Information that is volatile or specific to particular locations or groups is on the server.

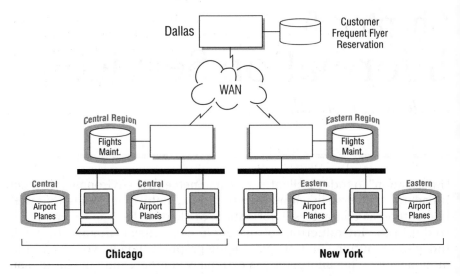

Exhibit 1. Example of Distribution of Information.

- Information that is accessed and updated throughout the organization is on the central system or the enterprise system.
- Most information (except, perhaps, for some static codes tables) is stored on the server, although the processing may be distributed across client and server.
- Putting information on a client may require information replication across clients (usually limited to codes tables) and could lead to synchronization and integrity issues.

CHARACTERISTICS OF INFORMATION IN NETCENTRIC COMPUTING

The example illustrates the primary characteristics of information in a client/server and netcentric computing environment.

Information Is Distinct from Processes

The most important characteristic of information is that it is kept distinct from the processes that access and use it. The chief function of the netcentric architecture is to isolate the business logic from the technology itself. Within the Information Services component of the architecture this isolation is achieved by maintaining two layers, a logical layer and a physical layer.

- From a logical viewpoint, an application issues a request for information, and elements of that information (e.g., location, formats, and management mechanisms) are transparent to the user. A single infor-

mation request is all that is necessary to retrieve the information, potentially from multiple sources, to support a business function.
- From a physical viewpoint, the information may actually be stored on, and retrieved from, many different sources that are being managed by many different database managers on many different platforms.

Information Is Usually Distributed

Distributed information can be defined formally as "information that is physically separated between locations or platforms." Netcentric computing does not imply distributed information nor does distributed information imply netcentric computing. However, most client/server and netcentric systems rely on some form of distributed information.

Client/server and netcentric computing implies more processing locations (geographic and platform) with local disk storage capabilities. Because information should reside close to the users who need to access that information, information distribution offers important advantages that will be discussed subsequently.

Information Is Spread across Multiple Environments

Because of the distributed nature of information in a netcentric computing environment, organizations often have to deal with a multivendor environment. This places demands on the networking and communications aspects of the netcentric architecture.

Information Is in Multiple Forms

The graphical environment of today's applications and the ability to send different types of information (e.g., data, graphic, image, voice, or video) directly to the desktop have made the information environment of client/server and netcentric computing much more complex.

Information May Be Replicated or Duplicated

Because information is generally distributed in the netcentric architecture, it often means that information must be replicated across multiple locations. The existence of multiple copies of information means that users must be especially concerned with keeping them synchronized and accurate.

Replication of information implies methods to perform the replication, additional disk resources, possible integrity problems because of multiple copies, and information management and ownership issues. These issues are addressed later in this chapter

Information Is Often Fragmented or Segmented

Because information accessed by an application is heterogeneous and dispersed, it is often fragmented. The information may be recombined in various ways, and so the Information Services component of the netcentric architecture must have a way of ensuring the integrity of the information in its various combinations.

ISSUES IN THE DISTRIBUTION OF INFORMATION

The ultimate goal of distributed information processing is to give every user transparent access to dispersed, disparate information. With client/server and netcentric computing, developers seek to isolate applications from knowledge of information location, information access methods, and information management products. At the same time, they seek to ensure that the information is reliable, i.e., that it has integrity.

When to Consider a Distributed Database Strategy

When particular business functions have certain characteristics, distributed information and distributed information processing may be considered:

1. *Geographical distribution.* The business functions are spread over several different sites, making it impractical to support some (or all) of the processing requirements from a central site.
2. *Local decision making and independence.* The organizational structure is distributed and the business has several local sites with the authority to make local decisions as to how to process and act upon its information.
3. *Performance.* The response time at the local site becomes unacceptable due to the transfer of data between the central and local sites.
4. *Scalability.* Business growth has caused the volume of data to expand, the volume of processing to increase, or has resulted in expansion to new sites.

Potential Benefits

The potential benefits for a distributed database strategy apply both to true distributed database management systems and to implementations that incorporate distributed data management strategies.

Organization. A distributed system may better reflect an organization's structure, which often is logically distributed (e.g., into divisions, departments, and projects) as well as physically distributed (e.g., into plants, warehouses, and branch offices).

Ease of Growth. Once installed, a distributed system is able to expand more gracefully than a nondistributed system. For example, if significant business growth has caused the volume of information to expand or the volume of processing to increase, it may be easier to expand the system by adding a new site to an existing distributed system than by replacing or extending an existing centralized system with a larger one.

Lower Costs. It may be less expensive for organizations to add another server or to extend the server than to add or extend a mainframe.

Local Autonomy. Distributing a system allows individual groups within an organization to exercise control over their own information while still being able to access information at remote locations when necessary.

Increased Availability. A distributed system may offer greater availability than a centralized system in that it can continue to function (though at a reduced level) even if an individual site or communication link has failed. Also, with the support of replicated information, availability is improved in that a replicated information object remains available as long as at least one copy of that object is available.

Increased Efficiency. Response times can be reduced because information in a distributed system can be stored close to its point of use, enabling most information accesses to be local.

Increased Flexibility. Information can be dynamically moved or replicated, existing copies can be deleted, or new information types can be added to accommodate changes in how the information is used.

Potential Challenges

Although distribution of information throughout a system has many benefits, it must overcome a number of challenges, as well.

Complex Architectural-Level Communications. In these systems, messages containing information, processing requests, and acknowledgments of previous requests are passed continuously among various remote sites. Coordinating this message flow is complex and can be costly.

Complex Update Control. If two users update the same piece of information, a method must be found to mediate conflicts. One way to ensure information integrity is to employ a locking mechanism. However, the locking strategy becomes more challenging as machines are added; network failure must be taken into consideration. Added complexity also arises with distributed transactions where one user updates two data sources simultaneously and both updates must occur in sync.

Network Dependency. When data are distributed across the network, reliable communications between sites are required or processing may be halted. This increased reliability may require expensive duplication of network resources to provide an acceptable amount of system availability for the users.

Complexity of "Location Transparency." In the ideal distributed information environment, the end user or application programmer has access to all required information without having to know where that information is physically located. This feature is known as location transparency and it is supported by some of the database management system (DBMS) products currently available. This places a substantial burden on the architecture and its designers to locate the information efficiently and to transport the information to the application on request, without excessive processing delays.

Location Transparency also Complicates User Support. A user problem within a single application may originate from any number of remote sites that are transparent to the user, making the problem more difficult to identify and resolve.

Information Synchronization. Maintenance of redundant information over multiple sites and processors increases the complexity of information synchronization routines. Complex time synchronization between separate machines may be required.

Organizations must be aware of what their synchronization requirements are. Timing is one example of a synchronization challenge. When does information need to be synchronized? In real time? Overnight? Several techniques for performing information synchronization efficiently are discussed later.

Changes in Organizational Structure. Changes in the existing organizational structure could invalidate the information design. With distributed information, one must build in flexibility to change as the organization changes.

Security. Managing access to information and preventing unauthorized access are greater challenges in client/server and netcentric computing than in a centralized environment. Complexity here is a result of the distributed nature of system components (hardware, software, and data).

Information Transformation. Because information is on multiple platforms and multiple management environments, the information must be transformed from one format or type to another. Some information types may be supported in one environment and not in another.

Information Management. Distributed information is more difficult to manage, creating challenges for backup and recovery of information and for overall information integrity.

Heterogeneous Environments. Client/server and netcentric information may be on multiple databases, file systems, and hardware platforms connected by multiple network protocols.

Rules for Design

"Location transparency" is a key to successful information design in client/server and netcentric computing. Database expert C.J. Date puts this principle another way: "To a user, a distributed system should look exactly like a nondistributed system. The user or programmer who accesses and manipulates information should be able to do so logically through a single access, as if it were all managed by a single DBMS on a single machine."

From this underlying principle, Date sets forth 12 related rules for distributed data design, or distributed information design. Date's guidelines are helpful in designing overall information access in a netcentric architecture, although it is unlikely that any system will conform to all 12 of these rules. Most organizations focus on the need to achieve local autonomy and the need for information independence.

The 12 rules are.

Local Autonomy. All operations at any particular site should be controlled by that site and not dependent on another site to function. Each local site owns and manages its own information, and each site is therefore responsible for the accuracy, security, and integrity of that information.

No Reliance on a Central Site. A corollary of the first rule , this rule is necessary to prevent bottlenecks and the potential vulnerability of relying on a central site.

Continuous Operation. Planned system shutdowns should never be necessary. Good design means that maintenance, database administration and operations, and upgrades should take place without shutting down the system.

Location Independence. Users and applications should be able to access remote information as if it were local. This simplifies application design and permits information to be moved around without causing changes to existing applications.

Segmentation Independence. If an information relation can be separated into segments for physical storage and access, the distributed database design should support storing the segments at the location where they are used most frequently. Users should be able to access any information logically as if it were not segmented at all.

Replication Independence. Replication of information should be transparent to the users and to the application. Access proceeds logically as if there is only one copy of the information.

Distributed Query Processing. Users should be able to make a single query across multiple physical information locations.

Distributed Transaction Management. The system should provide a single point of entry for the transaction, even if the transaction involves information from multiple sites to complete the business function.

Hardware Independence. Client/server and netcentric systems include a variety of machines. The system must be able to present a "single-system image" of the database to the user while allowing different hardware systems to participate as partners in the system.

Operating System Independence. Systems with heterogeneous hardware may use more than one operating system. The information should be able to allow all operating systems to participate in the same distributed system.

Network Independence. In a client/server or netcentric system, multiple communications systems must be able to operate together, transparently to users and application designers.

DBMS Independence. Many system installations have different types of DBMSs. Thus, it is vital that they all support the same interface and that they can interoperate.

Meeting these challenges of distributed information is the function of the Information Services component of the netcentric architecture.

INFORMATION SERVICES FRAMEWORK

A two-layer approach is useful to keep information distinct from the processes that access and use it: a logical layer and a physical layer. Within the

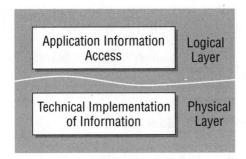

Exhibit 2. Logical and Physical Layers.

netcentric architecture, the information services component maintains this logical/physical distinction (Exhibit 2)

Logical Layer

The logical layer acts to isolate the physical aspects of information (e.g., location, storage format, and access language) from applications and applications developers. This layer provides all the detail services associated with information and with access to or from that information.

Physical Layer

The physical layer can be used within a netcentric architecture to isolate the detailed technical implementations of information. This layer insulates an organization and its applications from the rapid pace of change in information management technology. This layer can also be used to position legacy information sources into the netcentric computing environment, independent of migrating applications and implementing new applications.

DATABASE SERVICES

Database services are responsible for providing access to a local or remote database, maintaining integrity of the data within the database, and supporting the ability to store data on either a single physical platform or, in some cases, across multiple platforms. These services are typically provided by DBMS vendors and accessed via embedded or call-level SQL variants and supersets. Depending upon the underlying storage model, non-SQL access methods may be used instead.

Many netcentric applications today are broadcast-type applications designed to market a company's products and/or publish the company's policies and procedures. Furthermore, there is now a growth of netcentric applications that are transaction-type applications used to process a customer's sales order, maintenance request, etc. Typically, these types of applications require integration with a database manager. Database Services include Replication/Synchronization Services, Access Services, Security Services, Indexing Services, and Storage Services.

Replication/Synchronization Services

Replication Services support an environment in which multiple copies of databases must be maintained. For example, if ad hoc reporting queries or operational data stores can work with a replica of the transaction database, these resource-intensive applications will not interfere with mission-critical transaction processing. Replication can be either complete or partial. During complete replication all records are copied from one destination to another; during partial replication only a subset of data is copied as specified by the user or the program. Replication can also be done either real-time or on demand (i.e., initiated by a user, program, or scheduler). The following might be possible if databases are replicated on alternate server(s):

- Better availability or recoverability of distributed applications
- Better performance and reduced network cost, particularly in environments where users are widely geographically dispersed
- Improved access to wider ranges of data as data replicas may be more readily available

The terms "Replication" and "Synchronization" are used interchangeably, depending on the vendor, article, book, etc. For example, when Lotus Notes refers to Replication it means a combination of Replication and Synchronization Services described previously. When Sybase refers to Replication it only means copying data from one source to another.

Access Services

Access Services enable an application to retrieve data from a database as well as manipulate (insert, update, and delete) data in a database. SQL is the primary approach for accessing records in today's DBMSs.

Client–server and netcentric systems often require data access from multiple databases offered by different vendors. This is often due to integration of new systems with existing legacy systems. The key architectural concern is in building the application where the multivendor data problem is transparent to the application needing the data. This provides future portability and flexibility, and also makes it easier for application developers to write to a single database access interface. Achieving database access transparency requires the following:

Standards-Based SQL API. This approach uses a single, standards-based set of APIs to access any database and includes the following technologies: Open Database Connectivity (ODBC), Java Database Connectivity (JDBC), and Object Linking and Embedding (OLE BD).

SQL Gateways. These provide a mechanism for clients to transparently access data in a variety of databases (e.g., Oracle, Sybase, or DB2) by translating SQL calls written using the format and protocols of the gateway server or primary server to the format and protocols of the target database. Currently, there are three contending architectures for providing gateway functions.

Distributed Relational Data Access (DRDA). This is a standard promoted by IBM for distributed data access between heterogeneous databases. In this case the conversion of the format and protocols occurs only once. It supports SQL89 and a subset of the SQL92 standard, and is built on top on APPC/APPN and TCP/IP transport stacks.

IBI's EDA/SQL and the Sybase/MDI Open Server. These use SQL to access relational and nonrelational database systems. They use API/SQL or T-SQL, respectively, as the standard interface language. A large number of communication protocols are supported, including NetBIOS, SNA, DecNET, and TCP/IP. The main engine translates the client requests into specific server calls. It handles security, authentication, statistics gathering, and some system management tasks.

Security Services

Security Services enforce access control to ensure that records are only visible or editable by authorized people for approved purposes. Most DBMSs provide access control at the database, table, or row level as well as concurrency control. However, there may be severe limitations in the DBMS's ability to pass data needed for security authentication across a network, forcing the architect to build those services into the Security Services layer.

Indexing Services

Indexing Services provide a mechanism for speeding up data retrieval. In relational databases, one or more fields can be used to construct the index. Therefore, when a user searches for a specific record, the index is used to find the location of that record, which is faster scanning the whole table sequentially. Revolutionary advances in indexing techniques — such as bitmapped indexing, context indexing, and star indexes — provide rich capabilities for netcentric computing.

Storage Services

Storage Services manage the physical storage of data. These services provide a mechanism for saving information so that data will live beyond program execution. Data are often stored in relational format (an RDBMS) but may also be stored in an object-oriented format (OODBMS) or other formats such as IMS or VSAM.

DOCUMENT SERVICES

Document Services provide similar structure and control for documents that DBMSs apply to record-oriented data. A document is defined as a collection of objects potentially of different types (e.g., structured data, unstructured data, images, multimedia) a business user deals with. An individual document might be a table created using a spreadsheet package, a report created using a word processing package, a web page created using an HTML authoring tool, unstructured text, or a combination of these object types. Regardless of the software used to create and maintain the component parts, all parts together constitute the document, which is managed as a single entity.

Netcentric applications that are executed from a browser are particularly well suited for serving up document style information. If the web application consists of more than just a few HTML documents, integration with a document management system should be considered. Document Services include Replication/Synchronization Services, Access Services, Indexing Services, Security Services, Storage Services, and Versioning Services (see Exhibit 3).

Replication/Synchronization Services

Replication Services support an environment in which multiple copies of documents must be maintained. A key objective is that documents be shareable and searchable across the entire organization. Therefore, the architecture needs to *logically* provide a single repository, even though the documents are *physically* stored in different locations. Replicating documents on alternative server(s) may have some benefits: better availability or recoverability of a distributed application, better performance, reduced network cost, or increased information access and availability.

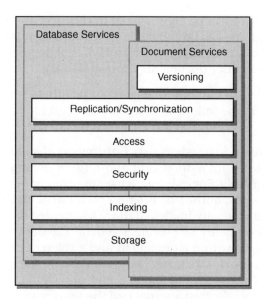

Exhibit 3. Information Services Framework.

Synchronization services perform the transactions required to make consistent information sources that are intended to mirror each other; they support the needs of intermittently connected users or sites. As with databases, these services are especially valuable for users of remote or mobile devices that need to be able to work locally without a constant network connection and then be able to synchronize with the central server at a given point in time.

Access Services

Access services support document creation, maintenance, and retrieval. These services allow users to capture knowledge or content through the creation of unstructured information, i.e., documents. Access Services allow users to effectively retrieve documents they created, and documents that were created by others. Documents can be comprised of many different data types including text, charts, graphics, or even audio and video.

Indexing Services

Locating documents, as well as content within documents, is a more complex problem and involves several alternative methods. The Windows File Manager is a simplistic implementation of a hierarchical organization of files and collections of files. If the user model of where documents should be stored and found can be represented in this way, the use of structure and naming standards can be sufficient. However, a hierarchical document-filing organization is not suitable for many types of document queries (e.g., retrieving all sales order documents for over $1000).

Therefore, most document management products provide index services that support the following methods for searching document repositories:

- *Attribute Search.* Scans short lists (attributes) of important words that are associated with a document and returns documents that match the search criteria. For example, a user may query for documents written by a specific author or created on a particular date. Attribute search brings the capabilities of the SQL-oriented database approach to finding documents by storing in a database the values of specially identified fields within a document and a reference to the document itself. To support Attribute Search, an index maintains document attributes, which it uses to manage, find, and catalog documents. This is the least complicated approach of the searching methods.
- *Full-text Search.* Searches repository contents for exact words or phrases and returns documents that match the search criteria. To facilitate Full-text Search, full-text indexes are constructed by scanning documents once and recording in an index file which words occur in which documents. Leading document management systems have full-text search services built in, which can be integrated directly into applications.
- *Context Search:* Searches repository contents for exact words or phrases. It also searches for related words or phrases by using synonyms and word taxonomies. For example, if the user searches for *auto*, the search engine should look for *car, automobile, motor vehicle*, etc.
- *Boolean Search:* Searches repository contents for words or phases that are joined together using boolean operators (e.g., AND, OR, or NOT). The same types of indexes are used for Boolean Search as for Full-Text Search.

Security Services

Documents should be accessed exclusively through Document Services. If a document is checked in, checked out, routed, viewed, annotated, archived, or printed, it should be done only by users with the correct security privileges. Those access privileges should be controlled by user, role, and group. Analogous to record locking to prevent two users from editing the same data, document management access control services include check-in/check-out services to limit concurrent editing.

Storage Services

Storage Services manage the physical storage of documents. Most document management products store documents as objects that include two basic data types: attributes and content. Document attributes are key fields used to identify the document, such as author name or created date. Document content refers to the actual unstructured information stored within the document. Generally, the documents are stored in a repository using one of the following methods:

- *Proprietary database.* Documents (attributes and contents) are stored in a proprietary database, one that the vendor has specifically developed for use with its product.
- *Industry standard database.* Documents (attributes and contents) are stored in an industry standard database such as Oracle or Sybase. Attributes are stored within traditional database data types (e.g., integer or character); contents are stored in the database's BLOB (Binary Large Objects) data type.
- *Industry standard database and file system.* Documents' attributes are stored in an industry standard database, and documents' contents are usually stored in the file system of the host operating system. Most document management products use this document storage method today because this approach provides the most flexibility in terms of data distribution and also allows for greater scalability.

Versioning Services

Versioning Services maintain a historical record of the changes to a document over time. By maintaining this record, these services allow for the recreation of a document as it looked at any given point in time during its evolution. Additional key versioning features record who made changes and when and why they were made.

DDBMS FRAMEWORK

The rest of this chapter discusses a critical component of managing information in a netcentric application: the distributed DBMS (DDBMS). The DDBMS promises a number of benefits for organizations, including the ability to expand a system more gracefully in an incremental fashion, local autonomy, increased availability and reliability of information, and increased efficiency and flexibility. With a DDBMS, users located in different geographical locations will be able to retrieve and update information from one or more locations in a network transparently and with full integrity and security.

CHARACTERISTICS OF DDBMS IN CLIENT/SERVER AND NETCENTRIC COMPUTING

Client/server and netcentric computing allow information to be kept distinct from the processes that use that information. Any DDBMS product used in a netcentric environment must be able to maintain this distinction. This section discusses a number of crucial characteristics of DDBMS products:

- Stored procedures
- Triggers
- Support for referential integrity
- Two-phase commit
- Support for nontextual or multimedia information
- Information replication
- Information gateways
- Disk mirroring

Stored Procedures

A stored procedure is a set of named SQL statements defined within a function that is compiled within the DDBMS for runtime execution by name. Essentially, it is information access logic coded into the database server for use by all clients.

Stored procedures can be compared to third-generation language (3GL) routines, but they are executed by DDBMS software and contain SQL statements. At runtime, the stored procedure is accessed through a 3GL or 4GL call.

Advantages of Stored Procedures. Stored procedures have a number of important advantages:

- *Information transfer volume is minimized.* Because the stored procedure can execute all SQL statements and information access logic, only required information is returned to the requesting process.
- *Speeds execution.* Stored procedures are usually compiled into the database engine (not the application) for fast execution, which generally improves DDBMS and information access performance.
- *Decreases lines of code.* Applications can have less code, and they do not need to include, within each application, information integrity or reused information access logic.
- *Eases some maintenance activities.* Applications have less data structure information; therefore, it is easier to change table sizes, column names, and so forth.

100

- *Promotes code reusability.* Stored procedures can be thought of as object processing for information tables; they modularize and encapsulate information operations into a library-like area. Each stored procedure can be reused when accessed by any application that has permission to use it.
- *Enforces distinctions between information and process.* All information access, location, format, and so forth can be addressed within the stored procedure and therefore removed from the application logic that processes that information.

Potential Drawbacks of Stored Procedures. The use of stored procedures has a number of potential drawbacks:

- *Each DDBMS vendor's implementation is different.* Once an organization chooses a particular DDBMS and uses that vendor's stored procedures, it may be locked in to that vendor or, at a minimum, those stored procedures have to be reimplemented.
- *Changes in a stored procedure can affect many applications.* The balance of application processing between the application and stored procedure must be understood. Like any library routine, changes require a test of all users.
- *System performance may be degraded by the inappropriate use of a stored procedure.* For example, a stored procedure may have to return multiple information types from multiple sources to respond to a single request.

When to Use Stored Procedures. Stored procedures should be used in the following cases:

- *When a set of SQL calls should be grouped logically for a single business operation.* A logical set of data operations, that performs a single business function and is executed frequently (such as "make reservation") provides a good base for a stored procedure.
- *When the same set of SQL calls are used in many applications.* As soon as the same SQL statements are used by more than one application, stored procedures are valuable for avoiding problems in updating several applications when changes are made, and for improving the consistency of SQL use within an organization or project.
- *When one wants to decrease information transfer from client to server in complicated information requests.* A stored procedure call is often a smaller information message from a client to a server than a complex SQL statement(s). However, when there is less information transfer, there are more MIPS used on the server.
- *When one wants to maximize processing on a server platform, balancing client processing.* Stored procedures add central processing unit usage

on the server and should be balanced against application processing on the client.

Triggers

Triggers are convenient "start" mechanisms to initiate stored procedures or SQL commands. Triggers can be based on either clock events or data events. A clock-based trigger might be, "At 1:00 a.m. each morning, replicate the AIRPORT entity to sites New York, Chicago, and Dulles with the AIRPORT_REP stored procedure." A data-based event might be, "When a new row is inserted into the RESERVATION table, initiate the RESERVATION_ACCOUNTING stored procedure."

Triggers have a number of advantages. They permit applications developers to remove event-based logic from applications or the infrastructure software, and they tie a data-driven event to the actual data that drives the event. However, it is difficult to know what will happen to the database if many triggers cascade on and on. Infinite loops may be possible if designers are not careful and do not conduct thorough testing.

Referential Integrity

Referential integrity is the correctness and consistency of relationships among data tables, and the correctness of information content. These are crucial issues in a relational database environment. The most important question with regard to referential integrity is whether it should be handled by the DDBMS or by the applications.

If the DDBMS enforces the integrity rules, integrity is centralized and not maintained in all application programs; integrity can be changed without modifying applications. However, DDBMS integrity enforcement used indiscriminately generates high overhead. Too much integrity checking slows down the system considerably.

In general, DDBMS-enforced referential integrity should be used when possible. The advantage is that the DDBMS enforces integrity more effectively than application logic. Furthermore, applications do not have to design and code the logic, and the logic can be centralized in the DDBMS. However, applications still have to test it.

There are two reasons to avoid DDBMS-enforced referential integrity:

1. The business rule that needs to be enforced is not a rule available from the DDBMS.
2. Using DDBMS-enforced referential integrity forces awkward constraints on application programs or on database maintenance processes.

It is vital to define all the business rules between tables before deciding how the relationship should be maintained. There are four ways to alter a referential relationship (insert a child, update the primary key of a child, update a foreign key of a parent, and delete a parent), and there are four possible business rules for how to retain referential integrity in each situation, for a total of 16 options. Most DDBMSs offer only six options. When one needs one of the missing options, the application must enforce it.

DDBMS-enforced referential integrity should not make program structures awkward or less maintainable. However, complex links between tables may force difficult management, loading, and unloading scenarios. For example, a credit card company wanted a 24x7 application to allow new credit card products to be defined online, in such a way that the new products were not available to customers until all rules regarding the new product were fully defined. The credit card products had many complex rules, which were to be split across many child tables under the main product table. The simplest way to guarantee that the product could not be used until it was complete was to insert all the children first, and insert the parent only when all the child rows were entered and validated. DDBMS-enforced referential integrity would not permit such a scenario, so application-enforced integrity was used instead.

Similarly, if too many tables are linked together through DDBMS-enforced referential integrity, backup/restore scenarios may become excessively difficult, so it is wise to keep less than about 15 referentially linked sets of tables.

When bulk-loading information into the database, referential integrity constraints should ensure that the database is consistent and accurate after loading. Some DDBMS products have a "backdoor" load that bypasses integrity constraints.

In general, DDBMS-enforced integrity should be used whenever it is justified by business events. However, the DDBMS should not be used to perform application integrity, for example, to validate codes against code tables. These values usually do not change often, and the constant validation is simply unnecessary overhead. Also, developers should not put more than a manageable number of tables into a single connected referential tree structure that must be maintained by the DDBMS. Developers must understand the characteristics of the specific DDBMS they are working with to determine what that manageable number is.

Two-Phase Commit

Two-phase commit (sometimes abbreviated 2PC) is a protocol used when a logical unit of work updates information in two or more recovery managers or "nodes." 2PC ensures integrity of information between nodes. It has been used for many years to ensure integrity between a transaction monitor and a DBMS running on the same processor.

In a client/server or netcentric environment, distributed 2PC is a technique for guaranteeing integrity across distributed processors. Exhibit 4 shows a timeline of activities associated with two-phase commit.

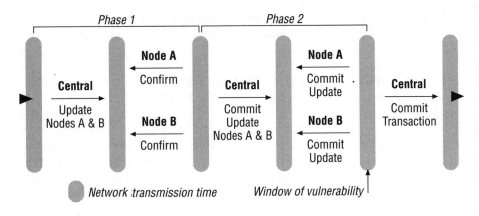

Exhibit 4. Example of Two-Phase Commit.

Phase 1. Phase 1, or the prepare phase, queries all the recovery managers to verify that they are ready to commit, that is, ready for updating. This phase initiates the cleanup tasks of the memory management facilities at each node.

If a participating node (not the coordinating node) is unable to receive the prepare message (and any subsequent rollback), it checks periodically for unreleased locks (or checks when communication/processing is restored) and queries the coordinator about the status of the transaction. The coordinator responds that the transaction was rolled back because all sites could not participate, and the participating site also rolls back, releasing all locks.

Phase 2. Phase 2, or the commit phase, tells each participating node to write a commit log record. If the commit is successful at all the remote nodes involved in the transaction, and the originating node receives a successful acknowledgment from each of the remote nodes, the transaction at the originating node is committed. If confirmation is not received from all nodes involved, the transaction is rolled back.

Advantages and Disadvantages. Two-phase commits have several advantages. A 2PC approach can ensure that multiple databases remain synchronous. If some other approach is used to guarantee synchronization, it must incorporate similar synchronization logic and could mean building a custom 2PC architecture.

Two-phase commits are DDBMS supported; the DDBMS product can enforce and control the protocol (e.g., sending the messages, waiting for receipt, confirming, committing, and rolling back). Also, 2PCs are application independent. Because they are controlled by the DDBMS, applications do not need to control the execution of the protocol.

However, the 2PC implementation does leave a window of vulnerability: there are gaps in transmission between the central/coordinating node and the nodes involved in the transaction. If the participating node commits but the initiating node does not receive acknowledgment of the commit, the initiating node does not know whether to commit or to roll back. As a result, the initiating node does not know what to do and data integrity may be lost, defeating the entire objective of 2PC. The probability of this occurring increases with the number and distance of sites involved in the transaction. It works extremely well between CICS and DB2 running on the same mainframe box where the distance between nodes is negligible. However, it is a different matter when the commit message must travel through space to a satellite and back en route between nodes. Two-phase commit can also affect overall system and application performance.

Distributed two-phase commit is a complicated strategy — time consuming and costly. It relies on complex synchronous messaging over the network. Communications failures can have a substantial impact on the practicality of this technique.

In addition, the common approach requires participation and success from all sites involved in the transaction. If one site cannot complete the transaction, the entire transaction fails. Some observers have described 2PC as a protocol that guarantees that failure at one node will be replicated to all nodes.

So, when is two-phase commit appropriate? Developers should avoid two-phase commits by designing applications so that information updated during a single logical unit of work is located within the same node. If they cannot avoid it, designers should use two-phase commits when they need to have some form of synchronization of information between nodes. However, they must remember that inconsistencies in information integrity are still possible, so they must either control the integrity problems with a "data check" program or with regular offline downloads or synchronizations.

Multimedia or Nontextual Information Storage

Support for more complex types of information is an important DDBMS capability to evaluate. This information goes by a number of different names: unstructured information, nontextual information, multimedia, and extended information. By whatever name, this information consists of such things as digital images, graphics, video images, voice, word processing documents, and spreadsheets.

The DDBMS has two primary methods by which it can handle these kinds of information: either defined within the database in data types called binary large objects (BLOBs), or defined outside the database structure with a pointer containing the file name where the information is contained within the DDBMS. The decision to use a BLOB or a file should be reviewed to determine application requirements, data administration requirements, and network impact.

BLOB storage has several advantages. The integrity of information is maintained by the DDBMS. Also, BLOBs are logically equivalent to other data types, which makes retrieval easier. However, a BLOB is a nonstandard SQL data type so the designer must be careful to ensure that the DDBMS supports it. Current performance levels may be poor as a result of the large size of the BLOBs.

An advantage of storing extended data types outside the database is that the file can be accessed independently of the DDBMS, through operating system services. This may lead to better retrieval performance. Disadvantages of this type of storage include the fact that the integrity of the pointer to the file, and of the information itself, must be maintained by the application. Also, backup and restore operations must use both the DDBMS and file procedures.

Information Replication

Information replication is a critical function of most mission-critical distributed information architectures. Replication is the synchronization of a database or subset of a database from one location to another. Replication can occur regularly or irregularly, automatically or manually. Replication works well for information that does not change frequently and for data that needs to be synchronized but not in real time. This is the case most of the time.

Replication provides faster access to information and less transfer of information across the network. However, a challenge to replication is keeping multiple copies of information synchronized. If the DDBMS cannot provide automatic synchronization, additional development time is necessary to provide and maintain this synchronization.

Hands-on experience to date suggests that recovery is very complex. In addition, replication can throw unpredictable loads on the network such that network administration groups are reluctant to allow the feature into the network.

Information Gateways (Middleware)

Information gateways (also referred to as DBMS middleware) are mechanisms that allow applications to access information from a variety of DDBMSs without extensive platform-specific or DDBMS-specific programming.

An information gateway may be a part of the DDBMS or it may be a separate product. The primary functions of the gateway include transparent routing of SQL calls and translating among various dialects of SQL. Gateways are particularly valuable when there is an existing installed base using a variety of DDBMSs.

An information gateway accepts an SQL statement from the client application and translates it into a format understandable by the target DDBMS(s). The gateway then sends the statement to be processed. After processing, the information gateway receives the results, translates them into a form that can be understood by the client, and then returns the information and status to the client.

Gateways allow access to information across multiple database management systems. The applications can use a consistent interface for all information, which saves development time and cost as well as training time for application designers and end users. However, gateways may result in a slower response time to queries because of the time required for formatting, protocol conversion, and other activities of the gateway. Some gateways offer read-only access, so updates must be processed differently. There are also potential information accuracy and integrity issues associated with the use of information gateways.

Disk Mirroring

Disk mirroring is a DDBMS-enforced "hot backup" disk capability within a single platform. It ensures that information is not lost in cases of disk failure. Generally, in a disk failure or disk crash, all information inserted since the last tape backup is lost. With disk mirroring, the backup disk is always up-to-date with respect to the primary disk. Disk mirroring also increases the availability of the DDBMS.

With disk mirroring, the DDBMS automatically transfers to the backup disk if the primary disk fails. It then automatically synchronizes the primary disk after the failure is cleared.

Disk mirroring provides obvious advantages to information security; in addition, it is transparent to applications controlled by the DDBMS. However, more disks are required in disk mirroring, and mirroring cannot be done over a LAN. Also, some minor performance decreases may result from mirroring.

MATCHING FUNCTIONS AND FEATURES

In any particular client/server or netcentric system, some features and functions of DDBMSs may be critical and others may not. When evaluating a DDBMS, it is important to find one appropriate for the specific system and business requirements. A matrix, such as the one in Exhibit 5, is a worksheet for matching functions and features to products under consideration.

	Product A	Product B	Product C
Stored Procedures			
Triggers			
Two-Phase Commit			
Referential Integrity			
Multimedia			
Replication			
Gateways			
Mirroring			

Exhibit 5. Matrix of Features.

CONCLUSION

Maximizing the benefits of client/server and netcentric computing presents some of the greatest challenges to designers and developers. One of the primary business benefits of netcentric computing is that knowledge workers have access to more and better types of information located throughout the enterprise. However, that access requires a methodical approach to enabling applications to access and manipulate information, whether it is stored locally or remotely in files or databases. Even the fact that we refer to this part of the netcentric architecture as information access (rather than its traditional name, data access) reveals an important part of the information challenge of netcentric systems.

In addition, a key technology in client/server and netcentric computing is the DDBMS. Although theoretically a distributed DBMS does not have to be relational, the relational model provides a simpler and more practical vehicle to support DDBMS functions than hierarchical or network models.

A relational DDBMS also tends to provide better support for the flexible, dynamic information requirements found in most netcentric applications. The major DDBMS products in the marketplace today are built on a relational framework, and the success of relational DBMSs has had a direct impact on spurring the development of DDBMS products. More and more, organizations will see distributed DBMS as a practical technology component that is needed to support their growing business needs.

Chapter 6
Communications Architectures
Andersen Consulting

Netcentric computing is an outgrowth of the increased importance and capabilities of the network as well as the associated communications that the network enables between computing environments and access devices. Netcentric computing implies being connected anywhere, anytime. It transforms the common phrase "The network is the computer" into "The network is everywhere." The popular and academic journals, professional gatherings, and our firm's work with organizations all bear witness to the fact that people have now realized the scope of communications issues in developing business solutions today.

In netcentric computing, the network is no longer simply a pipe that moves data from point A to point B. Instead, networks provide a rich set of services that are increasingly more sophisticated to keep pace with the requirements of netcentric applications.

This chapter explores an architectural framework that categorizes and defines the services that are provided by the network and discusses areas in which these services are evolving. Specific networking technologies that are evolving to support netcentric applications are discussed in Section III of this book.

WHAT IS A COMMUNICATIONS ARCHITECTURE?

The evolving role of a network can be seen in the advent of such concepts as "electronic commerce" and the "virtual enterprise." The network continues to support traditional types of data traffic in an individual corporate enterprise (i.e., local area networks (LANs) and wide area networks (WANs). However, nontraditional business flows (video, graphics, voice, etc.) also need to be supported as well as the new relationships created in the virtual enterprise. Companies that produce the final packaged product or service interact with their suppliers through a seamless information infrastructure. In addition, the need to support an ever-increasing base of public access from home and mobile locations further stretches and redefines the old network boundaries. As computing becomes more distributed and pervasive, the role of the network will grow to support and enable this exchange of content between any points that generate or use information. Exhibit 1 illustrates these key characteristics of the network.

What is a network? The domain of the network may be defined as the portion of the overall enterprise technology architecture that supports the movement of knowledge in a digital, electronic format between different locations. To provide this capability, the network is composed of communications hardware, software, and services. The network does not include the computing platforms, knowledge technologies, or business logic and applications. However, all network components must provide well-defined services and interfaces to interact effectively with these other technology components.

COMMUNICATIONS ARCHITECTURE GUIDING PRINCIPLES

How is this definition of a network any different from the way the role of the network has been perceived in the past? At first glance the answer may be, "Not much." However, some fundamental concepts are introduced here that are key to how network architectures will be viewed in the foreseeable future. While the following guiding principles affect all aspects of near-term computing architectures, they will have some very specific impacts on the network domain that will guide the characteristics of future communication architectures.

Netcentric Computing

A netcentric architecture is a standard architecture that allows internal users, customers, and business partners to use multiple electronic access devices (e.g., PCs, mobile computers, kiosks, telephones, etc.) to access disparate sources of information. Netcentric architectures employ open, commonly accepted standards for the network, client, and associated components (e.g., Internet, TCP/IP, web browser, ActiveX, COM, CORBA, Java, etc.). Web-based solutions are examples of netcentric architectures. A netcentric architecture requires an intelligent, flexible, standards-based network.

Individuals

The physical network infrastructure is shifting to support more dynamic human-to-human communications styles instead of the traditional, precise computer-to-computer communications. Until now, application requirements were the sole driver for network designs. Now, with interaction styles mimicking more human traits, networks must incorporate multime-

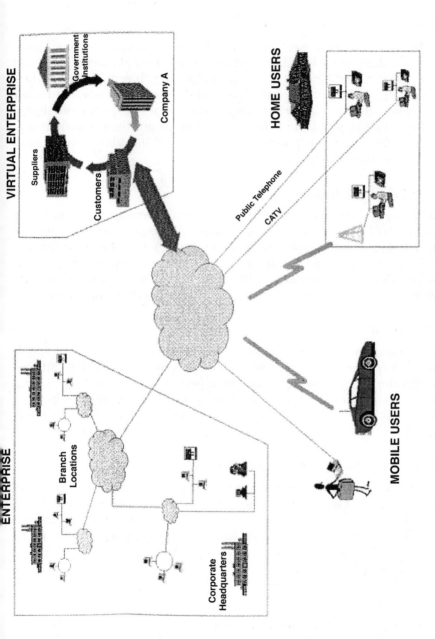

Exhibit 1. Key Network Characteristics.

dia, workflow, collaboration, and other qualities that better support the way different individuals use the network.

Mobility

As individuals drive out new requirements, an "anywhere, anytime" computing paradigm must be addressed to support new classes of personal devices. These new devices no longer follow the "bigger, better, faster" characteristics of legacy workstations and servers and hosts, but rather the "smaller, cheaper, faster" characteristics of phones, personal digital assistants (PDAs), and laptop computers. This forces the network to support more devices, more varieties of devices, and the added overhead of intermittent connectivity.

Distributed Computing

Although most enterprises are still hierarchical, some are flattening their processes by introducing more autonomy. This requires systems to support distributed data, applications, and infrastructure. Because the network is the only part of the infrastructure that has a logical and physical end-to-end view of all resources, the network architecture must provide services to help manage processes that transcend central implementation.

Public Access

Just as enterprise networks are extended to business partners to create virtual enterprises, the enterprise network may also be opened to interaction with the general public (customers, potential customers, etc.). Supporting public access (e.g., Internet access, access via public kiosks, etc.) and the resulting virtual communities requires specialized network services relating to security, directories, heterogeneous platforms, etc.

Open Network Services and Interfaces

The communication architecture must support common, open network services and interfaces that are easily shared. Not only must there be well-defined standards that can be shared between the client and server, but an "intelligent network" role will need to exist to help proxy capabilities as well. This will allow more rapid expansion of enterprises as they take advantage of virtualization.

The Virtual Enterprise

As more enterprises begin to partner and cooperate, networks will need to support relationships with services that never had to exist before. The challenge to the communication architecture is not in providing the connections but in enabling the end-to-end processes associated with them. Many of these

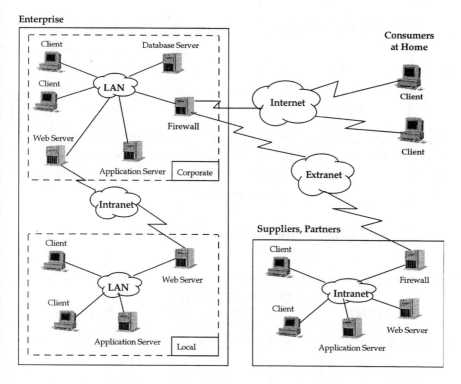

Exhibit 2. Basic Network Components.

processes will require the network to provide secure, independent, reliable, dynamic services that transcend organizational boundaries.

THE COMMUNICATIONS ARCHITECTURE

Exhibit 2 is a representation of the physical networking environment of netcentric solutions.

This physical environment is supported by a logical representation of a netcentric execution architecture discussed in Chapter 3 (Exhibit 3). The components of the architecture that represent the network architecture have been colored gray.

The Communication Services component on the client and server and the communication fabric component represent a high-level view of the communications architecture. The remainder of this chapter focuses on a description of the communication services and the communications fabric portions of the netcentric execution architecture. Exhibit 4 illustrates a further breakdown of the network-specific layers of a netcentric communication architecture.

115

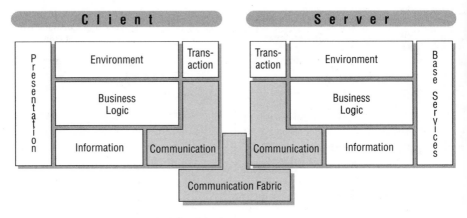

Exhibit 3. Netcentric Execution Architecture.

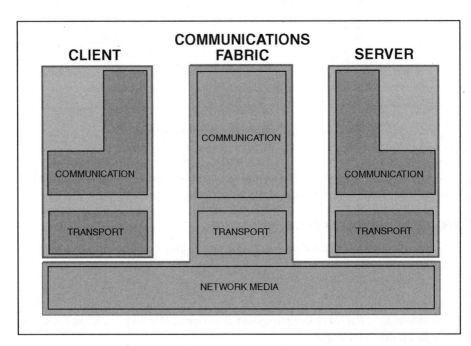

Exhibit 4. Network-Specific Layers of the Communications Architecture.

Each layer (e.g., communication services layer, transport service layer, and the network media layer) contains specific network-related services that are needed to deliver the necessary functionality. To be fully functional, a netcentric architecture requires services from each of the three layers.

Within a layer, individual services are selected to deliver the necessary functionality. The services provided in these three layers enable the applications and higher level services to be isolated from the intricacies of the low-level network (e.g., developing application interfaces directly with complex communications protocols).

Communication Services Layer

The communication cervices layer manages the interaction of distributed processes over the network. This layer enables an application to interact transparently with other applications regardless of whether they reside on the same computer or on a remote computer. The communication services layer performs four distinct functions:

- Manages communications between applications
- Initiates and manages the transfer of information between processes over the network
- Provides specialized interface and communication management capabilities based on the type of resource accessed so that network nodes can intelligently interact with distributed resources
- Provides interfacing and translation to ensure that information received is in a readable format for the local system

Transport Services Layer

The transport services layer provides capabilities for transferring data through the network to the ultimate destination. Its primary functions include transporting data (including reliability, security, and quality of service) and transporting voice calls.

Network Media Services Layer

The network media services layer performs the low-level transfer of data between network nodes, using physical media such as wiring. Its primary functions include:

- Performing low-level transfer of data between network nodes
- Managing low-level signaling across physical media
- Physical wiring, cabling, and radio frequency spectrum

Each of these layers plays a distinctive role in the delivery of information from one computing device to another. An analogy might better clarify their distinctive roles. Consider a passenger train moving toward its destination. The tracks, railroad switches, lights, and stations are performing similar functions as network media services in a communications architecture.The train itself — including engine, cars, and conductor — provides the transport services.

117

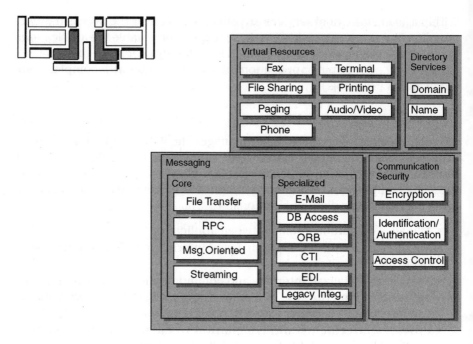

Exhibit 5. Communication Services.

Additionally, at the station, passengers have various services to choose from: the express train, dinner train, destination, and so forth. These services at the station are analogous to the communication services component of the architecture.

The rest of this chapter looks at each of these layers in more detail.

COMMUNICATION SERVICES

There are five primary communications services categories (Exhibit 5):

- Core Messaging services
- Specialized Messaging services
- Communications Security services
- Virtual Resource services
- Directory services

CORE MESSAGING SERVICES

Broadly defined, messaging is sending information or commands between two or more recipients. Recipients may be computers, people, or processes in a computer. To send this message, a protocol (or in some cases, multiple protocols) is used that both the sender and receiver can understand. A protocol is a set of rules describing, in technical terms, how two end points should exchange information. Protocols exist at several levels during the exchange of information. Protocols facilitate transport of the message carrying the information. Both end points must recognize and observe the protocol. As an example, a common protocol in today's networks is the Transmission Control Protocol/Internet Protocol (TCP/IP). TCP/IP is the principle method for transmitting data over the Internet. This protocol is responsible for ensuring that a series of data packets sent over a network arrives at the destination and is properly sequenced.

Messaging services transfer formatted information from one process to another. By drawing upon messaging services, applications can shield themselves from the complexity of the low-level transport services. There are three key messaging styles used to support Interprocess Communication (IPC): Store and Forward, Synchronous, and Asynchronous Messaging.

Store and forward messaging provides deferred message processing. For example, store and forward messaging may use an e-mail infrastructure upon which to build applications. Common uses would be for forms routing and e-mail.

Synchronous messaging allows an application to send a message to another application and wait for a reply before continuing. Synchronous messaging is typically used for update and general business transactions. It requires time-out processing to allow the application to reacquire control in the event of failure.

Asynchronous messaging allows an application to send a message to another application and continue processing before a reply is received. Asynchronous messaging is typically used for larger retrieval type processing, such as retrieval of larger lists of data than can be contained in one message.

Messaging styles are important because they serve as the primary link to the application and business requirements. For example, suppose a business process requiring a series of processing steps needs to be automated. Additionally, each step needs to be performed in sequence at real time. Before continuing to the next step of the process, an application must know if the previous step was successful. Because of the send-receive-continue nature of the business process, the more appropriate messaging style for this application is synchronous messaging.

In addition to the messaging styles, interprocess messaging is typically implemented in one of two ways:

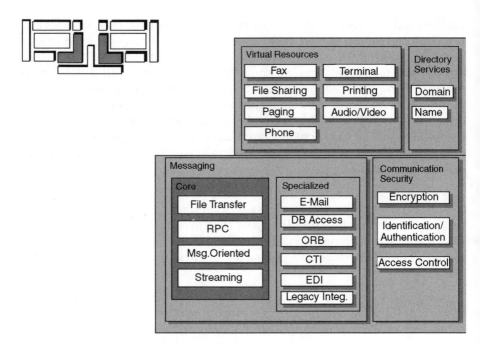

Exhibit 6. Core Messaging Services.

Remote Procedure Calls (RPC) Services

RPCs are a type of protocol by which an application sends a request to a remote system to execute a designated procedure using the supplied arguments and return the result.

- Function based: uses the subroutine model of programming. The message interface is built upon the calling program passing the appropriate parameters and receiving the returned information.

- Message based: uses a defined message format to exchange information between processes. While a portion of the message may be unstructured, a defined header component is normally included. A message-based approach is not limited to the call/return structure of the function-based model and can be used in a .conversational manner.

Core messaging services can be divided into the following services (Exhibit 6):

- File transfer services
- RPC (Remote procedure call) services
- message-oriented services
- Streaming services

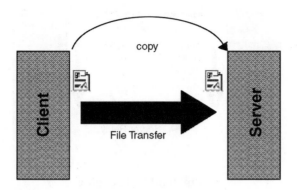

Exhibit 7. File Transfer.

File Transfer Services

File Transfer services enable the copying and receiving of files or other large blocks of data between two resources. Exhibit 7 depicts File Transfer, in which a bulk data transfer occurs (possibly in either direction). Note that a file transfer copies a file, resulting in a copy on both machines.

The following are examples of File Transfer protocols and standards.

File Transfer Protocol (FTP)

Allows users to upload and download files across the network. FTP also provides a mechanism to obtain file name, directory name, attributes, and file size information. Remote file access protocols such as Network File System (NFS) also use a block transfer method but are optimized for online read/write paging of a file.

Hypertext Transfer Protocol (HTTP). Within a web-based environment, web servers transfer HTML pages to clients using HTTP. HTTP can be thought of as a lightweight file transfer protocol optimized for transferring small files. HTTP reduces the inefficiencies of the FTP protocol. HTTP runs on top of TCP/IP and was developed specifically for the transmission of hypertext between client and server.

Secure Hypertext Transfer Protocol (S-HTTP). A secure form of HTTP, mostly for financial transactions on the web. S-HTTP has gained a small level of acceptance among merchants selling products on the Internet as a way to conduct financial transactions (using credit card numbers or passing sensitive information) without the risk of unauthorized people intercepting this information. S-HTTP incorporates various cryptographic message formats such as DSA and RSA standards into both the web client and the web server.

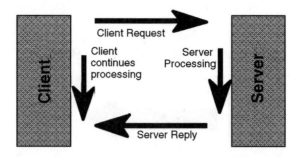

Exhibit 8. RPC Messaging.

File Transfer and Access Management (FTAM). The OSI (Open Systems Interconnection) standard is used for file transfer, file access, and file manExhibit 8 depicts RPC messaging, in which the message originator stops processing while waiting for a reply.

RPCs emulate the function call mechanisms found in procedural languages (e.g., the C language). This means that control is passed from the main logic of a program to the called function, with control returning to the main program once the called function completes its task. Because RPCs perform this mechanism across the network, they pass some element of control from one process to another, for example, from the client to the server. Because the client is dependent on the response from the server, it is normally blocked from performing any additional processing until a response is received. This type of synchronous data exchange is also referred to as blocking communications.

Exhibit 8 depicts RPC messaging in which the message originator stops processing while waiting for a reply.

Message-Oriented Services

Message-oriented services refers to the process of distributing data and control through the exchange of records known as "messages." Message-oriented services provide the application developer with a set of simple verbs (e.g., connect, send, receive, and disconnect) that are used to exchange information with other distributed applications.

For example, to send data to a remote process, the application developer uses a "send" verb. This verb, along with the appropriate parameters (e.g., data to be sent and the process's logical name), is included as part of the application code.

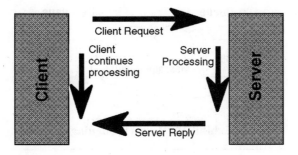

Exhibit 9. Message Passing.

Once the verb is called, the message-oriented services are responsible for managing the interface to the underlying communications architecture via the communications protocol APIs and ensuring the delivery of the information to the remote process. This interface may require that message-oriented services have the following capabilities.

- Translating mnemonic or logical process names to operating system compatible formats
- Opening a communications session and negotiating parameters for the session
- Translating data to the proper format
- Transferring data and control messages during the session
- Recovering any information if errors occur during transmission
- Passing results information and status to the application

An application continues processing after executing a message-oriented services verb, allowing the reply to arrive at a subsequent time. Thus, unlike RPCs, Message-Oriented Services implements a "nonblocking" messaging architecture.

message-oriented services products typically support communication among various computing platforms (e.g., DOS, Windows, OS/2, Macintosh, UNIX, and mainframes).

There are three types of message-oriented services commonly implemented:

- Message Passing
- Message Queuing
- Publish and Subscribe

Message Passing. This is a direct, application-to-application communication model. An application request is sent in the form of a message from one application to another. The communication method can be either syn-

123

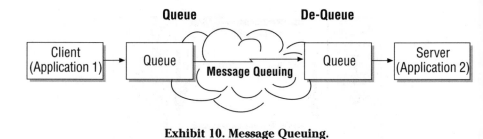

Exhibit 10. Message Queuing.

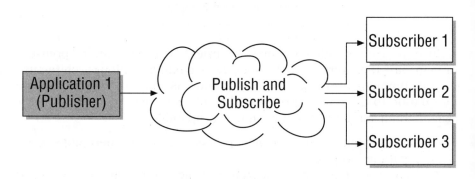

Exhibit 11. Publish and Subscribe Messaging.

chronous (in this case the sending applications waits for a response from the receiving application, like RPCs) or asynchronous (through callback routines). In a message-passing model, a direct link between two applications that participate in the message exchange is always maintained (Exhibit 9).

Message Queuing. Message Queuing (also known as Store and Forward) is an indirect application-to-application communication model that allows applications to communicate via message queues rather than by calling each other directly (Exhibit 10). Message queuing is asynchronous by nature and connectionless, meaning that the recipient need not be directly available when the message is sent. Moreover, it implies support for reliable, guaranteed, and assured (nonduplicate) message delivery.

Publish and Subscribe. Publish and Subscribe (also known as Push messaging) is a special type of data delivery mechanism that allows processes to register an interest in (i.e., subscribe to) certain messages or events (Exhibit 11). An application sends (publishes) a message which is then forwarded to all processes that subscribe to it.

Streaming Services

Streaming is the process of transferring time-sensitive data streams (e.g., video or audio) in real time. Streaming differs from the other types of core

124

Functionality	Sample Protocol options	Architecture Service
Controlling media delivery	RTSP or proprietary	Streaming messaging service
Monitoring data stream	RTCP or proprietary	Streaming messaging service
End-to-end delivery of stream	RTP or proprietary	Streaming messaging service
Message transport	UDP, Multicast UDP, TCP	Message transport service
Packet forwarding/Internetworking	IP, IP multicast	Packet forwarding/Internetworking service

Exhibit 12. Streaming Architecture Options

messaging services in that it delivers a continuous, one-way stream of data rather than the relatively short messages associated with RPC and message-oriented messaging or the large batch transfers associated with File Transfer. (While the media stream is one-way from the server to the client, the client can issue stream controls to the server.) Streaming may be used to deliver video, audio, and other real-time content across the Internet or within enterprise networks.

Streaming is an emerging technology. While some multimedia products use proprietary streaming mechanisms, other products incorporate standards. Data streams are delivered using several protocols that are layered to assemble the necessary functionality. The following are examples of emerging standards for streaming protocols.

Real-Time Streaming Protocol (RTSP). RTSP is the proposed Internet protocol for establishing and controlling on-demand delivery of real-time data. For example, clients can use RTSP to request specific media from a media server, to issue commands such as play, record, and pause, and to control media delivery speed. Because RTSP simply controls media delivery, it is layered on top of other protocols, such as the following.

Real-Time Transport Protocol (RTP). Actual delivery of streaming data occurs through real-time protocols such as RTP. RTP provides end-to-end data delivery for applications transmitting real-time data over multicast or unicast network services. RTP conveys encoding, timing, and sequencing information to allow receivers to properly reconstruct the media stream. RTP is independent of the underlying transport service, but it is typically used with UDP. It may also be used with Multicast UDP, TCP/IP, or IP Multicast.

Real-Time Control Protocol (RTCP). RTP is augmented by the RTCP. RTCP allows nodes to identify stream participants and communicate about the quality of data delivery.

Exhibit 12 summarizes the protocol layering that supports streaming.

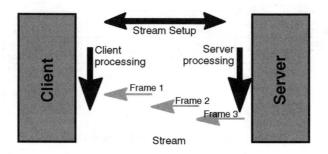

Exhibit 13. Streaming.

A key attribute of any streaming architecture is the adherence to a flow of time-sequenced data packets. Each series of packets contains the necessary information to play the next segment in a sound or video clip. Exhibit 13 highlights the one-way, time-sequenced nature of the flow of data packets for a streaming architecture.

SPECIALIZED MESSAGING SERVICES

Specialized messaging services extend the core messaging services to provide additional functionality. Specialized messaging services may extend core messaging services in the following general ways:

- Providing messaging among specialized systems by drawing upon basic messaging capabilities
- Defining specialized message layouts
- Defining specialized intersystem protocols
- Suggesting ways in which messaging draws upon directory and security services to deliver a complete messaging environment

An example of a specialized messaging service is E-Mail Messaging. E-Mail Messaging is an implementation of astore-and-forward message-oriented services, in that E-Mail Messaging defines specialized, mail-related message layouts and protocols that utilize store-and-forward messaging.

Specialized messaging services is comprised of the following categories (Exhibit 14):

- E-Mail Messaging
- CTI Messaging
- EDI Messaging
- Object Request Broker Messaging
- Database Access Messaging
- Legacy Integration Messaging

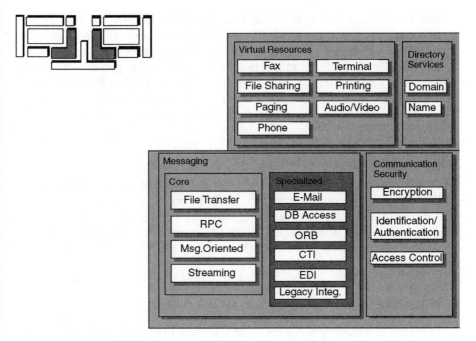

Exhibit 14. Specialized Messaging Services.

E-Mail Messaging Services

E-Mail Messaging services reliably exchange messages using the store-and-forward messaging style. E-mail message systems traditionally include a rudimentary form of directory services (discussed later). While some e-mail products use proprietary protocols, the following are examples of e-mail-related standards:

X.400. The X.400 message handling system standard defines a platform independent standard for store-and-forward message transfers among mail servers. X.400 is often used as a backbone e-mail service, with gateways providing interconnection with end-user systems.

Simple Mail Transfer Protocol (SMTP). SMTP is a UNIX/Internet standard for transferring e-mail among servers.

Multi-Purpose Internet Mail Extensions (MIME). MIME is a protocol that enables Internet users to exchange multimedia e-mail messages.

Post Office Protocol (POP). POP3 is used to distribute e-mail from an SMTP server to the actual recipient.

Internet Message Access Protocol, Version 4 (IMAP4). IMAP4 allows a client to access and manipulate e-mail messages on a server. IMAP4 permits manipulation of remote message folders, called "mailboxes," in a way that is functionally equivalent to local mailboxes. IMAP4 also provides the capability for an offline client to resynchronize with the server. IMAP4 includes standards for message handling features that allow users to download message header information and then decide which e-mail message contents to download.

Database Messaging Services

Database Messaging services (also known as Database Access Middleware, or DBAM) provide connectivity for clients to access databases throughout the enterprise. Database messaging software draws upon basic interprocess messaging capabilities (e.g., RPCs) to support database connectivity. DBAM can be grouped into one of three categories:

- Open
- Native
- Gateway

Open database messaging services typically provide single applications seamless access to multiple data sources, both relational and nonrelational, through a standard application programming interface (API) set. Examples include ODBC (Open Database Connectivity) and JDBC (Java Database Connectivity). ODBC is considered an industry de facto standard.

By contrast, *native* database messaging services are those services, usually proprietary, provided by the DBMS vendor. Examples include SQL*Net for Oracle DBMS and DB-LIB for Sybase DBMS.

Additionally, *gateway* database messaging services can be used to facilitate migration of data from one environment to another. For example, if data in a DB2 environment needs to be integrated with data in a Sybase environment, Gateway DBAM can enable the integration.

Object Request Broker (ORB) Messaging Services

ORB Messaging enables objects to transparently make requests of, and receive responses from, other objects located locally or remotely. Objects communicate through an ORB. An ORB enables client objects to access server objects either locally or remotely over a network and invoke operations (i.e., functions and methods) on them. ORBs typically provide interoperability between heterogeneous client and server environments across languages, operating systems, network protocols. In that respect, some have said that ORBs will become a kind of "ultimate middleware" for truly distributed processing. A standardized Interface Definition Language

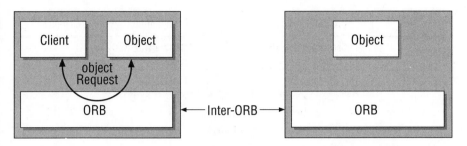

Exhibit 15. CORBA-Based Object Request Broker Messaging.

(IDL) defines the interfaces that applications must use to access the ORB Services. The two major Object Request Broker standards/implementations are

- Object Management Group's Common Object Request Broker Architecture (CORBA) (www.omg.org)
- Microsoft's (Distributed) Component Object Model (COM/DCOM) (www.microsoft.com)

CORBA. Common Object Request Broker Architecture (CORBA) is a standard for distributed objects being developed by the Object Management Group (OMG). The OMG is a consortium of software vendors and end users. Many OMG member companies are developing commercial products that support the CORBA standards or are developing software that use those standards. CORBA provides the mechanism by which objects transparently make requests and receive responses, as defined by OMG's ORB. The CORBA ORB is an application framework that provides interoperability between objects, built in different languages, running on different machines in heterogeneous distributed environments.

The OMG's Internet Inter-Orb Protocol (IIOP) specifies a set of message formats and common data representations for communication between ORBs over TCP/IP networks. CORBA-based Object Messaging is summarized in Exhibit 15.

Component Object Model. Component Object Model (COM) is a client/server object-based model, developed by Microsoft, designed to allow software components and applications to interact with each other in a uniform and standard way. The COM standard is partly a specification and partly an implementation. The specification defines mechanisms for the creation of objects and communication between objects. This part of the specification is paper based and is not dependent on any particular language or operating system. Any language can be used as long as the standard is incorporated. The implementation part is the COM library that

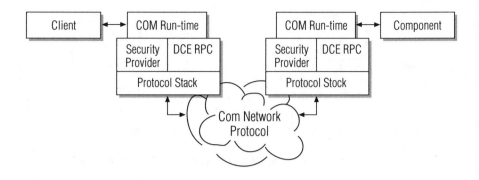

Exhibit 16. Microsoft COM/DCOM Messaging.

provides a number of services that support a mechanism that allows applications to connect to each other as software objects (Exhibit 16).

COM is not a software layer through which all communications between objects occur. Instead, COM serves as a broker and name space keeper to connect a client and an object but, once that connection is established, the client and object communicate directly without having the overhead of passing through a central piece of API code. Originally conceived as a compound document architecture, COM has been evolved to a full object request broker including recently added features for distributed object computing. DCOM (Distributed COM) contains features for extending the object model across the network using the DCE RPC mechanism. In sum, COM defines how components should be built and how they should interact. DCOM defines how they should be distributed. Currently, COM/DCOM is only supported on Windows-based machines. However, third-party vendors are in the process of porting this object model to other platforms such as Macintosh, UNIX, etc.

CTI Messaging Services

Computer-Telephone Integration (CTI) integrates computer systems and telephone systems to coordinate data and telephony activities. For example, CTI can be used to associate a customer's database entry with the customer's telephone call and route the call accordingly.

CTI Messaging supports communication among clients, CTI servers, PBXs/ACDs, hybrid platforms, networks, and external telephony devices. CTI Messaging relies upon proprietary PBX/ACD APIs, CTI vendor-specific APIs or message sets, and industry-standard APIs.

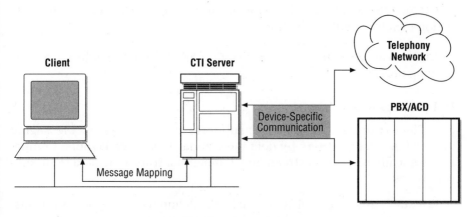

Exhibit 17. CTI Messaging.

CTI Messaging has two primary functions (Exhibit 17):

1. Device-specific communication
   Manages direct communications between telephony devices and data devices.
   Allows applications to control PBXs, key telephone systems, ISDN, analog PSTN, cellular, Centrex, etc., and supports features such as address translation, call setup, call answering, call dropping, and caller ID.
   Provides interface-to-carrier networks for call delivery and call-related messaging.
2. Message mapping
   Translates device-specific communication to generic API and message set

CTI products can be divided into the following categories:

CTI Platform-Specific Products. These can only be implemented on the hardware of a specific vendor.

CTI Telephony-Based API Products. These include proprietary PBX/ACD-based messaging sets which permit external devices to interface with the vendor's PBX/ACD call and station control logic.

CTI Server/Workstation-Based or Host-Based API Products. These operate on a particular computer vendor's hardware platform and provide call control and messaging functionality.

CTI Cross-Platform Vendors. These products have been ported to multiple hardware platforms/operating systems.

CTI Enabling Solutions. These focus solely on call control and call/application synchronization functions.

CTI Enterprise Solutions. These provide all CTI business functions to varying degrees.

EDI Messaging Services

EDI (Electronic Data Interchange) supports system-to-system messaging among business partners by defining standard message layouts. Companies typically use EDI to streamline commercial transactions in their supply chains.

EDI standards (e.g., EDIFACT, ANSI X12) define record layouts for transactions such as "purchase orders." EDI services include the generation and translation of EDI messages according to the various public message layout standards.

EDI messaging can be implemented via electronic mail or customized message-oriented architectures.

Legacy Integration Services

Legacy services provide gateways to mainframe legacy systems. Design techniques for integration with existing systems can be grouped into two broad categories:

- Front end access: access of information through screens/windows (this will be further discussed in the Terminal Emulation section in Virtual Resources later in this chapter).
- Back end access: this approach tends to be used when existing data stores have information that is needed in the client/server environment but accessing the information through existing screens or functions is not feasible. Legacy messaging services typically include remote data access through gateways. A database gateway provides an interface between the client/server environment and the legacy system. The gateway provides an ability to access and manipulate the data in the legacy system.

COMMUNICATION SECURITY SERVICES

As organizations open up their computing resources to business partners, customers, and a broader audiences of employees, security becomes one of the hottest topics in most discussions. This section focuses on network communications-related security. For a broader perspective on security in netcentric environments, refer to Chapter 28. This chapter will introduce some of the key communications architecture security concepts.

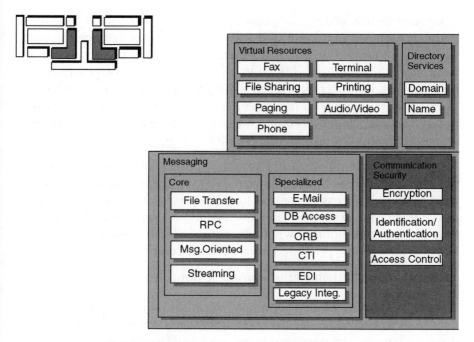

Exhibit 18. Communication Security Services.

Communications security services can be broken down into the following three categories (Exhibit 18):

- Encryption Services
- Identification and Authentication Services
- Access Control Services

Encryption Services

Encryption services encrypt data prior to network transfer to prevent unauthorized interception. (Note that encryption can occur within the Communication Services layer, the Transport Services layer, or the Network Media Services layer.) Within the Communication Services layer, encryption occurs at the top of the protocol stack and is typically performed in an application (e.g., in an e-mail application). This is an end-to-end approach that can leave the remainder of the protocol stack (i.e., the Transport Services and the Network Media Services) unaffected. Refer to the Transport Security topic in the Transport Services section for more information on security.

Identification/Authentication Services

Identification/Authentication services verify network access requests by validating that users are who they claim to be. For secure systems, one or more Identification/Authentication mechanisms can be used to validate authorized users and integrated with Access Control Services to verify which functions and data they have access to. Within the corporate network, Identification/Authentication services are often included in directory services products like Novell's NDS (NetWare Directory Services) or Microsoft's Windows NT Domain Services. These products require the user to have an established account and supply a password before access is granted to resources through the directory.

Identification/Authentication for accessing resources across the Internet or an intranet is not as simple and is a rapidly evolving area. web sites need to restrict access to areas of information and functionality to known customers or business partners. More granular Identification/Authentication services are required where sensitive individual customer account information must be protected from other customers.

Identification/Authentication can occur through various means:

Basic ID/Authentication. This requires that the web client supply a user name and password before a request is serviced. Basic ID/Authentication does not encrypt the password in any way, and thus the password travels in the clear over the network where it can be detected with a network sniffer program or device. Basic ID/Authentication is not secure enough for banking applications or anyplace where there may be a financial incentive for someone to steal someone's account information. It is, however, the easiest mechanism to set up and administer and requires no special software at the web client.

ID/Password Encryption. This offers a somewhat higher level of security by requiring that the user name and password be encrypted during transit. The user name and password are transmitted as a scrambled message as part of each request because there is no persistent connection open between the web client and the web server.

Digital Certificates or Signatures. These are encrypted digital keys that are issued by a third party "trusted" organization (i.e., Verisign). They are used to verify a user's authenticity.

Hardware Tokens. These are small physical devices that may generate a one-time password or that may be inserted into a card reader for ID/Authentication purposes.

Virtual Tokens. These are typically a file on a floppy or hard drive used for ID/Authentication (e.g., Lotus Notes ID file).

Biometric Identification. This involves the analysis of biological characteristics (such as fingerprints, voice recognition, or retinal scans) to verify an individual's identify.

Access Control Services

When a user requests access to network resources, the Access Control service determines if the user has the appropriate permissions or privileges and either allows or disallows the access. (This occurs after the user has been properly identified and authenticated.)

The following are examples of ways to implement Access Control services:

Network Operating Systems. Access Control services are bundled with all network operating systems to control user access to network resources.

Application Proxies. An application-level proxy, or application-level gateway, is a robust type of firewall. (A firewall is a system that enforces an access control policy between a trusted internal network and an untrusted external network.) The application proxy acts at the application level rather than the network level. The proxy acts as a go-between for the end user by completing the user-requested tasks on its own and then transferring the information to the user. The proxy manages a database of allowed user actions, which it checks prior to performing the request.

Filters. World Wide Web filters can prevent users from accessing specified content or Internet addresses. Products can limit access based on keywords, network addresses, time-of-day, user categories, etc. Filters are typically implemented on a firewall.

Servers, Applications, and Databases. Access Control can occur locally on a server to limit access to specific system resources or files. Applications and databases can also authorize users for specific levels of access within their control. (This functionality is within the Environment Services grouping in the execution architecture.)

DIRECTORY SERVICES

Directory services will play a major role in the future of netcentric computing, primarily because of the increasingly distributed and dynamic nature of netcentric environments. Directory services manage information about resources on the network and perform a variety of processes. These processes range from simple name-to-address resolution (e.g., when *www.ac.com* is typed in a browser connected to the Internet, that name resolves to IP address 204.167.146.195) to the logical integration of heterogeneous systems to create a common view of resources.

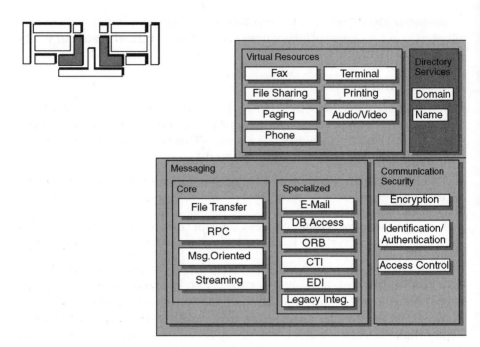

Exhibit 19. Directory Services.

Directory ervices typically perform one or many of the following functions:

- Store information about network resources and users, and track relationships
- Organize resource access information in order to aid in the location of and access to other resources throughout the network
- Provide location transparency, because resources are accessed through a directory rather than based on their physical location
- Convert between logical resource names and physical resource addresses
- Interact with Security services such as identification/authentication and access control services to maintain necessary access permissions and privileges
- Provide single network logon to file and print resources; in certain cases, provide single network logon for network applications integrated with the directory services
- Distribute and synchronize directory information throughout the environment (for reliability and location-independent access)

Directory services is comprised of two subservices: name services and domain services (Exhibit 19).

Name Services

The Name service creates a logical "pronounceable" name in place of a binary machine number. These services could be used by other communications services such as File Transfer, Message services, and Terminal services. A Name service can be implemented on its own or as part of a full-featured Directory service.

Domain Services

A network domain is a set of network nodes under common control (i.e., common security and logins, unified addressing, coordinated management, etc.). Domain services manage these types of activities for the network nodes in a domain. Domain services may be limited in their ability to support heterogeneous systems, and in the ability to scale to support the enterprise.

Most Directory services running today tend to eitherprovide limited functionality or to be highly proprietary. In fact, many organizations maintain multiple directories, from e-mail to printer and host information. In a netcentric environment, it is crucial to provide seamless location of, and access to, resources, individuals, and applications. Emerging Directory service technologies such as the Lightweight Directory Access Protocol (LDAP) may prove key in providing integrated, open Directory services for netcentric applications.

VIRTUAL RESOURCE SERVICES

Virtual Resource services proxy or mimic the capabilities of specialized, network-connected resources. This allows a generic network node to emulate a specialized physical device. In this way, network users can interface with a variety of specialized resources.

A common example of a Virtual Resource service is the capability to print to a network printer as if it were directly attached to a workstation.

Virtual Resource Services include the following (Exhibit 20):

- Terminal services
- Print services
- File Sharing services
- Phone services
- Fax services
- Audio/Video Services
- Paging services

Terminal Services

Terminal services allow a client to connect to a nonlocal host via a network and to emulate the profile (e.g., the keyboard and screen characteristics)

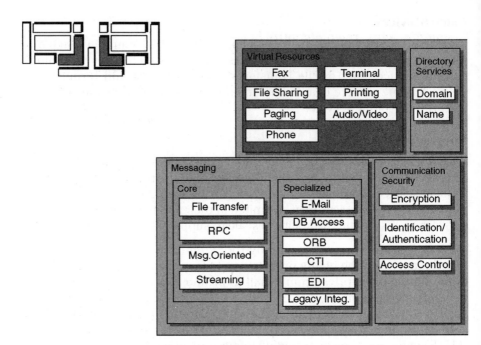

Exhibit 20. Virtual Resource Services.

required by the host application. For example, when a workstation application logs on to a mainframe, the workstation functions as a dumb terminal. Terminal services receive user input and send data streams back to the host processor. If connecting from a PC to another PC, the workstation might act as a remote control terminal (e.g., PC Anywhere).

The following are examples of Terminal services:

Telnet: a simple and widely used terminal emulation protocol that is part of the TCP/IP communications protocol. Telnet operates establishing a TCP connection with the remotely located login server, minicomputer, or mainframe. The client's keyboard strokes are sent to the remote machine while the remote machine sends back the characters displayed on the local terminal screen.

3270 emulation: emulation of the 3270 protocol that is used by IBM mainframe terminals.

tn3270: a Telnet program that includes the 3270 protocol for logging onto IBM mainframes; part of the TCP/IP protocol suite.

X Window System: allows users to simultaneously access applications on one or more UNIX servers and display results in multiple windows on a local display. Recent enhancements to XWS include integration with the web and optimization of network traffic (caching, compression, etc.).

Remote control: while terminal emulation is typically used in host-based environments, remote control is a sophisticated type of client/server Terminal service. Remote control allows a client computer to control the processing on a remote desktop computer. The GUI on the client computer looks as if it is the GUI on the remote desktop. This makes it appear as if the remote applications are running on the client.

rlogin: a remote terminal service implemented under BSD UNIX. The concept behind rlogin is that it supports "trusted" hosts. This is accomplished by having a set of machines that share common file access rights and logins. The user controls access by authorizing remote login based on a remote host and remote user name. This service is generally considered a security risk and avoided in most business system configurations.

Print Services

Print services connect network workstations to shared printers. The administration of Print services is usually handled by a print server. Depending on the size of the network and the amount of resources the server must manage, the print server may run on a dedicated machine or on a machine that performs other server functions. Print servers queue print jobs sent to network printers; the jobs are stored in the server's print buffer and then sent to the appropriate network printer as it becomes available. Print services can also provide the client with information, including print job status, and can manage in-progress print jobs.

File Sharing Services

File Sharing services allow users to view, manage, read, and write files that may be located on a variety of platforms in a variety of locations. File Sharing services enable a unified view of independent file systems. This is represented in Exhibit 21, which shows how a client can perceive remote files as being local.

File Sharing services typically provide some or all of the following capabilities:

Transparent access: access to remote files as if they were local

Multiuser access: distribution and synchronization of files among multiple users, including file locking to manage access requests by multiple users

File access control: use of Security services (user authentication and authorization) to manage file system security

Multiplatform access: access to files located on various platforms (e.g., UNIX, NT, etc.)

Integrated file directory: a logical directory structure that combines all accessible file directories, regardless of the physical directory structure

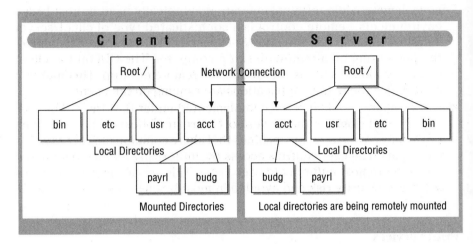

Exhibit 21. UNIX File Sharing Services Example.

Fault tolerance: use of primary and replica file servers to ensure high availability of file system

Scalability: ability to integrate networks and distributed file systems of various sizes

Phone Services

Phone virtual resource services extend telephony capabilities to computer platforms. For example, an application on a desktop computer can place and receive telephone calls for the user. Phone virtual resource services may be used in customer care centers, help desks, or any other environment in which it is useful for a computer to replace a telephone handset.

Phone services enable clients, servers, and specialized telephony nodes (PBXs, ACDs, etc.) to control the telephony environment through the following telephony controls:

- Call control
- Controls telephone features
- Controls recorded messages
- Manipulates real time call activities (e.g., make call, answer, transfer, hold, conference, mute transfer, release, route call, call treatments, and digits collected)
- Telephone status control
- Controls telephone status functions
- Logs users in and out of the system
- Sets ready, not ready, and make busy statuses for users

The following are examples of uses of Phone virtual resources.

PC Telephony. PC telephony products allow desktop computers to act as conduits for voice telephone calls.

Internet Telephony. Internet telephony products enable voice telephone calls (and faxing, voice mail retrieval, etc.) through the Internet. For example, an Internet telephony product can accept voice input into a workstation, translate it into an IP data stream, and route it through the Internet to a destination workstation where the data is translated back into audio.

Desktop Voice Mail. Various products enable users to manage voice mail messages using a desktop computer.

Fax Services

Fax services provide for the management of both inbound and outbound fax transmissions. If fax is used as a medium for communicating with customers or remote employees, inbound fax services may be required for centrally receiving and electronically routing faxes to the intended recipient. Outbound fax services can be as simple as supporting the sharing on the network of a single fax machine or group of machines for sending faxes.

Examples of Fax service functionality include the following:

- Managing incoming faxes
- Receiving faxes via the telephone network
- Queuing faxes
- Routing and distributing faxes
- Displaying or printing faxes
- Managing outgoing faxes
- Generating faxes
- Queuing faxes
- Transferring faxes via the telephone network

Fax services can provide centrally managed faxing capabilities, thus eliminating the need for fax modems on every workstation. A fax server generally provides Fax services to clients, such as receiving, queuing, and distributing incoming faxes, and queuing and sending outgoing faxes. Clients can view faxes and generate faxes to be sent.

Applications may compose and transfer faxes as part of notifying users or delivering information. For example, an application may use Fax services to add customer-specific information to a delivery receipt form and fax the form to a customer.

Audio/Video Services

Audio/Video services allow nodes to interact with multimedia data streams. These services may be implemented as audio only, video only, or combined audio/video.

Audio Services. Audio services allow components to interface with audio streams such as the delivery of music or radio content over data networks.

Video Services. Video services allow components to interface with video streams such as video surveillance. Video services can add simple video monitor capabilities to a computer, or they can transform the computer into a sophisticated video platform with the ability to generate and manipulate video.

Combined Audio/Video Services. Video and audio content is often delivered simultaneously. This may be accomplished by transferring separate audio and video streams or by transferring a single interleaved stream. Examples include video conferencing and television (traditional or interactive).

Audio/Video services can include the following functionalities:

- Streaming content (audio, video, or both) to end users
- Managing buffering of a data stream to ensure uninterrupted viewing/listening
- Performing compression and decompression of data
- Managing communications protocols to ensure smooth delivery of content
- Managing library of stored content or managing generation of live content

Audio/Video services draw upon lower-level services such as streaming (see Streaming Messaging services) and IP Multicast (see Packet Forwarding/Internetworking services) to efficiently deliver content across the network.

Paging Services

Wireless short messaging (i.e., paging) can be implemented through wireless systems such as paging networks, GSM voice/data networks, PCS voice/data networks, and dedicated wireless data networks.

Paging virtual resource services provide the message formatting and display functionality that allows network nodes to interface with wireless paging systems. This service emulates the capabilities of one-way and two-way pagers (Exhibit 22).

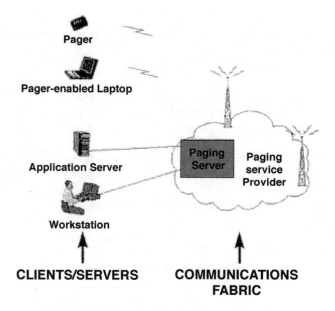

Pager

Pager-enabled Laptop

Application Server

Paging Server

Paging service Provider

Workstation

CLIENTS/SERVERS **COMMUNICATIONS FABRIC**

Exhibit 22. Use of a Paging Virtual Resource.

Paging systems allow pages to be generated in various ways:

- E-mail messages to a specified mailbox
- DTMF (touch tone) signaling to a voice response system
- Encoded digital messages transferred into a paging provider gateway
- Messages transferred to a locally attached two-way wireless pager

COMMUNICATION SERVICES LAYER SUMMARY

Overall, the Communication services layer provides the foundation for net-centric applications enabling client/server and virtual resource communications. Selecting the appropriate Communication services, that meet the business and applications requirements is a key step to ensuring a successful communications architecture. In addition, ensuring the required Transport services support the selected Communication services is important. Transport services are the subject of the next section.

TRANSPORT SERVICES

Transport services are the portion of the communications architecture that provides the movement of information across a network. While the communications fabric includes all the hardware, software, and services between the client and server nodes, Transport services play a key role

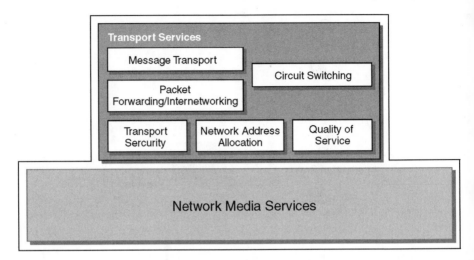

Exhibit 23. Transport Services.

performing network functions across the enterprise or between enterprises. Transport services include the following (see also Exhibit 23):

- Message Transport services
- Packet Forwarding/Internetworking services
- Circuit Switching services
- Transport Security services
- Network Address Allocation services
- Quality of Service services

Message Transport Services

Message Transport services are responsible for the end-to-end delivery of messages. They can include the following functionality.

End-to-End Data Transfer. The Message Transport service formats messages for sending and confirms the integrity of received messages.

Connection Control. The Message Transport service may establish end-to-end (client–server) connections and track addresses and other associated information for the connection. The service also tears down connections and handles hard connection failures.

Reliable Transfer. The Message Transport service may manage reliable delivery of messages through the use of acknowledgments and retransmissions.

Flow Control. The Message Transport service may allow the receiver to govern the rate at which the sender transfers data.

Multiplexing. The Message Transport service may define multiple addresses or ports within a single network node, allowing multiple processes on the node to have their own communications paths.

It is important to note that some transport services do not implement all of the listed functionalities. For example, the UDP protocol does not offer connection control or reliable transfer.

The following are examples of protocols that provide message transport:

- SPX (Sequenced Packet eXchange)
- TCP (Transmission Control Protocol)
- UDP (User Datagram Protocol)
- NetBIOS/NetBEUI (Network Basic Input/Output System/NetBIOS Extended User Interface)
- APPC (Advanced Program-to-Program Communications)
- AppleTalk

Packet Forwarding/Internetworking Services

Packet Forwarding/Internetworking services transfer data packets and manage the path that data takes through the network. They include the following functionalities:

Fragmentation/Reassembly. The Packet Forwarding/Internetworking service divides an application message into multiple packets of a size suitable for network transmission. The individual packets include information to allow the receiving node to reassemble them into the message. The service also validates the integrity of received packets and buffers, reorders, and reassembles packets into a complete message.

Addressing. The Packet Forwarding/Internetworking service encapsulates packets with addressing information.

Routing. The Packet Forwarding/Internetworking service can maintain routing information (a view of the network topology) that is used to determine the best route for each packet. Routing decisions are made based on the cost, percent utilization, delay, reliability, and similar factors for each possible route through the network.

Switching. Switching is the process of receiving a packet, selecting an appropriate outgoing path, and sending the packet. Switching is performed by routers and switches within the communications fabric. Switching can be implemented in several ways.

145

- For some network protocols (e.g., TCP/IP) routers draw upon dynamic routing information to switch packets to the appropriate path. This capability is especially important when connecting independent networks or subnets.
- For other network protocols (e.g., Ethernet, Token Ring) switching simply directs packets according to a table of physical addresses. The switch can build the table by "listening" to network traffic and determining which network nodes are connected to which switch port. Some protocols such as Frame Relay involve defining permanent routes (permanent virtual circuits, or PVCs) within the network. Because Frame Relay is switched based upon PVCs, routing functionality is not required.

Multicasting. The Packet Forwarding/Internetworking service may support multicasting, which is the process of transferring a single message to multiple recipients at the same time. Multicasting allows a sender to transfer a single copy of the message to the communications fabric, which then distributes the message to multiple recipients.

The following are examples of protocols that provide Packet Forwarding/Internetworking:

- IP (Internet Protocol)
- IP Multicast (emerging standard that uses a predefined set of IP addresses to instruct network routers to deliver each packet to all users involved in a multicast session)
- IPX (Internetwork Packet Exchange)
- ATM (Asynchronous Transfer Mode)
- Frame Relay
- X.25

The following are examples of network components that perform Packet Forwarding/Internetworking:

- Routers
- Switches
- ATM switches, Frame Relay switches, IP switches, Ethernet switches, etc.

The following are examples of protocols that maintain routing information tables within routers:

Distance Vector Protocols. Each router periodically informs neighboring routers as to the contents of routing table (destination addresses and routing metrics); routing decisions are made based on the total distance and other "costs" for each path:

- IP and IPX Routing Information Protocols (RIP)
- AppleTalk Routing Table Management Protocol (RTMP)
- Cisco's Interior Gateway Routing Protocol (IGRP) and Enhanced IGRP

Link-State Protocols. Each router periodically broadcasts changes to the routers directly on adjacent networks:

- Open Shortest Path First (OSPF)
- ISO's Intermediate System to Intermediate System (IS-IS)
- Novell's NetWare Link Services Protocol (NLSP)

Policy Routing Protocols. These allow Internet backbone routers to accept routing information from neighboring backbone providers on the basis of contracts or other nontechnical criteria; routing algorithms are distance vector:

- Border Gateway Protocol (BGR)
- Interdomain Routing Protocol (IDR)

Circuit Switching

While Message Transport services and Packet Forwarding/Internetworking services support the transfer of packetized data, Circuit Switching services establish physical circuits for the transfer of circuit-switched multimedia- and image-oriented content such as voice, fax, and video.

Circuit Switching services use an end-to-end physical connection between the sender and the receiver that lasts for the duration of the "call" transferred through brief, temporary, logical connections between nodes.

Circuit Switching services include the following functionality:

- Establishing end-to-end path for circuit (may involve multiple intermediate nodes/switches)
- Managing end-to-end path (quality, billing, termination, etc.)

The following are examples of Circuit Switching services:

- Analog dialup telephone circuit
- Cellular telephone circuit
- ISDN (Integrated Services Digital Network)

Transport Security

Transport Security services (within the Transport services layer) perform encryption and filtering.

Transport-Layer Encryption. Encryption within the Transport services layer is performed by encrypting the packets generated by higher level services (e.g., Message Transport) and encapsulating them in lower level packets (e.g., Packet Forwarding/Internetworking). (Note that encryption can also occur within the Communications services layer or the Network Media services layer.) Encryption within the Transport Services layer has the advantage of being independent of both the application and the transmission media, but it may make network monitoring and troubleshooting activities more difficult.

The following standards supportTransport-layer encryption:

- Poin-to Point-Tunneling Protocol
- Layer 2 Tunneling Protocol

Transport-layer Filtering. Network traffic can be controlled at the Transport services layer by filtering data packets based on source or destination addresses and network service. This ensures that only authorized data transfers can occur. This filtering is one of the roles of a packet filtering firewall. (A firewall is a system that enforces an access control policy between a trusted internal network and an untrusted external network.)

The IETF standard IPSec supports interoperability among security systems. IPSec allows two nodes to dynamically agree on a security association based on keys, encryption, authentication algorithms, and other parameters for the connection before any communications take place; it operates in the IP layer and supports TCP or UDP. IPSec will be included as part of IPng or the next generation of IP (IPv6).

Network Address Allocation Services

Network Address Allocation services manage the distribution of addresses to network nodes. This provides more flexibility compared to having all nodes assigned static addresses. This service assigns addresses to nodes when they initially power-on and connect to the network.

The following are examples of standards that implement Network Address Allocation and allow a network node to ask a central resource for the node's network address (e.g., IP address):

- DHCP (Dynamic Host Configuration Protocol)
- BootP (Bootstrap Protocol)

Quality of Service Services

Different types of network traffic (e.g., data, voice, and video) have different quality of service requirements. For example, data associated with video conferencing sessions is useless if it is not delivered "on time." On the other hand, traditional best-effort data services, such as file or e-mail transfer, are not affected by variations in latency. Quality of Service (QoS) services deliver a defined network throughput for designated traffic by allocating dedicated bandwidth, prioritizing data traffic, etc. (Note that, as an alternative to predefined throughput, some QoS protocols can also offer a best effort, i.e., variable, throughput QoS based on available network capacity.)

Exhibit 24. Quality of Service Parameters

Parameter	Description
Connection establishment delay	Time between the connection request and a confirm being received by the requester
Connection establishment failure probability	Chance that the connection will not be established within the maximum establishment delay
Throughput	Bits per second of transmitted data
Transit delay	Time elapsed between when sender transfers packet and recipient receives packet
Residual error rate	Number of lost or corrupted messages compared to total messages in the sampling period
Transfer failure probability	The fraction of the time when the throughput, transit delay, or residual error were not those agreed upon at the start of the connection
Connection release delay	Time between when one node initiates a release and the other node performs the release
Connection release failure probability	Fraction of release attempts which do not succeed
Protection	Specifies a secure connection
Priority	Indicates traffic priority over the connection
Resilience	Probability that the transport layer spontaneously terminates

Exhibit 24 provides a description of various Quality of Service parameters. Quality of Service can be achieved in various ways.

Specialized QoS Communications Protocols. These provide guaranteed QoS.

Asynchronous Transfer Mode (ATM). ATM is a connection-oriented wide area and local area networking protocol that delivers QoS on a per-connection basis. QoS is negotiated as part of the initial connection setup and as network conditions change. Because of the small size of ATM data cells, QoS can be better managed compared to protocols such as Ethernet that have large frames that can tie up network components. For ATM to deliver QOS to applications, ATM must be used end to end.

Resource Reservation Protocol (RSVP). The emerging RSVP specification proposed by the Internet Engineering Task Force (IETF) allows applications to reserve router bandwidth for delay-sensitive IP traffic. With RSVP, QoS is negotiated for each application connection. RSVP enables the network to reserve resources from end to end using Frame Relay techniques on Frame Relay networks, ATM techniques on ATM, and so on. In this way, RSVP can achieve QoS across a variety of network technologies as long as all intermediate nodes are RSVP capable.

IP Stream Switching. This improves network performance but does not guarantee QoS.

149

IP Switching. IP Switching is an emerging technology that can increase network throughput for streams of data by combining IP routing software with ATM switching hardware. With IP Switching, an IP switch analyzes each stream of packets directed from a single source to a specific destination and classifies it as short- or long-lived. Long-lived flows are assigned ATM Virtual Channels (VCs) that bypass the IP router and move through the switching fabric at the full ATM line speed. Short-lived flows continue to be routed through traditional store-and-forward transfer.

Tag Switching. Like IP Switching, emerging Tag Switching technology also improves network throughput for IP data streams. Tag Switching aggregates one or more data streams destined for the same location and assigns a single tag to all associated packets. This allows routers to more efficiently transfer the tagged data. Tag Switching is also known as Multiprotocol Label Switching.

Data Prioritization. This improves network performance for prioritized application traffic but does not guarantee QoS.

Although not an example of end-to-end QoS, various network components can be configured to prioritize their handling of specified types of traffic. For example, routers can be configured to handle legacy mainframe traffic (SNA) in front of other traffic (e.g., TCP/IP). A similar technique is the use of prioritized circuits within Frame Relay in which the Frame Relay network vendor assigns different priorities to different permanent virtual circuits.

Prioritization techniques are of limited effectiveness if data must also pass through network components that are not configured for prioritization (e.g., network components run by third-party network providers).

TRANSPORT SERVICES SUMMARY

Transport services continue to improve and evolve to new levels. Through enhanced quality, tighter security, improved management and control, and increased speeds, Transport services play an important role in moving key business information to an intended destination quickly, safely, and accurately. As netcentric computing continues to evolve, Transport services should continue to converge to an infrastructure based on open industry standard technologies that integrate the many physical networking options available today. The next section discusses these physical networking options in more detail.

NETWORK MEDIA SERVICES

The Network Media layer, which provides the core of the communication fabric from the overall communications architecture framework, offers the following capabilities:

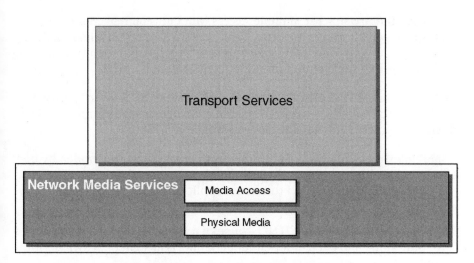

Exhibit 25. Network Media Services.

- Final framing of data for interfacing with the physical network
- Receiving, interpreting, and acting on signals from the communications fabric
- Transferring data through the physical network

Network Media services (Exhibit 25) perform two primary service functions:

- Media Access services
- Physical Media services

Media Access Services

Media Access services manage the low-level transfer of data between network nodes. Media Access services perform the following functions:

Physical Addressing. The Media Access service encapsulates packets with physical address information used by the data link protocol (e.g., Ethernet and Frame Relay).

Packet Transfer. The Media Access service uses the data link communications protocol to frame packets and transfer them to another computer on the same network/subnetwork.

Shared Access. The Media Access service provides a method for multiple network nodes to share access to a physical network. Shared Access schemes include the following:

CSMA/CD (Carrier Sense Multiple Access with Collision Detection). A method by which multiple nodes can access a shared physical media by "listening" until no other transmissions are detected and then transmitting and checking to see if simultaneous transmission occurred.

Token passing. A method of managing access to a shared physical medium by circulating a token (a special control message) among nodes to designate which node has the right to transmit.

Multiplexing. A method of sharing physical media among nodes by consolidating multiple, independent channels into a single circuit. The independent channels (assigned to nodes, applications, or voice calls) can be combined in the following ways:

Time division multiplexing (TDM) — use of a circuit is divided into a series of time slots, and each independent channel is assigned its own periodic slot.

Frequency division multiplexing (FDM) — each independent channel is assigned its own frequency range, allowing all channels to be carried simultaneously.

Flow Control. The Media Access service manages the flow of data to account for differing data transfer rates between devices. For example, flow control would have to limit outbound traffic if a receiving machine or intermediate node operates at a slower data rate, possibly due to the use of different network technologies and topologies, or due to excess network traffic at a node.

Error Recovery. The Media Access service performs error recovery, which is the capability to detect and possibly resolve data corruption that occurs during transmission. Error recovery involves the use of checksums, parity bits, etc.

Encryption. The Media Access service may perform encryption. (Note that encryption can also occur within the Communications services layer or the Transport services layer.) Within the Network Media services layer, encryption occurs as part of the data link protocol (e.g., Ethernet, Frame Relay). In this case, all data are encrypted before being placed on the wire. Such encryption tools are generally hardware products. Encryption at this level has the advantage of being transparent to higher-level services. However, because it is dependent on the data link protocol, it has the disadvantage of requiring a different solution for each data link protocol.

The following are examples of Media Access protocols:

• Ethernet
• Token Ring

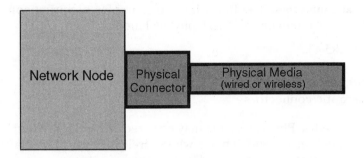

Exhibit 26. Subcomponents of Physical Media.

- FDDI (Fiber Distributed Data Interface)
- Portions of the ATM (Asynchronous Transfer Mode) standard
- HDLC (High-level Data Link Control)/SDLC (Synchronous Data Link Control)
- LAP-B (Link Access Procedure — Balanced)
- T-carrier, E-carrier (e.g., T1, T3, E1, E3)
- TDM and FDM (Time Division Multiplexing and Frequency Division Multiplexing; used on T-carriers, etc.)
- SONET (Synchronous Optical Network), SDH
- PPP (Point-to-Point Protocol), SLIP (Serial Line Internet Protocol)
- V.32, V.34, V.34 bis, etc.
- RS-232, EIA-232
- TDMA and FDMA (Time Division Multiple Access and Frequency Division Multiple Access; used on wireless links)

Specialized services convert between addresses at the Media Access level (i.e., physical addresses like Ethernet) and the Packet Forwarding/Internetworking level (i.e., network addresses like IP). The following protocols are examples of this functionality.

Address Resolution Protocol (ARP). ARP allows a node to obtain the physical address for another node when only the IP address is known.

Reverse Address Resolution Protocol (RARP). RARP allows a node to obtain the IP address for another node when only the physical address is known.

Physical Media Services

The Physical Media are divided into two categories (Exhibit 26):

- Physical connectors
- Physical media (wired or wireless)

Physical Connectors. The following are examples of wiring connectors used to connect network nodes to physical media:

- RJ-11, RJ-45
- BNC
- DB-9, DB-25
- Fiberoptic connectors

Physical Media. Physical Media may be wired or wireless. Wired Physical Media includes wiring and cabling, while wireless Physical Media includes antennas, connectors, and the radio frequency spectrum.

The following are examples of wired physical media:

- Twisted pair wiring
- Shielded twisted pair wiring
- Coaxial cable
- Fiberoptic cable
- Four-pair voice-grade wiring

The following are examples of wireless physical media:

- Cellular antennas and the associated radio frequencies
- Wireless local area network antennas and the associated radio frequencies
- Satellite antennas and the associated radio frequencies

NETWORK MEDIA SERVICES SUMMARY

Without the Network Media services (which we compared earlier to the interconnected train tracks, signals, and switches), information would not be capable of traveling to its intended destination. While this infrastructure is a complex network of numerous interconnected copper wires, fiberoptic cables, and radio antennas, continued change in Network Media services is likely to be slow. We are more likely to continue to see new technologies evolve to adapt and bridge the various physical network options. These technologies make up the essense of netcentric computing, which continues to expand the reach of client/server while delivering rich new content.

CONCLUSION

Today's advanced communications architectures permit organizations to take full advantage of the convergence of computing, communications, and knowledge. Netcentric computing applications provide more direct links with business partners and allow companies to respond quickly to fluctuations in customer demand. As communications architectures grow in sophistication, one should expect the network to enable almost total supply chain integration. Applications that manage and perform business-to-business processes will enable the ultimate virtualization of business: bringing together strategy, people, process, and technology in a unique configuration across multiple companies to serve the customer in a more powerful way than any one company could on its own. That will be the final convergence, one in which most barriers between companies and their customers have been removed.

Chapter 7

An Information Architecture for the Global Manufacturing Enterprise

Robert L. Sloan
Hal H. Green

The two most important responsibilities of leadership are to establish a vision or strategy for the organization and to put in place the systems, processes, and structures that enable the organization to progressively achieve that vision. One of the structures used by manufacturers to create competitive advantage is integrated information systems (IS). Competitive advantage, including cost and differentiation, can be won or lost by marginal differences in the speed, accuracy, and comprehensive nature of information being delivered to decision makers.

An organization's competence in timely decision support capabilities has been given impetus by the total quality movement; the Malcolm Baldrige criteria state that "the ability to access and act on timely, reliable business data is requisite to the achievement of quantitative continual improvement in the delivery of products and services."[1]

Michael Porter has described the importance of horizontal strategy as the interrelationship between business units. Integrated information and control systems support horizontal strategy, enabling independent business units to share key product and process information along the whole supply chain.

0-8493-9968-8/99/$0.00+$.50

HORIZONTAL BUSINESS INTEGRATION STRATEGY

Manufacturers are providing increased service levels in response to competitive pressure to create differentiation in product offerings. One trend is toward smaller, custom lot sizes on the part of the process manufacturer, and custom product configurations on the part of the discrete component manufacturer.

As manufacturing assumes these higher levels of service, the strategic model of the manufacturing organization is moving toward a professional context in which the operating work of an organization is dominated by skilled workers who use procedures that, though difficult to learn, are well defined.[2] In this model, empowered workers are given greater decision latitude. In other words, with increased automation of the manufacturing processes, the nature of the work in the plant or factory shifts from manually effecting the independent processes to using IS in support of customer-driven operating objectives related to production. The empowered worker equipped with business operating objectives makes decisions using information that previously was the purview of manufacturing management. IS, integrated with factory automation systems, therefore enables both differentiation and flatter organizational structures.

Compared with the conventional machine concept of the manufacturing organization, empowered or high-performance work teams typify a more people-centered, organic culture. This new manufacturing organization depends on high-speed access to high-quality information. For example, total quality management prescribes the use of statistical quality control (SQC) techniques. Manufacturers use SQC software to help workers process the sheer quantity of data required by the application of SQC principles in manufacturing, further illustrating the affinity among strategy, organization, and information technology (IT).

The IS organization within the global manufacturing enterprise must understand the impact organizational strategy has on the IT infrastructure. Furthermore, it must determine and create the optimum IT architecture to best support a horizontal business integration strategy.

DIFFERENTIATING INFORMATION SYSTEM
PRODUCTS AND SERVICES

Historically, IS has delivered custom computer applications to business functions to improve effectiveness and reduce cost. System projects were justified on their stand-alone return on investment. The IS management structure reflected project team independence and aligned applications development teams with their respective customers (i.e., manufacturing, finance, or distribution). This approach to systems development avoided the long-term need to integrate data between applications. Viewed separately, each system met its functional objective. Viewed collectively, they presented a set of conflicting interfaces and incompatible information, thereby constraining a horizontal business integration strategy.

As businesses flatten their organizations, their dependence on integrated information flow across worldwide boundaries increases. The IS organization must find ways to remove the functional and technical incompatibilities of existing computer systems that are barriers to business-centric information access.

Trends in Manufacturing

More business managers recognize that information-related service extensions to their product/service mix can affect their companies' ability to compete favorably in international markets. They are also beginning to recognize that existing computer systems were designed in a way that is inconsistent with the view of information as an asset to be managed by the corporation, which has led to concerns about the return on investment for older systems.

Plant-level IS, once the domain of process control engineers and production personnel, are being drawn into the scope of the IS function from the standpoint of integrating the operational data in these systems with horizontal supply-chain business strategy. The span of the IS organization's responsibility may expand to include multiple operational (e.g., manufacturing) systems from which enterprise information is collected and delivered. The charter of IS becomes focused on assimilating and combining manufacturing process data with other forms of business data to enhance the quality of customer service, to support integrated operations objectives, and to provide value-added decision support across the corporation.

QUANTITY OF MANUFACTURING DATA

IS is pervasive across the manufacturing supply chain. The entire manufacturing supply chain uses information, but the epicenter of IT in a modern industrial manufacturing company usually exists at the manufacturing plant site. Here, a variety of systems, using data at different levels of abstraction, are employed to control manufacturing processes, provide decision support to operations, and perform planning functions such as those offered by MRPII (material requirements planning) systems.

The problem of functionally integrating manufacturing software applications is exacerbated by the total volume of data employed in manufacturing. In the case of the process/batch manufacturer that employs process control systems, extensive quantities of process data may exist within the process control applications. Most of that data is needed by other parts of the manufacturing organization. It is common, for example, for a process manufacturing plant to generate 8 to 10 million pieces of information every 24 hours.

A central concern when manufacturing process data is integrated into enterprisewide IS is the requisite changes necessary to derive information from elemental process data. For example, a *Fortune* 100 diversified chemical company needs to maintain a complete history for each lot or batch of material made, including details of the processes used to make any given batch. A maker of an automobile safety device needs similar detailed information for each discrete component and assembly produced. In addition, the customer, the automotive industry, and proper business practice all specify that the detailed information be maintained indefinitely and be available on demand during the anticipated 20-year life of the product.

NATURE OF MANUFACTURING DATA

The problems outlined in each of these situations can be understood when the nature of manufacturing data itself is examined. Exhibit 1 identifies four categories of data that exist in manufacturing:

- Derived data needed for longer term business decision support
- Transaction-driven, product-oriented data
- Event-driven, operations-oriented data
- Real-time, process-oriented data

The columns in Exhibit 1 contrast the key attributes of these different data types. Nonsite-specific positioning of derived data is critical to successful horizontal business integration for the multisite manufacturing enterprise.

Process data possesses the lowest level of integration in manufacturing, whereas decision support data has usually been integrated or summarized to afford the user a basis for broad business and planning decisions. These two extremes can be illustrated by considering the questions the business user of manufacturing data might ask as compared with those asked by a process engineer concerned about the problem of manufacturing process optimization.

Business users of manufacturing data might want to know about the yield for a given product manufactured at all sites during the previous month. A typical process engineer might inquire about the historical trend of temperature for one or more tag (i.e., input/output) values related to a particular piece of equipment or process. Both questions have equal relevance and potential merit, but they are fundamentally different as they are based on the type of data needed to render a valid response.

KEY ATTRIBUTES OF DATA / CATEGORIES OF DATA	Example Data	Typical Orientation	Typical Use	Integration Scope	Typical Volume
Multisite Decision Support	Lot/Batch Quality Summary	Subject/Table	Multisite Read Only	Business	Low
Cross-Area Integrated Operations	Lot/Batch Quality Detail	Subject/Table	Transaction Driven	Site	Medium
In-Area Operations	In-Area Quality Result	File/Field	Event Driven	Area	Medium
Process/ Machine Control	Process/Quality Parameter	Tag or I/O	Real Time	Machine/Process Step	High

Exhibit 1. Manufacturing data framework.

The process-related question requires access to manufacturing (i.e., process control) data at its lowest atomic level. The product yield question requires access to data stored at a higher level of abstraction. Process data such as lot/batch yield must be collected and derived uniformly into a value for product yield at each site. This type of query represents a significant change in the level of abstraction and integration of the data across multiple plant sites.

The operations data presented at the middle levels of Exhibit 1 reflect the transformation of data from process (tag) to subject (table). An operations database often provides a repository for manufacturing data that is clearly outside the process domain but is still necessary for manufacturing. Operating conditions, procedures, recipes, and specifications—organized by product, equipment/cell/area, or manufacturing team—are often candidates for operations data. If MRP is employed, the operations information database is also often used to provide the MRP system order operations as they are completed by product, line, or plant.

DATA-DRIVEN MANUFACTURING APPLICATION FRAMEWORK

Past efforts to computerize manufacturing focused on the automation of isolated process steps or organizational functions. The success of the global manufacturing enterprise depends on new application architectures predicated on data integration, and the availability of derived production data for use in multisite business decision support. Using the categories of manufacturing data from Exhibit 1, a data-driven application framework can be constructed for a typical manufacturing site (see Exhibit 2). This framework takes advantage of the existing differences in data, provides for the horizontal separation of multiple manufacturing process steps, and recognizes the need for operational integration. The upper level in this manufacturing site application framework supports the business need for horizontally integrated, multisite production information access.

Adoption of a consistent manufacturing site application framework both enables multisite integration and presents a major cost reduction opportunity. The lack of a consistent framework for site applications all too often results in unique site applications that require expensive life cycle support. Use of a consistent framework enhances the prospects of multisite applications development (or commercial purchase), which significantly lowers life cycle support cost.

EFFECTIVE INFORMATION DELIVERY

In view of the strategic use of IT and the vast quantity of manufacturing data now available, what should the product of the IS organization be? What should the role of IS be in the world-class manufacturing organization?

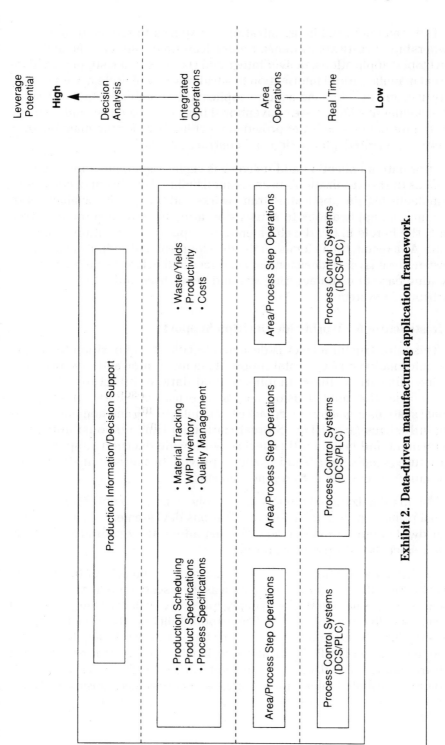

Exhibit 2. Data-driven manufacturing application framework.

The manufacturing IS organization is required to reduce total cost of ownership of software systems, reduce lead times, increase flexibility of developed applications, deliver integrated (i.e., customer, supplier, and internal manufacturing) information to a wide variety of users across the enterprise, and develop and acquire applications suitable for multiple sites. The manner in which these conventional business objectives and their implied information needs are provided must improve for the manufacturer seeking integrated information and control systems.

Information collection and delivery is replacing applications development as the IS organization's prime responsibility. The advent of consistent manufacturing site application frameworks and the growing availability of commercial applications to satisfy operational needs can reduce, over time, the IS role in the development and support of operational applications. As a result, IS can focus on the development and support of a new infrastructural layer of decision data services and networks built above the existing base of manufacturing site and centralized order entry/product distribution systems.

Infrastructure for Worldwide Decision Support

This infrastructural layer is designed to collect and position the requisite information for horizontal supply chain integration and worldwide decision support. William Inmon's unified data architecture with data warehouses that hold decision support information separate from operational systems is gaining acceptance in manufacturing and nonmanufacturing industries alike.[3] The IS organization's prime responsibility is to implement and maintain this secure worldwide decision support infrastructure (see Exhibits 3 and 4) and to provide business with effective information access and delivery mechanisms.

The IS organizational models have evolved so far to optimize its traditional primary product: custom applications development. To accomplish worldwide information delivery, IS must adopt an organizational model that reflects its new primary product.

As the IS organization changes from a custom manufacturer to a product distributor, with enterprise information as its essential product, the central focus of IS becomes information supply, inventory, regional warehouses, and business delivery mechanisms. The responsibility for this nonoperational data storage, structure, and content must be separated from applications development and controlled centrally or regionally, driven by the need for data integration, end-user data access, and enterprisewide data integrity (see Exhibit 5). Distributed information storage and access mechanisms, predicat-

An Information Architecture for the Global Manufacturing Enterprise

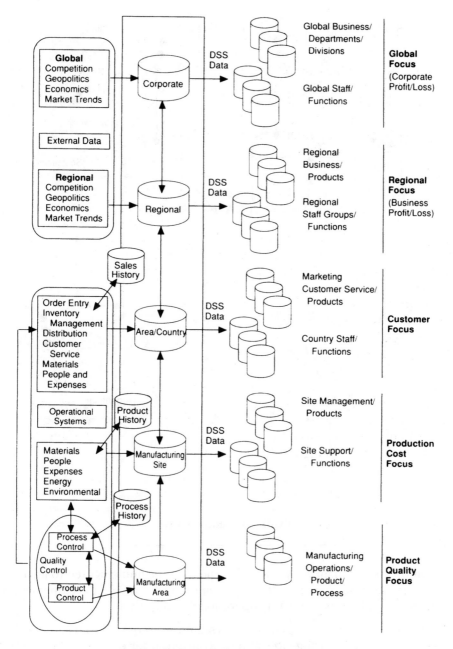

Exhibit 3. Data delivery architecture.

165

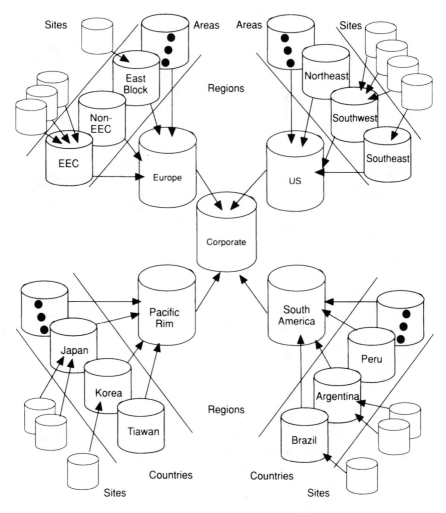

Exhibit 4. Global scope.

ed on the use of client/server technologies, can be implemented to insulate both the business users and decision support system (DSS) developers from the incompatibilities of existing operational applications.

New or reengineered operational systems are required to pass selected data from manufacturing sites and centralized order entry/product distribution operational systems to the infrastructure layer, thereby taking advantage of the ability of the infrastructure to provide data to decision support applications. New operational systems can be downsized and optimized to best meet the immediate operational tasks. History, nonoperational analysis, and reporting could be accomplished as extensions of the

166

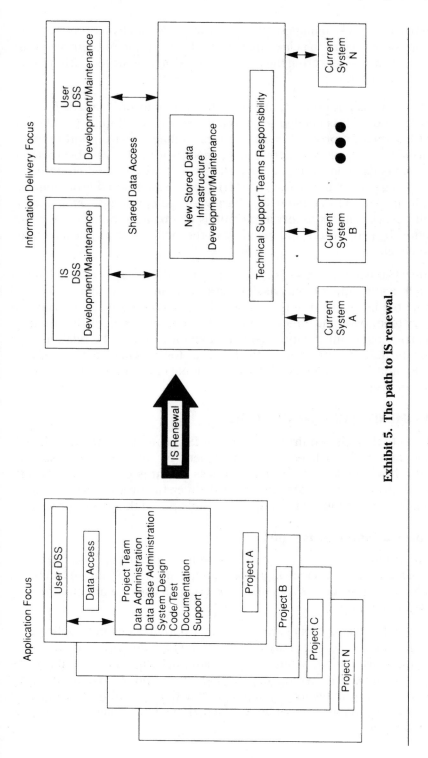

Exhibit 5. The path to IS renewal.

infrastructure layer using commercially available analysis tools. Such a strategy allows users to select analysis tools according to their own business needs, with IS ensuring the integrity of the data managed within the infrastructure layer.

Delivery Teams. A consistent set of development policies, principles, methods, and tools is needed to govern the secure development and delivery of information products and services. Online metrics relating to the performance of the infrastructure layer need to be made available to determine who is using information, as well as when, why, and where information is being used. A single (i.e., logical) decision support environment can provide insulation from underlying hardware and operating system incompatibilities. Decision support applications can be accomplished as a unified effort by IS or others, independent of the facilities or physical location of the developer.

A new IS business-focused organizational model emerges in which internal technical support teams assume responsibility to design, build, and support the infrastructure layer. Radiating from the core are information delivery teams working directly with the businesses to identify information needs and ensure information delivery. Exhibit 6 details the relationships among the different members of the business-focused information delivery team. Exhibit 7 shows the overall organizational model for optimizing information delivery.

RECOMMENDED COURSE OF ACTION

The actual steps required to move an IS organization toward the described information delivery paradigm depend on current IS business practice and how quickly the IS and business cultures can accept change. Although the individual paths forward will differ, the overall goal is to establish sustainable change in both the IS technology and the people processes.

Organize around Information Delivery

If the IS function is to be a provider of information as opposed to a provider of automation, then change is a prerequisite. The IS culture can begin by defining its purpose as that of empowering its user community through access to information.

Existing IS organizational structures that optimize custom applications development should gradually be replaced with structures that promote cross-application integration. Decision support capability should be removed as a task of individual applications development teams and organized as an enterprisewide infrastructural activity. Employee recognition and reward mechanisms must be redesigned to reinforce and sustain these new IS directions.

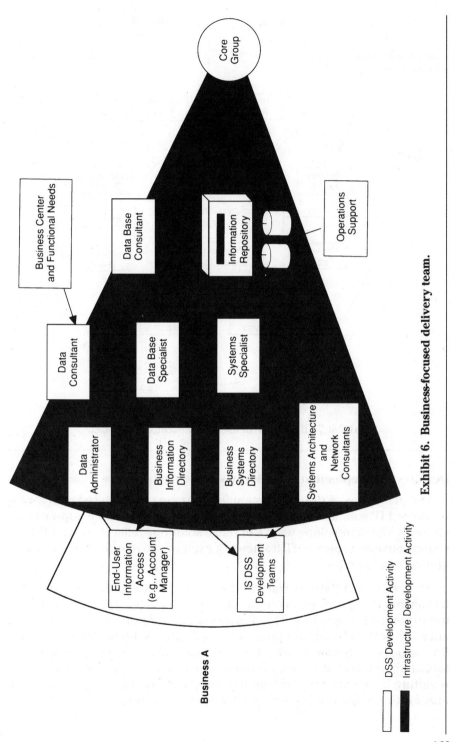

Exhibit 6. Business-focused delivery team.

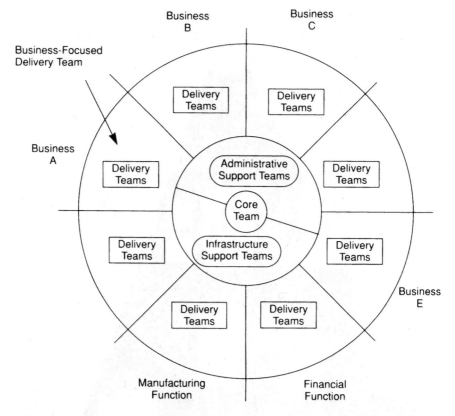

Exhibit 7. Business-focused organizational model.

Develop and Implement an Enterprisewide Architecture

The plant sites of the global manufacturer are often littered with locally optimized IT solutions that defy integration into a multisite supply chain strategy. The stand-alone nature of these solutions reflects the fact that no shared business rules or IT framework exist to provide the technical integration ground rules.

An essential IS path forward is the establishment of the architectural framework that provides a consistent technical context for horizontal business integration strategy. This framework should provide specific guidance for both existing and proposed applications, technology, and data. Data is not only a valid architectural consideration; it is fundamental to establishing integrated information delivery mechanisms. The data models resulting from data architecture development become the product catalogs for the IS function's information delivery business.

Information strategic planning offers a valid approach to designing the overall enterprise architecture. The deficiency in information engineering has been a lack of recognition of the fundamental differences and uses in manufacturing data at different levels in the architecture. Exhibits 1 and 2 reflect these differences and their implications for manufacturing systems. Exhibits 3 and 4 reflect the logical placement of the data warehouses in the global manufacturing architecture. The use of encyclopedia-based, computer-assisted systems engineering technology is strongly recommended in the development of the enterprisewide architecture. The distributed nature of this technology allows IS to both automate and share reusable software assets while teaming across geographical boundaries.

Notes

1. Malcolm Baldrige National Quality Award, U.S. Department of Commerce and the National Institute of Standards and Technology, Gaithersburg, MD.
2. Mintzberg, H. and Quinn, J.B., *The Strategy Process,* Englewood Cliffs, NJ: Prentice-Hall, 1991.
3. Inmon, W.H., *Building the Data Warehouse,* Wellesley, MA: QED Information Sciences, 1992.

Chapter 8
Server-Based Computing Architecture
Bosco Cheung

The advent of the computer revolution greatly expanded the universe of information and processing power available to the end user. The once simple stand-alone computer and the software that ran on it grew in complexity, creating a whole new set of problems for enterprise computing.

Faced with an ever-changing computing environment, IT professionals must improve the efficiency of business-critical application deployment. In order to reduce the total cost of computing ownership for their organizations, they must also leverage everything in their current computing infrastructure hardware, applications, networks, and training. And all of this must be accomplished along with:

- Managing and supporting users in a timely and cost-effective manner
- Extending access to business-critical applications to dispersed users, regardless of connection, location, or device
- Ensuring exceptional application performance
- Providing tight security for enterprise-level computing

These challenges have made enterprisewide application deployment even more daunting because the products developed to this point have only addressed one, or possibly two, of the obstacles discussed in this section.

Management

From a management perspective, traditional enterprise application deployment is often time-consuming, expensive, and difficult to maintain. Not only do administrators have to physically distribute applications to every client, but they also have to deal with version control issues, remote support, multiple system configurations, and data replication. When confronted with thousands of users, the cost of application ownership can quickly spiral out of control.

0-8493-9968-8/99/$0.00+$.50
© 1999 by CRC Press LLC

173

Access

Today's corporate computing landscape comprises a heterogeneous mix of desktop devices, network connectivity, and operating systems. Access to vital Windows-based applications is difficult—or, in the case of Internet/Intranet computing, nonexistent—and often involves costly upgrades, problematic emulation software, and complete application rewrites.

Performance

Most corporate applications today are designed for high bandwidth networks and powerful desktop computers. This type of application design puts tremendous strain on congested corporate networks and yields poor performance over lower bandwidth, remote connections. Because of this, many users simply avoid using the vital applications and data to get their work done. When this happens, redundant work and significant decreases in productivity are often the result.

Security

Security is also a challenge because in traditional client/server architectures, business-critical applications and data live on both the server and the client desktops spread throughout the world. Not only does this increase the risk of unauthorized access, but it also increases the risk of lost or stolen information.

A BETTER APPROACH: SERVER-BASED COMPUTING

Server-based computing is a model in which applications are deployed, managed, supported, and executed 100 percent on a server. It uses a multiuser operating system and a method for distributing the presentation of an application's interface to a client device.

With server-based computing, client devices, whether "fat" or "thin," have instant access to business-critical applications via the server without application rewrites or downloads. This means improved efficiency when deploying business-critical applications. In addition, server-based computing works within the current computing infrastructure and current computing standards, and with the current and future family of Windows-based offerings. This means improved returns on computing investments— desktops, networks, applications, and training. The end result: server-based computing is rapidly becoming the most reliable way to reduce the complexity and total costs associated with enterprise computing.

How Does Server-Based Computing Work?

The server-based computing model employs three critical components. The first is a multiuser operating system that enables multiple concurrent users to log on and run applications in separate, protected sessions on a single server. The second is a highly efficient computing technology that separates the application's logic from its user interface, so only keystrokes, mouse clicks, and screen updates travel the network. As a result, application performance is bandwidth-independent. The third key component, centralized application and client management, enables large computing environments to overcome the critical application deployment challenges of management, access, performance, and security.

Server-based computing is made possible by two Citrix technologies: Citrix Independent Computing Architecture (ICA®) and Citrix MultiWin. A de facto standard for server-based computing, the ICA protocol shifts application processing from the client device to the server. MultiWin, the technology licensed by Citrix to Microsoft to jointly create Terminal Server, enables multiple users to simultaneously access applications running on a server.

WHAT IS INDEPENDENT COMPUTING ARCHITECTURE (ICA)?

Independent Computing Architecture (ICA) is a Windows presentation services protocol from Citrix that provides the foundation for turning any client device—thin or fat— into the ultimate thin client. The ICA technology includes a server software component, a network protocol component, and a client software component.

On the server, ICA has the unique ability to separate the application's logic from the user interface at the server and transport it to the client over standard network protocols—IPX, SPX, NetBEUI, TCP/IP and PPP—and over popular network connections–asynchronous, dialup, ISDN, Frame Relay, and ATM. On the client, users see and work with the application's interface but 100% of the application logic executes on the server.

The ICA protocol transports keystrokes, mouse clicks, and screen updates over standard protocols to the client, consuming less than 20 kilobits per second of network bandwidth.

Role of ICA

ICA is highly efficient; it allows only keystrokes, mouse clicks, and screen updates to travel the network. As a result, applications consume just a fraction of the network bandwidth usually required. This efficiency enables the latest, most powerful 32-bit applications to be accessed with exceptional performance from existing computers, Windows-based terminals, network computers, and a new generation of business and personal information appliances.

With over two million ports in use worldwide, Citrix ICA is a mature, reliable technology and is fast becoming a de facto industry standard for server-based computing.

INTEGRATED ARCHITECTURES

Server-Based Computing Compared to Network Computing and Traditional Client/Server Computing

While all three computing models have a valid role in today's enterprises, it is important to note the differences between them. In traditional client/server architecture, processing is centered around local execution using fat, powerful hardware components. In the network computing architecture as defined by Sun, Oracle, Netscape, IBM, and Apple, components are dynamically downloaded from the network into the client device for execution by the client. But with the Citrix server-based computing approach, users are able to access business-critical applications—including the latest 32-bit Windows-based and Java™ applications—without requiring them to be downloaded to the client. This approach also provides considerable total cost of application ownership savings since these applications are centrally managed and can be accessed by users without having to rewrite them.

Basically, the server-based computing approach delivers all the benefits of both host computing and personal computing as follows:

- Host Computing Benefits
  Single-point management
  Physically and technically secure
  Predictable ownership costs
  Mission-critical reliability
  Bandwidth-independent performance
  Universal application access
- Personal Computing Benefits

  Thousands of off-the-shelf applications
  Low-cost and fast-cycle application development
  Standards-based
  Graphical, rich data and easy to use
  Wide choice of device types and suppliers

WHAT IS A WINDOWS-BASED TERMINAL?

A Windows-based terminal (WBT) is a thin client hardware device that connects to Citrix server-based system software. Because the applications it accesses are installed on the server, a Windows-based terminal is not the equivalent of a computer with its operating system and array of local applications. It is also not interchangeable with a network computer or NetPC because these devices download and run applications off the network.

The key criterion that distinguishes Windows-based terminals from other thin client devices, such as NCs or NetPCs, is that there is no downloading of the operating system or applications, and there is no local processing of applications at the client. All execution of the application logic occurs on the server.

176

Defining Characteristics of a Windows-Based Terminal

Windows-based terminals have the following characteristics:

- An embedded operating system such as DOS, Windows CE, or any real-time operating system

- ICA and/or Microsoft Remote Desktop Protocol (RDP) presentation services protocol to transport keystrokes, mouse clicks, and screen updates between the client and server

- 100 percent server-based execution of application logic

- No local execution of application logic at the client device
- A Windows-based terminal may incorporate third-party emulation software such as X, 3270, and 5250 for connection to other host systems

Fitting the Windows-Based Terminal within the Enterprise

The "thinness" of a Windows-based terminal and the many benefits of server-based computing make these thin clients ideal for certain types of workers and market segments. For example, task-based employees who primarily work with line-of-business applications such as order entry would be ideal candidates for a Windows-based terminal. Retail organizations operating point-of-sale terminals and branch locations of banks and stores are markets that are also rapidly adopting these thin clients. Windows-based terminals are also well suited for existing "green screen" terminal users moving to a Windows environment.

SERVER-BASED COMPUTING KEY FEATURES AND BENEFITS

While other approaches for deploying, managing, and supporting business-critical applications across the extended enterprise have been introduced, only the server-based computing model developed by Citrix provides today's growing enterprises with the tools and capabilities they need to be successful. This innovative software enables enterprises to:

- Bring server-based computing to heterogeneous computing environments, providing access to Windows-based applications regardless of client hardware, operating platform, network connection, or LAN protocol

- Offer enterprise-scale management tools to allow IT professionals to scale, deploy, manage, and support applications from a single location
- Provide seamless desktop integration of the user's local and remote resources and applications with exceptional performance

MIS rarely has the luxury of deploying mission-critical applications in a homogeneous environment, let alone from a centralized location. Instead, the enterprise network usually includes a wide variety of servers, client workstations, operating systems, and connections. The user base can include from dozens to thousands of local, remote, and mobile users.

Heterogeneous Computing Environments

Heterogeneous computing environments are a fact of life in the enterprise, comprising an installed base of many client devices, operating systems, LAN protocols, and network connections. However, for the enterprise interested in making Windows-based applications available to all users, server-based computing enables an organization to leverage its existing infrastructure yet still provide the best application fit for both users and the enterprise. This type of approach supports all types of hardware, operating platforms, network connections, and LAN protocols. As a result, organizations can deliver the same set of applications to virtually any client device anywhere with exceptional performance

Enterprise-Scale Management Tools

Organizations building application deployment systems will want the added benefits of server-based computing system software to gain robust management tools that help scale systems and support applications and users enterprisewide. With these tools, administrators will be able to significantly reduce the costs and complexities of deploying, managing, and supporting business applications across the extended enterprise.

Seamless Desktop Integration

With server-based computing, end users of both Windows and non-Windows desktops gain an enhanced computing experience through broadened application access with exceptional performance that is bandwidth-independent, as well as complete access to local system resources—even though applications are running remotely from the server.

SERVER-BASED COMPUTING SOLUTION SCENARIOS

With server-based computing, customers can increase productivity and develop a competitive advantage by gaining universal access to the business-critical applications they need to operate successfully, regardless of the connection, location, or operating systems they may be using.

The following solution scenarios demonstrate how server-based computing can help customers overcome the challenges of enterprise-wide application deployment.

Branch Office Computing

For manageable, secure application deployment and access over corporate WANs.

Problem. To better serve and support customers, many enterprises are opening branch offices. However, this is creating many difficulties for administrators who do not have the resources to adequately staff these new offices. One such problem is database replication. Many times, individual LANs are built for each branch office. Configuring and managing these branch office LANs and the information on them creates numerous management challenges. Another problem is application performance. Since most branch offices are connected by WANs to headquarters, vital data and applications must travel back and forth across the network. This type of setup creates numerous user delays and unacceptable application response. Previously, the only option was a bigger WAN connection which meant increasing costs, not just once but on an ongoing basis.

Solution. Server-based computing is a better solution because it minimizes network traffic, even for Windows-based, 32-bit applications. This approach allows applications to be deployed, supported, and managed from a central location.

Cross-Platform Computing

For Windows-based application deployment to non-Windows desktop users.

Problem. In today's era of global consolidation, many enterprises are buying and/or merging new companies into their organizations, as well as adding their own new employees and locations around the world. Typically, this has resulted in a widely diverse set of client devices, operating systems, processing power, and connectivity options across the enterprise.

For IT professionals, trying to leverage existing technology investments while deploying business-critical applications—especially the latest 32-bit Windows-based applications—to all users has become more and more difficult. As a result, organizations have had to resort to using problematic emulation software, purchasing additional hardware, or investing in costly application rewrites.

Solution. Server-based computing is a better, more cost-effective solution because it enables virtually any existing device in the enterprise to access Windows-based applications without special emulation software, changes in system configuration, or application rewrites. This means that enterprises can maximize their investments in existing technology and allow users to work in their preferred computing environments.

Web Computing

Allowing remote users to access full-function, Windows-based applications from web pages.

Problem. Web computing is taking off. But to deploy interactive applications on an intranet or the Internet, application development is required. The Java applet "download-and-run" model is not an extension of any current computing technology. New software, and often new hardware, is required to successfully deploy these solutions. Every time the application changes, the web-based application needs to change as well.

Solution. Server-based computing enables administrators to launch and embed corporate Windows-based applications into HTML pages without rewriting a single line of code. Plus, it eliminates the need to manage and maintain two separate sets of code.

Remote Computing

To give high-performance, secure access to business-critical applications over remote, dialup connections.

Problem. The changing work environment is allowing more and more employees to work away from the office—at home, hotels, customer locations, etc. This means that a wide variety of network connections is being used to access corporate applications. Unfortunately, the lower the bandwidth, the lower the application performance. Because of this, many remote users are avoiding corporate applications altogether, as they'd rather work than wait.

Another factor is application management and support for remote users. Administrators are forced to spend excessive amounts of time trying to diagnose and correct problems over the phone. Unfortunately, the problems are usually not resolved the first time.

Solution. Server-based computing works better for remote users because it keeps all application processing on the server, meaning less traffic is sent across the network. Plus, it's optimized for low-bandwidh connections so users can get LAN-like performance over analog or ISDN modems, WANs, wireless LANs, and even the Internet. By eliminating the need for on-site staff, server-based computing also makes it easier for administrators.

Thin Client Device Computing

Vital, Windows-based applications can be extended to newer, low-cost devices.

Problem . Traditional mini- and mainframe computing deliver some of the same "centralized computing" benefits as server-based computing. The problem is that these types of machines weren't designed for the thousands of GUI-based Windows applications that are available today. Furthermore, users of these types of machines are familiar with the text-based interface and are typically slow to adopt new operating systems.

Also, many of today's new devices—like Windows-based terminals, PDAs, wireless tablets, and information appliances—are not compatible with the Windows-based, business-critical applications being used in the enterprise unless rewrites are performed.

Solution. With server-based computing, the latest Windows-based programs can be extended to these thin devices without application rewrites. This enables users to work in their preferred environments and still access the Windows-based applications they need to work successfully. Plus, organizations can reap the benefits resulting from reduced overhead, lower acquisition costs, and fewer moving parts.

CONCLUSION

The server-based computing architecture model offers any size organization an alternative enterprise computing solution that reduces the total cost of computing ownership, leverages components of their current computing environment, and reduces the development and support hardships normally associated with implementing an enterprise solution.

Section III
Enabling Technologies

Chapter 9
Using Middleware for Interoperable Systems

Raymond J. Posch

The increasingly distributed nature of business locations and operations has led to a concomitant expansion of client/server computing from the department level to the enterprise level. Yet the successful implementation of client/server, or distributed, business applications depends on interoperability—the ability of applications to work together across a network to perform business functions. Systems integrators need to know exactly how a client application will talk with a server application before either can be designed or written. If they do not, unrealistic assumptions about applications-level connectivity can be project killers.

Because enterprises typically have many and diverse systems to meet their business needs, interoperability problems are almost always encountered as soon as applications on desktops, mainframes, midrange systems, and servers need to interact with each other. No products have emerged as clear-cut, widely supported standards, de facto or otherwise, for distributed enterprise applications. Systems integrators are tested to the utmost by the fact that these client/server applications must be developed with wide-ranging assortments of platforms, networks, databases, and tools.

The need for applications to be able to directly exchange information in real time in a distributed heterogeneous environment has led to the development of middleware—software that bridges the gap between business applications and systems-level services such as databases, network protocols, and operating systems. This chapter discusses the business issues in enterprise computing and the myriad interoperability problems associated with achieving distributed business applications. It then reviews how middleware is being used to solve these problems.

0-8493-9989-0/99/$0.00+$.50
© 1999 by CRC Press LLC

DISTRIBUTED APPLICATIONS DEFINED

A distributed application is an automated business activity broken down into multiple processing functions running on different computers and performed in a coordinated fashion by sending information across a network. Depending on the relationship of the components, such applications are also referred to as client/server or peer-to-peer applications. Because the application components must work together across the network, the applications are more generally referred to as cooperative processing applications.

The so-called two-tier client/server model divides the processing into a client portion, which interfaces with the user, and a server portion, which interfaces with the database. Execution of business rules is divided among the client or server components.

The three-tier model divides the work into presentation on the client platform, business rules on one or more application platforms, and database access on one or more database platforms. This model attempts (at least conceptually) to isolate the business rules to the middle tier so that client applications and database server applications are less affected by the frequent changes that occur in business rules. It is believed that this approach can lead to applications that are easier to maintain and that scale better as the volume of business transactions grows.

BUSINESS ISSUES IN ENTERPRISE COMPUTING

IT Infrastructure, Legacy Systems, and Changing Technology

Organizations invest in the IT infrastructure necessary for conducting business. This IT infrastructure comprises computers, software, and networks. An organization that has been in business for any period of time is likely to have legacy systems (i.e., hardware, software, and networks) that may not be easily replaced as newer capabilities become available. Such an organization is also likely to replace its computers or networks to increase speed and capacity, for example.

Because technology, especially information technology, changes continuously, organizations face at least two major challenges to their ability to manage their investments in IT infrastructure:

1. Ensuring that business-critical applications can easily adapt and remain in operation when computers, operating systems, and networks are changed or replaced for reasons of capacity, price/performance, or functional fit. This is very much an issue of managing assets and operating costs.
2. Choosing infrastructure components that allow for the quick use of new technologies. This relates particularly to applications software

because the cost efficiencies of operating the business are often directly related to the applications. New technologies often have steep learning curves and existing applications may not be easily adaptable. Although this is an issue of managing assets and costs, it is also one of business adaptability and responsiveness. It is especially important for a rapidly growing business.

Integration in a Distributed Business World

The challenges of managing an IT infrastructure are complicated further by the increasingly distributed nature of business organization and operations. Employees and business functions that were centralized in a single headquarters 10 years ago are now likely to be scattered in dozens or hundreds of locations around the globe. Departments that previously consisted of employees performing the same or similar functions are now often organized as distributed teams with team members in many different locations. This increasing physical distribution of people, functions, and supporting systems engenders at least three major challenges:

Integrating the business (internally) in a distributed environment. This issue actually breaks down into a series of related issues, such as:

- Ensuring that employees located in remote or branch offices have the information they need to do their work.
- Ensuring that employees across different locations can communicate effectively and work together as teams.
- Ensuring that employees across all locations understand critical objectives, are working together toward common goals, and receive the information feedback they need to evaluate and fine-tune their work. This is a huge problem and the reason that the concept of enterprisewide information systems is becoming more important.

Integrating externally with other entities. Companies that previously carried out business transactions with suppliers or customers primarily by phone or mail are now interacting through such electronic communications methods as *electronic data interchange (EDI)*, electronic mail (e-mail), and the World Wide Web. The question here is how to establish effective communication yet ensure that information is not shared inappropriately.

Providing a consistent—if not common or at least unified—supporting infrastructure. Such an infrastructure comprises voice communications, *fax*, networked computers, and information access and exchange across all locations.

INTEROPERABILITY: THE TECHNICAL CHALLENGE

Because organizations depend on the enabling tools of information technology, their business objectives for enterprise computing are accompanied by a host of technical issues. Interoperability, however, is most often the stumbling block to mission-critical client/server systems.

Large-scale client/server applications involve complex networks, usually with many local area networks (LANs) interconnected through a *wide area network (WAN)*. More often, such applications involve multiple *WANs* and multiple network protocols, such as IBM's *System Network Architecture (SNA)*, NetBIOS, *Transmission Control Protocol/Internet Protocol* (TCP/IP), and *Frame Relay*. They typically involve several different computing platforms, or different types of computers running different operating systems, such as PCs running Microsoft Corp.'s Windows; servers running Hewlett-Packard's HP-UX; and mainframes running IBM Corp.'s MVS and *CICS*. They often involve multiple databases, perhaps based on different database management system (DBMS) platforms such as Oracle Corp.'s *ORACLE* and IBM's DB/2 and *IMS*. And, they will certainly involve business applications on distributed platforms tied together in a number of different ways, such as by transaction monitors, message-oriented middleware, data access middleware, and *remote procedure calls* (RPCs), or sometimes by clumsier mechanisms like file transfers or sequential batch processing jobs.

Systems integration at the enterprise level entails getting many different information systems components to work together across the enterprise network. Because these myriad components must interoperate effectively, interoperability is the first key to success. But, interoperability is not simply a problem of network protocol compatibility—it exists at many different levels, such as:

- Network interoperability
- Platform interoperability
- Database or data access interoperability
- Object or software component interoperability
- Presentation interoperability—graphical user interfaces (GUIs) and multimedia user interfaces (MUIs)
- Workgroup/workflow/e-mail interoperability
- Applications interoperability

Network Interoperability

Today, many companies running very large networks use multiple network protocols. If they are or were large IBM shops, they typically have 3270 terminal protocol, plus one or more *SNA* protocols on their *WAN*; NetBIOS on their LANs; *TCP/IP* on their UNIX-based engineering networks; and perhaps even some Novell *IPX*. Multiple *network operating systems* may be a management issue, but at the application-to-application level (AAI) differing protocols and spanning across networks of varying types are usually the biggest problems. For example, on an *SNA LU* 6.2-only network, a client application can be written to invoke the APPC *application programming interface (API)* to establish a session and exchange information with a server application that also uses the APPC *API*. However, when one application is on an *SNA* network and the partner application is on a *TCP/IP* network, a major interoperability problem arises.

Platform Interoperability

Organizations striving to implement mission-critical distributed applications face the difficult challenge of interoperability among platforms of completely different types, such as *IMS* on IBM mainframes and UNIX platforms. Much of what has been done to date under the client/server classification involves decision support applications. Most mission-critical functions are performed primarily with the assistance of mainframe applications; yet, getting *IMS* or *CICS* to talk to non-IBM platforms, and especially nonmainframe platforms, is proving to be difficult.

Database Interoperability

This category of interoperability has to do with applications accessing information in databases located on multiple systems, in databases on different platform types, or—the most difficult of all—in databases of completely different types (such as *ORACLE* and *IMS*). The interoperability problem is somewhat lessened if all databases are relational databases using *structured query language (SQL)*, although not all *SQLs* are the same. It is definitely easier if all databases use the same DBMS product, but even then there may be difficulties between certain platforms or with certain network protocols. In any of these cases, database interoperability is a major consideration, especially when legacy systems are involved and are expected to work with newer systems.

Object/Software Component Interoperability

The advent of object-oriented systems in which data is encapsulated in objects allows information to be exchanged among applications as objects. The exchange is handled by an *object request broker (ORB)*, originally defined by the *Object Management Group*. *ORBs* are now available from multiple software companies.

Issues are surfacing, however, with *ORB* dependence on *remote procedure calls* when operating across enterprise networks, and with *ORB*-to-ORB interoperability—that is, getting different *ORB* products from different vendors, usually also involving different platforms, to work together. Applications built using other types of component-based software are also becoming more commonplace—with Microsoft's VBX (Visual Basic Custom Controls) being the most frequently cited type. The major issues are how such reusable components exchange information with other components, and how they can work consistently and compatibly on different platforms.

GUI/MUI Interoperability

Another issue concerns how applications using a *graphical user interface (GUI)* or *multimedia user interface (MUI)* can be written to work on different platforms. This is, in part, a portability problem rather than an interoperability problem.

The real interoperability problem with *MUI* applications, which are expected to proliferate in the future, is twofold. It concerns interoperation of *GUI* functions as part of client/server exchanges when different types of *GUIs* are involved—such as Windows, Presentation Manager, and Motif—and how to make *full-motion video* or interactive compound media information exchanges work across heterogeneous platforms and heterogeneous networks.

Workgroup/Workflow/E-Mail Interoperability

As *groupware* connectivity becomes more common, one workgroup using one *groupware* product will increasingly need to interoperate with other workgroups using different *groupware* products. This is especially true with intercompany connectivity. Workflow interoperability, therefore, is a problem of:

- Integrating different *groupware,* workflow, and e-mail products
- Supporting these types of applications across heterogeneous platforms and networks
- Integrating *groupware*, workflow, and e-mail applications with other types of applications
- Resolving differences in document formats so that, wherever possible, format conversion takes place automatically under the covers

Applications Interoperability

Distributed computing usually refers to distributing the processing among applications located on different systems. Enterprise computing extends distributed computing to a larger scale—across an enterprise network of LANs, *WANs,* and multiple kinds of platforms—but it may also go much further by integrating applications in different business disciplines, such as the employee skills database and corporate directory services. In both cases, at the level where things must happen based on business events, one application somewhere on the network must exchange data with another application somewhere else on the network. Interoperability in terms of client/server computing always comes down to AAI interoperability regardless of how many other kinds of interoperability issues are actually involved.

MIDDLEWARE SOLUTIONS

Nearly all cases of successful large-scale distributed computing applications involve the use of middleware to solve interoperability problems. Middleware, as the name is meant to imply, is software that sits between business applications and the systems-level services, or so-called platforms, that are the source of compatibility problems. Software layering, from which the middleware idea derives, is illustrated in Exhibit 1.

Exhibit 1. Layered software architecture.

Business Applications
Middleware
(Common Application Services)
System Services
(i.e., Database, Network, Operating System)

Because middleware is based on layering, with a new layer of software being inserted as a higher-level platform on which business applications will reside, it provides a degree of encapsulation or abstraction of the lower-level services. In fact, middleware typically introduces new *APIs* that are used to invoke the higher-level services. That is why it is common for applications designers and programmers to talk in terms of the new APIs—for example, Microsoft's *ODBC* or MAPI, or IBM's DRDA—when describing how applications will be interconnected and how one or more of the interoperability problems will be solved.

Because of the layering effect, middleware helps insulate business applications from changes in platforms, networks, or other systems services. IT executives can therefore change the underlying technologies, using more-effective and efficient ones, without changing the applications. The abstraction of services through the higher-level *APIs* also simplifies applications programming, enabling programmers to create or modify applications more quickly in response to business changes. By providing the means for linking applications together across a network, middleware provides a mechanism for applications interoperability and information access.

There are several types of middleware, including:

- X.400, MAPI, SMTP
- X.500, Streettalk

- ODBC, DRDA, distributed DBMS
- DCE, ONC
- CORBA/ORB, OLE2/COM, OpenDoc
- Gateways (such as SQL Server and OmniConnect)
- RPCs
- Message passing and queueing
- Transaction monitors

Most of these types of middleware are ultimately aimed at the AAI connectivity problem. Some are specific to e-mail interoperability (*X.400*, MAPI, *SMTP*); some are specific to database interoperability (*ODBC, DRDA*, distributed DBMS, database gateways); some are specific to object-oriented interoperability (ORB, OLE2, OpenDoc); and some are more generalized (*DCE, RPCs*, message passing and queueing).

All these types of middleware let one application exchange information with another. The exceptions are X.500 and Streettalk, which are directory services (i.e., middleware that addresses the problem of how applications are identified and actually found in large enterprise networks).

There are other interoperability solutions as well, such as protocol converters, bridges, gateways, data format translators, and other special-purpose hardware and software, but these often work at a system or network level and do not facilitate the AAI dialogues that are fundamental to client/server and other forms of distributed computing. The need for the direct exchange of information among applications in a heterogeneous environment has caused middleware to come into existence and to now play a dominant role in the IT architectures of progressive enterprises.

Message-Oriented Middleware

One particular type of middleware—message-oriented middleware—allows an application to send messages (i.e., data) to other applications and to receive messages in return. It encompasses message passing, message queueing, and transaction monitors. Messages in this context are any type of transaction or other exchange that might occur between distributed applications. The meaning and the format of the messages are defined by the structure and contents of the data to meet the requirements of each particular distributed application.

One example of commercial message-oriented middleware, and probably the earliest to be used in a mission-critical production environment, is the Communications Integrator (CI) of Covia Technologies (Englewood, *CO*). The Communications Integrator, first used in the computerized airline reservations system industry, was initially developed by United Airlines for its Apollo reservations network. CI originated in the mid-1980s to allow applications to become independent of network protocols, which in turn would facilitate moving applications to new servers/hosts within the network, allow new hardware and software platforms to be added to the network more readily, and simplify the complexities of programming for AAI communication.

The Apollo network was already a very large network with database server applications running on mainframes, new services being added regularly, and transaction volumes growing rapidly. Because plans were being made for PCs and LANs at customer sites, LAN servers, and PC-based LAN-to-WAN gateways to be added to the reservations network, a much more dynamic and adaptable approach was needed for dealing with distributed applications in a changing network environment. It is also interesting to note that between 1985 and the early 1990s when commercial message-oriented middleware was not yet available, many other companies with large networks in industries other than airline reservations were going through similar transitions and developing their own in-house message middleware.

The approach used in the CI, which was sold for the first time in industries other than the airlines industry beginning in late 1991, was to design an *API* having consistent functions, verb set, and options (i.e., parameters) across all platforms regardless of operating system, language used for the product implementation, or network protocols supported. The Communications Integrator *API* allows applications to register with the message service and then call a send routine to send messages or a receive routine to receive messages. Applications do not have to deal with the problems of network sessions because the Communications Integrator, running on each node, takes care of all session management under the covers.

When sending a message, applications take advantage of the CI's directory services to simply specify the name of the application to receive the message; select a message type (i.e., *asynchronous* or one-way, or synchronous or query with correlated reply); select other options such as priority, assurance level, and whether notification is requested; and then issue the send. When receiving a message, applications select the mode (i.e., blocking or nonblocking), select whether looking for a reply to a specific query or simply the next one available, and then issue the receive.

An Example of Middleware Use. Healthcare Data Exchange (HDX), headquartered in Malvern, PA, near Philadelphia, provides one example of how middleware is used in a large distributed application. Using the Communications Integrator, HDX has implemented a patient insurance eligibility and claims system for its multistate network of healthcare providers. Client applications resident in PCs at the admission desks of providers initiate requests for patient records, eligibility, and admissions based on information supplied by the patient. These requests are sent to appropriate server applications running on local servers or on mainframes at HDX data centers. Switching applications at intermediate servers may trigger multiple requests to systems both inside the HDX network (e.g., HDX claims processing on an IBM mainframe or HDX accounting systems on DEC mainframes) and outside (e.g., eligibility with Medicare or commercial insurance companies). Responses containing screen displays, printed patient records, admissions paperwork, or billing statements are sent back to the admission clerk's PC or to a print server application located nearby. Response times must, of course, be kept as short as possible.

The networked healthcare information business places great demands on client/server applications. In the HDX case, middleware provided flexibility and adaptability to deal with several different platforms, the possibility of future network changes such as from SNA to TCP/IP, and rapid growth, while at the same time simplifying programming through a higher-level message API.

Although the Communications Integrator is no longer being sold, other middleware products are now available. Some examples include MQSeries from IBM, DECmessageQ from Digital Equipment Corp., and Pipes from PeerLogic. In addition, distributed transaction monitors, such as Tuxedo from Novell and TopEnd from AT&T, are now also positioned as message-oriented middleware products.

TRENDS IN MIDDLEWARE DEVELOPMENT

Given the multiplatform, multiprotocol world in which most modern enterprises operate, middleware has come into existence in the last 10 years as a necessary means of providing applications with a degree of insulation from the differences across platforms and protocols. As such, middleware allows the applications to be less affected by changes in those platforms and protocols, while simultaneously providing interoperability across a heterogeneous IT environment.

There is a great explosion in products within each niche or type of middleware, and new types of middleware products are being developed to meet new needs and to solve new interoperability problems. The rapid growth of the Internet, for example, has generated new products for Internet-based applications, and middleware that allows applications on corporate desktops and servers to interact in real time with applications on Internet servers should be available soon. Middleware development is still in its growth stage, and the middleware marketplace has not yet seen much consolidation.

Ultimately, the market will determine which are the preferred middleware solutions. Such solutions will likely be strongly influenced by other IT trends, such as the development of object-oriented and multimedia technologies. In the end, the preferred middleware solutions must not only be embraced by end users, they must also be integrated by software vendors into the application and tool products that must interface with the end users' custom applications.

Critical issues to customers will be whether the middleware supports the customer's particular platforms and network protocols, is relatively easy to use, and is easy to manage—that is, whether and how easily the middleware can be installed, configured, and tuned in a distributed manner. The market must also contend with issues relating to the degree of integration and compatibility with other middleware products and with common applications, especially those used by each customer to conduct day-to-day business.

Although applications developers would like it to be otherwise, the evolution of middleware products, along with other client/server tools, will take time—maybe five to ten years. In the meantime, businesses must be able to solve their interoperability problems so that they can implement distributed computing solutions that meet business needs. In some cases these systems might be characterized as enterprisewide information systems that are used throughout the enterprise and allow the enterprise to act in a more integrated way in serving customers. There may also be smaller enterprise client/server applications that improve some business process, such as customer support, by automating and facilitating customer interaction in a consistent way across many different functions of the enterprise.

In any case, distributed systems today, and for at least the next several years, will likely use point solutions—middleware tools selected according to the unique requirements of the particular system being implemented—rather than integrated solution sets that are suitable for use in all distributed applications of the enterprise.

Given time, however, client/server software and middleware tools will inevitably achieve greater maturity, and integrated solution sets will be offered by the major software companies. Many software vendors, just like end users, are struggling to deal with diverse platforms and protocols and the related interoperability problems. Some vendors specialize only in selected software markets and systems, such as PCs or UNIX, but the most complete solutions will likely come from the software vendors who are now established players in enterprise networking, such as IBM or Computer Associates, or those who may be able to expand to that level, such as Microsoft.

RECOMMENDED COURSE OF ACTION

Because most situations in which organizations are striving to implement client/server applications are unique, IT staffs should research middleware options themselves or hire specialist consultants to find the best solutions to meet their specific requirements. In some cases, for example, a distributed DBMS such as ORACLE may fit the particular situation; in others, message-oriented middleware may provide the right interoperability solution.

Assessing and managing the risks involved in proposed solutions cannot be taken lightly, however. Proof of concept should be considered a necessary phase of any first-time undertaking or sizable project to ensure that the software and the hidden complexities that are part of large-scale and mission-critical client/server applications are fully understood. System requirements must address the adaptability and probable life of the middleware as part of the adaptability and probable life of the overall client/server application. These strategies can be used to manage middleware decisions and distributed application projects.

Many successful mission-critical applications have been implemented in recent years, and middleware tools supporting such applications should continue to evolve to meet the needs of the market. As the market matures, middleware products will have added functions and features, improve in performance, and become more proven in real business conditions. These are the attributes that enterprise-level client/server computing demands.

Chapter 10
Evaluating Object Middleware: DCOM and CORBA

T.M. Rajkumar and Richard J. Lewis, Jr.

OBJECTS IN THE FORM OF SOFTWARE COMPONENTS ARE CHANGING the way applications are developed and delivered. Component technology breaks the application into intrinsic components and then glues them to create the application. Using components, the application is easier to build, robust, and delivered quicker. A middleware is used as the object communication bus to enable distribution of these components across heterogeneous networks and operating systems.

The need for reliable distributed computing middleware environments is becoming pressing as three-tier client-server networks become commonplace. While much of the industry backs the Common Object Request Broker Architecture (CORBA) as the standard object bus, Microsoft is pushing its own Distributed Component Object Model (DCOM). Managers and system architects have to determine what object bus to use in their companies. This chapter reviews the two primary forces in distributed object technology, CORBA and DCOM. It discusses their individual strengths and weaknesses across a wide spectrum of categories, and gives some sensible advice on what technologies might be best applicable to current projects. Finally, it takes a look into what the future has in store for these architectures.

WHAT IS CORBA?

CORBA is a set of distributed system standards promoted by an industry standards group called the Object Management Group (OMG). The idea behind CORBA is to allow applications to communicate with one another no matter where they are located or who has designed them. The CORBA standard defines the ORB, a mechanism through which distributed software and their clients may interact. It specifies an extensive set of bus-related services for creating and deleting objects, accessing them by name,

0-8493-9979-3/99/$0.00+$.50
© 1999 by CRC Press LLC

storing them in persistent store, externalizing their states, and defining ad hoc relationships between them.

History

OMG has more than 700 member companies who have been working on the CORBA standard for eight years. CORBA 1.1 was introduced in 1991 by OMG and defined the Interface Definition Language (IDL) and the Application Programming Interfaces (API) that enable client/server object interaction within a specific implementation of an Object Request Broker (ORB). CORBA 2.0, adopted in December 1994, defines true interoperability by specifying how ORBs from different vendors can interoperate.

Since 1989, the Object Management Group has been working to create standards for object-based component software within the framework of its Object Management Architecture. The key component is the Common Object Request Broker Architecture (CORBA), whose specification was adopted in 1991. In 1994 CORBA 2.0 defined interoperability between objects in heterogeneous systems. Since then the world has seen a growing list of CORBA implementations come to market. Dozens of vendors have recently announced support for the CORBA Internet Inter ORB Protocol (IIOP), which guarantees CORBA interoperability over the Internet. Specifications of several generally useful support services now populate the Object Services segment of the architecture, and work is proceeding rapidly in specifying domain specific technologies in many areas, including finance, healthcare, and telecommunications.

CORBA Architecture

The four main elements of the object management architecture are shown in Exhibit 1 and are the following:

- **ORBs:** The ORB defines the object bus and is the middleware that establishes the client/server relationships between objects. The ORB provides interoperability between applications on different machines in heterogeneous distributed environments and seamlessly interconnects multiple-object systems.
- **Object Services:** These define the system-level object frameworks that extend the bus. They include services such as security, transaction management, and data exchange.
- **Common facilities:** These define horizontal and vertical application frameworks that are used directly by business objects. They deal more with the client than a server.

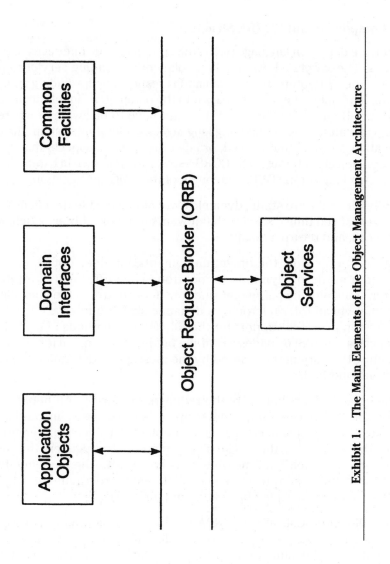

Exhibit 1.   The Main Elements of the Object Management Architecture

- **Domain interfaces:** These are interfaces like common facilities but are specific to a certain domain, such as manufacturing, medical, telecommunications, etc.
- **Application interfaces:** These objects are defined by the developer to solve the business problem. These interfaces are not standardized.

ORB Component and CORBA Structure

Interface definition language (IDL) stubs provide static interfaces to object services. These define how clients invoke corresponding services on the servers. The ORB intercepts the call and is responsible for finding an object that can implement the request, pass it to the parameters, invoke its method, and return the results. The client does not have to be aware of where the object is located, its programming language, its operating system, the communication protocol that is used, or any other system aspects that are not part of an object's interface. The CORBA structure as shown in Exhibit 2 specifies the workings of the ORB component of the OMG specification.

While IDL stubs are static, dynamic invocations enable the client to find (discover) at run time a service that it wants to invoke, obtain a definition, issue a call, and return a result.

On the server side, the object implementation does not differentiate between a static or dynamic invocation. The ORB locates an object adapter, transmits the parameter, and transfers control to the object implementation via an IDL skeleton or a dynamic skeleton interface (DSI). The IDL skeleton provides support for the IDL-defined methods of a particular object class. The DSI provides a runtime binding mechanism for servers by inspecting the parameters passed by the message to determine the target object and method.

The object adapter accepts the requests for service on behalf of the server objects. If necessary, it starts up server processes, instantiates or activates the server objects, assigns an object id (object reference), and passes the requests to them. The object adapter also registers the classes it supports and their runtime object instances with the implementation repository. Object adapters are specific to each programming language, and there can be multiple object adapters for every object.

Inter-ORB protocols allow CORBA products to interoperate. CORBA 2.0 specifies direct ORB-to-ORB interoperability mechanisms when the ORBs are resident in the same domain (i.e., they understand the object references, IDL type system, etc.). Bridge-based interoperability is used otherwise. The bridge then maps the ORB-specific information across domains. General Inter-ORB protocol specifies the transfer syntax and a set of standard message formats for ORB interoperation. Internet Inter-ORB Protocol is the implementation of this specification over a TCP/IP network. These

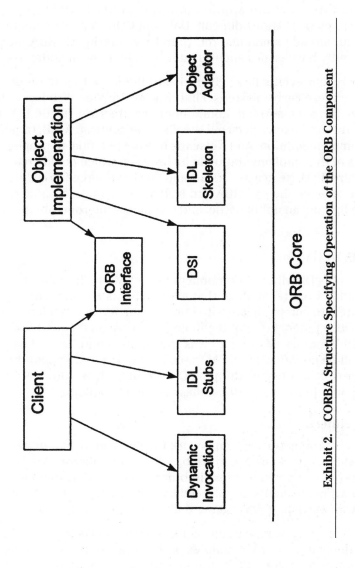

Exhibit 2. CORBA Structure Specifying Operation of the ORB Component

systems also support interobject references to locate and identify an object over the TCP/IP network.

CORBA IN THE REAL WORLD

CORBA has been around for a long time, but differences in early CORBA implementations made application portability and interoperability between implementations difficult. Different CORBA implementations fragmented an already small market, thereby rendering CORBA ineffective. Only recently have issues such as interoperability been addressed.

Other recent events have given rise to the hope that the industry can overcome these early missteps. First, the World Wide Web has created an incentive for a mainstream component architecture. Second, Netscape, Novell, and Oracle have licensed the Visigenic Software ORB, targeting one CORBA implementation. And Netscape has the potential to propagate large numbers of that implementation in its browser, which could create critical mass. Third, IBM, Netscape, Oracle, and Sun have agreed to ensure interoperability between their CORBA and IIOP implementations. Still, these vendors are fighting an uphill battle, and significant interoperability problems remain.

WHAT IS DCOM?

Microsoft's Distributed Component Object Model (DCOM) is object-oriented middleware technology that allows clients and servers in a distributed system to communicate with one another. It extends Microsoft's Component Object Model (COM) technology to work on the network. As is the case with Windows, Microsoft owns DCOM and controls its development. There will be no differing DCOM implementations to fragment the market, and Microsoft has begun shipping DCOM on both Windows NT and Windows 95. In other words, critical mass is quickly building.

COM Architecture

COM is an object-based framework for developing and deploying software components. COM lets developers capture abstractions as component interfaces and then provide binary classes that implement those interfaces. Encapsulation is enforced by COM such that client applications can only invoke functions that are defined on an object's interface.

COM interfaces define a contract between a COM object and client. It defines the behavior or capabilities of the software component as a set of methods and properties. COM interfaces are implemented by COM classes. COM classes are bodies of code that implement at least one COM interface. All COM classes implement two functionalities: lifetime management and interface management. COM classes may implement several interfaces. COM clients must explicitly request the interface they need. It also lets clients

202

widen their interface requirement at run-time or query whether a component supports an interface. Lifetime management is accomplished by reference counting.

COM classes reside in a server either as DLLs or EXEs. COM classes implemented as DLLs share the same address space (in-process) as their clients. COM classes implemented within EXEs live in different processes (out-of-process) than their client. Such out-of-process clients are supported via remote procedure calls.

COM classes are like meta classes. They create instances of COM classes, and also store static data for a class interface. For example, if a COM server has four different COM classes inside, that COM server will also have four class objects — one for each kind of COM class within the server.

OLE is a set of system services built on top of COM for constructing compound documents that is also used for supporting components. OLE Automation allows a component object to expose its methods through the Idispatch interface, allowing late binding of method calls. OLE Controls (OCXs) provide exposure to the interface of an object using method pointer tables called vtables.

COM's binary interoperability standard facilitates independent development of software components and supports deployment of those components in binary form. The result is that software vendors can develop and package reusable building blocks without shipping source code. Corporate application developers can use COM to create new solutions that combine in-house business objects, off-the-shelf objects, and their own custom components.

DCOM Architecture

DCOM, or Distributed Component Object Model, extends COM to the network with remote method calls, security, scalability, and location transparency. With COM, objects may be loaded into the client's process or launched in a separate process on the the same machine. DCOM extends this transparency to include location transparency, allowing objects to exist anywhere on the network. When the client and the object server are on different machines (see Exhibit 3), the remoting layer adds a proxy object in the client's process space and a stub process on the server's process space. The proxy object is then responsible for marshaling the parameters and making the function call. The stub unmarshals the parameters and makes the actual function call on the component object. The results are then marshaled and sent back to the proxy object where it is unmarshaled and given to the client. The entire process of creating the proxy and

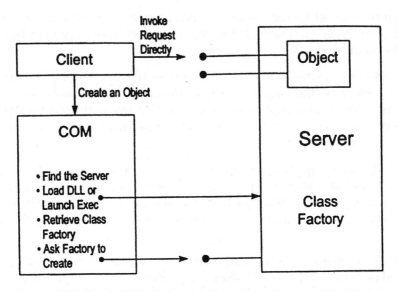

Exhibit 3.   A COM Object and an Invocation by a Client

stub is invisible to either the client or the server, and they use remote procedure call as the interprocess communication mechanism.

ARCHITECTURE: CORBA VS. DCOM

The member companies of the Object Management Group have shared one consistent vision of an architecture for distributed, component-based object computing since OMG's inception in 1989. The architecture is described in the Object Management Architecture Guide, first published in 1990, and has been incrementally populated with the specifications of the core interobject communication component (CORBA), and with common services for handling transactions, security, concurrency control, and other vital support functions for object-based applications. Both the architecture and the individual specifications are vendor-neutral, and control of their technical direction and definition is via a public process that ensures broad cross-industry consensus. The specifications are available to all (OMG members or not), and free rights to implement software using the specifications are guaranteed by the terms of the OMG's constitution.

DCOM, being a version of Microsoft's COM, has deep roots in the client desktop GUI side as well as the server side. However, CORBA's main focus has always been on the server side. ORB vendors were in the past expecting the now defunct OpenDoc to compete with Microsoft's COM on the client side. Today CORBA has no model specification to compete with desktop COM components for heterogeneous client GUIs. However, JavaBeans, a component technology from SUN, is being integrated to support client

204

components with CORBA. This technology is still evolving. Until COM is ported to other platforms, however, Microsoft's client side advantage exists only on 32-bit Windows platforms.

The CORBA Object Reference differs from DCOM's Interface Reference in several ways. CORBA supports multiple inheritance of object interfaces, whereas DCOM has a mechanism allowing multiple independent interfaces per object.

Interfaces. Both use the interface mechanism to expose object functionalities. Interfaces contain methods and attributes as a common means of placing requests on an object. CORBA uses standard models of inheritance from object-oriented languages. DCOM/ActiveX uses the concept of multiple interfaces supported by a single object. DCOM requires that multiple inheritance be emulated through aggregation and containment of interfaces.

Identity. Another difference is the notion of object identity. CORBA defines the identity of an object in an object reference that is unique and consistent. If the object is not in memory, the reference is used to reconstruct the object. DCOM in contrast defines the identity in the interface, but the reference to the object itself is transient. This may lead to problems when reconnecting because the previously used object may not be directly accessible.

Reference Counting. Reference counting is also different in both. A DCOM object maintains a reference count of all connected clients. It uses pinging of the clients to ensure that the clients are alive. CORBA does not need to do remote reference because its object-reference model allows the re-creation of the object if it has been prematurely deleted. CORBA does not attempt to track the number of clients communicating with a particular object. If a client releases the object on the server while another is using it, the object will be destroyed and an error will return to the other client on the next method call. Thus, it is up to the object implementation to provide life-cycle management if such behavior is unacceptable. Without a transaction manager integrated into the distributed system, it is very difficult to implement a reliable life-cycle management system.

APIs. CORBA uses two application protocol interfaces (APIs) and one protocol for object requests. It provides the generated stubs for both static and dynamic invocation. In addition, dynamic skeleton interface allows changes during runtime. DCOM provides two APIs and two protocols. The standard interface is based on a binary interface that uses method pointer tables called vtables. The second API, OLE Automation, is used to support dynamic requests through scripting languages.

PROGRAMMING DCOM AND CORBA

CORBA defines a finite set of primitive data types used for argument passing and structure definitions. CORBA interface definition language (IDL) files are similar in syntax to the C language, but deal only with interface-related details.

Two of the primary differences between COM and CORBA are structure and naming. A COM object consists of one or more categories of interfaces, where each one is named and has its own derivation hierarchy. A CORBA object follows a standard object model in that its interface is defined by its class and all the ancestors of that class. In the COM interface definition, the developer provides a universal identifier (UUID) that uniquely identifies the interface and class definitions. The UUID identifies classes instead of a class name so that you can have multiple classes with the same name but different vendors and functionality. CORBA, on the other hand, uses a naming system that includes the class name and an optional module name. Module names are equivalent to the C++ namespace concept, where class names can be scoped (assigned) to a particular module. The COM approach ensures that a collision will not occur. The CORBA version would allow a program to use two or more classes of the same name if their module scopes are different.

Error conditions and the amount of information they return is another difference. CORBA implementations provide an exception mechanism that returns errors as a structure embedded within another object called the Environment. A standard System Exception structure is defined for system-level and communications errors that can occur during a remote method call. Since CORBA is generally implemented with an object-oriented language, the exception systems of CORBA and the language can be tied together. Thus in C++, an error that occurs on the server will result in an exception being thrown on the client. In contrast, all methods in COM return an HRESULT integer value that indicates the success or failure of the call. This integer value is split up into a number of bit fields that allow the programmer to specify context, facility, severity, and error codes, making error handling more laborious.

The error-handling example is an area that CORBA is better at supporting than DCOM. Though both promote the aspect of location transparency, the reality that object implementations exist in other processes and the complications that can result from this are exposed in the way errors are handled. Developers like to know where an object exists when an error occurs. CORBA seems better, with its support for reporting system errors separate from application-level errors, which makes it easier for the developer to build appropriate exception-handling code.

206

Existing Services. To quickly implement distributed object technologies, it is important to have a built-in core set of components that applications can use. While DCOM comes bundled with a few more than CORBA, both suffer from a lack of existing components.

SECURITY

DCOM has a more flexible security implementation than does CORBA. DCOM provides multiple levels of security that can be selected by the administrator. DCOM uses access control lists (ACLs) on COM components. Administrators can use ACLs to determine who has access to the objects. DCOM methods can also programmatically control authorization of individual method invocations. By combining NT APIs and registry keys, a method can implement custom security. DCOM's security managers are platform-dependent, however, they employ readily available authenticators from third parties.

CORBA object services specify three levels of security. Level 0 specifies the authentication and session encryption using technology similar to that of the secure sockets layer (SSL) on web servers. This requires that the IIOP be secure, and object servers have to register themselves with the ORB as secure. Levels 1 and 2 are differentiated based on whether the CORBA clients and server objects are aware of the security layer. In Level 1 they are not aware, and in Level 2 they are aware of the security layer. Because CORBA's security specification has only recently been completed, ORB vendors have in the past had to come up with their own security implementations, which were incompatible with each other. Most vendors are currently only supporting SSL and Level 0 security.

SCALABILITY

Transaction Processing (TP) monitors help with scalability of any application by providing two critical services:

- Process management — starting server processes, filtering work to them, monitoring their execution, and balancing their workloads
- Transaction management — ensures atomicity, consistency, isolation, and durability (ACID) properties for all processes and resources under its control

Both DCOM and CORBA leverage TP monitors to provide for scalability and robustness.

DCOM is designed to work with the Microsoft Transaction Server, which began shipping in early 1997. Transaction Server is a transaction processing system that enables development, deployment, and management of multi-tier applications composed of COM and DCOM objects. DCOM is used for all object communication among machines. Transaction Server transparently

207

provides transaction support to objects; manages threads, processes, ODBC database connections, and sharing data among concurrently executing objects. Transaction Server has a tight integration with SQL Server, and it can be used with a wide range of databases. Transaction Server currently does not support failover and load balancing, though it is expected to in future releases. In addition, DCOM is scheduled to work with a next-generation Directory Services scheduled to ship with Windows NT 5.0. These services will provide a highly scalable store for object references and security information for DCOM.

CORBA has a specification called Object Transaction Services (OTS) that is designed to interoperate with X/Open-compliant transaction monitors. Hence, CORBA OTS is designed to work both with ORB-based and traditional TP transaction processing services. OTS offers the capability of supporting recoverable nested transactions that supports ACID and two-phase commit protocols. IDL interfaces can be used to provide a way to access the TP monitor application remotely. Integrating TP monitors within an ORB allows the CORBA components to be wrappers of existing business functionality and to support legacy data.

PLATFORM SUPPORT

DCOM will currently only run on 32-bit Windows platforms. It is currently integrated into Windows NT 4.0, both Server and Workstation, and is available free for Windows 95.

However, cross-platform support for DCOM is coming, with third-party ports coming for UNIX, including one for Linux, Digital UNIX, HP/UX, and Sun's Solaris, as well as IBM's MVS and DEC's OpenVMS. Microsoft is actively seeking partners to port DCOM to other platforms, although some are concerned that Microsoft will favor its Windows-based implementations over the published DCOM standards. Applications using DCOM running on non-Windows platforms are only able to invoke the services on the Windows platforms, as opposed to allowing applications to be built anywhere.

Among UNIX users, there is a driving need to have an easy means to connect application on the desktop and the server. Software AG, a developer of three DCOM-on-UNIX ports, estimates that of the 600,000 UNIX servers in production systems worldwide, about 80 percent need an easier way to bridge the worlds of UNIX and Windows.

Critics of DCOM point out that the DCOM component model isn't inherently distributed. It has to be ported to every platform where it is to be used in order to get portability. That is clumsier than CORBA, which was built from the ground up to be distributed.

In order for DCOM to be widely used for creating enterprise applications, cross-platform services such as Transactions Server and Message Queue Server must be in place. Although Microsoft is expected to provide versions of its COM-based messaging and transaction services on other platforms, directly or through a third party, no formal commitment has been made.

LANGUAGE SUPPORT

CORBA is well suited for use by object-oriented languages. The code is much cleaner because the bindings fully exploit the features of the host language. DCOM, on the other hand, has done nothing to provide management classes for the method arguments or a way to link error conditions to the C++ exception mechanism. CORBA also has a superior mechanism for handling arrays and sequences and provides an "any" data type for marshaling arguments whose type one does not know in advance. For object-oriented languages such as C++, the DCOM interface is cumbersome and requires more low-level code.

On the other hand, since DCOM supports OLE automation, applications can be developed with popular, nonobject-oriented languages such as Visual Basic or Delphi. If you are developing a PC-based application within these environments DCOM is definitely easier. For those dealing with object-oriented languages and significant object models, the CORBA model is more of a natural fit because of COM's inability to support polymorphism and framework development.

INDUSTRY SUPPORT

Although many key companies such as Netscape, Oracle, and Sun Microsystems have agreed to support the emerging CORBA standards, there is some doubt whether they are fully committed to the standard, or if they will shift to DCOM if it gains considerable market share. DEC has announced it will use more than one technology; HP has indicated interest in supporting COM on their versions of UNIX but remains uncommitted to DCOM. Others, such as IBM, seem to be firmly backing CORBA. IBM has introduced a CORBA-based development suite of middleware products, including Component Broker Connector and Component Broker Toolkit, which it plans to offer free with many of its products.

Tools vendors such as Oracle are hoping to find a middle ground in the battle for market share between DCOM and CORBA. Oracle has released a development environment that supports both native COM and CORBA components.

MATURITY

CORBA and DCOM have great potential for creating seamless distributed computing environments, despite the fact that CORBA is currently struggling to establish its standards and DCOM has yet to prove it can operate as a cross-platform solution.

A Complete Tool?

While both architectures can create the structure for enterprise-level applications, neither is capable of generating an actual enterprise-ready application, which requires other services such as transactions, event notification, concurrency control, and naming. While neither CORBA nor DCOM is a complete solution for network programming, CORBA offers good code for object-oriented languages. DCOM is easy to use with non-object-oriented languages such as Visual Basic.

PERFORMANCE

The network performance of DCOM is comparable to that of CORBA's IIOP, with each accomplishing reasonable request-reply response times. However, a standard method of communicating over an asynchronous transport is needed for both DCOM and CORBA. Currently, because of their highly synchronous operation, these technologies are limited to operating over LANs and server backbones. Internet use, or use over a company WAN, is not practical with the current technologies because of the high rate of synchronous request-reply activity required.

The OMG is in the midst of finalizing the Asynchronous Messaging service. This service extends CORBA's synchronous processes and provides a notion of "store-and-forward" processing with a variety of quality of service guarantees for messaging, reporting, and similar functions.

SUPPORT FOR THE WORLD WIDE WEB

Netscape has declared the Internet Inter-ORB Protocol (IIOP) as its standard for communicating between distributed objects and has included object broker technology in Communicator and SuiteSpot. Microsoft continues to position its Windows, DCOM, and ActiveX as its distributed object solution, and Explorer is the only browser to support ActiveX.

Notification services are being provided in conjunction with the asynchronous messaging services in CORBA to enable an object to subscribe and receive notification of changes. This is essential to support the various push technologies emerging on the Web. Along with Event services, this provides support for publish and subscribe to be effectively supported. Many CORBA vendors have provided support for this technology. However, they are not very scalable, since by their very nature the Event services use a point-to-point connection oriented approach.

PROTOCOLS SUPPORTED

DCOM supports several protocols, such as TCP/IP, IPX/SPX, and Named Pipes. Though not limited to IIOP, CORBA ORBs only support the TCP/IP-based Internet Inter-Orb Protocol (IIOP) or proprietary inter-ORB protocols. DCOM's core network protocol is called Object Remote Procedure Call (ORPC). It is based upon DCE RPCs (Distributed Computing Environment Remote Procedure Calls), with extensions such as the addition of a primitive data type to support object references.

EASE OF USE

DCOM has just a few key management tools and has based the transport and security mechanisms on familiar Distributed Computing Environment (DCE) standards. This has made managing distributed components much less of a challenge.

INTEROPERABILITY BETWEEN CORBA AND DCOM

Currently, the Internet Inter-ORB Protocol (IIOP) is the OMG-approved method of linking distributed CORBA objects. Microsoft says it has no plans to support IIOP in DCOM, and there is currently no built-in COM support in CORBA. This battle of standards is making the implementation of both CORBA and COM services difficult.

As most enterprises will have both COM and CORBA environments, it is necessary that the objects in each be able to communicate with each other. OMG published a specification two years ago called "COM/CORBA Interworking" (now part of the CORBA 2.0 specification), which defines standardized mappings between COM and CORBA objects. There are several companies shipping implementations of this specification, including IONA, HP, Digital, and Expersoft. Basically, one of two approaches is used: encapsulation or converter. In the encapsulation approach, a call to the server object system is wrapped in an implementation of the object from the client system. ORB vendors provide generators to create such a bridge from the interface description of the object. In the converter approach, conversation proxies are generated during runtime based on the interface description of the object it represents. Both support bidirectional calls to and from either object system.

THE FUTURE

Microsoft is about to release a new version of COM called COM+, which is designed to simplify the creation and use of software components. COM+ will provide a runtime and services that are readily usable from any programming language or tool. It is intended to enable extensive interoperability between components regardless of how they were implemented.

Where COM+ really shines, and where it most affects DCOM, is how COM+ will address the difficulties inherent in writing component-based distributed applications. COM+ will introduce an extensibility mechanism called interception, which will receive and process events related to instance creation, calls, returns, errors, and instance deletion. Services that the Microsoft Transaction Server provides today will become a part of COM+, and thus will be a core part of future Microsoft operating systems.

Similarly, OMG is defining and filling in the services required for most of the service layers, such as directory service, transactions, and security. Vendor implementations of these are starting to appear. Others such as persistence, concurrency, time, query, trader, collection, and versioning will slowly trickle in over the next couple of years. In addition, JavaBeans technology is being pushed as the client component technology, and Java support for CORBA is emerging. This may help provide additional support for CORBA on the desktop.

CONCLUSION

DCOM is more accessible than CORBA at this stage of the technologies because of Microsoft's experience and focus on the included DCOM management tools. For Microsoft-centric companies, DCOM is a solution that is tightly integrated with the Windows operating system. Customers have the most to lose in the object wars, and interoperability between CORBA and DCOM will likely be an important issue for many years. Where cross-platform capability or access to legacy objects is required, CORBA is currently the clear winner. CORBA provides companies with the highest degree of middleware flexibility through its extensive third-party support. More likely, all enterprises will use a mix of the two technologies, with DCOM at the desktop and CORBA at the enterprise level.

In essence, DCOM and CORBA provide similar enough services that debates on minor technical issues ought to be dismissed in favor of more practical concerns, such as scalability, openness, availability, and maturity. Other important issues to be considered are the operating systems and programming languages used in the current project. Availability of CORBA and DCOM bridges may render the choice moot, and users will not be aware or care whether it is DCOM or CORBA under the covers, because what they will use will be higher services (such as business facilities) built on top of either architecture.

Notes

[1] Object Management Group, 1997, "CORBA vs. ActiveX," http://www.omg.org/ activex.htm..

[2] Object Management Group, 1997, "What is CORBA?," http://www.omg.org/ omg00/wicorba.htm.

[3] T.M. Rajkumar, 1997, Client Server Development with Components.

[4] *InfoWorld,* August 4, 1997, v19 n31 p6(1), HP to Push DCOM as Part of CORBA, McKay, Niall.

[5] *Network Computing,* July 15, 1997, v8 n13 p98(5), Is DCOM Truly the Object of Middleware's Desire?, Frey, Anthony.

[6] *Network Computing,* July 1, 1997, v8 n12 p101(1), Three's a Crowd with Object Lessons, Gall, Nick.

[7] *InformationWeek,* May 26, 1997, n632 p122(1), Component Software War, Harzog, Bernd.

[8] *InfoWorld,* May 19, 1997, v19 n20 p51(2), Microsoft's Cross-Platform DCOM Plans to Raise Questions, Bowen, Ted Smalley.

[9] *PC Week,* May 12, 1997, v14 n19 p8(1), DCOM-to-Unix Ports on the Way, Leach, Norvin.

[10] *PC Week,* May 12, 1997, v14 n19 p93(1), Single Victor Unlikely in Object Protocol War, Lewis, Jamie.

[11] *Byte,* April 1997, v22 n4 p103(3), Programming with CORBA and DCOM, Pompeii, John.

[12] DBMS, April 1997, v10 n4 p26(6), Inside DCOM, Roy, Mark and Ewald, Alan.

[13] Object Management Group, 1997, IIOP, http://www.omg.org/corba/corbiiop.htm.

[14] Microsoft Corporation, 1997, "COM and DCOM," http://www.microsoft.com/ cominfo/.

[15] *Byte,* April 1997, v22 n4 p93, Distributing Components, Montgomery, John.

[16] *Microsoft Systems Journal,* 1997, v12 n11, Object-Oriented Software Development Made Simple with COM+ Runtime Services, Kirtland, Mary.

[17] *Object Magazine,* July 1997, p. 68-77. CORBA/DCOM interoperability, Kotopoulis, Alexander and Miller, Julia.

[18] BMS, March 1997. p. 43-50 CORBA Masterminds Object Management, Kueffel, Warren.

[19] *Application Development Trends,* October 97, p. 41-46. Deeper Inside CORBA, Dolgicer, Max.

Chapter 11
A Technical Primer for Getting Started with JavaBeans
Charles Dow

SOFTWARE ENGINEERS ALL OVER THE WORLD ARE TIRED OF WRITING THE SAME CODE over and over again. They want to be able to reuse with ease the bulk of the code required to build the plumbing of an application, then be able to concentrate on the business rules and data. To accomplish this, tested and reliable building blocks that can be plugged together using a common protocol are needed.

JavaBeans provides a key piece of the technologies needed for these building blocks. The fact that JavaBeans is simple to develop, uses a modern object-oriented language, and handles the Internet and its associated security issues, makes its appeal unquestionable.

JavaBeans technology is very much like all OO technology; it has rich layers that need to be peeled away like an onion. This chapter is designed to show readers a few of its layers and how easily they can be peeled. Remember, one does not need to know all of the layers to reap the rewards of this remarkable innovation of the recent past. More importantly, by applying a few coding standards, the benefit of using JavaBeans can be obtained without requiring additional effort by developers. JavaBeans are not just for GUI widgets. They can provide far more business value. Components at runtime can be nonvisual (i.e., they do not have a graphical user interface).

SOME HISTORY

JavaBeans 1.0 has been available in JDK 1.1 since February 1997. Apple, Baan, Borland, CI Labs, Corel, Informix, IBM, JUSTSYSTEM, Lotus, Microsoft, Netscape, Novell, Oracle, ParcPlace, Silicon Graphics, SunSoft, Sybase, Symantec, Texas Instruments, Visual Edge, plus many external reviewers participated in its development. JavaBeans is a Core API, which means one can expect it to be available on all the VMs.

0-8493-9976-9/99/$0.00+$.50
© 1999 by CRC Press LLC

ENABLING TECHNOLOGIES

TOOLABILITY

A key design goal for the JavaBeans technology was to provide components that could be manipulated visually by tools. JavaBeans allows developers to create reusable software components that then can be assembled together using visual application builder tools such as Sybase's PowerJ, Borland's JBuilder, IBM's Visual Age for Java, SunSoft's Java Workshop, Symantec's Visual Cafe, and many, many others. Visit the website, http://java.sun.com/beans/tools.html for a current listing of tools (available at the time of publication).

SIMPLE BEANS ARE FREE

Wouldn't it be nice to be able to concentrate only on writing the code needed to solve a particular problem and then be able to turn it into a component for others to use? That is possible in Java by following a few simple rules (a.k.a. design patterns) when writing code.

Before learning the name for those rules, follow some steps that will illustrate the process of bean-building.

Step 1. Write a Class

```
// A very simple example
// Time Bean class
// Time.java


import java.text.*;
import java.util.*;
import java.awt.Color;


public class Time {
Date currentDate;
SimpleDateFormat formatter;
String dateString;


public String getDateString () {
currentDate = new Date();
formatter = new SimpleDateFormat ("EEE, MMM d, ''yy");
```

```
dateString = formatter.format(currentDate);

return dateString;

}

public void setDateString (String newString) {

dateString = "No date as yet";

}

}
```

Note: A JavaBean does not have to be an applet or an application. It is a Java class, no more, no less. (Java classes do not have to be simple.)

Step 2. Compile the Class

D:\MyJavaSource\Time javac Time.java — javac is the compiler supplied with the JDK. One can download the JDK from http://java.sun.com/products/jdk/1.1/ (Web address accurate at time of publication). Do not forget to add a source directory to the CLASSPATH before compiling. Once that is done, execute javac from the source directory, as shown above.

Step 3. Create a JAR File for a Bean

A JAR file is the standard archive for Java code. There is one little twist that has to be applied if it is to contain a JavaBean. A manifest should be added. The manifest is a text file that needs to have at a minimum:

```
Name: Time.class

Java-Bean: True
```

Enter a command such as:

```
D:\MyJavaSource\Time jar cfm Time.jar Manifest.txt
Time.class
```

Note: Type jar by itself for a listing of the switches jar will accept. After running the command, you will have Time.jar.[1]

Step 4. Test the Bean

If one does not have the JavaBeans Development Kit (BDK), it can be downloaded from the following site: http://java.sun.com/beans/software/bdk_download.html (Web address accurate at time of publication).

Copy the new *Time.jar* file to the jars sub-directory of the BDK (...\BDK\jars).

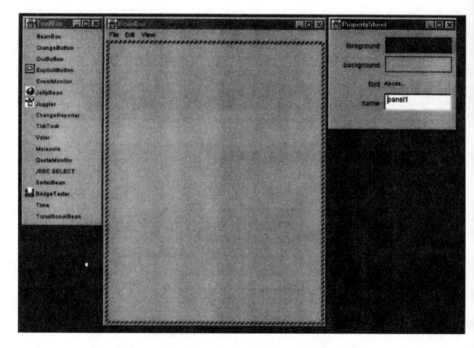

Exhibit 1. ToolBox, BeanBox, and PropertySheet.

Using the BeanBox[2] supplied for free by JavaSoft (part of the BDK), launch the BeanBox. On Windows NT, use the batch file provided ...\BDK\beanbox run.bat. On other operating systems, please read the documentation that came with the BDK.

The three windows (namely ToolBox, BeanBox, and PropertySheet) shown in Exhibit 1 appear on the screen.

The toolbox contains sample beans provided by JavaSoft. Ignore them at this time. Notice the Time bean is one of the options in the list provided by the Toolbox. This one will be used. Left mouse click on the Time entry in the Toolbox; crosshairs will appear. That signifies that the cursor is loaded. Move the cursor over the BeanBox and Left mouse-click. A button-like shape entitled *Time* will appear. Left mouse click on it to select it. Then choose *Edit, Report* from the menu. A report similar to the one shown in Exhibit 2 will appear.

The *setDateString* is the method to set the DateString property or attribute.

The *get DateString* is the method to get the DateString property. A *get without a set* is a read-only property and vice-versa.

```
C:\WINNT\System32\CMD.exe                                              [_][□][X]

H => Hidden
E => Expert
I => Indexed Property

Properties:
    class                   class java.lang.Class        getClass/
    dateString              class java.lang.String       getDateString/setDateString

Event sets:

Methods:
    public final native void java.lang.Object.notifyAll()
    public final native void java.lang.Object.wait(long) throws java.lang.InterruptedException
    public final void java.lang.Object.wait(long,int) throws java.lang.InterruptedException
    public java.lang.String java.lang.Object.toString()
    public void Time.setDateString(java.lang.String)
    public final native void java.lang.Object.notify()
    public boolean java.lang.Object.equals(java.lang.Object)
    public java.lang.String Time.getDateString()
    public native int java.lang.Object.hashCode()
    public final native java.lang.Class java.lang.Object.getClass()
    public final void java.lang.Object.wait() throws java.lang.InterruptedException
```

Exhibit 2.   Report 1.

Then a list of Event sets:

We have none at this time.

Then a list of Methods:

Notice, the above will appear for the class and all that it inherits. (This can be turned off.)

HOW DOES THE BEANBOX KNOW?

The BeanBox uses Introspection. Introspection simply put says, "If I know it is a bean (from the Manifest), then I will use the Java Core Reflection API that the JDK provides to allow us to dynamically obtain the fields, methods, and constructors of loaded classes from the class file."

The Introspection process can be better assisted by providing an associated BeanInfo class.

VOILA — OLD CODE INTO BEANS

But what if one did not know the few rules when writing one's code? Modify the method names, as shown below (Essentially getting rid of the get and set portions that the Reflection API recommends).

```
// A very simple example

// Time Bean class

// Time.java


import java.text.*;
```

```
import java.util.*;
import java.awt.Color;

public class Time {
    Date currentDate;
    SimpleDateFormat formatter;
    String dateString;

    public String obtainDateString () {
        currentDate = new Date();
        formatter = new SimpleDateFormat ("EEE, MMM d,
''yy");
        dateString = formatter.format(currentDate);
        return dateString;
    }
    public void replaceDateString (String newString) {
        dateString = "No date as yet";
    }
}
```

If the above is compiled, and placed in a Jar with the same manifest file as above, the report from the BeanBox that appears is shown in Exhibit 3.

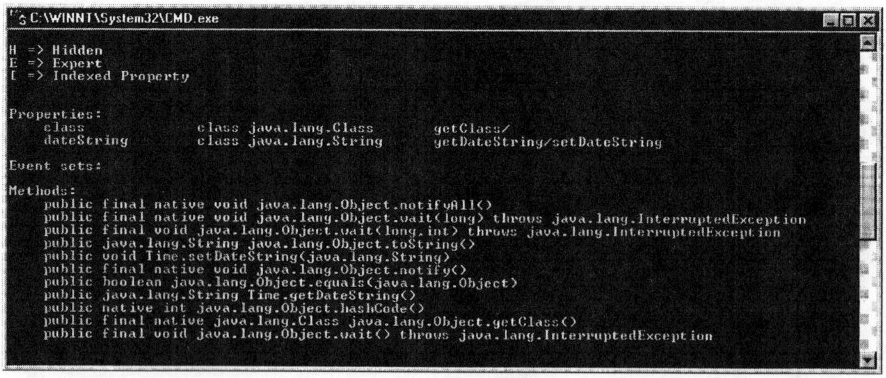

Exhibit 3.   Report 2.

Note: The only property that can be seen by Introspection is the inherited read-only property. All methods are found.

ADDING A BEANINFO CLASS

To make a bean smarter, the BeanInfo[3] class is provided. Developers are encouraged to use this facility. The BeanInfo class will return instances of XxxDescriptor classes to describe the Bean, e.g., BeanDescriptor, EventSetDescriptor, FeatureDescriptor, and others when sent the appropriate messages.

To allow one to only provide the information that he or she wants to specify, there is a helper class, SimpleBeanInfo class, that can be inherited from; it will provide appropriate defaults for any method not overridden. The PropertyDescriptor classes should be used so that the BeanBox can see the getter and setter. Following is the BeanInfo class used:

```
// The BeanInfo class that we associate with our Time Bean


import java.beans.*;

public class TimeBeanInfo extends SimpleBeanInfo {


    public PropertyDescriptor[] getPropertyDescriptors() {

        try { PropertyDescriptor aPropertyDescriptor =
        new

        PropertyDescriptor( "dateString," Time.class,

    "obtainDateString,""replaceDateString");

        PropertyDescriptor[] anArrayOfPropertyDescriptors =
        {

        aPropertyDescriptor};

        return anArrayOfPropertyDescriptors ;

        } catch (Exception e) {

            System.err.println("Exception occurred "+e);

            return null;

        }

    }

}
```

Compile as before and use the following command to create the Jar:

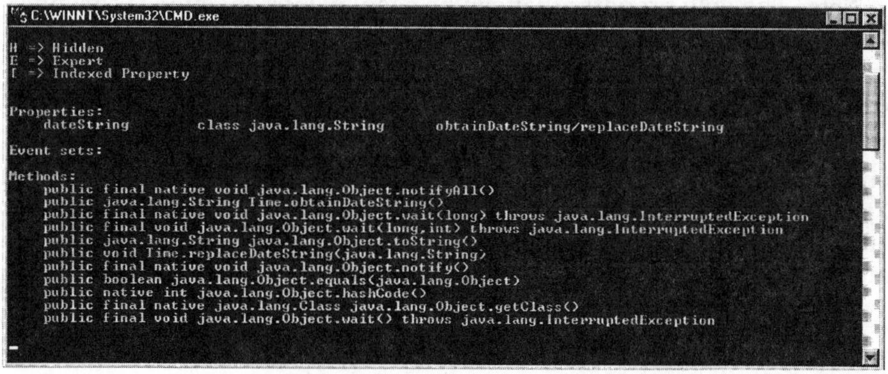

Exhibit 4. Report 3.

```
Jar cfm Time.jar manifest.txt *.class
```

Note: The manifest does not change because only Time.class is a bean. Run the BeanBox and get the report.

The report from the BeanBox now appears as shown in Exhibit 4.

Note: A more complex bean will have three parts, as follows:

• Properties
• Methods
• Events

There are many other features that Beans could use. After this taste of Beans, readers are encouraged to explore these further. Please note that for illustration purposes the code sample was trivial and broke many of the rules of a well-mannered Bean. The best reference that the author is aware of for JavaBeans Guidelines is a document produced by IBM's WebRunner team at http://www.ibm.com/java/education/jb-guidelines.html.

CONCLUSION

JavaBeans is a relatively easy-to-learn tool for building components that provide more functionality than mere widgets. Components provide both functionality and data management in reusable, easy-to-snap-together, little pieces that are combined to build sophisticated applications. The World Wide Web can be mined for many of the tools for getting started with JavaBeans.

References

Tremblett, P., Java Reflection, *Dr. Dobb's J.,* Jan. 1998, 36.

Morrison, M., Weems, R., Coffee, P., and Leong, J., How to Program JavaBeans, *JavaSoft's Beans Development Kit (BDK)*, ZD Press, Indianapolis, IN, May 1977.

Notes

1. For those with Winzip, you can quickly snoop at the jar file and the manifest.mf file contained within.
2. According to the BDK documentation, "the BeanBox is intended as a test container and as a reference base, but it is not intended as a serious application development tool."
3. Look at the documentation for the BeanInfo class.

Chapter 12
Javabeans™ and Java Enterprise Server™ Platform

David Wadsworth

A MAJORITY OF THE WORLD'S DATA RESIDES ON MAINFRAME SERVERS. This legacy poses many challenges to the information systems (IS) community as it struggles with the demands of business units for new and innovative solutions to business problems. Organizations need to adopt a flexible, secure, and cost-effective architecture that will enable them to remain competitive and enable breakaway business strategies. Adoption of Java™ computing realizes these benefits by providing key technology enablers.

JAVA TECHNOLOGY REVIEW

The Java programming language was introduced to the public in May 1995. Key features of the language such as platform independence and ease of programming made it an instant success in the software development community. Other features such as safe network delivery and baked-in security have made the language the *de facto* standard for the development and deployment of Web-based applications.

Applications written in the Java programming language are compiled to bytecode that can run wherever the Java platform is present. The Java platform is a software environment composed of the Java Virtual Machine and the Java Core Application Programming Interfaces (API's). Portability of applications is achieved because there is only one virtual machine specification, which provides a standard, uniform programming interface on any hardware architecture. Developers writing to this base set of functionality can be confident that their applications will run anywhere without the need for additional libraries. Core libraries include functional support for GUI development, I/O, database connectivity, networking, math, components (JavaBeans), multithreading, and many others.

0-8493-9976-9/99/$0.00+$.50

225

Sun's Java computing architecture is an implementation framework that uses standard, currently available network protocols and services to deliver the power of Java applications to the widest possible base of Java platform-enabled devices and users. With this architecture, transactions can be moved transparently to the most cost-effective, appropriate support channel within a network owing to the portable, Write Once, Run Anywhere™ nature of Java applications.

JAVA PLATFORM COMPONENT ARCHITECTURES

Designing and developing applications by means of components has been available for many years. The challenge has been to embrace and extend existing technology with new technology. Until recently, such an approach has been proprietary and difficult to deploy. The Java computing environment with JavaBeans, a component technology, and server architecture solution Java Enterprise Server, enables organizations to greatly simplify access to business systems. What follows is a description of the JavaBeans component model and an overview of the Java Enterprise Server platform.

JAVABEANS

A JavaBean is a reusable Java software component that can be visually manipulated and customized in a builder tool. These application building blocks are constructed so as to communicate easily with each other in a common environment. They also have the ability to store their state on the shelf to be revived at a later date. Because they are written in the Java programming language for deployment on any Java platform, JavaBeans are the platform-independent components for the network.

JavaBean components can range from simple GUI elements, such as buttons and sliders, to more sophisticated visual software components, such as database viewers. Some JavaBeans may have no GUI appearance of their own, but still can be manipulated in an application builder.

The JavaBean API has been designed to be accessible by builder tools as well as manipulated manually by human programmers. The key APIs, such as property control, event handling, and persistence, can be accessed by both hand-crafted applications and builder tools. As well as event handling, property control, and persistence, introspection and customization are distinguishing features of all JavaBeans.

Property Control

Property control facilitates the customizing of the JavaBean at both design and runtime. Both the behavior and appearance of a JavaBean can be modified through the property features. For example, a GUI button might have a property named "ButtonLabel," which represents the text displayed in the button. This property can be accessed through its getter and setter methods. Once properties for a bean are configured, their state will be maintained through the persistence mechanism.

Persistence

The attributes and behavior of a bean are known as the state of the bean. The persistence mechanism within the JavaBean API supports storage of this state once the bean is customized. It is this state that is incorporated into the application and available at runtime. This externalization can be in a custom format or the default. A custom external format allows the bean to be stored as another object type such as an Excel document inside a Word document. The default is reserved for those instances where the bean's state needs to be saved without regard to the external format.

Event Handling

Event handling is a simple mechanism that allows components to be connected based on their production of and interest in certain actions. A component or series of components can be sources of events that can be caught and processed by other components or scripting environments. Typical examples of events include mouse movements, field updates, and keyboard actions. Notification of these events generated by a component are delivered to any interested component.

The extensible event-handling mechanism for JavaBeans allows for the easy implementation of the model in application builder tools. Event types and propagation models can be crafted to accommodate a variety of application types.

Customization

Changing the appearance and behavior of a JavaBean is accomplished through the customization features of the JavaBean's API. Each JavaBean contains a list of exported properties, which an application builder can scan and use to create a GUI property editor sheet. The user can then customize the bean using this dynamically created sheet. This is the simplest form of customization.

Another layer of customization is possible by attaching to the bean a customizer class that acts as a properties wizard. This wizard will have a GUI that can be employed to tailor the properties for the related bean in a guided tour fashion. Such wizards are more likely to be found associated with complex beans such as calculator beans or database connection beans. Once customization is completed the properties will be stored using the persistence mechanism.

Introspection

The properties, methods, and events a JavaBean supports are determined at runtime and in builder environments by means of introspection. Introspection is a prescribed method of querying the bean to discover its inherent characteristics. Introspection is implemented using the Java programming language rather than a separate specification language. Thus, all of the behavior of the bean is specifiable in the Java programming language.

One introspection model supported by the JavaBeans API provides a default view of the methods, events, and properties. This simple mechanism does not require the programmer to do extra work to support introspection. For more sophisticated components, interfaces are available for the developer of the bean to provide specific and detailed control over which methods, events, and properties are exposed.

Default, low-level reflection of the bean is used to discover the methods supported by the bean. Design patterns are then applied to these methods to determine the properties, events, and public methods supported by the component. For example, if a pair of methods such as setColor and getColor are discovered during the reflection process, the property color is identified by the application of the get/set design pattern for property discovery.

More complex component analysis can be built into the bean by the use of a BeanInfo class. This class would be used by a builder tool to discover the bean's behavior programmatically.

Security

JavaBeans are governed by the same security model as all other Java applets and applications. If a JavaBean is contained in an untrusted applet, then it will be subject to the same restrictions and will not be allowed to read or write files on the local file system or connect to arbitrary network hosts. As a component in a Java application or trusted applet, a JavaBean will be granted the same access to files and hosts as a normal Java application. Developers are encouraged to design their beans so they can be run as part of untrusted applets.

Runtime vs. Design-time JavaBeans

Each JavaBean must be capable of running in a number of different environments. The two most important are the design time and runtime environments. In the design environment a JavaBean must be able to expose its properties and other design-time information to allow for customization in a builder tool. In some cases wizards contained in the bean may be employed to simplify this process.

Once the application is generated the bean must be usable at runtime. There is really no need to have the customization or design information available in this environment.

The amount of code required to support the customization and design-time information for a bean could be potentially quite large. For example, a wizard to assist in the modification of bean properties could be considerably larger than the runtime version of the bean. For this reason it is possible to segregate the design-time and runtime aspects of a bean so it can be deployed without the overhead of the design-time features.

JavaBeans Summary

JavaBeans are the component object model for the Java platform. These device-independent components can be customized and assembled quickly and easily to create sophisticated applications.

JAVA ENTERPRISE SERVER PLATFORM

As organizations adopt Internet technologies to enable new business strategies, they are faced with the task of integrating all of their legacy applications, databases, and transaction services with Web-based services. Traditional applications designed in the client/server model do not deploy well in an Internet/extranet environment. Although not new, multitier architectures for application development and deployment are best suited for extending the reach of a company's infrastructure to partners, suppliers, customers, and remote employees. The Java Enterprise server platform provides such an architecture in an open and standards-based environment that it incorporates existing infrastructure while extending their reach to intranets, extranets, and even the Internet. An extensible architecture, the Java Enterprise server platform contains the API's products and tools necessary to construct new enterprisewide applications and integrate with existing systems.

Traditional mission-critical applications are written to the APIs of the underlying operating system, thereby tying the application to a single operating system. Porting of the application to a new operating system is both difficult and expensive. These same applications may rely on a service, such as a transaction monitor. Access to this service will be through the software vendor's proprietary APIs creating another platform lock and presenting a barrier to moving to a different service provider.

The Java Enterprise server platform is designed to address these platform-lock issues. It extends the notion of "write once, run anywhere" to include "and integrate with everything." Based on a layer and leverage model, the Java Enterprise server platform can be built on top of existing legacy systems such as transaction monitors, database access, system

```
┌─────────────────────────────────────────────────────────┐
│              Platform Neutral Development                 │
│                                                           │
│     Enterprise JavaBeans Components Model                 │
│  ┌────┬─────┬──────┬─────┬─────┬─────┬───┬──────┬──────┐  │
│  │Web │Nam- │Mess. │Dist.│Secur│Mgt  │DB │Trans-│      │  │
│  │Serv│ing  │      │Obj. │ity  │     │   │action│      │  │
│  └────┴─────┴──────┴─────┴─────┴─────┴───┴──────┴──────┘  │
│              Java Virtual Machine                         │
│  Solaris  NT  HP-UX  AIX  MVS  IRIX  MacOS ... others     │
│                                                           │
│  Network Serv.  TCP/IP  SPX/IPX  SNA  DECnet  LanMgr      │
│                                                           │
│                 Physical Network                          │
└─────────────────────────────────────────────────────────┘
```

Exhibit 1. Java Enterprise server platform architecture.

---

management, naming and directory services, and CORBA (Exhibit 1). Interfaces to these services, as well as a component model that provides for application encapsulation and reuse, are integral to the Java Enterprise server platform. The component model includes JavaBeans components for the client, and Enterprise JavaBeans (EJB's) components for the server.

All of the benefits of rapid application development, scalability, robustness, and security of the JavaBeans component architecture are extended to the Java Enterprise server platform. EJBs also have the ability to provide transactional services. Coupled with these benefits is an open architecture capable of providing ease of development, deployment, and management.

Enterprise JavaBeans, an extension of the JavaBeans architecture, provide a distributed component architecture for developing and deploying component-based, multitier applications. Business logic is encapsulated in the Enterprise JavaBeans promoting a high degree of reuse. Access to low-level services such as session management and multithreading is simplified such that developers building applications do not need to deal directly with these functions.

Distributed applications developed with Enterprise JavaBeans can be deployed on any other platform without modifications. Support for transactions and messaging integrate with existing legacy systems and middleware.

The heart of the Enterprise JavaBean platform is the Enterprise JavaBean executive (Exhibit 2). This runtime executive is used to execute the components that provide the services required by an application. Through

Enterprise JavaBeans

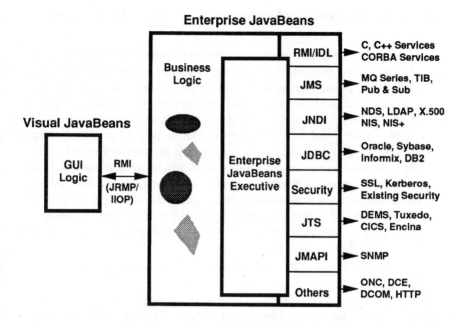

Exhibit 2.   Enterprise JavaBeans framework.

its components, the executive manages load balancing and handles multi-threading, transaction management, security, and connection management. This frees programmers to focus on developing the components that contain business logic.

Communication between the client and server in an application does not need to rely on any particular protocol. Both the client and server sides of the application are coded using the Java programming language. At deployment time the underlying communication stubs are generated automatically. The Java programming language introspection of the application class files is used to generate the communication stubs.

Unlike JavaBeans which use the Java event model, Enterprise JavaBeans use the distributed CORBA event model. The event model supported by the Java programming language is well-suited for local, tightly integrated applications, but does not perform as well in a networked environment where high latency and insecure networks are common. Enterprise Java-Bean events are propagated across the network over CORBA's Internet InterORB Protocol (IIOP) to other components.

Enterprise JavaBeans can be configured automatically as CORBA objects, then accessed through IIOP by clients. These client applications do not have to be written in the Java programming language to access the components. EJB's also can function as COM/DCOM objects for Windows clients.

Access to several key services are offered as part of the Enterprise Java-Bean specification (Exhibit 2). These services are offered through specific Java platform APIs such as JavaIDL/RMI for accessing CORBA, DCE, or ONC services; Java Message Service (JMS) for access to messaging systems such as MQ Series; Java Naming and Directory Interface (JNDI) for accessing multiple naming and directory services such as LDAP and NDS; Java Database Connectivity (JDBC) for connecting to various relational and nonrelational databases; Java security API's providing for encryption and authentication; Java Transaction services (JTS) providing a Java programming language binding to the object transaction services (OTS) of CORBA; Java management API (JMAPI) providing for the management of networked resources such as workstations and routers; and Web services through the Java Server API. Each is detailed below.

JavaIDL

The Java Interface Definition Language (IDL) provides standards-based interoperability and connectivity with CORBA. Through these interfaces, Java applications are able to access existing infrastructure written in other languages. This is one of the key interfaces for legacy system integration. JavaIDL is part of the Java platform core API set and is, therefore, available across multiple platforms.

Java Message Service

Java Message Service (JMS) provides an interface to messaging systems that provide publish/subscribe and message queue services. This platform-independent interface also will support the emerging push/pull technologies.

Java Naming and Directory Interface

Many different kinds of naming and directory services exist in today's enterprises. Directory services such as LDAP, NIS, and NDS provide networkwide sharing of information about the users, systems, applications, and resources that exist on an intranet or the Internet. User information can include login IDs, passwords, security access, and electronic mail addresses. System information can include network addresses and machine configurations. The Java Naming and Directory Interface (JNDI) is independent of any specific naming and directory service implementation. Application developers can access multiple namespaces easily through JNDI. A single interface simplifies the access to composite namespaces as well as enabling an application to be portable across different platforms.

Java Database Connectivity

One of the earliest and now core APIs is the Java database connectivity API (JDBC). This is a SQL-based, database-independent API that frees developers from writing database vendor-specific code in their applications. JDBC supports the common database functionality such as remote procedure calls, SQL statements, database connection, and result sets. Because JDBC is implemented via a driver manager, which itself can be implemented in the Java programming language, applets can be delivered to the client with the database connectivity built in. Implementation drivers for all the major RDBMS are already available for JDBC, and a JDBC-to-ODBC bridge is standard in the Java Developer's Kit Version 1.1. JDBC drivers for object-relational DBMSs as well as IBM's IMS are also currently available.

Java Security API

Security is an integral part of the Java Platform and extends to the Java Enterprise Server architecture. There are four key areas that are supported by various security APIs: authentication, authorization, privacy, and integrity.

Authentication is the system's ability to verify or recognize a user. Typically performed at application access or system sign-on, authentication is the first line of defense present in a comprehensive security model. The JavaCard APIs allow smart cards to be employed as secure user authentication devices. These physical cards combined with a secure personal identification number (PIN) enable users to be recognized by the target system. Digital signatures, another authentication method, also are supported through the Java Virtual Machine.

Authorization is the means of determining which data, systems, and services a user can access. The Java Security APIs and access control lists (ACL) are available for managing who can access what. ACLs can be built for each Enterprise JavaBean and consulted whenever the bean is accessed. Based on the user's role some form of access can be given or denied. Transaction servers installed in the application enforce the ACL at runtime. Because ACLs are not a static structure they can be moved around the network with an EJB object. These embedded ACLs then can be accessed by the application developer.

Privacy concerns are raised in the context of transmission of sensitive data across public networks. To protect data such as credit card numbers, encryption typically is employed. The Java language cryptography APIs provide application or session-level encryption. This interface can support any encryption implementation including DES.

As data passes through a network, be it private or public, there is a chance for malicious or accidental modification. To prevent such actions it is necessary to be able to guarantee the integrity of the transmission. The same mechanisms for insuring privacy can be used for maintaining integrity of network communications, namely session and application encryption.

Java Transaction Services

Java Transaction Services (JTS) within the Enterprise JavaBean framework are a low-level API not meant as an application programmer interface. JTS programming is targeted to the resource managers and TP monitor programmers. Currently available implementations include BEA Systems, Jolt product for Tuxedo access, or IBM's JavaCICS for access to mainframe CICS applications.

Java Management API

The Java Management API (JMAPI) is a set of interfaces for the development of distributed network, system, and application management applications. JMAPI is designed to be incorporated into a variety of devices, across diverse network protocols and numerous operating systems. With support for the Simple Network Management Protocol (SNMP), JMAPI can communicate directly with a variety of existing devices. In the future, device manufacturers will incorporate the JMAPI directly into their products. System administrators using applications developed on this foundation are able to easily manage their network, applications, or other systems from any Java platform located anywhere on the network.

Java Server API

The Java Server API is an extensible framework that can be employed to develop network-centric servers quickly. These servers are capable of providing network-based services, such as Web services, file and print services, proxy services, and mail services. To extend the functionality of a Java server a developer can create servlets using the Java Servlet API. Java servlets are programs that can be local to the server, or downloaded across the network, and then executed on the Java server. These servlets are perfect for processing form data from HTML pages, replacing the platform-dependent CGI-bin scripts in use by many organizations.

SUMMARY

The ability to integrate with legacy systems and extend enterprise services to the network with platform-independent technologies are key benefits of developing a Java Enterprise Server strategy. Enterprise JavaBeans, the component architecture for the Java Enterprise Server, provide a software- and hardware-independent method to access these systems and make them available to business components. These components can easily access services, such as transaction monitors and message systems, DBMSs, and naming services with the assurance of the Java Platform's "write once, run everywhere."

Chapter 13
Distributed Objects and Object Wrapping
Hedy Alban

ADVANCES IN SYSTEMS INTEGRATION OVER THE PAST DECADE have resolved connectivity issues at lower layers of the Open Systems Interconnection (OSI) network model. Solutions exist for connecting systems at the hardware level or the transport level. Communications networks, phone lines, cables, and fiber are available to connect systems to local area or wide area networks, hubs, and switches. Connectivity between most operating system platforms is similarly available.

Data sharing among disparate platforms and applications is largely resolved as well. The common architectural features among relational database management systems (DBMSs) enable middleware products to mix and match data from heterogeneous sources, and SQL Access interfaces allow nonrelational data architectures to participate also.

A variety of replication techniques can enhance access. New and better solutions for data reconciliation among platforms come to market almost daily. A similar variety of approaches is available for preserving transaction integrity in distributed environments.

Although integration solutions are available in the lower layers of the OSI networking model, analogous interoperability at the application level remains elusive. Processing routines are locked into specific applications environments and cannot be invoked except through that specific application. Stored procedures are buried within the proprietary languages of DBMS products, uninvoked during heterogeneous data access so that they cannot deliver on their promise of universality and consistency. Object-oriented programming fares no better; object systems are not compatible with one another.

As a result, a vast treasure of useful intelligence is trapped within specific contexts. Imagine that the fastest routine for cursor movement was devised for a vertical application that caters to a small number of users. Theoretically, such a function could revolutionize the user interface for other applications that are installed on the same machine or network; however, it may be trapped inside the specific vertical application and remain unavailable for use in other applications. Thus, the customer actually owns an outstanding capability but cannot put it to use except in a very small context.

Sometimes, the dependence of individual processing routines on the proprietary applications that contain them cripples the very mechanisms that have been built up over the years to impose consistency and administrative order at the application level. For example, stored procedures contain processing routines that should be enforced consistently each time a data element is accessed. They are a means for enforcing business rules such as maximum credit limits, ensuring consistent enforcement no matter what application accesses them.

Unfortunately, however, the language of stored procedures is proprietary to each DBMS. When a developer tries to write a multivendor DBMS application or a user tries to access multiple DBMSs through a query tool, the stored procedures fall by the wayside and consistent enforcement disappears.

For these reasons, then, application interoperability is regarded widely as the next step in the evolution toward enterprisewide networking capability. The requirement is for cooperation among heterogeneous equipment and software applications that are currently installed.

ACHIEVING MULTIPOINT CONNECTIVITY

At present, the remote procedure call (RPC) is the most common technology for application-level interoperability. RPC is the favored technique for implementing cross-platform DBMS stored procedures. It is the mechanism chosen for the Distributed Computing Environment (DCE) architecture promoted by the Open Software Foundation, and the basis for the Sun Solaris network file server (NFS). Currently, there is not a more robust approach than DCE for heavy production environments. It is not the best theoretical answer, but it is the most mature of the developed distributed approaches.

Nevertheless, RPCs are not optimal for many enterprise solutions because they are point-to-point solutions. They are able to connect an individual application with another. As the network becomes more complicated, however, a more comprehensive solution is required.

With a more comprehensive solution and with broad multipoint connectivity throughout the network, it will be possible to enforce business rules consistently, to locate data consistently, to reuse helpful routines in multiple contexts, and to consistently apply application routines to the data.

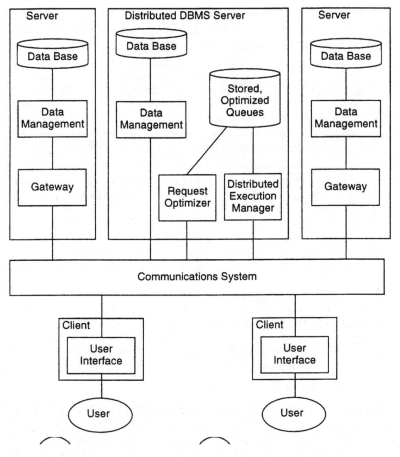

Exhibit 1. Point-to-point vs. multipoint connectivity.

Many theorists and practitioners believe that distributed object technology provides the solution for these problems. Distributed object technology promises to overcome the current obstacles to enterprisewide client/server implementation. The object request broker (ORB), the engine of a distributed object environment, provides a universal layer for multipoint connectivity (Exhibit 1). The RPC mechanism and the object request broker are explained and contrasted in this chapter and in Exhibit 2.

WHAT ARE DISTRIBUTED OBJECTS?

Distributed objects represent the next generation of client/server facilities. In this context, an object is a chunk of code that represents a business

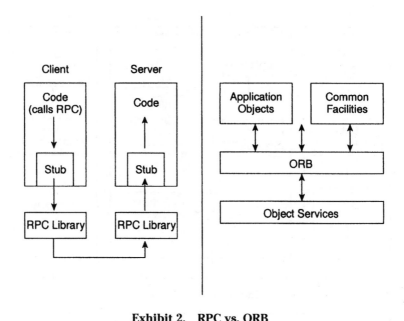

Exhibit 2. RPC vs. ORB

function. A distributed object is an object that can be accessed from anywhere on a network, across platforms, programming languages, and application systems.

Distributed object computing allows developers to build applications as a series of components or services that can be designed and stored across a network and brought together only when needed to perform a specific business function. Developers essentially snap together complex client/server systems simply by assembling and extending reusable distributed objects. A systems builder could select objects from several vendors and connect them as easily as audio components are connected at home today. Individual programming modules (objects) would exist independent of the application for which they were created, free for recombination with other modules in new contexts and for new applications. With distributed object computing, component developers and users can locate code without knowing its location in advance.

Outgrowth of Compound Document Applications

Distributed object technology appeared first in compound document applications. Compound documents contain more than one data format — for example, they may contain a combination of text, charts, and graphical material.

In early practice (which continues, for the most part, even today), each component was created in the tool most appropriate for it (e.g., text in a word processor, charts in a spreadsheet, and graphics in a drawing program) and then assembled into a single whole, usually in a desktop publishing package. To edit the document, users would access the appropriate component via its source application (i.e., the spreadsheet) and then reassemble the edited components into the complete document.

With the advent of distributed object technology, returning to the source application became unnecessary; each component of the document came with its own tools for editing and manipulating it. Thus, for example, the creator could edit a spreadsheet within the same environment that he or she edited the text or drawing. In Microsoft parlance, the compound document is created in a container application that accepts component processing modules from various applications; the function of the component modules appears to the user as selections in a menu bar.

For compound documents, the convenience to the end user of application integration is obvious and important. The significance of application integration goes far beyond this specific application, however. The true significance of application integration comes forth in a networked environment, where it comes into play for the administration and maintainability of the system. It also dovetails with other current practices, like business rules and stored procedures and maintaining consistency across the enterprise.

OBJECT-ORIENTED PROGRAMMING AND DISTRIBUTED OBJECTS

Object orientation is becoming increasingly popular for the benefits of code reuse, adaptability, and the ability to make the computer environment look and feel like the real world as never before. In the context of object-oriented programming, an object generally is defined as a software entity that contains both data and the processing code to manipulate that data.

By definition, classical software objects possess the qualities of inheritance, polymorphism, and encapsulation (although the details of these terms are irrelevant to this discussion). A distributed object, in contrast, is defined and evaluated in terms of its context independence — that is, its ability to function independent of the application (e.g., context) from which it was created.

Therefore, a distributed object need not possess the qualities of the classical software object; instead, it may be a standard sequence of coded statements that are isolated and enveloped in such a way as to become available for interaction with other objects. In modern parlance, a software module can be transformed into a distributed object by encapsulating it in

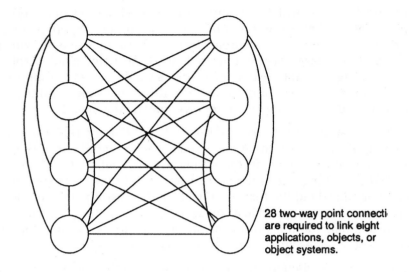

28 two-way point connecti
are required to link eight
applications, objects, or
object systems.

Exhibit 3.   Object with wrapper.

---

a wrapper (Exhibit 3), thereby exposing it to other distributed objects on the network.

Once a software module is transformed into an object, it can be accessed and executed as if it were a primitive. Object programmers and users no longer view the module or its code. Instead, they view the object as a basic computing element. They manipulate the object itself, not its internals.

Object Wrapping

The chief mechanism for integrating legacy applications into the distributed object environment is wrapping. The simplest form of wrapper, with which most readers are familiar, is the Windows icon. A user can access a DOS application within a Windows environment simply by clicking on its icon. In this situation, the icon is the wrapper for the DOS application, permitting it to be treated like a Windows application; the internals of the application, however, function like a DOS program and not a Windows program.

Technically speaking, it is possible to convert an entire application into a single object by this means. All applications can be converted into distributed objects by this means. Optimally, however, conversion to distributed objects exposes individual application components in a more granular way.

Most applications require a better level of integration, where individual functions of an application are made universally available within the object environment. For example, a programmer might wish to integrate the data access routines of one application into the user interface of another application. The original access routine performs unchanged, but as a whole the routine will be merged into a second application. To accomplish this, the programmer must wrap the required routine and then make it accessible (i.e., expose it) to other objects in the environment.

Wrapping is possible only when clear boundaries exist between objects. In other words, the distributed object must contain all information required for the computer to execute it. In the previous example, if the original application were written in a modular fashion, then it would be easier to isolate the routine for integration into the new application. But even so, the process is not really a clean-cut one.

A typical application, even if it is well-written, modular, and well-organized, will still have dependencies among various portions of the code. At the very least, the definition of variables and working storage areas are defined outside a programming module. The wrapper must accommodate this to operate.

Bridging Legacy and Distributed Object Environments. An object wrapper serves as an interoperability bridge between the legacy system and the object environment. On one side of the bridge, the wrapper links up to the legacy system's existing communication facilities. On the other side of the bridge, the wrapper defines the legacy system to the object environment, exposing it within the object environment and bringing specific services, such as security.

During the process of object wrapping, a development team may decide to perform other system enhancements at the same time. For example, an installation may collect metadata at the same time that it performs its analysis for object wrapping, preparing the system for future maintenance projects. Reverse engineering may be in order, or data migration into a more modern DBMS architecture. Sometimes object wrapping may be used to subdivide a large project into modules with clear boundaries for future enhancements on a component-by-component basis.

Each legacy system presents a unique integration problem with its own constraints. Some legacy systems may have no API at all, and others may have an extensive proprietary API. Access mechanisms can be sockets, RPCs, or something else. The object wrapper hides these idiosyncracies and presents a consistent and clear interface.

Object wrapping occurs when an organization migrates existing applications into a distributed object environment. During this process, it is wise to seek a path that avoids extensive software rewriting. It is also wise to keep the target environment firmly in mind, to choose wrappers that con-

243

form to a set standard so that objects will interoperate once the task is complete.

Wrapping Techniques. Wrapping greatly simplifies and empowers client/server computing. Individual objects within the system are inconsistent internally but, given a uniform interface, can interoperate seamlessly. Some techniques for wrapping include:

- *Layering*: Layering is a basic form of wrapping wherein one form of API is mapped onto another. For example, one can layer a CORBA-based interface over RPC services. This technique is applicable where the existing object already has a clearly defined API and well-defined services.
- *Encapsulation*: Encapsulation is a general form of object wrapping where the original code remains largely intact. An encapsulation is a black box where only the input and the output are revealed externally; underlying implementation is hidden. Encapsulation separates interface from implementation. Encapsulation is a convenient way to wrap legacy systems where source code is inaccessible or nonexistent.
- *Object gateways*: Object gateways implement the most generic form of encapsulation and are used in worst-case situations, where the legacy system provides no API, no access to code, and no scripting interface. With this form of wrapping, all processing occurs within the closed system using that system's menus, user interface, and toolset. The user interacts with the application using the facilities provided by the legacy system. Object gateways can be handy tools for quickly loading multiple legacy applications unchanged into the new object environment.

OBJECT REQUEST BROKERS

The object request broker (ORB) is the engine of the distributed object environment, enabling communication among objects both locally and across the network. ORBs can make requests to other ORBs and can process responses. They hide all differences between programming languages, operating systems, object location, and other physical information that is required for interobject and internetwork communication. All these processes happen behind the scenes, hidden from the user and the client/server application.

Common Object Request Broker Architecture (CORBA)

CORBA is a specification for an object-oriented universal middleware that supports application interoperability in three-tier client/server environments (Exhibit 4). CORBA-compliant tools permit objects to communicate with one another, even if they reside on different platforms and are written in different languages using different data formats. The CORBA

Employee 1		Site 1
Name	**Salary**	**Department**
Ackman	5000	Car
Baker	4500	Car

Employee 2		
Name	**Salary**	**De**
Carson	4800	To
Davis	5100	To

Employee 2		Site 3
Name	**Salary**	**Department**
Carson	4800	Toy
Davis	5100	Toy

Exhibit 4.   Three-tier client/server architecture.

---

specification provides a language for multiple object systems to communicate with one another.

CORBA Specifications and Implementation. CORBA-compliant products provide a uniform layer encapsulating other forms of distributed computing and integration mechanisms. CORBA can accept many different implementations.

The RPC, which is the basis for interprocess communication under DCE, is one implementation model. Message-oriented middleware (MOM) is another implementation. Some vendors, like Iona Technologies, are basing CORBA on Open Network Computing (ONC)-compatible RPCs. Other vendors, such as Hewlett-Packard, are using OSF/DCE; some others, like Sun-Soft, are bypassing the RPC layer and implementing CORBA at low layers. CORBA is designed to accept all of these models as well as future solutions that might arise. CORBA-compliant software completes the interoperability task through well-defined interface specifications at the application level.

CORBA defines a high-level facility for distributed computing, the object request broker (ORB). CORBA is a specification for creating ORBs. The ORB functions as a communication infrastructure, transparently relaying object requests across distributed heterogeneous computing environments.

CORBA also defines an Interface Definition Language (IDL), a technology-independent language for encapsulating routines. A universal notation for defining software boundaries, IDL, can be mapped to any programming language. Mappings to C, C++, and Smalltalk, as approved by the Object

Management Group (OMG), are currently available. The mapping is contained within the header files of IDL.

Finally, CORBA includes a set of specifications for common facilities, object services, and application objects. Common facilities define high-level services such as printing and e-mail. Object services define lower-level services such as object creation, event notification, and security. Application objects are all other software, including developer's programs, commercial applications, and legacy systems.

The Object Transaction Service (OTS) subspecification of CORBA is of particular interest to database programmers. OTS defines how atomic transactions can be distributed over multiple objects and multiple ORBs. OTS was designed to interact simultaneously with both ORB-based and traditional TP monitor-based transaction services. OTS can support recoverable nested transactions, even in a heterogeneous environment, that fully support ACID and two-phase commit protocols. OTS is based on technology developed by Transarc Corp., inventors of the Encina transaction processor, which usually functions on top of their DCE product.

Typically, commercial ORB products provide facilities for creating objects and wrappers. The developer first creates an object and defines its boundaries. The developer then submits this IDL code to the ORB product. The compiler in the product translates the IDL code into the target language (e.g., C++). The compiler generates the header files, stubs, and skeleton programs for each interface, exposing the object to other objects within the environment. In an environment where objects use OMG IDL interfaces and are otherwise CORBA-compliant, these objects discover each other at run time and invoke each other's services.

Note that CORBA is a specification, not an actual product. It does not deliver an accompanying reference implementation (i.e., source code) in the way that DCE and UNIX do. Furthermore, CORBA specifies only interfaces among objects; it does not define the object system itself.

Individual vendors build their own products and their own ORBs. CORBA-compliant ORBs interoperate with one another as long as they are referencing version 2 of the CORBA specification. (The various releases of version 1 are too general to guarantee interoperability.) Most object vendors provide developer support for implementing linked library code using OMG IDL interfaces.

Significance of the CORBA Standard. The significance of CORBA will grow as object-oriented systems gather critical mass within the corporate information resource. At present, many corporations already have begun pilot projects and small-scale systems using object technology. They may be working with VBX and OLE 2.0 in the context of their desktop workstations, exploring Internet and intranet applications using Java, and developing some applications with C++ as well. Right now these environments operate as discrete units, but dependencies among them are inevitable. What will bind them together?

Point-to-point solutions provide a quick fix but add complexity to the system. A standard such as CORBA is required if systems builders are to create a flexible, layered structure for connectivity between object systems and avoid point-to-point connectivity. In point-to-point connectivity, one object system requires a specific protocol to connect with, for example, Microsoft's DCOM (Distributed Component Object Model), another to connect with Java, a third to connect with IBM's System Object Model (SOM), and so on. True, it is faster and easier to create point solutions to satisfy immediate requirements, but the market must keep the long view in mind as well.

Fortunately, several of the products just mentioned do indeed comply with CORBA. The only way that a rational format for interoperability will take place is through market pressure. If customers insist on CORBA compliance, then vendors will deliver it; if not, then CORBA will die.

Distributed Computing Environment (DCE)

The Distributed Computing Environment (DCE) provides the means and the tools to transform a group of networked computers into a single coherent computing engine. It is a large and complex middleware product that enables communication among multiple heterogeneous platforms, masking differences among computer platforms. It enables the development of distributed applications that make optimal use of existing computer resources such as storage devices, CPUs, and memory.

DCE enables cooperation among these computer resources and, at the same time, provides tools to deal with such problems as data protection, time and event synchronization, reconciliation of data formats and file-naming schemes among platforms, and so on. An appropriately configured DCE environment allows end users to access multiple computers with a single log-on and to access remote data with the same ease that they access local data.

DCE can be described in terms of its benefits to the end user, the programmer, and the network administrator.

DCE's Benefits for the Network Administrator. DCE provides facilities for organizing an enterprise into administrative units (called cells) and then creating directory services to help programs locate resources within this organization. Following installation, network administrators can move files from one location to another without modifying programs or notifying users.

DCE delivers the following features:

- Multihost replication of files and applications, so that programs can continue to operate even when systems go down and servers are moved around.
- DCE Security Service for cross-system protection by means of authentication.
- DCE Distributed File Server (DFS) for tracking programs and data when they are moved from one computer to another, so that programs need not be recompiled with the new address and users need not be aware of the move.
- DCE Directory Service for look-up capability, so that users and applications can communicate with people and resources anywhere in the network without knowing their physical location.

Although not itself object-oriented, the Distributed Computing Environment can support interoperability among different object strategies. For example, DCE can provide a transport layer above which ORBs communicate with one another. In fact, DCE provides explicit support for ORBs through its DCE Common InterORB protocol.

DCE's Benefits for the Programmer. For applications developers, DCE provides the RPC and threads.

Remote Procedure Calls. The remote procedure call is a mechanism for interprocess communication that ties the client and server application code together. It handles the lower levels of interprocess connectivity, shielding the programmers from the details of that connection. It performs data conversion and manages all lower-level aspects of communication and, when programmed to do so, provides automatic recovery from network or server failure.

The RPC invisibly hides the differences in data formats between heterogeneous computers, reconciling differences in byte ordering, data formats, and padding between data items. It hides these differences by converting data to the appropriate forms needed by the destination system.

To integrate legacy applications into the DCE environment, the programmer can wrap the application with an interface definition. The wrapped application will be available within the DCE environment to all supported systems, but it must be rewritten into a client/server style (i.e., it must be rewritten in modular fashion or given a client/server interface through a DCE-compatible screen scraper or similar tool) to reap the benefits of distributed computing.

Threads. DCE threads enhance performance by allowing the programmer to specify threads for the purposes of task separation and task division. In task separation, the programmer can designate slow-moving tasks (e.g., routines that require user input or retrieval from a slow data storage device) to be performed in a separate thread, so that the flow of the application can continue simultaneously with the slow operation. In task division, a large task can be broken into several smaller tasks and assigned to different processors.

DCE's Benefits for the End User. The end user on a DCE system enjoys the benefits of distributed computing often without being aware of it. In a well-implemented DCE environment, the end user experiences better performance when the workload is better distributed among available resources. The end user also derives benefit from the client/server application that permits a more user-friendly interface and greater end-user autonomy in accessing corporate data. Finally, the end user experiences reduced downtime as a result of DCE's high-availability features. DCE permits access to the entire distributed environment with one log-on.

DCE and CORBA Contrasted

DCE and CORBA share a similar concept of the distributed enterprise, promising a seamless distributed computing environment with transparent interoperability among applications. They share concepts, some facilities, and even terminology. They are so similar, in fact, that many regard CORBA as the next generation of DCE.

In many ways CORBA and DCE are complementary. They are also remarkably similar in the way that they work. Both are developed by a consortium of vendors: DCE is promoted by the Open Software Foundation (OSF); CORBA is endorsed by the Object Management Group (OMG). Both depend on the consensus of their members, and both evaluate technologies that are submitted by their members for adoption. The overlap in membership between the two organizations could explain their remarkable similarity in concept.

Important differences exist as well, as summarized in Exhibit 5.

Exhibit 5.   Differences Between CORBA and DCE

CORBA	DCE
Object-based	Nonobject-based
Provides specifications for interfaces only	RPC provides complete specifications and source code for the network computing system
Not yet a fully implemented specification	High level of product maturity and robustness for large-scale, high-security, heavy-transaction systems
Addresses OSI application layer	Addresses OSI presentation and session layers

OSI Model Support. Most important, CORBA and DCE address different layers of the OSI model, and they express the application environment at different levels of abstraction. In fact, CORBA and DCE are considered complementary precisely because they address different layers of the OSI seven-layer mode.

CORBA addresses the application layer of the OSI model, whereas DCE addresses the presentation and session layers. Therefore, DCE contains a lot of the lower-layer information and processing that is necessary for system interoperability to take place.

CORBA, in contrast, does not deal with these low-level details at all. Instead, it specifies a mechanism by which objects can interoperate, even if they are built on disparate low-level processes. CORBA's aim is to provide interfaces between objects so that they can interoperate. CORBA works at the application layer, reconciling incompatibilities between two or more object-oriented systems so that the objects deriving from two or more development systems will interoperate.

A derivative benefit of this application-level interoperability is simplicity or, in analyst jargon, abstraction. CORBA specifications require programmers to examine applications and functions at a higher level of abstraction than any other tool for distributed computing. This high level of abstraction makes it easier for people to grasp the big picture. It insulates the programmer and user from technical details of the computer environment. The resulting applications are flexible, adaptable to change and new technologies, as well as to layering and a divide-and-conquer approach to applications development and reengineering.

Furthermore, CORBA adds a comprehensive layer of support for object-oriented programming. Specifically, it aims to provide interoperability among different object systems. Its primary purpose is to deliver interORB interoperability.

CONCLUSION

Many analysts have jumped on the object bandwagon, proclaiming object-oriented programming to be the breakthrough technology that will enable the industry to upgrade software as quickly as hardware. Like many technologies that are excellent in theory, however, the upfront effort for large-scale conversion is enormous. A golden rule is always to balance theory and practice.

To move from current information structure into the object paradigm requires a enormous rewrite of all code. Although object wrappers could provide a quick fix, wrapped objects do not provide the full benefit of more granular objects.

At the same time, object technology is penetrating every organization, at least to some degree. This is because the technology is infiltrating off-the-shelf applications software, especially at the client level. Similarly, object technology likely will become the norm for developing applications to run on the ubiquitous Internet, where upfront reengineering costs do not come into play and infrastructure issues are largely predefined.

Given the inevitably of object orientation, it is important for object systems work together. A standard for interoperability at the application level, like CORBA, is a necessity.

Nevertheless, CORBA has traveled a rocky road. CORBA had a bad reputation from its initial release. OMG members with different interests slowed down consensus. Because of these delays, many vendors implemented their products ahead of the specification and later were reluctant to retrofit their work for the sake of compliance. In addition, the public was slow to understand the benefits of CORBA beyond DCE. Probably most important, CORBA's viability was shaky because Microsoft products, which account for 80% of the object market, are noncompliant.

Vendors and users seem, at last, to be rallying around CORBA. The growth of the Internet probably has a strong role here — as the market takes off, vendors perceive an opportunity and are more likely to cooperate. They also need the compliance to enhance their own marketability. CORBA has won Microsoft's support for moving its DCOM object infrastructure into compliance with CORBA.

In conclusion, object technology and distributed objects may not be the cure-all for distributed computing issues, but when combined with other integration strategies — most notably the Internet — it can become a practical solution for many specific applications. With a growing market for object technology and Microsoft support in hand, the outlook for CORBA looks better than ever.

Chapter 14
Integrating Package Processes Over Multiple Application Platforms

Ido Gileadi

The key to successful business process integration over multiple application platforms is to utilize an additional layer, in the n-tier model, for storing the common data between applications and implementing the business process using logic in the layer. By achieving such an architecture, the business process and data are isolated from the applications, thereby making the integration easy to manage and monitor through middleware, also called processware.

INTRODUCTION

Companies and people are relying more than ever on computerized systems to run their businesses. Traditional computing tasks such as finance, human resources, and contact management are now extended to include additional areas where the business is seeking to gain a competitive advantage. Computerized systems are viewed by management as the primary tool for gaining advantage over the competition.

The introduction of multiple applications at all levels of the organization and the executive attention these applications are receiving highlight a well-known problem. All applications must work in tandem, communicate with each other, and, most importantly, pass meaningful data that can then be rolled up for management reporting.

Information technology (IT) organizations have been integrating packages for many years. The integration programs of the past were like bridges connecting disparate islands — point-to-point connections transferring subsets of data, typically in ASCII file format, on a predefined schedule.

0-8493-9968-8/99/$0.00+$.50
© 1999 by CRC Press LLC

This type of point-to-point integration required detailed knowledge of each application and did not provide a satisfactory solution when real-time access to data and functionality was required.

With the introduction of enterprise resource planning (ERP) systems came the promise of support for integrated business processes. The idea was that the ERP systems would cover most aspects of computerization in an organization. Because ERP was one integrated package, it would allow complete start-to-end business process integration. The reality is that ERP packages cannot address all of an organization's business requirements in a satisfactory manner. We can therefore see a combination of packaged software as well as legacy and custom-made software residing alongside each other, each providing a solution to a portion of the business process.

Once again, IT organizations are faced with the challenge of integrating multiple application platforms into one coherent business process.

THE CHARGE

An organization undergoing a major package implementation such as SAP, Baan, Oracle, or PeopleSoft will typically start with identifying the scope of the project. The scope of the project may include complete business process reengineering that will result in new and improved business processes. The project may take the approach of implementing existing processes; this approach may minimize the benefits of implementing new packaged software because a great deal of the benefit is in the reengineering and tuning of existing processes.

The project's business team will be charged with redefining the business processes. The IT team will be charged with identifying the best application platforms to support the business processes and integrating these various applications into one end-to-end seamless process.

An example of an integrated business process and the multiple application platforms that may be supported is depicted in Exhibit 1, which shows a simplified order-taking process. Order header information is first created in the ERP system. Line-by-line information is then entered. As the lines are entered, the line items must be configured and priced. These tasks are accomplished by a configuration and pricing application. For each line and for the overall order, an available to promise (first date when this order can be completely manufactured) is calculated by the scheduling application. All of the data collected from the various applications is used to complete the order and submit all the order lines into the ERP system.

It is evident in Exhibit 1 that we are dealing with a process that is supported by multiple application platforms and that there is a need to integrate the applications in real time to support the process.

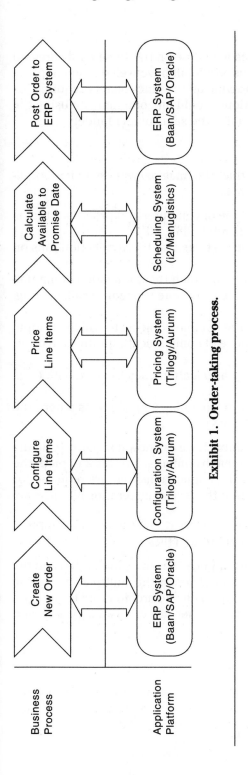

Exhibit 1. Order-taking process.

THE PERFECT WORLD

In a perfect world, all applications would be on the same hardware and software platforms. The applications would all have well-defined application programming interfaces that provide all the functionality required for the business process. The applications would all communicate using the same communication standards and use the same object models.

THE REAL WORLD

The real world is more complex than the imaginary perfect view. Applications can differ in the following areas:

- *Hardware platform.* The actual type of computer and processor that is used to run the application (e.g., Intel, RISK, MF)
- *Software platform.* The operating systems that the application runs on (e.g., HP UX, NT, MVS, Solaris)
- *Communication method.* The way in which the application communicates with external applications (e.g., remote procedure call, messaging, distributed objects)
- *Object model.* The definition of the common objects to which all applications will adhere for the purpose of communicating with each other (e.g., CORBA, COM/DCOM)
- *Database.* The database that the application uses to store data (e.g., Oracle, Sybase, Informix)
- *Network protocol.* The network protocol used on systems where the application resides (e.g., TCP/IP, IPX)

Looking back at the example in Exhibit 1, we can now concentrate on the differences between the application environments. Exhibit 2 depicts the different platforms used to support the applications that are required for the order-taking process. It is clear that the task of integrating all these applications is quite complex.

SELECTING AN APPROACH AND ARCHITECTURE

Once we have a clear picture of the applications to be integrated and the business process that should be integrated across the multiple application platforms, we are ready to select an approach and architecture for integration. The following should be considered when selecting an approach and architecture:

- Platform information:
  - Hardware platform
  - Operating systems
  - Object models
  - Communication methods
- Real-time versus batch processes

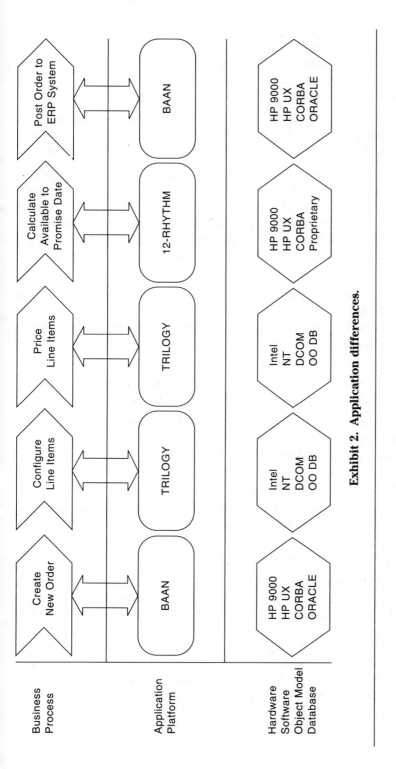

Exhibit 2. Application differences.

- Future software upgrades.
- Future addition of new applications
- Ongoing management of integration code
- Error handling and transaction monitoring
- New skills requirements

The above considerations will help to make a decision on the architecture and the integration objectives. This in turn will drive the selection of middleware software that will facilitate integration between applications.

The traditional approach of point-to-point integration will not deliver the required functionality for this process. An order entry clerk cannot wait for batch processes to kick in and perform file transfers while keying in an order. A realtime processware approach is required. An approach where the process is defined within a middleware/processware product and the applications act as servers providing the required functionality is more appropriate.

Let's examine two approaches to processware implementation. The first approach is based on object definitions and a process definition that acts on these objects. The second approach is based on event definitions and rules agents that trigger the events in a sequence related to the business process.

Stepping back, let's examine the various operating models of typical applications. A typical application can be divided into three layers:

- *Presentation layer.* The screens with which the user interacts to view and enter data
- *Business logic layer.* The processing logic that is triggered by user actions
- *Database layer.* Storage and retrieval of persistent data over time

Most applications consist of all three layers. The primary difference between applications within the scope of this chapter is the degree of distribution of these layers. Exhibit 3 illustrates the various options that are available for distributing the layers.

Exhibit 3 depicts the most common models for application distribution. In the single-tier model, all three layers reside on the same machine. The application can be accessed directly on the single machine or through multiple terminals. The two-tier (client/server) model has a separate database layer on a server designed and configured to run a database engine. The business logic and the presentation layers are still lumped together into what is known as a fat or thick client. The three-tier model separates each layer. The presentation layer can run on a Windows-based client or a browser, the business logic can run on an application server, and the database can run on a database server. The database server and the application server can be con-

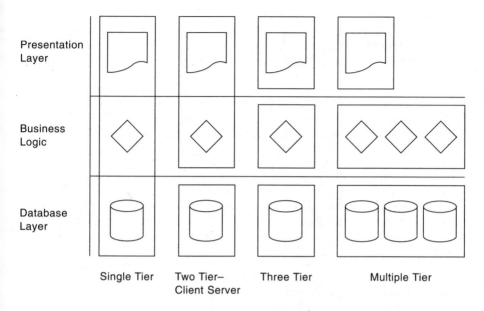

| Presentation Layer | Single Tier | Two Tier–Client Server | Three Tier | Multiple Tier |

Exhibit 3. Application distribution.

figured differently to accommodate the special requirements for running logic and database activities. The multitier model accommodates further distribution of the database and the application logic on multiple servers. Distribution of the computing layers allows for better load balancing.

The goal of business process integration over multiple application platforms is to create an additional business logic layer that contains common data structures that all applications can access and populate through a set of agreed-upon calls. The business logic layer can be implemented using distributed object models such as DCOM and CORBA or an event-based system where the common data can be implemented. Both approaches are examined in Exhibit 4.

In Exhibit 4, in addition to the familiar multitier architecture, there is a new layer for business process integration. This layer defines objects or events that contain common data structures. The business logic layer or the presentation layer can activate methods for these objects as well as access data contained in the objects. The object data structures contain the data required to support the integrated business process. This layer may be implemented using events that can be published or subscribed to. Any application business logic or presentation layer may publish an event and populate all or part of the data structure for that event. Once an event is published, all the applications that subscribe to the event are notified and processing is triggered.

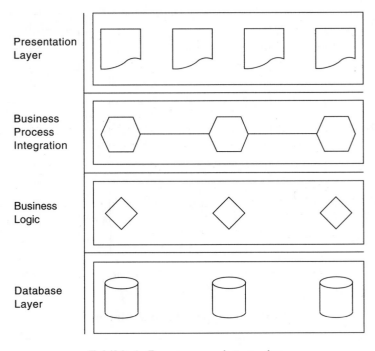

Presentation Layer

Business Process Integration

Business Logic

Database Layer

Exhibit 4. Processware integration.

The preceding architecture supports the creation of an additional process logic layer. The key to successful business process integration over multiple application platforms is to utilize this new layer for storing the common data between applications and implementing the business process using logic in the layer. By achieving such an architecture, the business process and data are isolated from the applications, thereby making the integration easy to manage and monitor. It will also be easier to modify specific pieces of the integration, replace applications, or update them to new versions.

CONCLUSION

In summary, the new concept of processware was introduced in this chapter. Processware is middleware software that facilitates the creation of an additional computing layer called the business process integration logic. This layer can be implemented using distributed objects or events to encapsulate the common data structures and the business process. Among the benefits of this approach and architecture are

• Isolation of integration business logic from the applications

- Creation of common data structures to communicate information between applications
- Easy migration of integration code upon upgrade or replacement of any of the applications involved
- Ability to manage and monitor the integration of the various applications
- A set of tools that facilitates the creation of the integrated business process and takes care of the communication and networking layer, thereby allowing users to focus on coding the business logic

Several products in various stages of development are suited to support processware. In some cases, portions of the products have already been released. Each of these products takes a somewhat different approach to implementation. Time will tell which of these products will thrive and become a major player in this emerging market.

Section IV
Development in an Integrated Environment

Chapter 15
Developing New Applications in a Heterogeneous Environment
Raj Rajagopal

As mentioned earlier in the handbook, there are many organizations that have heterogeneous computing environments and will probably continue to have them for the foreseeable future. Developing new applications in these organizations invariably raises a number of environment related issues that need to be addressed.

In planning or developing new applications, the following few questions probably will be raised:

- Should a Windows application or a UNIX application be developed?
- If one environment is chosen for the long term, is there a way to easily make it work in another environment in the short term?
- Should the traditional languages and APIs be used or should new application development tools be chosen?
- Should object-oriented frameworks be used?
- How are legacy applications interfaced with and how is the data that resides in the corporate databases accessed?
- What language is best to develop the application?

This chapter is not intended to be a primer on new application development, but will look at developing new applications from a Windows, UNIX, NetWare coexistence and migration viewpoint. Applications can be developed that will execute across platforms in a number of ways:

- The application can be developed once using a proprietary API and run in different environments

0-8493-9989-0/99/$0.00+$.50
© 1999 by CRC Press LLC

- APIs can be developed for one environment (such as Win32 for Windows NT) and executed in another (such as UNIX) using porting tools. Porting applications was covered earlier in the handbook.
- Distributed applications can be developed in a heterogeneous environment.
- Applications can be developed using 4GL products or object-oriented frameworks.
- Standard 3GL languages, such as C/C++, and compile switches to isolate environment-specific code can be used.

Besides executing in different environments, applications also must be able to:

- Interface with legacy applications
- Access the data that resides in the corporate databases
- Perform transaction processing across heterogeneous systems

CROSS-PLATFORM APPLICATION DEVELOPMENT

API-based applications that can run in both Windows NT and UNIX can be developed in one of three ways:

1. Proprietary APIs. This can be done in one of three ways.
   a) Layered APIs that reside on top of native APIs
   b) Layered APIs plus extensions
   c) Emulated APIs
2. Use Win32 and port to UNIX
3. Use POSIX and port to Win32

The API-based approach is covered later in this chapter.

The development can be moved a level higher than APIs and 4GL tools and other application generators can be used. Finally, Portable Object-Oriented Frameworks can be used. 4GL tools such as PowerBuilder are well known in the industry. 4GL products and Portable Object-Oriented Frameworks are covered later in this chapter.

If 4GL or other development tools that come with their own language(s) and script(s) are not being used, then the common development languages for which many cross-platform toolkits and porting tools are available are C and C++. Even when developing applications using C and C++, some constructs can be used to facilitate the generation of cross-platform applications. A detailed list of C and C++ differences was covered earlier in the handbook and compilations can be used conditionally to generate the executable for the chosen platform as shown below:

```
#ifdef   unix

    int   dfile;  /*  file  descriptor  */
```

```
#endif

#ifdef _MSC_VER HANDLE dfile; /* file handle */
#endif

.

.

.

#ifdef unix
    if ((dfile = open(DataFile, O_RDWR |
        O_CREAT)) == -1)
#endif
#ifdef _MSC_VER /* using Visual C++ */
    if ((dfile = CreateFile(DataFile, GENERIC_READ |
    GENERIC_WRITE, FILE_SHARE_READ, NULL,
    OPEN_ALWAYS, FILE_ATTRIBUTE_NORMAL, NULL)) ==
    INVALID_HANDLE_VALUE) #endif
```

In developing web-based applications, Java, HTML, etc. will most likely be used which, for the most part, are portable across platforms. Mainframe-based applications must be interfaced with, or data must be accessed from, mainframe-based databases.

Although COBOL is the language most commonly used in mainframe applications, mainframe applications can still be interfaced with using any language desired.

Cross-Platform Development Using Proprietary APIs

There are three variations of proprietary APIs — Layered APIs supporting the least common subset, Layered APIs plus extensions, and Emulated APIs.

Here are a few advantages and disadvantages of using proprietary APIs.

The advantages are:

• Applications can be easily ported to different environments, in many cases transparently to the application. Thus, operating systems can be switched with very little change to the applications themselves. This is one way to avoid standardizing on Windows or UNIX but allowing the applications to run on either.

- It is easy to have a common source for developing applications that will eventually run on multiple hardware/software platforms, particularly if applications eventually need to run in multiple environments.

The disadvantages are:

- Proprietary APIs are tightly linked to the vendors that provide them. If all applications in an organization are written to a proprietary layer, the organization becomes dependent on that API and the API vendor.
- The number of environments the application will work on and the features the application can support depend on the number of environments and features supported by the API vendor.
- If the API vendor discontinues the API or goes out of business, it may be difficult to update an application to take advantage of enhancements to underlying OS and maintain the application.
- It is one more layer of software, which increases the chances of introducing bugs and interface problems.
- There may be a performance penalty (unlike a native application that does not use the APIs but uses OS calls directly) but the penalty may vary.
- Programming support usually comes from the software vendor and others using the software through newsgroups, etc. While vendor support depends on the vendor, support from others using the software depends on the popularity of the product.
- Proprietary APIs, as shown, avoid the differences among APIs of different platforms and operating systems by providing the least common subset of the underlying native APIs. The least common subset limitation can be overcome by providing additional proprietary APIs, as discussed below.
- If a proprietary API approach is chosen, managers may want to check availability and price of the API vendor's source code (either delivered outright, or at least held in escrow and deliverable in case the vendor goes out of business). While the source code may not be the best solution in case the API vendor goes out of business, it is at least one option to be exercised.

Layered APIs supporting least common subset. Proprietary APIs allow for the development of applications that are independent of target systems. As shown in Exhibit 1, proprietary APIs provide a layer of abstraction and map the APIs invoked by the applications to those provided in the native environment. Thus, the application always makes the same calls regardless of the target operating system.

"Layered APIs" is a reference to the fact that the APIs provide a cross-platform layer on top of a native OS layer. The main problem is that the

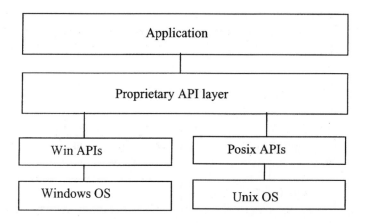

Exhibit 1. Layered APIs supporting the least common subset.

---

proprietary APIs, as shown above, support only functions that are common to the underlying environments, i.e., the APIs support the least common subset of the functions in the underlying environments.

Layered APIs plus extensions. The least common subset problem mentioned above can be overcome by the API vendor providing its own APIs for functions not supported in the native APIs. There are two ways in which this can be done. One way is use the native APIs wherever possible and provide extensions for unsupported functions.

Another method is to avoid using any native APIs, but instead provide a replacement API library for the native APIs. The second method is commonly called "emulated APIs" and is covered later in this chapter. The layered APIs plus extensions approach is shown in Exhibit 2.

Although the least common subset problem is solved, the proprietary extensions introduce diversity between the proprietary implementation and the operating system provider's native implementation. An application that uses the vendor's extension will not run natively.

Emulated APIs. Many operating environments include a set of low-level calls and a library of high-level calls that are built on top of the low-level calls. For example, Motif uses xlib calls for performing many user interface functions such as displaying a window.

When an application needs to display a window, it can call Motif or it can call xlib directly. If a third-party library, as a replacement for Motif, implements whatever Motif supports plus other functions available in other environments such as Windows but not in Motif (example Notebook controls), such a library would be an emulated API library.

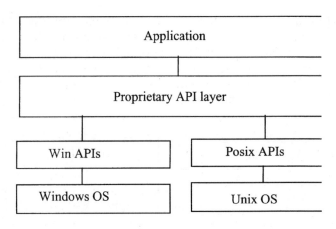

Exhibit 2. Layered APIs plus extensions.

There are advantages and disadvantages to the emulated API approach. The advantages are that porting applications across supported platforms tends to be relatively simple and an emulator can opt to provide a completely consistent look and feel across all platforms as it doesn't use the native functions.

However, since emulated APIs replace all the native high-level functions, the code size tends to be much higher than the layered APIs. And it may not be possible to use an enhancement to APIs made by the native OS vendor until an equivalent enhancement is made by the emulated API vendor. An example of proprietary API would be AppWare from Novell, although Novell is de-emphasizing this product.

CROSS-PLATFORM GUI DEVELOPMENT

Many vendors provide cross-platform development tools that allow development of both GUI and non-GUI code. Regardless of which vendor is chosen, it is a good idea for to segment applications into GUI and non-GUI portions. Segmenting applications provides a number of benefits:

- It is easy to extend an application to another GUI environment as well as drop support for a GUI environment, if necessary.
- Developing, testing, and debugging applications is easier.
- Segmenting provides the option of implementing the GUI portion natively, particularly if performance is an issue.

While segmenting allows the source to be partitioned, when opting for native implementation of GUI, separate source libraries must be maintained for the different GUIs chosen. The cost of managing multiple sources for development and maintenance must be weighed against the performance benefits and potential cost benefits (of not using a porting toolkit). In addition, developers familiar with the environments chosen to go native will be needed, as well as developers familiar with the porting toolkit (if one is used).

DEVELOPING APPLICATIONS USING WIN32 API ON UNIX

Instead of proprietary APIs, there are tools that provide the Win32 API support on UNIX and thus enable Windows applications to run on UNIX. These tools assume the role of Windows in such systems, providing the function calls, messages, device contexts, and controls that Windows provides for application programs. Microsoft offers a licensing program called WISE to facilitate development using the Win32 API and subsequent porting to UNIX.

Examples of companies that have used WISE include MainSoft, Bristol Technology, Insignia Solutions, and Locus Computing. This approach offers cross-platform development capabilities starting with the WIN32 API instead of a proprietary API. This approach also helps in porting current Windows applications (whose source is available) to UNIX, as covered earlier in the handbook.

Microsoft WISE. The Microsoft Windows Interface Source Environment (WISE) is a licensing program from Microsoft to enable customers to integrate Windows-based solutions with UNIX and Macintosh systems. WISE solutions come in two forms — WISE SDKs and WISE emulators.

WISE SDKs

WISE SDKs provide source code compatibility and the application source code must be recompiled for the different systems the application needs to run on. WISE SDKs are available on Macintosh and UNIX systems. A WISE SDK consists of tools to port code from a PC and libraries to compile Windows code on the Macintosh or UNIX systems.

An overview of WISE SDK is shown in Exhibit 3.

WISE SDKs typically include source code preprocessor, makefile generator, Windows libraries, resource compiler, MFC for UNIX, and online help.

- Source code preprocessor — the source code preprocessor changes PC source code to make it compatible with a UNIX system. For example, the source code preprocessor changes separators in a path name from \ to /. The preprocessor removes the carriage return character from each line to make the file compatible with a UNIX system.

- Makefile generator —automatically generates makefiles.
- Windows libraries — these libraries provide the same services to applications that Windows provides to Windows applications. Libraries can be built low-level (using xlib functions) or at a higher level (using Motif functions).
- Resource compiler — the resource compiler is used to compile Windows resource script files (and associated files) that specify details of resources such as menus, dialog boxes, icons, cursors, strings, and bitmaps on the UNIX system and generate a UNIX version of the resource file.
- Microsoft Foundation Classes (MFC) for UNIX-WISE SDKs — include support for MFC on UNIX systems.
- Online help — programmers can port rich text format files and help instructions from a PC and use the WISE SDK help compiler to compile and generate a UNIX system help file. The help engine displays the help file to a user.

Examples of WISE SDKs include MainWin from Mainsoft and Wind/U from Bristol.

WISE Emulators

WISE emulators provide object code compatibility and enable shrink-wrapped Windows-based applications to run unmodified on UNIX and Macintosh systems. A WISE emulator intercepts Windows calls from a Windows application and translates them into calls that can be satisfied by the host system's services. Examples of WISE emulators include SoftWindows from Insignia and Merge from Locus.

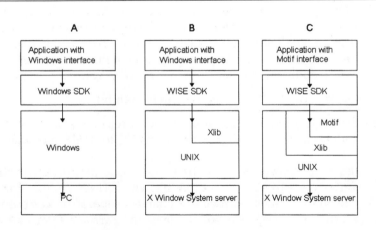

Exhibit 3. WISE SDK overview.

DEVELOPING APPLICATIONS USING 4GL TOOLS

Rather than adopting an API approach of writing to Win32 or POSIX or a proprietary API, applications can be developed using 4GL tools. 4GL tools come with versions that run on Windows as well as UNIX. Thus, if applications are developed using a 4GL tool in one environment, it should be possible to reuse the 4GL source for the other environments. The advantages and disadvantages mentioned for proprietary APIs apply to 4GL tools as well. One advantage that applies to 4GL tools that does not apply to proprietary APIs is that, in general, it is faster to develop applications using 4GL tools than with the more traditional programming language/APIs-based approach.

As shown in Exhibit 4, there are several categories of 4GL application development tools. Ranging from GUI builders to CASE and Integrated CASE (ICASE), these categories can be differentiated by their support for application complexity and the scalability of users and transactions.

Exhibit 5 summarizes common products and vendors for each of the 4GL categories.

If a 4 GL product is being used for application development, the vendor should be consulted as to whether the resulting 4 GL application will execute in other environments that may be of interest.

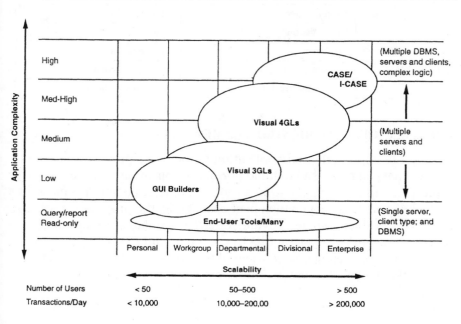

Exhibit 4. Categories of 4GL applications.

Exhibit 5.   4 GL products and vendors.

4GL Category	Products	Vendor
GUI Builders	Galaxy	Visix Software
	Elements Environment	Neuron Data
Visual 3 GLs	InterBase	Borland
	Visual Basic	Microsoft
	VisualWave	ParcPlace-Digitalk Systems
Visual 4 GLs	ApplixWare	Applix
	Sapphire/Web	Bluestone
	Axiant	Cognos
	UNIFACE SIX	Compuware
	DIGITAL Application Generator	Digital Equipment Corp.
	Forte Application Environment	Forte Software
	FOCUS	Information Builders
	APTuser	International Software Group
	Magic	Magic Software
	Elements environment	Neuron Data
	Oracle Designer/Developer	Oracle
	JAM 7	Prolifics
	PROGRESS	Progress Software
	Sapiens Ideo	Sapiens USA
	Unify Vision	Unify
	uniVerse	Vmark Software
CASE/ICASE	Foundation Design/I	Andersen Consulting
	Composer by IEF	Texas Instruments

PORTABLE OBJECT-ORIENTED FRAMEWORKS

Portable object-oriented application frameworks provide a set of C++ classes that can be reused to build portable applications and functions for print, file, and other application services. Some application frameworks have the same least common subset problem as the proprietary APIs. To avoid this problem, some provide code that emulates the missing functions. Frameworks are attractive to customers interested in developing new applications using object-oriented techniques and interested in portability. Some object-oriented frameworks are covered below.

DSC++

Information on DSC++ is available online at http://www.xvt.com.

XVT's Development Solution for C++ (DSC++) helps in cross-platform development by building applications in one platform, and then porting them easily to other platforms. DSC++ uses C++ which, after compilation, results in native applications.

The core of DSC++ is an application framework that contains a full set of functions common to all GUI-based applications, including documents, windows, scrolling views, visual interface objects, graphical primitives, geometry management, data managers, and inter-object communication. DSC++ also includes Rogue Wave Tools.h++ data structures.

The framework's visual tool allows users to design and interconnect reusable GUI components with clicks of the mouse. DSC++'s visual tool guides the user through the development process from defining architecture and laying out the interface to writing code and building the final application. Project files containing portable GUI application interface information be displayed and edited on any XVT-supported platform.

DSC++ generates C++ source code, application resources, and makefiles that can be used with a built-in development library to make an application natively.

Platforms supported by DSC++ include:

• Microsoft Windows, including Windows NT
• Power Macintosh and Macintosh
• OS/2
• OSF/Motif (on many systems)

Allegris

Information on Allegris is available online at http://www.intersolv.com.

Allegris includes the following product series:

• Allegris Workshop
• Allegris Constructor
• Allegris Object Repository
• Allegris DataDesigner

The Allegris Series can be deployed on a product-by-product basis or as a complete integrated development environment as shown in Exhibit 6.

Allegris Workshop. Allegris Workshop is a complete OO development environment for building reusable components and client/server applications. Allegris Workshop combines a GUI developer offering full Windows 95 controls with Allegris Foundation, a class library of more than 170 cross-platform components.

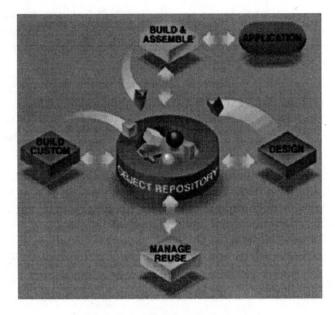

Exhibit 6.   Allegris product series.

Windows 95 controls include notebooks; portable fonts and colors; enhanced status bar; flexible, dockable toolbar; multilevel undo/redo; interactive property sheets; menu editor; and online help editor.

The class library includes classes for GUI design, event processing, data management, transparent internationalization, file handling, and OLE 2 support. Allegris Workshop provides double-byte character support (DBCS) across all platforms using UNICODE as a basis. Allegris Workshop is built on a foundation of true object technology and offers the full object-orientation of the Smalltalk Model View Controller.

Allegris Workshop facilitates developing interoperable cross-platform applications using portable resource formats which support multiple languages from a single executable without recompiling, and geometry management features. Allegris Workshop can be used in conjunction with the INTERSOLV DataDirect Developer's Toolkit for C++ to provide ODBC access to over 30 relational databases.

Allegris Workshop provides full ActiveX container support (linking, embedding, activation, and automation). Allegris Webshop, available as an add-on to Allegris Workshop, provides additional C++ classes for building web-server applications, and the Portable Resource Workshop can generate HTML forms.

Allegris Workshop is currently available for Windows 95, Windows NT, Windows 3.1, OS/2, SunSoft Solaris, IBM AIX, HP-UX, and DEC UNIX.

Allegris Constructor. Allegris Constructor is a component-based development environment that enables developers to build and assemble scalable components from departmental applications to enterprise applications and Internet/intranet applications. Developers use point-and-click, drag-and-drop painters to build application components and control application behavior using scripts written in an object-oriented extension of standard BASIC. For example, components are distributed across clients and servers through simple drag-and-drop.

Allegris Constructor delivers applications as compiled C++ applications. Allegris Constructor comes bundled with the command-line version of the Borland C++ compiler, linker, and debugger. Applications created using Allegris Constructor can access data from Oracle, Sybase, Informix, SQL Serve,r or any other ODBC-compliant data source. Mainframe databases are accessed through DataDirect SequeLink.

ActiveX insertables, controls, and servers can be imported into the Allegris Object Repository for use in developing applications with Allegris Constructor. The capability to deploy components built with Allegris as ActiveX components is planned for the future.

Allegris Constructor can be hosted on either Windows 95 or Windows NT. The Allegris Object Repository (AOR) is supported by Oracle, Sybase System 10 or 11, SQL Server, Informix, or Sybase SQL Anywhere databases. Upon installing Allegris Constructor, a stand-alone, single-user version of the Sybase SQL Anywhere repository is created.

Allegris Object Repository. The Allegris Object Repository (AOR) is a scalable repository that is tightly integrated with the other products in the Allegris Series and serves as the backbone for the Allegris development environment. It provides a workgroup-management framework to store, manage, and reuse software components.

The AOR leverages INTERSOLV's DataDirect data connectivity technology and the BLOB (Binary Large Object) storage capability of major relational databases.

The Allegris Object Repository can be hosted on top of many popular databases such as FoxPro 3, Sybase SQL Anywhere, Sybase System 10 or 11, Oracle, SQL Server, Informix, and DB2/2.

Components stored in the AOR—whether built with Allegris Constructor, designed with Allegris DataDesigner, or imported as ActiveX components or DLLs—are assigned categories and given descriptions, and these categories and descriptions, along with component types, can be used as search criteria when attempting to locate components for reuse.

Allegris DataDesigner. Allegris DataDesigner is the analysis and design component of Allegris that enables the design of static object models and relational databases for distributed object applications. Relational models are used in Allegris to automate access to data. Object models in Data-Designer are built using the Unified Modeling Language (UML) notation.

DataDesigner can import existing database definitions from SQL DDL or directly via ODBC.

zApp Developer's Suite 3

Information on zApp is available online at http://www.roguewave.com.

zApp Developer's Suite 3 includes the following components:

- zApp Application Framework
- zApp Interface Pack
- zHelp
- zApp Factory

The zApp Application Framework provides a hierarchy of more than 200 classes for standard application objects. The zApp Interface Pack adds components such as bitmap buttons and 3-D controls. The zApp Application Framework also includes a spreadsheet-like table object with a variety of cell types to display any kind of data in matrix format. zHelp is an online help system based on HTML.

zHelp includes a portable help viewer and supports popular features like hypertext links, inline images, and multiple fonts. zApp Factory is a visual development environment for zApp. zApp Factory features a WYSIWYG application generator that allows drag-and-drop construction of complete applications and generates the corresponding zApp source code. zApp factory features an integrated application development environment including the following:

- Project Manager — displays all application components in an organized, hierarchical fashion
- Modeless Object Manager — displays and edits an object's properties
- Window Designer — supports object alignment, sizing, spacing, and positioning, as well as drag-and-drop capability for adding controls, tool buttons, status items, icons, and bitmaps
- Code Generator — produces commented zApp source code, resources, make files, and project files for all supported environments

Code Generator includes incremental and selective code generation and protects user code, so custom routines are preserved on code regeneration

The zApp factory includes integrated and stand-alone test modes to let programmers run their prototype within the zApp Factory environment, or as a discrete application without compilation. It is possible to execute specific user-written code either through a link to user source code that is triggered as a response to a particular event, or by embedding source code in blocks within the source file in constructs called protect blocks.

zApp is source-code portable across 12 operating environments, including X/Motif, OS/2, and 16- and 32-bit Windows. zApp provides a method of porting resource files across all supported platforms. zApp supports the current version of all major compilers for each platform and integrates with third-party development tools, such as editors, debuggers, and version control systems.

The zApp family of tools is built on Rogue Wave's Tools.h++. zApp's source code is included free of charge.

Systems Toolkit from ObjectSpace

Systems Toolkit is a C++ object library. More information on Systems toolkit is available online from ObjectSpace at http://www.objectspace.com.

Systems Toolkit is not a complete application development system as are the other frameworks. It provides operating system independence for many of the difficult-to-implement subsystems. One of the things keeping it from being a complete application development system is the lack of functions for building the user interface.

CROSS-PLATFORM APPLICATION DEVELOPMENT USING JAVA

The most recent trend in business application development is to use Java and iwebntranets. Java provides a way to implement and script components that run on webweb browsers. The webweb server becomes the application engine, and the browser is the portable user interface.

For Java applications, portability is determined by the browser's ability to provide a Java runtime environment consistent with the Java specification. As with other computer standards, there are differences among Java implementations. Not all browsers implement Java while conforming strictly to the specification.

Besides the web browsers such as Netscape and Internet Explorer, many operating systems have started providing Java support as well.

DEVELOPING DISTRIBUTED APPLICATIONS IN A HETEROGENEOUS ENVIRONMENT

Some of the application development tools covered earlier in this chapter support the development of distributed applications. These tools permit developing client/server applications where clients and servers are distributed. Developing distributed applications involves the development of an application where portions of the application could reside on heterogeneous systems at different nodes in a network, but work together to fulfill the functions of the application.

To accomplish this, the applications need an environment that will provide distributed services, a mechanism to pass messages between applications, functions to accomplish distributed transaction processing, ability to access data from different databases, and a mechanism to facilitate communication among objects in a distributed environment. This section covers the distributed application environment and services. The other topics are addressed later in this chapter.

Open Software Foundation (OSF)

Information about OSF is available online from its home page at http://www.osf.org.

The Open Software Foundation (OSF) is an industry consortium of hardware and software vendors that aims to advance the cause of distributed computing. The goal of distributed computing is to make the network and other supporting software running on different hardware as transparent as possible to an application. OSF's vision for distributed computing is its Distributed Computing Environment (DCE) specificatio, produced in 1990. The current DCE version is DCE 1.2.2.

OSF produced an Application Environment Specification (AES). AES consolidated DCE components from different vendors into one standard specification. AES is a reference implementation. AES includes source code and a Validation Test Suite (VTS). Vendors are expected to use AES to come up with their own DCE-compliant product offering.

DCE

There are six core services that are part of a distributed application and these services are provided by DCE cells (A cell is a unit of one or more computers).

1. Remote Procedure Call (RPC) services to allow an application to access services provided by another computer on the network
2. Distributed directory services to locate any named object on the network using a single naming model
3. Threads service to be able to execute multiple threads

4. Distributed time services to maintain one time across all computers on the network by synchronizing the system clocks of different computers
5. Security services to authenticate users, authorize access to resources, and provide user and server account management on a distributed network
6. Distributed File Services to access files anywhere on a network

All the above services may not be available when developing distributed applications. The most important service from the above is the RPC service.

DCE, UNIX, and Windows NT

DCE services have been available on many UNIX environments for a while. Information on porting a UNIX DCE application to run on Windows NT is to be found in the chapters on porting presented earlier in the handbook.

To develop distributed applications and Windows NT as part of a chosen environment, it should be noted that Windows NT, natively, includes only full RPC support. Microsoft is working on providing directory services. At this time, third-party software is necessary to provide the other services.

For example, Digital has a product known as Digital DCE Services for Windows NT that provides RPC services, Cell Directory Services, DCE Threads services, Distributed Time Services, and DCE Security Services. Gradient Technologies has DCE products that provide the core DCE services as well as distributed file services.

Digital DCE Services for Windows NT

Information on Digital DCE Services for Windows NT is available online at http://www.digital.com.

The Digital DCE for Windows NT is a product family that is an implementation of OSF DCE Release 1.0.3 adapted and enhanced for Windows NT with some additional capabilities from the OSF DCE R1.1 and R1.2 releases.

The Digital DCE for Windows NT product family consists of four separate products, each one of which is supported on both the Intel and Alpha platforms. The products are summarized below.

1. Digital DCE Runtime Services for Windows NT
2. Digital DCE Application Developer's Kit
3. Digital DCE Cell Directory Server for Windows NT
4. Digital DCE Security Server for Windows NT

Let us briefly look at these products.

DEVELOPMENT IN AN INTEGRATED ENVIRONMENT

Digital DCE Runtime Services for Windows NT. Every system within a DCE cell must run the DCE Runtime Services. The Digital DCE Runtime Services is a fully integrated set of services that provides applications with the essential capabilities required to use DCE's distributed services. The Digital DCE Runtime Services for the Windows NT product makes the following DCE features available to distributed applications:

- OSF DCE RPC including:
  a) Transparent mapping to the Microsoft RPC API calls so that applications that conform to the DCE RPC API can easily be ported to Windows NT
  b) Translation of the Microsoft RPC status codes to the standard DCE RPC status codes
  c) Use of the DCE Cell Directory Service for location-independent naming of application services
  d) Use of the DCE Security Service for authentication, authorization, and secure communication
- Distributed Time Services
- DCE Security Services
- DCE Name Services
- DCE Threads

The Runtime Services kit also includes new Windows-based DCE management tools:

- DCEsetup for configuring and managing the DCE services on a system
- DCE Director for managing DCE cells. It presents an object-oriented view of the DCE environment. The top-level object is the cell. Objects in the cell that a user can manage include users, groups, hosts, CDS directories, and servers. DCE Director makes it easy to perform management tasks such as creating, deleting, and modifying cell objects.
- In addition, the DCE Director allows access to the standard DCE control programs (rgy_edit, cdscp, acl_edit, and dtscp), while providing new functions, such as allowing authorized users to preconfigure host machines in a cell and manage user accounts.
- Visual ACL Editor for graphically managing DCE ACLs, which is integrated with the DCE Director or can also be used as a standalone tool

The Digital DCE for Windows NT product supports all the network transports that are supported in Windows NT. In addition, DECnet is supported if PATHWORKS for Windows NT is used. The Digital DCE Runtime Services for Windows NT kit must be installed first and is a prerequisite for installing and using the DCE Application Developer's Kit, the CDS Server kit, and the DCE Security Server kit.

Developing New Applications in a Heterogeneous Environment

The Digital DCE Application Developer's Kit for Windows NT. The Digital DCE Application Developer's Kit for Windows NT includes the tools and files required for the development of distributed applications: it includes:

- IDL compiler, which generates RPC interface stubs for C and C++ applications
- Standard DCE and additional Windows-based sample applications
- All public DCE application programming interfaces, including the DCE RPC API, DCE Threads API, DCE Security API, DCE name services API, and the DCE Time Services API

Digital DCE Cell Directory Server for Windows NT. Digital DCE Cell Directory Server for Windows NT, which provides the distributed repository supporting the DCE name services. The kit includes a Cell Directory Services (CDS) server and a Global Directory Agent (GDA) server. The CDS server provides naming services within a DCE cell.

A DCE cell must have one master CDS server and may add any number of read-only replica CDS servers to improve performance and reliability. The optional GDA server provides a means of linking multiple CDS namespaces via either X.500 or the Internet Domain Name Server (DNS BIND).

Digital DCE Security Server for Windows NT. Digital DCE Security Server for Windows NT provides the repository of security information in a cell used to protect resources from illegal access and allow secure communication within and between cells. The DCE Security Server accomplishes this through three services:

- DCE Authentication Service allows users and resources to prove their identity to each other. The DCE Authentication Service is based on Kerberos, which requires that all users and resources possess a secret key.
- DCE Authorization Service verifies operations that users may perform on resources. A DCE Registry Service contains a list of valid users. An Access Control List (ACL) associated with each resource identifies users allowed to access the resource and the types of operations they may perform.
- DCE Data Integrity Service protects network data from tampering. Cryptographic checksums automatically generated by RPC enable DCE to determine whether data has been corrupted in transmission.

There must be one master security server in every DCE cell. Additional read-only security servers, called replicas, can be installed in a cell to improve performance and reliability.

The core DCE functionality provided in the Digital DCE for the Windows NT product family can be summarized as:

- DCE Remote Procedure Call (RPC): Provides the OSF DCE RPC API used to create and run client/server applications. It allows direct calls to application procedures running on remote systems as if they were local procedure calls. Authenticated (secure) RPC calls are supported through the use of the DCE Security facility provided in the Runtime Services. On Windows NT, the DCE RPC is layered on the native Microsoft Windows NT RPC. The Microsoft RPC is fully interoperable with DCE RPC running on all other DCE platforms.
- DCE Distributed Time Service (DTS): Synchronizes time on individual hosts in a distributed network environment.
- DCE Security Service Client: Provides access to DCE security services. It enables secure communications and access via authorization and authentication services. This access can be used by either the client or the server side of a DCE application.
- DCE Cell Directory Service (CDS) Client: Provides access to CDS name services allowing location-independent naming of resources. This access can be used by either the client or the server side of the user's application.
- The Interface Definition Language (IDL) Compiler: IDL is the language used to define remote procedure calls.
- DCE Threads Service: Provides user-context multiprocessing functionality. This provides a simple programming model for building applications that perform many operations simultaneously. The DCE Threads service has been integrated with the Windows NT kernel threads facility.

PC-DCE and DFS for Windows NT

Information on PC-DCE and DFS for Windows NT is available online at http://www.gradient.com.

Gradient Technologies produces DCE products for all Windows Operating Systems, many UNIX Operating Systems, Mac, etc. PC-DCE provides the core DCE services such as RPC, Security, etc., and DFS for Windows NT provides distributed file services. The PC-DCE architecture including DFS is shown in Exhibit 7.

PC-DCE for Windows NT and Windows 95 product family components are:

- PC-DCE Runtime for Windows NT and Windows 95
- PC-DCE Application Developers Kit (ADK) for Windows 95 and Windows NT
- PC-DCE Cell Directory Server (CDS) for Windows NT
- PC-DCE Security Server for Windows NT
- Regii Remote Configuration Tool for Windows 95 and Windows NT

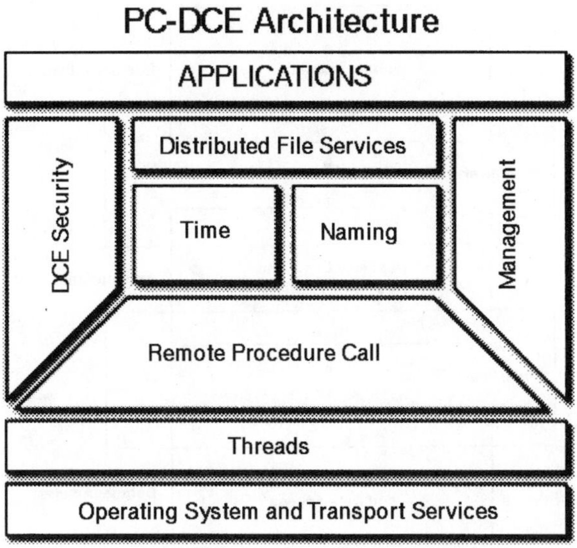

PC-DCE Architecture

Exhibit 7. PC-DCE architecture.

Middleware Products for Distributed Applications

Middleware consists of both application programming interfaces (APIs) and protocols that support the mapping of applications to the resources they use in a distributed environment. Also, because middleware works across heterogeneous environments, it enables the integration of applications across those environments. See Exhibit 8.

Message-Oriented Middleware

Message-oriented middleware (MOM) provides reliable communications among the components of a distributed application. MOM allows applications to communicate asynchronously, meaning that the sender and receiver do not have to be available on the network at the same time, and that the sending program does not block while waiting for a response. MOM provides guaranteed message delivery even when a process, node, or network fails.

MOM may also provide queue-based semantics to provide other application benefits, such as having multiple writers and multiple readers of a queue. These features allow an application to prioritize messages, to perform publish/subscribe operations, and to do dynamic load balancing. If a queue is backlogged with messages, additional servers can be started up to pull messages off the queue.

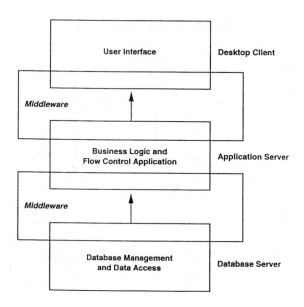

Exhibit 8. Middleware facilitates distributed client/server application development.

MOM has been used to integrate legacy applications with new applications, and is especially effective in dealing with distributed, heterogeneous environments. MOM has achieved great success in manufacturing, telecommunications, health care, and financial services environments.

DECmessageQ (DmQ) is the MOM product based on the message queuing paradigm. DmQ provides application developers with a simple, easy-to-use mechanism to integrate applications across multiple platforms — both DIGITAL and non-DIGITAL. It is primarily used when business solutions require asynchronous communications, high reliability and performance, quick development turnaround, and little to no training of expensive IT staff.

DECmessageQ provides a suite of distributed communication features such as publish and subscribe (message broadcasting), guaranteed delivery, priority selection, global naming, self-describing messages, and flexible configuration (failover and fail-back).

Accessing Distributed Databases

There are products that provide transparent access to distributed heterogeneous databases such as Oracle Rdb Distributed Product Suite from Oracle.

The Rdb Distributed Product Suite is data access and integration software that provides transparent, seamless integration of heterogeneous data for applications that run on OpenVMS, UNIX, Windows, and Windows/NT desktop systems. The Rdb Distributed Product Suite tool set includes:

- Rdb Distributed Option (formerly known as DEC DB Integrator or DBI, now included with Oracle Rdb)
- The Rdb Transparent Gateways to Oracle, DB2, Sybase, RMS, CODA-SYL DBMS, PC Data, and Custom Drivers (all purchased separately)
- Rdb Replication Option (formerly known as DEC Data Distributor, now included with Oracle Rdb).
- The DataBase Integrator (also formerly known as DEC DB Integrator, but purchased separately by customers who do not use Oracle Rdb)

With the Rdb Distributed Option, users transparently read/write data regardless of database management system, data formats, or the data's physical location. For example, legacy RMS files can be accessed on OpenVMS/VAX, an enterprise Rdb7 database on an OpenVMS Alpha, an Oracle7 on UNIX, and virtually any PC data on Windows or Windows NT like a single relational database. Multiple local and remote Rdb databases appear as a single Rdb database to the application.

The Rdb Distributed Option's unique query optimizes and analyzes both network costs and the capabilities of the source databases to enhance parallel query performance.

The read/write Rdb Transparent Gateways can be used separately or with the Rdb Distributed Option to integrate non-Rdb data sources. The Rdb Transparent Gateways can access Oracle and Sybase data on any platform supported by these database managers. The Rdb Transparent Gateway to PC data can read and write to all popular ODBC data sources, including Microsoft SQL Server, Microsoft Excel, Microsoft Access, dBase, Btrieve, FoxPro, Paradox, and ASCII files. The Rdb Transparent Gateway to Custom Drivers allows fast development of a Transparent Gateway to any custom data source on OpenVMS or DIGITAL UNIX.

The Rdb Replication Option can be used to provide scheduled and on-demand full or partial database replication on a single system or over the network. The Rdb Replication Option can transfer data among Rdb databases and, with the Rdb Distributed Option and Rdb Transparent Gateways, it can transfer distributed and heterogeneous data. For full replication or incremental transfers, the source database must be Rdb and the target database can be either Rdb, Oracle7, DB2, Sybase, or a relational PC data source. For data transfers (on-demand or scheduled), sources can be Rdb or any database accessible through the Rdb Transparent Gateways. Targets are Rdb, Oracle7, DB2, Sybase, or a relational PC data source.

DEVELOPMENT IN AN INTEGRATED ENVIRONMENT

Distributed Objects

Distributed applications that are object-oriented can be developed using distributed objects that interact with each other through an object request broker. Distributed objects is a very active topic and the technologies that are relevant here include:

- Common Object Request Broker Architecture (CORBA) from the Object Management Group (OMG)
- Active X and the Distributed Component Object Model from the Open Group (Microsoft has provided these technologies to the Open Group to standardize these technologies)
- Java-based applets and applications

Some of the products that are available for developing distributed object-oriented applications in a heterogeneous environment include:

- ObjectBroker from Digital Equipment
- PowerBroker product family from Expersoft
- Orbix from Iona Technologies

There are still many mainframe applications in use today — by some estimates, over 80 percent of corporate data still resides on mainframe-based data storage. Following are some options that will allow users to interface with mainframe-based legacy applications and access legacy data.

MAINFRAME LEGACY APPLICATION INTERFACING AND DATA ACCESS

In developing new applications, a situation may arise where an application needs to interface with mainframe-based existing applications as well as retrieve data from mainframe-based databases. This section will look at some of the tools for Windows, UNIX, and NetWare environments that provide these functionalities. That is, the section will talk about applications access. When users on Windows or UNIX machines need to access mainframe applications, solutions like terminal emulation are available and these are covered later.

Microsoft BackOffice

Microsoft BackOffice is a suite of products based on Windows NT server for a number of server functions including interfacing with mainframes. The following is an extract of extensive data available at http://www.microsoft.com/backoffice. The products in the BackOffice family that pertain to mainframe interface include:

- Microsoft SNA Server — Integrates existing operational systems with the Internet and intranet for host connectivity.

288

- Microsoft SQL Server — A database server that supports large Internet and intranet web databases
- Microsoft Transaction Server — formerly known by its code name, "Viper" — is a new product that combines the features of a TP monitor and an object request broker

Later, this chapter will examine these products briefly.

SNA Gateways

SNA gateways are used for interfacing with mainframe applications including interactive access from a heterogeneous LAN attached workstation, program-to-program access, and file and data transfers. Exhibit 9 shows an SNA gateway. The gateway routes all client traffic to the mainframes and provides protocol and data translation where necessary.

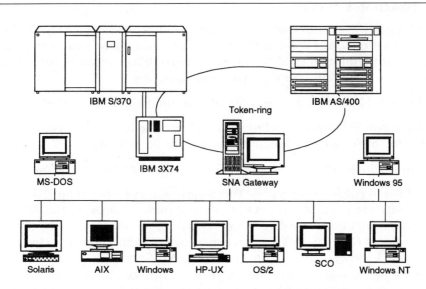

Exhibit 9.   SNA Gateway to interface with mainframes.

The SNA TCP/IP gateways can be implemented in one of three ways:

- Branch-Based Deployment — The branch-based deployment is the traditional way to deploy SNA gateways. SNA servers are placed in the branch and communicate with the host using native SNA protocols either via dedicated SDLC lines or tunneled over DLC/802.2. Routers can be used to direct the traffic to the central site, or MPR support of NT 4.0 can be used in lieu of a router.

- Centralized Deployment — Channel-attached or Token-Ring-attached SNA servers are placed at the data center and connect to the host using native SNA protocols. The centralized SNA servers provide split-stack or TN3270 service for local and remote systems via TCP/IP. Additionally, client-based LU0 or LU6.2 applications can connect anywhere on the TCP/IP WAN.
- Distributed Deployment — Combines the two approaches. Branch-based SNA servers funnel TCP/IP-encapsulated traffic to centralized SNA servers. It is not required for each branch to have an SNA server; they may be distributed strategically throughout the network. The most significant advantages of distributed deployment over centralized deployment are improved host response times for users in the branch and reduced traffic load on the WAN.

Distributed deployment of SNA gateways is shown in Exhibit 10.

Microsoft SNA Server

SNA gateways are available from many vendors. Microsoft's SNA Server, which runs on top of Windows NT server, provides many built-in functions that let it perform as an SNA gateway to allow Windows and UNIX clients to access mainframe applications and data.

Exhibit 11 shows an overview of the Microsoft SNA Server.

Microsoft SNA Server includes a number of built-in or third-party software for SNA gateway functions as shown in Exhibit 12.

The main features of the SNA Server are summarized below.

- Shared Folders Gateway — This feature allows PCs with no SNA client software installed to access "shared folders" files on the AS/400. Implemented as a native Windows NT Server file system, the Shared Folders Gateway (SFG) service makes AS/400 files appear to users as just another drive on the Windows NT Server.
- Single Sign-on — The single-sign-on feature of SNA Server 3.0 automatically provides SNA host account information when starting an SNA application on a client.
- TN5250 Service — This feature enables any TN5250 emulator to connect to the AS/400 via SNA Server without installing TCP/IP on the AS/400.
- SNA Server Manager — A graphical console used as the single point of control for configuring and managing all SNA Servers, host connections, sessions, users, security, auditing, and other functions in a Windows NT domain. SNA Server Manager integrates the administration of SNA Server, TN3270 Service, TN5250 Service, SNA Print Service, Shared Folders Gateway, and Host Security into a single interface.

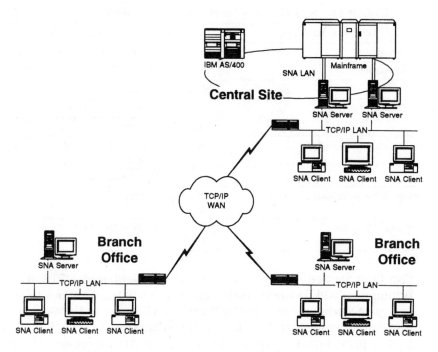

Exhibit 10. Distributed deployment of SNA gateways.

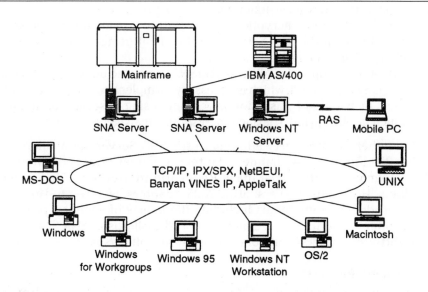

Exhibit 11. SNA gateway functions using Windows NT SNA server.

Exhibit 12. SNA Gateway functions in Microsoft SNA server.

Gateway function	SNA Server 3.0 solution
3270 emulation	tn3270-server, tn3270E
5250 emulation	tn5250-server
Printing	SNA Print Service
File Transfer (m/f)	IND$FILE (from tn3270 client)
	FTP-to-AFTP gateway
File Transfer (AS/400)	Shared Folders (i.e., FTP to a shared folder on the NT server)
	FTP-to-AFTP gateway
Remote Administration	SNA Remote Access Server (i.e., TCP-over-SNA), w/ MPR
Program-to-Program	Parker Software's SNA/APPC Client for UNIX

- SNA Print Service — This feature provides server-based 3270 and 5250 printer emulation, allowing mainframe and AS/400 applications to print to any LAN printer supported by Windows NT Server or NetWare. Mainframe printing supports both LU1 and LU3 data streams, including transparent print jobs sent by host-based print preprocessors. AS/400 printing supports standard SCS line printing as well as pass-through support for host-based 3812 graphics printing emulation by using the IBM Host Print Transform function.
- SNA Client-Server Encryption — This feature provides encryption of all data between the SNA Server and the client using the RSA RC4 data encryption standard.
- Sync-Point Support for APPC — The SNA Server includes support for the APPC Syncpoint API, which is necessary to implement robust, cross-platform distributed transaction processing using host-based databases (such as DB2) and transaction resource managers (such as CICS).

A number of third-party add-ons to the SNA Server are available for 3270/5250 Emulation—Channel adapters, Channel Attached Gateways, Coax/Twinax Adapters, Database Replication/Gateways, File Transfer Products, Host Print Servers, SDLC/X.25 Adapters, webweb to Host, and other products. More details including the names of vendors, products, and product descriptions are included on the Microsoft SNA Server web page http://www.microsoft.com/products/backoffice/sna.

SNA Client for UNIX

SNA Client for UNIX is an implementation of Microsoft's SNA APIs for the UNIX environment by Parker Brothers. SNA Client supports the SNA interfaces APPC, CPI-C, LUA/LU0, and CSV for program-to-program

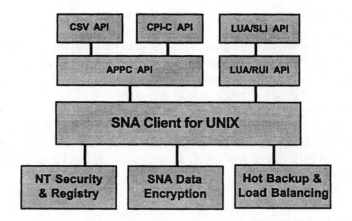

Exhibit 13. SNA Client for UNIX architecture.

communication to IBM mainframes and AS/400s. SNA Client utilizes an NT/SNA Server gateway to provide the underlying SNA transport mechanisms between UNIX and IBM systems. The architecture of SNA Client is shown in Exhibit 13.

APPC support includes syncpoint support. CPI-C Level 1.2 is supported, with many Level 2.0 extensions. LUA/LU0 support includes both the low-level RUI and high-level SLI interfaces. CSV includes character-set conversion tables and an industry-standard programmatic interface to IBM's NetView. The SNA Client utilizes advanced SNA Server features such as load balancing and client/server encryption. Emulation support includes TN3270E, printing, HLLAPI, scripting, and X/Motif.

Versions are available for Solaris, HP-UX, AIX, and SCO. The SNA Client requires Microsoft SNA Server as a gateway (running on NT). SNA Client makes it possible to support Windows, DOS, OS/2, and UNIX clients from the same NT server.

As an alternative to using an SNA/APPC client, the IBM ANYNET product can be used. There are significant differences in the approaches between the two. See the white paper from Microsoft and Parker Brothers for more details.

Microsoft SQL Server

The Microsoft SQL Server is a database management system featuring support of standards such as ANSI SQL-92, SNMP, and ODBC.

The main features of the SQL server are summarized below.

- Distributed Transaction Coordinator to manage transactions that span two or more SQL Server systems
- Built-in heterogeneous data replication of text and image data types to enable distribution of data to non-SQL Server systems
- Dynamic Locking to reduce contention among users trying to insert rows on the same page simultaneously
- SQL Server systems can send and receive information via the Internet or intranets through tight integration with Microsoft Internet Information Server and other third-party web servers. A Web Assistant generates HTML pages from SQL Server data on a scheduled or trigger-driven basis.
- SQL Server provides scalability through support for standard symmetric multiprocessing with automatic workload balancing across multiple processors.
- Integrated with C2/E3 security in Windows NT
- Distributed Data Warehousing
- Data warehousing functions including OLAP query support, CUBE, ROLLUP, and a new *Insert Exec* function that allows SQL Server to programmatically retrieve information from multiple sources and populate SQL Server tables with the results
- Mail Integration to send and receive electronic mail using Microsoft Exchange, or populate Exchange public folders with data from SQL Server. SQL Server can also send optional attachments automatically when the data changes or on a scheduled basis using the built-in scheduling capabilities of SQL Executive

Microsoft Transaction Server

The Microsoft Transaction Server is a recent addition to the Microsoft backoffice family. Some of the functions of the transaction server are:

- Developers can build Transaction Server applications as software components using tools that support ActiveX, including Microsoft Visual Basic, Visual C++, and Visual J++.
- Transaction Server includes a component packaging service to facilitate integration, installation, and deployment of many components as a single application.
- Transaction Server manages a pool of ODBC connections to a database.
- Transaction Server automatically provides transparent transaction support to applications running on the server. The application does not need to use low-level transaction control primitives to accomplish this.
- Transaction Server uses DCOM for component-to-component communications across a network. Microsoft is trying to license DCOM as an open-industry standard through the Open Group.
- Transaction Server works with many resource managers—including relational databases, file systems, and image stores—that support a

transactional two-phase commit protocol. This enables businesses to leverage existing investments in UNIX and mainframe data stores.

• Win32 "fat" clients and HTML "thin" clients can access Transaction Server applications concurrently.

• Administrators can easily partition an application across multiple servers by deploying an application's components into several packages, with each package running on its own server.

Besides the BackOffice family products that are relevant to interfacing with mainframes, the BackOffice family includes many other products for Mail support (Microsoft Exchange), Internet/intranet support (Internet Information Server and Proxy Server), Systems Management support (Systems Management Server), etc. The BackOffice series runs as an integrated family on the Windows NT server platform. More details on Microsoft BackOffice is available online at http://www.microsoft.com/backoffice/.

Novell NetWare for SAA

Information about Novell NetWare for SAA is available from http://www. novell.com. The following is a brief extract.

NetWare for SAA is a result of a strategic alliance between Novell and IBM. It is a gateway for integrating NetWare and IntranetWare networks with IBM host systems (S/390s and AS/400s). It lets NetWare clients access applications and data on SNA-based IBM hosts via IPX/SPX, TCP/IP, and AppleTalk. The clients could be DOS, Mac, Windows 3.1, Windows 95, Windows NT, or OS/2 clients.

NetWare for SAA includes TN3270E emulation support. It provides support for a variety of server-to-host link types and adapters including SDLC multipoint, Frame Relay, and high-speed FDDI. It includes functions to administer desktops, gateways, and host links from NetWare, remotely or from the host. It includes support for Lan-to-Host and Host-to-Lan printing. It comes in two flavors (NetWare for SAA 2.2 and NetWare for SAA: As/400 Edition). It uses Novell's directory services-NDS.

More than 100 third-party applications are available supporting NetWare-to-host integration with NetWare for SAA. Applications include host printing, software distribution, database access, centralized data backup, network management, and integrated security. Software development tools are also available for creating custom applications for 32-bit clients and NetWare platforms.

Some of the functions that can be performed using NetWare for SAA include:

• File Transfer — A networked client can download or upload files from and to MVS or AS/400 systems. The client can use IP on the network to communicate with the SAA gateway. The gateway then communicates with the MVS using APPC, thereby eliminating the requirement for TCP/IP on the mainframe.

- Self Defining Dependent Logical Unit (SDDLU) Support — SDDLU support allows a customer to activate a dependent LU without VTAM definitions on the host. By activating the LU only when it is needed, a big list of VTAM definitions need not be predefined and an LU can be added without requiring VTAM generations.

Besides some of the commercial products and add-ons mentioned above, there is public domain software that performs some of the functions provided by the commercial products. Public domain software is typically free and is not guaranteed. Support in many cases is by the author(s) and is on a best effort basis. Such an approach makes it difficult for public domain software to be used for many business applications.

HETEROGENEOUS DATABASE ACCESS

There are database-access products that let an application access data from any type of PC databases, server databases, or even mainframe-based databases located anywhere on the network. Using these heterogeneous database servers, an organization can decide on the optimal data distribution strategy for the enterprise data and pick the optimal combination for the location of the data that satisfies data access and integrity requirements.

Empress

The Empress Heterogeneous Database Server from Empress is a fully distributed database management system that lets users and applications running Empress and UNIX access data from any database. The database could be PC-based, workstation (server)-based, or even mainframe-based. Details on Empress Heterogeneous Database Server are available online at http://www.empress.com

EDA

EDA, which stands for Electronic Data Access, is a family of client/server products from Information Builders that provides SQL-based access to more than 60 relational and nonrelational databases that reside on 35 different hardware platforms. More details on EDA/SQL are available online at http://www.ibi.com.

The EDA product family includes:

- EDA Client (EDA/Link communications, API/SQL, ODBC driver)
- EDA Server Engines (MVS, VM, Digital, Tandem, UNIX, AS/400, OS/2, and Windows NT) include the following components:

— EDA Hub Server
— EDA Transaction Server (CICS, IMS/DC)
— EDA Relational Gateway (DB/2, Oracle, Informix, Sybase, Rdb, Ingres)
— EDA Nonrelational Gateway (IMS, VSAM, IDMS, RMS, ISAM, etc.)
— EDA Stored Procedure Gateway
• Oracle Transparent Gateway to EDA
• EDA Web Client Services
• EDA Open Database Gateway
• EDA Enterprise Copy Manager Overview and White Paper
• EDA Data Extenders (DB2, Oracle, Informix, Lotus DataLens, DDE)
• EDA Communication Gateways (OS/2, Windows NT, Novell NetWare)
• EDA Governing Services

Omni SQL Gateway

OMNI SQL Gateway from Sybase offers transparent read/write access to data across many heterogeneous data sources. OMNI SQL Gateway is part of Sybase's middleware product family called EnterpriseCONNECT.

Hyperstar

Hyperstar from Vmark Software provides a set of ODBC driver products that enable transparent read/write access to corporate databases on more than 30 different platforms that include popular database systems. Hyperstar works in conjunction with Vmark's relational database management system called UniVerse.

The HyperStar Fast Path Server for UniVerse is a middleware product designed specifically to provide fast, reliable, seamless access to data stored in UniVerse from 16- or 32-bit Windows-based third-party tools, programming languages, or an RDBMS running on a UNIX server using ODBC.

This allows users of Excel, Lotus 1-2-3, Microsoft Word, and many more desktop productivity tools to access UniVerse data more conveniently and transparently, as well as to integrate the data into their applications. The HyperStar Fast Path Server is fully ODBC compliant, providing maximum flexibility in enterprise connectivity tasks. It also features built-in support for many TCP/IP stacks, allowing existing networks to be used without the need to purchase additional networking or TCP/IP products.

The combination of UniVerse and HyperStar supports the use of UniVerse tables, views, and files with D, S, and A dictionary types. This eliminates the need to make UniVerse data files appear more SQL-like to facilitate high-performance ODBC read-and-write access. The combination also takes full advantage of UniVerse multivalued data structures and extended features, such as select lists and I-types.

With HyperStar Fast Path server, UniVerse users can implement an ODBC solution today and gradually migrate to using the full UniVerse SQL interface with its security and declarative integrity features.

INTERFACING LEGACY APPLICATIONS WITH INTERNET

Legacy applications can be implemented from the Internet or intranet using middleware such as BEA Jolt.

BEA Jolt

BEA Jolt, from BEA Systems, Inc. is software for enabling companies to make powerful, secure transaction systems running mission-critical or legacy applications immediately accessible from the Internet or an enterprise intranet, with no additional application programming.

Through BEA Jolt, mission-critical, legacy, or Internet applications can easily share business transactions in the Java environment, which is critical for Java to be used effectively across the enterprise.

BEA Jolt is based on the BEA TUXEDO middleware. BEA Jolt and BEA TUXEDO provide the infrastructure for ensuring that mission-critical and legacy applications can easily interoperate in an environment such as the Java Computing model.

CONCLUSION

This chapter looked at different ways to develop applications so that the applications will execute in different environments. Low-level API-based approaches or high-level 4GL or Object framework-based approaches can be used. We also covered techniques to interface with legacy applications and data from the applications being developed.

Chapter 16
Component-Based Development

Nancy Stonelake

INTRODUCTION

COMPONENT-BASED DEVELOPMENT is being touted as the solution to the latest software crisis. What is it and how true is the hype? The objectives of this article are shown in the following list:

- To define component-based development
- To describe its benefits and weaknesses
- To examine the basic architecture and popular component models
- To examine alternatives and component-based developments in conjunction with current technology and data management
- To examine some of the challenges facing IT shops that want to move to a component approach

DEFINITION

Component-based development differs from traditional development in that the application is not developed completely from scratch. A component-based application is assembled from a set of preexisting components. A component is a software bundle that performs a predefined set of functionality with a predefined API. At its simplest level, a component could be a class library or GUI widget; or it may be as complex as a small application, like a text editor; or an application subsystem, like a help system. These components may be developed in-house, reused from project to project, and passed between departments. They may be purchased from outside vendors who specialize in component development, or bartered between other companies in similar lines of business.

Components can be divided into two broad "types": business components and framework components. Business components encapsulate knowledge of business processes. They may be applied in a vertical industry sector such as banking, or in a cross-industry standard business function like accounting or e-commerce. Framework components address specific software architecture issues like the user interface, security, or reporting functions.

DEVELOPMENT IN AN INTEGRATED ENVIRONMENT

BENEFITS

How is component-based development better than traditional development practices? If we compare developing enterprisewide applications to auto manufacturing, current application development is like machining each part from scratch for every automobile being assembled. This is time-consuming and expensive when most of the parts are the same or similar in configuration. Henry Ford revolutionized manufacturing by standardizing parts and having workers specialize in small aspects of construction. Component-based development works on the same principles and reaps similar benefits.

Due to the similarity among all software applications, using components can reduce design time. Almost all applications have some security system, error handling, and user help functionality. Why are we wasting our time deciding how to provide help to users when the real question is what level of help users need? Components can provide framework solutions that can be tuned to our business requirements. This has the additional benefit of allowing us time to focus on the business logic, which is the key to fulfilling requirements.

Implementation time is reduced because components are already built. Additional coding may be required to integrate the component into the system, but the required functionality is already there.

These two main facts have additional implications. Since components are prebuilt, testing time is reduced. Components are already unit tested; they only require integration testing within the application. Overall, with components we require less design, development, and testing resources. This means we need fewer people with highly specialized and hard-to-find skill sets, and we can leverage the people we have to do the things needed in the application.

Additionally, the cost of developing the components can be leveraged over many buyers. Since we acquire components from other departments in the company and pass our components on to them, they share in the costs. Vendors sell to multiple users and they all share in the development and maintenance costs. Component developers can afford to have designer/developers devoted to each component over its life cycle, and these resources can become specialists in the component piece.

WEAKNESSES

Component development is an immature industry. This has several effects and implications, primarily: limited vendors, products, and skilled human resources.

At this time there are limited choices in component vendors, and company stability may be an issue. While there is a stable set of GUI component vendors, the offerings in true business components are limited. The lack of availability also limits competitive advantage. If all our competitors are using the same business logic, are we doing anything better than they are or are we just matching the pace? Product stability is also an issue. It is important that the API of a component remain constant, otherwise we may incur heavy maintenance costs when integrating new product releases.

Component-based development requires a different approach to software development and there are few people who have actually done it. It requires people who can discern what parts of an application may be useful to other applications and what changes may need to be made to support future applications. In other words, you need a good designer/architect with a good crystal ball. To successfully reuse components, you must have designers/implementers who are familiar with the component library so they don't spend all their time looking for components that don't exist. They must also be able to adapt components to fulfill the requirements.

In addition, there must be supporting corporate strategies to promote reuse. No benefit is gained by crafting components that remain unused. Designers and developers need some impetus to change, and the resources to support component development must be provided. This means taking the time to develop and locate components and promoting awareness of their availability.

BASIC ARCHITECTURE

Component architecture is based on locating components where they can best serve the needs of the user. This must account for several factors: speed, processing power, and accessibility. One possible architecture is shown in Exhibit 1.

GUI widget components sit on the client, however business logic may be required locally for complex applications, or on the server for transactional applications. These components can be placed wherever the architect sees fit. Component-based development does not provide an architecture so much as it permits good architectural choices to be implemented.

In distributed environments components can follow the CORBA or DCOM models. Components can be wrapped as CORBA objects or have a CORBA object interface. This makes them accessible through an ORB, permitting ready distribution. Alternatively, components can conform to the COM model and be distributed using the DCOM specifications. While these two distribution models can interwork, that is beyond the scope of this discussion.

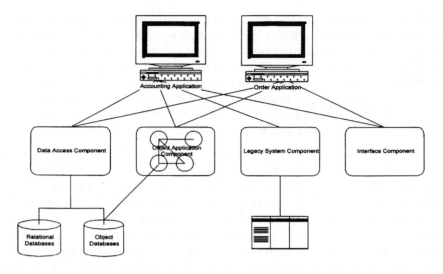

Exhibit 1.   Component architecture.

A component architecture can be described as a service-based architecture, as in the SELECT Perspective, where components act as the interface to a "service" which is a black box encapsulation of a collection of related functionality that is accessed through a consistent interface. Services are shared among applications to provide the application functionality. The system is then distributed according to business requirements rather than software limitations.

COMPONENT TYPES

As mentioned previously, different components address different areas of functionality. These can be divided into framework components and business components. Framework components can be further broken down into data access components, user interface components, and subsystem components. Business components include business logic components and application components. These groupings allow us to place components based on the best configuration for our environment.

Data access components handle database interaction, including creation, deletion, query, and update. While data access components generally access a relational database, components can also access flat files, object databases, or any other persistent storage mechanism. This allows us a mechanism to change the back-end data storage without impacting the delivered applications. It also allows us to deliver the same application using different databases with minimal change. The data component is replaced to suit the new environment.

User interface components handle user interaction and define the look and feel of the application. Separation of this component allows us to change the interface so that applications can take on the look and feel of the deployment environment. This helps to reduce training time by offering the user a consistent paradigm across applications.

Subsystem components provide functionality like error handling, security, or user help. They allow for standardization across applications.

Business logic components encapsulate the policies of a business. By separating them from general application or data logic, we can easily change applications to reflect changing business policies such as offering discounts to large customers or recommending complementary products.

Application components are small applications that contribute to the functionality of a larger piece, text editors, for example. Application components include legacy applications that are wrapped to provide a standard interface for interaction with other components or use within applications.

COMPONENT MODELS

Currently there are two primary component models: JavaBeans and ActiveX. These two models can interact over bridges or by wrapping one as the other.

JavaBeans is the component model for the Java programming language. Because Beans are written in Java they run on any platform. A Bean may implement any functionality but it must support the following features: introspection, customization, events, properties, and persistence. JavaBeans are intended to be integrated with visual development environments and they should have some visually customizable properties, although they may not have a visual representation themselves.

ActiveX is based on the Component Object Model (COM) and was developed by Microsoft. While ActiveX has been a proprietary technology, Microsoft plans to transition it to an industry standards body. ActiveX enables developers to embed event-driven controls into web sites by optimizing the COM model for size and speed. While ActiveX components implemented in different languages can interact, ActiveX components are compiled into platform-specific formats. The most common ActiveX implementation is for "Windows-Intel," limiting ActiveX to a Microsoft environment.

The OMG is currently in the process of defining a distributed component model based upon the Object Management Architecture. This will define a CORBA component and make integrating CORBA Components significantly easier.

COMPONENTS, OO, CLIENT SERVER, AND NETWORK COMPUTING

Component-based development has its roots in object-oriented technology and client/server development and can act as an enabler for network computing.

Components extend object technology and object methodologies. Like objects, components should be developed in an iterative, incremental fashion. Components must be identified from existing applications and reworked to apply to new applications. Components and objects incorporate the idea of encapsulation and black box accessibility. With components, as with objects, we are not concerned with how a service is performed internally, only that it is performed correctly. Components are refinements of objects in that the API is defined in a language-independent standard. Components, like objects, communicate through industry standard middleware: CORBA or DCOM. This middleware acts as a layer of abstraction so that components can be called in the same fashion, regardless of their function. This further hides the component's implementation, whereas direct object communication can rely on implementation-specific calls.

Components act as service bundles, relying on tightly coupled object or legacy applications to implement their functionality. Components are then loosely coupled to form applications.

Components can be used to develop stand-alone applications, or assembled in a traditional client/server fashion, with components providing server functionality like database access or client functionality on the user interface. Additionally, components allow us to move one step beyond. Components are designed to provide a limited service, and so allow for a true separation of the interface, business logic, and persistence. This allows them to be assembled in a multitier relationship and locate the components/tiers in the best place to run them.

Components can also enable network computing. Network computing allows for dynamic deployment, execution, and management of applications. Network computing architectures feature cacheable dynamic propagation, cross-platform capabilities, automatic platform adjustment, and runtime context storage. Since components are small units of work they are easily cacheable. Components written in Java using the JavaBeans specification are cross-platform, and ActiveX components can run on any Microsoft-friendly platform. Components can be dynamically managed, running on whatever server is appropriate given the current load.

ALTERNATIVES

As shown, component technology can work with client/server and network computing architectures as well as object-oriented development.

The primary alternatives to component-based development are traditional "from scratch" development and package implementation.

Component-based development is superior to "from scratch" in that we anticipate reduced design, development, and testing time, with a lower bug ratio since components are prebuilt and pretested. We spend our time developing new components that are missing from our library, and crafting and testing the links between components.

Component-based development is superior to package implementations in its flexibility. We have more control over what features are included based on our needs; additionally, we can change those features as our needs change.

CHALLENGES

It looks as if component-based development is a good thing. It saves time and money. How can we use components effectively in our own development environments? We will examine several areas: design, component acquisition, implementation, and maintenance.

Remember the idea behind component-based development is to free up our resources to concentrate on finding solutions for business problems. This can take us down several alleys. We may have to make a paradigm choice. If the application needs to be distributed or if the components are developed in multiple languages, we will have to decide whether to use DCOM or CORBA. The environment the application will run in and the available components will influence this choice. When working in an all Microsoft environment DCOM is the obvious choice. Where heterogeneous operating systems are used CORBA is a better choice.

Acquiring components has its own challenges. If they are to be acquired from internal sources, channels for reuse have to be set up. This means components have to be described in a way so that other departments can use them easily. There must be a mechanism for publishing their availability, and accounting systems must reflect the costs of component development and recapture on reuse. In short, the whole corporate structure may have to change.

Purchasing components has other problems that may be influenced by corporate culture. While the ideal is that components can be replaced at will, the reality is that an application may become dependent on a component. Corporations may not desire this dependence. When purchasing components, the financial stability of the provider company and the product stability must be considered. Will the product be supported in the future, and will its functionality and API remain consistent? Resources must be allocated to identify suitable components and evaluate the risk and future considerations that may impact their use.

Integrating components into an application presents challenges to developers and project managers. If the component is a class library, the object model will be affected. Library considerations can affect the subclass relationship. There may be conflicts between releases if you override methods in a subclass or make extensions to the purchased library.

Components also require good configuration management. You may not just be dealing with your own code releases but also with the code releases of vendors, and your releases will impact users of your components. Code releases should be scheduled so downstream users can schedule regression testing. Vendor releases should be integrated into the application release and should undergo full regression testing. While there will be lag time, efforts to keep everyone on the same release should be made, otherwise the releases may diverge into separate products. This will lead to confusion about what the component should do and will require additional maintenance resources.

Another issue for project managers is developer resentment. Many developers feel that code that is not developed in-house is not as good. In addition, there is the old hacker mentality of trying to get into the guts of the component instead of using the interface. This will make integration of vendor-supplied software updates more difficult because the component has lost its "black box" functionality. Staff who can act as advisors on component use are required. The advisors will work with the development teams to recommend components for use on specific projects, and will harvest new components. Rotating development staff through the advisory positions will build knowledge about the component library and development process and help in identifying functionality that is used across development teams.

Finally, there are long-term maintenance considerations. If a component is developed in-house, who is responsible for maintaining it? Is it the developer of the component, or the user who may require modifications to apply it? Organizational change may again be necessary. A software library, with its own dedicated staff, is a good solution to this problem. The library staff is responsible for maintaining the components and managing potential conflict between multiple users. For purchased components, maintenance is also an issue. Vendors may be slow to correct problems, and you may find yourself maintaining the component and feeding the fixes back to the vendor. Even with prompt vendor response, the component must be regression tested and fed into the release schedule.

CONCLUSION

Component-based development offers an environment that can facilitate multitier architecture and allow a true separation of data, business logic, and user interface. It has the potential to increase developer productivity and lower costs, but it is not an approach without risk. The advantages must be weighed against the risks over the entire software life cycle.

References

ActiveX FAQ, Microsoft Corporation, 1996.
Allen, Paul and Frost, Stuart, *Component-Based Development for Enterprise System: Applying the SELECT Perspective,* Cambridge University Press and SIGS Books, 1998.
Austin, T., *Is Network Computing Just a Slogan?* Gartner Group, 1997.
Hamilton, Graham (Ed.), *JavaBeans API Specification Version 1.01,* Sun Microsystems, 1997.
Natis, Y., *Component Models Move to the Server,* Gartner Group, 1997.
Smith, D., *Microsoft Bolsters ActiveX: Developers Should Use Caution,* Gartner Group, 1996.

Chapter 17

Programming Components: COM and CORBA

T.M. Rajkumar and David K. Holthaus

DATABASE TECHNOLOGIES HAVE EVOLVED from the 1970s' hierarchical databases to relational database management systems in the 1980s, and to object databases and client/server systems in the 1990s. While the shift from central processing to client/server did not fully leverage object technology, Internet-based technologies promise to provide the infrastructure for objects. Web-based browsers are poised to become the universal clients for all types of applications. These applications increasingly depend on components, automation, and object layers linking systems.

During the same period, it became less and less possible for software developers to quickly, efficiently, and inexpensively develop all of the functions and modules demanded by customers. Therefore, software development methodologies for Internet and web applications are increasingly focused on component technologies. Component technology breaks the application into intrinsic components and then glues them to create an application. Using components, an application is easier to build, make robust, and deliver quickly.

WHAT IS A COMPONENT?

A component is an independently delivered package of software services. A component is language independent and allows reuse in different language settings. Software components can be either bought from outside or developed in-house. Implementation requires that it be possible to integrate them with other applications using standardized interfaces. They must implement the functionality specified in the interface efficiently. Components may be upgraded with new interfaces.

A component encapsulates methods (i.e., behavior) and data (i.e., attributes). Component must provide encapsulation, but inheritance is not as rigid a requirement. Components may include other components. Components do not necessarily have to be object-oriented, though a large

309

majority of them are because it provides mechanisms to hide the data structure (i.e., encapsulation). Using objects makes components easier to understand and easier to create.

Components may be classified in many different ways. One such classification is based on their function within applications: business or technical components.

Business components usually include the logic that supports a business function or area. These must be developed in-house because it forms part of the core knowledge of an organization. In addition, business knowledge required to create them generally does not exist outside. They are also difficult to develop because organizations must standardize in some manner. There must be a common vision for the organization, and a common architecture must be present to develop business components.

Technical components are represented by elements that are generic and that can be used in a wide variety of business areas. These typically come in the form of GUI components, charting, or interapplication communication components.

A second classification is based on granularity of components. Fine-grained components such as class libraries and encapsulated components are typically small in size and are applicable in a wide range of applications. Although they have large reuse across multiple applications, they are close to code and provide limited productivity to a developer in large-scale applications.

Large-grained components provide broader functionality, but they have to be customized for use. A framework is an example of a large-grained component. Frameworks provide two benefits: flow of control and object-orientation. A framework can be thought of as groupings of components packages or components that belong to a logically related set and together provide a service. They provide a substrate or lattice for other functional components, and a framework can be composed of other frameworks. They also provide the flow of control within components. This helps in the scale of the solution developed.

Object orientation of frameworks helps with the granularity of the components. Ideally, during the assembly stage one wants a small number of large components. However, to increase generality of the solution created, one wants a large number of small components. Large components must be customized prior to delivering needed functionality. Frameworks allow developers to modify and reuse components at various levels of granularity. Frameworks are examples of "white-box" components (i.e., you can look inside the components to reuse them). With inheritance, the internals of parent classes are visible to subclasses in a framework. This provides a developer with the flexibility to modify the behavior of a component. Thus,

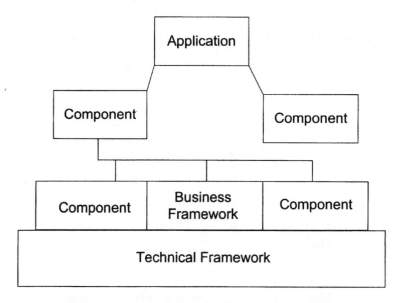

Exhibit 1. Application Integration with Components

frameworks enable customization, allowing developers to build systems quickly using specialized routines.

Frameworks come in two categories: technical and business. Technical frameworks encapsulate software infrastructure such as operating system, graphical user interface (GUI), object request broker (ORB), and transaction processing (TP) monitor. Microsoft Foundation Class (MFC) is an example of such a framework. Business frameworks contain the knowledge of the objects in a business model and the relationships between objects. Typically, they are used to build many different components or applications for a single industry. Technically, while not based on components, Enterprise Resource Planning (ERP) and software such as SAP are examples of business frameworks. An application is generally built with both technical and business frameworks (see Exhibit 1).

CLIENT/SERVER COMPONENTS

Client/server systems typically use three tiers — presentation layer, business layer, and data or server layer (see Exhibit 2). The objective behind the three tiers is to separate the business layer from the presentation and data layers. Changes in one layer are isolated within that layer and do not affect others. Within component technologies, the business layer communicates to the presentation layer and the data layer through an object bus, which is typically an object request broker (ORB). This layering makes the system very scalable.

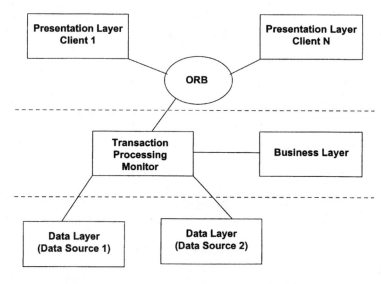

Exhibit 2.   Three-Layer Client/Server Architecture

An ORB is a standard mechanism through which distributed software objects and their clients may interact. Using an ORB, an object and its clients can reside on the same process or in a different process, which they can execute on different hosts connected by a network. The ORB provides the software necessary to convey the requests from clients to objects, and responses from object to client. Since the ORB mechanism hides the details of specific locations, hosts, and conversion of data representation, and hides the underlying communication mechanism, objects and clients can interact freely without having to worry about many details. Thus, distributed applications can incorporate components written in different languages, and are executable on different host and operating system platforms. This flexibility allows the data layer to be composed of both legacy software and relational, object databases.

Business logic may reside on multiple server computers and data may reside on multiple servers. A TP monitor must be used to manage the business logic to provide centralized control. A TP monitor also manages the logic on the serves by providing an array of mission critical services such as concurrency, transactions and security, load balancing, transactional queues, and nested transactions. A TP monitor can prestart components, manage their persistent state, and coordinate their interactions across networks. TP monitors thus become the tool to manage smart components in a client/server system with components.

The real benefit of components in client/server applications is the ability to use the divide-and-conquer approach, which enables clients to scale through distribution. In this approach, an application is built as a series of ORBs. Since an ORB is accessible by any application running on a network, logic is centrally located. Developers can change the ORB to change the functionality of the application. If an ORB runs remotely, it can truly reflect a thin client. ORBs are portable and can be moved from platform to platform without adverse side effects to interoperability, and can provide for load balancing.

COMPONENT STANDARDS

Object models such as ActiveX, which is based on COM, CORBA, and Java Beans define binary standards so that each individual component can be assembled independently. All component standards share the following common characteristics:

- A component interface publishing and directory system
- Methods or actions invocable at run time by a program
- Events or notifications to a program in response to a change of state in an object
- Support for object persistence (to store such information as the state of a component)
- Support for linking components into an application

The following paragraphs describe each standard.

ActiveX, COM, and DCOM

ActiveX is based on COM technology, which formally separates interfaces and implementation. COM clients and objects speak through predefined interfaces. COM interfaces define a contract between a COM and its client. It defines the behavior or capabilities of a software component as a set of methods or properties. Each COM object may offer several different interfaces but must support at least one unknown. COM classes contain the bodies of code that implement interfaces. Each interface and COM class have unique IDs, IID and CLSID, which are used by a client to instantiate an object in a COM server. There two types of object invocations:

- In-process memory (DLLs), where a client and object share the same process space
- Out-of-process model, where a client and object live in different processes

Clients can call either easily. A remoting layer makes the actual call invisible to a client. An ActiveX component is typically an in-process server. An actual object is downloaded to a client's machine. DCOM is COM extended for supporting objects across a network. DCOM allows objects to be freely distributed over several machines, and allows a client to instantiate objects on remote machines.

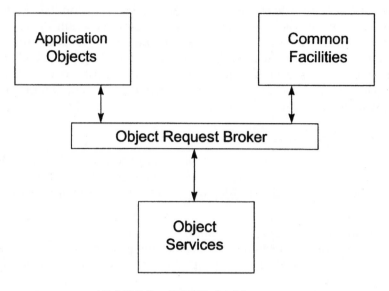

Exhibit 3. CORBA Architecture

CORBA

The Common Object Request Broker Architecture (CORBA) is a set of distributed system standards promoted by an industry standards organization, the Object Management Group. It defines the ORB, a standard mechanism through which distributed software and their clients may interact. It specifies an extensive set of bus-related services for creating and deleting objects, accessing them by name, storing them in a persistent store, externalizing their states, and defining ad hoc relationships between them.

As illustrated in Exhibit 3, the four main elements of CORBA are the following:

- *ORBs*. This defines the object bus.
- *Services*. These define the system-level object frameworks that extend the bus. Some services are security, transaction management, and data exchange.
- *Facilities*. These define horizontal and vertical application frameworks that are used directly by business objects.
- *Application objects*. Also known as business objects or applications, these objects are created by software developers to solve business problems.

A Comparison of CORBA and DCOM

Both CORBA and DCOM use an interface mechanism to expose object functionalities. Interfaces contain methods and attributes as a common means of placing requests to an object. CORBA uses standard models of inheritance from object-oriented languages. DCOM/ActiveX uses the concept of multiple interfaces supported by a single object. DCOM requires that multiple inheritance be emulated through aggregation and containment of interfaces.

Another difference is the notion of object identity. CORBA defines the identity of an object in an object reference, which is unique and persistent. If the object is not in memory, it can be reconstructed based on the reference. DCOM, in contrast, defines the identity in the interface, the reference to the object itself is transient. This can lead to problems when reconnecting because the previously used object cannot be directly accessed.

Reference counting is also different in both. A DCOM object maintains a reference count of all connected clients. It uses pinging of clients to ensure that all clients are alive. CORBA does not need to do remote reference because its object reference model allows the re-creation of an object if it had been prematurely deleted.

CORBA uses two application program interfaces (APIs) and one protocol for object requests. It provides the generated stubs for both static and dynamic invocation. In addition, dynamic skeleton interface allows changes during runtime.

DCOM provides two APIs and two protocols. The standard interface is based on a binary interface that uses method pointer tables called *vtables*. The second API, object linking and embedding (OLE) automation, is used to support dynamic requests through scripting languages. OLE automation uses the IDispatch method to call the server.

CORBA is typically viewed as the middleware of choice for encapsulating legacy systems with new object-oriented interfaces, since it provides support for languages such as COBOL and mainframe systems. DCOM has its roots in desktop computing and is well supported there.

JavaBeans

JavaBeans enables the creation of portable Java objects that can interoperate with non-Java object systems. Unlike ActiveX, which predominately operates in Windows environments, JavaBeans is intended to run in diverse environments as long as there exists a Java Virtual Machine that supports the JavaBean API. JavaBeans provides the standard mechanisms present in all the component technologies. This standard is still continuing to evolve.

Comparison of Java and ActiveX

A trusted JavaBean has all the capabilities of a Java application. However, if you run a JavaBean that has not been signed by a digital source, its

315

capabilities are limited like any other applet. Java also has limited multimedia support. In contrast, ActiveX objects cannot run from the Web unless they are trusted and have access to all of Windows' capabilities. Hence, ActiveX supports multimedia.

ActiveX and Java both use digitally signed certificates to protect against malicious attacks. In addition, JavaBeans is available for a large number of machines and has cross-platform capability. ActiveX is most widely available on the Windows desktop.

Irrespective of the technology standard, bridges, available from different vendors, can translate between standards. Hence, organizations should choose a standard in which they have the greatest expertise for analysis, design, and development.

HOW TO DESIGN AND USE COMPONENTS

As shown in Exhibit 1, applications are built from the composition and aggregation of other, simpler components, which may build on frameworks. Application design is broken into component and application development. Component development is divided into component design and implementation. A good knowledge of an application's domain is necessary to develop frameworks and components. In general, the steps of domain definition, specification, design, verification, implementation, and validation must be done prior to application. The following sections explain these steps.

Domain Definition. This defines the scope, extent, feasibility, and cost justification for a domain. An organization must define the product it plans to build as well as define the different business and technical areas that must be satisfied through the use of software.

Domain Specification. This defines the product family (i.e., framework) used for application engineering. It includes a decision model, framework requirements, and a hierarchy of component requirements. The decision model specifies how components will be selected, adapted, and reused to create complete application systems. Product requirements are arrived at by analyzing similarities in functions, capabilities, and characteristics as well as variances among them. The component part of the product family is represented hierarchically. When an organization considers components, it must consider not only what the component will do for the domain now but also in the future.

Domain Design. A domain expert must work with a component designer to use a modeling methodology and extract the design patterns that occur in that domain. Design patterns are repeatable designs used in the construction of an application. The architecture, component design, and generation design are specified here. Architecture depicts a set of relationships among the components such as hierarchical, communication, and database. Component design describes the internal logic flow, data flows, and dependencies. Generation design is a procedure that describes how to select, adapt, and compose application systems using the decision model and architecture.

Domain Verification. This process evaluates the consistency of a domain's requirements, specification, and design.

Domain Implementation. During this procedure, components are either developed or acquired off the shelf to fit the architecture. Each component must be tested within the common architecture it supports as well as any potential architecture. Certification of components must be acquired when necessary. It must also decide how to store it in repositories, the implementation of application generation procedures, and how to transition to an assembly mode.

Domain Validation. This evaluates the quality and effectiveness of the application engineering support. Application engineering consists of the following:

- *Defining requirements.* In this process, an application model that defines a customer's requirements is defined. This model uses the notation specified in the domain engineering steps. Typically, a use case model can be used to identify requirements. Use cases are behaviorally related sequences of transactions that a user of a system will perform in a dialogue
- *Selecting components and design.* Using rules in the decision model, reusable components are selected based on the component specification (capabilities and interfaces) and design (component logic and parameters).
- *Generating software.* The application is then generated by aggregating components and writing any custom software.
- *Testing.* Testing involves the testing of use cases and, components, and integration testing and load testing.
- *Generating documentation.* The application documentation is created.

MANAGING THE COMPONENT LIFE CYCLE PROCESS

Developing with components means an organization must move from doing one-of-a-kind development to a reuse-driven approach. The aim is to reorganize the resources to meet users' needs with greater efficiency. The steps in this process are discussed in the following sections.

Establishing a Sponsor. This involves identifying component reuse opportunities and shows how their exploitation can contribute to an organization's IS goals. Sponsors must be identified and sold on the various ideas.

Exhibit 4. Assessment of Component Potential for Reuse

Concern	What to Ask
Domain potential	In the given domain, are there applications that could benefit from reuse?
Existing domain components	Are expertise and components available?
Commonalities and variables	Is there a sufficient fit between need and available components? Can they be customized?
Domain stability	Is the technology stable? Do the components meet stable standards? Are the components portable across environments?

Exhibit 5. Assessment of an Organization's Capability to Reuse Components
Columns

Application Development	Component Development	Management	Process and Technology
Component identification for use in application	Needs identification, interface, and architecture definition	Organizational commitment, planning	Process definition and integration
Component evaluation and verification	Components needs and solutions	Managing security of components	Measurement and continuous process improvement
Application integrity	Component quality, value, security, and reusability determination	Intergroup (component and application) coordination	Repository tool support and training

Developing a Plan. This plan should guide the management of the component development process. The plan includes the following:

1. *Reuse assessment.* This assessment should evaluate the potential opportunity for reuse, identify where the organization stands with respect to reuse, and evaluate the organization's reuse capability Exhibits 4, 5, and 6 can be used to conduct the assessment.
2. *Development of alternative strategies.* On the basis of the assessment, an organization can develop a strategy to implement and align the process, as well as choose the appropriate methodologies and tools.
3. *Development of metrics.* In the planning stage for implementation, metrics must be used to measure success.

Exhibit 6. Organizational Reuse Capability Model

Stage	Key Characteristics

Opportunistic	• Projects individually develop reuse plan
	  – Existing components are reused
	  – Throughout project life cycle, reuse of components is identified
	  – Components under configuration and repository control

Integrated	• Reuse activities integrated into standard development process
	  – Components are designed for current and anticipated needs
	  – Common architectures and frameworks used for applications
	  – Tools tailored for components and reuse

Leveraged	• An application-line reuse strategy is developed to maximize component reuse over a set of related applications
	  – Components are developed to allow reuse early in the life cycle
	  – Process performance is measured and analyzed
	  – Tools supporting reuse are integrated with the organization's software development efforts

Anticipating	• New opportunities for reuse of components build on the organization's reuse capability
	  – Effectiveness of reuse is measured
	  – Organization's reuse method is flexible and can adapt to new process and product environment

Implementation. The organization finally implements the plan. Incentives can be used to promote reuse by individuals and the organization.

CONCLUSION

Component technology is changing the way client/server applications are being developed. Supporting tools for this software environment are rapidly emerging to make the transition from regular application development to a component-based development. With proper training of staff, planning, and implementation, organizations can smoothly transfer to this new mode of development and rapidly develop and efficiently deliver client/server applications.

Chapter 18
Managing Object Libraries
Polly Perryman Kuver

SOFTWARE REUSE IS A CONCEPT that has been bounced around in the industry for years and years; still, information systems developers are searching for ways to master its implementation. The principles of object-oriented design and development have shown themselves to be a starting point for developing reusable software. Application of the principles, however, only offers a partial solution since compliance with the principles and the development of objects does not automatically result in reusability. It requires a great deal of planning and effective management of object libraries. This is because until the commonality of the object types is defined and effectively managed, the value of software reuse cannot be realized.

Many companies miss out on valuable opportunities to streamline processes while improving product because they do not have a cohesive plan to implement object library management. Other companies lose out because they think object library management is a practice limited to documented object-oriented design methodologies. Still other companies use clumsy procedures intending to promote software reuse without ever realizing the importance of planning for software reuse, which is itself a form of object library management. When the essential components of object library management are understood and implemented, these missed opportunities can knock again.

One of the biggest mistakes companies make is "throwing" objects into a library without a scheme for making sure the team benefits from them. For example, a company had a practice of telling coders if they develop a routine that others can use, to put it in Library X. This was so everyone could access and use the code. This had a major impact on one project. Several developers faithfully added routines to a common library that indeed saved development time for database access, output, and a number of other common functions. A young fellow we will refer to as Sam contributed a particularly well-used routine. The problem was that while Sam's common object executed beautifully, it was unfortunately a resource hog, and when it was used by other developers it created problems. The impact of modifying the object to correct and improve the performance issues and retest the 50-plus

0-8493-9979-3/99/$0.00+$.50
© 1999 by CRC Press LLC

programs using the object was significant. The schedule delay was unacceptable to the customer; funding for the project was withdrawn.

On another project where the "throw-it-in" approach to object library management was used without a master plan, coders duplicated efforts by individually creating their own renditions of routines for common use. The object library became so convoluted with multiple objects for similar types of functions that no one was able to use it. The benefits gained by the concept were preempted entirely by the approach.

So how can object library management be implemented effectively without impinging on the creativity of talented staff? It basically depends on three things to be successful. The first is appointment of a design authority. The designated design authority assumes full responsibility for establishing the highest classification for objects, the characteristics for base objects within the classification, and determining which objects possess commonality to the system for potential reuse within the application, upgrades, and related products. The person who takes on the role of the design authority must communicate beyond the structure of the objects, making certain that the development team understands the standards and methods used to structure, document, build, and subsequently maintain the object library.

The second area for success lies in the effective use of basic configuration management functions such as version control and release management. The implementation of the configuration management functions may use any of the configuration management tools in the market today, such as Rational-Atria ClearCase or Intersolv's PVCS, that have been upgraded to work with large objects. The configuration management functions may also be implemented using internally developed tools and methods when purchase of these tools would strain the budget.

The third area for success is quality control and testing. The quality control and testing that must be performed covers more than the demonstration that the coded object works to specifications. It must also ensure that development personnel are complying with the structure established for object management that allows for improvement in the processes used by development personnel using the object library.

Object library management can and should be practiced regardless of the development methodology being used because it offers direct benefits to developers and customers alike. The most direct benefit of object library management is better product at lower cost. While this may sound like a television commercial for every imaginable product on the market, from baby diapers to automobiles, the positive effects of object library management can demonstrate improved productivity through team-focused procedures and higher quality through uniformity, consistency, and, most importantly, meaningful design controls.

With the components of success identified, it is important to note that as languages, systems, and user applications become increasingly complex to program, the need for object management takes on greater implications in the life of a product. As many companies are finding out, the effects of poor object library management impacts not only initial development of a product but results in spiraling chaos with the maintenance and upgrade of the product.

THE DESIGN AUTHORITY

The design authority is a role rather than a position. The role may be filled by a single individual, such as the engineering manager, the lead design engineer, the system architect, or by a group of people who work together to satisfy the goals of object library management. The critical point is to define the role and fill it. It is important not to confuse the design authority role with the responsibilities of a configuration control board whose function is quite different.

Once the design authority role has been assigned, the work of managing object libraries can begin in earnest. Using input from the users, a rudimentary framework for objects can be set up. It is here that the design authority may elect to use the Unified Modeling Language (UML). Whether UML or some other method is used, it is of particular importance that the system requirements are clearly defined, analyzed, and documented. They are the basis upon which all of the design and system testing are based and they must be clearly understood by all parties. The initial object framework can and probably will be a hodgepodge of objects and classifications both at the highest level and at base levels. The reason for this is that the users will be providing their input at different levels. For instance, one or two of the users may be listing specific types of reports they need to generate on a cyclical basis, while other users may be stating their desire to employ animation and sound without specifying what type of animation or sound. The result is that input will be provided on various levels and the design authority must be able to determine the value to place on the information.

This may be better explained by referring to some of the early discussions about object-oriented programming (see the Recommended Reading list at the end of this chapter) in which a classic shape example was used for clarification. In the example, shapes became the classification for managing objects that performed functions on a shape, such as changing the shape's size or moving it. The type of shapes — circles, squares, and triangles — inherit the capabilities of the objects. This allows functions to be performed on any type of shape, thus setting up the ability for reuse of the functions on shape types added to the system at later dates.

323

It is the design authority who begins to set up a framework for new and continuing development. Decisions will need to be made as to whether the input falls into the circle/square category, the perform-on category, or the shapes category. If it is a shape category it will hold objects. If it is an object it will do something. It is the objects, then, that need to be constructed. It is the classification and management of these objects that takes the design authority to the next critical work effort.

In order for an object to do something, it needs to possess both the data and function qualities necessary to perform. Peter Coad and Edward Yourdon expressed these qualities as an equation: Object-oriented = Objects + Classification + Inheritance + Communication with Messages.[1] The design authority, in maximizing the potential of solid object library management, must be able to cross-reference and promote the use and reuse of these qualities in the development environment. For instance, objects in an edit classification may include copy, move, and delete. The construction of the object must permit these functions to be performed on any designated text or graphic unit. As such, the design authority can, within the object library management structure, ensure the reuse of these objects from one product to another and from one upgrade to the next. In planning the object libraries, the design authority must also consider those types of objects that will more likely be upgraded in the short and long terms. While the quickness of advancing technology may make this step seem like crystal ball engineering, the design authority will have responsibility for working with management to minimize technological risks and keep development moving in a forward rather than circular direction.

It is not the role of the design authority to determine how the defined object structure is implemented within the configuration system. That function is performed by specialists in configuration management.

CONFIGURATION MANAGEMENT

Configuration management is a function best performed by a specialist who has three principal tasks. The first is making certain the version control mechanisms sustain the object classifications and hierarchy structure laid out by the design authority. The second is ensuring that the version control mechanisms put into place support the application development staff in easy retrieval and storage of objects. The third is tracking the correct object versions and building them into defined releases of the product. Whether your organization has a configuration management tool in place or not, when the decision to implement an object library management plan is made, a serious comparative capability evaluation of the existing tool and those available in today's market must be made.

Most of the recognized configuration management tools available today will at a minimum provide version control and support release builds.

Nearly all of the tools allow text, graphic, and multimedia object storage. The trick in selecting and using a tool for object library management is in evaluating the available tools in relationship to the scope of the efforts it will be supporting and the manpower investment the company is willing to make to ensure the successful implementation of the tool. It is critical that during this evaluation focus is maintained on the design structure and intended reuse capabilities desired. This means it needs to be evaluated not only for what it will do today, but whether it will meet the needs of your organization in terms of future growth. For example, current plans for your product over the next 5 years are to support both Windows and Macintosh users. The tool that best fits the design structure and size requirements for the project only runs in a UNIX environment today. The question as to how the developers will effectively be able to take advantage of the version control features of the tool must be addressed, as does how clean the build feature of the tool really stays.

A similar dilemma presents itself when an organization uses off-site developers for various pieces of the system. One example can be taken from a company whose off-site animation staff developed its product, which was eventually embedded within the company's primary product. It turned out that the operating system used by the off-site developers was not compatible with the configuration management tool being evaluated. A number of work-arounds were drafted and discussed, but the bottom line was that each of them made the version control and build processes cumbersome and less reliable. A lesser known configuration management tool offered the necessary interface for this off-site work and provided all of the other features in a somewhat diminished capacity. The question that had to be asked and answered was which tool was going to best meet the goals of the organization now and in the future. If the organization was willing to fumble through for a while and gamble that the interface for off-site programming was going to be constructed, or the off-site programmers could be transitioned to a different compatible operating system, then perhaps the more well-known tool would be a good choice. If the need for better object management was immediate and the organization was willing to gamble on the eventual expansion of the lesser known tool's capabilities, then the less sophisticated tool would be a good choice.

These examples are merely representative of the types of questions that must be part and parcel of a configuration management tool evaluation. Other important questions include, but are not limited to:

- What support does the vendor supply in configuring the tool in your organization's environment?
- If interfaces are going to be constructed by the tool vendor, will they become part of the configuration management tool product line or

stay a customized piece of software your organization will become responsible for maintaining?

- What training is required by your organization's staff to set up and operate the tool effectively?
- How many man-hours must be devoted to maintaining the tool in order to ensure its successful use?

Even when the current in-house tool meets the technical specifications for object library management and object development, there are still set-up factors to be considered in assessing the planned design authority structure in relationship to the current configuration of the tool. New areas may need to be prepared and a different hierarchy may need to be defined to support the build features of the tool. This work cannot be overlooked during the evaluation process.

Another stumbling block to successful object library management is in the planning of releases. Here the design authority and configuration management specialists need to work closely to define the contents and status of each release. It is not sufficient for the design authority to send an e-mail that says include x, y, and z. Success is based on knowing not only that x, y, and z are in the release, but also knowing the problem state of x, y, and z within the overall scheme of the object library management plan. In other words, the plan for Release A will include version 2.2 of x, version 2.3 of y, and version 4 of z, and we know that version 2.3 of y includes a few glitches that should be fixed before the release date but will not crash the software if they are not fixed. However, version 4 of z may cause some problems, in which case the fallback plan is to use version 2.8 of z because version 3 of z had to be recalled. This is the type of information that becomes part of the release plan composed by the design authority and the configuration management specialist. This, of course, brings us right to the third component needed for successful object library management, quality control and testing.

QUALITY CONTROL AND TESTING

How did the design authority and configuration management specialist make the decision on which version of z to use if the possible problems with z surfaced during the release build? The answer is that version 2.8 was a thoroughly tested and proven object within the system and it did not have a relationship with either x or y. It would not need to be retested. It could just be used because the quality control supporting solid object library management includes traceability, predictability, and uniformity, which are achieved by testing the design, the constructed objects, the object relationships, and the object system. Keep in mind that objects that have been tested can be used and used and used without having to test and test and test. New development will occur in a more orderly manner because the structure laid out within the object library management plan will lend itself to a clearer and more logical next step. The quality controls are essential in taking the management of objects from basic reuse in the initial product to a viable expanded product vision.

Working with the design authority, quality control personnel complement the object library management plan while imposing and enforcing these controls, because the structure of the objects and the communication from the design authority to the development staff ensures that everyone is working toward the same goal. The quality group does the testing of the object and ensures that it meets the construction and use guidelines established. Quality control accomplishes this by being a part of the development rather than an appendage to development, validating the object structure and conducting walkthroughs where questions and issues can be raised and resolved. The quality group should work closely with the configuration management specialists to ensure the integrity of the released product by validating both the configuration of the tool being used for version control and release management, and verification of the product release plan.

SUMMARY

The goal is to maximize an organization's competitive edge in the marketplace. The components for successful object library management presented in this chapter can be raised to whatever level of sophistication best fits your organization. The important thing is to plan and manage the objects constructed.

On a small project the biggest problem may appear to be people resources. Keep in mind that there are three roles that need to be played for success. This may mean that the lead designer is also the design authority and a developer and the configuration management specialist. The quality control and testing role, however, must be performed by someone other than this person. If necessary, even a nontechnical project manager can perform the quality control and testing role as long as the concepts and goals of the project are clearly stated and the basics of object library management are understood. The greatest benefit to the small project is that communication between the design authority and developers is stronger and the setup of the configuration management tool is generally much easier.

On a large project there are larger problems. There, the design authority may be a team of people for which some protocol and tie-breaking mechanisms need to be laid out from the start in order to keep the design moving. Communication between the design authority and the developers is more difficult to maintain. The setup of the configuration management tool may take several weeks, and training sessions may need to be conducted to ensure that developers fully understand what is expected of them. And quality control and testing is more involved and necessary. The biggest benefit in a large project is the value of being able to gain a greater long-range vision for the application or product, and in being able to cross-train personnel in many areas.

The point is to take action whether the project is the conversion of a legacy system to the new technology, or the development of new systems with existing and future technology. Begin by committing in black and white what your organization needs to accomplish. Then establish an organization to assess and plan for that accomplishment. Once the plan is formulated, provide training whether it is vendor-supplied, seminars, or in-house group sessions. Success can be repeated over and over again when there is a plan to implement and an understanding of the technology. Then appoint the design authority, start evaluating configuration management tools, and prepare a testing strategy that will meet your organization's goals for object management.

Notes

1. Coad, Peter, and Yourdon, Edward, *Object-oriented Analysis*, Prentice-Hall, Engle-wood Cliffs, NJ, 1990.

Recommended Reading

Jacobson, Ivar, Griss, Martin, and Jonsson, Patrik, *Software Reuse*, ACM Press, pp 60-61, 117, 356 and 436, 1997.

Entsminger, Gary, *The Tao of Objects, A Beginner's Guide to Object Oriented Programming.* M & T Publishing, Inc., 1990.

Chapter 19
Java Application Development Including Database and Network Integration

Nathan J. Muller

Developed by Sun Microsystems and introduced in 1995, Java is described by the company as "a simple, robust, object-oriented, platform-independent, multi-threaded, dynamic, general-purpose programming environment."

Simply put, Java is a scaled down version of the C++ programming language that omits many rarely used, poorly understood, and confusing features. It is used for creating applets for use on the Internet, intranets, and any other complex, distributed network. Java provides the capability for distributing specific software functions to end-users in the form of applets, regardless of their location, hardware platform, hardware storage space, or processing power.

While Java is a compiled general purpose language that can be used to build a variety of business applications, JavaScript is a creation of Netscape Communications and is an interpreted scripting language that is focused on manipulating documents on the World Wide Web. JavaScript provides the means of adding interesting features to documents published on the Web, particularly those rendered by Netscape Navigator (version 2.0 or above). The scripts are embedded in the HTML document itself.

The hypertext markup language (HTML) provides a set of tags that tell web browsers how to render various elements of a document so it will be viewed as the author intended. A script placed between an HTML document's <HEAD>and </HEAD> tags can add such things as simple animations, a scrolling banner, a digital clock, and other features to the web page. It can also be used to open additional windows from within the browser's main window.

With browser software that is Java-enabled, the user has access to the functionality provided by Java applets and Java scripts. A browser that is "Java-enabled" is one that has a built-in Java interpreter. If the browser software is not Java-enabled, the applets and scripts are not available to the user and, in most cases, will be hidden from view. However, JavaScript offers limited functionality and it is not to be confused with Java.

JAVA APPLETS

Applets are distributed programs that are sent from web servers to web clients (i.e., PCs equipped with browsers) that have built-in Java interpreters. Applets can reduce hardware requirements at the desktop for many casual end users because both applications storage and processing take place at the server.

With the exception of the browser, software is maintained only at the server site, reducing the burden on IS staff. Applet technology can also help reduce the learning curve because casual users are given access to only the features they need for completing specific business transactions.

Applets provide World Wide Web users with ready access from their local systems to additional web page content that can be delivered in a more visually compelling way, such as through the use of animation. The user can view and interact with an applet—such as requesting that a product image rotate to provide a fuller view of its appearance—and then discard it when it is no longer needed. Applets reside on a web server and are called from within a hypertext markup language (HTML) document. This allows the same applet to be used by many users. Applets also provide many other functions, such as access to corporate databases.

For example, through an electronic requisition applet, users can have easy access to central databases for online corporate and vendor catalogs. Users can also download an electronic form for requesting purchases. Once the user has completed a request, it is automatically routed for approval and processing through a workflow application. Casual users of the procurement system can access the applet via a browser without running a copy of the client application on their desktops.

DEVELOPING CORPORATE APPLICATIONS WITH JAVA

Whether Java is a good choice for corporate applications development depends on how well Java can contribute to improvements in the following key areas of IS:

- Speed of applications development
- Applications effectiveness and efficiency
- Program and programmer portability
- Development costs
- Maintenance and support
- Technical training

Speed of Applications Development

The Java language was designed as an object-oriented language from the ground up. The needs of distributed, client/server-based systems coincide with the packaged, message-passing paradigms of object-based software.

To function within increasingly complex, network-based environments, programming systems must adopt object-oriented concepts. The Java language provides a clean and efficient object-based development environment.

A key feature of object-oriented programming is code extensibility, a characteristic of objects that lets application developers reuse them to build, maintain, and enhance applications without having to access the program's source code. The ability to create new objects from existing objects, change them to suit specific needs, and otherwise reuse them across different applications offers an effective means of developing applications faster.

Applications Effectiveness and Efficiency

Large corporate applications development environments stress effectiveness over efficiency. Getting the work done is valued more than getting the work done efficiently. Being a simpler language than C++, Java allows programmers to concentrate on the application instead of the mechanics of building the application.

For example, programmers need not worry about managing memory allocation, freeing memory, and keeping track of what memory can be freed because Java self-manages memory. Automatic garbage collection is an integral part of the Java language and runtime system. Once an object has been allocated, the runtime system keeps track of the object's status and automatically reclaims memory when objects are no longer in use, freeing memory for future use.

Java's memory allocation model and automatic garbage collection make programming tasks easier and cut down on program bugs, crashes, and memory leaks that inhibit performance. In general, these Java features provide better performance than would be obtained through explicit memory management.

Freeing programmers of this and other tedious responsibilities allows work to be done efficiently as well as effectively.

Program and Programmer Portability

Most large corporations use a mix of computing platforms. Although a common application programming interface (*API*) can reduce the cost of corporate applications in heterogeneous computing environments, it is inadequate for the development of network-centric applications. Consequently, many programmers have given up on them, preferring instead to specialize in developing applications for one platform or another.

With a ported Java runtime environment for every platform architecture and a rich set of class libraries, programmers are finding it easier to develop applications that can run on multiple platforms. Applications written with Java are platform-independent because the code is entirely portable.

The Java *virtual machine* is based on a well-defined porting layer, primarily based on the Portable Operating System Interface for Unix (POSIX) interface standard, an industry standard definition of a portable system interface. Porting to new architectures is a relatively straightforward task.

Not only are the programs portable, the programmers are portable as well. This means the corporate applications group can develop programs for any architecture. Because the client and server parts of an application can both be written in the same language, there is no longer a need for special groups scattered throughout the enterprise, such as the Sun Solaris C++ group in research, the PC Visual Basic programmers in document distribution, or the GNU developers working on special projects. Java requires only a corporate applications group.

Development Costs

Traditionally, the cost of developing applications on a workstation has been high. Although the overall hardware and long-term maintenance costs of a Sun Solaris workstation, for example, are very attractive to big businesses, the additional cost of software development with C++ is prohibitive to all but the largest companies.

The use of the corporate intranet and Java-based applications development tools can lower the cost of corporate computing considerably.

Java tools are priced at affordable PC levels. The success of the Internet has leveled the pricing of software to the point where software for high-powered Unix workstations costs nearly the same as versions that run on PCs. This is a pricing trend that should become more prevalent with Java-based software tools.

With the growing public-domain and shareware tools communities that routinely include source code, corporate programmers have a rich selection of tools from which to choose. The introduction of Java has spawned a whole new market for tools that enable programmers and non-programmers to create, test, deploy, and document network-aware applications.

Program Support and Maintenance

An ongoing requirement with corporate software is the demand for program support. Although Java is not a panacea, it has several features that make certain tasks easier for programmers.

Javadoc is a component of the Java Development Kit (JDK). If programmers use certain commenting conventions in their Java source code, Javadoc will scan the code for these comments and create *HTML* pages that can be viewed with a browser. This eases the job of creating programmer documentation.

With regard to maintenance, Java applications can run on the server. If there are changes to the applications, they are made at the server. Programmers and network administrators do not have to worry about distributing changes to the PC. The next time users log in, they automatically get the most current applet. With Java, network administrators do not have to worry about runtime licenses or the distribution of dynamic-link libraries (*DLLs*) to all the PC clients.

Technical Training

A primary goal in the development of Java was to make it a simple language that could be programmed without extensive training and would be roughly attuned to current software practice. The fundamental concepts of the Java language can be grasped quickly, allowing programmers to be productive from the start.

Making the Java language a minimal subset of C++ while simultaneously retaining its look and feel means that programmers can migrate to the Java language easily and be productive quickly. The Java language learning curve can be as quick as a couple of days.

Programmers with knowledge of C++ who have some experience programming with a *graphical user interface (GUI)* library will be able to learn it quickly. If a programmer does not know C++ but knows another object-oriented programming language, it might take longer to learn the essentials of Java, but it is not necessary to learn C++ before learning Java.

If a programmer does not know any object-oriented language, the essentials of object-oriented technology must be learned before anything else. This knowledge can then be applied to Java.

New gateway software is designed to aid applications developers by translating C++ components into Java automatically. The gateway software operates during the build stage of an application, enabling a Java-based program to recognize C++ components and automatically generate a Java interface. Not only will this kind of software greatly reduce the Java learning curve, it will speed the migration of legacy applications to network-aware Java applications.

JAVA FOR NON-PROGRAMMERS

There are now Java development tools designed for web authors instead of programmers. These tools provide a visual interface builder for Java that automatically generates Java code, allowing applications to be created simply by dragging and dropping typical controls such as buttons, list boxes, and menus. The generated source code can be used as provided or modified.

Other products allow users to build Java-based animations for web pages. Users can build their own or customize animations selected from a library that comes with the development kit.

Visual authoring tools for creating Java applets allow users to create media-rich Java applets without the need for programming or scripting. Users work in a what-you-see-is-what-you-get (*WYSIWYG*) page-layout environment, visually specifying òliveó objects through a series of drag-and-drop actions.

INTEGRATING JAVA AND THE DATABASE

An important issue among Java developers is how to access corporate data necessary to support Java applications. Numerous solutions are becoming available to connect web-based Java applications to the data on servers and hosts. That connection is critical if Java is to be more than just a technology for building small applets that can be downloaded to and run inside a web browser. Until Java applets can make use of corporate data, their usefulness is limited.

To remedy this situation, Sun Microsystems' JavaSoft unit, which develops and markets Java tools, has come up with the Java Data Base Connectivity (JDBC) specification, which is intended to compete with Microsoft's *Open Data Base Connectivity (ODBC)* solution for allowing Java applets to connect to different vendors' SQL databases. The JDBC specification is expected to enable the building of large-scale Java-based application servers in corporate client/server networks. Without this type of interface, programmers would have to master a different interface for each database used by their company.

Bridges to ODBC and CORBA

The JavaSoft unit even offers a bridging tool to link Java applications to databases that support Microsoft's *ODBC* interface. With the bridge, Java developers need only work with JDBC to build database applications that can also access existing *ODBC* data. The bridge is fully compatible with existing *ODBC* drivers.

In the future, as JDBC drivers are built for specific databases—such as those from Ingres, Oracle, and Sybase—developers can choose a pure JDBC link to databases or use the bridge to *ODBC.* JDBC will support interchangeable database drivers by means of a driver manager that would automatically load the proper JDBC driver for connecting to a specific database.

Third-party middleware solutions are emerging that link Java objects over the network using the Internet Inter-ORB Protocol (IIOP) specified in the *Common Object Request Broker Architecture (CORBA).*Through this *CORBA* connection, developers can connect new Java applets to existing C or C++ programs. With the addition of an "object wrapper," this connection also links Java applets to host transactions and data.

At this writing, Sun's JavaSoft unit has announced plans to add new code that lets Java objects on different computers easily work with each other without additional middleware such as an object request broker (ORB). Javasoft is also developing the added capability of letting Java objects interact across a firewall. Firewalls control public Internet access to corporate backbones, but also prevent client/server applications from working across broad portions of the Net.

INTEGRATING JAVA WITH AN OPERATING SYSTEM

Because Java is an interpreted language that relies on easily ported underlying code to talk to the operating system, it can easily run on Windows, Unix, and other common operating systems. Efforts are underway by the major operating system vendors to integrate Java into their systems, providing a way to make Java more accessible to developers and users. Developers will have easier access to Java programming on their platform of choice, and users will be able to run Java applets and applications outside of their web browsers.

DEVELOPMENT IN AN INTEGRATED ENVIRONMENT

Microsoft is embedding Java into future versions of Windows 95 and Windows NT. Apple will integrate Java into its Macintosh, Pippin, and Newton operating systems, as well as into its authoring technologies, Internet servers, client software, and CyberDog Internet suite. Silicon Graphics (SGI) plans to embed Java in its IRIX operating system, and Sun will embed it in Solaris. IBM Corp. is embedding Java in all its client and server product lines this year, including Lotus Notes and Merlin, its forthcoming new version of OS/2, as well as *AIX*, OS/400, and OS/390 (formerly MVS).

Other companies that plan to integrate Java into their operating systems include Hewlett-Packard, Hitachi Ltd., Novell, Santa Cruz Operation, and Tandem Computers.

Native Applications

Putting the Virtual Machine—Java's native operating environment—inside the operating system will give Java applications the speed of those written in a compiled language and still allow them to run cross-platform. In addition to speed, the benefits to users of a Java-embedded operating system include access to a greater number of applications that they can run natively, with or without a browser.

What remains to be seen is whether the operating system vendors will make extensions and additions in the form of *APIs* that could result in serious interoperability problems. If this happens, not only is the goal of Java's portability defeated, but the industry could see Java fragment into a multitude of flavors reminiscent of UNIX.

JAVA SECURITY

The Java language was designed to operate in distributed environments. With security features designed into the language and runtime system, the Java language enables construction of tamper-free programs. In the networked environment, Java programs are secure from intrusion by unauthorized code attempting to get behind the scenes and create viruses or invade file systems.

Java's networking package provides the interfaces to handle the various wide area network protocols, including *hypertext transfer protocol (HTTP), file transfer protocol (FTP)*, and *Telnet*, among others. The networking package can be set up to:

- Disallow all network accesses
- Allow network accesses to only the hosts from which the code was imported
- Allow network accesses only outside the firewall if the code came from outside
- Allow all network accesses

MAKING DUMB TERMINALS SMART

Several vendors, including IBM, offer *HTML* gateways that give users of 3270 and 5250 terminals easy access to the Web and corporate intranets. The gateway converts 3270 or 5250 datastreams into *HTTP* to call up Internet or intranet hosts.

SNA Integration

With *HTML* and other web protocol support, 3270 and 5250 users will be able to participate in the Java environment as well. In essence, Java makes dumb terminals smart.

IBM estimates that more than 50 percent of its Systems Network Architecture (*SNA*) users will need Internet or intranet access. But with more than $20 trillion invested in *SNA* applications and about 40,000 *SNA* networks worldwide, users are not quite ready to throw away their *SNA* networks just yet.

Equipping 3270 and 5250 terminals to handle *HTML* and Java allows users to choose between web browsers or terminal emulators when accessing host data. Browsers are appropriate for accessing host programs and data over intranets. Web browsers give users a structured, graphical view of data that facilitates intuitive point-and-click navigation through large databases.

In many cases, terminal emulation offers faster response time for data retrieval than graphically oriented web browsers. For some applications, terminal emulators may be the preferred tools because familiar function keys provide a fast way to navigate files and initiate processes. Furthermore, certain types of legacy data are easier to import into desktop applications than web-formatted data.

With access to *Transmission Control Protocol and Internet Protocol* (TCP/IP) and *SNA* networks, the huge investment in terminals and legacy applications can be extended while giving users access to the Web and Java-enabled applications.

CONCLUSION

The early success of the C++ programming language owes a great deal to its ability to access legacy code written in C. Likewise, Java preserves much of C++ and offers a number of compelling benefits: it is portable, high-level, secure, and easy to master. Together, these and other benefits of Java have the potential to free companies from the dependence of long applications-development cycles and let them adapt to changing business needs faster.

Once written, Java applications can be run unchanged on any operating system to which the Java interpreter has been ported. The code for an application written for Solaris-based SPARCstations, for example, can be copied to a Windows 95 Pentium workstation and will run with no recompilation. In contrast, programming in C with various cross-platform tools promises portability, but generally there is still some code to rework before the application can work on another platform.

Java does have some shortcomings. IS departments that are planning to deploy critical production systems built with Java must weigh its benefits against its shortcomings. For example:

- *There are differences in the way Java applications are displayed in different GUIs.* For example, a scroll bar works on UNIX but not on Windows NT. These are the kinds of problems that can be expected in the first release of an applications-development tool and that will be ironed out in future releases of Java.
- *Security is still evolving.* Java's security does not let a downloaded Java application read or write to the local hard disk. This prevents a virus written in Java from being able to infect the computer's data and programs. The Netscape browser further restricts the application so that it can only communicate back to the server from which the data came, so a downloaded Java application cannot raid other servers. Yet these protections also limit what the application and end user can do. For example, spreadsheet users would not be able to update a local image of their spreadsheet from a central source because of the security restrictions in Java. Ultimately, Java will need to permit users to configure trusted applications.
- *Heavy-duty processing is limited.* Although Java's performance is adequate for the kinds of applications it is being used for now—interactive client applications—it must become faster at the server where heavy application processing is done. Java's code uses an interpreter as the application is being executed, so performance is slower than compiled third-generation code, such as C. The introduction of just-in-time (JIT) compilers for the Java clients and machine-code compilers for Java servers will make Java comparable in performance to raw C code.

Section V
Integrated Databases

Chapter 20
Distributed
Database Design
Elizabeth N. Fong
Charles L. Sheppard
Kathryn A. Harvill

A DISTRIBUTED DATABASE ENVIRONMENT ENABLES A USER TO ACCESS DATA residing anywhere in a corporation's computer network without regard to differences among computers, operating systems, data manipulation languages, or file structures. Data that are actually distributed among multiple remote computers will appear to the user as if they resided on the user's own computer. This scenario is functionally limited with today's distributed database technology; true distributed database technology is still a research consideration. The functional limitations are generally in the following areas:

- Transaction management
- Standard protocols for establishing a remote connection
- Independence of network technology

Transaction management capabilities are essential to maintaining reliable and accurate databases. In some cases, today's distributed database software places responsibility for managing transactions on the application program. In other cases, transactions are committed or rolled back at each location independently, which means that it is not possible to create a single distributed transaction. For example, multiple-site updates require multiple transactions.

CURRENT DBMS TECHNOLOGY

In today's distributed database technology, different gateway software must be used and installed to connect nodes using different distributed database management system (DBMS) software. Therefore, connectivity among heterogeneous distributed DBMS nodes is not readily available (i.e., available only through selected vendor markets).

0-8493-9976-9/99/$0.00+$.50
© 1999 by CRC Press LLC

In some instances, distributed DBMS software is tied to a single network operating system. This limits the design alternatives for the distributed DBMS environment to the products of a single vendor.

It is advisable to select a product that supports more than one network operating system. This will increase the possibility of successfully integrating the distributed DBMS software into existing computer environments.

In reality, distributed databases encompass a wide spectrum of possibilities, including the following:

- Remote terminal access to centralized DBMS (e.g., an airline reservation system)
- Remote terminal access to different DBMSs, but one at a time (e.g., Prodigy, CompuServe, and Dow Jones)
- Simple pairwise interconnection with data sharing that requires users to know the data location, data access language, and the logon procedure to the remote DBMS
- Distributed database management with a generic data definition language and a data manipulation language at all nodes
- Distribution update and transaction management
- Distributed databases with replication that support vertical and horizontal fragmentation
- "True" distributed DBMSs with heterogeneous hardware, software, and communications

The definition of distributed DBMSs lies anywhere along this spectrum. For the purpose of this chapter, the remote terminal access to data as discussed in the preceding list is not considered a distributed DBMS because a node on the distributed DBMS must have its own hardware, central processor, and software.

Limitations of Commercial Products

Some of the problems that currently frustrate managers and technicians who might otherwise be interested in exploring distributed data solutions include the following:

- A distributed database environment has all the problems associated with the single, centralized database environment, but at a more complex level.
- There are no basic, step-by-step guidelines covering the analysis, design, and implementation of a distributed database environment.

A distributed DBMS offers many benefits. However, there are also many architectural choices that make the applications design for distributed databases very complex.

To ensure an effective and productive distributed database environment, it is essential that the distributed environment be properly designed to support the expected distributed database applications. In addition, an effective design will depend on the limitations of the distributed DBMS software. Therefore, implementing today's distributed database technology requires identifying the functional limitations of a selected commercial product. Identification of these limitations is critical to the successful operation of an application in a distributed database environment.

DISTRIBUTED DATABASE DEVELOPMENT PHASES

Effective corporationwide distributed database processing is not going to happen overnight. It requires a carefully planned infrastructure within which an orderly evolution can occur. The four major development phases are planning, design, installation and implementation, and support and maintenance.

The Planning Phase. The planning phase consists of high-level management strategy planning. During the planning phase, an organization must consider whether it is advantageous to migrate to a distributed environment. This chapter assumes that migration to a distributed environment is desirable and feasible and that the corporate strategy planning issues and tasks have been identified. The result of this phase is the total management commitment for cost, resources, and a careful migration path toward a distributed database environment.

The Design Phase. The design phase is concerned with the overall design of the distributed database strategy. The overall design task involves the selection of a distributed DBMS environment in terms of the hardware, software, and communications network for each node and how these elements are interconnected. The design of the distributed database environment must incorporate the requirements for the actual distributed database application. The overall design divides into two main tasks: the detailed design of the distributed database environment and the detailed design of the initial distributed database application. In certain cases, the initial application may be a prototype that is intended to pave the way for the full-production distributed database application.

The Installation and Implementation Phase. This phase consists of the installation and implementation of the environment that provides basic software support for the distributed DBMS application. The task of developing the distributed database application could occur in parallel with the installation of the environment.

The Support and Maintenance Phase. The support and maintenance phase consists of support for the distributed DBMS environment and the support and maintenance of the application. Although these support and maintenance tasks can be performed by the same people, the nature of the tasks and responsibilities are quite distinct. For example, the distributed application may require modification of report formats, whereas the distributed environment may require modification to add more memory.

CORPORATION STRATEGY PLANNING

The main task during the strategic planning phase is to obtain the commitment of senior management. The measure of this commitment is the amount of resources — both personnel and equipment — necessary for the development of a distributed DBMS. The factors that must be considered during the strategy planning phase are as follows:

- What are the objectives of the organization's next 5-year plan?
- How will technological changes affect the organization's way of doing business?
- What resources are needed to plan for the development of, and migration to, a distributed DBMS?
- How will outcomes be measured relative to the impact on the organization's competitive position?

The corporate strategy plan must include detailed specifications of the total system life cycle. It must also include a realistic timetable of schedules and milestones. Important consideration must be paid to the allocation of costs for new acquisitions, training personnel, physical space requirements, and other tangible items.

During the strategic planning phase, information must be gathered on the organization's business functions and goals, related constraints and problem areas, and the organization's user groups. Only after the needed information has been gathered is it possible to develop high-level information categories and their interrelationships.

The process of developing the distributed database plan is iterative. The activities involved are performed by IS managers. Although these individuals often have the vision to recognize the long-term benefits of a distributed DBMS environment to an organization, they must rely on the participation and input of those in the organization who are directly involved with the business functions and use information to make decisions and manage operations. There must be considerable interaction among many different people in the organization, each of whom provides feedback to validate and refine the plans.

Strategic planning must first provide a sufficient justification for the expenditure of resources necessary to migrate to a distributed environment. Only after this justification has been accepted and fully approved by senior management can the task of initiating projects to design, develop, and implement a distributed DBMS environment and application start.

OVERALL DESIGN OF DISTRIBUTED DATABASE STRATEGY

A distributed database environment consists of a collection of sites or nodes connected by a communications network. Each node has its own hardware, central processor, and software, which may or may not include a DBMS. The primary objective of a distributed DBMS is to give interactive query and application programs access to remote data as well as local data.

Individual nodes within the distributed environment can have different computing requirements. Accordingly, these nodes may have different hardware and different software, and they may be connected in many different ways. Some of the variations possible in the distributed database environment are discussed in the following sections.

Client/Server Computing

The most basic distributed capability is remote database access from single users at a node. A node may be a mainframe, a minicomputer, or a microcomputer (personal computer). The node that makes the database access request is referred to as a client node, and the node that responds to the request and provides database services is referred to as a service node. The association is limited to the two parties involved — the client and the server. Exhibit 1 represents several different configurations available under a client/server computing environment. The following are descriptions of the different configurations shown in the exhibit.

Client Single-User Node. The operating environment of an individual can be single user or multiuser, depending on the operating system of that node. In a single-user operating environment, a node can be only a client. Such a node may or may not have databases. For non-database client nodes, the software typically consists of front-end application programs used to access remote database server nodes. This front-end software is generally in the form of end-user interface tools (e.g., a query language processor, a form processor, or some other application-specific program written in a third-generation language).

DESIGNING AND MANAGING DATABASES

The front-end software formulates and issues user requests. It processes user requests through its established links with appropriate communications software. The front-end software only captures a user's request and uses communications software to send that request to a remote database node requesting its DBMS to process the request. In addition to the capabilities outlined, single-user nodes with databases allow local data to

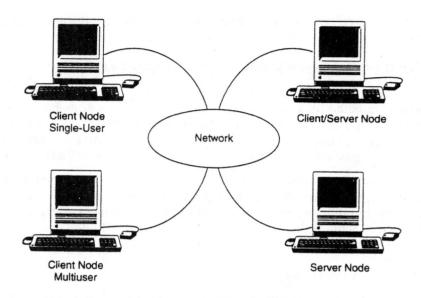

Exhibit 1. Client/server computing.

be included in the same query operations specified for remote data. Therefore, operationally, the query results will appear as if all data are coming from a central database.

Client Multiuser Node. The functional capabilities outlined for the client single-user node are expanded in the client multiuser node because of the presence of a multiuser operating system at the user node. Such a configuration generally has several user processes running at the same time. At peak use time, the presence of several user processes can cause slower response time than is experienced in a client single-user node. The client multiuser node is more cost-effective, however, because it can allow multiple remote database access at different sites by different users at the same time. This is made possible through an identifiable list of remote server node locations. In addition, as with the client single-user node, the client multiuser node can include local database access in conjunction with access to remote databases.

Server Node. The server node is capable of providing database services to other client requests as well as to itself. It is a special multiuser node that is dedicated to servicing remote database requests and any local processes. This means that incoming requests are serviced, but it does not originate requests to other server nodes. The functional capabilities of a server node are as follows: this node must be included in the server list of some remote client node, there must be an operating DBMS, and there must be a continuously running process that listens for incoming database requests.

Client/Server Node. A node with a database can be a client as well as a server. This means that this node can service remote database requests as well as originate database requests to other server nodes. Therefore, the client/server node can play a dual role.

Homogeneous Distributed DBMS Environment

A completely homogeneous distributed DBMS environment exists when all the nodes in the distributed environment have the same DBMS but not necessarily the same hardware and operating system. However, the communications software for each node must use the same protocol to send or receive requests and data.

Design and implementation of a homogeneous distributed DBMS environment need involve only a single vendor. Any data request issued at a client node does not require translation because the database language and data model are the same across all nodes in the network.

Heterogeneous Distributed DBMS Environment

In a truly heterogeneous distributed DBMS environment, the hardware, operating systems, communications, and DBMSs can all be different. Different DBMSs may mean different data models along with different database languages for definition and manipulation. Any database request issued at a client node would have to be translated so that the server node responding to the request would understand how to execute the request.

Various degrees of heterogeneity can exist. For example, within the distributed environment, different DBMSs can still be compatible if they all support the relational data model and understand SQL, a relational query language that is an ANSI and ISO standard. Presently, however, even among SQL-conforming systems, there is no general communications software that will accept generic SQL statements from any other SQL-conforming DBMS. This is an area in which the pending remote data access standards are needed.

DISTRIBUTED ENVIRONMENT ARCHITECTURE

The design of a distributed database environment can be evolutionary — by incremental interconnection of existing systems, or by developing a totally new distributed DBMS environment using the bottom-up approach. Some of the design issues in adopting either approach are described in the following sections.

Interconnection of Existing Systems

Not all organizations have the luxury of developing the distributed database environment from scratch. Already-existing database management applications are costly investments that are not likely to be replaced all at once by new distributed systems. The existing environment, including hardware, software, and databases, can be preserved by providing a mechanism for producing federated systems (i.e., systems composed of autonomous software components).

The federated approach is a practical first-step solution toward a distributed database environment. It accommodates a legacy of existing systems while extending to incorporate new nodes. Therefore, it is important to select distributed DBMS software that supports existing computer hardware and allows for expansion. Within a federated system, pairs of nodes can be coupled in ways that range from very loose (i.e., each node is autonomous) to very tight (i.e., each node interacts directly with the other). The various forms of coupling affect the design, execution, and capability of the distributed applications.

The mode of coupling affects the number of translations required to exchange information between each site. Zero translations are needed when both components use the same representations. Some systems may choose to translate the data produced by one site directly to the format required by the other site. A more common method is to translate the data into a neutral format first, and then translate into the target format.

Loose Coupling. Loosely coupled systems are the most modular and in some ways are easier to maintain. This is because changes to the implementation of a site's system characteristics and its DBMS are not as likely to affect other sites. The disadvantage of loosely coupled systems is that users must have some knowledge of each site's characteristics to execute requests. Because very little central authority to control consistency exists, correctness cannot be guaranteed. In addition, loosely coupled systems typically involve more translations that may cause performance problems.

Tight Coupling. Tightly coupled systems behave more like a single, integrated system. Users need not be aware of the characteristics of the sites fulfilling a request. With centralized control, the tightly coupled systems are more consistent in their use of resources and in their management of shared data. The disadvantage of tight coupling is that because sites are independent, changes to one site are likely to affect other sites. Also, users at some sites may object to the loss of freedom to the central control mechanisms necessary to maintain the tight coupling of all the systems.

Cooperation Between Sites

For a truly distributed DBMS environment, a variety of methods are available to specify cooperation between sites. One way of classifying the distributed environment is to define the amount of transparency offered to the users. Another way is to define the amount of site autonomy available to each site, and the way sites interact cooperatively.

Degrees of Transparency. Transparency is the degree to which a service is offered by the distributed DBMS so that the user does not need to be aware of it. One example of transparency is location transparency, which means users can retrieve data from any site without having to know where the data are located.

Types of Site Autonomy. Site autonomy refers to the amount of independence that a site has in making policy decisions. Some examples of policy decisions include ownership of data, policies for accessing the data, policies for hours and days of operation, and human support. In addition, all modifications to the site's data structures must be approved by the cooperating federation of data administrators.

Interconnection of Newly Purchased Systems

An organization will have much more freedom if it decides to establish a distributed database environment from scratch. Currently, vendors are offering homogeneous distributed DBMSs with a compatible family of software. This approach, however, can lock the organization into a single vendor's proprietary products.

Other distributed architecture choices are as follows:

- Identical DBMS products at each node, with possibly different hardware environments but a single proprietary communications network to interconnect all sites
- Standard conforming DBMS products at each node that rely on standard communications protocols
- Different DBMSs, using the same data model (e.g., relational), interconnected by a single or standard communications protocol
- Different DBMSs, using different data models (e.g., relational or object-oriented), interconnected by a single or standard communications protocol

Some distributed DBMS vendors offer a bridge (gateway) mechanism from their distributed database software to any foreign distributed database software. This bridge (gateway) may be obtained at additional development cost if it has not already been included in the vendor's library of available software.

In the design of a totally new distributed DBMS product, it is advisable to consider a mixture of standard conforming DBMSs and communications protocols. Because the technology and products are changing quickly, the designed architecture must be continuously reviewed to prevent it from being locked into an inflexible mode.

CONSIDERATION FOR STANDARDS

As the trend toward distributed computing accelerates, the need for standards, guidance, and support will increase. Application distribution and use will be chaotic unless there is an architectural vision and some degree of uniformity in information technology platforms. This is particularly true in client/server and workstation environments. To achieve this goal, a systems architecture incorporating standards to meet the users' needs must be established. This architecture must isolate the application software from the lower levels of machine architecture and systems service implementation. The systems architecture serves as the context for user requirements, technology integration, and standards specifications.

The benefits of standardization for both the user and the vendor are many. The number and variety of distributed DBMS products are increasing. By insisting that purchased products conform to standards, users may be able to choose the best product for each function without being locked into a specific vendor. Therefore, small to midsize vendors may effectively compete in the open marketplace. For effective planning and designing of a distributed DBMS environment, it is important for the designers to consider what standards already exist and what standards will be emerging to be able to incorporate standardized products.

There are many areas of distributed DBMS environment in which standards should be applied. Some of the standards relevant to the design of a distributed DBMS include communications protocols, applications programming interfaces, data languages for DBMSs, data representation and interchange formats, and remote data access.

Communications protocol standards are necessary so that systems from different products can connect to a communications network and understand the information being transmitted. An example of a communications protocol standard is the Government Open Systems Interconnection Profile (GOSIP).

The application programming interface (API) standard is directed toward the goal of having portable applications. This enables software applications developed in one computing environment to run almost unchanged in any other environment. An example of an application programming interface standard is the Portable Operating System Interface for Computer Environments (POSIX).

The data languages commonly supported by a DBMS are the data definition language, the data manipulation language, and the data control language. An example of a standard data language for the relational DBMS model is SQL.

To exchange data among open systems, a standard interchange format is necessary. The interchange format consists of a language for defining general data structures and the encoding rules. An example of a standard data interchange language is Abstract Syntax Notation One (ASN. 1).

An important standard for the distributed processing environment is the remote access of data from a client site to a database server site. A specialized remote data access protocol based on the SQL standard is currently under development.

SUMMARY

To start the overall design process, a review of the organization's existing facilities should be conducted. This review is done to determine whether the new distributed database environment can use some or all of the existing facilities. In the decision to move into a distributed environment, requirements for additional functionalities must be identified. Such organizational issues as setting up regional offices may also be involved. The distributed architecture must take into consideration the actual application operating, the characteristics of the user population, and the workloads to be placed on the system. Such an architecture must also incorporate standardized components.

Chapter 21
Component Design for Relational Databases

Ashvin Iyengar

INTRODUCTION

Component-based object-oriented architectures are becoming increasingly popular in building industrial strength applications. However, relational databases are not going to be replaced by object databases in the foreseeable future. This paper explores the ramifications of component-based designs on data management and offers strategies which could be deployed in the use of relational centralized databases with object-oriented component-based application architectures.

WHY RELATIONAL DATABASES ARE HERE TO STAY

From a pure application design perspective, object-oriented databases would be much more suitable for use with object-oriented component-based application architectures. However, the business realities are more complex and include the following considerations:

- Object-oriented databases are not mature enough to be entrusted with the job of managing large corporate data;
- It is more difficult to find professionals with experience in administration as well as the design of object-oriented databases;
- The vast majority of corporations are currently using relational databases to manage business information; and
- Most current live applications have been designed and developed to work with relational databases.

MOVING TOWARDS A COMPONENT-BASED ARCHITECTURE STANDARD

The subject of object-oriented design and programming involving relational databases has been well explored. More often than not, the data

0-8493-9968-8/99/$0.00+$.50
© 1999 by CRC Press LLC

model is constructed using pure relational database modeling techniques with little if any consideration for object-oriented design techniques. This necessitates the use of impedance matching techniques to allow object-oriented applications to interact with relational data models.

Application architectures are becoming increasingly component based to satisfy the need for flexible as well as manageable systems. The effort to move away from large monolithic applications has been underway for a number of years. This has resulted in the adoption of client-server-based architecture as the de facto standard in the industry. However, with lack of proper design, client-server architectures became just as monolithic as mainframe applications and thus inherited all the maintenance problems associated with large monolithic applications. Object-oriented design techniques and multitiered architectures were adopted in order to solve this problem. Component design is a natural next step in the evolution of application architectures since it combines the principles of object-oriented design with multitiered application architecture. In addition, industry-wide acceptance of the incremental and iterative software development methodology over the old waterfall development methodology has provided an additional thrust towards component-based design.

Some of the other factors contributing towards making component-based application design the de facto standard are:

- The maturing of technologies like DCOM (distributed component object model) and CORBA
- The plethora of new technologies encouraging the design and deployment of components over the Web (e.g., JavaBeans)
- The ability to design, develop, and deploy components using high level, widely used applications like Visual Basic
- The potential for using third-party components along with in-house applications in order to fulfill specific needs (e.g., a professional third-party charting component)
- The resulting relative ease of component replacement

BACKGROUND OF MULTITIERED ARCHITECTURES

The current thrust is towards the use of distributed, component-based application architectures. The ever-increasing need to deploy applications over the Web and the resulting security considerations have led to an n-tiered architecture, using, at the very least, three distinct tiers:

- Web server
- Application server
- Database server

Whereas, a number of studies have shown that pure object-oriented applications are difficult to design and develop and that the payoffs information technology (IT) executives had hoped for in terms of reuse are seldom realized, multitiered architecture is here to stay. Three-tiered architecture is, in fact, the industry standard and a wide variety of application development environments from Smalltalk to Visual Basic support and encourage the use of this standard architecture.

In general, a three-tiered architecture has the following layers:

• Interface layer
• Business layer
• Data layer

The driving force behind three-tiered architecture is the need to support both flexibility and robustness in applications. Decoupling the interface layer from the database offers the advantage of changes in the database that need not affect the interface layer directly, thereby isolating the effects of a change in either layer. The interface layer describes how the application interacts with the outside world. If the outside world is comprised of end users, then the interface layer refers to a user interface. Alternatively, if it is comprised of client applications, it refers to an application interface.

Arguably, the main payoff involved in object-oriented architectures is not reuse but rather change management. Effective change management is also the goal of three-tiered architectures. Since three-tiered architectures are easier to implement with object-based (if not object-oriented) systems, new life has been extended to object-based systems. In this article, a distinction is being made between object-oriented and object-based systems. Object-based systems implement classes and objects, but do not permit other aspects of object-oriented programming like inheritance and polymorphism. So whereas the three pillars of object-oriented programming can be said to be encapsulation, inheritance, and polymorphism, object-based programming mainly concerns itself with encapsulation.

A leading example of an object-based application development is Visual Basic. Visual Basic is to the client-server world what Cobol is to the mainframe world. Since classes in Visual Basic are implemented using DCOM (distributed component object model), it is extremely easy to develop and deploy components using Visual Basic.

An object-based component can be described as a set of objects collaborating to provide a common functionality and implementing a common interface. Thus, an object-based component improves the encapsulation aspect of object-based applications. By virtue of this it also increases the flexibility as well as robustness of an object-based application, since changes to the component are isolated.

It has already been argued that the main thrust towards three-tiered architecture is coming from a need for effective change management. Change management, as used in this paper, encompasses the concepts of flexibility and robustness. It has also been argued that object-based applications by virtue of their support for encapsulation are a natural choice for the implementation of business solutions with underlying multitiered architectures. Since a component-based architecture enhances the ability of multitiered architectures to deliver on its promise, it would be logical to conclude that component-based multitiered architectures are here to stay.

So the prevalent application development environment can be said to have the following features:

- Multitiered architecture
- Relational databases
- Object-based applications
- Component-based application architecture

APPLICATION ARCHITECTURE EXAMPLE

Now this article will take an example where a set of three tables provides a certain functionality (e.g., hold information pertaining to interest rates in a portfolio management system) and three discrete applications interact with these three tables. It will start with a simple two-tiered application architecture example and note the problems in the chosen context. Then it will move to a more object-oriented version of the same problem and again note the problems with the approach. Finally, it will illustrate a solution to the same problem using a data-component approach.

In Exhibit 1, Application A1 is responsible for displaying and maintaining information in M1 (the set of tables T1, T2, and T3 constituting a subdata model). Applications A2 and A3 use the information in M1 to do their processing. Note that Application A1 interacts with all the tables in M1, whereas Applications A2 and A3 interact with only T3.

The shortcomings of two-tiered applications have already been noted. In this case, the tight coupling between the applications and the data is obvious and, consequently, flexibility is severely compromised. Also, there are three different applications interacting with the same data, so complexity is increased since a change in data storage/design would necessitate a change to all the client applications.

To make this design more object-oriented, now move to Exhibit 2 which illustrates a three-tiered object-oriented architecture. Applications A1, A2, and A3 contain their own relational-to-object mapping layer (also known as impedance matching layer). Now consider that new business rules necessitate a change to M1. M1 is a subdata model corresponding to functionality F1 (e.g., performance history of various investment options in a portfolio management system). If the new data model involves changing

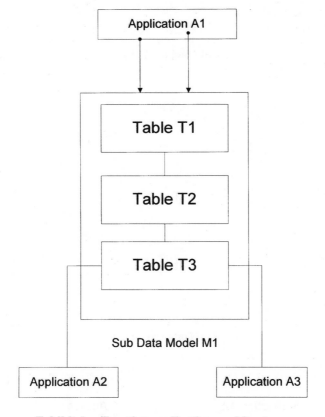

Exhibit 1. Two-tier application architecture.

the way information is represented in T3, then all applications involving T3 (in this case Applications A1, A2, and A3) have to be updated. In addition to requiring duplication of effort, this design increases the risk of application malfunction since it is possible to miss updating an application which needs updating. Also note that even aside from complicating change management, this design involves duplication of effort in terms of data access as well as relational-to-object mapping.

In order to solve the above-mentioned problems, modify the design to produce a more object-oriented approach by introducing components. Exhibit 3 introduces a component C1 that encapsulates subdata model M1. This makes C1 a data-component. Consequently, the methodology illustrated in Exhibit 3 is referred to as the data-component approach.

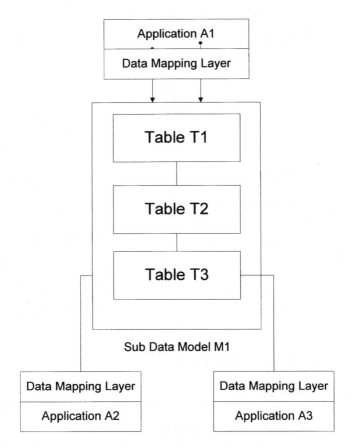

Exhibit 2. Three-tier application architecture with data-mapping layer.

ADVANTAGES/FEATURES OF THE DATA-COMPONENT APPROACH

The data-component approach, as illustrated in Exhibit 3, offers the following features and advantages:

- Applications do not access the tables directly but use the interface functions provided by the interface layer in C1.
- Satisfies an important OOD (object-oriented design) requirement: keep function and data together.
- Eliminates redundant data access as well as data mapping.
- Separates the GUI from the business logic — an important requirement of three-tier client server computing.
- Allows implementation of n-tiered architecture since C1 can be deployed on an application server.
- Provides much better change management (which, as elaborated before, is an even greater benefit of object-oriented development than re-

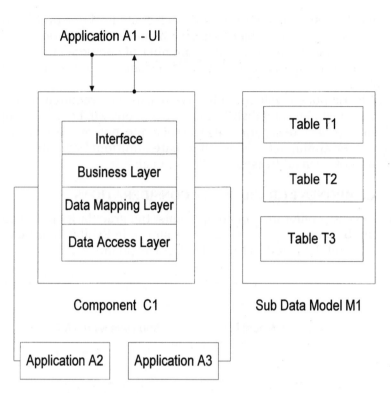

Exhibit 3.   Application architecture example using data-component approach.

use) since changes in the data model no longer affect client applications directly. The only time the client applications are affected is when changes to the data model/functionality affect the interface between C1 and the client applications.

- Allows implementation of multiple interface or different views of data, thus adding a new twist to the classic MVC (Model View Controller) object-oriented architecture.
- Provides data source independence since changing the source of the data will affect only the data access and data mapping layers of the component and the client applications will be insulated from any such change.
- Reduces the effort involved in allowing new applications to access the data.

DISADVANTAGES/LIMITATIONS OF THE DATA-COMPONENT APPROACH

The data-component approach as illustrated in Exhibit 3 has the following possible disadvantages or limitations:

- If used indiscriminately, this approach could lead to a proliferation of components, thereby increasing the number of applications.
- Large applications using a large number of components could experience performance degradation, especially while loading the application.
- Each component will possibly have registration requirements, so the task of installing and distributing applications will be more complex.
- This approach deals primarily with discrete, non-overlapping use cases. Overlapping use cases will create additional complexities that have not been addressed in this approach.

DATA-COMPONENT GRANULARITY CONSIDERATIONS

To prevent proliferation of components, the granularity of the components can be increased. For example as shown in Exhibit 4, use cases U1 and U2 use subdata models M1 and M2, correspondingly.

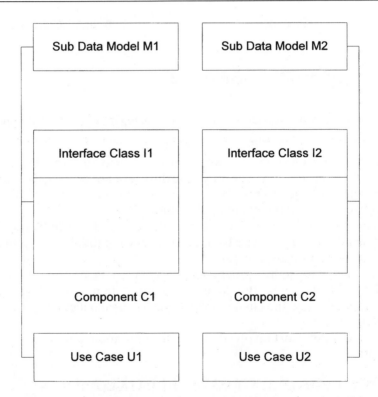

Exhibit 4. One-to-one component to subdata model example.

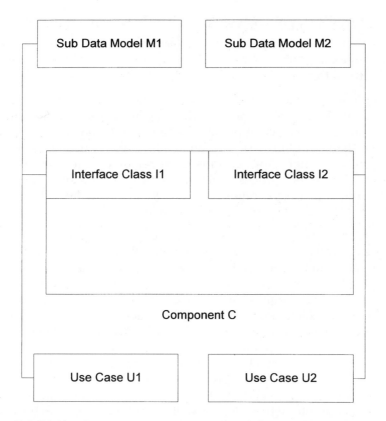

Exhibit 5. One-to-many component to subdata model example.

Instead of having components C1 and C2 that correspond to use cases U1 and U2, if U1 and U2 are closely related, a single component C (with interfaces I1 and I2) can serve U1 and U2, as illustrated in Exhibit 5.

The same exercise of combining related use cases into components could be carried out through the application design space, thereby bringing component proliferation under control.

IMPLEMENTATION OF THE COMPONENT-BASED DESIGN USING MICROSOFT'S ARCHITECTURE

Even though the component technology war between CORBA and DCOM is far from over, the fact remains that DCOM (in some form) has been around longer and is used widely in the industry. It also has, arguably, more opportunities to mature into a stable, industrial strength technology. Consequently, Microsoft's DCOM platform is discussed in the implementation of the data-component approach illustrated in Exhibit 3.

In Microsoft's DCOM technology there are two main types of components:

1. ActiveX Exe
2. ActiveX DLL

The difference between the two types of components is that the ActiveX Exe is an out-of-process component while the ActiveX DLL is an in-process component. In-process components usually offer significantly better performance than out-of-process components. However, in-process components and their client applications must reside on the same physical machines. With out-of-process components there is no such restriction, therefore out-of-process components offer greater flexibility in terms of deployment at the cost of application performance.

The choice between in-process and out-of-process components would therefore depend on the physical architecture. Note that three-tier software architectures can be deployed using two-tier physical architectures. In a two-tier implementation, the database runs on a database server and the user interface layer as well as the business layer runs on the client desktops. This kind of implementation is also called fat-client, since most of the applications are deployed on individual workstations. Whereas this might be sufficient for a small shop, for larger shops, distribution as well as maintenance of all the various components on individual workstations can prove to be a daunting as well as error-prone task. For this reason, larger shops may prefer to implement a physical three-tier architecture which would involve client workstations interacting with an application server which in turn would interact with a database server. While this approach alleviates some of the distribution problems inherent in the two-tier architecture, a new problem is created with multiple workstations accessing the same application on the application server concurrently. Clearly, it would be counterproductive to start up a new copy of the application for every workstation that needs it. Therefore, some sort of a queuing solution is inevitable. It is in this respect that the DCOM architecture is yet to mature. Microsoft's solution to the problem involves use of MTS (Microsoft's transaction server), but that may not be a universally viable solution for every situation.

It is also worth noting that even though it is technically easy to convert an ActiveX DLL to an ActiveX Exe, there are other considerations involved which might necessitate knowledge of the physical architecture in advance. The main consideration is network traffic. With out-of-process components, performance requirements usually dictate the use of fewer but longer messages, whereas with in-process components frequencies of messages do not result in performance penalties.

If the generic architecture example illustrated in Exhibit 3 were to be implemented on a Microsoft platform, the following notes might apply:

- The interface layer of component C1 interfaces with Applications A1, A2, and A3. Since A2 and A3 are inquiry-only applications, they can share a common interface. So, we would have two interface classes, I1 and I2. I1 will implement the interface needed for A1 and I2 would implement the interface needed for applications A2 and A3. In some cases, classes I1 and I2 could be implemented in a separate ActiveX DLL. This has the advantage of providing decoupling between the client and server applications. In practice, this has to be weighed against the cost of distributing this additional component. There will also be a minor performance penalty involved in separating the interface classes in a separate component since an additional program will have to be loaded.
- Another factor to be considered while designing the interface layer is the number of parameters needed for the component to query and present the information. Assume, for starters, a method M1 in component C1 where the number of input parameters is n and the method returns only one value. A change in the input parameters would entail changing method M1 and therefore changing the interface. Therefore, except for trivial methods, it would make sense to encapsulate the data flowing between the component and its client applications, in classes. In this example a class C1M1 would contain all the input parameters as well as result values for method M1 in Component C1. M1 now would be passed a reference to object OC1MI (corresponding to class C1M1). With this approach, if method M1 were to need a new input parameter or need to return an extra result value, the interface would remain unchanged and changes would be restricted to class C1M1 and its usage.
- The business layer of the component should contain most of editing rules and the business logic. Including the editing logic in the business layer of the component goes a long way towards ensuring data integrity since applications that update the data maintained by the component have to use the interface layer of the component. Note that the business layer is not exposed directly to the outside world. External applications can only use the methods exposed by the interface layer, which in turn will interact with the business layer. Also, since the interface layer does not directly interact with the data layer of the component, the business layer has a chance to enforce its business rules and ensure logical integrity.
- The data layer of the component typically consists of two internal layers, namely a relational-to-object mapping layer and a data access layer. The data access layer is responsible for the actual interaction with the database. The data mapping layer is responsible for mapping relational data into objects. Each record in a relational database is essentially an array of values. If a query returns more than one record (a RecordSet in Microsoft-speak), then we are dealing with a two-dimensional array. The data-mapping layer typically converts a single record to an object, and a RecordSet to a collection of objects. Also, for per-

sistent data, the object in the data mapping layer must know how to access the objects in the data access layer in order to store updated data. It is also worthwhile noting that the data access layer could be implemented as a separate component in itself. That way multiple applications can use the data access layer to manage their interactions with the physical database.

Following are examples of the architectures discussed in this paper:

1. The business layer has classes B1 and B2 that correspond to the interface layer classes I1 and I2. B1 and B2 interact with classes R1,R2,...., RN which implement various business rules. B1 and B2 also interact with corresponding classes DM1 and DM2, which belong to the data mapping layer of the data layer. DM1 and DM2 in turn interact with classes DA1, DA2, and DA3, which access/update data in Tables T1, T2, and T3.
2. Instead of having separate classes B1 and B2, depending on the application, a single class B may suffice.
3. Again, depending on the application, a single class DA may provide the functionality provided by DA1, DA2, and DA3.
4. Note that DM1 and DM2 provide the business view of the data model and this case is basically driven by the choice of B1 and B2 as the business classes. Depending on the requirements, classes DM1, DM2, and DM3 could correspond to DA1, DA2, and DA3 or any other combination that makes sense.
5. Note that classes DM1 and DM2 could create and return a variety of objects. For example, object O11 might correspond to a specific record in the table T1. Object O12 might correspond to a collection of records. Alternatively, O12 may be implemented as an object containing a collection of O11 objects. Similarly, objects O21 through O2N might correspond to Table T2. Alternatively, O21 through O2N might correspond to data linked between Tables T2 and T3, if appropriate.

The possibilities are endless. The examples listed previously illustrate some of the considerations that might come into play during the design of the component. To reiterate one of the main points in this article, effective change management, assume that a change is to be made to this design. Instead of accessing data in Tables T2 and T3 directly, applications must use a View instead. In this case, only relevant classes in the data access layer and maybe the data mapping layer will need to be changed. All other classes in the business and interface layers of the component can remain unchanged. Also, the client applications using the component remain unaffected. Thus use of a multitiered component-based architecture has provided for flexibility (providing ease of change by restricting the area of change) as well as robustness (limiting the scope of the effect of change).

DATA-COMPONENT MINING

Data-component mining is the process by which an existing data model can be analyzed and broken up into subdata models with associated data-components. One approach to component mining is to study the data model to identify loosely coupled sets of entities. Each such set of entities can be called a subdata model. Each such subdata model is a good candidate for a component and more so if the subdata model is used by more than one application. Use cases have become a standard way of defining requirements/functionality in object-oriented design. A list of existing as well as future use cases can also provide a valuable perspective during data-component mining design. Related use cases can be combined to help identify subdata models and, consequently, corresponding data components.

For example, in a portfolio management system, analysis of the ERD (entity relationship diagram) of the data model might suggest that the set of entities containing historical performance data could constitute a subdata model M1. Similarly, the set of entities pertaining to investment choices in a client's portfolio could constitute another subdata model M2. There is now a potential use for two data components: C1 corresponding to model M1 (historical performance data) and C2 corresponding to model M2 (client's investment choices). Alternatively, it could start with use cases. For example, consider the following use cases:

- U1 — Provide inquiry of client's investment elections.
- U2 — Provide investment election change update/change.
- U3 — Provide inquiry of investment performance data.
- U4 — Provide update of investment performance data.
- U5 — Calculate portfolio values for a given client.

U1 and U2 deal with the same information (a client's investment choices). Similarly, U3 and U4 deal with the same information (investment performance data). U5 deals with the client's investment choices as well as investment performance data. Since investment performance data is independent of a client's investment choices, the entities in the data model corresponding to investment performance data can be said to be loosely coupled with the entities pertaining to client investment elections. Therefore, investment performance data as well as client investment choices are both candidates for subdata models with corresponding data components. The implementation of U5 would then involve use of both data components.

CONCLUSION

The data component approach to data management can be valuable in an environment involving object-oriented applications and relational databases. The primary advantage provided by this approach is ensuring that the application responsible for updating information is responsible for pro-

365

viding inquiry of the same information, thereby providing for superior change management. This approach can be used in any environment that allows development of component-based applications.

Chapter 22
Using CORBA to Integrate Database Systems
Bhavani Thuraisingham and Daniel L. Spar

INFORMATION HAS BECOME THE MOST CRITICAL RESOURCE in many organizations, and the rapid growth of networking and database technologies has had a major impact on information processing requirements. Efficient access to information, as well as sharing it, have become urgent needs. As a result, an increasing number of databases in different sites are being interconnected. In order to reconcile the contrasting requirements of the different database management systems (DBMSs), tools that enable users of one system to use another system's data are being developed. Efficient solutions for interconnecting and administering different database systems are also being investigated.

There are two aspects to the object-oriented approach to integrating heterogeneous database systems. In one approach, an object-oriented data model could be used as a generic representation scheme so that the schema transformations between the different database systems could be facilitated. In the other approach, a distributed object management system could be used to interconnect heterogeneous database systems. This chapter explores the distributed object management system approach by focusing on a specific distributed object management system: the object management group's (OMG) Common Object Request Broker Architecture (CORBA).

INTEROPERABILITY ISSUES

Although research on interconnecting different DBMSs has been under way for over a decade, only recently have many of the difficult problems been addressed. Through the evolution of the three-tier approach to client/server, the capability of integrating DBMS's has improved significantly. The traditional two-tier client/server approach included the layers of

1. Client
2. Server

For small systems, the two-tier approach works reasonably well. For larger systems with greater numbers of connected clients and servers, and greater levels of complexity and requirements for security, there is a substantial need for three-tier architectures. Two-tier systems are notorious for their development of the "fat client," where excessive amounts of code running business logic are required to be loaded onto the client machine.

The three-tier approach breaks client/server components into the layers of:

1. Client (presentation layer)
2. Middleware (business logic)
3. Server (data and resource management)

The result is much more efficient use of resources, and greater "plug and play" capabilities for both clients and servers. Clients can be superthin browsers running JAVA applets, and servers can be efficiently integrated and load-balanced.

With the advent of web servers, the three-tier model becomes "n-tier" since a web server is often placed between the client and middleware layers.

Schema Heterogeneity. Not all of the databases in a heterogeneous architecture are represented by the same schema (data model). Therefore, the different conceptual schemas have to be integrated. In order to do this, translators that transform the constructs of one schema into those of another are being developed. Integration remains most difficult with the older legacy databases that are prerelational.

Transaction Processing Heterogeneity. Different DBMSs may use different algorithms for transaction processing. Work is being directed toward integrating the various transaction processing mechanisms. Techniques that integrate locking, timestamping, and validation mechanisms are being developed. However, strict serializability may have to be sacrificed in order to create a heterogeneous environment. Independent transaction processing monitor (TP monitor) software is now readily available in the distributed systems marketplace. TP monitor software has been used for years on mainframes, and is now of great assistance in high-volume systems such as Internet commerce. Examples include web-based stock brokerage trading sites.

Query Processing Heterogeneity. Different DBMSs may also use different query processing and optimization strategies. Research is being conducted to develop a global cost model for distributed query optimization.

Query Language Heterogeneity. Query language heterogeneity should also be addressed, even if the DBMSs are based on the relational model. Structured query language (SQL) and relational calculus could be used to achieve heterogeneity. Standardization efforts are under way to develop a uniform interface language.

Constraint Heterogeneity. Different DBMSs enforce different integrity constraints, which are often inconsistent. For example, one DBMS could enforce a constraint that all employees must work at least 40 hours, even though another DBMS may not enforce such a constraint. Moving these business rules over to the application servers on the middle tier and away from the DBMSs on the third tier will also help isolate and correct business rule inconsistencies.

Semantic Heterogeneity. Data may be interpreted differently by different components. For example, the entity address could represent just the country for one component, or it could represent the number, street, city, and country for another component. This problem will be difficult to resolve in older systems that combined multiple domains in a single database field and often assigned cryptic names to tables and fields that do not reveal their content.

THE COMMON OBJECT REQUEST BROKER ARCHITECTURE (CORBA)

CORBA was created to provide an object-based central layer to enable the objectives of three-tier distributed systems, especially in the area of interoperability.

The three major components of CORBA are the object model, the object request broker (ORB) and object adapters, and the interface definition language (IDL).

The Object Model

The object model describes object semantics and object implementation. Object semantics describe the semantics of an object: type, requests, object creation and destruction, interfaces, operations, and attributes. Object implementation describes the execution model and the construction model. In general, the object model of CORBA has the essential constructs of most object models.

The Object Request Broker (ORB)

The ORB essentially enables communication between a client and a server object. A client invokes an operation on the object, and the object implementation provides the code and data needed to implement the object. The ORB provides the necessary mechanisms to find the object implementation for a particular request and enables the object implementation to receive the request. The communication mechanisms necessary to deliver the request are also provided by the ORB.

In addition, the ORB supports the activation and deactivation of objects and their implementation as well as generating and interpreting object

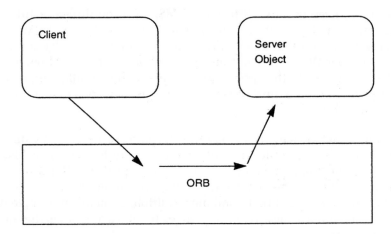

Exhibit 1.   Communication through an Object Request Broker (ORB)

references. Although the ORB provides the mechanisms to locate the object and communicate the client's request to the object, the exact location of the object, as well as the details of its implementation, are transparent to the client. Objects use object adapters to access the services provided by the ORB. Communication between a client and a server object using the ORB is illustrated in Exhibit 1.

INTERFACE DEFINITION LANGUAGE (IDL)

IDL is the language used to describe the interfaces that are called by client objects and provided by object implementations. IDL is a declarative language; client and object implementations are not written in IDL. IDL grammar is a subset of ANSI C++ with additional constructs to support the operation invocation mechanism. An IDL binding to the C language has been specified, and other language bindings are being processed. Exhibit 2 illustrates how IDL is used for communication between a client and a server. The client's request is passed to the ORB using an IDL stub. An IDL skeleton delivers the request to the server object.

INTEGRATING HETEROGENEOUS DATABASE SYSTEMS

Migrating legacy databases to new generation architectures is difficult. Although it is desirable to migrate such databases and applications to client/server architectures, the costs involved in many cases are enormous. Therefore, the alternative approach is to keep the legacy databases and applications and develop mechanisms to integrate them with new systems. The distributed object management system approach in general, and the CORBA approach in particular, are examples of such mechanisms.

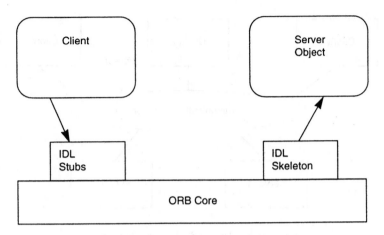

Exhibit 2. Interface Definition Language (IDL) Interface to Object Request Broker (ORB)

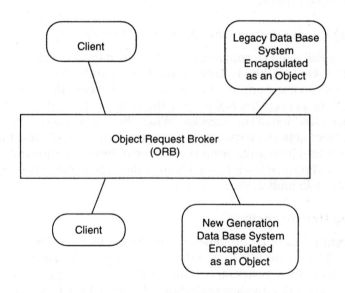

Exhibit 3. Encapsulating Legacy Databases

Although the major advantage of the CORBA approach is the ability to encapsulate legacy database systems and databases as objects without having to make any major modifications (see Exhibit 3), techniques for handling the various types of heterogeneity are still necessary. The CORBA approach does not handle problems such as transaction heterogeneity and semantic heterogeneity. However, the procedures used to handle the types

371

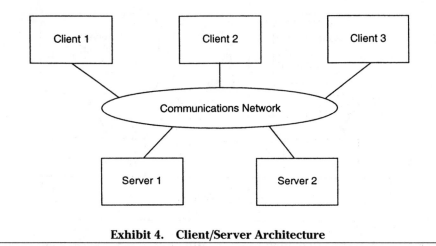

Exhibit 4. Client/Server Architecture

of heterogeneity can be encapsulated in the CORBA environment and invoked appropriately.

Handling Client Communications with the Server

A client will need to communicate with the database servers, as shown in Exhibit 4. One method is to encapsulate the database servers as objects. The clients can issue appropriate requests and access the servers through an ORB. If the servers are SQL-based, the entire SQL query/update request could be embedded in the message. When the method associated with the server object gets the message, it can extract the SQL request and pass it to the server. The results from the server objects are then encoded as a message and passed back to the client through the ORB. This approach is illustrated in Exhibit 5.

Handling Heterogeneity

Different types of heterogeneity must be handled in different ways. For example, if the client is SQL-based and the server is a legacy database system based on the network model, then the SQL query by the client must be transformed into a language understood by the server. One representation scheme must be transformed into another. The client's request must first be sent to the module that is responsible for performing the transformations. This module, the transformer, could be encapsulated as an object. As illustrated in Exhibit 6, the client's SQL request is sent to the transformer, which transforms the request into a request understood by the server. The transformed request is then sent to the server object. The transformer could directly transform the SQL representation into a network representation, or it could use an intermediate representation to carry out the transformation.

372

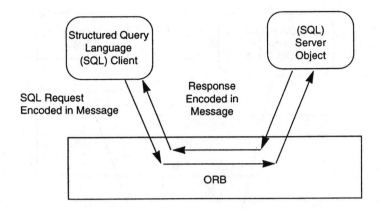

Exhibit 5. Common Object Request Broker Architecture (CORBA) for Interoperability

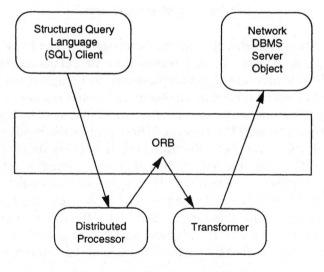

Exhibit 6. Handling Transformations

Handling Transformations

The distributed processor could also be used to perform distributed data management functions. The distributed processor is responsible for handling functions such as global query optimization and global transaction management. This module is also encapsulated as an object and handles the global requests and responses. The response assembled by the server is also sent to the transformer to transform into a representation understood by the client. Response delivery is illustrated in Exhibit 7.

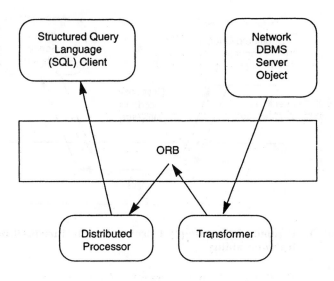

Exhibit 7. Delivering Responses

Semantic Heterogeneity. If semantic heterogeneity has to be handled, a repository should be maintained to store the different names given to a single object or the different objects represented by a single name. The repository could be encapsulated as an object that would resolve semantic heterogeneity. For example, a client could request that an object be retrieved from multiple servers. The request is first sent to the repository, which issues multiple requests to the appropriate servers depending on the names used to denote the object. This approach is illustrated in Exhibit 8. The response may also be sent to the repository so that it can be presented to the client in an appropriate manner. The repository could be an extension of the transformer illustrated in Exhibit 6. All the communications are carried out through the ORB. This example highlights some of the benefits of separating the business logic from the actual data stored in the DBMS servers.

CONCLUSION

The rapid growth in distributed systems has placed two key demands on IT managers:

1. How can the most efficient and effective design — the three-tier model — best be implemented to manage a very heterogeneous environment?
2. How can the semantic meaning of the legacy data elements be best understood so they can be shared across systems?

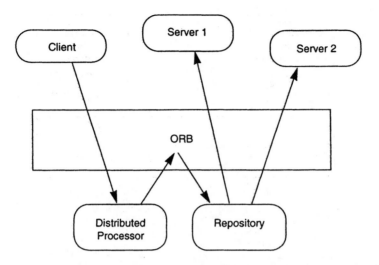

Exhibit 8.   Handling Semantic Heterogeneity

The CORBA approach is an excellent means of addressing heterogeneity, especially with respect to queries, languages, transactions, schemas, constraints, and semantics. However, although CORBA is useful for integrating heterogeneous database systems, there are still several issues that need further consideration. For example, should a server be encapsulated as an object? How can databases be encapsulated? Should an entire database be encapsulated as an object or should it consist of multiple objects? Should stored procedures be encapsulated also?

Although there is still much work to be done, the various approaches proposed to handle these issues show a lot of promise. Furthermore, until efficient approaches are developed to migrate the legacy databases and applications to client/server-based architectures, approaches like CORBA and other distributed object management systems for integrating heterogeneous databases and systems are needed.

Chapter 23
Middleware, Universal Data Servers, and Object-Oriented Data Servers

James A. Larson
Carol L. Larson

RELATIONAL DATABASE MANAGEMENT SYSTEMS are used widely to store and access an enterprise's data. The data elements managed by relational DBMSs are simple data types such as integers, floating point numbers, short character strings, and dates. However, relational DBMSs do not manage complex data types that may be important to an enterprise. Complex data types include multimedia data types such as text, images, audio, and video, and compound data types such as dates and time series. Until recently, relational DBMSs could not deal with these data types, which left enterprises with file systems or manual systems to manage their nonrelational forms of information.

Different enterprises have different requirements for complex data types. Some enterprises need multimedia data types, some need compound data types, and some need both. Although many enterprises depend heavily upon relational database technology, others rely primarily on file systems, and still others rely on manual procedures to manage noncomputerized multimedia data. It is doubtful that a single mechanism can satisfy these differing requirements.

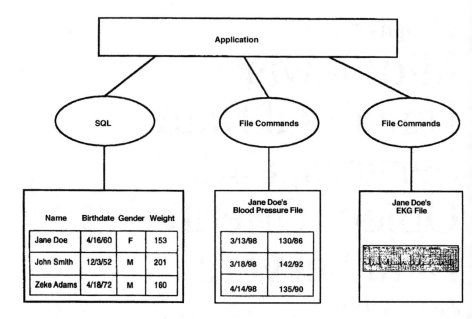

Exhibit 1.   Data extraction mechanism.

THE CHALLENGE OF COMPLEX DATA TYPES

Exhibits 1 through 4 illustrate four different mechanisms for dealing with complex data types. To illustrate the differences among the four approaches, a simple medical information system containing three types of data will be used.

Relational data includes the patient's name, unique identifier, address, date of birth, height, and weight. Typically, this information is stored in a Patient Information table managed by a relational DBMS. In an object-oriented DBMS, the information is contained within the Patient object.

Compound data includes daily blood pressure readings taken over several weeks. For the data extraction and middleware mechanisms, this information may be stored as a file consisting of several records, each containing the <date> and <reading> values. With a universal data server, the information is stored as a single data type, called a time series, consisting of a sequence of <date, reading> pairs. In an object-oriented data server, the information is represented as a Blood Pressure subobject of the Patient object.

Multimedia data includes the electrocardiogram (EKG) of the patient's heartbeat. With the data extraction, middleware, and universal data server approaches, the EKG is stored as a bit map in a file. In the object-oriented

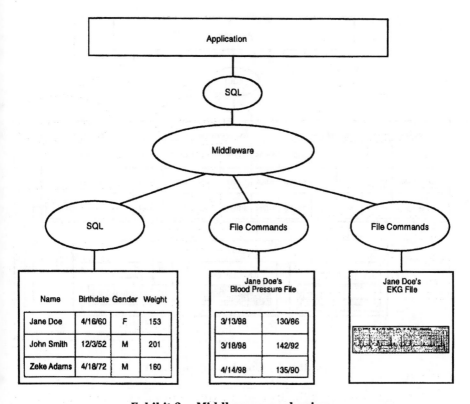

Exhibit 2.   Middleware mechanism.

data server mechanism, the EKG is represented as an electrocardiogram subobject of the Patient object.

Of course, a real medical database would have much more information than illustrated in each exhibit, but the examples will serve to illustrate the differences among the four mechanisms. For this discussion, assume that all data reside on the same computer.

The issues of distributed data are complex and beyond the scope of this article. Please see *Software Architectures for Distributed DBMSs in a Client/Server Environment* by J. A. Larson and C. L. Larson (Auerbach Publication, in press) for more information.

MECHANISMS SUPPORTING COMPLEX DATA TYPES

The first two mechanisms illustrated in Exhibits 1 and 2 enable applications to access existing data structures without migrating data to new types of servers.

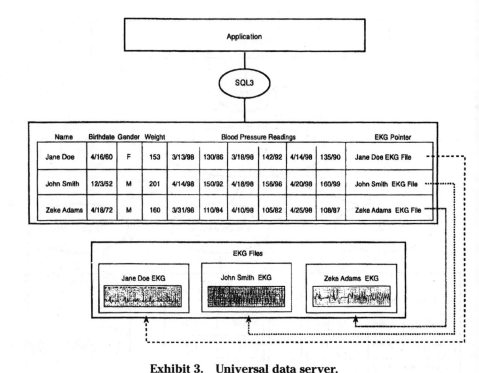

Exhibit 3.   Universal data server.

Data Extraction

In Exhibit 1, applications extract and integrate data from a relational database and a file system. To access relational information about Jane Doe, the application issues an SQL request to the relational DBMS, which returns the Patient Information about Jane Doe by accessing the Jane Doe Blood Pressure and EKG files. The application then merges and formats the information before presenting it to the user.

Middleware

With this approach, commercial middleware acts on behalf of the application to extract multimedia data from files and data from a relational data server. As shown in Exhibit 2, the application first issues an SQL request to the middleware, which passes it on to the relational DBMS, which in turn accesses the database and returns the Patient Information about Jane Doe. Next, the application issues SQL requests to the middleware, which converts the SQL request into file accesses applied to the file system and then returns the Jane Doe Blood Pressure file and the Jane Doe EKG file to the application. The application is responsible for merging the data from the database and the files before presenting it to the user.

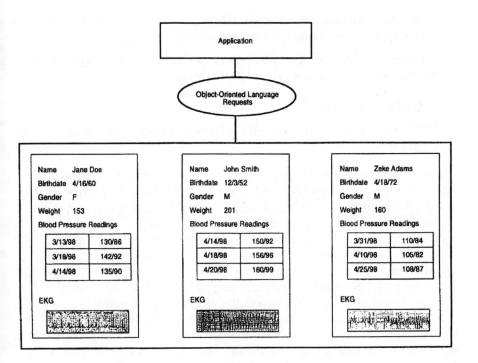

Exhibit 4.   Object-oriented data server.

A special type of middleware, called gateways, enables users to formulate requests in a language that is converted by the middleware to another language for processing. For example, when the application submits a request using SQL, the middleware translates the request to the format required by the underlying data server. Example gateways include the following:

- CrossAccess Data Delivery System from Cross Access Corporation. This system translates DB2 SQL to IMS, IDMS, Model 204, and file systems.
- EDA/SQL from Information Builders Incorporated. This software translates SQL into nonrelational data commands.
- OLE DB and Open Database Connectivity (ODBC) from Microsoft Corporation. These application program interfaces (APIs) and associated implementations enable applications to access many relational data servers, file systems, and other data sources.
- DB2 DataJoiner from IBM. DB2 DataJoiner is a translator that converts SQL requests into the format required by nonrelational data sources. It also performs other functions, including cross-database joins and

data conversions. Unlike most gateways, it has an optimizer to optimize queries involving data from multiple sources.

Gateways enable applications to access existing data sources without migrating the data to a new type of data server.

NEW DATA SERVERS

DBMS venders have introduced two new data servers to manage complex data types.

Universal Data Server. Exhibit 3 illustrates a universal data server, which contains extensions to relational data servers that store, search, and retrieve complex data types. These systems are called object relational, extended relational, multimedia, and universal data servers. The term universal data server is used frequently to indicate that a relational data server has been extended to support a variety of new data types. The application issues an SQL request to the universal data server, which returns Jane Doe's Patient Information, including the Blood Pressure complex data type, to the application. The universal data server uses pointers in the EKG column to access the bitmap containing Jane's EKG from the file system. Unlike the data extraction and middleware mechanisms, the universal data server integrates data from the file system and the universal database before returning the integrated results to the application, which in turn formats it and presents it to the user.

Object-oriented Data Server. As shown in Exhibit 4, this server stores, retrieves, and searches complex data types. In the object-oriented data server, the complex data types are called objects; they contain data to which the user may apply object-specific functions. Some objects may be similar to tables in relational DBMSs, and other objects may be complex data objects containing multiple nested subobjects. In the medical example, the object-oriented data server retrieves the Patient object for Jane Doe, as well as subobjects EKG and Blood Pressure. The application formats and presents the information to the user.

MECHANISM SELECTION AND EVALUATION CRITERIA

The four mechanisms differ in the features they support and are summarized in Exhibit 5.

Programming Language Support. When using data extraction, middleware, or universal servers, application programs use an Application Program Interface (API) to open a database, submit a request, and retrieve the results. These approaches do not support a programming language that accesses the database directly. However, applications written in an object-oriented language, such as C++ or Java, access objects in an object-orient-

Exhibit 5. Comparison of Mechanisms

| | Mechanism | | | |
Criteria	Data Extraction	Middleware	Universal Data Servers	Object-Oriented Data Servers
Programming language support	No	No	No	Yes
Extensible data type support	No	No	Yes	Yes
User-defined functions	No	No	Yes	Yes
Integrated backup and recovery	No	No	Yes	Yes
Automatic optimizers	No	No	Yes	Yes
SQL access	No	Yes	Yes	Yes
Multimedia access	Yes	Yes	Yes	Yes

ed data server directly. Object-oriented data servers enable programmers to access the database using the programming language without using special I/O commands, such as read and write.

Extensible Data Type Support . With the extracted and middleware approaches, programmers must implement new data types in the application and map the new data types to the data types supported by the underlying data sources. These tasks are taken over by database administrators for the universal and object-oriented data servers. For the universal data servers, database administrators define new data types by defining their representation, storage structure, and access methods using SQL 3. (Although SQL and SQL2 both describe tables, SQL3 describes tables and other complex data types that may be nested.) For object-oriented data servers, database administrators use an object-oriented language to define new data types.

New Functions . Part of defining a new data type is defining new functions involving the new data type. In the extracted and middleware approaches, programmers implement these new functions as part of the application. For universal and object-oriented data servers, database administrators define new functions to operate on the new data types. These functions can enforce business rules on the data, implement new functions required by application programs, and optimize queries.

Integrated Backup and Recovery . With the data extraction and middleware approaches, there is no integrated backup and recovery for both the file system and database. However, both universal and object-oriented data servers provide automatic backup and recovery mechanisms so that the entire database can be backed up and restored.

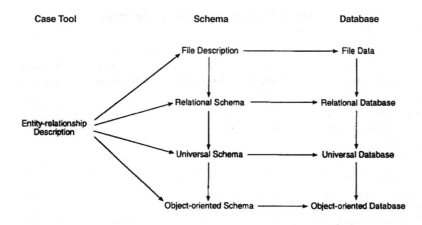

Exhibit 6. Mappings and conversions among schemas and databases.

Automatic Optimizers . For the data extraction and middleware ap-́ proaches, the application programmer must code all optimizations direct- ly into the application. Any global query optimization also must be done by the programmer. With the universal and object-oriented data servers, the database administrator specifies optimization procedures for execution by the data server. These optimization procedures are reused by each request submitted to the server.

SQL Access . Although the extraction approach includes a relational DBMS that supports SQL requests, all accesses by applications to the file system must be expressed using traditional file I/O commands. The re- maining three mechanisms support SQL requests for accessing all data. With the middleware approach, the middleware translates SQL requests into file I/O commands. The universal data server accepts and executes SQL requests against all data. Objects in most object-oriented data servers can be viewed as tables and, thus, support SQL requests. In addition, ob- ject-oriented servers also support requests expressed using an object-ori- ented language. These requests may include data type-specific functions.

Multimedia Access . All of the mechanisms support access to complex data types.

MIGRATING SCHEMA AND DATA

Exhibit 6 illustrates data models and databases involved in the conver- sion from files to relational or universal servers and, finally, to object- oriented data servers. Many enterprises use CASE tools to develop con- ceptual models of the enterprise's data. For example, several CASE tools use the entity-relationship modeling technique to represent the enterprise's data and a database schema for a relational or universal data server. Other CASE tools generate object-oriented syntax for creating object classes for an object-oriented data server.

When migrating from files to relational or universal data servers, file descriptions must be converted into relational schema. Some CASE tools are able to accept file descriptions and generate SQL syntax for creating equivalent relations. However, most database administrators perform this step manually. Chapter 25, "Migrating Data to an Integrated Database," gives suggestions for mapping files into relational schema.

When migrating to a universal server, most relational schema do not need to be converted; however, some schema may need to be extended to describe new media and complex data types. CASE tools should be used to modify the enterprise's conceptual schema and, then, to generate a revised relational schema. If the CASE tool does not support media or complex data types, the database administrator may need manually to modify the SQL generated by the CASE tool to incorporate these new data types into the relational schema.

When migrating from relational or universal servers to object-oriented servers, the database administrator must decide whether to model existing data as relations or as more complex objects. To minimize changes to existing applications, most data remain modeled as relations. However, some data should be modeled as objects, especially the new media and compound data types that provide the motivation for switching to an object-oriented data server. Some CASE tools generate either relational or object-oriented schema, which enable the database administrator to avoid manually converting a relational or universal schema into an object-oriented schema. If the enterprise does not have such a CASE tool, then the database administrator must generate object-oriented schema for all new data and existing relational data.

After the schema are in place, the database administrator must populate the new data server with data from the old files and/or databases. This involves writing conversion software that extracts data from the source files or databases, changes the format to conform to the new data schema, and inserts the data into the new data server. Any new data also must be captured and entered into the new data server. This conversion software may be quite complex when migrating from files into relations, especially when integrating data from multiple files. The conversion software is quite simple when converting relations from a relational or universal data server into relations in an object-oriented data server. Capturing and loading new media and compound data into the object-oriented data server may, however, be quite complex. Most database server venders provide conversion software to assist database administrators when migrating data to a new server.

RECOMMENDATIONS

The four mechanisms represent four steps of a migration path from independent relational data servers and file systems (which are integrated by applications that extract data) to integrated object-oriented data servers (which perform the most data management functions). For enterprises requiring complex data types, the long-term goal is clearly to employ an object-oriented data server. The other approaches can be used as intermediate stepping stones before migrating to an object-oriented data server.

If only a handful of applications require complex data types, the data extraction approach is preferred because it provides no disruption for legacy applications.

The middleware approach adds SQL support, which may be desirable for end users who are able to use GUI interfaces to generate SQL requests to all of the data. This positions the data for later upgrade to universal data servers, which support SQL directly.

Universal data servers provide integrated data management support for the new data types, as well as integrating them with the traditional tables of relational data systems. For relational data servers users, this is a reasonable alternative because most major relational data server vendors support universal data servers. The upward migration from relational to universal data servers is straightforward if the enterprise does not switch vendors.

The object-oriented data server promises to provide the most features and functions. However, some experts feel that object-oriented data servers do not provide performance superior to the relational data servers with their optimizers. In time, the optimizers of object-oriented data servers will improve just as optimizers for relational data servers have improved over the past ten years. Universal data servers appear to be in a safe holding pattern, providing access to complex data types, until object-oriented data servers provide the features and performance required by users.

Recommended Reading

Barry, D.K., *The Object Database Handbook : How to Select, Implement, and Use Object-Oriented Databases,* John Wiley & Sons, New York, 1996.

Cattell, R. G. G., *Object Data Management: Object-Oriented and Extended Relational Database Systems,* Addison-Wesley, Reading, MA, 1991.

Chamberlin, D., *DB2 Universal Database : IBM's Object-Relational Database Systems,* Morgan Kaufman Publishers, San Francisco, 1988.

Colonna-Romano, J. and Srite, P., *The Middleware Source Book,* Digital Press, Burlington, VT, 1995.

Finn, M., Use OLE DB to Integrate Your Data, *Databased Web Adv.,* Nov. 1997, 64–66.

Francett, B., Middleware on the March, *Software Mag.,* April 1996, 71–76.

Middleware, Universal Data Servers, and Object-Oriented Data Servers

Goddard, D., How Middleware Can Help Your Enterprise, *Databased Web Adv.*, May 1996, 100–107.

Larson, J. A. and Larson, C. L., *Designing an Integrated Data Server*, Auerbach Publication No. 22-01-95 (1997).

Larson, J. A. and Larson, C. L., *Migrating Files to Relational Databases*, Auerbach Publication No. 22-01-29 (1996).

Larson, J. A. and Larson, C. L., *Software Architectures for Distributed DBMSs in a Client/Server Environment*, Auerbach Publication (TBA 1998).

Larson, J. A. and Larson, C. L., *Why Universal Data Servers*, Auerbach Publication (TBA 1998).

Loomis, M. E. S. and Chaudhri, A. B., Eds., *Object Databases in Practice*, Prentice-Hall, Upper Saddle River, NJ, 1997.

Making Connections Across the Enterprise: Client-server Middleware, *DBMS*, January 1993, 46–51.

Recommended Websites

For more information about the products mentioned in this chapter, see the following Web pages:

Cross Access Corp. (Cross Access Delivery System), Oakbrook Terrace, IL, http://www.crossaccess.com/

IBM DB2 DataJoiner: http://www.software.ibm.com/data/datajoiner/

IBM Home Page: http://www.ibm.com/

Information Builders Inc. (EDA/SQL), Two Penn Plaza, New York, NY 10121-2898, 212.736.4433, Fax 212.967.6406, http://www.IBI.com/

Microsoft Corporation, Redmond, Washington, http://www.microsoft.com/

Microsoft Open Database Connectivity (ODBC), http://www.microsoft.com/data/odbc/

Microsoft OLE DB, http://www.microsoft.com/data/oledb/

Chapter 24
Designing an Integrated Data Server

James A. Larson
Carol L. Larson

An enterprise's information may be scattered across multiple, isolated information islands in a sea of computers and database systems. To use enterprise data, users must locate, access, and integrate data from multiple databases and files that may be located in different data systems on different computers and possibly separated geographically.

The evolution of an enterprise and its databases contributes to the scattering of data. Many companies encourage their enterprise units (i.e., divisions, departments, and subsidiaries) to be independent from each other. Independent enterprise units evolve differently with different data requirements, applications, and systems. Each enterprise unit designs its database to meet its particular needs. Databases of different enterprise units often contain different information used for different purposes.

WHEN SHOULD DATA BE INTEGRATED INTO A DATA SERVER?

The proliferation of PCs has greatly aggravated the data dispersion problem. The widespread use of PCs has resulted in many files and databases that are frequently stored on floppy disks. These off-line databases make it even more difficult to access all of the enterprises's data. To be useful, data must be available when users need it. Furthermore, users may not know what data are available or how to find it.

In such an environment, users must perform three essential actions to obtain meaningful information:

- *Locate information.* Users must determine if relevant data are available somewhere among the computing resources of the enterprise. Then, they must locate the appropriate computer containing the relevant data.

- *Access information.* Users must be able to formulate separate requests to access each data source.
- *Integrate information.* Users must integrate the results of their requests into an integrated format so they can review and use the data to make decisions.

If users are not able to access the data they need or are not aware of what data they need, they cannot make the necessary decisions or perform their jobs optimally. This results in poor performance for both the individuals and the enterprise as a whole. Data should be integrated into a centralized server if the cost of poor performance is greater than the expense of integrating the diverse databases and files into a centralized database server.

DATA INTEGRATION FROM MULTIPLE SOURCES

The term *source tables* refers to tables to be integrated. Target tables are the result of the integration. Exhibit 1 illustrates bottom-up and top-down approaches to integrating data from multiple sources. The bottom-up approach consists of four steps:

- *Inventorying existing data.* Source database tables and files to be integrated into a target centralized database server must be identified.
- *Modeling individual databases.* The entities and their relationships within each source database must be identified.
- *Converting all schemas to relational schemas.* All entities and relationships must be expressed in a common format.
- *Integrating source schemas into a target schema.* Structural and format inconsistencies among data from different source databases must be identified and resolved.

The top-down approach consists of two steps:

- *Designing the target schema.* Data elements needed in the target schema must be determined.
- *Constructing cross-references.* Cross-references are essential from each source schema to the target schema. Mappings between the source and target schemas must be defined.

After using the bottom-up approach, the top-down approach, or a combination of these approaches, the database administrator migrates and integrates source data from the various source databases into a target relational database server. Erroneous and inconsistent data should be identified and resolved.

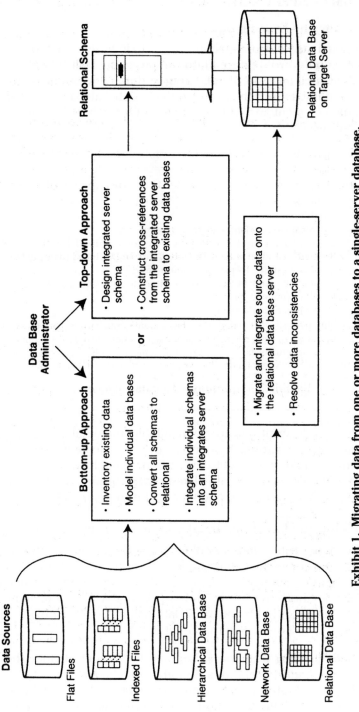

Exhibit 1. Migrating data from one or more databases to a single-server database.

THE BOTTOM-UP APPROACH

Step 1: Inventorying Existing Data

The first step in the bottom-up approach is to identify every source data element that should be integrated into the target centralized data server. Exhibit 2 illustrates an example of a source data element. From this description, the database administrator quickly determines the meaning of the source data element and whether it should be included in the centralized database server.

English name:	class
COBOL name:	class
Fortran name:	class
C name:	class
Type:	short integer
Values:	1 = freshman (student with fewer than 45 hours)
	2 = sophomore (student with 45 or more hours and with less than 90 hours)
	3 = junior (student with 90 or more hours and with less than 135 hours)
	4 = senior (student with 135 or more hours)
	5 = graduate student (formally admitted to graduate school)
	6 = other (none of the above)
Source:	student record in student file
Calculation:	automatically calculated from the student's transcript record on the second week of each semester. The value includes the number of hours the student actually earned the previous semester. This field is not updated automatically when incomplete grades are changed to final grades.

Exhibit 2. Description of a data element.

If data element descriptions are not available, the database administrator must examine applications that access the data elements to determine their meaning. If the data element descriptions do not exist, the database administrator should create a data element description for each data element and form a data element dictionary for future reference.

Step 2: Modeling the Individual Databases as Schemas

A data model describes database objects and their relationships, as well as each data element in each source database or file. In addition, the data model describes the elements of the target database. Using the same data model to describe both the source and target database objects allows the database administrator to identify the relationships between objects in the source databases and objects in the target database.

Popular Data-Modeling Techniques. Popular data models include the relational data model, entity-relationship data models, and object-oriented data models. To facilitate a comparison of objects in different databases, it is desirable to use a single data model to describe all databases and files.

Database administrators differ in their choice of data models and often argue the advantages and disadvantages of the various data models. Here, the relational data model is used because it is the data model used by the target database management system.

Step 3: Integrating Schemas into an Integrated Server Schema

One strategy for schema integration is to identify the relationship between pairs of source tables and then construct the appropriate target table. The bottom-up approach uses the following four steps to define a target schema:

Identify Pairs of Source Tables as Candidates for Integration. Database administrators should use heuristics to identify candidate pairs of source tables. One possible heuristic is to consider only pairs of source tables that have the same name, nearly the same names, or names that are synonyms. Another possible heuristic is to consider pairs of source tables that have several columns with the same name, nearly the same name, or names that are synonyms.

Determine the Relationship of the Rows of the Source Tables. Database administrators should determine the relationships between pairs of source tables. The five tables in Exhibit 3 describe each of the four possible relationships — logical containment, logical equivalence, logical overlap, and logically disjoint — between any pair of source tables, referred to as tables A and B. These relationships are defined as follows:

- *Logical containment.* If each row in A always corresponds to a unique row in B, then B logically contains A. For example, every SmallAircraft row always corresponds to a row of Aircraft. Therefore, Aircraft logically contains SmallAircraft.
- *Logical equivalence.* If each row in A always corresponds to a unique row of B and each row in B always corresponds to a unique row in A, then B is logically equivalent to A. For example, every CarValue row always corresponds to a CarRegistration row and every CarRegistration row always corresponds to a CarValue row. Therefore, CarValue is logically equivalent to CarRegistration.
- *Logical overlap.* If some of the rows in A correspond to some of the rows in B and some of the rows in B correspond to some of the rows in A, then A and B logically overlap. For example, some Truck rows are found in CarRegistration, and some CarRegistration rows are found in Truck. Therefore, CarRegistration and Truck logically overlap.
- *Logically disjoint.* If none of the rows in A corresponds to any of the rows in B and none of the rows in B corresponds to any of the rows in A, then A and B are logically disjoint. For example, no rows of Aircraft are found in CarRegistration, and no rows of CarRegistration are found

Aircraft (Source Table)

Owner	RegNumber	Flight Rating Level
Able	14	2
Baker	23	1
Gilbert	67	3

Small Aircraft (Source Table)

Owner	RegNumber	Flight Rating Level	Range
Able	14	2	600
Baker	23	1	800

Car Value (Source Table)

RegNumber	Year	Manufacturer	Model	Price
37	95	Plymouth	Voyager	15000
42	92	Ford	Taurus	7000
54	95	Jeep	Cherokee	17000

Car Registration (Source Table)

Owner	RegNumber	Year	Manufacturer	Model
Carson	37	95	Plymouth	Voyager
Davis	42	92	Ford	Taurus
Elgin	54	95	Jeep	Cherokee

Truck (Source Table)

Owner	RegNumber	Load Limit	Year	Manufacturer	Model
Able	14	2000	94	Dodge	Ram
Elgin	54	1000	95	Jeep	Cherokee

Exhibit 3. Sample source tables.

in the Aircraft table. Therefore, Aircraft and CarRegistration are logically disjoint.

The database administrator must determine which of the candidate pairs of source tables to integrate. Two source tables may be integrated if they are logically equivalent, one logically contains the other, or they logically overlap. If two source tables are disjoint, they should only be integrated if the database administrator determines that they represent the same type of entity. For example, the Aircraft and CarValue tables should not be integrated based on logical analysis alone.

Create the Integrated Tables. For each pair of source tables to be integrated, the database administrator must determine how many target tables to create as a result of the integration. There are three general approaches.

No-Table Approach. The database administrator should not integrate the two source tables. For example, because Aircraft and CarRegistration (see Exhibit 3) are logically disjoint, they should not be integrated into a single table. However, these tables may be integrated if the database administrator determines that several applications will access both tables for the same purpose.

Single-Table Approach. A single target table should be created to replace a pair of source tables to be integrated. The single target table contains the union of the columns from the two source tables with columns suitably renamed. Some rows of the target table may contain nulls in the columns that are not common to both of the source tables.

An example of the single-table approach is CarValue's logical equivalence to CarRegistration. The database administrator should create a single-target table, Car, to replace CarRegistration and CarValue by constructing the columns of the Car table to be the union of the columns of CarValue and CarRegistration. The Car target table should appear as shown in Exhibit 4.

Owner	RegNumber	Year	Manufacturer	Model	Price
Carson	37	95	Plymouth	Voyager	15000
Davis	42	92	Ford	Taurus	7000
Elgin	54	95	Jeep	Cherokee	17000

Exhibit 4. Car (target table).

As another example, the Aircraft table (see Exhibit 3) logically contains the SmallAircraft table. The database administrator should construct the columns of the target table, Airplane, to be the union of the columns of the source tables, Aircraft and SmallAircraft. The Airplane target table appears in Exhibit 5.

Owner	RegNumber	Flight Rating Level	Range
Able	14	2	600
Baker	23	1	800
Gilbert	67	3	(null)

Exhibit 5. Airplane (target table).

There is no value in the Range column for the airplane with RegNumber 67 because it is not a small aircraft and the Range column is not common to both source tables. Some database administrators dislike the single-table approach because a missing value implies additional semantics; in this case, Airplane 67 is a small aircraft.

Multiple-Table Approach. Multiple target tables should be created to replace the two source tables to be integrated. One target table contains the columns and the rows common to both source tables being integrated.

Each of two additional target tables contains the key from the source table and the columns from the source table not common to the two source tables to be integrated. In the multiple-table approach, the extra target tables represent rows that are in one but not the other source table.

For example, the Truck and CarRegistration source tables logically overlap. Three target tables can be constructed from the source tables CarRegistration and Truck. The Vehicle target table contains the common columns of the Truck and CarRegistration source tables, as shown in Exhibit 6.

Owner	RegNumber	Year	Manufacturer	Model
Carson	37	95	Plymouth	Voyager
Davis	42	92	Ford	Taurus
Elgin	54	95	Jeep	Cherokee

Exhibit 6. Vehicle (target table).

The Truck target table contains the columns of the source Truck table minus the columns of the Vehicle target table; as shown in Exhibit 7. The Car target table contains the columns of the CarRegistration source table minus the columns of the Vehicle target table, as shown in Exhibit 8.

RegNumber	Load Limit
14	2000
54	1000

Exhibit 7. Truck (target table).

RegNumber	Price
37	15000
42	7000
54	17000

Exhibit 8. Car (target table).

Some database administrators dislike the multiple-table approach because they feel the target tables are overnormalized or broken into too many tables, which may result in complex operations. For example, the Vehicle, Car, and Truck tables must be joined to access all the data associated with a vehicle. When a vehicle is removed from the database, rows of multiple tables must be deleted.

The choice between the single-table and multiple-table approaches must be made by the database administrator based on the anticipated use of the resulting tables. Generally, the single-table approach is used if the primary usage will be retrieval; the multiple-table approach is used if the primary use will be update.

TOP-DOWN APPROACH

Step 1: Designing the Target Schema

The database administrator designs a centralized database, such as the following two source tables:

- Aircraft (which contains Owner, RegNumber, FlightRatingLevel, and Range).
- Vehicle (which contains Owner, RegNumber, Year, Manufacturer, Model, Price, and LoadLimit).

Step 2: Constructing Cross-References Between the Integrated Server Schema to Existing Databases

This step requires that the database administrator define the mappings between the source and target schemas. For each column in a source table, the corresponding column in a target table must be identified. In Exhibit 9, these correspondences are illustrated by arrows. The database administrator should review the mappings and check for the following situations:

- *New value.* If a data element in a target table has no mapping, then there will be no way for it to contain any values. The database administrator can either specify the manual process for supplying values to this data element or delete it from the schema.
- *Potential inconsistent value.* If a column in a target table has two or more mappings, then it will receive data from two or more source tables. There is a possibility of inconsistencies when data is obtained from the two source tables. These inconsistencies must be detected and resolved by the database administrator.
- *Missing data element.* If a data element in a source table is not mapped to a data element in any target table, the database administrator should verify that the missing data element will not be used by applications accessing the source database. If an application does access the data element, then the missing data element should be inserted in the appropriate target table.

CENTRALIZED DATABASE SERVER POPULATION AND INCONSISTENT DATA RESOLUTION

After using a combination of the bottom-up and top-down approaches, the structural relationships between the source and target data elements

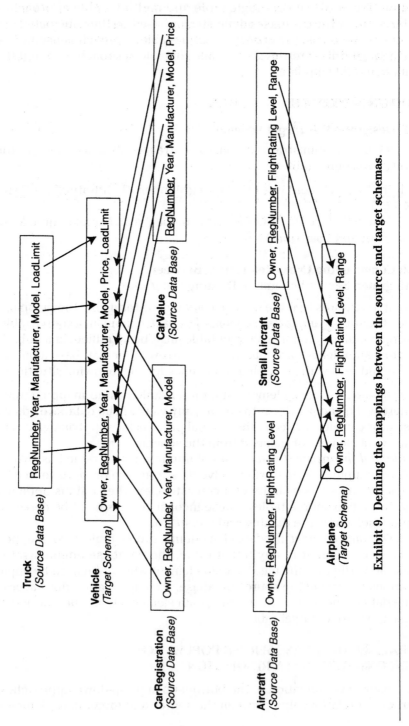

Exhibit 9. Defining the mappings between the source and target schemas.

should be identified. The database administrator should identify and resolve structural inconsistencies such as naming issues, differing levels of abstractions, inconsistent coding structures, and inconsistent data formats. If a target data element has multiple source elements, value inconsistencies should be detected and resolved.

RECOMMENDED COURSE OF ACTION

Users must perform three essential actions to obtain meaningful information:

- Locate relevant data and the computer that contains the data.
- Formulate separate requests to each data source to access the data.
- Integrate the results of the users' requests into an integrated format that users review and use to make decisions.

Data should be integrated into a centralized server if the cost of poor performance is greater than the expense of integrating the diverse databases and files into a centralized database server.

The bottom-up approach for schema integration creates an inventory of existing data and identifies the local databases and files to be integrated into a centralized database server, models individual databases, converts all schemas to relational schemas, and integrates source schemas into an integrated target schema.

The alternative top-down approach first designs the target schema and then defines the mappings from the source schemas to the target schema. Most practitioners use a combination of the top-down and bottom-up approaches.

Chapter 25
Migrating Data to an Integrated Database

James A. Larson
Carol L. Larson

Relational database management systems (RDBMSs) are a great boon to data access. However, migrating data into a unified relational database can be quite challenging. To perform a successful migration, database administrators need to know how to:

- Detect and resolve structural inconsistencies.
- Detect and resolve value inconsistencies.
- Balance the trade-off between the cost of maintaining an accurate database with the cost of mistakes due to inaccurate data.

STRUCTURAL INCONSISTENCIES

Inconsistencies among data files can be classified as either structural or value. Structural inconsistencies are incompatibilities among the schemas or file descriptions and should be identified and resolved before migrating data between the source and target files. Value inconsistencies are differences in values of corresponding schema items and can be identified only as data are moved and integrated from multiple sources into a single target file. Database administrators deal with each of these two inconsistencies in very different ways.

Structural inconsistency is the situation where the organization and formats of the target schema are different from the organization and formats of the source schema. Types of structural inconsistencies include naming issues, different abstraction levels, inconsistent coding structures, inconsistent data formats, and unneeded or missing data.

Naming Issues

The first task facing database administrators in determining how the data items of a source file relate to the data items of a target file is the identification of corresponding data elements. Database administrators often

0-8493-9968-8/99/$0.00+$.50
© 1999 by CRC Press LLC

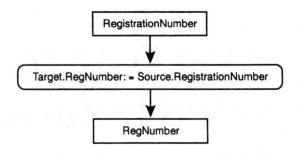

Exhibit 1. Indicating the correspondence between a source data element and a target data element.

use data element names as clues to map data elements of a source file into the data elements of a target file. Exhibit 1 illustrates the notation used to indicate how a data element (i.e., RegistrationNumber) in the source file maps to a data element (i.e., RegNumber) in the target file.

Frequently, the names of two corresponding data items in the source and target files are similar, and therefore the database administrator has no trouble identifying the correspondence. However, at times, data elements with the same name or nearly the same name may have very different meanings. For example, "date" may have several different meanings, including start date, end date, date the data was entered, publication date, date of issue, or date something becomes active. Database administrators must understand how the data will be used to determine precisely if two data elements really mean the same thing.

Sometimes data elements with different names mean the same thing, as in title and job, level and class, rank and position, and location and address. Again, database administrators must understand how data will be used to determine whether data items with different names are equivalent.

Different Abstraction Levels

Two similar data items may represent similar information at different levels of abstraction. For example, the data item BirthDate is more specific than BirthYear because BirthDate includes the month and day of birth. In another example, the data element Author is binary and indicates only whether a person has written one or more books. However, the element NumberBooksAuthored is much more specific; it indicates that a person is an author and the number of books authored.

It is always possible to define a mapping from the specific to the more general data element. Exhibit 2 illustrates the mappings from BirthDate to BirthYear and from NumberBooksAuthored to Author. However, additional

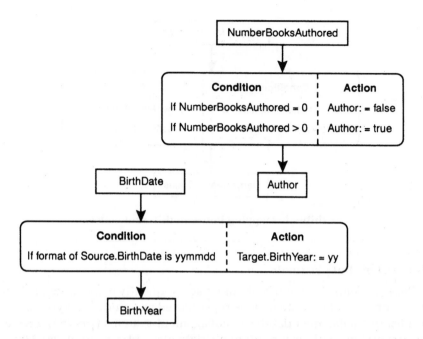

Exhibit 2. Mapping specific data elements to general data elements.

information is required to map a general data item to a more specific data item. Retaining as much specificity as possible is recommended, so information from the source database is not lost as it is migrated to the target database.

Inconsistent Coding Structures

The values used to represent information may differ between two data items. As illustrated in Exhibit 3, the source data element may use "S" for single and "M" for married, and the target data element may use "1" for single and "2" for married. In this case, mapping between the two coding structures is straightforward.

In some cases, one coding structure is more specific than another. For example, the source data element uses "U" for undergraduate and "G" for graduate and the target data element uses four different codes ("F" for freshman, "S" for sophomore, "J" for junior, and "R" for senior) for undergraduates and two codes ("M" for master's and "P" for Ph.D.) for graduate students. Retaining the more specific coding structures is recommended. As the mappings in Exhibit 4 illustrate, additional information is necessary to map the general codes (G and U) to the specific codes (F, S, J, R, M, and P).

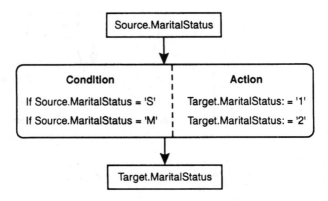

Exhibit 3. Mapping between different codes.

Inconsistent Data Formats

Data elements from different databases frequently use different data formats. For example, a date may be represented as mm/dd/yy, yy/mm/dd, or in Julian formats. Most database management systems (DBMSs) have utility conversion routines for automatic data format translation, as shown in Exhibit 5.

Occasionally, multiple data items from one file map to a single data item in another file. For example, BirthMonth, BirthDay, and BirthYear map to BirthDate and, as illustrated in Exhibit 6, LastName and FirstName map to CompleteName.

Unneeded or Missing Data

Database administrators should pay special attention to data that is contained in the source file but missing from the target file. Missing data may indicate that an application using the target file may have been overlooked during the analysis. Because the required data is missing from the integrated database, these applications cannot be executed. Database administrators should validate that the data in the source file is not needed in the target file.

Database administrators should also pay special attention to data in the target file that is not present in the source file. This data represents new database requirements and may indicate that an expensive data collection effort may be necessary to populate the new data item so applications accessing the new data can be executed.

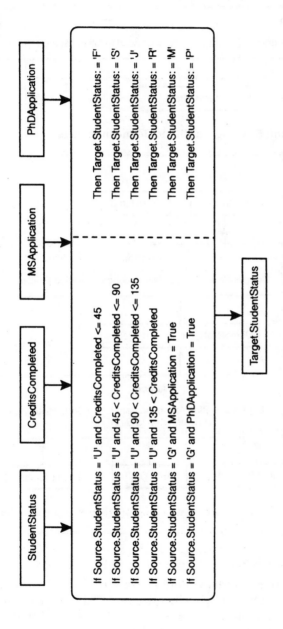

StudentStatus   CreditsCompleted   MSApplication   PhDApplication

If Source.StudentStatus = 'U' and CreditsCompleted <= 45   Then Target.StudentStatus: = 'F'
If Source.StudentStatus = 'U' and 45 < CreditsCompleted <= 90   Then Target.StudentStatus: = 'S'
If Source.StudentStatus = 'U' and 90 < CreditsCompleted <= 135   Then Target.StudentStatus: = 'J'
If Source.StudentStatus = 'U' and 135 < CreditsCompleted   Then Target.StudentStatus: = 'R'
If Source.StudentStatus = 'G' and MSApplication = True   Then Target.StudentStatus: = 'M'
If Source.StudentStatus = 'G' and PhDApplication = True   Then Target.StudentStatus: = 'P'

Target.StudentStatus

Exhibit 4. Deriving values for a more specific data element.

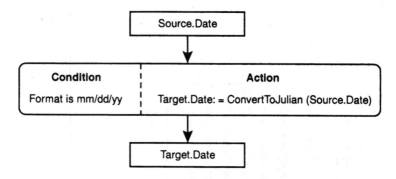

Exhibit 5. Using a utility to define mappings.

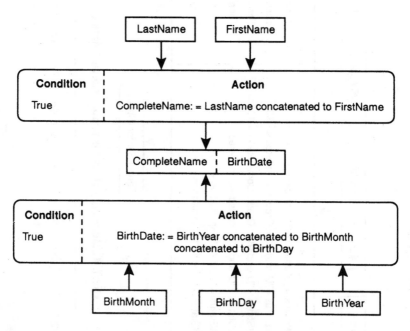

Exhibit 6. Combining two source data elements to create a single target.

VALUE INCONSISTENCIES

Whenever there are two independent sources of values for a data item, it is possible that the values may be inconsistent. Exhibit 7 includes an algorithm for detecting such inconsistencies. It is assumed that the first source of values has already been migrated to the target Vehicle file. Exhibit 7 also illustrates the pseudocode for detecting inconsistencies between

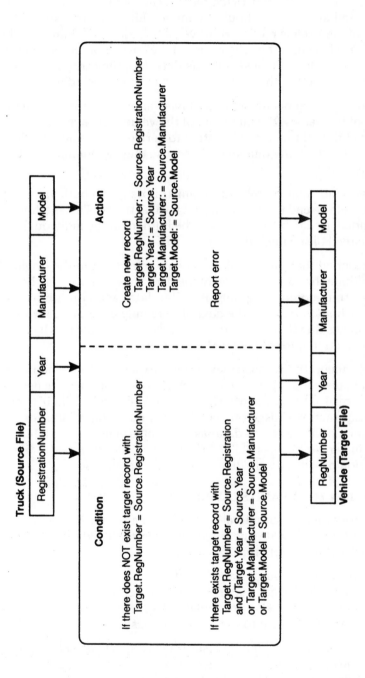

Truck (Source File)

| RegistrationNumber | Year | Manufacturer | Model |

Condition

If there does NOT exist target record with
Target.RegNumber = Source.RegistrationNumber

If there exists target record with
Target.RegNumber = Source.Registration
and (Target.Year = Source.Year
or Target.Manufacturer = Source.Manufacturer
or Target.Model = Source.Model

Action

Create new record
Target.RegNumber: = Source.RegistrationNumber
Target.Year: = Source.Year
Target.Manufacturer: = Source.Manufacturer
Target.Model: = Source.Model

Report error

| RegNumber | Year | Manufacturer | Model |

Vehicle (Target File)

Exhibit 7. Representing an algorithm to detect value inconsistencies.

records of the source Truck file and the target Vehicle file. If there is no matching Vehicle record for the Truck record, then a new Vehicle record should be created and values should be moved into the corresponding data elements of the Vehicle record. However, if there is a matching Vehicle record for the Truck record, then the values of the corresponding elements should be compared. If an inconsistency is detected, the error should be reported right away so that the inconsistency can be corrected manually.

When inconsistencies occur, some database administrators calculate the maximum of the values, the minimum of the values, the average of the values, or some other automatic calculation to derive a single target value. These approaches are not recommended because they do not improve the accuracy of the data.

On the other hand, some database administrators retain both values in the database to let the end user choose which value to use. This method is not recommended, either, because it puts the burden on the individual using the data instead of the individual entering the data.

It is recommended that the owner of the data refer back to the original source to determine the accurate value of the data. However, this can be an expensive and time-consuming activity. The database administrator should consider how to balance the cost of obtaining accurate data with the cost of mistakes due to inaccurate data to determine how much effort should be expended to correct known database errors.

A completely accurate database may be very expensive to maintain because of the cost of validating each data item. However, this may be necessary for databases that may have serious implications when their users take inappropriate actions based on inaccurate or out-of-date data. For example, errors in a police warrant database or a pharmacy's drug interaction database may result in loss of life, but errors in a holiday card mailing list or a television broadcast schedule are not life-threatening.

DATA MIGRATION TOOLS AND SERVICES

Many tools are available for migrating data from a source database to a target database. Generally, data migration tools assist the database administrator in constructing scripts that:

- Extract data from the source database files.
- Convert data to the format required by the target database.
- Detect inconsistencies between similar data from two sources.
- Insert the extracted data into the target database.

Some data migration tools contain a scripting language used to specify the four migration operations (i.e., extracting the data, converting the data, detecting inconsistencies, and inserting the extracted data). The scripting language can also be used to execute the scripts. After executing the scripts, the database administrator examines reports generated by the scripts and resolves any errors and data inconsistencies detected.

Some tools use a graphical user interface (GUI) to display the data elements from the source schema and the proposed data elements in the target schema. Using drag-and-drop operations, the database administrator identifies and specifies each of the migration operations. The GUI interface then generates the scripts. The database administrator may then edit the scripts to include additional functions and operations.

Despite the variety of data migration tools available, most tools only work with specific DBMSs. Vendors often provide tools for migrating data from files or from other DBMSs to their products, but rarely provide tools for migrating data from their products. The migrating tool marketplace is dynamic; new tools are announced frequently, and existing tools become outdated quickly.

Users can contact DBMS vendors for an up-to-date list of migration tools that work with particular DBMSs and solicit the vendor's recommendation about the usefulness of each tool. Costs for the tools vary. Some tools may be available at no cost from the vendor.

Because database administrators are familiar with the meaning and use of each data item, it is recommended that they perform their own data migration. However, if it is difficult to obtain and learn to use migration tools, hiring a service organization to migrate the data may be cost effective. Database administrators should work closely with the service organization to develop the appropriate mappings between the source and target data and to resolve the data inconsistencies when detected.

RECOMMENDED COURSE OF ACTION

Database administrators should identify structural relationships between the source and target data elements. If the corresponding data elements are structured differently, pseudocode should be written for mapping the source data elements to the target data elements. From this pseudocode, code can be written or generated to migrate the source table to the target table. When migrating data to a data element already containing values, values should be checked and corrected according to the enterprise's general policy for tolerating and correcting erroneous data.

Bibliography

Brodie, M.L. and Stonebraker, M., *Migrating Legacy Systems: Gateways, Interfaces and the Incremental Approach*, Morgan-Kaufman, San Francisco, 1995.

Chapter 26
Mobile Database Interoperability: Architecture and Functionality

Antonio Si

Wireless networks and mobile computing have opened up new possibilities for information access and sharing. The need to interoperate multiple heterogeneous, autonomous databases is no longer confined to a conventional federated environment.

A mobile environment is usually composed of a collection of static servers and a collection of mobile clients. Each server is responsible for disseminating information over one or more wireless channels to a collection of mobile clients. The geographical area within which all mobile clients could be serviced by a particular server is called a cell of that server.

In this mobile environment, databases managed by database servers of different cells might be autonomous. Information maintained in a database will usually be most useful to clients within its geographical cell. In this respect, information maintained by databases of different cells might be disjointed or might be related. A mobile client, when migrating from one wireless cell to another, might want to access information maintained in the database server and relate it to the information maintained in its own database. Such an environment is termed a mobile federation, to distinguish it from a conventional federated environment. The database managed by a mobile client is termed a mobile database, while the database managed by the server is a server database. Using similar terminology, the database system managed by a mobile client is referred to as a mobile component and the database system managed by a server is referred to as a server component.

0-8493-9968-8/99/$0.00+$.50
© 1999 by CRC Press LLC

It is not clear if existing techniques can address interoperability in this newly evolved computing environment. This chapter presents a reference architecture for a conventional federated environment, proposes a set of functional requirements that a federated environment should support, and examines existing techniques for a federated environment with respect to each functional requirement in the context of the newly evolved mobile federation.

A WORKING SCENARIO

A tourist would like to discover information about attractions and accommodations within a certain area. With a portable computer equipped with a wireless communication interface, each mobile client (tourist) can receive travel information from the server over a wireless channel. Such an application might be called an Advanced Traveler Information System (ATIS).

In practice, each server database would maintain traveler information restricted to its own cell. For example, a server database serving the city of Los Angeles might provide vacancy information for all hotels within the Los Angeles area, such as the Holiday Inn near the Hollywood Freeway. A user might query the server database to obtain all hotels that have vacancies. Information maintained by different server databases might, to a large extent, be disjoint in this application domain, but there might still be some information overlap among different server databases.

For example, a Holiday Inn within the Los Angeles region might decide to maintain partial information on Holiday Inns in other regions, such as Pasadena. It is also important to note that different server databases will, in general, be autonomous, each employing different database management tools and even different data models to manage its own information. Exhibit 1 illustrates a snapshot of the information maintained in different server databases and a mobile client who accesses information via a wireless channel.

It would be useful to have a high-level capability that allows structured units of information to be identified from a server database and incorporated into a local database managed by a mobile client. For example, a client might want to maintain information on all hotels in Cell 1 and Cell 2, since he or she travels to these two areas the most. A client visiting Cell 1 (as shown in Exhibit 1) might issue a query to obtain all hotel information. When the client visits cell 2, the hotel information incorporated into his or her database will have to be interoperated with the existing information that the client previously incorporated from the server database in Cell 1. This allows a mobile client to query the information using his or her own familiar database management tools. These various server databases, together with the local database of the mobile client, form a mobile federation. It is interesting to

412

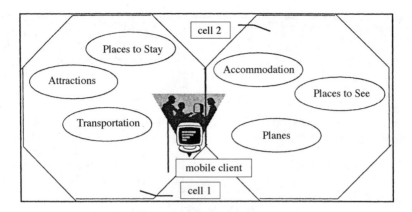

Exhibit 1.   Snapshot of ATIS databases.

note that the local database maintained in a mobile client is, in effect, a data warehouse since its data is constructed by integrating data from various data sources.

The objective of a mobile federation is similar to a conventional federated database environment. Both environments are trying to share information among multiple autonomous databases. In a mobile federation, the sharing of information is implicit; the information is shared within the context of a mobile client. In a conventional federated system, the information is shared among the databases themselves. Obviously, the server databases of various cells could also share information among themselves, in which case the server databases form a conventional federated environment as well.

FEDERATED ENVIRONMENT ARCHITECTURE

Exhibit 2 illustrates a typical federated environment. As the exhibit shows, a collection of independent database components is interconnected via a communication network. Each component consists of a database and a schema. A database is a repository of data structured or modeled according to the definition of the schema, which can be regarded as a collection of conceptual entity types. (The implementation of an entity type, of course, depends on the database model employed by the component; it may be a relation in a relational model, or it can be an object class, if an object-oriented model is employed.)

Information-Sharing Techniques

Sharing of database information in this federated environment could be achieved at three different levels of granularity and abstraction:

413

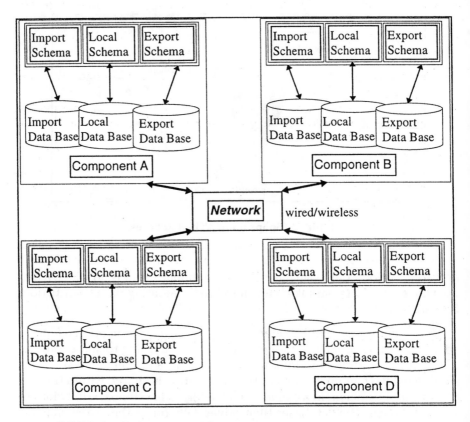

Exhibit 2.   Reference architecture for a federated environment.

- Entity types belonging to the schema of individual components could be shared such that modeled real-world concepts could be reused.
- Data instances stored in individual components' databases (the implementation of which also depends on the database model employed) could be shared such that information of modeled real-world entities could be reused.
- Applications developed on a component's database could be shared among any other components. For example, if the server database in Cell 1 in Exhibit 1 develops a pathfinder application that allows a mobile client to search for the shortest route to a destination, it could be reused by a mobile client in searching paths within Cell 2 as well.

The simplest way to achieve information sharing in a database federation is for a component to simply browse through the content of a nonlocal (i.e., remote) component's database. In this respect, an explorer should be provided. Alternatively, a component could integrate remote information into its local database. The newly integrated information could be reused by the component in the future. To support such reuse of information, the database of a component, say X, is logically partitioned into three different subsets, as shown in Exhibit 2:

- *Local database.* The local database refers to the set of data instances originally created by X.
- *Import database.* The import database refers to the set of remote data instances that X retrieves from the export databases of remote components.
- *Export database.* The export database is a subset of the union of the local database and import database, which represents the set of data instances the component is willing to share with other components. In other words, a component should be able to export its imported data instances if the access privilege constraints specified on the imported instances are not violated.

Similarly, from the reference architecture in Exhibit 1, the schema of a component X is also partitioned into three different subsets. The local schema refers to the entity types originally created by X and is used to model the local database. The import schema, which refers to the entity types X retrieves from the export schema of remote components, is used to model the import database. Finally, the export schema, which is the subset of the union of the local schema and the import schema, is used to model the export database.

Integrating a remote application belonging to a remote component, say Y, into X's local system is difficult because X's local computer system might be different from that of Y. One possibility (proposed by D. Fang et al.) is to integrate the signature of the remote application into X's local system. To execute the application, X's local data is passed to component Y; the application is run on the remote component using X's data and the results are returned back to X. The Java virtual machine could make application sharing easier.

CHARACTERISTICS OF A FEDERATED DATABASE ENVIRONMENT

Each component within a federation is usually heterogeneous and autonomous in nature. Heterogeneity is a natural consequence of the independent creation and evolution of autonomous databases; it refers to the variations in which information is specified and structured in different components. Autonomy means each component is under separate and independent control.

Heterogeneity

In general, a spectrum of heterogeneities of different levels of abstraction could be classified.

Database Model Heterogeneity. Each component may use different database models to describe the structure and constraints of its data.

Conceptual Schema Heterogeneity. Each component may model similar real-world concepts in different ways, such as the different schema used by the different database components of the multiple ATIS databases depicted in Exhibit 1. This is also referred to as semantic heterogeneity. This conceptual schema heterogeneity could be further divided into three discrepancies, each of which can be explained as follows:

- *Naming mismatch.* Two entity types from different components modeling the same real-world concept might use different naming conventions in representing the attributes. In the ATIS database in Exhibit 1, the ranking of a hotel might be modeled by an attribute called "rank" of Places to Stay in component A, while the same information might be modeled by an attribute called "number of stars" of Accommodation in component B.
- *Domain mismatch.* The same attribute of two entity types from different components might be represented in different domains. For example, both Attractions and Places to See of components A and B, respectively, in Exhibit 1 might have an attribute "zip code." However, component A might represent the attribute as an integer, while component B might represent it as a string.
- *Schematic discrepancy.* Data in one database might be represented as entity types in another database. In Exhibit 1, entity type Planes of component B might be represented as an attribute of Attractions in component A.
- *Data specification heterogeneity.* Each component may model similar real-world entities in different units of measure. One component might represent the distance of an attraction in meters, while another component might represent it in miles.
- *Update heterogeneity.* Since each component is under separate and independent control, data instances modeling the same real-world entity in different databases might be updated asynchronously. When the daily rate of a hotel is updated, databases A and B in Exhibit 1 might be updated at different times.
- *Database tools heterogeneity.* Each component may use different tools to manipulate its own database. For example, different components might use different query languages.

Types of Autonomy

Orthogonally, each component can exhibit several different types of autonomy.

Design Autonomy. This refers to the ability of a component to choose its own design on the data being managed, the representation of the data instances, the constraints of the data, and the implementation of the component's database system.

Association Autonomy. This refers to the ability of a component to decide to what extent the component would like to participate in the interoperability activity. A component is free to share its schema, data, or applications with other components; a component can even decide not to participate in the sharing activity at all.

Control Autonomy. This refers to the ability of a component to control the access privileges of any remote component on each of its exported information units (entity types or instances). In general, four types of access control privilege could be granted by a component to a remote component on each of its exported information units:

- Read (R) access to the database instances
- Read definition (RD) access to entity types
- Write (W) access to database instances
- Generate (G) access for creating database instances

These four access privileges form a partial order such that W > G > RD and W > R > RD. Neither G nor R dominates the other. For instance, if component X grants W access privilege to remote component Y on one of its exported entity types, component Y is allowed to read the instances of the entity type as well. By contrast, if X only grants R access privilege to Y on the entity type, Y is not allowed to modify any instances of the entity type.

If an exported unit of a component, say X, is imported from another component, Y, the capability of X to control the access privileges on the exported unit will depend on whether the unit is imported by copy or imported by reference from Y.

Execution Autonomy. This refers to the ability of a component to execute local operations without interference from external components. For example, component X might run an application on behalf of remote component Y. This autonomy implies that X can run the application as if it is a local execution (i.e., X can schedule, commit, or abort the application freely).

FUNCTIONAL REQUIREMENTS OF A FEDERATED DATABASE ENVIRONMENT

From the perspective of a component, X, several functional capabilities need to be supported in order to be able to participate in the interoperability activity with other components.

Information Exportation

Component X must be able to specify the information it is willing to share with other components. Such a facility should allow the component to specify the export schema, the export database, or any application that the component would like to be sharable. Furthermore, X should be able to specify the access privileges of each remote component on each of its exported information units.

A mobile federation is comparatively more dynamic than a database federation, connecting and disconnecting from the wireless network frequently. A mobile component also enters and leaves a cell frequently. It is difficult for a server component to keep track of which mobile components are currently residing within the cell under its management. Furthermore, a cell can potentially have many components visiting at any moment. Therefore, it is not possible for a server component to indicate the access privileges of each mobile component. An access control mechanism that is scalable with respect to the number of mobile components is necessary. Due to the dynamic nature of a mobile component, it is not always possible to incorporate information from a mobile component.

Information Discovery

Before component X can access or use any remote information, X must be aware of the existence and availability of the information in which it is interested. A facility must be provided to allow X to discover any remote information of interest at various granularity or abstraction, including schema, data, or applications.

In general, there are two ways information could be discovered by component X. One possibility is that X can formulate a discovery request for its interested information, in which case a facility must be provided to identify the components containing information units that are relevant to the request. Another possibility is for component X to navigate or explore the exported information space of each remote component and look for the interested information. An explorer must then be provided for such a navigation purpose.

Information Importation

Once interested information units from remote components are discovered, component X can import the information units into its local database. Through importation, component X can reuse the discovered information in the future. In general, three importation capabilities are required: schema importation, data importation, and application importation.

Schema Importation. This refers to the process of importing remote export schema into X's local schema. This process is further composed of two activities — heterogeneity resolution and schema integration. Hetero-geneity resolution is the process of resolving any conflict that exists be-tween X's local schema and the remote schema.

Since different components might use different database models to specify the data, a facility must be provided to translate the remote sche-ma from the remote database model to the one used in X's local system. Furthermore, since different components might model similar real-world concepts differently, another heterogeneity that must be resolved is to identify the relationship between X's local schema and the remote schema.

Referring back to the ATIS federation in Exhibit 1, two entity types be-longing to two different schema might model the same real-world concept, such as the Attractions information of component A and the Places to See information of component B. Alternatively, two entity types might model related information, such as the Transportation information of component A and the Planes information of component B. Finally, two entity types might model different concepts, such as the Attractions information of component A and the Planes information of component B.

Data Importation. Similarly, data importation refers to the process of importing remote export database information into X's local database. This process is composed of two activities: instance identification and data integration.

Instance identification refers to the process of identifying the relation-ship between the remote database and the local database. Two data in-stances from different databases might model the same, related, or different real-world entities. This process is complicated because, on the one hand, instances from different databases cannot be expected to bear the same key attributes; on the other hand, merely matching nonkey at-tributes may lead to unsatisfactory results because data instances model-ing different entities may possess the same attribute values. This process is further complicated by possible update heterogeneity that might exist between the two instances.

Once the relationship between the remote database and X's local data-base is identified, the remote database can be integrated into the local da-tabase. Again, the remote database should be integrated such that its relationship with the local database is reflected.

There are two different paradigms for integrating a remote data instance from a remote component, Y, into X's local database: imported by copy and imported by reference.

When a remote instance is imported by copy, the data instance is copied into the local database. The copied data instance becomes part of the local database. Any access to the imported instance is referred to its local copy.

When a remote instance is imported by reference, a reference to the remote instance is maintained in the local database. Any access to the imported data instance requires a network request to Y for up-to-date data value. When a remote data instance is imported by copy, the local component, X, has complete control on the local copy of the imported instance and is allowed to specify the access privileges of other remote components on the local copy of the imported instance. However, when a remote data instance is imported by reference from component Y, Y still maintains its control over the imported instance. Component X is still free to export the imported instance; however, X cannot modify the access privileges specified by Y on this imported data instance.

Application importation can only be achieved to a very limited extent due to the possible differences in the computer systems of the different components. However, with the advent of Java mobility code, this could soon become a reality.

In a mobile federation, communication between a mobile component and a server database is usually over an unreliable wireless channel. It is more efficient for a mobile federation to import an instance by copying since a component does not need to rely on the network to obtain the data value of the instance. A mobile component, in general, has less storage space than a federated component. A mobile component, therefore, might not be able to import all data instances and will have to maintain only those instances that it accesses most frequently.

Information Querying and Transaction Processing. Component X should be able to operate its imported information in its local system. The operation on the imported information should be transparent in the following manner:

- *Functional transparency.* All existing local tools of component X, such as its query language and database management system (DBMS) software, should be operational on the imported information units in the same manner as they operate on the local information units.
- *Location transparency.* Users and tools operating on the imported information units should not be aware of their original locations and remote nature.

Very often, there is a conflict between supporting the described functional capabilities in a component and preserving the autonomy of the component. To preserve the autonomy of a component, modifying any component of the DBMS software is not recommended.

TECHNIQUES FOR DATABASE SHARING

To support database-sharing functional capabilities, data model heterogeneity must be resolved. This is usually addressed by employing a common canonical model, which provides a communication forum among various components. Schema and instances represented in the local data model are required to convert to the canonical model. Most research prototypes use an object model as the canonical model because of its expressive power. Most corporations, however, use relational models. ODBC from Microsoft and JDBC from Sun Microsystems are generally considered the industry standards.

Information Exportation

Information exportation can be easily achieved using database view mechanisms. Exhibit 3 illustrates the management of exported information. A subhierarchy rooted at class Exported-Classes is created under the root of the class hierarchy (i.e., OBJECTS). To export a class, O, a class name E_O is created as a subclass of Exported-Classes. To export an attribute of O, the same named attribute is created for E_O; this allows a component to specify exported information at the granularity of a single attribute.

Each exported instance is handled by a multiple-membership modeling construct of the object model, relating the original class to which the instance belongs to the E_ counterpart. In effect, classes belonging to the subhierarchy rooted at Exported-Classes represent the export schema, and the instances belonging to the subhierarchy represent the export database (depicted by the shaded region in Exhibit 3).

In Exhibit 3, only class Places to Stay is exported because only Places to Stay has a corresponding E_Places to Stay class. All attributes of Places to Stay have the corresponding ones defined on E_Places to Stay. Furthermore, two instances of Places to Stay are exported, relating via a multiple membership construct to E_Places to Stay. A component employing a relational data model could use a similar technique to specify its exporting information units since the export schema and database are, in effect, a view of the database.

Access control mechanisms for exported information are limited and especially difficult to achieve in a mobile federation. It is difficult for a server component to keep track of which mobile components are within the cell under its management and specify their individual access privileges. A multilevel access control mechanism is more applicable in this domain.

In a multilevel system, database information units are classified into privilege levels. The privilege levels are arranged in an order such that possessing a privilege level implies possessing all its subordinate levels. For example, a typical multilevel system contains four privilege levels:

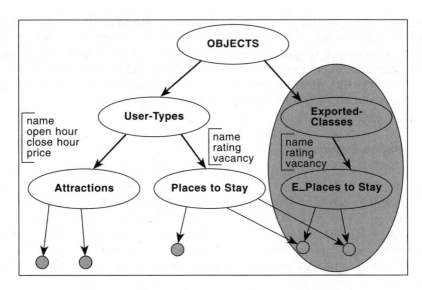

Exhibit 3. Information exportation via object view.

top secret, secret, confidential, and unclassified. A typical database system could have an arbitrary number of privilege levels. To access an information unit, the user needs to obtain a clearance at least equal to the privilege level of the unit. In a mobile federation, a mobile component could join a privilege level that will inherit the database information units that it could access from the server database.

Information Discovery

Information discovery can be achieved by exploring the exported information of a database component. A typical device that explores the content of several databases is depicted in Exhibit 4. This explorer is implemented on the Netscape Navigator, providing a platform-independent browsing capability because of the availability of Netscape in UNIX workstations, Macintosh computers, and PCs.

The explorer in Exhibit 4 allows a component to explore multiple databases at the same time. It employs a relational model as the canonical model. Exported information units are viewed as relations. The explorer has windows to browse four separate databases of remote components, and a window to the local database of a component.

An alternate approach to discovering remote information units that are interesting to a particular component is to specify the requirements of the interested information units. Remote information units that are relevant to the discovery specification will be identified. Specification could

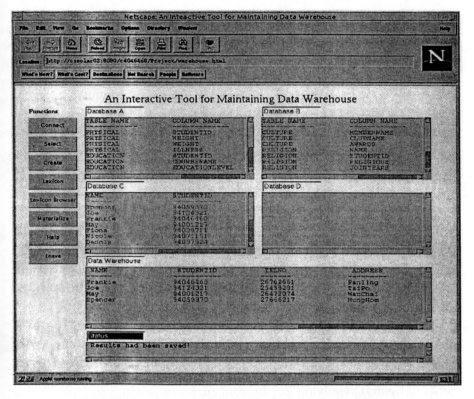

Exhibit 4.   A sample information discovery explorer.

be initiated in an ad hoc manner. Following are three different types of discovery requests:

- A component can request remote entity types (instances) that model the same real-world concept (entity) as a local entity type (instance).
- A component can request remote entity types (instances) that model a complementary view of a local entity type (instance).
- A component can request remote entity types (instances) that model an overlapping view of a local entity type (instance).

To support these three types of discovery requests, one approach is to use a probability model to determine the extent to which two entity types (instances) from different databases modeled the same real-world concept. The probability model is based on two heuristics derived from the common attributes of the two entity types: intraconcept similarity indicator and interconcept dissimilarity indicator.

Intuitively, an intraconcept similarity indicator refers to the probability that the common attributes will be modeled in related entity types. Intercon-

423

cept dissimilarity indicator refers to the probability that the attributes will be modeled in unrelated entity types. Two entity types from different databases will have a high probability of similarity if their overlapped attributes have a high intraconcept similarity indicator as well as a high interconcept dissimilarity indicator. The use of these heuristics is based on the observation that different databases might model complementary or even disjointed views of the same concept; on the other hand, different databases might model different concepts similarly.

A more general specification could be achieved using first-order logic like language. Each component will thus require a mediator that understands the specification language and identifies information units relevant to the specification.

In a mobile federation, it is not important if a server database returns all information relevant to a discovery request; rather, it is much more important that the returned information units are indeed relevant because of the typically low bandwidth on a wireless channel. One approach to ensure this is to create a profile that captures the interests of each component.

Information Importation

Schema Importation. As mentioned previously, a component, X, can import (partial) remote schema from a remote component, Y, into its local schema by first resolving any heterogeneity between X's local schema and Y's schema.

One common approach to resolve schema heterogeneity between X's local schema and Y's remote schema is through a common knowledge base that contains various real-world concepts. Entity types from different databases are required to match with the concepts in the knowledge base. If both entity types map to the same concept in the knowledge base, they are regarded as modeling the same real-world concept. The knowledge base also provides instructions that define how a remote entity type could be integrated into the schema of a component's local database. The instructions could be specified in the form of rules or in a logic-like syntax. The former is easier to understand but is less flexible. The latter is more flexible, but is less user friendly.

In a mobile federation, it is difficult to specify a knowledge base that is applicable to all mobile components because there is a potentially unlimited number of mobile components visiting a wireless cell. It is perhaps more appropriate for a mobile component to provide its own knowledge or its personal profile, containing its own view for integrating remote schema into its own local schema.

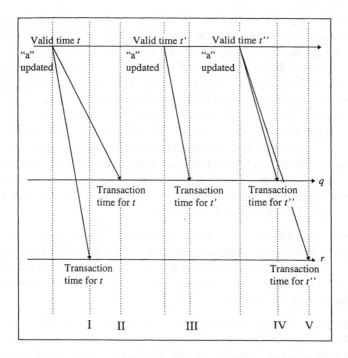

Exhibit 5.   Update heterogeneity in a database federation.

Instance Importation. To identify the relationship between instances from two databases, one needs to address the data specification heterogeneity and the update heterogeneity problems. Data specification heterogeneity is usually resolved, again, via a knowledge base, indicating how the representation of a remote instance could be converted into the representation of the local database.

Exhibit 5 illustrates the importance of update heterogeneity in identifying the relationship between instances from various databases. In Exhibit 5, valid time denotes the time in which a fact was true in reality, while the transaction time denotes the time in which a fact was captured in a database.

One approach to addressing update heterogeneity is to use historical update information on the instances to determine their degree of similarity. The historical update patterns of each instance represent the changes of states of the instance since its creation, inherently capturing its behavioral properties. This allows the instance identification to be performed based on behavioral property in addition to structural property, as is done traditionally. The historical update information of an instance could be easily obtained through a transaction log.

As mentioned previously, instance integration could be performed via import by copy or import by reference. Using an object model as a canonical model, it is quite easy to support these two integration paradigms within one general framework. Exhibit 5 illustrates the partial conceptual schema of two components, A and B, of the ATIS databases from Exhibit 1. Instances x and y of component B are imported from class Accommodation of component A. The class Remote-Classes is created in component B to hold the object instance of definitions of the imported instances and the address of components from which the instances are imported (i.e., address of component A in the example). These two types of information are placed in the attributes r_oid and r_host, respectively. A class called R_Accommodation is created in component B as a subclass of Remote-Classes to model the imported instances.

In effect, the subhierarchy rooted at Remote-Classes represents the import schema and the instances belonging to the subhierarchy represent the import database; this is depicted by the shaded region in Exhibit 6. Notice that the structure of the import subhierarchy mirrors that of the export subhierarchy mentioned previously.

Attributes of classes belonging to the Remote-Classes subhierarchy are user-defined methods. To obtain the attribute value for attribute "a" of an imported instance, x, the method "a" will obtain the "r_oid" of x and initiate a remote request to the remote component, whose address is specified in "r_host" of x, to obtain the attribute value for the instance. This achieves the effect of import by reference. To support import by copy, the imported instances are added to a local class via multiple-membership construct. The additional inherited attributes could be used as placeholders for the copied attribute values of the imported instance. This is illustrated in Exhibit 6. The obtained value of an attribute of an instance returned from the corresponding method could be stored in the additional attributes inherited.

In a mobile federation, the connection between a mobile component and the server component could be disconnected at any moment, either due to the unreliability of a wireless channel or due to the movement of a mobile component to another cell. It is, thus, more appropriate for a component to import an instance by copy rather than by reference. This also has the effect of caching the instance into the local database of a mobile component. In this respect, one could regard the local database of a mobile component as a data warehouse since the local database is derived from multiple database sources.

Information discovery and importation could be provided within a uniform framework or interface. This allows discovered remote information units to be imported into the local database of a component. The explorer in Exhibit 4 also provides functions for information importation as well. In this particular system, a relational model is employed as a canonical mod-

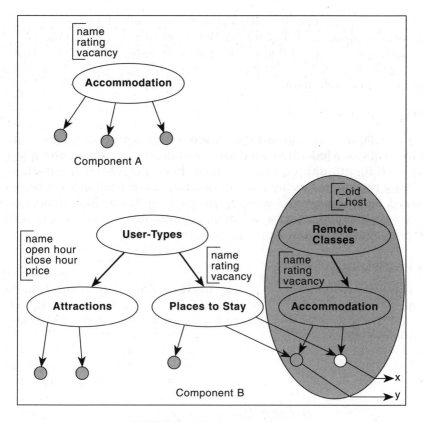

Exhibit 6. Data integration.

el. The integration of information units from several databases is basically achieved via the "join" operation in this explorer. A component could also create a lexicon containing relationships among attributes of different databases. This resolves the conceptual heterogeneity. This lexicon acts as a localized profile of the component, capturing the perspectives of the component on the relationships among information units from different databases.

Information Querying and Transaction Processing

The notion of transaction is supported weakly in existing database federation prototypes. The reason stems from the fact that it is very difficult to support all the properties of transaction processing in a federated database system without seriously violating the autonomy of individual components and without rewriting the DBMS software of individual components.

Consider a situation in which a component X submits a transaction T to a remote component Y. The transaction T, when executed in component Y, is simply a local transaction of component Y. Component Y is free to abort the transaction without notifying component X. Component X thus might obtain inconsistent data.

CONCLUSION

This chapter has presented a reference architecture and functional requirements for a federated database environment. Techniques for addressing each functional requirement have been presented. Limitations of existing techniques in the domain of a mobile federation have been discussed, and proposed solutions have also been briefly illustrated. Experience with real applications in a mobile federation is necessary to further pinpoint additional problems that require research.

ACKNOWLEDGMENTS

This work is supported in part by the Hong Kong Polytechnic University Central Research Grant Number 351/217. Part of the materials in this chapter are the results of the Remote-Exchange project at the University of Southern California.

Chapter 27
Integrating EDMSs and DBMSs

Charles Banyay

DATABASE MANAGEMENT SYSTEMS (DBMS) HAVE BEEN AN INTEGRAL PART OF INFORMATION TECHNOLOGY (IT) and the systems development life cycle since the 1960s. The database, especially the relational database, has received ever-increasing visibility during the past decade due to the mass availability of very cost-effective PC-based DBMSs. As a result, the relational database has become ingrained as the natural metaphor for an information repository with most organizations that utilize IT.

With the advent of the electronic document or, to be more precise, the electronic document management system (EDMS) as a significant new metaphor for an information repository, it is useful to juxtapose the two approaches and to explore their relative advantages. First, it is necessary to discuss the traditional process of using a DBMS in managing data. Second, it is necessary to evaluate the unique properties of documents as opposed to structured data and the challenges associated with managing information using this metaphor. Having considered these two, it is possible to discuss how the DBMS can be used cooperatively with the new metaphor for information repositories — the electronic document or EDMS.

THE DATABASE MANAGEMENT SYSTEM

The majority of IT professionals would not consider developing even the most simple of applications without employing some kind of DBMS to manage the data. The traditional approach to utilizing database technology, regardless of the application, involves some form of data analysis. Data analysis generally consists of four stages called by different names, by the various methodologies, but they all involve some form of:

- Data collection and normalization
- Entity-relationship mapping

0-8493-9976-9/99/$0.00+$.50
© 1999 by CRC Press LLC

- Transaction analysis
- Data modeling

At the end of this process, once the type of database management system to be utilized is determined, one has enough information with which to begin a physical and logical database design. The data analysis activities should provide enough information to enable a design which will have a high degree of predictability in terms of data access performance and data storage size.

Data collection and normalization within any organization begins with the analysis of the data as it exists currently. Various methodologies emphasize different approaches to this analysis. Some emphasize beginning with the analysis of source documents, while others advocate analyzing the data as it is presented to the users. For this discussion it is irrelevant where one starts a project, what is important is that a "functional decomposition" process is followed in all instances. Functional decomposition attempts to distill the relevant data from some source (e.g., data collection documents or presentation documents). As recently as one year ago, one could have safely assumed that the documents would have been on paper; today that may not necessarily be so. For the purposes of this discussion, however, the medium is irrelevant.

Once this distillation process or functional decomposition is finished, one proceeds with a truly data-driven approach to analysis. The next step involves grouping the data into logical groups called entities. Using a process called normalization, one then proceeds to remove as much data redundancy as possible from these entities, sometimes producing more entities in the process. There are many good references on data normalization techniques, and for the purposes of this article there is no requirement to go into any more depth than this.

Once the entities are in their normal form, one generally proceeds to associate each entity with the other entities using some entity-relationship mapping technique. Entity-relationship mapping is, in general, an attempt to reconstitute the data back into something that is meaningful to the business where the data originated. A thorough understanding of the business functions and processes that use the data is crucial for creating meaningful entity-relationship maps. During this mapping process some form of quantification of the entities also occurs.

The next step in data analysis is the transaction analysis. Transaction analysis involves listing all of the business events that could trigger access to the information within the as yet undesigned database, and mapping the flow of the transaction through the entities as it satisfies its requirement for information. The transaction flow is dependent on the entity relationships. Once all the transactions are mapped in this way and the quantity of each transaction is determined, one has a good idea of how the data should be ordered and indexed.

The final step in the data analysis activity is to construct the data model. Constructing the data model involves quantitative analysis. Using the structure from the relational map and the number of accesses identified in the transactional analysis, one derives a new structure for the model. This new structure may result in new entities that may reduce the number of entities that need to be accessed for certain high-usage transactions. The first data model generally proves to be inadequate. Data analysis is therefore an iterative process. As one proceeds through the iterations, one learns more about the data. The new information may indicate that decisions made earlier in the process may not have been optimal and may need to be revisited.

The ultimate database design will not only depend on the results of the data analysis activity but also on the choice of DBMS. Good design does not just depend on knowledge of the specific data requirements of a particular application or the general information requirements of an organization. These are critical elements of the design, but almost as important is a good understanding of the particular DBMS, its architecture, and its design constraints.

The critical aspect to understand about data analysis for the purposes of this discussion is the process of functional decomposition. Functional decomposition is a process that is extremely important to data analysis. It is the process by which reality or a body of knowledge is decomposed, summarized, or reduced into its most fundamental, elementary components. This decomposition is generally from the one perspective that is important to the particular application being considered. These elementary components are the data items that ultimately make up the database, such as those shown in Exhibit 1.

An important consideration in Exhibit 1 is that any process of reduction or distillation results in a tremendous amount of other "stuff" that does not make it into the final version. This stuff is lost. Consequently, one advantage offered by functional decomposition is that the process reduces reality or a body of information to its elementary components that represent one or at least a very limited perspective on this body of information. This enables the construction of a database. The "bad" aspect of functional decomposition also relates to its strength, namely, that the process reduces reality or a body of information to its elementary components that represent one or at least a very limited perspective on this body of information. Much of the original body of information can be lost in the process.

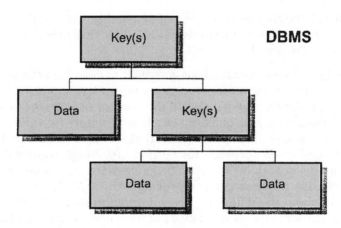

Exhibit 1.   Elementary components.

THE ELECTRONIC DOCUMENT

Before comparing the DBMS with the electronic document management system as an information repository, it is useful to build a common understanding of the definition of a "document" in the context of this discussion.

The first thing that most people think of in any discussion of a document is paper. This is due to the fact that most of today's generations have grown up with paper as the most common medium on which documents have resided. A piece of paper or a collection of pieces of paper is usually referred to as a document, especially if it has a collective purpose. Paper, however, is very limiting and is just one method of representing a document. It is certainly not the only way. Even if one disregards the electronic medium for the moment, there is a myriad of ways that documents have existed and do exist. There are stone tablets, scrolls, hieroglyphics, paintings, carvings, and more recently film, just to mention a few. Even the scented letter is a document that is more than just scribbled words on a piece of paper. The scent can convey more information than the words.

If one includes the electronic medium, then a document can be much more than is allowed in the limited paper medium or in anything that has been described above. A document can contain voice-annotated video, graphics, still images, and drawings with backup text. One can imagine the vast information content of a document of this nature.

The second feature that people think of when discussing documents is the concept of a page. This is also due, in all probability, to the association of documents with paper. People, in general, have an optimum quantum of information on which they can focus at any one moment. This is an aspect of what psychologists call bounded rationality. A page is probably an optimum quantum of information. Represented on paper, information could appear in the format that is most familiar; however, in some other form it could be quite different. The concept of a page is useful and will probably evolve as the understanding of documents evolves, and as this understanding moves beyond paper as the common representation of a document. It will suffice for the purposes of this discussion to think of a page as a component of information and of a document as containing one or more pages or one or more quantums of information.

So, in summary, what is a document? The word *document* is both a verb and a noun. To document is to record (e.g., to record an event or to tell a story). It follows that anything that records an event or tells a story can be called a document. A document can and generally does contain many different types of entities. Generally there is either text or an image, but if people expand their horizon beyond paper, a document can contain voice, video, or, in the world of virtual reality, any combination of tactile stimuli. In the most general definition, a document is a representation of reality that can be reproduced and sensed by any combination of the five senses.

The preceding may stretch human creative capabilities somewhat, so for the purposes of this discussion the definition of a document can be limited to a collection of images and textual information types. The information can be coded or uncoded. The essence of the definition of the document, as a representation of reality that can be reproduced and sensed, is really the crucial aspect of the definition that is most germane to this discussion. The representation of reality implies that a document captures information at a quantum level or quantum levels higher than simple data.

The best illustration of this is the well-known "A picture is worth a thousand words." A picture in one entity can represent a thousand data elements or more. An illustration may convey this idea better. Suppose one is creating a document describing an automobile accident report for a property and casualty insurance company. The document would begin with a notice of loss, which could be an electronic form that is created initially by an agent within a call center. The agent would record all relevant information about the accident, including the name and policy number of the policyholder, the date and time of the accident, the date and time of the call, and all particulars of the loss, such as damages to the car, etc.

The agent then sends a compressed version of the document to the adjuster with some comments and instructions. The information to this point is in coded data format and could be through any traditional data system. The new capabilities of a document-based system allow the adjuster, when the document is received, to attach a few still photo shots of the automobile along with further comments and the detailed cost estimates supplied by the body shop. In addition, the adjuster can scan in the police report of the accident and attach it to the document. The claims document now contains a much more complete description of the entire event. This more complete description could produce a very different result by the end of the claims process. This more complete description is not possible through just simple coded data or traditional relational DBMS systems.

It is not necessary to describe the insurance claims process any further. What it illustrates is the wealth of information contained in a document-based approach to information processing. One needs to contrast this to an approach enabled by an application system containing only coded data in a relational format.

FUNCTIONAL DECOMPOSITION AND DATA DISTILLATION

The primary reason that traditional application systems oriented around a DBMS have sometimes failed to meet the expectations of the business community, and the reason that much of the business information today still resides on paper, is the failure of these applications to capture the entirety of the multifaceted information pertaining to an event. That is a real mouthful, but what it says is that if in capturing information electronically a business user only manages to capture the bare essentials focused on a certain perspective and loses most of the other peripheral information which may be central to other perspectives, then the business user will, in general, not be completely satisfied. The business user is forced to keep other, nonelectrical repositories of information and continue to work with information in nonelectrical media. This generally adds up to a lot of paper and a lot of traditional, inefficient, and ineffective business processes.

As discussed at the end of the data analysis activity, in any process of reduction or distillation there is a tremendous amount of other peripheral information that does not make it through the process. Reality is reduced to a very limited perspective based on what is retained. This process may leave out information of interest to other perspectives. The result is a very narrow perspective on the information, general dissatisfaction, and alternative repositories of information within the organization.

THE DBMS AND THE EDMS

So why not just discard DBMSs, and why not rely totally on documents as the new metaphor for an information repository? The above discussion seems to imply that database systems are bad and documents are good — far from the truth. Documents, despite having a tremendous capability of holding a great deal of multifaceted information, have their own weaknesses. Years ago one would have begun the list of these weaknesses with the fact that documents tend to take up vast amounts of storage space, require a great deal of bandwidth for transmission, and generally require expensive equipment for good presentation, such as large, high-resolution monitors and multimedia processors. Today, these weaknesses seem to be fading in importance, although not as quickly as one had hoped and would like. Bandwidth is increasing, storage costs are plummeting, and high-resolution monitors are dropping in cost.

The real weakness of documents, and this has little to do with storage or display technology, is that they are difficult to search. Because most of the information content of a document is uncoded, and because there is very little in the way of search engines for uncoded data, documents are difficult to search. Once stored, they are difficult to find unless they have been indexed with exactly the criteria for which one is searching. Unfortunately, information is of little use if it cannot be found readily when needed.

It seems, then, that there is an impasse. On the one hand, a DBMS is a tool that has tremendous capabilities to search and reproduce information to which it has access, in the combinations that users generally require. The weakness of the DBMS, however, is that it generally has access to only a limited perspective on a small body of information. On the other hand, an EDMS is a tool that can house vast amounts of content about a body of information from a multitude of perspectives. The primary weakness of an EDMS, however, is that once the information is stored it is difficult to find.

Neither one of the tools on its own seems capable of meeting the expectations for comprehensive information management. They do, however, have complementary strengths. With the DBMS, information is relatively easy to find, and, with the EDMS, information content is vast and rich. If one could successfully combine these strengths, then one would have a tool that might better meet the expectations of the business community. The combination might not meet all of the expectations, but would certainly be superior to either tool in stand-alone mode. The whole promises to be greater than the sum of the parts in this case.

The logical question arises, "Why use a DBMS to store data?" Why not use the EDMS to store the information, and use the DBMS to store the data about the EDMS or metadata? This would enable one to search the DBMS for the combination of information that one requires contained in the EDMS. This is exactly the approach that many leading vendors of document management applications, such as FileNet and Documentum, have taken. Both vendors use a relational database, such as Oracle or Sybase, to store the metadata that points to various data stores, such as magnetic or optical disks, that house the documents.

The DBMS in many of these document management systems has evolved beyond simple metadata which just houses pointers to content documents. These second-generation document management systems have developed the concept of the virtual document. The virtual document illustrated in Exhibit 2 is more than a collection of pointers to content

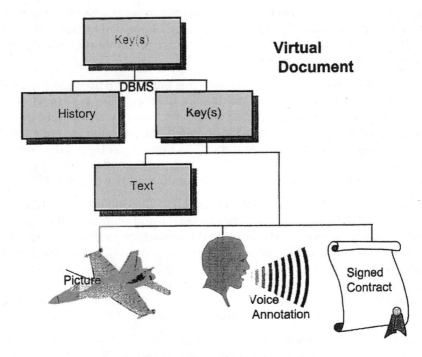

Exhibit 2. The virtual document.

documents. The metadata in second-generation document management applications also contains far richer information, such as a comprehensive history of the virtual document. The history may contain work-in-process information or information about each member document, such as the time each was added to the document collection, who entered it, and from which application.

CONCLUSION

The combination of DBMS and EDMS certainly offers advantages over either in stand-alone mode; however, the degree of the advantage can be deceptive. The metadata in the database is just that, data about the document and not about all of the information within the document. Here is the crux of the matter. What is metadata but distillation? If the only way to find a wealth of information is through the limited perspective of its metadata, then the information is not nearly as valuable as if one could find it from the multitude of perspectives contained within the information itself.

The challenge facing most document management application vendors today is how to minimize even this more expanded data distillation. The development of new search engines may be part of the answer. Development of such technologies as pattern-recognition applications, which can scan the uncoded components of documents, may be another part.

Whatever the solution to reducing the effects of data distillation, it is not something that will be totally eliminated within the near future. Combining the strengths of a DBMS and an EDMS, however, definitely provides better access to a larger volume of information than if either one is used alone. The combination is by no means a panacea, but it is a step or a number of steps in the right direction toward solving the information-processing problems that knowledge workers face every day.

As the marriage between the DBMS and the EDMS evolves further, there may be a new dawn for IT. This new dawn will be true electronic information processing rather than electronic data processing. The real payoff in this evolution and in developments of this nature is that it may eventually solve the seeming paradox of information processing in the office environment. This paradox is that, even though there has been a tremendous investment in information technology in the office, office productivity has not risen as dramatically as expected during the past 20 to 30 years.

Chapter 28

Interfacing Legacy Applications with RDBMSs and Middleware

Dan Fobes

TODAY PROGRAMMERS HAVE A WIDE RANGE OF OPTIONS when developing applications. There is an endless number of tools and techniques associated with simply writing a program. Hardware advances deliver what used to be the power of a mainframe on a programmer's desktop. Given the pace of software and hardware advances, it should follow that programmer productivity has grown equally as fast. This is not the case, because for many new applications being developed there is one constraint — it must plug into an established world of corporate data and the processes that manage them. For many companies, the processes that manage their enterprise data were written 10 to 15 years ago. These applications are also referred to as legacy systems. Rewriting legacy systems would solve the technology gap experienced today, but the cost and risks are usually too great. This chapter outlines some options available for interfacing legacy systems with the latest technology, enabling a company to continue to compete in a rapidly changing field.

CLIENT/SERVER AND DECENTRALIZED IS

In the 1970s and early 1980s IBM dominated IS with mainframes, and IS programmers wrote largely in COBOL. All programs were defined by users, then written by IS. As a result, all mission-critical applications were coded by one group and executed on one machine. In the mid to late 1980s, the PC started to replace terminals as companies moved to empower the user with word processors and spreadsheet applications. Nontechnical users could move data from the mainframe to their desktop and do some additional client processing within a spreadsheet without the aid of IS. Network operating systems (NOSs) provided a means to connect PCs in a local area network allowing for users to share both the raw mainframe data and PC-processed data, hence the birth of client/server. As a result, companies had distributed their mission-critical data processing from a centralized IS throughout the enterprise.

The Failure of Client/Server

All applications can be broken down into three groups of code (or tiers):

1. Presentation Tier — get user information
2. Business Tier — process user information
3. Data Tier — write processed information

When applications were written by one group and run on one machine, these layers were usually intermixed. It was not uncommon for one programmer to write one program that contained all three. With the advent of modular programming, large programs could be broken down into a collection of shared modules, reducing both the time required to finish an application and the risk of writing entire applications from scratch. Unfortunately, the immediate IS benefit of reusing modules would often come at the expense of large modules with large numbers of parameters instructing them how to behave for different types of invocations. However, modular programming presented the opportunity to separate the presentation tier from the business and data tiers.

With client/server applications, there is a requirement to distinguish among the presentation, business, and data tiers. There are two computers involved in client/server applications — the client and the server. The client application executes on the client PC, with all presentation input being received locally from the user. However, some data are read from and written to the server for the purpose of information sharing. As a result, unlike a mainframe application, a client/server application is separated from some of its data by a network — the slowest part of any computer.

For applications such as simple spreadsheet calculations the client/server model works fine. However, many corporations, lured by the low cost of client/server technology and a need to standardize, attempted to move all IS applications to a client/server architecture. After investing lots of time and money, many companies found that the tools enabled them to re-create the applications, but the client/server model made it impossible to implement them. No matter how fast the client and server hardware is, the network is a bottleneck. With the business tier executing on the client and saturating the network with file I/O requests, it was not uncommon to see a complex client/server application become unusable when 25 to 50 users began to use it — something a mainframe could handle easily.

SUCCEEDING WITH DISTRIBUTED DATA PROCESSING

The scalability problem that exists with client/server applications has many proposing a return to mainframes and centralized IS. However, given that data is distributed throughout an enterprise and applications exist on various platforms, others would benefit if the data and the processes that manage them can be tied together. Currently available are several options that provide for both types of solutions:

- Relational Database Management Systems
- Remote Procedure Call
- Messaging

As stated above, most legacy mainframe applications contained all three tiers. Clearly the presentation must be rewritten for the PC. For each of the technical solutions above, consider a simple PC application, PCDEPOS, that collects user information such as an account number and amount of money to deposit. The goal is to have PCDEPOS call an existing COBOL program on a mainframe, MFDEPOS, which performs the transaction (i.e., it represents the business and data tiers only).

RDBMS

One solution to the fragmentation of mission-critical data and their processes is to centralize them to one or more relational databases. Data access through a relational engine can be much faster because data contained within files located across various platforms is moved under the control of a technology built to manage it. Files are moved to tables, and selected columns within tables can be indexed. Furthermore, business logic, usually in the form of COBOL programs, can be recoded as SQL-based stored procedures that are compiled and then executed within the RDBMS engine for optimal performance. Additionally, most databases support some form of replication whereby tables from one database can be replicated to others, facilitating information sharing. Finally, Transaction Processing (TP) monitors are available for most RDBMSs. A separate product, TP monitors interface a client application to an RDBMS and increase performance where large numbers of users require data access. It does this by creating a pool of costly connections to the RDBMS and having the application use a connection from the pool only when necessary.

For the example application, PCDEPOS is created to collect information from the user using middleware, called an open database connectivity (or ODBC) driver, supplied by the RDBMS vendor to facilitate communication between the client and the server. Files that MFDEPOS wrote to and read from, or the data tier, must be moved into RDBMS'$ tables. There are two options for MFDEPOS'$ data processing logic (the business tier) — it can be rewritten as a stored procedure within the RDBMS or modified to perform I/O against SQL tables instead of files.

There are two problems with this solution. For one, it increases the cost and complexity of applications. An RDBMS requires the purchase of an RDBMS, additional server hardware, and one or more dedicated database administrators (DBAs) to install, design, tune, and maintain it. The other problem is risk. Simple applications may be easy to move to a RDBMS; however, no legacy application is simple. Many companies will be required to spend a large amount of resources normalizing or breaking up the data within records as they move from files to RDBMS tables. This is because an RDBMS table has a limit of 255 columns and no row can exceed 2 kilobytes in size — legacy applications typically exceed this. Also, not all data maps over from a file to a table (e.g., dates), and for each of these, a translation is required. Time and staff must be allocated to not only normalize data and map data types, but also verify that existing data moves cleanly into the RDBMS. Part of the migration to an RDBMS is the modifications to the existing business tier code. In the example application, rewriting the MFDE-POS business tier as a stored procedure introduces significant risk because of the differences between the languages (a form of SQL and COBOL). The alternative of replacing file I/O within the COBOL program with RDBMS I/O is usually not feasible because of the scalability issues (requires the COBOL code to execute on the PC).

An RDBMS solution has many benefits, however the costs and risks associated with moving the data and recoding the business logic must be weighed.

REMOTE PROCEDURE CALLS

For most, there is a significantly smaller risk in tying together existing systems that work. What is needed is a form of interprocess communication (IPC) to have one process send and receive data to another. One form of IPC is Remote Procedure Call (RPC).

Using RPC, a program calls a procedure that is executed on a different machine. There is always a one-to-one relationship, and the calling program blocks until the called procedure returns. This sounds simple enough, but since the applications are residing in different address spaces, the only data that each share are the parameters they pass, not global variables within the applications. For an RPC across different machines, data mapping must be addressed because not all hardware supports the same byte-order (i.e., it stores numbers differently). Finally, either or both machines can crash at any point and recovery must be addressed.

Some vendors of development systems provide proprietary RPC mechanisms that address some of the above issues. There are also standards such as the RPC protocol used by the Open Group's Distributed Computing Environment (DCE). Additionally, third-party vendors provide Object Request Brokers (ORBs) for RPC services. The most common ORB is called CORBA. A standard created by the Object Management Group (OMG), CORBA facilitates RPCs across different machines. Unfortunately, the CORBA standard is just that — a standard. Because CORBA is similar to UNIX, each vendor has a slightly different implementation of that standard, and until very recently different CORBA implementations could communicate with each other. Microsoft has a competing technology called the Distributed Component Object Model (DCOM). Many vendors support both CORBA and DCOM as their RPC mechanism, and although both CORBA and DCOM are complex to program, they are options that should be considered when evaluating distributed processing via RPC.

MESSAGE-ORIENTED MIDDLEWARE

Another form of IPC is messaging. Vendors of message-oriented middleware provide a mechanism to send and receive messages asynchronously from one process to another. A message is simply a string of bytes the user defines. There are two approaches to messaging: message queues and publish/subscribe. In a message queue environment, an application sends messages to and receives messages from queues. In a publish/subscribe model, an application broadcasts and receives messages via a subject. The sender specifies the subject of the message and the receiver specifies the subject(s) it wants to get messages for. There are pros and cons to each; however, both are sufficient for most environments.

As stated above, a message is a user-defined string of bytes — there is no standard that needs to be followed. A typical messaging application sends and receives messages asynchronously across multiple platforms. The messaging subsystem handles the routing with most vendors supporting the concept of guaranteed and assured delivery (i.e., the message will get to the receiver and only once). One of the strengths of messaging, which differentiates it from RPC, is that the sender need not block or wait until the receiver responds. Another strength is that one message may be delivered to multiple listeners.

For the example application, messages would contain the arguments to the MFDEPOS program. To facilitate messaging, a new server application called MFLISTEN is required, and the client application must be modified to send and receive messages to it. MFLISTEN listens for client messages and calls the server application with the arguments specified in the message. Once completed, MFDEPOS returns control back to MFLISTEN, which sends the arguments back to the client via a message.

Since there is no enforced message type, defining one that is flexible becomes a challenge. Different requests for different server applications will likely require a different message, and over time this may become unmanageable as each request begins to change. There are two ways to solve this problem: message versioning and self-describing messages.

To accomplish the deposit application using message versioning, a message could simply contain the linkage to MFDEPOS with each parameter separated by a delimiter (see Exhibit 1).

Exhibit 1. Message Containing Parameters with @@ as a Delimiter for MFDEPOS.

```
-------------------------------------------------
| Parameter 1@@Parameter 2@@Parameter 3@@ ...
-------------------------------------------------
```

Exhibit 2. Simple Message with Segments Supporting Message Versions.

```
| 4 bytes | 2 bytes | 2 bytes | 2 bytes | 2 bytes | ...
-----------------------------------------------------------------------------
| MessageID | Segment Count | SegmentID | Segment Version | Segment Size | Parameter 1...
-----------------------------------------------------------------------------
                    | SegmentID | Segment Version | Segment Size | Parameter 1...
                    ------------------------------------------------------------
```

Although this works, it requires a dedicated MFLISTEN program for each server program such as MFDEPOS. A more flexible approach would be to break up the message into multiple segments and then build a header to contain segment information (see Exhibit 2). Designing messages around segments is not new — a standard called Electronic Data Interchange, or EDI, is also based on segments.

Here, MessageID represents the format of the message, Segment Count is the number of segments in the message, SegmentID is the start of the segment and represents the program name (e.g., 1 for MFDEPOS), Segment Version represents the format of the parameters (number, order, datatypes), and the parameters follow. The parameters can be delimited or fixed length — their layout is defined by SegmentID and Segment Version. The benefit to moving the program name and version down to the segment is that it allows for one MFLISTEN program to serve as an interface to multiple server programs. The only problem with this design is when MFDE-POS'$ linkage changes, the format of the segment changes and the segment version must be incremented. Sending applications such as PCDEPOS would need to be changed to send the new message. Receiving applications such as MFLISTEN would need to be modified to verify the new message version and call the updated version of MFDEPOS.

To accomplish the deposit application using self-describing data, the version number within the message is replaced by field descriptors. Specifically, each parameter value in the message is prepended with a field name that defines it (see Exhibit 3).

With self-describing data, the segment remains the same, but each parameter has two components: a descriptor and a value. These two components can be fixed length or delimited (they are fixed length in Exhibit 3). The benefit to this structure is that it automates the process of calling legacy

Exhibit 3.   Segment Supporting Self Describing Data.

2 bytes	2 bytes	2 bytes	8 bytes	?	8 bytes
SegmentID	Segment Version	Segment Size	P1 Descriptor	P1 Value	P2 Descriptor	...

applications. The best case scenario with versioning saw one listener program created to serve multiple server applications. However, the sending applications (PCDEPOS) and the listener application (MFLISTEN) require an update when there is any change to the server application's linkage (MFDEPOS). With self-describing fields, we can reduce this maintenance to a batch scan on the server. An application on the mainframe can be written to scan a COBOL program and extract the linkage to a table that contains each name and type. The sending applications would then use the names in the COBOL linkage to describe their data, followed by the value of that field. The MFLISTEN program, upon receiving a message, can extract the program name and map the linkage in the message to the linkage in the database automatically, then make the call. New versions of MFDEPOS can be scanned and the database updated. No changes are required to MFLISTEN or PCDEPOS in most cases.

Some message systems allow for field mapping within the message. This allows the MFLISTEN application to query the message for fields instead of parsing it directly. This simplifies MFLISTEN and combines with self-describing data, which provides the optimal messaging solution.

Not all is golden with a messaging solution. Although guaranteed delivery insures a message gets to its destination, it may be possible that one transaction is composed of several messages. Additionally, one message may require the execution of multiple listener programs. In either case, a program would have to initiate a transaction locally, send the messages, subscribe to the responses, and roll back if any of them failed. Another possible issue with messaging is security. With messages traveling back and forth on a network, a hacker can easily listen in, make a change, and send messages back out. Here, encryption is required.

RECOMMENDED COURSE OF ACTION

The above technologies are not mutually exclusive, and in fact, it may turn out that a combination of all three is the best solution. For example, a client may communicate with a server using RPC, the server may use messaging to perform IPC with another server, and one or both of these servers may interact with an RDBMS.

In general, all programs should be separated into three tiers and corporate data should be managed by an RDBMS. Business logic should be

445

coded in a high-level language such as COBOL, which calls a minimum of stored procedures for I/O intensive requests. Finally, the presentation should be coded in a rapid application tool that supports an RDBMS such as Visual Basic. For companies that require a high volume of transactions, middleware in the form of a transaction server or a TP monitor combined with an ORB should be considered.

Migrating an enterprise to this configuration involves many steps and differs for different companies. Avoid the all-or-nothing approach. Risk can be reduced by using a divide-and-conquer approach that targets subsystems. Below are some high-level steps for accomplishing such a migration:

1. Identify a logical subsystem of the enterprise.
2. Form a team composed of programmers who understand the subsystem, and others who understand the target technology.
3. Identify the data of the subsystem.
4. Identify existing applications that manage the data, then tie them together using messaging. This will uncover redundant data and data processing within the subsystem.
5. Design the RDBMS solution (tables, stored procedures, etc.).
6. Create a listener program that listens to the messages created in Step 4 and performs the requests on the RDBMS.
7. Once the RDBMS can service all of the messages of Step 4, it can be phased in.
8. Go to Step 1.

Some applications may span subsystems. Messaging supports this requirement well and should be used. Although most RDBMSs support replication, this usually requires one server to stream over tables of information to another server at scheduled intervals. Not only does this introduce a delay across servers, it does not scale for large databases — messaging the updates as they happen addresses both shortcomings.

When the RDBMS phase-in is complete, new applications should go directly against the RDBMS. Most new technology being introduced provides for access to RDBMSs. The legacy applications can continue using messaging, be modified for direct RDBMS access, or be rewritten.

Section VI
Data Warehousing

Chapter 29
Developing a Corporate Data Warehousing Strategy

Manjit Sidhu

As recently as three years ago, data warehousing was the domain of a few large organizations with deep pockets. In these early initiatives, data warehousing projects took two to three years to implement. The hardware costs alone were measured in the millions. The software and human resource costs to implement these warehouses were at least as much again, if not more. A generally acceptable strategy was to implement a data warehouse in an iterative-phased approach with each phase taking from four to nine months for completion.

As the tools and technologies matured and improved in performance, data warehousing became available to the mainstream. Many organizations have started to implement data warehouses and mini-data warehouses in the form of data marts. Individual business units have started implementing these solutions by themselves or with the help of consultants who are independent of the corporate IT groups. This was done without due regard for the overall needs of the enterprise as a whole. A multitude of data mart implementations with disparate technologies, uncoordinated data models, and metadata has sprung up in organizations. In the rush to implement applications, organizations are not taking the time to first develop a well-thought-out data warehousing strategy and architecture which can subsequently be used to guide the development of data warehousing initiatives within the organization.

DEFINING A DATA WAREHOUSE

For the purposes of this paper, we will use the terms "Data Warehousing", "Data Warehouse", and "Data Mart" as described in Exhibit 29.1.

Although much debate has raged over the differences between data warehouses and data marts, for the purpose of this paper we will use the term "data warehouse" or "data warehousing" to include data marts.

0-8493-9979-3/99/$0.00+$.50
© 1999 by CRC Press LLC

✤ **Data Warehousing**
  - _Data warehousing_ is a discipline which results in applications that provide decision support capability, allow access to business information, and create business insight.

✤ **Warehouse Structures**
  - A _data warehouse_ is a (mainly) read-only time-variant database in which data is transformed, integrated, summarized and organized by subject area to be used effectively for decision support.
  - A _data mart_ is a smaller data warehouse with a limited focus. The focus can be limited functionally (financial analysis, fraud detection, etc.) or it can be cross-functional, but limited in scope (by line of business, by region, etc.).

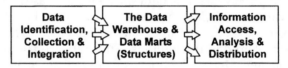

Data Identification, Collection & Integration	The Data Warehouse & Data Marts (Structures)	Information Access, Analysis & Distribution

Exhibit 29.1

Where a distinction needs to be made between warehouses and marts, we will state that:

1. Data is sourced from multiple independent operational "legacy" systems and possibly from external data providers (e.g., Dunn and Bradstreet, Nielsen, and Census data).
2. This data is then cleansed (bad data corrected) and homogenized (codes and values made consistent, e.g. one system may have "M" for male and "F" for female while another may have "0" for male and "1" for female).
3. It is then loaded into data structures to produce a consistent integrated view of the data, allowing for _insight_ and analysis through "query" processing.
4. This data is generally not updateable, except through a predefined update cycle that keeps it synchronized with the source systems that feed it.
5. Metadata, that is data that describes the data, is created and maintained throughout the process.

The major components of a data warehousing process are shown in Exhibit 29.2.

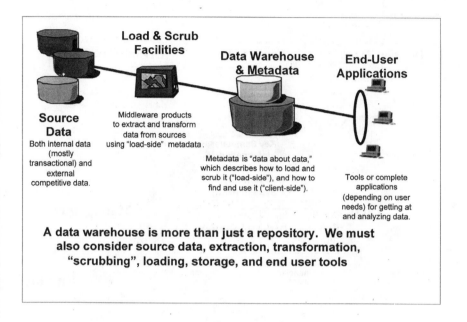

Load & Scrub Facilities

Data Warehouse & Metadata

End-User Applications

Source Data
Both internal data (mostly transactional) and external competitive data.

Middleware products to extract and transform data from sources using "load-side" metadata.

Metadata is "data about data," which describes how to load and scrub it ("load-side"), and how to find and use it ("client-side").

Tools or complete applications (depending on user needs) for getting at and analyzing data.

A data warehouse is more than just a repository. We must also consider source data, extraction, transformation, "scrubbing", loading, storage, and end user tools

Exhibit 29.2

There are different information requirements at various levels of an organization. Executives require very concise, highly summarized information, whereas those running the day-to-day operations require detailed transactional level information. Middle management requires information that is summarized to a level between the transactional and the highly summarized levels.

Exhibit 29.3 shows the various levels of information requirements that exist in a typical organization.

DEVELOPING A DATA WAREHOUSING STRATEGY AND ARCHITECTURE

A data warehousing strategy is a blueprint for the successful introduction, ongoing support, and enhancement of data warehousing in an organization, i.e., for the provisioning of information to users at all levels. This information is used primarily for decision making, and is generally sourced from operational data used for the ongoing operations of the organization.

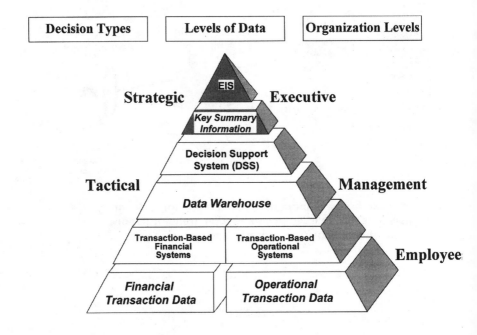

Exhibit 29.3

The strategy serves to provide a common vision for availing information aligned with business objectives, strategies, and goals. It provides a platform for common definitions and an understanding of data and business terms, and for ensuring a consistent approach among the many initiatives that will arise. The strategy also serves to focus IT and the business towards specific, long-term business objectives and away from purely technical considerations, while providing a robust and flexible foundation for meeting these evolving needs.

The development of a data warehouse strategy can be thought of like planning a journey. It describes where you want to go, why you want to go there, and what you will do when you get there. The strategy acts as an itinerary and roadmap for getting there. It also describes the means (the technology and tools) that will be required for getting there safely and expediently.

452

Just as a travel plan does not require the need to define internal technical specifications for all vehicles required on the journey, strategy and architecture describes the important characteristics of the technologies, but not the specific "nitty gritty" details. The details are left for subsequent technology selection projects.

There is no single definitive strategy on how to implement data warehousing in an organization. Decisions about data warehousing strategies need to be based on the specific needs of an organization.

A data warehousing strategy needs to take into consideration an organization's vision, structure, and culture. Therefore, it is important to keep in mind that the strategy needs to address not only information and technology considerations, but what will work in the organization from organizational, skills, infrastructure, cultural, and political perspectives. In particular, the cultural perspective should not be underestimated. Many technically sound strategies have failed because of the cultural and political environments within an organization.

It is important that all of the individuals involved in implementing data warehousing projects work with the same goals in mind. Part of understanding the goals involves ensuring that there is consistent use of terminology such as the difference between a data warehouse and a data mart, the meaning and purpose of an operational data store, and the definition of Metadata. The strategy should define how information should be organized in data marts versus a data warehouse, and the level of detail that needs to be stored. The strategy should also provide a glossary of terms for data warehousing.

FRAMEWORK FOR A DATA WAREHOUSING STRATEGY AND ARCHITECTURE

Exhibit 29.4 is a pictorial representation of a framework for the development of a data warehousing strategy and architecture. The significance of presenting the framework as a pantheon is that, built correctly, the strategy should survive change occurring in a business for a long time, just as pantheons survive generations.

The steps of the pantheon represent the foundation required as the base for the strategy. It establishes a baseline understanding of the business and technology that the data warehousing strategy needs to support. The columns represent individual components of the strategy. The "Information Delivery" column represents how information will be delivered to the organization, and the implementation component defines how the strategy will be implemented.

ramework for Data Warehousing Strategy and Architecture

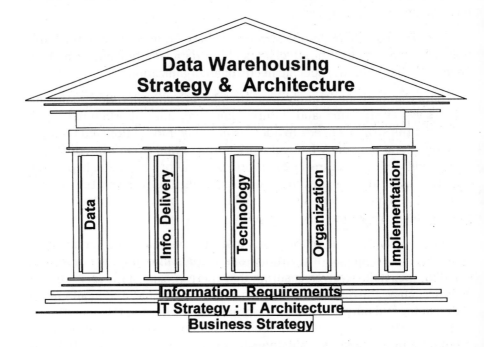

Exhibit 4

PROJECT STRUCTURE

The data warehousing strategy and architecture project should be conducted by two to three individuals with data warehousing experience. The team leader should possess solid data warehousing experience, and should have participated in a previous strategy and architecture development project. All members of the team should have practical experience in the design and implementation of data warehouses.

The team members should be knowledgeable about the business and know the informational needs of that type of business. The informational needs of a high technology manufacturer, for example, are significantly different from those of a government branch. The team should be augmented on at least a part-time basis with industry-specific subject matter specialists who bring expertise on where the industry is headed, and other future considerations that the team may not always be able to glean from interviews with users from the business community. The team should also have access to technical staff from the organization who can provide information on current and planned technology, systems, and data.

The project typically lasts between one to three months depending on the size of the organization, the scope of the mandate (enterprisewide or for a specific part of the organization or subject area), and the level of detail required. There is a danger that a longer project could lose focus and executive interest. Besides, there is no need to go into deep levels of detail at the strategy level.

The strategy usually does not delve into specific details behind tools and technology selections, although certain recommendations concerning tools and technologies need to be made, especially if the choices are clear. For example if the organization has already selected a DBMS and that DBMS is clearly sufficient for the data warehouse project, then that recommendation can be made. The mandate of the strategy is to provide rules and guidelines around the selection of tools and technologies.

ESTABLISHING A BASELINE UNDERSTANDING

At the outset of the strategy, a baseline understanding of the situation needs to be established. This provides an overall context of the environment for which the strategy is being developed, and helps to quickly establish an understanding of the "as is" situation so that a "to be" can be defined.

Understanding Business Objectives

At the beginning of the process, relevant documents should be obtained and reviewed to gain a baseline understanding of the business mission, vision, goals, and objectives. The strategy must be supported, and support these business goals and objectives of the organization. This baseline understanding should be used as a reference point to ensure that the requirements and strategy are aligned with business objectives. If a major deviation is detected or there is a lack of clarity as to how data warehousing will support the business objectives, then the project should be paused and a quick review conducted.

Understanding Existing Technical Strategy and Environment

The data warehousing strategy team should also gain a baseline understanding of the technical strategy of the organization. This includes the current or evolving technical standards and technologies employed at the organization and how they are meant to support the business strategy. This should be used as a reference point to ensure that the strategy and architectural recommendations resulting from the work are in compliance with and support the technical strategy.

DATA WAREHOUSING

The technology component of the data warehousing strategy should support and comply with the technical architecture of the organization. We say "should", as it is sometimes possible that the architecture development process may discover that the technology architectural standards employed are not adequate to support the data warehousing initiative and need adjustment. This sometimes happens when a particular platform standard, such as the Data Base Management System (DBMS) or the server standard for operational systems, may not be adequate to support the very large data volumes and complex queries that the data warehousing solution may require. In such cases, an alternative DBMS or server technology will need to be introduced.

Understanding Current and Planned Initiatives

The data warehousing strategy team should gain an understanding of current or planned initiatives underway that will impact the strategy. This information is sometimes not as straightforward to obtain as the other baseline information mentioned earlier. Some digging may be required, and it is not unusual to discover some hidden "skunk work" projects of which management was not aware. It is important to determine the scope of these projects, subject areas covered, and technologies used. This information can serve three purposes:

- It can be an eye-opener for management as to what is really going on, providing an added impetus to develop and enforce a coherent strategy.
- It serves to demonstrate the plethora of technologies that may have "sneaked in" and need expensive licensing and support to maintain.
- It can show how the overlapping of subject areas across these independent initiatives may be leading the organization down the path towards silos of data warehousing data.

Understanding Organizational Readiness

An assessment should be conducted on organization readiness to implement, support, and use data warehousing. The assessment should consider whether the organization has the mindset to use and leverage the data warehouse, uses common data definitions, and has the skills and readiness to implement, and support the data warehouse.

BUSINESS REQUIREMENTS

Once a baseline understanding has been achieved around the business and technical strategies, the requirements-gathering phase can begin.

The business requirements phase involves the interviewing of key business users of the data warehouse, and should involve individuals from across all areas of the organization. The "business discovery" phase, as it has been characterized in some methodologies, is followed by "data discovery", whereby the data required to support the informational needs is determined and assessed for availability and quality.

There are a number of techniques for requirements gathering. This can range from individual interviews to JAD (joint application development) group sessions, where users or "stakeholders" from various areas are brought together to define and prioritize requirements. The requirement identification phase should include senior management as well as middle management.

Sometimes it is not a good idea to include people from different levels of the organization in the same meeting, to avoid feelings of intimidation that may lead some people to hold their opinions and experience private. Power and casual users who will use the information on a day-to-day basis as part of their jobs should also be involved. Sample reports currently used should be obtained and analyzed.The strategy at this point should clearly lay out the business requirements and gain agreement from key stakeholders and sponsors of the project before proceeding on to the next phase.

BUSINESS BENEFITS

One of the most difficult tasks in the development of a data warehousing strategy is the identification of business benefits. Business benefits are the core of a business case that management looks for in order to judge the merits and value of proceeding with the data warehouse.

Traditionally, management looks to the business case to identify tangible benefits and costs for the data warehouse. This requires clear identification and quantification of benefits and costs. Although the costs are relatively easy to assess, the benefits are much harder to quantify.

The data warehousing project by definition is one whose exact nature and usage is unpredictable. There are a lot of "soft" benefits that accrue from its usage that are not easily quantifiable. For example, what is the dollar value of making faster decisions because the information will now be readily available? To determine the benefit of having consistent, accurate data for making informed decisions, one must estimate the cost to the organization of making all the bad decisions that are being made with bad data! And no one will own up to that!

One of the difficulties with developing a business case is that the business community understates the benefits they can achieve. There are three reasons for this:

- They will have to take accountability for delivering on those benefits once the data warehouse is implemented. If they don't deliver, they look bad.
- Their budget may be adjusted based on the benefits they identified. For example, if they identified two clerks who spend much of their time gathering information that could be readily available in the data warehouse, then they may lose those clerks when the data warehouse is implemented.
- They may look bad if they claim they have had all this inefficiency in their organizations and have not done anything about it until now.

There are a number of approaches for analyzing benefits, and some consulting companies have developed methodologies to do this. Whatever approach is used in the final analysis, the benefits must be documented, and an agreement must be obtained from stakeholders and sponsors before moving on to the next stage.

DATA STRATEGY

Data strategy is concerned with defining the high-level data architecture to support business requirements. This includes the following:

- Determining subject areas that will be part of the data warehouse and the order in which they should be implemented
- The granularity or level of detail stored
- The placement of data at various locations with the topology
- The modeling constructs used, i.e., entity-relational modeling, dimensional modeling or a combination
- Identifying the main types and sources of the data from a high level, with the details being left to the data warehouse development projects

Subject Areas

Subject areas are broad categorizations of an area of interest to the organization. Some examples of subject areas include the following: Customer, Product, Supplier, Expenses, Assets, and Organization. An analysis of requirements will determine the subject areas to be included in the data warehouse and the order that these subject areas should be implemented. Subject area data is often spread among many different applications, and data stores in operational systems and the data warehouse brings data for a subject area together from these sources. Subject areas and their relationships to one another can be represented schematically in a high level E-R (Entity Relationship) type model. (See Exhibit 29.5.)

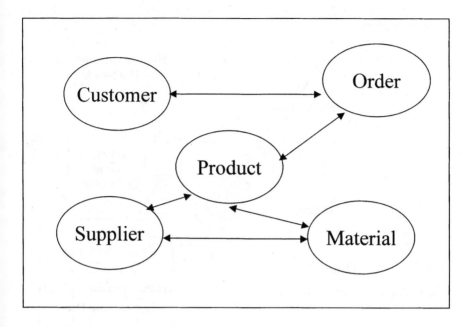

Exhibit 29.5

Granularity

Data granularity refers to the level of detail that will be stored in the data warehouse. Data can be stored from an individual atomic (transactional) level to lightly summarized to highly summarized. It is important to establish the level of granularity required at this stage since the implications on the architecture can be profound. Storing detailed "atomic" data can magnify the size of the warehouse exponentially, and require changes in the topology and architecture, i.e., where to place detailed data and how and when to summarize data for physical access by various levels of usage.

The level of granularity can only be established by careful examination of requirements. It is important at this stage to separate the real needs from the wants. It is quite common for users to answer, "I want all the details," when asked what data they need and at what detail to do their job. There can be differences in the orders of magnitude of disk storage requirements between storing detailed or summarized data, resulting in the difference between success and failure of the project.

In addition, the level of detail depends on the particular manner in which the data will be used. Exhibit 29.6 shows the various levels of detail at which data needs to be stored for various analytic purposes.

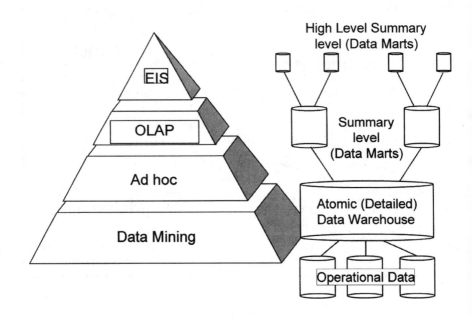

Exhibit 29.6

History

One of the distinguishing characteristics of a data warehouse is the "time variant" element of the data. The time variant nature naturally leads to the need for storing historical data in the data warehouse, which can cause an explosion in terms of volumes of data. The impact of this is not only on the larger storage space required to house the data but, more significantly, on the negative impact on performance as queries will need to plow through larger and larger volumes of data. The requirements gathering should clearly draw out the real historical needs of the organization; once more separating the needs from the wants. The strategy should provide direction on how much history should be loaded into the data warehouse.

Time Element

The time elements stored in a data warehouse differ significantly from the time elements stored in transactional systems. Transactional systems usually "time-stamp" transactions in terms of date, hours, minutes, and seconds. This is mostly for tracking exactly when an event occurred, and for the purpose of sequencing transactions. Time characteristics in a data warehouse are defined and used differently. It is common for the time element to be stored at the date level with characteristics such as day of week, weekday or weekend, holiday, and season. This allows for analysis such as, "How do sales volumes of a product compare within a week of a major holiday to a week following the holiday?"

Data Model

In the data warehousing arena, a debate has been raging for a long time about whether a data warehouse should contain normalized or denormalized data. The debate centers around the use of a normalized entity-relationship type of model to a heavily denormalized dimensional model. Vendors of hardware and software products favor one over the other, often based on how well their product handles one type of model over the other.

The issue is one of balance between flexibility and performance. The strategy needs to address this and define what type of modeling will be employed at the various locations within the data warehouse, and where data will be stored. This may include an operational data store, an enterprise data warehouse, data marts, or any combination of the above. There is usually room for both types of constructs within the data warehouse. The strategy must clearly address this and provide guidance for a consistent development approach for data warehousing within the organization.

Data Quality

The data quality issue is of paramount importance to data warehousing, and many a data warehousing effort has resulted in failure for one simple reason—failing to realize the poor data quality of the source systems, and not having implemented programs in advance to do something about it.

The strategy is not the place to assess detailed data quality, but it is a place for defining data quality policies and metrics. The strategy should include policies on the necessary evaluations that must be conducted before data can be introduced into the data warehouse. Various techniques ranging from statistical sampling to complete analysis can be deployed, and there are many tools on the market to assess as well as cleanse data.

Data Extraction, Transformation, Transportation, and Loading

The data extraction, transformation, and loading (ETL) tools support the capturing, transferring, receiving, cleansing, transforming, and loading of data from operational and external data sources into the data warehouse. This is the most complex and time-consuming process in the development of a data warehousing project. It is estimated that 60 percent to 70 percent of the effort and cost of building data warehouses is the extraction and transformation of data. It is also an area where data warehousing projects typically fail. To be successful requires the adoption of a proper strategy and consistent approach and set of tools. The tools and processes required

461

to support this must be tightly integrated with the entire data warehouse and will need to interface with many of the source systems and technologies within a typical environment.

The lack of a coherent strategy can create the risk of individual business units sourcing and "staging" data independently of each other, leading to inconsistencies in the way business rules are implemented and how the data is loaded into the data warehouse environment. It can also add to the load on the source system platforms as the source systems are being accessed multiple times instead of in a coordinated fashion. The strategy should clearly lay out the process that needs to be followed to minimize "going to the well" too often, and ensure the enterprise uses tools that can be integrated within the overall environment.

Data Staging

Data warehousing architectures typically employ some form of data staging strategy where an image of the data is copied to an intermediate location after being extracted from source systems, and before being loaded into the data warehouse tables where it will be accessed by users.

The reasons for staging data include:

- Centralizing the data before it is "homogenized" in terms of standardization of structures and codes
- Ensuring a low impact on production process windows
- Providing the ability to audit "raw" data before it is altered during transformation

The techniques that can be employed for staging data depend on a number of factors, including the frequency and the location of the data. The project should take these and additional considerations into account and define an overall data staging strategy. This includes rules around the need for staging, the length of time staged data can be retained, access to the staged data, and the possibility of archiving of the "raw" staged data for audit purposes.

Information Management

The successful implementation and long-term success of the data warehouse depends on effective management of the data through information management policies, procedures, and practices. These practices are usually established, maintained, and enforced by an Information Management Function within the organization. The strategy needs to define information management roles, responsibilities, and accountabilities within the organization, and ensure the promotion and maintenance of the following data characteristics, which are of paramount importance to the successful implementation of data warehousing.

- *Data Integrity and Accuracy*—the usefulness of the data warehouse is dependent on the accuracy and completeness of the data and on the confidence that the data is what it is represented to be. The level of data accuracy and quality must be ascertained, published, and understood by the user community.
- *Data Consistency*—there is enterprise wide semantic and syntactic consistency of data definitions. The definitions must be available to all who need them in a consistent, coherent, easy to use format
- *Managed Data Redundancy*—unmanaged data duplication leads to reduced accuracy, questionable integrity, and increased costs. The goal should be to have as few copies of data as possible.
- *Data Accessibility*—there is significant value in data and in its shareability across the organization. Data should be easily accessible to anyone who requires it for the purpose of executing their job function except where privacy or legal implications prohibit it.
- *Manage Data as an Asset*—data is an important corporate asset and its creation, usage, retention, security, and final disposition should be managed as such. Roles and responsibilities for the usage and management of data should be defined, understood, and accepted by both the systems groups and business users. All data must have an "owner" defined for the purpose of having functional accountability for the definition and management of the data.

Information Management includes the following points:

- Creating and communicating the corporate data strategy
- Creating, enforcing, and monitoring adherence to data standards
- Developing and publishing metadata management standards
- Developing and publishing a high level enterprise information model to be developed to more detailed levels through systems development efforts
- Monitoring data for consistency and accuracy and publishing data quality assessments
- Implementing and monitoring a data management "roles and responsibilities" model within the organization

Metadata management

A strategy to support the proper capture, management and provision of metadata, "data about data," is essential for the successful implementation of data warehousing.

There are three types of Metadata that need to be managed:

- Technical metadata, which describes the technical characteristics of the data within the warehouse; for example, the length of a particular data item and its format

- Business metadata, which describes data in terms of business understanding and usage; for example, the definition of net profit and the formula for calculating it
- Operational metadata, which describes operational aspects of the warehouse, such as the last time the data was refreshed

The metadata strategy needs to address how the metadata will be managed and provide high level policies and guidelines for a follow-on project to develop. The strategy should provide direction for the selection of metadata management tools.

Methodology

Traditional systems usually implement a "waterfall" methodology through which requirements can be accurately defined so that an action and the result of that action is both predictable and repetitive. Decision support systems by their very nature are not predictive in the sense that often the questions or queries posed to the system are of an ad hoc type and not easily predictable. The formulation of at question usually depends on the results from a previous question, leading to what's often described as "drilling down" to more detailed levels for answers to findings obtained at a higher level of summarization.

Managers charged with overseeing the development of the data warehousing are often comfortable with working with a rigorous and "safe" systems development methodology, where exact requirements are clearly documented and "frozen" before development begins. They are sometimes uncomfortable with the system being developed in small pieces where the data content and capability of each phase isn't precisely known and is open to change from one iteration to the next. They feel a lack of control in not knowing "exactly" what they will get at the end of the "deliverable". Data warehousing projects are most successful when implemented in an iterative manner, with each iteration taking four to six months, and the deliverables subject to change during the follow-on iteration.

The strategy should address the methodology issue carefully and recommend an iterative approach to implementation. A particular methodology should be recommended if possible, or at least a follow-on methodology selection project should be identified and scheduled.

CONCLUSION

This article examined key components and approaches for assembling a data warehousing strategy for an enterprise.

Chapter 30
A Framework for Developing an Enterprise Data Warehousing Solution

Ali H. Murtaza

THE DECISION TO BUILD A DATA WAREHOUSE IS NOT FOR THE FAINT OF HEART — many critical issues must be understood early or the project will fail. An enterprise data warehousing project is generally a huge, time-consuming investment. In many cases, the benefits are not immediately quantifiable and require a leap of faith to justify. While there are many reasons to build a data warehouse, the two most common reasons are to optimize control of current operations or to gain significant competitive advantage. For instance, a complex, geographically distributed organization may decide that it needs to identify its most profitable customer segments for target marketing programs. This is accomplished by extracting customer data from multiple production systems into a single, consolidated data warehouse. On the other hand, a niche company may architect a data mart as the first stage of a large data mining effort — revealing insightful purchasing patterns that could be leveraged for additional revenue. In both cases, the data warehouse defines itself as an integrated, non-volatile catalog of organizational data that is convertible into actionable information for strategic decision-making.

There are numerous advantages to maintaining such a central perspective over the business that allow the end user to monitor both departmental and corporate performance, access all customer account information,

0-8493-9976-9/99/$0.00+$.50
© 1999 by CRC Press LLC

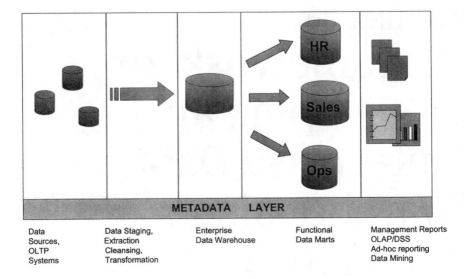

| Data Sources, OLTP Systems | Data Staging, Extraction Cleansing, Transformation | Enterprise Data Warehouse | Functional Data Marts | Management Reports OLAP/DSS Ad-hoc reporting Data Mining |

Exhibit 1.   Enterprise data warehouse model.

increase managerial control, make proactive business decisions, and create sales opportunities. Although an IDC study reported an average data warehousing implementation cost of $3 million, this expensive investment also produces a three-year average return-on-investment (ROI) of 401 percent. Exhibit 1 shows a standard enterprise data warehouse architecture.

CONSIDERING THE CHALLENGES

An enterprise data warehousing initiative is one of the most daunting projects an organization can tackle; a typical effort requires high levels of executive sponsorship, close cooperation between the business and IS communities, cross-functional expertise, and significant time and capital investments. In fact, the high risk of failure prompts experts to depict unsuccessful data warehousing projects as characteristic rites of passage for new project managers; experts state that approximately one out of every five DW projects actually runs to completion. This can easily make a project manager's decision to develop a data warehouse a risky move — often the key to success is the simple ability to neutralize the negative elements that could otherwise sabotage the project.

Before embarking on any data warehousing journey, a clearly defined enterprise strategy with specific goals and objectives must be presented to the project sponsors and stakeholders. Also, the project's objectives must align with those of the organization or the project will fall short; the main driving force of any data warehousing effort is to assist decision-making in achieving corporate objectives. Any project that focuses on achieving strategic objectives that differ significantly from the parent organization will be rejected by senior executives and teach a painful lesson to the project manager.

A data warehousing venture differs from most technology projects in having a high level of executive involvement. There should be no misconceptions about which group is driving a data warehouse project: the business users. Business users define the information requirements, validate the enterprise data model, and access the data for queries and reports. If the business user cannot easily navigate or understand the detailed, summarized, and historical data stored in the warehouse, the benefits are minimized. Frequent communication between the business and IS communities is mission-critical during all project phases to ensure that both groups are aligned and that the development plan meets the original business objectives.

Furthermore, the overall project structure and individual responsibilities must be clearly identified from the start to prevent any confusion among team members. If appropriate technical expertise is not available within the organization to staff the desired roles, the project manager should consider external consultants to fill in the skill gaps. Often, these consultants can provide valuable industry knowledge and vendor relationships important during the data modeling and tool selection stages. Regular meetings should be scheduled at all levels to keep everyone up-to-date and to uncover any potential roadblocks. A mandatory high level of sponsorship ensures political support and reduces resistance from any of the business units. As the project progresses, the project manager must be aware of all organizational or resource issues and raise them immediately to the project sponsor. Clear communication among the different project teams maintains high morale and strong levels of commitment to project objectives. Many data warehousing projects last over 18 months — albeit in manageable three- to six- month iterations — but their benefits are realized even later, and maintaining the executive commitment and sponsorship becomes a serious challenge. The project manager must be aware of any cultural sensitivities to sharing data among the different functional units. Any political vendettas, power struggles, or personal conflicts should be identified early and handled quickly before they can become destructive. The key to success is constant involvement — business involvement in generating user requirements, creating the logical data models, and choosing the end-user tools, and IS involvement for the hardware/software selection, data extraction, physical implementation, and performance tuning.

A typical driving factor behind data warehousing projects is competition within the industry. As competitors take the lead in implementing their own corporate data warehouses and start to make sizable gains in market share and improvements in their bottom lines, many companies naturally follow and expect dramatic results in performance, and significant gains in competitive advantage. Consequently, it becomes critical to understand the stability of the organization's industry — potential acquisitions or mergers could leave behind a lot of unfinished work, greater confusion surrounding corporate data, and wasted capital expenditures for both organizations. Today, many vendors are offering vertical solution sets for data-rich industries such as financial, telecommunication, and health care services. These solutions are sought desperately by organizations for common business requirements and data models essential for effective analysis to be done. External consultants are also being leveraged for their vertical expertise and familiarity with vendor tools in addition to their project-related experience.

STAGE 1 — BUSINESS REQUIREMENTS

In the first stage of a data warehousing project, business requirements for enterprise information are gathered from the user community. This process generally consists of a series of interviews between the end users and the information technology teams in order to understand the informational needs and gaps in the organization. The consolidated results of these interviews drive the content of the data models and establish specific objectives for the new data architecture. The selection of business facts, dimensions, aggregations, level of granularity, historical depth, hierarchies, predefined queries, and standardized reports are all driven by the business users. Once the final version of the information requirements is approved by both the business and IS functions, functional data models are created with the granularity, historical detail, and summarization needed to allow end users access to the data while minimizing the performance effects of common table joins and complex queries. Specific vertical knowledge is most valuable here in customizing the data model to handle industry-specific analysis. Every piece of data in the target data model should have some business value attached to it or it is useless to the business and should be dropped from the model. Lack of trust in the data raises a red flag and severely hinders the success of the project. However, the users must have realistic expectations of the kind of information that will be available to them in the new world. Sample reports or vendor demonstrations can help in this stage to train inexperienced users to visualize the types of querying results and analytical capabilities of the data warehouse front-end tools.

The degree of summarization and size of the data being retained determines whether the data should be stored in a relational or multidimensional database. While the relational DBMS is well-established, commonly understood, and can support very large databases, the multidimensional

DBMS is growing in popularity by offering quicker access to pre-aggregated data and multidimensional analysis capabilities. Multidimensional hypercubes are memory-intensive but reduce the number of physical joins for queries and take advantage of hierarchical and historical information in the schema to roll-up through dimensions. Many organizations are discovering the need for a hybrid schema; both technologies are used by loading the data first for longer term retention into "near normal" relational models subsequently used to build specific views or dimensional models. All external feeds that are required for additional information must also be mapped into the enterprise model in this phase.

STAGE 2 — DATA SOURCING

Companies with data-intensive businesses typically have great difficulty in accessing their operational data. Somewhere in the depth of the multiple legacy systems lie valuable nuggets of business information that can never be capitalized upon because of generally poor data quality and integrity. Consequently, this second stage, which involves extracting, cleansing, and transforming the data from the multiple sources to populate the target data warehouse, is vital and often tends to be the most time-consuming part of the project. Further compounding this problem is the possible discovery that the technical resources supporting these legacy systems are no longer employed in the organization, so cryptic data definitions and programs are left to be deciphered for extraction when they are required. The task of cleaning up enterprisewide data from different functions and departments is often underestimated and can add significant delays to the project timelines. Increased complexity of the data makes the extraction process all the more difficult and laborious. Also, another issue to consider is the capacity of the transactional systems to scale in order to capture larger data volumes or external feeds that might be required in the target warehouse. Tool selection in this data staging layer must be well-researched to integrate with the proprietary systems and the target warehouse.

STAGE 3 — TARGET ARCHITECTURE

The initial IS task to design a target architecture for the data warehouse can create religious, ideological wars among the architects; debates have raged over the tactical deployment of data marts and operational data stores as compared to the complete vision of an enterprise data warehouse. Some organizations will not take the risk of a failed project that could consume three years of their best resources. The scope of the business vision can also dictate the architecture approach: a short-term vision would require a lower budget, quick ROI implementation with small resource requirements offered by data marts, while more strategic objectives of long-term gain and full organizational control would necessitate the full-blown enterprise data warehouse architecture. The most popular architecture choices outside the enterprise data warehouse model are the operational data store, virtual data warehouse, DSS data warehouse, and the data mart.

An operational data store is a rudimentary data store that provides a consolidated view of volatile transactional data from multiple operational systems. This architecture often provides realtime operational data that removes the redundancy and resource costs of creating a separate data warehouse. Analysis can be done with basic querying and reporting without impacting the performance of the production systems. This architecture also offers a shared view of the data, with regular updates from the operational systems. It contains current-valued data which is volatile yet very detailed. Unfortunately, operational data is not designed for decision support applications and complex queries may result in long response times and heavy impact on the transactional systems.

A virtual data warehouse is quick to implement and usually less risky than a traditional data warehouse. It involves data access directly from operational data stores without creating a redundant database. This method gives the user universal access to data from any of the multiple sources; however, the extensive process of cleaning up the data to transform it into actionable information cannot be avoided. There are obvious time and cost savings from not having to consolidate the data or introduce infrastructure changes, but the tradeoff exists in the reduced usability of the data from the multiple systems. If there is a lot of data duplication in the various systems, this will easily confuse the end user and remove any confidence they have in the information. Also, if the data distribution across the legacy systems requires cross-functional information between non-SQL–compliant data sources, the load, complexity, and access time will be impacted on the OLTP systems and network, even if the query can be performed. This architecture also requires more intelligent analysis from the end user to understand the results of multiple queries instead of just one. Distributed query processing software must be in place to decide where and when the queries should be performed in the transactional systems. Once results are obtained, significant data validation may be required to make sense of the business information that was not cleansed or integrated. Also, the end user will not have access to historical snapshots which are among the most valuable strategic decision-making tools offered by a data warehouse. Finally, the results will not be repeatable as the data is continuously changing.

The decision support data warehouse architecture simply consists of snapshots of corporate information consisting of low-level or highly summarized data. This method has the advantages of minimal infrastructure costs, access to nonvolatile data, quick deployment time, and no repetitive

470

data stores. However, the main flaw of this architecture is its inherent lack of flexibility to handle complex decision support analysis expected from a fully architected data warehouse; the data structures are not changed, merely stored periodically as snaphots for comparative analysis. This technique provides good historical information but fails to optimize access to the data. In fact, the snapshots of data are ideal for independent business intelligence and data mining approaches to unearthing customer patterns and trends.

Another potential architecture is the popular data mart or functional data warehouse that captures a subset of the enterprise data for a specific function, business unit, or application. Data marts require less cost and effort to deploy, and provide access to functional or private information to specific organizational units. They are suited for businesses demanding a fast time to market, quick impact on the bottom line, and minimal infrastructure changes. Data marts are essentially mini-data warehouses without the huge cost, long-time investment, high risk of failure, and high level of corporate approval; they are ideal for a rapid, iterative, prototype deployment. Data marts store nonvolatile, time-variant, and summarized information used to serve the information needs of the business unit. However, data marts should not be used as a cheaper solution to a data warehouse; they should simply represent an initial step towards an enterprise data warehouse. If data marts are introduced first, they should be designed to integrate with a future enterprise data warehouse, or much rework will have to be done over the long term. As other business units notice the benefits, data marts must not be allowed to propagate freely throughout the organization or the situation will spell disaster when attempting to integrate them into a single corporate warehouse. When data marts are introduced after the successful implementation of a data warehouse, they can be deployed quickly by replicating required subsets of the corporate database.

STAGE 4 — ACCESS TOOL SELECTION

The level of sophistication of the intended user should be a main driver in the reporting tool selection process. Exhibit 2 illustrates the many levels of query, reporting, and OLAP tools in the marketplace with functions ranging from basic management reporting to complex, drill-down, pass-through analytical processing. It is crucial that the user be comfortable in navigating through the newly consolidated data. Otherwise, this huge capital investment will result in the same scenario the organization started with namely, lots of data with no perceived method to access it. Sample reports and demonstrations are good aids in assessing the results and the capabilities of the business intelligence tool.

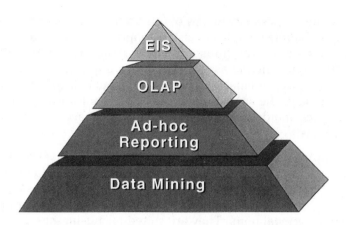

Exhibit 2. User access tools.

In fact, careful training should be provided for the end users to ensure that they understand the various capabilities of the tools. Instead of producing monthly management reports, they should be encouraged to make ad-hoc queries and "slice and dice" through the multiple dimensions and navigate throughout the available information to isolate the specific set of information they require. Once the user taps into the metadata layer (see Exhibit 1) and understands the type of data and relationships that exist in the warehouse, he or she is better equipped to perform meaningful analysis and extract valuable information about the business. Newly evolved data mining technologies promise to bring even greater benefits by performing complex statistical analysis on historical records to uncover business patterns, customer trends, organizational inefficiencies, and even potential fraud.

STAGE 5 — DATA WAREHOUSE ADMINISTRATION

One of the most commonly neglected issues is the administration of the data warehouse after it is built. The appropriate technical resources must be assigned to monitor query load and performance, to handle dynamic changes to the data structures, and to ensure platform scalability with increased user demands. External data may be needed (e.g., stock feeds, Web downloads) and so the architecture must have an open interface to incorporate these new requirements. As users become more sophisticated in their use of the decision support tools, the frequency and complexity of the queries and reports will significantly impact the query performance. A "query from hell" can destroy perceived levels of performance if not identified and managed carefully. Consequently, a dedicated administrator is needed to maintain constant supervision of the query performance and to prevent the data warehouse from grinding to a halt.

Generally, data warehousing projects use the prototype approach to development, and much of the initial success of the prototype will determine the overall success of the project. The data model should be designed against an extensive range of end-user queries and target reports showing enhanced analytical business information, and should be designed to maintain buy-in from the executive sponsors during the pilot demonstration. Most importantly, the information must be accurate, or at least more accurate than the pre-data warehouse data to increase the user's confidence in the information. If the user has unwavering faith in the data, the project has a greater chance to succeed.

CONCLUSION

A common point of debate arises when measuring the overall investment impact of a particular project — the added value of business information is hard to translate into cost savings or generated revenue. The difficulty in quantifying these benefits is one of the most problematic issues facing the project manager in keeping corporate buy-in and team commitment. How can one measure business value? As shown in Exhibit 1, an answer lies in a well-developed metadata repository that allows the business user to easily understand and navigate through the large amounts of corporatewide data contained in the new warehouse. Each piece of data selected for the new data model should be clearly defined in the metadata and perceived as adding business value. If the end user sees no value in it, he or she will not use it and it should be omitted from the new data model. The remarkable change in the business analyst's job is represented by the drastically reduced time needed to gather organizational data — much more time is dedicated to garner meaningful information that will drive the sustained growth and operational efficiency of the corporation.

The designed architecture of the metadata and data warehouse must be scalable enough to support future changes to information needs and analytical requirements (e.g., Web-based delivery). Ongoing management of the data warehouse with minimal adjustments to the data architecture and business users excited about their data are true indicators of project success. Business value is reflected by the enhanced corporate control, lowered costs, increased revenue, strong market share, and new opportunities that are all direct results of the information delivery architecture called the data warehouse.

References

Bachteal, P., Data warehouses: professional management key to successful implementation, *Can. Man.*, 22: 22, 20-21, Summer 1997.
Barquin, R. C., *An Introduction to Data Warehousing*, Barquin and Associates, The Data Warehousing Institute, 1997.

DATA WAREHOUSING

Benson, B. and Von Hollen, C., *Case Study III: Strategies for a Successful Data Warehouse*, May 28, 1997.

Bischoff, J. and Alexander, T., *Data Warehouse Practical Advice from the Experts,* Prentice-Hall, New York, 1997.

Evans, J., Need for analysis drives data warehouse appeal, *Health Man. Tech.*, 18: 11, 28-31, Oct. 1997.

Foley, J., Data warehousing pitfalls, *Inform. Week,* May 19, 1997.

Hackney, D., *Understanding and Implementing Successful Data Marts*, May 28, 1997.

Stedman, C., Turning to outside warehousing help," *ComputerWorld.*

Waltner, C., Ready-made warehouses," *Inform. Week,* 655, 100-108, Nov. 3, 1997.

Chapter 31
Web-Enabled
Data Warehouses
Mary Ayala-Bush
John Jordan
Walter Kuketz

DELIVERING DATA WAREHOUSE ACCESS VIA WEB BROWSERS HAS A VARI-
ETY OF BENEFITS. Inside a corporate intranet, web-enabled data warehouses can increase ease of use, decrease some aspects of training time, and
potentially cut costs by reducing the number of proprietary clients. Upgrades can also be accelerated given a standard client, and data warehouses can more easily integrate with other applications across a common
platform. Extended to corporate trading partners via a so-called extranet
(a secure extension of an intranet outside a firewall), the information contained within a data warehouse may be of sufficient value to become a revenue source. While such internal and external benefits may be appealing,
they do not come without complicating issues.

In these traditional implementations, data warehouses have been used
by a small population of either highly trained or high-ranking employees
for decision support. With such a small audience having the warehouse application on their desktop, access control was straightforward: either the
end-user could access a given table or not. Once the warehouse begins to
be accessed by more people — possibly including some outside of the
company — access may need to be restricted based on content. Security
concerns also change as the user population increases, with encryption
over the public Internet being one likely requirement. Because web-based
access to a data warehouse means expanding the community of people
who will access the data, the types of queries will most likely be more varied. Better business intelligence may thereby be derived, but once again
not without complications.

In addition to security, performance (and therefore cost) issues become
immediately relevant, dictating reconsideration of everything from replica-

tion patterns to login requirements. This article explores how web-enabled data warehouses change the strategy, architecture, infrastructure, and implementation of traditional versions of these applications

STRATEGY

Business Relationships

The strategy for a web-based data warehouse should answer at least two questions:

- Who is being granted access?
- Why are they being granted access via the web model?

Answering these two questions will supply important information for the cost justification of broader access. Possible justifications might include getting better service from vendors, facilitating better relationships with customers, shortening time of products in the supply chain, and receiving revenues from an internal application. The implications of broader access include having to design an architecture flexible enough to allow for new audiences with needs and requirements that may not be well identified. In addition, going into the information business can distract a company from its core focus: how are pricing levels determined? How does revenue derived from a potentially unexpected external source change payback and ROI models? What are the service level agreements and how are they determined? Who becomes the customer service liaison, especially if the IS organization is already running at full capacity for internal constituencies?

Access Control and Security

Security is a primary consideration when contemplating web access to sensitive corporate information. Authentication can be required at three separate stages, allowing administrators to fine-tune who sees what when, while encryption (typically through the use of the secure sockets layer, or SSL) protects both queries and responses from being compromised in transit. Initially, the web server can require either name and password login or the presence of a certificate issued by the data warehouse administrator. This grants access to the site and triggers the SSL encryption if it is implemented. Once inside the data warehouse, the user might also be required to authenticate himsel or herself at the query server, which allows access to the appropriate databases. This might be a dedicated data mart for a vendor, for example, that precludes Vendor A from seeing anything pertaining to Vendor B, whose information is held in a logically (and possibly physically) separate data mart. Finally, authentication may be required by the database to limit access within a given body of data: a clerk at Vendor A can see only a selected portion of the A data mart, while A's president can see that company's entire data mart.

The logistics of security can be extensive. Maintaining certificates requires dedicated resources, while planning for and executing multitiered logins is a nontrivial task. At the same time, limiting access can imply limiting the value of the data warehouse, so security must be designed to be flexible and as friendly to legitimate users as possible.

New Components

Broader access to a data warehouse introduces a number of new elements into the traditional application model. What happens to the query engine vendor's pricing model as its proprietary desktop clients are no longer required? Where are the skill sets and hardware to implement web servers and connect them to the query engine? How much will data be transformed (and by whom) if it is moved out of a central data warehouse into data marts for security, performance, or other reasons?

ARCHITECTURE

If strategy is concerned with goals and objectives, architecture is the unifying conceptual design or structure. It defines a system's component parts and relationships. Good architectures ensure that the component hardware and software pieces will fit together into an integrated whole.

A web-enabled data warehouse introduces additional components within a system architecture, which must be expanded to include:

- The web server component.
- The components that connect the web server to the query engine.
- The component that formats the results such that they are viewable by a web browser.

The system architecture may also need a component for integrating data marts.

Even given these elements, the architecture must be flexible enough to change rapidly, given both the pace of innovation in the Internet arena and the evolving place of data warehouses in contemporary business. The warehouse components may change due to increasing numbers of people using it, changing aggregations based on security or performance requirements, new access paths required by technological or organizational evolution, etc.

New design considerations are introduced by each of the above components. web servers introduce new complications, particularly in regard to scalability issues. Secure transactions over a dialup connection can be painfully slow, but detuning the security at either the firewall or the web server can expose the corporate network to risk. Middleware between the web server and the query server can dramatically affect performance, particularly if common gateway interface (CGI) scripts are used in place of APIs. Database publishing to HTML is reasonably well advanced, but even here some of the newest tools introduce Java programming into the mix, which may cause implementation problems unless the skills are readily available. Java also presents the architect with new ways to partition the presentation layer and the application logic, with implications (for the network and desktop machines in particular) that are only beginning to be experienced in enterprise computing.

The system architecture must support competing enterprises accessing the data sources. One challenge is to support competing vendors where access control is data dependent. Both vendors can query the same tables; for example, by product, by region, by week. If a given retail outlet sells both vendors' products, and people from the sales outlet are allowed to query the data warehouse, they will need access to both vendors' histories.

A good system architecture must include the facility for access control across the entire web site, from the web server through to the database. If a mobile sales force will be given access while they are on the road, the architecture must have a component to address the types of connections that will be used, whether they are 800 dialup services, local Internet Service Providers (ISPs), or national ISPs such as CompuServe or AOL.

INFRASTRUCTURE

The infrastructure required to support the web-enabled data warehouse expands to include the web site hardware and software, the hardware and software required to interface the web server to the query server, and the software that allows the query server to supply results in HTML. The corporate network may have to be altered to accommodate the additional traffic of the new data warehouse users. This expansion increases the potential complexity of the system, introduces new performance issues, and adds to the costs that must be justified.

The web-enabled warehouse's supporting infrastructure also introduces new system administration skills. Because the warehouse's DBA should not be responsible for the care and feeding of the web site, a new role is required — the web site administrator, often called the webmaster. This term can mean different things to different people, so clarity is needed as the position is defined. Depending on the context, corporate webmasters may or may not be responsible for the following:

- Designing the site's content architecture
- Writing and/or editing the material
- Designing the site's look and feel
- Monitoring traffic

- Configuring and monitoring security
- Writing scripts from the web server to back-end application or database servers
- Project management
- Extracting content from functional departments

The amount of work that may have to be done to prepare for Internet or intranet implementation will vary greatly from company to company. For example, if the warehouse is going to be accessible from the public Internet, then a firewall must be put in place. Knowing the current state of web-based application development is essential: if organizational factors, skills, and infrastructure are not in place and aligned, the data warehouse team may either get pulled from its core technology base into competition for scarce resources or be forced to develop skills largely different from those traditionally associated with database expertise.

Web Site

Web site components include the computer to run the web server on and the web server software, which may include not only the web listener but also a document manager for the reports generated from the warehouse. One of the web protocols, called the Common Gateway Interface, allows the web browser to access objects and data that are not on the web server, thereby allowing the web server to access the data warehouse. The interface used does not access the warehouse directly but will access the query engine to formulate the queries; the query engine will still access the warehouse. The CGI has been identified as a bottleneck in many web site implementations. Because the CGI program must incur the overhead of starting up and stopping with every request to it, in high-volume systems this overhead will become pronounced and result in noticeably slow response times. API access tends to be faster, but it depends on the availability of such interfaces from or in support of different vendors.

Application Query Engine

The infrastructure must support the application query engine, which may run on the same computer as the data warehouse or on a separate computer that is networked to the data warehouse computer. This component must be able to translate the query results into HTML for the server to supply to the browser. Some of the query engines will present the results in graphic form as well as tabular form. Traditional warehouses have supported relatively small user communities, so existing query engines will have to be monitored to see how their performance changes when the number of users doubles, triples, or increases by even larger multiples. In addition, the type and complexity of the queries will also have performance implications that must be addressed based on experience.

DATA WAREHOUSING

Data Warehouse

The infrastructure for the data warehouse is not altered simply because web browsers are being used; instead, the expanded number of users and new types of queries that may need to be executed will likely force changes to be made. When a data mart architecture is introduced for performance or security reasons, there may be a need to change where the mart will be located: on the same machine as the warehouse, or on a separate machine. The infrastructure will have to support both the method of replication originally specified and new patterns of replication based on DASD cost considerations, performance factors, or security precautions.

Security

Web server access. Access to the web server can be controlled by: 1. requiring the user to log onto the web site by supplying a user name and password, 2. installing client certificates into the browsers of the clients to whom access is granted, or 3. specifying only the IP addresses that are allowed to access the web site. The client certificate requires less interaction on the user's part because they will not have to supply a user name and password to access the system. The client's certificate is sent to the web server, which will validate the certificate and grant the user access to the system. (Part of the process of enabling a secure web site is to install a server certificate. This must be requested from a third party, called a certificate authority, which allows one to transmit certificates authenticating that someone is who they say they are.) A less secure strategy is to configure the web server to allow connection from a selected number of computers, with all others being categorically denied access. This scheme will allow anyone from an authorized computer — as opposed to authorized persons — to access the web site. Because this method is based on IP address, DHCP systems can present difficulties in specifying particular machines as opposed to machines in a particular subnet.

Communication transport security. Both the query and especially the information that is sent back to the browser can be of a sensitive nature. To prevent others along the route back to the browser from viewing it, the data must be encrypted, particularly if it leaves the firewall. Encryption is turned on when the web server is configured, typically via the Secure Socket Layer (SSL) protocol.

Query server application. To access the query server, the user may be asked to supply a user name and password. The information supplied by the certificate could be carried forward, but not without some custom code. There are various approaches to use for developing the user names and passwords: one can create a unique user name for each of the third parties who will access the system (allowing the login to be performed on any machine), or create a unique user name for each person who will access the warehouse. Each approach has implications for system administration.

Database access. Database access can be controlled by limiting the tables users and user groups can access. A difficulty arises when there are two competing users who must access a subset of the data within the same table. This security difficulty can be solved by introducing data marts for those users where each data mart will contain only the information that particular user is entitled to see. Data marts introduce an entirely new set of administrative and procedural issues, in particular around the replication scheme to move the data from the warehouse into the data mart. Is data scrubbed, summarized, or otherwise altered in this move, or is replication exact and straightforward? Each approach has advantages and drawbacks.

IMPLEMENTATION

The scope of implementing a web-enabled data warehouse increases because of the additional users and the increased number of system components. The IS organization must be prepared to confront the implications of both the additional hardware and software and of potentially new kinds of users, some of whom may not even work for the company that owns the data in the warehouse.

Intranet

Training will need to cover the mechanics of how to use the query tool, provide the user with an awareness of the levels (and system implications) of different queries, and show how the results set will expand or contract based on what is being asked. The user community for the intranet will be some subset of the employees of the corporation. The logistics involved with training the users will be largely under the company's control; even with broader access, data warehouses are typically decision-support systems and not within the operational purview of most employees.

Implementing security for the intranet site involves sensitizing users to the basics of information security, issuing and tracking authentication information (whether through certificates, passwords, or a combination of the two), and configuring servers and firewalls to balance performance and security. One part of the process for enabling a secure web server is to request a server certificate from a certificate authority. Administratively, a corporation must understand the components — for example, proof of the legal right to use the corporate name — required to satisfy the inquiries from certificate authority and put in place the procedures for yearly certificate renewal.

Monitoring a web-based data warehouse is a high priority because of the number of variables that will need tuning. In addition, broader access will change both the volume and the character of the query base in unpredictable ways.

Intra/Extranet

In addition to the training required for internal users, training is extended to the third parties that will access the warehouse. Coordination of training among the third parties will likely prove to be more difficult: competing third parties will not want to be trained at the same time, and paying customers will have different expectations as compared with captive internal users. In addition, the look and feel within the application may need more thorough user interface testing if it is a public, purchased service.

Security gets more complex in extranet implementations simply because of the public nature of the Internet. It is important to keep in mind the human and cultural factors that affect information security and not only focus on the technologies of firewalls, certificates, and the like. Different organizations embody different attitudes, and these differences can cause significant misunderstandings when sensitive information (and possibly significant expenditures) are involved.

Monitoring and tuning are largely the same as in an intranet implementation, depending on the profiles of remote users, trading partner access patterns, and the type and volume of queries.

In addition, a serious extranet implementation may introduce the need for a help desk. It must be prepared to handle calls for support from the third parties, and combine customer service readiness with strict screening to keep the focus on questions related to the data warehouse. It is not impossible to imagine a scenario in which the third-party employees will call for help on topics other than the warehouse.

CONCLUSION

Because web browsers have the ability to save whatever appears in the browser, in web-enabled data warehouses, information that appears in the browser can be saved to the desktop. Protecting information from transmission into the wrong hands involves a balancing act between allowing for flexibility of queries and restricting the information that can potentially move outside corporate control. Legal agreements regarding the use of information may need to be put in place, for example, which tend not to be a specialty of the IS organization. Pricing the information can be another tricky area, along with managing expectations on the part of both internal and third-party users.

By their very nature, however, data warehouses have always been more subject to unintended consequences than their operational siblings. With changing ideas about the place and power of information, new organizational shapes and strategies, and tougher customers demanding more while paying less, the data warehouse's potential for business benefit can be increased by extending its reach while making it easier to use. The consequences of more people using data warehouses for new kinds of queries, while sometimes taxing for IS professionals, may well be breakthroughs in business performance. As with any other emerging technology, the results will bear watching.

Chapter 32
Distributed Integration: An Alternative to Data Warehousing
Dan Adler

DATA WAREHOUSING HAS, PERHAPS, BEEN THE MOST COSTLY systems development in the history of financial services. The concept of data warehousing grew out of regional and departmental consolidation projects in which large relational databases were used to store relatively large quantities of data and make these data available to standard query tools such as SQL and various SQL-based interfaces. These queries were very useful in helping departments track customer behavior, P&L, and, in combination with applications written in VB, C++, and S-PLUS, they helped departments and regional entities within financial institutions track market trends, manage risk, and develop predictions.

Many managers, however, when they saw the success of the special-purpose database, were inspired to take this concept to the next level. "If we can do so much with a relational database in one department, I wonder how much value we could extract by representing our entire firm in a relational database?" went the reasoning. And, for expanding global trading businesses that needed to control the risks associated with numerous local portfolios composed of complex financial instruments, the centralized data warehouse containing "everything" was particularly appealing.

At most financial institutions, however, extending numerous departmental and regional data collection projects to create a "firmwide" data warehouse representing a firm's entire global business just did not work. Wall Street — and retail banking's Main Street — are littered with tales of multi-year, multimillion-dollar data warehousing projects that were killed because they did not produce anything near what their architects promised. Problems include: transforming data stored in numerous formats, ensuring the data is "clean" and correct, developing and maintaining a firmwide data model describing interrelationships between different types of data, managing various types of middleware to transport data from place to place, limited network resources, etc. And, of course, users became frustrated waiting for the "warehouse" and its associated promised functionality.

Still, extracting value from firmwide information and controlling global market risk remain top priorities for financial institutions and their information technology departments, which are struggling to develop alternatives to data warehousing. One of the most promising such developments is Distributed Integration.

Distributed Integration is a new approach to integrating both firmwide data and analytics based on Internet technologies, such as cascaded Internet servers and data caching. The "Distributed" refers to data and analytics that reside in numerous physical locations. The "Integration" refers to users' ability to access these disparate data and analytics through an *analytic browser,* which can be any application residing on any desktop which maintains an active connection to one or more *Distributed Integration servers.*

This chapter will describe how Distributed Integration solves some data integration problems that data warehousing projects do not always successfully address, and show how Distributed Integration leverages existing desktop and intranet technologies to deliver this integrated data (and analytics) to large communities of internal and external users at a very reasonable price point.

THE HISTORY OF DATA WAREHOUSING

The firmwide relational data warehouse has been proposed as a solution to numerous business issues facing financial institutions during the 1980s and 1990s.

First, in wholesale banking, per-trade margins have steadily declined in the mature foreign exchange and interest rate markets as the number of market participants increased and interest rate markets became more liquid. To respond more nimbly to market movements and to identify long-term trends, "data mining" — in which information is collected and analyzed to identify underlying patterns — became extremely popular. The data warehouse has been proposed as means of conveniently storing large quantities of historical and realtime data in order to facilitate the data mining process.

An important subset of the data mining issue for wholesale bankers and money managers is the management of time series data. These are data that are periodically collected and time stamped. This sort of data is very difficult to store in relational formats because time series records — when expressed in tabular format — are very repetitive. Likewise, time series data are collected more or less continuously. Therefore, they tend to rapidly overpopulate relational databases and reduce performance. So, time series records are more often stored in file format for convenience. Blending time series and relational data for data mining purposes has often been an objective of data warehousing initiatives.

Another trend in wholesale banking has been the development of complex derivative instruments in response to the shrinking margins described above. These more complex instruments, often developed by local trading offices in response to specific customer demands, have raised control issues highlighted by a spate of "derivatives losses" stories in the mid 1990s as banks, corporations, and investment managers recognized the importance of, first, understanding their derivatives exposures in the context of their whole portfolios and, second, keeping a close eye on rapidly expanding foreign offices. Indeed, the downside of extreme decentralization was dramatically illustrated by the failure of U.K.-based Barings Bank. In the wake of the Barings scandal, many financial institutions turned to data warehousing as a solution to their "control and security" issues.

In retail banking, the consolidation and acquisition of numerous banks meant fierce competition, and product innovation and sales became ever more critical. Data mining became very popular in the retail deposit and credit card businesses, wherein effectively dissecting the customer's spending and living habits equals better product development and sales.

Finally, both retail and wholesale financial services providers became increasingly concerned with the rapid distribution and analysis of so-called "real time" data. Indeed, the global bull market, while providing satisfying returns across the board, also makes it more difficult for investment managers to differentiate themselves from the pack or from benchmark indices. Data warehousing capable of handling real data, then, became a Holy Grail for many firms.

CHOOSE YOUR WEAPONS

While data warehousing seemed like a sound solution to many of the above-mentioned business challenges at the conceptual level, the actual implementation of data warehousing solutions did not live up to the initial promise. First, this is because of the many difficulties associated with obtaining, converting, and transporting data that effectively limit the scalability of most data warehousing solutions.

Second, if it is possible to get data into a warehouse, it is often challenging to get the data out of the warehouse and into the hands of end users who need it.

For example, traditional relational data warehouses are built in conjunction with implementation of a large, costly "enterprise" system. Such enterprise systems are typically limited to a certain number of high-priority users. Providing general access to such a system is usually too costly due to licensing fees. And, if the enterprise system performs crucial operations functions, analysts and other nonoperations staff may not be allowed to apply query tools to the data warehouse; if they did, they could slow down mission-critical processes. When general queries are permitted against the data warehouse, they are often very slow. In most cases, specialized query tools must be purchased in order to identify, copy, and manipulate the relevant portion of warehoused data.

There are three major types of data warehousing implementations, and each has different benefits and drawbacks; these are listed below. However, while all of these solutions have been successfully implemented at the local level, none has successfully scaled up to the enterprise level.

Options for Data Warehousing

Numerous Interfaces. This is the classic, old-style data warehouse in which numerous "interface" programs are developed to create even more numerous download files which, in turn, may be uploaded to a centralized data warehouse during nightly, weekly, or monthly batch processing. While the interface method does possess a certain conceptual simplicity and, in fact, is sometimes the only option available to handle extremely proprietary — or antiquated — bits of data, it traditionally has a low success rate. This is because the sheer number of interface programs which must be successfully run and kept in sync is usually so large. This creates problems because, first, if something goes wrong in any one of these procedures, the entire data warehouse may become inaccurate. Second, these interfaces are often difficult to fix because they are often proprietary and, wherever there is IT turnover, impenetrable and undocumented.

Replication. Data replication can be used to create both a data warehouse and numerous redundant data sources by periodically copying new records across a suitable WAN. For example, let's say Bank X, headquartered in New York, has a London office and a Singapore office. Let's also say the data warehouse resides in New York. As new trades are entered in London and Singapore, they are both stored in local relational databases and copied or "replicated" and sent through the WAN to the data warehouse in New York. The same replication procedure can be used to populate a backup data warehouse located in, say, London. While this method is straightforward and has worked well for medium-sized and smaller portfolios, it also has distinct scalability problems. This is often due to excessive network traffic created by the constant copying and transmission of each and every transaction. As the network slows down, it becomes difficult to keep the data warehouse up to date, and network failures can result in corrupt, incorrect, or incomplete data.

Middleware. Middleware is a catchall term referring to "plumbing" software that is typically transparent to the user and may function as an engine for any or all of the following: data transformation, data integrity checking, transaction monitoring, data transformation, data distribution, and/or object/application communication. Some financial institutions have attempted to populate large physical data warehouses through the innovative use of multiple forms of middleware. Others have attempted to link together various types of middleware in order to create their own "virtual data warehouse" in which middleware supplies applications with RAM copies of relevant data.

Regardless of which sort of warehouse one is attempting to create, managing numerous forms of middleware has some substantial drawbacks. These include the extensive effort required to ensure that different middleware packages are compatible with each other and with critical data sources, scalability limits associated with various types of middleware (particularly ORBs when used in conjunction with a "virtual" warehouse), maintenance associated with upgrades, etc.

The Data Mart Variation

In response to the limitations of data warehousing, many financial institutions have abandoned multiyear data warehousing projects in favor of what is known as the "data mart" approach. Basically, the data mart approach refers to a data warehousing project that is based on a number of local, regional, or functional implementations. The prime benefit of this approach is that, unlike the traditional "big bang" style of warehouse building, users in specific regional or functional areas can actually see results within a more predictable period of time. And, for this reason, data mart projects have found a friendlier reception in financial institutions than "old style" data warehousing.

However, the final step of a data mart project is generally to combine all the data marts into a data warehouse by periodically copying these local databases in their entirety into a centralized, relational data warehouse. Often, it is easier to create a data warehouse from data marts than to build one from scratch because data marts are usually built with consistent technology, thus avoiding the need for massive data conversions.

However, these data mart-based warehouses do not usually work well for realtime analysis, in which constant data-copying would compromise performance both at the warehouse and data mart levels. And, a data mart-driven warehouse still comes up against the challenge of distributing the contents of the warehouse in a usable format to those who need them.

489

DISTRIBUTED INTEGRATION: A NEW WAY

Distributed Integration is a new way to integrate global financial data, analytics, and applications, and quickly distribute them to a large community of users. Unlike most traditional data warehousing solutions, this does not require all data to be physically co-located in a single huge database. Instead, the Distributed Integration architecture relies on Internet technologies to create a virtual data warehouse that is optimized for both scalability and the cost-effective delivery of critical data to large user communities.

Data and analytics residing in multiple physical locations behave like a single, integrated virtual environment through web-enabled *Distributed Integration servers*. These servers take advantage of Internet server cluster organization and data caching techniques and thus are configured for extreme scalability.

End users access the distributed integration virtual environment through a *Distributed Integration workstation,* which simply refers to any desktop which has a direct Internet connection to one or more Distributed Integration servers.

Almost any application (such as Excel™) residing on a distributed integration workstation can be enabled to view and manipulate integrated data and analytics; such applications are referred to *analytic browsers.*

Indeed, for the numerous highly paid analysts at most financial institutions who spend the majority of their time gathering relevant information to feed into their spreadsheets and then verifying that this information is clean, consistent, and correct, the analytic browser is truly a revolutionary concept.

Exhibit 1 provides a quick illustration of distributed integration. It depicts a global financial organization with two or more physical locations separated by a WAN or Internet connection.

The top location, say New York, has an equities group that maintains a database of equities using Sybase. They use a distributed integration server to make the data available to their own clients. They deliver analytics to traders at home through analytic browsers. They also have a group of analysts who write specific analytics and incorporate them into the Distributed Integration server, thus making them available to other analysts and to managers for control purposes.

The bottom location, say London, has a number of other groups that maintain an FX database in FAME and a commodities database in ORACLE. They make the data available to their own traders and analysts through their own Distributed Integration server, which also includes proprietary analytics. This group is also servicing some external clients who are con-

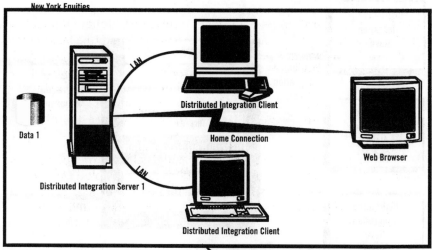

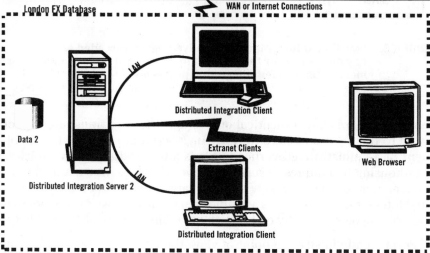

Exhibit 1. A sample of Distributed Integration architecture.

nected to them through the Internet, and get data, analytics, and web-based applications from them.

LEVERAGING INTERNET/INTRANET TECHNOLOGY

Since the Distributed Integration servers in these two locations can be cascaded, as shown in Exhibit 2, each set of endusers can see the data in the other location. Moreover, since the Distributed Integration architecture is characterized by transparent caching, the access times for local and

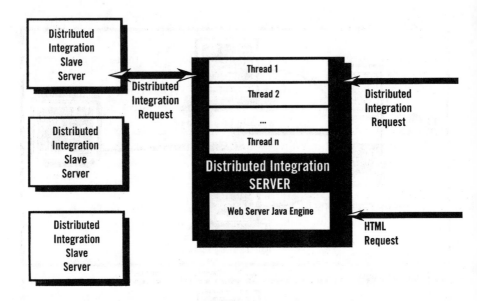

Exhibit 2. **Distributed Integration takes advantage of cascaded server technology developed for the Internet to ensure fast and efficient management of Distributed Integration processes.**

remote data are almost identical on average. Data are transparently replicated to the location where they are used without significant IT involvement or administrative overhead; this is a far cry from the various data warehousing techniques described above, which require extensive IT resources to implement. As new locations are added with their own Distributed Integration servers, it is a simple step to make those servers known to the existing ones, thereby creating global multidirectional connectivity.

From an administrative point of view, the data, analytics, and applications are being maintained by the group that originated, and most "cares" about them, and they maintain it in whichever database they have chosen. However, because these data are integrated on the server side, local administration and autonomy does not come at the price of effective controls. This is a critical point for risk managers, HQ treasury managers, and compliance managers, who are often strong advocates of data warehousing initiatives which centralize data and, in theory, enhance controls.

The Distributed Integration server caching will "equalize" the access speed such that the back-end database does not become a bottleneck even if it's a small ACCESS database running on someone's desktop PC. Distributed Integration makes it possible to then selectively share data, analytics, and applications across the entire organization without any additional integration work.

This architecture is highly scalable, since no single point can become a bottleneck as the number of locations increases. Thus, Distributed Integration avoids the scalability pitfalls associated with replication-based data warehousing solutions that tend to "clog up" a company's network.

For optimal scalability, the Distributed Integration server should be configured as a server cluster. This means it is not physically limited to a single process on a single machine. Such a server solution is implemented as a front-end, multithreaded, cluster manager process, with any number of symmetrical back-end servers that share the same configuration. Moreover, such clusters can always be cascaded among themselves, so there truly is no limit to the scalability of the Distributed Integration platform.

THE DISTRIBUTED INTEGRATION SERVER

Distributed Integration servers integrate historical and realtime data, metadata (i.e., data describing data), analytics, and applications. Because the server is capable of handling complex metadata and, by extension, almost any sort of data transformation, Distributed Integration is particularly well suited to address financial institutions' need for integrating time series and relational data.

In order to handle web-based applications naturally and efficiently, Distributed Integration servers must also, by extension, be Internet servers. Indeed, Distributed Integration servers have been built as plug-ins to preexisting Internet servers. As is consistent with Distributed Integration's reliance on the web and web-related technologies, it is most efficient to organize Distributed Integration servers as server clusters.

These Distributed Integration server clusters are stateless and connectionless, just like most web servers, and should be capable of supporting the HTTP 1.1 keep-alive option for multiple related requests with a single connection for best utilization of network resources. This is also important from a user-functionality perspective; once data have been requested and cached, a user should be able to query that data without recopying it across the network. Likewise, incremental changes should be transmitted without the necessity of replicating the entire data set in which the changes originated.

The server cluster organization is one important reason why Distributed Integration can scale beyond traditional data warehousing solutions. As displayed in Exhibit 2, the front-end Distributed Integration server funnels each request to a number of preconfigured slave servers that actually handle the data and analytical requests.

Scalability is achieved by the fact that any number of slave servers can be added to a cluster, and they are automatically load-balanced by the master server. Fault tolerance is achieved by virtue of the fact that slave servers can be distributed on multiple machines, thereby reducing the chances that a single machine failure will halt the system.

A separate spool of threads handles standard web server requests such as getting HTML pages, downloading Java applets, etc. This integrated architecture means that application, content, and data can be freely mixed to create a powerful application development and deployment model that is web-centric and leverages the currently existing infrastructure.

Distributed Integration, it is important to note, performs best in a reasonably consistent hardware environment in which the server machines may be considered more or less interchangeable, and all the slave servers must have access to all the same data and analytics. This implies a shared configuration, as well as shared metadata and data caches. Thus, the user sees the entire cluster as a single server, with one URL address. And this URL address, then, becomes the user's gateway to the firm's total knowledge base.

The Distributed Integration server cluster architecture delivers:

- Performance — through the use of multiple machines coupled with load balancing
- High availability — through redundancy of slave servers
- Scalability — you can add more processes and machines as the number of users increases

THE GATEWAY TO DISTRIBUTED INTEGRATION

Once one or more Distributed Integration servers have been configured to create a single point of integration for data and analytics, the next critical step is to cost-effectively distribute information to a large community of users. This has, in fact, been a challenge for those traditional data warehousing projects that have managed to get off the ground. A Java interface — or Distributed Integration gateway — can be used to connect desktop machines to integrated data and analytics residing on Distributed Integration servers.

When the gateway is active, a machine becomes a Distributed Integration workstation that is capable of "browsing" through all the information that is part of the Distributed Integration environment. Data and analytics can be accessed through a standard web browser or by building software that connects existing desktop applications to the Distributed Integration environment. Applications that have access to Distributed Integration are called analytic browsers. It is possible to develop Distributed Integration add-ins capable of converting almost any application into an analytic browser.

In the financial services industry, however, one of the most useful applications of the analytic browser will be to connect spreadsheets to the Distributed Integration environment, thus allowing analysts to access integrated data without having to convert files or otherwise participate in the data-cleaning and -collection process. More advanced analytic applications will also become much more powerful when combined with Distributed Integration; indeed, one of the likely benefits of dynamically connecting endusers to an integrated environment is to speed up the pace of financial innovation.

LONG-TERM IMPLICATIONS OF DISTRIBUTED INTEGRATION

Distributed Integration, as it is implemented on a more widespread basis throughout the financial services industry, is likely to have important, even revolutionary, effects on how banks, brokerages, etc. do business in the future. And, as early adopters, the experiences of these financial services firms will serve as a model for other industries. Long-term implications of the Distributed Integration model include the following advantages.

Facilitates Financial Innovation

The desktop PC is synonymous with the modern workplace, and the PC-based spreadsheet application is synonymous with modern finance. However, the demands of today's businesses are straining the practical limits of PC-based spreadsheet analysis. A common illustration of this phenomenon is the fact that numerous highly paid financial analysts spend the majority their time gathering relevant information to feed into their spreadsheets and then verifying that this information is clean, consistent, and correct.

By providing integrated firmwide data and analytics accessible through spreadsheets — such as Excel™ — Distributed Integration frees financial analysts from time-consuming data management duties and allows them to focus on value-added tasks. End users will also benefit from the opportunity to view and use the sum total of their firms' intellectual capital; they may combine this information in new and profitable ways.

Thus, the widespread adoption of Distributed Integration is likely to foster a new period of rapid financial and business innovation as analysts are simultaneously freed from the demands of data gathering and provided with accurate, integrated information.

Encourages a New Form of Corporate Organization: The Internet Management Model

As the number of web-enabled workstations within corporations reach critical mass, organizations will be able to learn from the Internet and adopt new ways of managing themselves that go beyond the traditional trade-offs between centralization and decentralization. The Internet Man-

495

agement Model (IMM) is one such method. It applies the Internet philosophy — that information and services are made globally available by the special interests that cherish them at low or no cost across a system which, to the customer, looks consistent, unified, and available on demand — to the corporate organization.

Distributed Integration, which allows local offices to manage and maintain their own mission-critical information while giving everyone access to the entire firm's intellectual capital, is an ideal vehicle for implementing IMM. Thus, rapid growth is sustained while top managers and business analysts have unprecedented access to the "big picture" presented by their firms' collective data and information systems. Islands of data ownership are eliminated.

By allowing firms to track individual and departmental contributions to firmwide intellectual capital, it becomes possible to identify high- and low-performing areas. Simultaneously, IMM gives individuals and functional units much greater freedom to incorporate new data and analytics into their business activities without obtaining time-consuming approvals from central IT and business planning groups.

Allows Corporations and Financial Institutions to Manage the WHEN Dimension

As businesses' profitability becomes increasingly dependent on the timeliness and quality of the information which serves as the basis for key production, marketing, and strategic decisions, the ability to view, manipulate, and analyze data by time will become a matter of "life and death." Time-centric data, however, is often repetitive and difficult to store in conventional database formats. The Distributed Integration architecture is optimized for the rapid storage, transmission, and analysis of time-centric data as part of an integrated systems environment.

Section VII
Enterprise Resource Packages

Chapter 33
Choosing your ERP Implementation Strategy

Marie Karakanian

The enterprise resource planning (ERP) project interfaces with all aspects of an organization: people, process, technology, systems, structure, skills, culture, and definitely available technology funds. Executives responsible for such projects must develop a very clear understanding of the tasks they are about to undertake, ensure that all the relevant variables are accounted for in the planning process, and that time and effort are dedicated to them during and after the implementation. To be more specific, the strategy should focus on the following aspects of the project:

- Drivers
- Resources
- Visibility and profile
- Components of the ERP technology to be implemented
- Package functionality business fit
- Existing technology platforms, systems, and data
- Users
- Implementation logistics
- Budget and available funds

It is noteworthy to mention that, although ERP implementations are categorized as projects— a one-time set of activities with a defined beginning and end and finite resources and deliverables— in reality, they have become perpetual jobs in the current state of affairs. This is because of ongoing technology upgrades, technology change dependencies, mergers and acquisitions, de-mergers, and, of course, recycling of people from one project to another. Holding people down to one job they have learned to become good at has become a very difficult task to achieve in today's ERP labor marketplace. So, an implementation strategy should also take into account project staff resourcing and retention strategy.

0-8493-9981-5/99/$0.00+$.50
© 1999 by CRC Press LLC

PROJECT DRIVERS

What instigated the project to start with? A proper understanding of the project, the reasons behind it and the demands on the organization must be understood very clearly by those who sponsor and run the project long before they initiate it. During the last four or five years, the following were among typical drivers for ERP projects:

- Lack of business systems integration
- Multiple technologies requiring multiple sets of tools, skill sets, and vendors to deal with
- Lack of shared corporate information
- Inconsistency of data
- Strategic information to executives
- Data duplication and "multiplication"
- Lack of Year 2000 compliance in existing systems
- Business globalization
- Centralization of corporate data
- Decentralization of regional or business unit data

Today, as the Y2K specter is quickly losing its weight, a large number of organizations still believe the demand for useful strategic information is greater than ever before in some business processes, such as human resources. A recent survey conducted by Deloitte & Touche and Lawson Software discovered that 67 percent of the surveyed HR executives believe that the demand for HR to provide useful strategic information is greater than ever before. Corporate disciples of such downplayed disciplines continue on, trying hard to play the strategic partner game with their corporate board members. Their challenge is converting the value of a not-so-easily-definable asset—human resources—into palatable figures by the means of technology. The journey has been long; however, it continues.

While most of the previous drivers still hold true for a number of organizations, more recent drivers such as shared services, employee self-service, and electronic commerce also impact ERP projects or the systems that build upon them. The nature of the driver will impact the formulation of the implementation strategy. For example, the need for Y2K compliance by the year 2000 can overrule a fundamental business process redesign, which can be undertaken at a later date.

RESOURCING

One key decision at the start of the implementation process involves project resourcing. The choice is between the acquisition of external consulting resources who have the required experience, skill sets, and know-how, versus internal resources who do not necessarily have the required expertise, but do have the promise of learning and internalizing a knowledge base that will remain within the organization after the conclusion of the project. Usually, resource selection is driven by the availability of project budgets, criticality of deadlines, and the promise of knowledge transfer.

Recent experiences that organizations have had vary significantly due to what appears to be high expectations from specialized consulting partners. The lack of true expertise is revealed quickly, and some organizations have had the sour taste of providing a learning platform to consultants who professed prior expertise in a given ERP package implementation. For this reason, organizations should conduct proper research and interviews before hiring their consulting partners.

An additional challenge organizations have faced, and are still facing, is the loss of their own staff to better paid jobs once the accumulation of new knowledge is at a level which is sought after in the labor markets. In some cases, organizations have rehired their own staff at much higher costs after they have defected into ERP consulting. Thus, the "internalization" of the new knowledge base has been proven to be very shaky. Project executives should try and develop retention strategies that the organization can deal with, which hopefully also has a certain level of internal equity.

VISIBILITY AND PROFILE

The ERP project needs to have its place among hundreds of concurrent projects it is competing with for executive attention. In smaller organizations, the champions of such projects are the executives themselves. The project should make sure that the appropriate communication plans and change–management mechanisms are put in place right from the start of the project. Also, the project manager should ensure that time and budget are allocated to such activities within each phase of the project, as the need for visibility heightens throughout the lifecycle of the project.

In large organizations most executives, although accountable at the end, are detached from such projects until disaster time comes along. To prevent such occurrences, appropriate links and status-reporting procedures should be established, at least with the line executives, to keep them informed of project progress, impact, risks, and challenges. Executive management should also be informed about various alternative solutions and be part of the decision-making process for preferred solutions, especially those that have critical impact on the operations of the organization.

COMPONENTS OF AN ERP PACKAGE

Before developing an implementation strategy, one area to concentrate on is the package itself and its components. Simply speaking, this can involve the following three areas at a minimum:

1. The various application modules included in the package, such as financials, distribution, human resources and payroll
2. Various tools such as reporting, importing data, and upgrades
3. Various API's that help integrate the package to various platforms of potentially different technologies, such as scanners, and interactive voice response systems

The strategy should address the potential modularity of the implementation. Considering the number and variety of the business processes that these applications enable, as well as the legacy data conversion and legacy systems integration, it may simply be impossible to come up with a true "big bang" approach and attempt to implement all components concurrently. Normally, such implementations are staged based on a number of considerations, including:

- The application dependencies within the new technology. Are there any mandatory modules that must be implemented before others?
- Optimization of the benefits of the new technology right from the beginning. Where can quick hits be identified that can start bringing some return on the technology investment?
- What currently manual business process can be automated whose manual operation costs the organization highly today?
- Are there internal resources available to the project to enable the concurrent implementation of some applications, such as general ledger, payroll, distribution, etc?
- Is the bundling of the package functionality suitable enough to replace and decommission some of the existing systems right away and stage the rest in a manageable manner? This will facilitate the decommissioning of the existing systems and potentially rid the organization of their maintenance costs.
- From package perspective, does it make sense to conduct a proper "proof of concept" of mission-critical modules with a representative group of business units before charging ahead with complete implementation?

Finding and developing the answers to these questions is not necessarily easy and straightforward; however, making the effort up front will help clarify the package and the organizational environment better and, therefore, contribute to a more informed strategy.

PACKAGE FUNCTIONALITY BUSINESS FIT

The selection of an off-the-shelf package for an organization implies that this package is a reasonable fit for the organization and its business requirements. However, ERP clients generally come to realize during implementation that the way they do business is somewhat different from the way the package expects them to. This creates a conflict that must be addressed in one way or another during the implementation. One option for addressing this gap is customizing the package to the client's requirements, with the assumption that the package vendor also provides the customization tools. Another option would be changing the way the client conducts its business. This is easily said, yet not so easily implemented. Apart from the challenges of managing change in organizations which have done certain things in specific ways for several decades, the potential impact of change can extend to collective agreements and union renegotiations which can take years, to say the least.

Normally, a compromise is reached with some customization and some process change. Some "flexible" ERP packages come bundled with their own proprietary tools that are used to perform the customizations. People-Soft is one good example that provides flexible and user-friendly tools. The customizations, however, must be done with the longer term in view, considering the impact on upgrades and the basic application structure.

EXISTING PLATFORMS, SYSTEMS, AND DATA

This aspect of the ERP implementation project should never be underestimated. Often legacy data is not in good shape and requires purification or a cleanup process. With respect to the data, a number of decisions need to be made with a view to the implementation. History conversion is one aspect that needs to be thought of during strategy formulation in order to plan accordingly. The possibility of storing historical information in different ways, as well as converting at a later phase, should be considered with a view to the business requirements.

Although ERP implementations are expected to replace the existing platforms, it does not necessarily happen in all cases. And when it happens, it doesn't take place in one shot, meaning that the project needs to integrate the new technology with the old technology and, therefore, recruit resources with the right expertise to the project . The total decommissioning of the existing platforms is normally driven by a lack of Y2K compliance; however, projects may find that interfaces are required for various legacy, mission-critical systems not addressed by the new ERP. These systems may be in the process of being re-hauled or patched up for Y2K compliance.

USERS

As users are on the front line, it is crucial to know their numbers and evaluate their needs, profiles, skill sets, and orientation towards the project and the new technology. They are the targets for the training, communication, and change management strategies of the project. An organization that is going to rollout an ERP system for the first time to managers as end users will have a different approach than the one that is replacing an existing system from its current users, such as accountants or payroll data entry clerks. A project team considering phased rollout will have a different training strategy than the one targeting for a big bang, one-time implementation approach.

An organization replacing a mainframe system with a client server, Windows-based system will need to consider training the users in Windows first, if required, before training them in the ERP system. Similarly, at the technical and operational user level, a client server technology will introduce different challenges to operational staff, who will require targeted, specific-knowledge transfer plans and intensive sessions from the project team. Some of these training sessions may require one-on-one instruction for long periods of time, or actual time on the project.

IMPLEMENTATION LOGISTICS AND SCHEDULING

This could vary significantly from one organization to another. Usually, multilocation, multibusiness unit organizations implement and roll out in a phased fashion. This could mean phased system handover to the user community or phased functionality rollout. This strategy will support organizations that may have fairly decentralized operations that are independent operations of each other, so that the phasing of the functionality and the rollout schedule are negotiated and well-coordinated with other business unit-specific projects.

If it happens that different units within an organization have different requirements in common areas such as payroll, the system design and configuration timeline can be developed in co-ordination with the rollout strategy.

The timing and scheduling of the implementation should take into account not only the readiness of the project team and the user community, but also other corporate projects. The high profile of the project should not be marred with problems arising from inadequate scheduling of concurrent projects. Decisions and agreements should be reached at the executive levels to ensure a smooth implementation where the focus of all parties involved can be directed towards the ERP project, at least for a temporary period of time.

BUDGET AND AVAILABLE FUNDS

The ERP project is one of the few winners among those competing for rare corporate resources. The size of the budget is a reflection of the expectations made from the project and its results. Therefore, it must be handled with extreme care and control.

The project manager should establish a budget monitoring process and a project reserve fund right from the start. Different budget buckets should be established, including those for the consulting partner, independent contractors, implementation-specific tools, project space, and team-building activities. He or she should make sure that the return on financial investment meets expectations, and that budget gaps are highlighted and brought forward to executive attention on a timely basis.

CONCLUSION

As a last word, it is a good practice to monitor and review the implementation strategy at each milestone of the project. Unfortunately, projects hardly ever finish as started. Changes occur constantly, project sponsors get reassigned, consulting partners move on, project resources depart, corporate priorities shift, and technology performance does not meet expectations. Therefore, a strategy review process should be built into the project plan, especially for longer-term ERP projects.

Chapter 34
Critical Issues Affecting an ERP Implementation

Prasad Bingi, Maneesh K. Sharma, and Jayanth K. Godla

Implementing an ERP causes massive change that needs to be carefully managed to reap the benefits of an ERP solution. Critical issues that must be carefully considered to ensure successful implementation include commitment from top management, reengineering of the existing processes, integration of the ERP with other business information systems, selection and management of consultants and employees, and training of employees on the new system.

The Enterprise Resource planning (ERP) software market is one of the fastest growing markets in the software industry. It has seen a rocky start with several project failures and a huge shortage of skilled and experienced workers. The ERP market is predicted to grow from a current $15 billion to a gigantic $50 billion in the next five years. The estimated long-term growth rates for ERP solutions are a stratospheric 36 percent to 40 percent. Some estimates put the eventual size of this market at $1 trillion. Recently, major ERP vendors such as SAP AG, Baan, and Oracle have reported significant financial results. Contributing to this phenomenal growth is the estimation that 70 percent of the Fortune 1000 firms have or will soon install ERP systems, and the initiatives by ERP vendors to move into medium to small tier industries with gross revenues less than $250 million. ERP vendors are aggressively cutting deals with these industries to make their products more affordable. For example, SAP, one of the leading ERP vendors, recently started selling its products to customers in the $150 million to $400 million revenue range.

Companies could spend hundreds of millions of dollars and many years implementing ERP solutions in their organizations. Once an ERP system is implemented, going back is extremely difficult; it is too expensive to undo the changes ERP brings into a company. There are several failed ERP attempts, and companies lost not only the capital invested in ERP packages and millions paid to outside consultants, but also a major portion of their business. Recently Unisource Worldwide, Inc., a $7 billion distributor of paper products, wrote off $168 million in costs related to an abandoned nationwide implementation of SAP software.[12] FoxMeyer Drug, a former $5 billion drug distributor, went bankrupt in 1996 and has filed a $500 million lawsuit against SAP. FoxMeyer charged that the ERP giant's package was a "significant factor" that led the firm into financial ruin.[14] Dell Computer Corp. has recently abandoned a much-publicized SAP implementation following months of delay and cost overruns. Dow Chemical, after spending half a billion dollars over seven years of implementing SAP R/2, the mainframe version, now has decided to start all over again on the new client/server version (R/3). Implementing an ERP system is a careful exercise in strategic thinking, precision planning, and negotiations with departments and divisions. It is important for companies to be aware of certain critical issues before implementing any ERP package. Careful consideration of these factors will ensure a smooth rollout and realization of full benefits of the ERP solution.

ERP SOLUTIONS

An ERP system can be thought of as a companywide information system that integrates all aspects of a business. It promises one database, one application, and a unified interface across the entire enterprise. An entire company under one application roof means everything from human resources, accounting, sales, manufacturing, distribution, and supply-chain management are tightly integrated. This integration benefits companies in many ways: quick reaction to competitive pressures and market opportunities, more flexible product configurations, reduced inventory, and tightened supply-chain links. The Earthgrains Co. implemented SAP R/3 and reports that its operating margins improved from 2.4 to 3.9 percent and pushed its on-time product delivery rate to 99 percent in 1997.[13] The company also reports better management information and happier customers. Similarly, at Par Industries in Moline, IL, an ERP system allowed management to base production on current customer orders rather than forecasts of future orders. The delivery performance improved from 60 percent on time to more than 95 percent, lead times to customers reduced from six weeks to two weeks, repair parts reduced from two weeks to two days, work-in-process inventory dropped almost 60 percent, and the life of a shop order dropped from weeks to mere hours.[1] IBM Storage Systems division, after implementing an ERP system, was able to reprice all of its products in five minutes compared with five days prior to the implementation. It also reduced the time to ship a replacement part from 22 days to three days, and the time to perform a credit check from 20 minutes to three seconds.[2]

The first tier players in the ERP market are SAP, Baan, Oracle, and PeopleSoft, while the second tier players are vendors such as J.D. Edwards, Lawson, and QAD. SAP, a German company, holds about one-third of the market share and is the leading vendor of ERP products. SAP's ERP product is R/3, and the current commercial version is release 4.0 b. Worldwide, there are more than 16,500 SAP R/3 installations. The product has a strong international appeal with capabilities to support multiple currencies, automatic handling of country-specific import/export, tax, and legal and language needs. The complete suite of SAP R/3 applications is available in 24 languages, including Japanese (Kanji) and other double-byte character languages.

The current ERP systems have an open client/server architecture and are realtime in nature, i.e., clients can process information remotely and the results of a new "input" will "ripple" through the whole "supply-chain" process. The appeal of such systems for businesses is that all employees of a company will have access to the same information almost instantaneously through one unified user interface. ERP systems such as SAP/R3 include not just the functional modules that "crunch" the numbers but also the most advanced technologies and methodologies. Implementing such a system results in benefits from the "integrated" nature of the system as well as from the "reengineering" of the business practices and the entire "culture" of the business, all at the same time.

The popularity of ERP programs can be attributed to an increasing trend towards globalization, mergers and acquisitions, short product life cycles, and the fear of looming disasters from aging legacy systems that cannot handle dates beyond the end of this century (commonly know as the Y2K problem). To be successful, a global enterprise must have accurate real-time information to control and coordinate the far-flung resources. ERP systems have the capability to integrate far-flung outposts of a company along with the supply-chain activities. This integration allows sharing of information in a standard format across many departments in the home country as well as across the national borders regardless of language and currency differences. In this era of global competition and uncertain markets, companies are merging for competitive advantage. In the United States, the past couple of years have seen about $1 trillion in mergers annually, many of which involved overseas firms. These newly formed corporations often have very little in common other than a corporate logo. To achieve synergy across national boundaries and product lines, these businesses must implement a set of standard business applications and consistent data definitions across all business units. ERP packages are extremely useful in integrating a global company and provide a "common language" throughout the company. Digital Equipment Corp. is implementing PeopleSoft's human resources system across its 44 locations worldwide. Digital is not only implementing a standardized human resources application but is also moving to a common architecture and infrastructure. For many companies, a global software rollout is a good time to do some serious housecleaning and consolidation of their IT infrastructure around the world. Digital is expecting a return on investment of 27 percent from this global rollout.[5] If the merging companies have already implemented the same ERP solution, then they will save a tremendous amount in cost and time when integrating their systems. Recently, Daimler-Benz AG and Chrysler Corp. merged to form Daimler Chrysler AG. The new company could dodge five to ten years of integration work because the companies use the same computer-aided design systems and SAP financial applications.[15]

Companies are also finding that the ERP solutions help them get rid of their legacy systems, most of which are not Year 2000 compliant. Sometimes it costs less for companies to replace their dinosaur systems than fix them. AlliedSignal Turbocharging Systems, a California-based turbocharger manufacturer, had more than 120 legacy systems, and the average age of the company's legacy systems was 18 years. In addition to these legacy systems, the company had several homegrown applications that had little or no source code documentation. These systems were so disparate and inefficient that running them not only drove IT costs up, but also increased the time to fill customer orders. AlliedSignal is implementing SAP R/3 to replace its 120 legacy systems in 15 of the company's 17 facilities worldwide. Company officials estimate a full payback on the $25 million project in a little more than two years. It has already started seeing the benefits of the ERP implementation in the first sites that went live with the new system. It is able to reduce the order fulfillment process to just a day from its previous weekly procedure.[8]

CRITICAL IMPLEMENTATION CONCERNS

Even in a single site, implementing ERP means "Early Retirement Probably." An ERP package is so complex and vast that it takes several years and millions of dollars to roll it out. It also requires many far-flung outposts of a company to follow exactly the same business processes. In fact, implementing any integrated ERP solution is not as much a technological exercise but an "organizational revolution." Extensive preparation before implementation is the key to success. Implementations carried out without patience and careful planning will turn out to be corporate root canals, not competitive advantage. Several issues must be addressed when dealing with a vast ERP system, and the following sections discuss each of them in detail.

Top Management Commitment

The IT literature has clearly demonstrated that for IT projects to succeed top management support is critical.[4] This also applies to ERP implementations. Implementing an ERP system is not a matter of changing software systems, rather it is a matter of repositioning the company and transforming the business practices. Due to enormous impact on the competitive advantage of the company, top management must consider the strategic implications of implementing an ERP solution.[2] Management must ask several questions before embarking on the project. Does the ERP system strengthen the company's competitive position? How might it erode the company's competitive position? How does ERP affect the organizational structure and the culture? What is the scope of the ERP implementation — only a few functional units or the entire organization? Are there any alternatives that meet the company's needs better than an ERP system? If it is a multinational corporation, the management should be concerned about whether it would be better to roll the system out globally or restrict it to certain regional units. Management must be involved in every step of the ERP implementation. Some companies make the grave mistake of handing over the responsibility of ERP implementation to the technology department. This would risk the entire company's survival because of the ERP system's profound business implications.

It is often said that ERP implementation is about people, not processes or technology. An organization goes through a major transformation, and the management of this change must be carefully planned (from a strategic viewpoint) and meticulously implemented. Many parts of the business that used to work in silos now have to be tightly integrated for ERP to work effectively. Cutting corners in planning and implementation is detrimental to a company. The top management must not only fund the project but also take an active role in leading the change. A review of successful ERP implementations has shown that the key to a smooth rollout is the effective change management from top. Intervention from management is often necessary to resolve conflicts and bring everybody to the same thinking, and to build cooperation among the diverse groups in the organization, often times across the national borders. Top management needs to constantly monitor the progress of the project and provide direction to the implementation teams. The success of a major project like an ERP implementation completely hinges on the strong, sustained commitment of top management. This commitment when percolated down through the organizational levels results in an overall organizational commitment. An overall organizational commitment that is very visible, well-defined, and felt is a sure way to ensure a successful implementation.

Reengineering

Implementing an ERP system involves reengineering the existing business processes to the best business process standard. ERP systems are built on best practices that are followed in the industry. One major benefit of ERP comes from reengineering the company's existing way of doing business.

All the processes in a company must conform to the ERP model. The cost and benefits of aligning with an ERP model could be very high. This is especially true if the company plans to roll out the system worldwide. It is not very easy to get everyone to agree to the same process. Sometimes business processes are so unique that they need to be preserved, and appropriate steps need to be taken to customize those business processes. Hydro Agri North America, Inc. implemented SAP R/3 in 1994, and since then the company has been fighting against the integration SAP provides because some of the company's processes are very unique. Trying to fit the SAP mold resulted in a lot of pain and fewer benefits. Now Hydro Agri will either build a different front-end application or use a different package whenever their processes clash with that of the SAP.[7] The companies also face a question as to whether to implement the ERP software "as is" and adopt the ERP system's built-in procedure or customize the product to the specific needs of the company. Research shows that even a best application package can meet only 70 percent of the organizational needs. What happens to the rest? An organization has to change its processes to conform to the ERP package, customize the software to suit its needs, or not be concerned about meeting the remaining 30 percent. If the package cannot adapt to the organization, then organization has to adapt to the package and change its procedures. When an organization customizes the software to suit its needs, the total cost of implementation rises. The more the customization, the greater the implementation costs. Companies should keep their systems "as is" as much as possible to reduce the costs of customization and future maintenance and upgrade expenses.

Integration

There is a strong trend toward a single ERP solution for an entire company. Most companies feel that having a single vendor means a "common view" necessary to serve their customers efficiently and the ease of maintaining the system in future. Unfortunately, no single application can do everything a company needs. Companies may have to use other specialized software products that best meet their unique needs. These products have to be integrated along with all the homegrown systems with the ERP suite. In this case, ERP serves as a backbone, and all the different software are bolted on to the ERP software. Third-party software, called middleware, can be used to integrate software applications from several vendors to the ERP backbone. Unfortunately, middleware is not available for all the different software products that are available in the market. Middleware vendors concentrate only on the most popular packaged applications, and tend to focus on the technical aspects of application interoperability rather than linking business processes. Many times, organizations have to develop their own interfaces for commercial software applications and the homegrown applications. Integration software also poses other kinds of problems when it comes to maintenance. It is a nightmare for IS personnel to manage this software whenever there are changes and upgrades to either ERP software or other software that is integrated with the ERP system. For every change, the IT department will be concerned about which link is going to fail this time. Integration problems would be severe if the middleware links the ERP package of a company to its vendor companies in the supply chain. Maintaining the integration patchwork requires an inordinate and ongoing expenditure of resources. Organizations spend up to 50 percent of their IT budgets on application integration.[9] It is also estimated that the integration market (products and services) equals the size of the entire ERP market.[3] When companies choose bolt-on systems, it is advisable to contact the ERP vendor for a list of certified third-party vendors. Each year, all the major ERP vendors publish a list of certified third-party vendors. There are several advantages to choosing this option, including continuous maintenance and upgrade support.

One of the major benefits of ERP solutions is the integration they bring into an organization. Organizations need to understand the nature of integration and how it affects the entire business. Before integration, the functional departments used work in silos and were slow to experience the consequences of the mistakes other departments committed. The information flow was rather slow, and the departments that made the mistakes had ample time to correct them before the errors started affecting the other departments. However, with tight integration the ripple effect of mistakes made in one part of the business unit pass onto the other departments in real time. Also, the original mistakes get magnified as they flow through the value chain of the company. For example, the errors that the production department of a company made in its bill of materials could affect not only the operations in the production department but also the inventory department, accounting department, and others. The impact of these errors could be detrimental to a company. For example, price errors on purchase orders could mislead financial analysts by giving a distorted view of how much the company is spending on materials. Companies must be aware of the potential risks of the errors and take proper steps, such as monitoring the transactions and taking immediate steps to rectify the problems should they occur. They must also have a formal plan of action describing the steps to be taken if an error is detected. A proper means to communicate to all the parties who are victims of the errors as soon as the errors are detected is extremely important. Consider the recent example of a manufacturing company that implemented an ERP package. It suddenly started experiencing a shortage of manufacturing materials. Production workers noticed that it was due to incorrect bills of materials, and they made necessary adjustments because they knew the correct number of parts needed to manufacture. However, the company did not have any procedures to notify others in case any errors were found in the data. The domino effect of the errors started affecting other areas of business. Inventory managers thought the company had more material than what was on the shelves, and material shortages occurred. Now the company has mandatory training classes to educate employees about how transactions flow through the system and how errors affect the activities in a value chain. It took almost eight weeks to clean up the incorrect bills of materials in the database.

Companies implementing electronic supply chains face different kinds of problems with integration of information across the supply-chain companies. The major challenge is the impact automation has on the business process. Automation changes the way companies deal with one another, from planning to purchasing to paying. Sharing and control of information seem to be major concerns. Companies are concerned about how much information they need to share with their customers and suppliers and how to control the information. Suppliers do not want their competitors to see their prices or order volumes. The general fear is that sharing too much information hurts their business. Regarding controlling information, companies are aware that it is difficult to control what they own, let alone control what they do not own. Companies need to trust their partners and must coordinate with each other in the chain. The whole chain suffers if one link is slow to provide information or access. The management also must be concerned about the stress an automated supply chain brings within each organization. For instance, a sales department may be unhappy that electronic ordering has cut it out of the loop, while manufacturing may have to adjust to getting one week's notice to order changes and accommodate those changes into its production orders.

ERP Consultants

Because the ERP market has grown so big so fast, there has been a shortage of competent consultants. The skill shortage is so deep that it cannot be filled immediately. Finding the right people and keeping them through the implementation is a major challenge. ERP implementation demands multiple skills — functional, technical, and interpersonal skills. Again, consultants with specific industry knowledge are fewer in number. There are not many consultants with all the required skills. Since the ERP market in the United States started approximately five years ago (and is growing at an astronomical rate), there are not many consultants with three or more years of experience. This has sent the compensation for skilled SAP consultants through the roof. One year's experience brings in $70,000 to $80,000 annually. Three to five years' experience could command up to $200,000 annually. One might find a consultant with a stellar reputation in some areas, but he may lack expertise in the specific area a company is looking for. Hiring a consultant is just the tip of the iceberg. Managing a consulting firm and its employees is even more challenging. The success or failure of the project depends on how well you meet this challenge.[10]

Implementation Time

ERP systems come in modular fashion and do not have to be implemented entirely at once. Several companies follow a phase-in approach in which one module is implemented at a time. For example, SAP R/3 is composed of several "complete" modules that could be chosen and implemented, depending on an organization's needs. Some of the most commonly installed modules are sales and distribution (SD), materials management (MM), production and planning (PP), and finance and controlling (FI) modules.

The average length of time for a "typical" implementation is about 14 months and can take as many as 150 consultants. Corning, Inc. plans to roll out ERP in ten of its diversified manufacturing divisions, and it expects the rollout to last five to eight years.[11] The length of implementation is affected to a great extent by the number of modules being implemented, the scope of the implementation (different functional units or across multiple units spread out globally), the extent of customization, and the number of interfaces with other applications. The more the number of units, the longer implementation. Also, as the scope of implementation grows from a single business unit to multiple units spread out globally, the duration of implementation increases. A global implementation team has to be formed to prepare common requirements that do not violate the individual unit's specific requirements. This involves extensive travel and increases the length of implementation.

The problem with ERP packages is that they are very general and need to be configured to a specific type of business. This customization takes a long time, depending on the specific requirements of the business. For example, SAP is so complex and general that there are nearly 8000 switches that need to be set properly to make it handle the business processes in a way a company needs. The extent of customization determines the length of the implementation. The more customization needed, the longer it will take to roll the software out, and the more it will cost to keep it up-to-date. The length of time could be cut down by keeping the system "plain vanilla" and reducing the number of bolt-on application packages that require custom interfaces with the ERP system. The downside to this "plain vanilla" approach is conforming to the system's mold, which may or may not completely match the requirements of the business.

For small companies, SAP recently launched Ready-to-Run, a scaled-down suite of R/3 programs preloaded on a computer server. SAP has also introduced AcceleratedSAP (ASAP) to reduce implementation time. ERP vendors are now offering industry-specific applications to cut the implementation time down. SAP has recently outlined a comprehensive plan to offer 17 industry-specific solutions, including chemical, aerospace and defense, insurance, retail, media, and utilities industries. Even though these specific solutions would be able to substantially reduce the time to implement an application, organizations still have to customize the product for their specific requirements.

Implementation Costs

Even though the price of prewritten software is cheap compared with in-house development, the total cost of implementation could be three to five times the purchase price of the software. The implementation costs would increase as the degree of customization increases. The cost of hiring consultants and all that goes with it can consume up to 30 percent of the overall budget for the implementation. According to Gartner Group, total cost of an outside SAP consultant is around $1600 per day. Going for in-house SAP-trained technologists creates its own worries. Once the selected employees are trained after investing a huge sum of money, it is a challenge to retain them, especially in a market that is hungry for skilled SAP consultants. Employees could double or triple their salaries by accepting other positions. Retention strategies such as bonus programs, company perks, salary increases, continual training and education, and appeals to company loyalty could work. Other intangible strategies such as flexible work hours, telecommuting options, and opportunities to work with leading-edge technologies are also being used. Many companies simply strive to complete the projects quickly for fear of poaching by head-hunting agencies and other companies.

ERP Vendors

As there are about 500 ERP applications available and there is some company consolidation going on, it is all the more important that the software partner be financially well off. Selecting a suitable product is extremely important. Gartner Group has the BuySmart program, which has more than 1700 questions to help a company choose a suitable ERP package. Top management input is very important when selecting a suitable vendor. Management needs to ask questions about the vendor, such as its market focus (for example, midsize or large organization), track record with customers, vision of the future, and with whom the vendor is strategically aligned. For a global ERP rollout, companies need to be concerned if the ERP software is designed to work in different countries. Also, management must make sure the ERP vendor has the same version of the software available in all the countries the company is implementing the system. Vendor claims regarding global readiness may not be true, and the implementation team may need to cross-check with subsidiary representatives regarding the availability of the software. Vendors also may not have substantial presence in the subsidiary countries. It is important to evaluate whether the vendor's staffers in these countries are knowledgeable and available. If there is a shortage of skilled staff, bringing people from outside could solve the problem, but it would increase the costs of implementation.

Selecting the Right Employees

Companies intending to implement an ERP system must be willing to dedicate some of their best employees to the project for a successful implementation. Often companies do not realize the impact of choosing the internal employees with the right skill set. The importance of this aspect cannot be overemphasized. Internal resources of a company should not only be experts in the company's processes but also should be aware of the best business practices in the industry. Internal resources on the project should exhibit the ability to understand the overall needs of the company and should play an important role in guiding the project efforts in the right direction. Most of the consulting organizations do provide comprehensive guidelines for selecting internal resources for the project. Companies should take this exercise seriously and make the right choices. Lack of proper understanding of the project needs and the inability to provide leadership and guidance to the project by the company's internal resources is a major reason for the failure of ERP projects. Because of the complexities involved in the day-to-day running of an organization, it is not uncommon to find functional departments unwilling to sacrifice their best resources toward ERP project needs. However, considering that ERP system implementation can be a critical step in forging an organization's future, companies are better off dedicating their best internal resources to the project.

Training Employees

Training and updating employees on ERP is a major challenge. People are one of the hidden costs of ERP implementation. Without proper training, about 30 to 40 percent of front-line workers will not be able to handle the demands of the new system.[6] The people at the keyboard are now making important decisions about buying and selling — important commitments of the company. They need to understand how their data affects the rest of company. Some of the decisions front-line people make with an ERP system were once the responsibility of a manager. It is important for managers to understand this change in their jobs and encourage the front-line people to be able to make those decisions themselves. Training employees on ERP is not as simple as Excel training in which you give them a few weeks of training, put them on the job, and they blunder their way through. ERP systems are extremely complex and demand rigorous training. It is difficult for trainers or consultants to pass on the knowledge to the employees in a short period of time. This "knowledge transfer" gets hard if the employees lack computer literacy or have computer phobia. In addition to being taught ERP technology, the employees now have to be taught their new responsibilities. With ERP systems you are continuously being trained. Companies should provide opportunities to enhance the skills of the employees by providing training opportunities on a continuous basis to meet the changing needs of the business and employees.

517

Employee Morale

Employees working on an ERP implementation project put in long hours (as much as 20 hours per day) including seven-day weeks and even holidays. Even though the experience is valuable for their career growth, the stress of implementation coupled with regular job duties (many times employees still spend 25 to 50 percent of their time on regular job duties) could decrease their morale rapidly. Leadership from upper management and support and caring acts of project leaders would certainly boost the morale of the team members. Other strategies, such as taking the employees on field trips, could help reduce the stress and improve the morale.

CONCLUSION

ERP solutions are revolutionizing the way companies produce goods and services. They are a dream come true in integrating different parts of a company and ensuring smooth flow of information across the enterprise quickly. ERP systems bring lot of benefits to organizations by tightly integrating various departments of the organization. Even though ERP solutions have been popular in Europe for some time, North American companies have been using them for only about five to six years. Some of the factors that have contributed to ERP growth are the trend towards globalization, Year 2000 problems, and mergers and acquisitions.

ERP systems are very large and complex and warrant careful planning and execution of their implementation. They are not mere software systems; they affect how a business conducts itself. How a company implements an ERP system determines whether it creates a competitive advantage or becomes a corporate headache. The top contributor for a successful ERP implementation is strong commitment from upper management, as an implementation involves significant alterations to existing business practices as well as an outlay of huge capital investments. The other important factors are the issues related to reengineering the business processes and integrating the other business applications to the ERP backbone. Upper management plays a key role in managing the change an ERP brings into an organization. Organizational commitment is paramount due to possible lengthy implementation and the huge costs involved. Once implemented, an ERP system is difficult and expensive to undo. Since no single ERP solution can satisfy all the business needs, organizations may have to implement custom applications in addition to the ERP software. Integrating different software packages poses a serious challenge, and the integration patchwork is expensive and difficult to maintain.

Selecting and managing consultants pose a continuous challenge due to the shortage of skilled consultants in the market. ERP vendors are bringing out industry-specific solutions and newer methodologies to cut the length and costs of implementation. Organizations could reduce the total cost of implementation if they reduce customization by adapting to the ERP's built-in best practices as much as possible. Selecting the right employees to participate in the implementation process and motivating them is critical for the implementation's success. Finally, it is important to train the employees to use the system to ensure the proper working of the system. ▲

References

1. Appleton, E., "How to Survive ERP," *Datamation*, October 9, 1998.
2. Davenport, T., "Putting the Enterprise into the Enterprise System," *Harvard Business Review*, July August 1998, Vol. 76, No. 4, pp. 121–131.
3. Edwards, J., "Expanding the Boundaries of ERP," *CIO*, July 1, 1998.
4. Johnson, J., "Chaos: The Dollar Drain of IT Project Failures," *Application Development Trends*, January 1995, pp. 41–48.
5. Horwitt, E., "Enduring a Global Rollout — and Living to Tell About It," *Computerworld*, Vol. 32, No. 14, March 1998, pp. S8–S12.
6. Koch, C., "Surprise, Surprise," *CIO*, June 15, 1996.
7. Melymuka, K., "ERP is Growing from Being Just an Efficiency Tool to One That Can Also Help a Company Grow," *Computerworld*, September 1998.
8. Needleman, T., "AlliedSignal Turbocharges its Systems," *Beyondcomputing*, September 1998.
9. Radding, A., "The Push to Integrate — Packaged Applications Promise to Speed Integration and Cut Costs," *InformationWeek*, No. 671, March 2, 1998.
10. Schwartz, K., "Putting Consultants on Your Team," *Beyondcomputing*, Vol. 7, No.6, August 1998.
11. Stedman, C., "Global ERP Rollouts Present Cross-Border Problems," *Computerworld*, Vol. 32, No. 47, November 1998, p. 10.
12. Stein, T., "SAP Installation Scuttled — Unisource Cites Internal Problems for $168 M Write-off, *InformationWeek*, January 26, 1998.
13. Sweat, J., "ERP — Enterprise Application Suites are Becoming a Focal Point of Business and Technology Planning, *InformationWeek*, No. 704, October 26, 1998.
14. Tiazkun, S., "SAP Sued for $500 Million," *Computer Reseller News*, August 26, 1998.
15. Wallace, B., "Now it's Cost-Cutting Time," *Computerworld*, Vol. 32, No. 47, November 1998, pp. 1 & 82.

Chapter 35
Risk Management Skills Needed in a Packaged Software Environment

Janet Butler

More organizations than ever are licensing software, contracting out development projects, and using purchased components in their development efforts. Such innovations can speed development time, reduce project costs, and enable an organization to prosper with a smaller development staff. However, the new development techniques also pose risks. IS managers can help mitigate the danger to their organizations by honing their hard-won abilities, applying them to the new software environment, and learning some new skills.

Traditional, customized development has in many cases become too expensive, and protracted development times may cause organizations to miss business windows of opportunity. The purchase of packages and off-the-shelf components, as well as contracted development, can greatly reduce costs and speed delivery. Due to the competition in every quarter, organizations would be far more vulnerable to major business risk if they did not seek alternatives to traditional development. But the new approaches pose many dangers.

WHY PACKAGES?

There is little doubt that organizations are increasingly moving to packaged software for major applications. The term coined for packages in industry is enterprise resource planning (ERP) software; in government it is commercial off-the-shelf (COTS) software, which may, however, simply refer to purchased components.

0-8493-9981-5/99/$0.00+$.50
© 1999 by CRC Press LLC

A recent study reported an equal number of applications bought versus those built in-house. Those conducting the study predict an imminent change to a ratio of 3 to 1 in favor of purchased software.[1]

Government Computer News also recently conducted a survey of 127 managers, who agreed that commercial software is the wave of the present and the future. Of the respondents, 58.3 percent said they use commercial software for one or more of these purposes: financial accounting, human resources, procurement, and electronic commerce. In addition, 85.7 percent of 42 respondents said customizing commercial software has saved them money.[2]

Many analysts have attributed the "feverish" pace of package purchases to the Year 2000 (Y2K) crisis. By this view, users running out of time to fix Y2K problems have chosen instead to install packaged software which is already Y2K-compliant. If this assessment is accurate, purchases of ERP applications should soon slow down as the Y2K market reaches saturation.

Recently, however, this premise has been refuted. While few doubt that avoiding Year 2000 fixes on homegrown applications has fueled the package market, users are voicing many other business reasons for buying packaged software.

In fact, Year 2000 fixes were not even mentioned in a recent survey by Forrester Research, Inc. in Cambridge, MA, that asked users why they buy packaged software. Instead, the 50 information technology executives surveyed gave these business reasons for replacing an application with packaged software: more flexibility as business needs change (26 percent), the ability to use common technology across business units (24 percent), the ability to facilitate business process reengineering (18 percent), tighter integration among applications (8 percent), the ability to standardize applications after acquisitions (6 percent), and other (18 percent).[3]

It appears that purchased software is here to stay, and the market will continue to grow unabated. Packages allow an organization to deliver a complex system in a relatively short time. In addition, common applications are available in many languages and for many platforms. There is also a large installed base of users, accompanied by a proven track record of success. And purchased software provides extensive documentation.

Furthermore, once the purchased software is installed, the organization spends far less money, time, and effort for ongoing maintenance than it would for in-house-developed software. And the organization need not redefine requirements for legal or other new requirements. Instead, it is the vendor's job.

The benefits of purchased software derive largely from economies of scale. The vendor need only develop the software once and can then distribute the cost of development and ongoing maintenance over a large installed base.

But there are downsides to purchased software. For one, it is just as difficult for a software supplier to develop software as it is for an in-house organization. In addition, commercial software is generally developed for the most widely accepted/installed technology. So it might not run efficiently on a particular computer or operating system. In fact, commercial software might use obsolete technology.

Furthermore, purchased software is slow to evolve. It is very expensive for a vendor to make major functional changes to commercial software. By a kind of "reverse economy of scale," as the cost of development and maintenance decreases because it is spread across a large installed base, the cost of implementing major improvements increases.

Another negative of purchased software is the use of multiple programming languages. To reduce maintenance and improve flexibility, vendors tend to write all or part of their software using homegrown report writers or fourth-generation languages (4GL). This might work well for the first package an organization buys, but it becomes a linguistic nightmare with subsequent purchases.

Say each vendor provides at least one language that may, however, differ from package to package. And the in-house development group purchases one or more general-purpose 4GLs. The multiple languages generally do not talk to one another. The languages present a major headache, given their learning curves, requirements for cross-training, and dependence on trained personnel.

Databases have also become an issue when an organization purchases software. Since packages are seldom designed for a specific database management system, an organization might have to choose software based either on functionality or database compatibility. It therefore becomes difficult for an organization purchasing software to have a single-image corporate database of information. In turn, this limits the organization's ability to fit its software to the business's changing requirements.

Risks associated with purchased software also include such vendor-related issues as vendor stability, mergers, acquisitions, and nonperformance. Organizational issues include software modifications, training requirements, budgeting considerations, and installation standards.

Despite its downsides, purchased software is being hailed as among the few viable solutions to meeting an organization's market needs. Given its productivity benefits, packaged software enables companies to deliver complex systems in a relatively short time.

A new skill for the development function, then, is the effective selection of purchased software. This means the organization must thoroughly understand its requirements, both functional and technical.

HOW TO DEFINE REQUIREMENTS-PLUS

The traditional software development life cycle consists of requirements analysis, software design, code, test/implementation, and maintenance/enhancement. Of these phases, the first and last, respectively requirements and maintenance , are the stages most relevant to the purchase of packaged software. But the concerns are somewhat different than with in-house software.

As noted above, the key to successful software selection is establishing requirements. Although requirements definition has always been a critical phase in the software development life cycle, the steps must be expanded. Of course, functionality remains number one on an organization's checklist of requirements, whether it is developing its own software, buying a packaged application, or contracting with a supplier to have a custom system built. However, an organization purchasing a package must not only determine its functional requirements, but it must also analyze available software and compare and weight the functional characteristics of each product to the requirements.

In this process, similar requirements can be grouped into these general classifications:

- *Product capabilities* — functional requirements for the type of software required, be it operating system or application software
- *Technical support information* — including product documentation and operating systems supported
- *Implementation information* — including report set-up, hardware requirements, software prerequisites, implementation effort, and complexity to change
- *Miscellaneous* — including pricing and maintenance schedules, discounts, the installed base of users, vendor information, and user group information[4]

As many companies are well aware, the major software vendors are formidable negotiators. So software purchasers must understand both their opponents' and their own requirements. They must know, for example, the type of software they need, how it will be used, how many users will access it, and how frequently. They must also know whether the software will be deployed locally or globally, how soon it might be migrated to a different hardware platform, and if an outsourcer will at some point take charge of the software.

To date, few companies have much experience in replacing applications developed in-house with integrated commercial packages. So they rarely agree on the percentage of requirements that must be met out of the box.

However, if users customize commercial software to a great degree, they will suffer the consequences when they upgrade to the vendor's next release. Customization should never be undertaken lightly, then, because customized functions might no longer work after a patch or a new system release.

In addition, those purchasing software must realize that choosing a package involves many compromises. Some required functions might be only partially met, while others will be missing entirely.

Unfortunately, software purchasers often do not understand their own requirements, so they select software based on specifications presented by a single vendor.

HOW TO NEGOTIATE A SOFTWARE LICENSE

Compared with those who bought technology in the past, today's software purchasers are far more sophisticated, possessing both financial and legal knowledge about software licensing issues. In addition, software is now becoming more of a buyer's than a seller's market, due to the competitive nature of the software market and the growing rate of technology change.

Information technology buyers must still anticipate difficult negotiations with vendors, however, due to the growing complexity of the marketplace. When mainframes and minicomputers were the only existing platforms, applications were licensed based on the box and/or terminals. While this changed dramatically with client/server computing, traditional licensing models completely broke down with the advent of World Wide Web-based computing.

Software is generally licensed rather than sold, since the product consists of intellectual property, plus the media it is printed on. Because the developing vendor technically retains ownership of the application, it negotiates a license governing its use with the purchaser.

When IBM unbundled software from computer hardware in 1969, it became common practice for software vendors to explicitly price software licenses. However, both maintenance costs and license prices were based primarily on vendor experience with computer hardware maintenance or the cost of the original software development.

By the 1980s, the major software pricing method had become tiered pricing, which was done in two ways. In the first, users paid a fixed price to start and paid a monthly or annual maintenance fee for license renewal and support, usually between 5 and 10 percent annually of the original fee. With the second tiered-pricing method, users paid a fixed initial fee for a specified term of use, and a subsequent monthly or annual maintenance fee for support.

Support in tiered pricing usually referred to corrections or bug fixes as well as upgrades. These new versions included perfective and adaptive changes. If little or no maintenance fee was charged, bug fixes were generally free; installable patches and upgrades were handled separately. Installation of the upgraded or corrected software was seldom included.

Beginning in the early 1990s, the primary software licensing model became 99-year or perpetual right-to-use licenses for a user or organization. However, there are many types of software licensing plans in use today. While software is sometimes licensed for use by a particular user, client/server applications that operate on a network might be priced based on the number of PCs that have access.

Purchasers might pay for software based on concurrent or named users or on site-specific or global use. Alternatively, licenses might be based on servers, networks, or even on the customer's annual revenue. In general, organizations use a transaction-oriented approach when buying software licenses.[5]

Software buyers will have an edge if they know the vendor's motivations and the industry environment in which it competes. Such an understanding can prevent miscommunications and misunderstandings. In addition, buyers can attempt to leverage volume by licensing software on a corporatewide basis, rather than by divisions or business units.

In purchasing software, buyers would be wise to do the following:

1. Obtain competitive bids from several vendors. This helps determine a market price to use in negotiations.
2. Deal with a vendor executive.
3. Understand the vendor's business model.
4. Use a professional arbitrator.
5. Demand clauses for maintenance and support.
6. Try to use their own standard contract.
7. Create a standard licensing process within their organization.

Although obtaining the best price for software is important for the purchasing organization, flexibility should take precedence. After all, there are many organizational changes taking place that might in turn change the way the software is used. For example, the organization might undergo a merger, an acquisition, data center consolidation, or centralization.

When such an organizational change takes place, users might have to buy a new license, unless the contract specifies otherwise. In fact, some analysts have estimated a 70 percent probability that corporations that do not so specify will have to repurchase their software license within three years.[1]

In addition, an initial software license fee may account for only 10 to 15 percent of the total cost of ownership of software over five years. So the purchasing organization might have opportunities for savings in usage rights, audit clauses, maintenance, and the rights to new versions.

In selling or licensing software, vendors initially try to sell the product for the highest price; they then attempt to earn more money on the sale over time. Because it gains them the most money, they try to make the license as restrictive as possible, giving them more control. Conversely, it is the purchasing organization's goal to obtain a less restrictive license.

The software license is the first product the vendor sells, but software maintenance is often a separate issue. Thus, in software maintenance as in new development, there are classic choices of "do" or "buy." The choices might apply differently, depending if the maintenance is corrective, perfective, or adaptive. Most vendors offer a contract for maintenance or service or a warranty. In this way, maintenance can become a marketable product and a source of revenue.[5]

HOW TO MANAGE SOFTWARE MAINTENANCE

Maintenance contracts specify how a buyer will receive software upgrades and provide terms for warranty and bug-fix remedies. With such contracts, vendors can profitably lock in customers for the long term. In fact, one major trend in software purchasing is software vendors' continuing, increased dependence on maintenance revenue. Therefore, organizations would be wise to negotiate software maintenance terms as part of the initial license agreement.

It might surprise buyers that maintenance contracts can be more expensive than software licenses in the long run. If, as is usual, maintenance contracts cost 12 to 20 percent of the initial license fee per year, a contract with a 15 percent annual fee for a $100,000 license will exceed the software's original cost after six years.

Software buyers have better leverage if they negotiate the first maintenance contract at the same time as the initial license. It also helps with long-range planning if the organization knows the total life cycle costs.

In negotiating maintenance, organizations should clearly define the meanings of "upgrade" and "new product." Otherwise, vendors might call a software release a "new product," which is not covered by the maintenance agreement.[1]

Sometimes customer and vendor needs can give rise to a win–win situation. For example, software tool vendor Cadence Design Systems, Inc. modified its licensing focus from selling software to contributing to users' productivity. In moving from traditional licensing and maintenance fee practices to the "flexible access model," the vendor changed its software maintenance model.

Thus, in some instances, Cadence now amortizes the fee for software maintenance services over the licensing period. The customer's right to receive software updates (perfective and adaptive modifications), bug fixes (corrections), and help desk support is negotiated as part of the initial license. No longer is software maintenance dependent upon or paid for through the maintenance fee. Instead, vendor updates, corrections, and help desk support depend on the terms of the contract.

While the traditional maintenance goal is to maximize usage, with the new model, it now enhances productivity. Whereas maintenance was formerly licensed per unit, the contract now covers all users. The monthly maintenance fee was generally 1 to 1.5 percent of the initial fee, but it now depends on particular features. As a result, customers gain flexibility, while the vendor has a multiyear financial commitment for maintenance.[5]

Of course, purchase and maintenance of individual software products differs considerably from that of COTS or ERP systems. In purchasing the latter, organizations must determine if the components will adapt to future needs, and, if so, how and by whom that adaptation will occur.

An organization that depends heavily on COTS component or ERP functionality may be at high risk. If the software functionality is not precisely what the organization needs over time, it can be expensive to have the vendor customize the product. If the organization creates "wrappers" or patches as substitutes for real source-code-based maintenance, this can produce instability in the system quality.

Furthermore, the vendor might drop the product. Therefore, organizations would be wise to get a guarantee from the supplier that if the product is dropped, the organization will gain rights to the source code. Even in this case, however, the organization must maintain software not written in-house, and it might have to hire developers who are expert in that code.

Organizations should make some key management decisions related to software maintenance before they opt for COTS or ERP software. They should determine if they can afford the dependency on the vendor, and they should decide if they can accept the risk.[7]

If maintaining COTS or ERP software is risky, some find it hard, at best, to envision. They cite IS' traditional 50 to 80 cost percentage in maintenance, with 60 percent of those costs in enhancement. Finally, they state, "Enhancement of a standardized, generalized product is both undesirable and nearly impossible."[8]

HOW TO EVALUATE SOFTWARE VENDORS

Mergers, competition, and falling software prices are corroding standard software support and services. In this marketplace, purchasing organizations should add new requirements when evaluating software vendors. They should consider the following:

- **Human factors** — Before purchasing packages, organizations should judge the vendor's quality of interaction with human beings for software support and customer service. They might even call the technical support line, timing how long it takes to get through and assessing how difficult questions are handled.
- **Corporate structure** — Purchasing organizations should determine if the vendor is a publicly or privately held corporation. If the former, the vendor might aim at maximizing shareholders' investments. If the latter, its goal might be customer satisfaction. In addition, the buyer should determine if the software being evaluated is the vendor's primary offering or only one of many products, how much the vendor has invested in development, how often it issues new releases, how committed it is to the product, and what the effect would be if support were lost.
- **Size in relation to customer focus** — Smaller companies tend to place more emphasis on customer care than larger ones.
- **User input into product development** — If the software is strategic to the purchaser's business, the buying organization should determine what impact it can have on future product development. For example, it should find out how the vendor responds to customer input, if the organization can take part in beta programs, and how the vendor handles customer feedback on enhancements and improvements. After all, the buying organization can best protect its software investment if it can influence product development.[6]

•CONCLUSION

For whatever reason, users are buying packaged software. The fact remains that commercial software has great and growing appeal. There are several trends in software purchasing that call for action on the part of purchasing organizations.

For starters, ERP package solutions will continue to replace user-developed applications, so buyers should develop flexible enterprise agreements to meet their business needs. In addition, software vendors are increasingly dependent on maintenance revenue, so buyers should see it as a strategic imperative to negotiate maintenance terms as part of the initial license agreement.

Furthermore, buyers should be wary of the increased risk in software contracts resulting from the continued consolidation of vendors. Enterprises should also seek multinational software agreements to address global requirements. Finally, with the Internet accelerating the rate of change in technology, purchasers should aim at increased flexibility in their software license agreements.[7]

Packaged applications are becoming strategic to many businesses. Therefore, software buyers should attempt to form strategic relationships with these types of suppliers versus those who sell commodity-type products, such as Netscape Communications Corp. and Microsoft Corp. It pays dividends for an organization to have a good rapport with a package supplier since the buyer depends on the vendor for products.

In short, today's software development environment has new skill requirements, including the selection of computer software, the negotiation of licenses, and the choice of and partnership with vendors. Savvy developers would be wise to buff up and enhance their skills to deal with these new needs posed by package acquisition, deployment, customization, and maintenance.

To ensure job security in a changing environment, developers would be wise to take immediate action. Since requirements are so critical in successful package and vendor selection, developers' first step should be to **become proficient at establishing requirements.** In this effort, a spreadsheet could be helpful in spelling out the functional requirements, listing the available software, and comparing and weighing the functional characteristics of each product in terms of requirements.

Next, because license negotiation is so critical, developers should **learn negotiation skills.** To this end, developers can take a class in negotiation given by a business school, an adult education provider, or a private organization.

For the best outcome in negotiations, developers should also **develop a standard contract** for their company, which includes a maintenance clause. Finally, because so much effort is generally involved in "reinventing the wheel," they should help **create a standard licensing process** within their organization.

References
1. "Don't be a licensing lightweight!" Rick Whiting, *Software Magazine*, January 1998, pp. 20–2+.
2. "Agencies want their apps off the shelf, survey reveals," Florence Olsen, *Government Computer News*, September 29, 1997, p. 1, 8.
3. "ERP more than a 2000 fix," Craig Stedman, *Computerworld*, August 3, 1998, p. 1, 84.

4. "Selecting computer center software," Howard Miller, *Enterprise Management Issues*, September/October 1997, pp. 19–21+.
5. "Software licensing models amid market turbulence," Cris Wendt and Nicholas Imparato, *Journal of Software Maintenance*, 9, 1997, pp. 271–80.
6. "Does size really matter?" John Lipsey, *AS/400*, February 1998, pp. 19–20+.
7. "COTS software: The economical choice?" Jeffrey Voas, *IEEE Software*, March/April 1998, pp. 16–19.
8. "SAP — Aligning IS with the enterprise takes on a whole new meaning!" Robert L. Glass, *Managing System Development*, April 1997, pp. 10–11.

Chapter 36
Managing SAP Knowledge Transfer

Guy Couillard
Ralph Booth
André Boudreau

This chapter discusses the knowledge transfer requirements of large system integration, especially in the context of enterprise resource planning projects. It is based on independent research and observations made while helping organizations manage the education and training dimensions of SAP R/3 implementations. The authors identify emerging best practices and suggest a process for managing enterprise resource planning knowledge transfer.

ENTERPRISE RESOURCE PLANNING SOFTWARE AND SAP R/3

Enterprise resource planning (ERP) and enterprisewide software packages have become important drivers of system integration. As a business concept, ERP extends manufacturing resource planning (MRP II) to the integration of an organization's core business processes and information assets. The sharing of enterprise information in an automated, process-oriented environment has become a competitive requirement in many industry sectors. This environment, although not limited to an organization's entities, must also increasingly include external trading partners.

Many organizations have implemented ERP concepts in their internal systems. Without the benefit of an overall data and process architecture, however, these organizations have found it daunting to integrate and enhance information systems developed over many years, often on incompatible technology platforms. This explains why a growing number of companies from diverse sectors have chosen to respond to integration and enhancement challenges by acquiring ERP business software packages from vendors such as SAP AG, Oracle, Baan, and PeopleSoft, as well as a growing number of smaller vendors. It also explains the development of substantial ERP consulting practices among all of the major consultancies.

ENTERPRISE RESOURCE PACKAGES

Client/server software packages that integrate finance, logistics, and human resources are a relatively recent phenomenon. Typical motivations to buy off-the-shelf solutionsrather than build are breadth of functionality (including multilanguage and currency support), embedded industry best practices (including global supply chain management with end-to-end business processes beyond enterprise boundaries), scalability to a large number of users, centralized as well as decentralized deployment options, flexibility (some ERP solutions can be reconfigured to address changing business requirements), and vendor research and development. Over the last two years, ERP solutions buyers have also had to consider the large cost of migrating legacy systems to the year 2000 — an expense that does not yield any additional business functionality and which cannot be capitalized as an asset in the U.S. (FASB Ruling, Issue 96-14, July 18,1996).

SAP AG's R/3 business process software is the leading supplier of ERP systems, with a 31 percent market share in enterprise business solutions (IDC, 1996). With approximately 8000 installations in over 50 countries, R/3 is popular with multinationals, large corporations (six of the top ten on the *Fortune* 500 list), and, increasingly, smaller firms with less than $200 million in annual revenues. This success has made R/3-based knowledge one of the most sought-after areas of expertise in the information technology (IT) industry, a phenomenon that is compounded by SAP's aggressive and continuous enhancement of R/3's functionality for a variety of industry sectors.

KNOWLEDGE TRANSFER IN ERP PROJECTS

ERP software strongly supports existing trends toward increased speed as the central competitive force of the 21st century. However, the deployment of ERP concepts, such as distributed access to enterprise information (integrated cross-functional business transactions sharing the same data or global, realtime management information) represents a major technical and organizational challenge. Most participants in ERP projects report that their ERP implementation effort represents the largest business or IT-related project their firms have ever attempted.

ERP software packages enable the deployment of very large quantities of business application functionality throughout the organization at a pace unheard of in custom software development. Naturally, configuring ERP applications to the needs of the organization, and developing interfaces, not to mention business process reengineering, can be long and laborious. Individuals with experience in both custom-developed and packaged ERP implementations, however, say that as long as the project remains within the general boundaries of a package's functionality, implementation times can be greatly reduced. Unfortunately, implementation is too often understood as installation and does not address the reality that organizations need to acquire new knowledge and attitudes to benefit from the powerful functionality of their ERP software package.

Many ERP implementers refer to their projects as learning journeys, both for themselves and their organizations. For some organizations, it is an easier journey than for others. Executive sponsors and, by extension, project teams that do not recognize the learning implications of ERP implementation tend to have a harder time. The ERP knowledge transfer process is not limited to the project team and the end users; it must also address the knowledge requirements of the executives and line managers who will govern the implementation. Lack of understanding of ERP concepts and ineffective executive governance of implementation are more frequent and serious problems than technical issues are. At all levels, efficient management of the knowledge transfer process improves the quality of the implemented solution, reduces cost, and accelerates the reaping of business benefits.

Knowledge transfer lessons from SAP implementations are good examples and are generally applicable to other ERP offerings. From a knowledge management perspective, most ERP solutions:

- Are large scale, providing an organizationwide learning effort for executives, project team members, line managers, and end users
- Require individuals who represent different functions within the organization to arrive at a common view of their operations within the conceptual framework of a software package
- Allocate a large percentage of implementation cost to knowledge acquisition through training and consulting
- Require rapid knowledge transfer (many implementations, including SAP, are completed in less than 12 months, and in even less than 6 months for smaller organizations)

The second point in this list is crucial. One cannot underestimate the challenges and complexities of arriving at a common view of operations when a multiplicity of organizational perspectives need to be accounted for. Project team members from different parts of the organization and external consultants must jointly develop a common frame of reference. This common frame of reference translates into a vision of how the organization will operate. From a knowledge acquisition standpoint, this is no different than custom application development projects. The difference resides in the ERP functionality framework (i.e., what the software can do and how it does it) that must be learned before or during the design and configuration process. This places a considerable, and often exhilarating, knowledge acquisition responsibility on members of the project team. Tremendous learning takes place in a relatively short time.

ENTERPRISE RESOURCE PACKAGES

ERP implementation projects have a way of raising issues and prompting decisions, many with far-reaching consequences on such issues as ownership of business processes, distribution and transparency of information, employee empowerment, and long-term IT strategy. Because concepts can be prototyped quickly using the ERP package, decisions appear more tangible at the design stage than with traditional business process re-engineering activities.

This chapter explores some of the actions that accelerate organizational learning and knowledge transfer. To better understand the dynamics of organizational learning and knowledge transfer, one must first look at the sequence and context in which ERP and, in particular, SAP knowledge transfer are accomplished.

Phases of SAP Knowledge Transfer

SAP implementations can be divided conceptually into four phases, with specific knowledge transfer activities occurring in each.

Opportunity Evaluation. In this phase, ERP solutions are evaluated, typically in the context of the business and IT strategy. The decision to proceed with implementation triggers the planning process which defines scope, effort, and required capabilities. Executive and project team training begins.

Design and Development. The design and development phase covers detailed business specifications, data, process and infrastructure configuration, prototyping, and development of interfaces to other systems. SAP project team training continues and production of end-user training materials takes place.

Deployment. Deployment refers to rollout of the SAP system, as well as the implementation of the new or redefined jobs for end users.

Continuous Learning and Enhancement. Once the system has been deployed, the focus of effort shifts from development to continuous measurement and fine-tuning of the SAP application and the human performance system.

OPPORTUNITY EVALUATION

A significant amount of knowledge transfer must take place even before the decision to acquire an ERP solution such as SAP is made. Because ERP projects have organizationwide implications, managers and key staff who have to support the implementation need to become involved in knowledge-building activities.

At this stage, knowledge building focuses on the organization's business and IT strategic drivers, industry best practices, ERP basic concepts, and implementation approaches. Responsibility for facilitating the learning process during this stage rests with the sponsor of the opportunity evaluation process.

Experience shows that team learning is more effective than individual learning, especially at the management level. A large portion of the learning that needs to take place at the opportunity evaluation phase has to do with challenging and expanding the organization's paradigms and frames of reference. This type of attitudinal change is best effected in group settings where new information is introduced and participants are given the opportunity to confront it. Misunderstandings, disagreements, and dissension have to be addressed explicitly as early in the process as possible because ERP implementations place great pressure on even the most sophisticated, intelligent organizations. Consensus and commonality of purpose are required to successfully go through transition pains.

Individuals learning together become involved in a process of knowledge building and knowledge sharing. Interestingly, this same process is at the heart of ERP. If it cannot be accomplished at the management team level; this may be an early warning sign that knowledge building and sharing will be difficult to implement at the organizational level.

A lack of involvement and knowledge of key stakeholders at this stage will result in insufficient commitment in the following phases and may significantly slow down the implementation process. SAP implementations trigger a large number of important questions. A lack of understanding will make it difficult for the executive team or steering committee to make timely decisions and ask appropriate questions.

Selecting Core Team Members

In addition to the executive team and operations people, a core team representing the IT and business communities must be involved in the opportunity evaluation phase. The core team is made up of experts from each of the functional areas that will be involved in SAP implementation. Some selection criteria for the core team members are:

- A detailed understanding of the nuances and quirks of the existing as-is business processes
- Credibility within the organization
- Analytical skills and the capacity to define scope and prioritize requirements
- An understanding of similar business practices in related businesses

Early in the opportunity evaluation phase, existing or "as-is" company practices need to be viewed from two perspectives: which practices are currently in place and where those practices need to be assessed, fixed, enhanced, or eliminated. This knowledge is a prerequisite for core team

ENTERPRISE RESOURCE PACKAGES

members. At this stage, external consultants are best able to bring benefits to the project when they are familiar with the organization's industry sector and business processes.

Industry best practices examine what other organizations in the same sector are doing to achieve optimal results. They also provide rationales for selecting the industry best practices embedded in ERP business process software.

SAP R/3's extensive features make it a technically challenging product to learn, especially at the detailed functionality level. Yet organizations consistently report that their most important implementation asset was an intimate knowledge of their own business and the best industry practices that SAP models. An understanding of current business practices transcends organizational seniority or even a position on the organization's departmental chart. For example, a middle-level business analyst who has been instrumental in developing existing systems may have acquired the depth and breadth of as-is knowledge and industry best practices, and possess the analytic skills to quickly model the required SAP configuration.

Methods of Learning for Executives

Methods of learning for senior executives during the opportunity evaluation phase must facilitate fact finding and decision making. Experience has shown that executive retreats and workshops, with an emphasis on strategic business drivers, business simulations, and benchmarking, are very effective. Conferences, site visits, and seminars with hands-on demonstrations complement executive knowledge transfer programs.

Methods of Learning for Core Team Members

As part of the opportunity evaluation phase, core team members should have at least an overall understanding of SAP and develop some knowledge of the specific functionality of one or two modules that will be implemented (e.g., finance and controlling or materials management and sales and distribution). This understanding is necessary to do the mapping between current business practices and the best business practices model used by SAP. The as-is/to-be gap must be known before the feasibility and scope of an SAP implementation can be evaluated.

As it is rare, except in the largest organizations, to have resources in-house with sufficient SAP expertise to do a gap analysis, external consultants are often involved at this stage. However, surrendering the information-gathering process completely to consultants does not contribute to knowledge building. A more effective approach is to have external consultants facilitate structured workshops where core team members and key executive stakeholders are walked through the business processes targeted for implementation and the applicable SAP functionality.

538

How the core team is organized also has an impact on the efficiency of the knowledge transfer process. The natural tendency to create functional subteams of finance, production, or sales should be resisted. It tends to recreate the functional boundaries within which an integrated enterprise system should not be. A more synergistic and effective approach is to organize the subteams along core business processes, such as the buy-it team, the make-it team, the sell-it team, and the measure-it team.

THE DESIGN AND DEVELOPMENT PHASE

At the beginning of the design phase, the core team's first tasks are to produce an analysis of current business processes as well as role maps of who does what, which are typically only sketched in the previous phase. Documentation of the current situation should not be overemphasized, especially when the problems with the as-is are well known by the project team.

The focus at this stage should be on:

* More accurate measures of scope, effort, and costs, and review of the risks and opportunities
* Provision of the team's first real task, which itself becomes a team-building intervention and ensures a common understanding of the project's key objectives

Once a proposal or plan has been submitted and approved, team members should:

* Map business practices into R/3
* Identify data and system interfaces
* Analyze and design the future hardware/network configuration
* Install the R/3 development, testing, and production systems

There tends to be a natural overlap between the work done in the opportunity definition and the design and development phases. For example, the identification of risks and opportunities is typically done in the first phase and revisited during the design and development phase. This iterative process allows for incorporation of the insights gained by the project team members into the ERP product and their own organization. Managing this process requires very strong project management skills. Otherwise, there is a risk of the project succumbing to scope creep or "paralysis through analysis."

ERP solutions are often catalysts for business process reengineering (BPR) activities. BPR with SAP requires three things. First, it requires an understanding of BPR and industry best practices. Second, it requires an awareness of why BPR is being undertaken within SAP. Third, it requires detailed design knowledge, more specifically, how tables are configured within SAP to define how the business operates.

The results of these parallel design tasks come together to form the detailed design. Once approved, the core team begins work on scenarios, which provide detailed scripts of the future work flows.

Each step in the scripts is mapped into a set of tables. These tables define how SAP models the work flow. These scripts are also used in defining tasks and jobs and become instrumental in creating job descriptions, training, and user documentation. In SAP, as in most ERP implementations, scripts and the information associated with them are among the simplest ways of making knowledge explicit. Managing this knowledge in a paper format quickly becomes overwhelming. An emerging best practice is to implement a knowledge management strategy and environment where business scripts, work scenarios, and other system information are captured electronically and organized so that they may be easily transformed into an online system that incorporates training documentation. Because ERP systems are designed to dynamically support organizational processes and, by extension, organizational learning, system documentation and training should be equally dynamic.

There are more than 125 courses with an average duration of three days in the SAP project team education catalog. Surveys indicate that formal SAP application training for core team members, regardless of their backgrounds, takes four to six weeks of classroom training. One of the first goals in any SAP implementation is for organizations to reduce dependency on consultants and develop knowledge self-sufficiency. When the ever-necessary but costly consultants are contracted, it must be made clear that their role is not only as expert, but also as mentor or trainer. System development at this phase is dependent on human development.

Another type of knowledge is required beyond SAP functionality. It concerns configuration and integration skills. Those skills are typically found in SAP implementation consultants. Experience has shown that transferring those skills to core team members augments the productivity of the project team and the quality of the implemented solution while reducing dependency on external consultants. Usually, the best way to develop configuration and integration skills is through intensive workshops or "boot camps," where participants have to configure a case study in a structured, team-oriented learning environment. At the moment, SAP relies on specialized external vendors to provide this type of training.

In addition, core team members will require informal practice using the system. Softer, people-oriented skills in organizational change management, group decision making, conflict resolution, and teamwork are often required. These skills can be provided by external consultants or by leveraging the company's training and organizational development expertise. Soft skills training is especially effective when integrated into the overall curriculum of the project team and delivered just-in-time. All ERP implementation project teams go through people-centered crises. Rarely, if ever, do projects fail for technical reasons alone.

Developing End-User Training

In parallel with design and development activities, end-user training must be developed to coincide with the SAP deployment. SAP itself recommends that 14 percent of the total budget be allocated for training. Most of the budget will be spent during this phase on delivering project team training and developing end-user training materials. It is important that a number of training issues be addressed. The first is that adult learning principles be followed to ensure effectiveness and efficiency of the knowledge transfer process. As with any large system implementation, the following adult learning principles should be followed:

- Learners perceive the training as related to their needs.
- Practice and experimentation are integrated.
- New skills are applied on the job immediately after training.

In many traditional systems implementations, end-user training — and, to some extent, documentation — are afterthoughts, cobbled together during implementation. In most cases, this is not because of sloppy planning. Traditional system-focused training design cannot begin until the system itself is completed. With SAP, it is possible to initiate training development activities in parallel with configuration. A human performance needs analysis can parallel and even enhance the as-is/to-be design. Allocating the training effort (i.e., how much time should be assigned to each task) begins with a high-level description of the tasks and assigning priority to them based on business needs rather than system structure. When training is aligned with business needs, it becomes possible to link investments in knowledge transfer and human performance to the achievement of business objectives. This exercise is frequently done in parallel with a review of human resources management policies.

The needs analysis must also identify the various audiences for which training materials will need to be developed. Much attention should be given to the special requirements of executives and operations managers. These requirements typically revolve around the modes of decision making made possible by the ERP application, measurement of business process performance, and access to information.

Technology-Assisted Learning

Once the training content and task order are defined, the method of delivery can be selected. Given a large number of end users and scheduling and resource challenges, many organizations are attracted to technology-enabled learning methods.

Even though videoconferencing and computer-based training (CBT) offer some real advantages, the needs analysis and preliminary design process are the same for classroom instruction as for computer-based methods. After that point, however, development costs for CBT are significantly higher. Common development ratios state that if CBT supported by hands-on exercises requires 30 hours to develop 1 hour of instruction, CBT will take between 100 and 200 hours to develop 1 hour of self-instruction.

Off-the-shelf SAP CBT programs can be acquired from specialized vendors. However, given the extreme customizability of SAP R/3, ready-made CBT is best suited for generic navigation skills and functionality overviews. Some vendors and specialized SAP training consultants also offer to customize their CBT titles to their clients' specific requirements. When large numbers of users need to be trained, custom CBT development can be cost effective.

Electronic performance support systems (EPSS) and online manuals are other means of transferring knowledge at the desktop. EPSS is particularly interesting in that it offers assistance at the moment the user needs it. EPSS tools are appearing on the market that take advantage of R/3's extended help function and make it possible to attach context-sensitive support and training materials to the application itself. Once again, large numbers of end users (typically more than 1000) are required to justify development costs. One advantage of EPSS over stand-alone CBT is that it more easily supports a coherent knowledge management strategy since it is easier to manage and enhance knowledge objects that are linked to the application. It is also possible to integrate multimedia knowledge objects or CBTs into some EPSS environments.

However, technology-assisted learning methods cannot completely replace instructor-led classroom instruction. All organizations implementing SAP surveyed by the authors stated that some classroom training was required for almost everyone. Essentially, classroom learning is the best way to address initial fears, questions, and change issues. Also, training groups of people together has the added advantage of fostering user communities. These informal groups can play a crucial support role following the initial deployment.

DEPLOYMENT

During deployment, the major task of the project team members is to go from being information collectors to being information disseminators. Most team members, in one way or another, become trainers. Senior management, core team members, and the "super-users" involved in design all shift from the role of learners and developers to trainers and coaches. The shift is not as simple as changing hats and will have started formally or informally long before the actual "go live" date.

542

Deploying end-user training on a large ERP application throughout the organization is a logistical challenge that is often underestimated. Poor deployment of a superb application still leaves a bad aftertaste. It can also delay future rollouts of the application. The root cause of most deployment problems can be found in inadequate resources and planning in the earlier phases of the project. Unfortunately, the attitude of many implementers is often, "We will deal with training once we have solved our configuration issues." The problem is that there will always be configuration issues to be dealt with.

Training Is Not Learning

Ensuring that learning takes place begins with the effective design of end-user training materials that are well-structured, include job aids and "cheat sheets," and are actually usable by the target audiences. This is followed by effective delivery of the subject matter by a competent, credible instructor who can put the information in context. It is also essential to provide plenty of opportunities to apply the new skills and knowledge in a safe environment. Learning labs available during and after working hours are of considerable value.

A train-the-trainer course should provide theory and practice in the three roles that a trainer must play: presenter, coach, and facilitator. Even in the event that end-user training is delivered in self-study mode, there will always be a need for human learning support in the form of a course administrator during end-user training, help desk staff, or colleagues.

In addition to receiving the same "how-to" training as the actual end users, managers and supervisors must be trained as support resources. The goal of this training is to allow them to be proactive troubleshooters, anticipating individual and group difficulties and providing encouragement, etc. This is especially important when users are forced to abandon legacy systems for an ERP application which initially may not have the same functionality as the system it is replacing.

Learning Communities

Human beings have a remarkable capacity to learn and adapt to new environments. Experience shows that social interactions play a major role in this process. ERP implementers often overemphasize structured learning and "programs" and neglect more informal but equally effective channels. Internal user groups, learning communities, affinity groups, and system ownership teams are all different ways of labeling these communities. These communities should not be confused with help desks, even though their roles may overlap. Learning communities are most effective at capturing and distributing new knowledge that comes from using the system over a period of time and dealing with unforeseen problems. In many ways, they are similar to "news groups" on the Internet.

Fostering them requires a relatively small investment, and they are frequently most effective when they are self-regulated, grass-roots phenomena. Simple means of fostering learning communities involve:

- Facilitating interaction and communication among the members of the group through e-mail channels, conference rooms, and sponsored meetings
- Fostering a sense of identity among the user community, even if it is spread geographically
- Ensuring that requests from the user community are taken into consideration by implementation teams and are acted on

CONTINUOUS LEARNING AND ENHANCEMENT

Once the training has been completed and the SAP system is in place, the process of knowledge management shifts from capture and delivery to enhancement. The first task is to collect real-world data on whether the task breakdowns and productivity levels were accurate and to report on any fine-tuning required. Data will be collected for help desk use, staff will be polled to evaluate how well the training prepared them for their jobs, and multilevel recommendations will be made for future training.

Managing Knowledge as an Asset

Capturing knowledge in each phase, including assumptions that led to design decisions, facilitates maintenance of documentation and training materials. Unfortunately, this type of activity is rarely perceived as adding value. Even though management often says that knowledge is essential to the organization, it is rarely managed as an organizational asset. This attitude, however, is evolving. Many organizations have realized that knowledge is a key ingredient in the productivity equation and have appointed chief knowledge officers. Their key responsibility is to identify core knowledge assets, both implicit and explicit, and define strategies that directly link knowledge management to organizational performance. Because it is probably the most knowledge-intensive project an organization can undertake, ERP provides an ideal opportunity for initiating a formal approach to knowledge management.

Chapter 37
Maximizing ROI by Leveraging the Second Wave of ERP

Judy Dinn

A surprisingly large number of companies that have implemented Enterprise Resource Planning (ERP) systems are not seeing the expected returns on their Information Technology (IT) investment. Many companies are actually experiencing an initial dip in performance and, realizing that if they want to maximize their ROI, they will need to stabilize the systems' environment, optimize business processes, and conquer lingering change management issues. These new initiatives are collectively called the "Second Wave".

ROI ON IT EXPENDITURES

Realizing Return on Investment (ROI) on IT initiatives has come to be a difficult process. During the last decade, businesses have made significant IT investments, either in implementing new supporting applications and infrastructure or adopting new technologies in hopes of creating new business opportunities.

In the 1990s, IT expenditures consumed a large percentage of corporate yearly budgets. To resolve Year 2000 compliance issues and to meet the growing informational demands of the business, companies throughout the world participated in the implementation of Enterprise Resource Planning (ERP) systems. Information technology and business project sponsors accepted full responsibility for creating organizational chaos, firmly believing that the countless opportunities would clearly be illustrated once they went "live". Now these sponsors are perplexed as they see that some benefits are coming to fruition while others are not even beginning to blossom. These project sponsors concede that in order to realize all the benefits they promised, it will mean more money, more organizational change, and more effort.

THE LIFECYCLE OF APPLICATIONS

The evolution of applications has been dynamic over the last three decades. Applications originated as custom-built systems that met the immediate needs of a unique business group. They matured, becoming large, complex, packaged systems supporting numerous enterprisewide business processes. The growth of the application lifecycle is described in the following stages.

Stage 1: Isolated/Homegrown Systems

In the 1970s, each department was supported by custom-built applications. Each application was built specifically for an individual function: General Ledger, Accounts Payable and Accounts Receivable, among others. Users were isolated from having to consider or include the requirements of other functional areas.

Stage 2: Integrated Functionality

The introduction of *Business Process Reengineering* emerged in the 1980s, and companies slowly attempted to adopt the notion of aligning their organizations by business processes as opposed to functional silos. In support of this movement, applications were redesigned around functional processes including Financials, Manufacturing, and Distribution, etc. This was accomplished by building complex interfaces to existing applications, or through the selection and implementation of Functional Package Applications.

Stage 3: Enterprise Applications

Throughout the 1990s, integration efforts continued and business processes were redefined to become end-to-end solutions, for example Order-to-Delivery. IT environments consisted of a collection of complex interfaces and multiple platforms. Business, at this time, was asking for a single system to support end-to-end business solutions while IT was attempting to simply support efforts and achieve cost efficiencies. In response, the market introducted a single integrated system.

An integrated system is defined as a single application that supports businesswide end-to-end processes and utilizes a common database. The market's solution was a packaged application called an Enterprise Resource Planning (ERP) system. An ERP system is an enterprise-integrated system consisting of linked applications which coordinate business activities and support the flow of information across the enterprise.

ERP systems focus specifically on integrating BackOffice functions (i.e., Finance, Procurement, Manufacturing, and Distribution) to achieve efficiencies across business processes. They minimize the complexity of IT environments, meet the requirements of the business, and address the issue of Y2K compliance. Companies view ERP systems as the answer to a number of their organizational issues.

Stage 4: Bolt-On/Decision Support, Late 1990s

With the BackOffice completely integrated and data collected centrally, bolt-on applications were introduced to the market. Bolt-on applications satisfy those functions not supported by traditional ERP applications. Bolt-ons interface with ERPs to further collect and support business information in order to provide real-time decision support. Bolt-ons include front-office applications like Sales Force Automation, e-Commerce, Production Planning, etc.

Stage 5: Integrated/Decision Support, Late 1990s – 2000+

Now that all business data is captured and collected centrally, more focus and investment is spent on information analysis and decision support tools. Information exchange is platform-independent throughout the geographically distributed enterprise via the intranet.

WHERE IS THE ROI ON ERP INVESTMENTS?

Both technology and operational problems motivated companies to undertake ERP systems implementation. The most compelling reasons at the beginning of the decade included not only Y2K compliance, but also disparate systems, poor IT performance, and limited visibility and accessibility to business information.

A 1998 survey by Benchmarking Partners, Inc., the Deloitte Consulting Second Wave Survey, set out to understand ERP post-implementation issues and trends. The respondents of the survey were manufacturing and consumer businesses, the two industries that are farthest along in the ERP implementation cycle. One of the more interesting survey questions asked of the 62 Fortune 500 Companies was, "are companies realizing the expected benefits from their ERP investments?" The findings illustrated that only 37 percent of the respondents expressed that they had achieved or were on track to achieve the specific, quantified benefits they expected. Some of the more disappointing post-implementation situations include:

- Financial and operational returns are lower than expected, whereas project and maintenance costs are higher than expected.
- Many elements of the "As Is" processes are still in place, therefore "best practice" efficiencies are not being utilized.
- The ERP implementation triggered new operational issues, and many users do not know how to use the system effectively.
- Y2K compliance is achieved, but the value of the systems is unclear.

Given the size and visibility of ERP initiatives within an organization, it is easy to comprehend why its ROI is on the radar of executive management. Now that the system is "live" and the immediate results are disappointing, when can we expect to see returns?

THE NEXT STEP: EXECUTING THE SECOND WAVE

The implementation of ERP systems is now being referred to as the "First Wave" of the ERP journey. Companies are realizing that, to capitalize on their ERP investments and realize business opportunities, they need to embark on a Second Wave.

The Second Wave deals specifically with process optimization. Throughout the First Wave, ERP implementations were strained by aggressive deadlines or the organizations' inability to make aggressive changes and key decisions. The result, implementations adopted "As Is" processes instead of best practices, data was not properly sanitized, leading to the conversion of "dirty" data, and training and change management were minimized; therefore users took longer to accomplish normal tasks. The Second Wave deals specifically with these issues by revisiting people, process, and technology.

In executing a Second Wave initiative, the organization is maximizing ROI by aggressively pursuing and measuring benefits. This involves stabilizing the current environment, realizing efficiencies, and engaging new opportunities made available by the ERP implementation. The Second Wave utilizes an organization's existing resource investment and knowledge and does *not* create a new solution; it simply reworks an existing solution to maximize an investment.

APPROACH

The Second Wave initiative starts once a company goes live with its ERP solution. It analyzes the status of the system and attempts to manage the expected dip in performance after going live. It identifies short-term stabilization needs (i.e., system tuning, support organization), quick-hit opportunities (i.e., conduct more training, modify process), and longer-term business benefits. The three stages for implementation described by Deloitte Consulting (2) address each area of potential benefit.

Stage One: Stabilize. Secure the base.

Once the implementation is live, the next step is to stabilize the technology and people processes. Stabilization may need anywhere from three to nine months to secure and sustain the core ERP functionality. It is during this time that companies may experience a dip in performance. The challenge is to manage the dip by fine-tuning new processes and mastering change in the organization. The result is improvement in speed and cost reduc-

548

tions in handling routine business transactions. Without this stage the organization cannot progress in successfully achieving additional capabilities.

Stage Two: Synthesize. Build for the Future.

Utilizing the stable ERP backbone, organizations can now start building new capabilities. During the next six to eighteen months, non-ERP applications are brought into the mix, process improvements are engaged, and additional education is deployed to further motivate people to undertake the next level of change. This stage deals with realizing effectiveness from the ERP Investment.

Stage Three: Synergize. Achieve Value in Use.

This is the future state that the organization envisioned achieving when they made their first investment. The organization has put in place an infrastructure which can dynamically support new business strategies and competencies. The people, processes, and technology are not only able but willing to adopt sweeping changes which benefit the company's success, and allow the company to transform itself to meet market pressures and customer demands. This stage is expected to last from 12 to 24 months.

CONCLUSION

When will technology cease to be an expensive infrastructure support-tool? The advantages that each era of technology boast of never fully come to fruition before companies are pressured to move on to the next trendy technology gadget. In the case of ERP implementation, companies are learning that the size and complexity of such a project is overwhelming. It is quite an accomplishment for those organizations that have gone live, but it is not surprising to find that not all parts of the implementation take advantage of all the opportunities available.

The Second Wave is a necessary step in ensuring that the original investment is fully realized. Executives should understand the quantitative and qualitative benefits that they are achieving now are just the beginning. Continual investment and rework of the solution are needed if the organization is to utilize all the possibilities that ERP presents.

REFERENCES

1.1998 survey by Benchmarking Partners, Inc., the Deloitte Consulting Second Wave Survey.
2.Deloitte Consulting, Second Wave Approach, 1999.

Chapter 38
ERP Packages: What's Next?

Conghua Li

In the past decade, companies from all around the world have spent tens of billions of dollars in licensing, customizing, installing, maintaining, and upgrading Enterprise Resource Planning systems (ERP). These systems have been applied in all conceivable industries, from banks and insurance companies to airlines and telecommunication companies; from manufacturing and utility companies to retail and hotel chains; from health care organizations and media companies to universities and government organizations, etc.

ERP packages, including SAP, PeopleSoft, Oracle, and Baan, have made tremendous contributions to the world of business. They have made a wide range of businesses from large to small more efficient by providing them with much information they need. This information includes sales figures, financial results, information on customers/clients, information on suppliers, inventory levels, distribution flow, production volumes, procurement volumes, and much more. This information gives businesses worldwide a clear overview and detailed understanding of their current performances, almost any time and anywhere. It enables management at all levels, from the CEO to the lowest operational units, to make business and operational decisions efficiently and effectively.

However, this information is mostly limited to "internal information". It does not cover "the other half" of most businesses. It does not include information about the market, the competitors, the industry, the clients of the segment, the customers of the segment, and the distribution channels, for example. Is this information not important to the success of a business? The answer is clearly, "Yes, it is critical!" Why is it not included in the scope of the existing ERP/Data Warehousing initiative that has cost companies around the world tens, if not hundreds, of billions of dollars to date? Because, historically, it has always been this way.

The past decade has been an area of process reengineering. Emphasis has been on the internal efficiency and effectiveness of a business. As a result, the ERP wave has caught the interest and attention of businesses around the world. CIOs have been required to play a key role in improving internal efficiency. On the other hand, the millenium is rapidly approaching. Information systems developed in the early days cannot survive without significant restructuring and debugging. CIOs have also been wrestling with the Y2K problems for years now.

However, now that most of the businesses in the advanced world have already implemented ERP systems in their operations or are at least in the process of implementing one, and the Y2K problems are mostly under control, the question inevitably turns to, "What's next?"

WHAT'S NEXT?

External focus! The "next" will need to be "External Focus." It will be for IT functions must take on the role of "corporate antennae". The intrinsic characteristic of doing business is like conducting warfare. In military operations, information technology has been applied not only to facilitate internal communication and control, but also, more importantly, to gather and process external information – like the antennae of an army. No army can win any battle or war if its information system is only applied to internal efficiency; for example, to accurately indicate how much ammunition is available or how fast its troops can move. To win any battle or war, the army must understandunderstand, accurately and in a timely manner, the moves of its opponents, the environment of the battlefield, and many other categories of external information.

Unfortunately, in the corporate world IT has been mainly applied for internal data gathering and processing. Due to the development of technologies, including information technology and the changing order of the global economy, today's industry and market are changing at an unparalleled rate of speed. This requires businesses to continuously monitor and take decisions against the changes in the industry and the marketplace. Historical approaches to strategic planning, which took place once every year or every couple of years, are dead. To enable businesses to compete effectively in the future, the interests and attention of CIOs of businesses around the globe will need to, and will be forced to, shift from an internal focus to an external focus. The "next" may be called "TIS", i.e. Total Information Solutions, or "EIM", i.e. External Information Management.

Today's businesses need to understand, monitor, process, and apply information on their industry, their competitors, and their customers, and a large amount of other information on an ongoing basis. The era is long gone in which strategic adjustments were done once every one to five years by the senior management only. And external information is collected, analyzed, and kept only by some strategists and senior management members.

The rise and fall of great companies is now proceeding at an unprecedented rate in corporate history. These ups and downs have hardly been due to how well they have managed their internal information. Instead, they are mostly due to how well they have managed and reacted to changes in their external conditions. No effort purely focused on internal efficiency can save an organization; however, efforts to adapt to external conditions can. Peter Drucker, a father of modern management, recently pointed out: "The forces that most influence organizations come from outside the organization, not from within." Today's businesses have to collect, process, and apply external information on the fly. Otherwise, a great business will be landed in no time.

As a result, today's business management is like flying a jet fighter. The jet fighter, with its complex internal operations controlled by its sophisticated systems, needs to actively search, collect, and process external conditions and information on the flight. In fact, the information that is shown on their instruments about the external conditions is so important that the pilots need only operate based on what their instruments tell them, instead of what their intuition or feelings tell them. Although managing a business is not exactly flying a jet fighter, the importance of collecting, processing, and using external information has increased to a level without previous comparison.

Although many companies have made significant efforts in developing customer and supplier databases in the past, they were mainly focused on the indirect customers and suppliers. While these databases have made considerable contributions, they limited the companies to a tunnel vision of their external interfaces.

The TIS will enable businesses to systematically monitor and collect data about broadly ranged external business conditions, integrate the external data with the internal data, and build or extract business intelligence for all adequate levels of management.

The external data will cover, but will not be limited to, such data as:

- consumer or customer trends of the target markets and their relevant segments:
  their changing preferences
  their changing demands
  their changing composition
  their changing distribution

- trends of the relevant industries:
  technology adaptation: "The technologies likely to have the greatest impact on a company and its industry are technologies outside of its own field"
  industry economics
  best practices

changing landscape of supply and distribution systems and mechanisms

- competitors:
  key competitors
  their market positioning
  their competitive approaches
  their competitive results

- competitive products or services:
  product or service innovations
  the benefit of these innovations to the customers
  their competitive positions
  the potential threat of these innovations to the company

Traditionally, this information was collected and processed by such corporate functions as strategic planning and marketing. By providing ongoing data collection and processing, the contribution and involvement of IT will bring a revolution to the ways in which external data are collected and processed, as well as to the ways in which business decision-making processes are organized.

WHO NEEDS THE EXTERNAL INFORMATION?

Like in a military operation, almost everyone in the army will need to access information and intelligence about the external conditions. While in the past many companies prospered with only a small elite having access to some fragmented and discontinuous external information, businesses of the future will wonder how they can even conduct the most basic tasks without understanding the external context.

Although almost everyone in any business entity in the future will need to access external information and intelligence on an ongoing basis, the following are some of the most critical areas where people will need to have efficient and effective access to this information and intelligence:

- strategy management
- product development
- product management
- marketing
- advertising
- public relations
- branding
- distribution
- sales
- customer services

The wide range of people who need the external information will pose a great challenge to data integration, distribution, and intelligence extraction. To cover external data will be far more challenging than covering internal data. If fuzzy logic may make "intelligent computer" come true, TIS may well make "intelligent enterprise" come true. Of course, in the case of an intelligent enterprise, decisions will still be made by human beings instead of computers.

For IT to take on some major responsibilities for collecting, processing and distributing external information is not to undermine the importance of the corporate planning function. In fact, it is to reinforce the effectiveness of this function by providing corporate antennae—ongoing data collection, processing, and distribution.

WHAT ARE THE CRITICAL ISSUES IN DEVELOPING "CORPORATE ANTENNAE"?

The critical issues of dealing with external data will be focusing on the following key areas:

- what data to collect
- where and how to collect the data
- how to process the data
- to whom and how to distribute the data
- what are the organizational or process implications

What Data to Collect?

First and foremost, critical issues will involve identifying the relevant data that are needed by the enterprise. This will be determined by the industry and the company itself. All information necessary to "fly the jet fighter" will need to be collected. Of course, 20 percent of information will fulfill 80 percent of the need. The key will be to identify the 20 percent of relevant information, particularly in the oversupply of information present today.

It is vital to understand that IT should not completely take over the role of collecting external data from the functions that have traditionally borne those responsibilities; functions such as planning, marketing, etc. IT will be focusing on the data that can be effectively collected on an ongoing basis.

Where and How to Collect

Companies need to identify suitable sources and determine effective ways to collect key information. There will be many possible sources for data collection, such as

- employees
- customers
- distributors
- suppliers

- strategic partners, such as among Star Airline members
- business information reporters such as Bloomberg, Reuters, Dow Jones
- online information providers such as Yahoo Finance, E-Trade
- business analyses from banks, brokerage houses, stock exchanges
- business studies from associations, government organizations, and research institutes

While team effort and partnerships are highly developed in most areas of today's business world, in the area of external information collection and processing, teamwork and partnership approaches are still in the Dark Ages. Team efforts and partnerships will be the keys for effectively establishing corporate antenna functions in the future.

It is also important to realize that collection and process of external data must be continuous and systematic. A jet fighter cannot fly without continuous collection of external data. Any interval in external monitoring may lead to catastrophe. Only structured data can be effectively integrated with the relevant internal data. And only effective integration of internal and external data can generate business intelligence that an enterprise needs to survive and to grow.

How to process?

Integration of external and internal data will be the key. While an oversupply of data and information exists, a short supply of intelligence persists in today's business world. It is critical to extract intelligence from the combination of external and internal data. The speed of processing needs to be high. Results need to be clear. Intelligence needs to be effective. It will not fulfill the mission simply to put information onto the intranet. The Internet phenomenon, in which people get billions of bits of data but can hardly find a relevant one, must be avoided.

As in data collection, processing must be on an ongoing basis. Purpose-oriented processing needs to be emphasized. Mr. Miles Au Yeung, an IT expert with Deloitte Consulting, pointed out when reviewing this article recently, "Despite some companies collecting external data today, they cannot turn data in real time into decision-making support. External data is not fed into operational systems for realtime adjustments. It still involves a lot of human effort to separate noise from useful data, and to process the data into information."

To Whom and How to Distribute?

It will be a significant challenge to determine what information will be accessible by whom, and how intelligence will be extracted. Virtually every department, operational unit, and individual will need to extract intelligence from a wide range of information. The scope will be far larger than the context of internal information. Also, the intelligence to be extracted will be far broader than intelligence that has been extracted from the internal data only. However, this will be the price that a business will have to pay if it wants to survive in the next millenium. Data distribution will be increasingly important. Only with effective data distribution can business intelligence be effectively extracted where and when it is needed.

What Are the Organizational or Process Implications?

In today's knowledge economy, information processes drive organizational structure. Along with the way in which external information is collected and processed, and the way in which business-decision making shifts, the organizational structures will be forced to change. This may well represent a new wave of worldwide corporate restructuring. This restructuring will go far beyond the simple change of IT organizational structures. It will cover most corporate organizations. As the way of business decision-making and organizational structures shifts, the organizational culture also will be forced to shift.

The change will be big. Challenges will be daunting. However, companies will have no choice but to go through it as this process will select the future winners and determine the future losers.

What Will Be the Role of CIOs?

Although CIOs will need, and will be forced, to shift their interests, attentions, and roles, the process will not be smooth. The CIOs will not only need to be more business-oriented in their future approach, they will also need to help the company to transit to new ways of doing business. They will need to assist the next wave of process reengineering and corporate restructuring. This wave of process reengineering and corporate restructuring will be focusing on building "Intelligent Enterprises." As in other significant changes in previous corporate history, tremendous resistance will occur.

Are today's CIOs prepared to take on these challenges? How much do they understand about strategic positioning? How much do they understand about business processes? How much do they understand about corporate organizational structures? How much do they understand about change management? What do they need to do if they are not yet equipped with the capabilities to take on these future challenges? Time will be of the essence. The challenges are already approaching and CIOs do not have much time left to get ready for them. While the roles of accountants and CFOs have matured, the true role of CIOs is just about to be born.

CONCLUSION

With the burden of Y2K, ERP, and Data Warehousing out of the way, and in the new landscape of global competition, companies will have the resources, and will be forced to start, to deal with external information processing issues. "Growth and survival both now depend on getting the organization in touch with the outside world," warned Peter Drucker. What is after ERP will be external data-focused! It might be TIS , EIM , or some other fancy term.

The corporate world has been talking about strategic IT for a long time. Now IT is going to cap its strategic importance for the first time in history by developing Corporate Antennae—transforming decision-making processes, and, hence, establishing Intelligent Enterprises.

Section VIII
Networking

Chapter 39
The Essentials of Enterprise Networking
Keith G. Knightson

Enterprise networks and enterprise networking are buzz-phrases on every salesperson's lips, together, of course, with "open" and "open systems." Many products are glowingly described with these phrases. Creating an enterprise network, however, requires more than just a knowledge of the buzzwords. This chapter explains the basic subtleties of an enterprise network and the challenges of establishing one.

THE NEXT GENERATION OF ENTERPRISES

An enterprise is nothing more than a fancy name for a given company or organization. It conveys, however, the notion of a geographically dispersed, multifaceted organization, an organization comprising many branches, departments, and disciplines (e.g., marketing, manufacturing, finance, administration).

In the past, the networking and information technologies deployed in an enterprise were many and disjointed. In some cases, this was because of local departmental or workgroup autonomy, or simply because of ignorance among different parts of the enterprise as to what information systems were being used, or it was an artifact of historical equipment acquisition procedures.

The allegiance of specific departments to particular vendors was also a factor. When acquisition of capital equipment is performed gradually (rather than implemented all at once, across the board), it is difficult to make sure that all equipment is mutually compatible. Finally, the lack of an enterprisewide view, strategy, or policy with respect to networking and information technology—and the possible convergence solutions—are contributing considerations.

0-8493-9989-0/99/$0.00+$.50
© 1999 by CRC Press LLC

Consolidating the Network

In the same sense that the word "enterprise" conveys the totality of an organization's operations, the phrase "enterprise network" means combining all the networking and information technology and applications within a given enterprise into a single, seamless, consolidated, integrated network. The degree of integration and consolidation may vary; total integration and consolidation may not be always achievable.

For example, an organization may have an SNA network from IBM Corp. and a DECnet from Digital Equipment Corp. In all probability, these two networks have their own communications components; there might be one set of leased lines serving the SNA network and another completely independent set of leased lines serving the DECnet.

It would be useful if all the IBM users could intercommunicate with all DEC users, but a first and evolutionary step might be to have both the SNA network and DECnet share the same leased lines. Now, only one physical network has to be managed instead of two separate ones, and more efficient and cost-effective sharing of the physical communications plant can be achieved.

A second step might be to interconnect the mail systems of the two networks to achieve at least the appearance of a single enterprisewide electronic-mail system.

A third step might be to unify the data and information and its representation as used within the organization. This would enable basic forms of data to be operated on by many applications.

The challenges of building an enterprise network fall into two distinct categories: getting the data (i.e., information) from A to B, and enabling B to understand the data when it receives it from A. These two categories are referred to in this chapter as the "networking challenge" and "beyond the networking challenge." In this context, the network is used as it is in the Open Systems Interconnection (OSI) reference model—that is, Layer 3 and below.

THE NETWORKING CHALLENGE

The networking part of the problem has three major components:

- Choosing from and integrating the many network technologies
- Selecting from the many vendor solutions
- Moving information from a local to a global environment

Integrating Network Technologies

The first basic problem with networks is that there are so many of them. In this context, networks are taken to mean the raw network technologies—leased lines (i.e., T_1 and T_3), X.25, ISDN, frame relay, asynchronous transfer mode (ATM), and the many and various LAN access methods.

If all the users in an enterprise are connected to the same network technology, there is no problem. Unfortunately, this is not always the case. Communication between users on dissimilar networks (e.g., two different LANs) is where the problem occurs.

Each network technology has its own characteristics and inherent protocols. From an enterprise viewpoint, this is bad news. For example, users connected to an X.25 network cannot easily be connected to those already connected to a LAN. For example, how would the X.25 user indicate the destination's media access control (MAC) address, and vice versa? X.25 networks understand only X.25 addresses and LANs understand only MAC addresses. The differences between network technologies and native protocols almost invariably prevent their direct interconnection.

Differences in addressing schemes present another difficulty. Addressing considerations alone usually dictate the use of a network interconnection device (NID) at the point at which two network technologies come together.

Exhibit 1 illustrates several network technologies, represented by N_1, N_2, N_3, N_4. Each of these technologies has its own native protocol (i.e., P_1, P_2, P_3, P_4). A way must be found to integrate all these disparate technologies into a single supernetwork, with globally uniform and globally understood characteristics and a single addressing scheme.

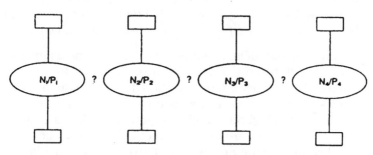

Notes:
- For every (sub)network N_i, there is a network-specific protocol P_i.
- All P_i's are different and thus not directly interconnectable.
- A way to make all the different networks look the same must be found, if the enterprise network is to appear as a single seamless network.

Exhibit 1.   The interoperability problem.

This is achieved by operating an integrating, unifying protocol (shown in Exhibit 2 as Px), sometimes known as an Internet protocol, over the top of all the possible basic communications networks. The Internet protocol (IP) of TCP/IP is one such protocol. The connectionless network layer protocol (CNLP) specified in the OSI International Standard 8473 is another. Proprietary systems have their own Internet protocols—for example, Novell uses its Internetwork Packet Exchange (IPX) and Banyan uses Vines.

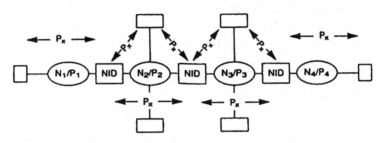

Notes:
NID   Network interconnection device
• A neutral protocol P_x is run over the top of every subnetwork.
• Because P_x is now the basis of the enterprise network, the individual networks are called subnetworks.
• P_x operates at the top of the network layer and is usually called an internet protocol.
• Several Px's exist (i.e., IP, CNLP, IPX).

Exhibit 2.   The interoperability solution.

From the architectural standpoint, the technical term for such an Internet protocol is subnetwork independent convergence protocol (SNICP). The protocols used on real-world communications networks (e.g., leased lines, X.25, frame relay, LANs) are known as subnetwork access control protocols (SNACP). The basic internetworking architecture is shown in Exhibit 3.

Unification does not mean simplification. Two protocols operating over a given subnetwork still require two address schemes. Routing tables are then needed in the network interconnection device to map the global enterprise address to the address to be used by the network interconnection device for the next link in the composite path. Exhibit 4 is a simplification of how the two addresses are used. In practice, the "next" address may be more complex, depending on the internetworking protocols under consideration. A network interconnection device of this type is called a router.

Selecting Vendor Solutions

The second basic problem is that each system vendor has a vendor-specific idea of how to build the supernetwork—the type of supernetwork

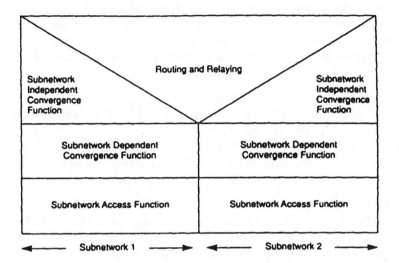

Exhibit 3. Network layer architecture.

protocol, the global addressing scheme, and the internal routing protocols to be used. At worst, this leads to a multiprotocol network, which amounts to several separate internets operating in parallel over the same physical communications plant.

Dealing with Multiple Protocols. An alternative to the multiprotocol network is to choose a single protocol for the entire enterprise supernetwork.

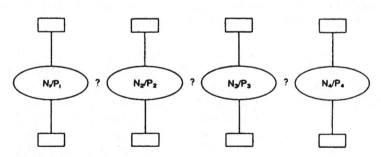

Notes:
• For every (sub)network N_i, there is a network-specific protocol P_i.
• All P_i's are different and thus not directly interconnectable.
• A way to make all the different networks look the same must be found, if the enterprise network is to appear as a single seamless network.

Exhibit 4. Simplified view of addressing.

565

This inevitably requires finding techniques to accommodate the systems that do not inherently operate this chosen protocol. Techniques include encapsulation (sometimes called tunneling) at the edges of the single-protocol network, or other techniques such as transport service interfaces and application gateways.

However, even with a single protocol, tunneling permits only the coexistence of incompatible systems; there can be little or no interaction between each of the tunneled applications. The major advantage of tunneling is that the core of the network is unified, optimizing network management and networking skills. The disadvantage is the effort required to set up the tunneling configurations at the edges.

The best solution is for all vendors to use the same Internet protocol. Increasingly, the protocol of choice for this purpose is TCP/IP. Although not a networking panacea, TCP/IP is the protocol of choice for most networking challenges involving multiple protocols.

Going Global

Many LAN-based systems include internal protocols that advertise the existence of various LAN- based servers. Such a protocol is sometimes known as a service advertising protocol (SAP). Protocol exchanges, frequently broadcast over the LAN, ensure that the availability and addresses of various servers are known throughout the LAN user community. This is useful when the geographic area is confined to a work group or a floor of a building; for example, the knowledge of a set of available printers is useful only in the area that has ready access to one of them. Thus, local messages must be constrained to local environments by putting adequate filtering at the point of access to the wide area portion of the enterprise network. There is no point in telling a user on a LAN in New York that there is a printer available on a LAN in Seattle.

WAN Transit Delays. Another global problem relates to the extra transit delay involved in transport over a WAN, especially for nonroutable protocols. Many protocol stacks used in local environments do not contain a network layer protocol—in other words, they have no routing layer. Such protocols cannot be routed directly in a router-based enterprise network. Where it is necessary for such an application to be networked outside a particular local environment, the local protocol stack must be encapsulated within an internetworking protocol. Then it can be launched onto the wide area part of the enterprise network.

Many of the local or nonroutable protocols are designed for very rapid acknowledgment. The transfer of these types of protocols across a wide area may cause problems; applications may prematurely time-out or suffer poor throughput because of the lack of a windowing mechanism adequate for the wide area transit delay.

To accommodate such applications, it is necessary to "spoof" the acknowledgments. This means that acknowledgments must be generated by the local encapsulation device. This requires the extra complication of adding a reliable transport protocol on top of the internetworking protocol across the wide area portion of the enterprise network. Once a local acknowledgment has been given, the originator will discard the original so it is no longer available for retransmission. Having given the local acknowledgment, the spoofing device must ensure reliable delivery to the remote end by employing a transport protocol of some sort (e.g., TCP or OSI Transport Class 4). The scheme, shown in Exhibit 5, avoids the end-to-end round trip delay T_r for every packet of data by providing an acknowledgment at time T_1.

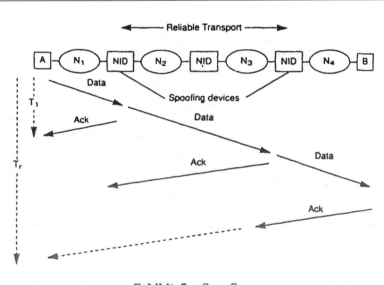

Exhibit 5. Spoofing.

Addressing. Going global also poses some challenges in the area of network layer addressing, particularly with regard to achieving enterprisewide uniqueness and structuring addresses for scalability and ease of routing.

Usually, addresses of stations within a local workgroup are allocated locally. This can present problems when, subsequently, the local workgroups must be integrated into a single enterprisewide address scheme. If several workgroup addresses—or parts of an address (e.g., an area or server name)—are the same, some changes will have to be made. From an operational perspective, changing addresses is not a trivial matter. It is best to avoid address allocation clashes right from the outset by having an enterprisewide address registration authority set up within the organization.

Some addressing schemes do have some hierarchy associated with them that can be used to avoid address encoding clashes by ensuring that local addresses are only the low-order part of the total address. Even in this case, however, an enterprisewide perspective is necessary to avoid clashes in the high-order part of the address.

Some vendors achieve uniqueness by allocating unique addresses when the equipment is shipped. However, this usually results in a flat, random address space that makes routing considerably more complex because there is no structure in the address to help "scale" the enterprise network from the routing perspective.

If the enterprise is to be permanently connected to the Internet (as opposed to using a dialup connection), IP addresses must be obtained from an appropriate addressing authority. Until recently, all addresses were dispensed directly from the Internet Network Information Center (InterNIC). More recently, in response to a number of problems associated with addressing practices in the past, IP addresses have begun to take on a more hierarchical form. As such, the enterprise may need to obtain a block of addresses from its Internet Service Provider (ISP), in effect obtaining a subset of the addresses that ISP has obtained from the InterNIC.

This practice ensures that the appropriate hierarchical relationships are maintained, allowing improved routing, and it has the added benefit of more efficiently allocating the available addresses. The primary drawback from the perspective of the enterprise is that addresses obtained in this fashion are no longer considered permanent. That is, if the enterprise changes ISPs, the addresses may also have to be changed.

Hierarchical Schemes. The most widely documented and hierarchically administered address available today is the OSI address space available for OSI Network Service Access Point (NSAP) addresses. A more recently developed scheme is the next generation of IP, now known as IP version 6 (IPv6), described in RFCs 1883-1886. NSAP addresses can consist of up to 40 digits, and IPv6 addresses can be up to 128 bits, either of which allows good scaling potential and simplified routing.

The reason that a hierarchical (i.e., scaled) address scheme is so important has to do with the way that routers operate and the size of the associated routing tables. If addresses were allocated completely randomly but uniquely from a large address space, every router would need a table with every address in it. Not only would the table be extremely large, but the time needed to find an entry could also be a problem. Routing is thus better arranged on the basis of hierarchical distinctions that are implicit in the address scheme.

To service a local workgroup or other limited geographical area, a local router must know only whether the destination address is internal or external. If it is internal, the router knows how to get the message to the destination; if it is external, the router can pass it on to the next-level router. This leads to the concept of areas, groups of areas, domains, and countries being components of a hierarchical address.

When legacy systems must be accommodated with conflicting address schemes and reallocation of addresses is impossible, tunneling may have to be employed merely to avoid interaction between the conflicting addresses. Because conflicting networks are divided into separate virtual private networks, the protocol under consideration cannot be routed natively even if the backbone routers are capable of doing so.

Routing Protocols. To reduce the amount of time devoted to setting up routing tables manually, and to allow dynamic rerouting and a degree of self-healing, routing protocols are often employed to distribute routing information throughout the enterprise network. These protocols are in addition to the internetworking protocol itself, but are related to it.

For every internetwork protocol routed in a multiprotocol network, there may be a specific routing protocol (or set of protocols). This also means in general that there will also be a separate routing table for each internetworking protocol. The situation in which several routing protocols are used simultaneously, but independently, is sometimes known as a "ships in the night" situation, because sets of routing information pass each other and are seemingly oblivious to each other even though there is only one physical network.

Some router manufacturers operate a single proprietary routing protocol between their own routers and convert to individual protocols at the edges of the network. There have been some attempts to define a single standard routing protocol based on the International Standards Organization's intermediate system to intermediate system (IS-IS) standard.

In an enterprise network, end systems (e.g., terminals, workstations, mainframes) usually announce their presence and their own addresses to the nearest local router. The local routers record all the local addresses within their area and inform all neighboring higher-level routers of their own area address. In this way, a router at the next and higher level in the hierarchy only needs to know about areas. Recursive application of these principles to a hierarchical configuration can lead to efficient routing by minimizing the amount of routing information to be transmitted and by keeping the size of routing tables small.

As the process of promulgating routing information proceeds across the network, every router in the enterprise network will obtain a table of reachability that it can then use for choosing optimum routes. Route optimality may be based on a number of independent metrics (e.g., transmit delay, throughput, monetary cost). Invariably, a shortest path first (SPF) algorithm is used to determine the optimal route for any particular metric chosen as the basis for routing. Both the Internet and OSI routing protocols use an SPF algorithm.

ROUTERS

Routers are the key interconnection devices in the enterprise network; subsequently, the router market has been one of the key growth areas during this decade. Some router vendors have grown from small $10 million companies to $1 billion companies.

In most cases, routers are purpose-built communications processor platforms with hardware architectures specifically designed for high-speed switching. Several possible pitfalls await the unwary purchaser of routers. Such a purchase involves four important considerations:

- The capacity and architecture in terms of the number of ports accommodated and throughput achievable
- Internetwork protocols supported and their associated routing protocols
- Support of technologies for the connected subnetworks
- Interoperability between different vendors

Capacity and Architecture

The number of ports required determines to a large extent the size of the router required, which in turn affects the architecture and throughput of the router. Physical size of circuit boards dictates how many ports can be placed on a single board. The greater the number of ports, the greater the number of boards required and the more critical the architecture.

Routing between ports on the same board is usually faster than routing between ports on different boards, assuming that there are on-board routing functions. Boards are usually interconnected by means of some kind of backplane. Backplane speeds can vary greatly between vendors. Routing functions and tables may be distributed across all boards or may be centralized. The bottom line is that the architecture affects the performance, and performance figures are sometimes slanted toward some particular facet of the architecture. Thus, some routers may be optimal for certain configurations and not so good for others.

Many of the router manufacturers make several sizes of router, which could be referred to as small, medium, and large. All of one vendor's routers may, regardless of size, offer the same functions, but the circuit boards may not be interchangeable between the different models. This can make a big difference when it comes to stocking an inventory of spare parts. There may also be differences in network management capabilities.

When making comparisons, the data communications manager must carefully analyze vendor throughput and transit delay figures. Although worst cases are helpful for the user and network designer, some vendors specify either the best cases or averages. Other metrics involved in measurement may also be different (e.g., packet size assumed, particular internetwork protocol, particular subnetwork).

Other architectural considerations include extensibility and reliability. For example, is hot-swapping of boards possible? If the router must be powered down and reconfigured to change or add new boards, the disruption to a live network can have severe ripple effects elsewhere in the network. Can additional routing horsepower be added easily as loads increase by simply inserting an additional routing processor?

The question of using stand-alone or hub-based routers may also be relevant. This is a difficult problem because of the traditional split between the hub and router manufacturers. Hub vendors tend not to be routing specialists, and router vendors tend not to be experts at hub design. Alliances between some vendors have been made, but the difference in form factors (of circuit boards) can result in some baroque architectures and poor performance. Except in the simple, low-end cases, purpose-built stand-alone routers usually perform better and are more easily integrated with the rest of the network.

Some stand-alone routers can directly handle the multiplexed input streams from T1 and T3 links, making voice and data integration possible. This is unlikely to be the case for a hub that has been designed mainly for operation in a LAN.

Internetwork Protocols Supported

Most router vendors claim that they support a large number of internetworking protocols. In some cases, however, there may be restrictions on the number of protocols that can be supported simultaneously. There may also be restrictions on the use of multiple protocols over certain network technologies, or hidden subnetwork requirements. An example of the latter might be the need for a separate X.25 permanent virtual circuit (PVC) for every individual protocol, as opposed to operating all the protocols over a single PVC.

Some vendors may also use a proprietary routing protocol scheme for internal routing, only making the standard protocols available at the periphery of the network. This makes it difficult to mix different vendors' router products on the same backbone or within a single routing domain.

Network Technologies Supported

Most manufacturers provide interfaces to a large number of network technologies (e.g., X.25 ISDN, frame relay, T1, T3, Ethernet, Token Ring). The method of support may also vary. For example, in the case of leased circuits, it may or may not be possible to directly connect the carrier's line to the router. Some routers may accept the carrier's framing mechanism directly; others may require an external converter to provide a simple serial interface (e.g., V.35) before connection can be achieved. Buyers should remember that the interaction between these interfaces and the multiple internetwork protocols may not be clearly reported by the vendor.

Interoperability

In the not too distant past, there was little interoperability between routers from different vendors. The reason most often cited was lack of standards for operating multiple protocols over a given subnetwork topology. Fortunately, the Internet community has made substantial progress subsequent to its definition of the Point-to-Point Protocol (PPP), which originally defined encapsulation and discrimination methods for multiprotocol operation over leased circuits. More recently, the utility of PPP has been extended with numerous enhancements. For example, it can now be used over switched services, including dialup, ISDN, and Frame Relay, and it can be used in a multilink configuration. It can operate with or without authentication, and with or without compression.

This plethora of options has led to the widespread support for PPP, both in terms of the number of protocols standardized for use with PPP, and in terms of the number of vendors building compatible routers. As such, interoperability among routers of different vendors is much more common than it was just a few years ago.

Network Management

It is extremely unlikely that a common set of management features will apply to all vendors' routers. Thus, if several manufacturers' routers are deployed in a given enterprise network, several management systems probably will be required. In the best case, these systems can be run on the same hardware platform. In the worst case, different hardware platforms may be required.

Filtering

The degree of filtering that can be applied—to prevent local traffic uselessly flooding the enterprise network—may vary with the manufacturer. Various parameters can be used as the basis for filtering—for example, source address, destination address, protocol type, and security codes. The disadvantage of using filtering is the labor involved in setting up the filter tables in all the routers.

BEYOND THE NETWORKING CHALLENGE— THE APPLICATIONS

Gateways, Tunneling, and Transport Service Interfaces. All the considerations discussed so far apply to the internetworking protocols. Multiprotocol networks serve only to share bandwidth; they do not allow applications to interoperate. Where that is necessary, with completely different stacks of protocols, an application gateway must be used. Exhibit 6 shows an OSI-based mail (X.400) application interoperating with a TCP/IP-based mail application over an application gateway.

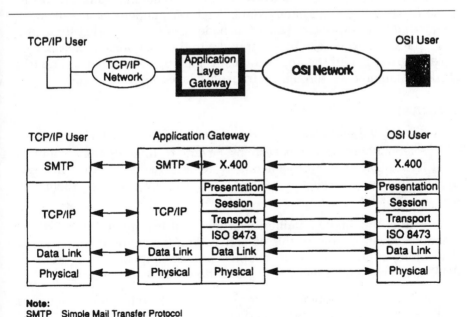

Note:
SMTP Simple Mail Transfer Protocol

Exhibit 6. Mail application gateway.

Such gateways may be sited either centrally or locally. The use of local gateways makes it possible to deploy an application backbone with a single standard application operating over the wide area portion of the enterprise network (e.g., an X.400 mail backbone). This reduces the number of gateways needed for conversion between all the different applications. Only one conversion is necessary for each application (i.e., to the one used on the backbone). A considerable number of different local systems could interoperate through the "standard" backbone application.

The encapsulation technique already mentioned in the context of IP tunneling allows the applications that can be so configured to operate across the enterprise network. A tunneled SNA application is shown in Exhibit 7.

Another solution that may help in the future is the availability of transport service interfaces for end systems (e.g., workstations, terminals, servers). A transport server interface allows a given application to be operated over any underlying communications protocol stack. In other words, applications and communications stacks can be mixed and matched as necessary. The so-called open operating systems (e.g., POSIX and X/Open) adopt this approach.

The transport layer is a fundamental dividing line in the system architecture. Network-related functions are separate from application-related functions so that applications work with many communications protocols. Exhibit 8 shows an end system containing both an open OSI/TCP/IP stack (shaded) and a proprietary stack (unshaded). Within an end system, protocol stacks can generally be separated into the communications-specific lowerlayer parts and the application-specific upper-layer parts. The two stacks communicate through a transport layer interface (TLI).

SUMMARY

In practice, legacy systems or other requirements result in the existence of a variety of heterogeneous systems. Several techniques can be applied to at least make the heterogeneous systems networkable over a single physical network. Varying degrees of interoperability between them may also be possible.

TCP/IP is the single common protocol that has made the most tremendous advances toward this objective. With the continued progress in developing Internet protocols, coupled with the impending migration to IPv6, the multivendor networking situation will only improve.

Nonetheless, developing an enterprise network architecture continues to pose significant challenges. An overall plan for the network minimizes confusion and puts in place a timed migration strategy toward a completely integrated network. Central control has fallen into disrepute, but

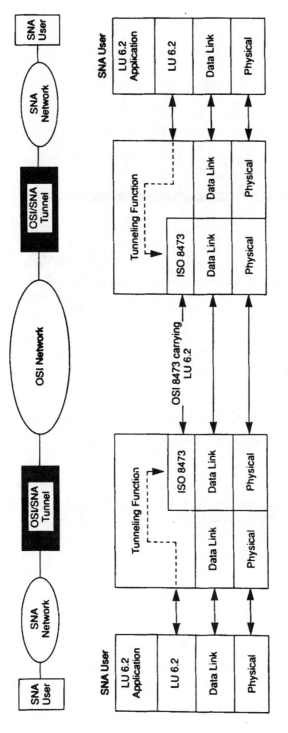

Exhibit 7. Tunneled SNA application.

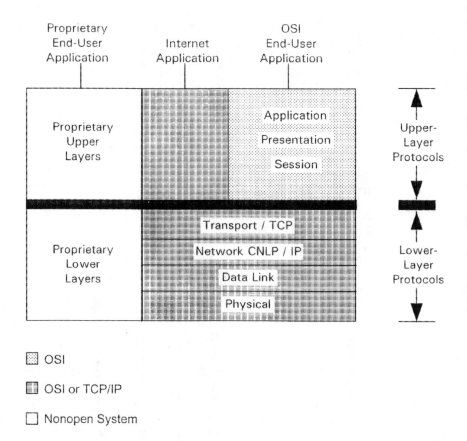

Exhibit 8. Transport layer interface.

without some control over how networking is to be achieved, all the real benefits of an enterprise network will not be realized. Finally, it is probably fair to say that enterprise networking is still something of a black art and is bound to present all data communications managers with some surprises and disappointments.

Chapter 40

Planning, Designing, and Optimization of Enterprise Networks

Roshan L. Sharma

INTRODUCTION

Network planning, design, and optimization should be an important component of a network management process despite its benign neglect by most network managers. Such a benign neglect resulted from the fact that network design was traditionally accomplished through the use of powerful mainframe computers. Since these computers required the use of large tariff-related databases, a great deal of time was spent in entering input data. A great deal of time was also spent on interpreting the output data that invariably came in the form of a thick stack of computer printouts. Lack of graphics provided no illustration of network topologies. Furthermore, the user was always kept out of the computer room. This made the network design process a mysterious effort, scaring even the most experienced network manager. Most of the modern network design tools still employ the old philosophy, which prevents the network managers from deriving the full benefits of new innovations in computer hardware and software.

The VLSI (Very Large Scale Integration) technology has now made the availability of very powerful personal computers, desktop or laptop variety, within reach of every network designer and planner. However, the lack of a user-friendly software for network design and planning had prevented the network managers from making use of the latest desktop hardware. Several new software packages have been created to make use of the new PC hardware platforms. The author has developed one such package called EcoNets as fully described in Reference 1. We will make use of EcoNets later and show how the network planning, design, and optimization process can be simplified to a level unimagined before. In fact, EcoNets can now be treated as a new type of scientific calculator bringing simplicity and ease of use to every networking specialist.

Any network planning and design effort can be broken into the following distinct tasks:

1. Creating a database for all locations and types of dumb terminals (e.g., telephones), intelligent workstations (WSs), customer premise equipment (CPE such as PABX or data LAN), and communication facilities serving those locations
2. Modeling all types of end-to-end multihour traffic flows between all locations
3. Modeling traffic growth during a life cycle of the network system,
4. Defining end-to-end performance requirements for all forms of communications
5. Designing strategic and tactical network alternatives using available technologies
6. Selecting the best alternative based on cost, cutover, and performanc,
7. Testing the performance of a post-cutover network implementation,
8. Updating the analytical tools and getting ready for next design cycle
9. Documenting the results

A cursory look at the above tasks will suggest that any network manager must accomplish these tasks in an iterative and a clear fashion. One will need a judicial combination of just plain old perseverance (for Tasks 1 and 9), traffic engineering practices (for Tasks 2 and 3), defining performance requirements (for Task 4), availability of a user-friendly and highly interactive design tools (for Tasks 5 and 8), systems engineering skills (for Task 7), and marketing savvy for selling the final solution to the upper management (for Task 6). Such capability requirement for a typical network manager is not that formidable if the right traffic analysis and network design tools are available. We will now describe each of the capabilities that must be controlled by the network manager. The capabilities required for Tasks 6, 7, and 9 are discussed in other appropriate chapters of this book.

THE ENTERPRISE DATABASE (EDB)

The first task is by far the most time-consuming. An enterprise database (EDB) should at least list the exact mailing address; ten-digit telephone numbers; associated Vertical and Horizontal (V&H) coordinates; all CPEs with vendor's name, date of installation, single point-of-contact for maintenance, the utilization level of each CPE, and type and number of communication facilities serving each location; and associated point-of-presence (POP) central offices of local exchange carriers (LECs) and inter exchange carriers (IECs) with their V&H coordinates. The list can grow into a very large one when the database must also classify the users at each location with their interlocation communications needs. Despite the difficulty of creating the EDB, many network managers and top company officials have already discovered the importance of such a database. In any case, *the task of network planning, design, and optimization is impossible without the availability of such an EDB.*

TRAFFIC ENGINEERING TECHNIQUES AND TOOLS

The next three tasks demand a capability for traffic modeling and traffic analysis. Before we define the traffic engineering efforts, we must first introduce some basic traffic-related concepts.

Basic Traffic Concepts

There are two types of traffic encountered in enterprise networks:

1. Well-behaved voice and video traffic
2. Bursty data traffic

It always is assumed that connection-oriented voice traffic behaves in a predictable fashion which implies that, 1. the call holding times can be expressed by at least first two moments (i.e., an average and a variance) and , 2. the finer structure of traffic flows don't require rapid changes in network resource deployment. But a close observation of speech energy over the duration of a talk will show that there are many pauses. Furthermore, two of the four-wire access lines (ALs) and trunks are always idle since only one party can talk at a time. These facts have helped long-distance carriers send more calls over expensive ocean cables than are possible over available trunks using pure circuit switching by using the time asynchronous speech interpolator (TASI) technology. Such a technology was never cost-effective over cheape,r land-based leased line. With the availability of Asynchronous Transfer Mode (ATM) or Broadband ISDN, one will be able to get the same benefit through the use of Variable Bit Rate (VBR) capability. The connection-oriented video traffic should not yield this benefit since intelligent WSs can maintain a full-duplex connection.

The data traffic between two CPEs is always bursty. This is caused by the complex rules of data communication protocols. Very small control messages may be involved in both directions before user information can flow. Although a full-duplex connection can be maintained, shared transmission lines in a packet-switched network can carry variable-length packets from many sources concurrently, thus muddying the picture in a hurry. The faster the transmission lines, the burstier the transmission will appear. It becomes clear that a notion of an average message length over a transmission line becomes rather vague.

One can now devise ways to measure traffic intensity considering the above aspects of two major types of traffic encountered in enterprise networks.

Circuit-switched (CS) voice and video traffic intensity is measured in *erlangs,* which is equal to the average number of circuits busy during a so-called busy hour (BHR) between two network nodes. We will define such a BHR later. To illustrate, if 15.5 conversations are observed concurrently between two network nodes (e.g., between a PABX and a voice switch or over an access line bundle) during a BHR, then the voice traffic intensity is 15.5 erlangs. The older measure of CS traffic intensity was *hundred call seconds (CCS).* But such a measure was almost useless since it did not represent any physical truth, such as the number of conversations observed.

Packet-switched data traffic intensity can be measured as the traffic rate in bits per second (bps) during a so-called busy hour. Only data rate in bps can describe the bursty nature of data traffic. Experienced network specialists have been using the concept of data erlangs for many years for defining the average data traffic intensity between two network nodes. This is obtained by dividing the observed BHR data rate (R) by the capacity (C) of each separate transmission line. For example, if the BHR data rate between two nodes is 392,000 bps and the capacity of a transmission line is 56,000 bps, then the data traffic intensity is 7 erlangs.

Modeling Traffic Flows in an Enterprise Network

Basically there are two kinds of network systems that present unique situations for modeling traffic flows within an enterprise network: 1. a *brand new* network system and, 2. an *existing* network system.

Modeling Traffic Flows in a Brand-New Enterprise Network. Many network specialists feel helpless in modeling traffic flows for a brand-new system. Many approximate methods have been devised over the years for predicting traffic intensities (TIs) between all major CPEs. To illustrate, a voice LAN (or PABX) generates about $0.1*N_s$ erlangs of BHR traffic where N_s is the number of active subscribers served by the PABX. Similarly, a data LAN generates about $(2/3)(WSC)*N_s$ where WSC is the BHR traffic intensity (in bps) generated by each *active* station on the LAN. A breakdown of these traffic expressions into intranodal and internodal traffic should be determined by the known pattern observed at each enterprise. Some network designers employ the 70/30 breakdown that implies that 70 percent of the traffic remains within the site (voice/data LAN) and 30 percent of the traffic goes to other CPEs as internodal flows. These TI values can then be entered into an input file that defines each site ID, the related V&H coordinates, and the total traffic (in and out) intensity handled by the site. The EcoNets tool calls such a file the VHD file.

The next task is to model the internodal traffic flows (i.e., exact traffic intensities handled by all the nodes and links in the path of a CPE-CPE connection). These computations are generally performed by the network planning/design software package for each assumed network topology (i.e., number of network switches and the link types employed at each network hierarchy). Some tools employ some critical design parameters to determine the fraction of traffic handled by ALs (connecting CPE and a switch) and trunks (connecting two switches). Eventually, the tool provides the total traffic intensity handled by each resource (node or link) of each network topology considered during a typical busy hour.

Modeling Traffic Flows in an Existing Enterprise Network. One can model exact traffic flows by using the detailed traffic data gathered by intelligent network nodes (e.g., PABX or LAN). The source ID, the destination ID, the call originating time, and the call duration for each connection is recorded in Station Message Data Recording (SMDR) tapes of voice network. Similar data is recorded by the data LAN for the packetized traffic. Simple traffic analysis packages are obtainable for analyzing the exact internodal traffic patterns between all pairs of CPEs. Such data can then be entered in a From-To-Data File (FTF) to define CPE traffic as simple vectors (From-Node ID, To-Node ID, and the BHR traffic intensity) for each CPE-nodal pair. This effort eventually provides actual traffic flows (i.e., the actual traffic intensity handled by all resource, nodes, and links) of each network topology studied during a typical BHR.

Modeling Time-Consistent Averages (TCAs) of Traffic Flows. Choosing a busy hour can be a very important task. No network can be economical if one selects the hour with the highest traffic. It may provide the required grade-of-service (GOS) during the busiest hour, but at all other hours of the day (especially during the evening and night hours) it becomes overkill. Nobody can afford such a network. If one selects an hour with the least traffic during the day, the network manager will hear complaints all day long. Therefore, one needs a proven methodology to select the so-called TCA traffic intensity for network design. There are two methodologies — one used in North America and one used by the other countries.

The first methodology requires the selection of a typical month and creating a matrix (30×24) of traffic intensities (TIs) for each network resource for that month. Next, it computes the average traffic intensity for each hour of the day over all 30 days of the month. This process is repeated for each of the 24 hours. The TCA traffic is the maximum value of all 24 TCA values. This value, as it will shown later, determines the size of the resource (number of AL and trunks in the bundle connecting two nodes or the computing power of an intelligent node). Again, one needs either the use of a software package for computing TCA traffic intensity (TI) values or a simple approach for approximating the TCA TI values.

The second methodology requires the observation of the 36 highest TI values over an entire year and then computing the average of these values to get a TCA value. This must be done for all resources.

Both of these methodologies are known to yield economical networks. It should be emphasized that no single methodology can predict an exact traffic pattern for the future. Traffic values behave like the stock market fluctuations. A single catastrophe, such as an earthquake or a major terrorist-bomb explosion somewhere, can also change the traffic patterns drastically. The objective of a good traffic engineering practice is to synthesize a cost-effective enterprise network using a consistent approach.

Modeling Traffic Growths during a Life Cycle of a Network System. In order to estimate the total costs incurred during the life cycle of a network system, one must first model the traffic intensities for each of the life cycle year. Experience shows that the so-called Delphi Approach (based on Socratic approach) works the best. Through interviews of all general managers, one can build good models of traffic growth during every year of the life cycle. There are times when one may find that some division may disappear altogether, either through divestiture or pure attrition. The data from all of the interviews must be collected, weighed, and processed to create a meaningful model.

PERFORMANCE ISSUES

Before one can define performance requirements for all the communication needs of an enterprise, one must first study the available concepts of performance and then study the exact enterprise needs in each of their business areas.

Concepts of Network System Performance

It is a commonly known fact that most of the existing network systems were implemented without any regard to their performance. As long as they satisfy the basic needs for communications, everyone is happy. No effort is expended in 1. predicting or measuring the actual performance of the system and 2. making any measured systemwide improvements after the system is operational. The lack of any concerted effort in defining and measuring performance of network system may lie in ignorance of concepts related to system performance. One can define the performance of a network system in four ways:

1. Total system costs computed on a monthly basis
2. System throughputs in terms of all types of transactions handled during a unit time
3. Systemwide quality-of-service (QOS)
4. Systemwide grade-of-service (GOS)

Total Monthly Costs. Transmission facilities determine the majority of total monthly costs of MANs and WANs. Since such costs are always paid on a monthly basis (just like our utility bills) to Local Exchange Carrier (LEC), Inter Exchange Carriers (IECs), and Other Common Carriers (OCCs), it simplifies matters a great deal. The other major items are one-time hardware costs and recurring costs of network management and control (NMC). It is a simple matter to convert the one-time hardware costs into equivalent monthly costs considering the life cycle duration (7 or 10 years depending on the enterprise) and cost of loaning money. It is similar to computing the monthly payment for a mortgage. The NMC costs related to spares can be handled just like one-time hardware costs. The remaining NMC costs on a monthly basis can be the same as either the monthly salaries paid to the NMC specialists or the monthly bills paid to an outsourcing company. It is therefore a simple task to compute the total monthly cost of a network system.

System Throughput. System throughput is measured the rate at which the various types of transactions are handled per unit time (usually second or minute). It is equal to the number of call attempts or calls completed per second for a voice network. It is equal to the number of packets handled per second or total bits (in and out) per second handled during a second. The throughput capability of each node is generally defined by the vendor of the equipment. The challenge lies in measuring the system throughput. By enumerating the exact paths of each transaction, one can estimate the system throughput. Consult Reference 1 for additional insight.

System Quality-of-Service (QoS). Performance aspects dealing with transmission quality, perceived voice quality, error-free seconds, data security, and network reliability (mean time between system failures) fall into the QoS criterion. Most of these are very hard to compute for the entire system. One can measure these performance aspects for some critical resource to get a feel. See Reference 1 for greater insight.

System Grade-of-Service (GoS). The GOS criterion deals with end-to-end blocking for a voice network and average response time (measured as the elapsed time between the moment the send key is pressed and the moment the return reply is discerned by the user) for a data communication. Analytical tools are available (Reference 1) for estimating such GoS parameters for voice, data, and integrated networks.

Defining Performance Goals for an Enterprise

Performance goals of a enterprise network should be developed by the corporate strategic planners. A typical strategic planning cycle lasts several years and it entails the following activities:

1. Continuous evaluation of the needs of the enterprise and its competitors. This activity defines the relationship of system response times to information workers' productivity for each of the transactions.
2. Studying the evolving new technologies, CPEs, and networking standards and finding ways to deploy these to achieve cost-effective enterprise networks and enhancing the productivity of its workers. This activity provides the cost and performance attributes of new hardware (e.g., ATM switches and LAN switches).

In order to perform its duties successfully, a strategic planning group should be properly structured to act in close cooperation with the corporate Information Technology (IT) department, and it should be provided with all the necessary resources and tools. Furthermore, a mechanism should be in place to properly reward all the members of this important group.

All future enterprise networks will have to deal with the ever-increasing demand for 1. voice, video, image, and data communications; 2. multiplexing of digitized voice, image, and video signals with regular data traffic at all hierarchies of enterprise locations through modern switches (e.g., ATM switches); and 3. unscheduled or varying demands for digital bandwidth at all hours of a day on a dynamic basis.

In order to design such an integrated enterprise network, the strategic planning group needs a user-friendly tool for evaluating alternative solutions very quickly. Such an approach should be an extension of the so-called "back-of-the-envelope" method employed by network managers of yesterday. They were generally concerned with designing only voice networks. The older "back-of-the-envelope" approach is no longer useful due to the complexity of modern integrated, hybrid, multilevel enterprise networks. It has been found that most of the hunches based on the so-called "common sense" are generally wrong when predicting the performance of an integrated network system. A user-friendly tool should help the strategic planning group to get "ball-park" solutions iteratively and interactively in order to fulfill its charter. See Page 587, *An Example of Planning and Design of an Integrated Enterprise Network Using Econets*, for an illustration of a "what if" approach required for rapid planning and designing or obtaining quick conceptual solutions by both the strategic and tactical planning teams.

NETWORK PLANNING AND DESIGN TOOL

Before we review the old and the new network design technologies, it should also be useful to discuss some major network design issues.

Major Network Design Issues

The current published literature dealing with networking is very confusing, at best. Most of the published articles are generally characterized by buzz words, a good deal of hype, lots of possible solutions, and no single recommendation. Although a part of the problem may lie in the fact that no single approach is ideally suited for all enterprises, no one can defend a lack of clarity that characterizes most published articles. While some articles recommend all virtual lines for enterprise voice networks, other articles emphasize the need for an integrated network management technique. While some articles recommend full freedom in designing departmental LANs and interconnections of these LANs through bridges and routers, other articles show the need for Frame Relay, SMDS and B-ISDN, or ATM in order to realize economies-of-scale in integrated enterprise networks. Most of the articles attempt only to expound a new type of switch technology or hardware. They rightfully leave up to the reader to assess the usefulness of the new technology or networking hardware to his or her enterprise.

Network design process is basically concerned with two issues: 1. topological optimization, which determines the way network nodes are connected to one another (including the type of connections) while satisfying a set of critical design and performance constraints, and 2. system performance dealing with end-to-end response times, path congestion, and availabilities.

Recurring network cost is generally the most important performance criterion and it is mainly determined by its topology. Network topology also determines the remaining performance issues such as response times and availability. Each network design package analyzes these performance issues in only an approximate manner.

Closed-form solutions for end-to-end system performance have been getting harder and harder to obtain ever since the first day a network was installed. Some of the current excitement about the interconnections of data LANs ignores the tribulations involved during the 70s when voice LANs (i.e., PABXs) were being interconnected to create enterprise networks with consistent topologies. Unfortunately, data internetworks encourage point-to-point type connections between LANs. This approach creates an undue network complexity for large networks. This in turn increases costs of NMC. The new ATM technology should eventually reduces this complexity by enforcing a consistent network topology and architecture.

NETWORKING

The Old Network Design Technology

The many older network design tools handled only voice or multidrop data networks. Some of the tools that came later handled only interconnections of data LANs to achieve an enterprise data WAN. Furthermore, most of these tools required mainframes. The use of a mainframe introduced an unnecessary curtain between the network designer and the host processor. The network design jobs were entered invariably via the "batch" approach, and the outputs came in the form of large printouts after a good deal of delay. Each change of a design parameter or study of a new technology required a new noninteractive, unfriendly delay. The absence of network-related graphics from outputs caused additional delays in interpreting the significance of results.

The old design technology also required the use of an extensive database of tariffs. These tariffs have been increasing in number and changing quite rapidly since the divestiture in 1984. The complexity of the tariff database was probably the main reason behind the need for mainframes. If such a database is incorporated into a desktop minicomputer or a PC-based workstation, one will experience sizable processing delays. In any case, one will be prevented from getting a truly interactive tool.

Since enterprise networks are planned and designed for a future period, this preoccupation with utmost accuracy in tariffs is uncalled for. Furthermore, since network topologies do not change with perturbations in any given tariff (they change only with varying design parameters and technologies), using a simplified set of existing or new tariffs will yield optimized networks in rapid succession even on a user-friendly desktop workstation. These topologies can be studied for a detailed cost analysis at a later period using one of the many available PC-Line Pricer (PCLP) units. This two-step approach should create a separation between the network design algorithms and the ever-changing tariffs. There should be no need to update the network design package just because a tariff changed slightly.

Network design tools based on the older technology were not only noninteractive, but they also were nonfriendly to use. A lack of a good graphical user interface (GUI) required lengthy training and a prolonged hands-on design experience to become familiar with the tool. A good design package should be an intuitive tool in the hands of an expert network designer and no more. A good hammer and a chisel alone will never guarantee beautiful furniture — one also needs a good carpenter. It should not be hard to understand why the vendors of network design tools have always had a hard time marketing these unfriendly network design tools. Most vendors have gone in and out of business several times under different names.

Some vendors (Reference 2) market software packages based on computer simulation for evaluating system performance. LANs (voice or data) and WANs consisting of interconnected data LANs can be evaluated for performance through computer simulation. A good deal of time must be spent on 1. writing the simulation program based upon the exact network topology and the underlying communication protocols, and 2. debugging the software before one can evaluate all of the performance metrics such as throughput and end-to-end response times. Since typical enterprise networks require exorbitant runtimes, a simulation tool is no longer an ideal way for synthesizing an optimum network topology. A network topology optimization package based on analytical tools is always the best approach. The resulting topology can be evaluated for studying detailed system response times and availabilities using an expensive simulation tool.

The New Network Design Technology

The new desktop workstation technology now provides several platforms for a user-friendly, interactive tool for optimizing network topology in an iterative fashion while varying the values of critical design parameters rapidly. Some well-known tools for network design also provide special menus for computing end-to-end response times for unusual operational conditions. Some packages even provide special tools for analyzing subsystem security and reliability.

Many new tools based on the graphical-user-interface (GUI) can evaluate any mix of CPEs, transmission facilities, and network topologies very rapidly in an intuitive manner. But in no way can this new technology eliminate the need for an expert network designer or an architect. Since the expert designer is always involved with "what-if" type analyses at all times through the graphical-user-interface, the solutions remain always meaningful and topical only if the network design tool provides such solutions rapidly. This approach is becoming an ideal one since the tariffs as we have known them are about to disappear. The modern tools allow the entry of approximate tariffs quickly. Next, we will describe one network planning and design package called EcoNets, and we will describe an example illustrating the network planning and design process associated with EcoNets.

Capability Highlights of the EcoNets Network Planning and Design Package

Inputs are in the form of flat, sequential files. Results are provided in the form of 1. graphics illustrating network topology with summary costs of communications facilities and response times (if applicable), and 2. output files containing detailed cost distributions and critical performance data.

The most important input file is called the VHD file listing the site/node ID, Vertical and Horizontal (V&H) coordinates, and total busy hour (BHR), time-consistent traffic intensities in bits per second (for data) or millierlangs (for voice) for each location of the enterprise. A from-to-data (FTD) file can also be used to represent exact traffic flows. Another file called the daily traffic profile relates the BHR intensities to the other 24 hours of the day for computing the costs on a daily/monthly basis. For an enterprise with many time zones, several BHR models can be used. The second most important LINK file defines the link-type that serves each location.

The third most important input file, called the NLT file, defines the link type, capacity (C), allowed maximum data rate (W_m), multiplexing factor (MF defining the equivalent number of voice conversations carried by the link), corresponding tariff number, and the multiplying factor for a privately-owned facility (F_{pf}), if applicable. Up to ten link types and corresponding C, W_m, MF, tariff number and F_{pf} can be defined by the NLT file. The Tariff file can define up to ten manually entered tariffs, each modeled by 17 parameters. Several Link, NLT, and Tariff files can be prepared to model many combinations of links and tariffs at all levels of network hierarchy. An input file called the system design file (SDF) defines the design parameters required to model/design the network.

The input file called the FTF defines the BHR from-to traffic for all significant pairs if such data is known. Other input files define the LATA numbers and names associated with each location. Several specialized input files are also employed for modeling/designing ACD networks employing a mix of virtual facilities and leased FX lines.

The File Menu allows the creation and viewing/updating of all input/output files. The Networking Menu allows the modeling/designing of multilevel voice, data, and IV/D network using the appropriate star data, directed link and multidrop data network topologies, and voice networks based on star topology. One can also model, design, and optimize backbone networks on an iterative manner. The Networking Menu also allows the designer to find optimum locations for concentrators/switches by starting with good solutions and improving these through a fast iterative process. By specifying the design parameters, one can model and design traditional data networks based on IBM's SNA (System Network Architecture); traditional packet-switched networks based on CCITT's X.25 standard; and fast packet-switched networks based on Frame Relay and ATM technology.

By specifying the design parameters, one can model hybrid voice networks using all types of leased and virtual facilities with or without multiplexing. One can also optimize a backbone network topology and model any given topology (for cost and routes). The Analysis Menu allows the designer to model/analyze any point-to-point and several multilink paths for congestion/queuing delays, LAN performance, and reliability. An Analysis Menu item also allows the computation of equivalent monthly cost of hardware and payoff periods for privately owned hardware and transmission facilities.

AN EXAMPLE OF PLANNING AND DESIGN OF AN INTEGRATED ENTERPRISE NETWORK USING ECONETS

An enterprise has 17 sites scattered throughout the United States. Its headquarters are in Las Colinas, Texas. It is engaged in the manufacture, distribution, marketing, and maintenance of highly specialized intelligent workstations. Two separate networks serve the enterprise. A voice network connects all its 17 locations (or PABXs) to a voice switch located at Las Colinas with leased voice-gradelines (VGLs). A separate data network connects workstations located at all of its locations to a host using the SNA-BSC protocol and 9600 bps lines. The newly appointed network manager wants to study the feasibility of a new network architecture. A consultant is engaged to study the problem.

A database (a subset of the EDB) for network design was created. It is illustrated in Exhibit 1. The 17 sites, their V&H coordinates, and BHR TCA of traffic intensities are shown for both voice (in millierlangs) and data (in bps). Also shown are their names according to a six-symbol city-state (CCCCST) code. Next, a Node-Link-Type (NLT) file is defined for four link types: VGL, 56Kbps line, T1 line, and T3 line. The simplified tariffs are defined for these links types next.

The consultant first modeled the existing voice and data networks. The monthly costs for these two separate networks were computed to be as $60,930 and $10,017, respectively. For a comparison, the EcoNets tool was then employed to study various topologies consisting of 1,2,3,4,5 switches and three links types for voice, and only the 9600 bps line for data (higher-speed lines resulted in no improvements).

The results are shown in Exhibit 2. The optimum voice-network topology (Exhibit 3) consisted of two switches (as determined by the EcoNets' center-of-gravity [COG] finding item of Networking Menu) and 56Kbps lines, each of which carries eight digitally-encoded voice conversations. The one-time cost of 17 special hardware boxes that perform voice encoding and multiplexing in the same box did not influence the optimum network topology. The optimum data network topology (Exhibit 4) also consisted of the same two switches as for the voice network and 9600bps lines. The cost of these optimum networks was found to be $37,546 and $9,147, respectively. This represented a monthly saving of $23,254 (or about 32.8 percent of existing costs). No matter which way one looks at this figure, it is a substantial saving.

Exhibit 1. **Enterprise database (EDB) 17-node network design (voice/data applications).**

			Nodal Definition Data			
N#	–V–	–H–	Load	Lata (BPS/MEs)	Link	Name
1	8438	4061	40000	552	0	LCLNTX
2	8436	4034	5000	552	0	DALLTX
3	8296	1094	1300	952	0	SRSTFL
4	8360	906	1300	939	0	FTMYFL
5	6421	8907	1300	674	0	TACMWA
6	6336	8596	1300	676	0	BELVWA
7	4410	1248	1400	128	0	DANVMA
8	6479	2598	1300	466	0	VERSKY
9	9258	7896	1300	730	0	TOAKCA
10	9233	7841	1400	730	0	NORWCA
11	9210	7885	1400	730	0	WLAXCA
12	7292	5925	1400	656	0	DENVCO
13	7731	4025	1300	538	0	TULSOK
14	7235	2069	1300	438	0	NORCGA
15	5972	2555	2500	324	0	COLMOH
16	9228	7920	2500	730	0	STMNCA
17	8173	1147	2500	952	0	TMPAFL
Total BHR Traffic = 68500						

Node-Link Type

Link Type	Link Capacity	MaxLink Rate
1	9,600 bps	6,300 bps
2	56,000	48,000
3	1,544,000	1,440,000

Tariff No. 1

Average Local Loops Charges ($)=294					
Mileage Bands	50	100	500	1000	10000
Fixed Costs ($)	72.98	149.28	229.28	324.24	324.24
Cost Per Mile ($)	2.84	1.31	0.51	0.32	0.32

Tariff No. 2

Average Local Loops Charges ($)=492					
Mileage Bands	50	100	500	1000	10000
Fixed Costs ($)	232	435	571	1081	1081
Cost Per Mile ($)	7.74	3.68	2.32	1.3	1.3

Tariff No. 3

Average Local Loops Charges ($)=2800					
Mileage Bands	50	100	10000	10000	10000
Fixed Costs ($)	1770	1808	2008	2500	2500
Cost Per Mile ($)	10	9.25	7.25	7.25	7.25

Tariff No. 4

Average Local Loops Charges ($)=8000					
Mileage Bands	10000	10000	10000	10000	10000
Fixed Costs ($)	16600	16600	16600	16600	16600
Cost Per Mile ($)	47	47	47	47	47

Daily Traffic Profile

Hour Numbers and Corresponding Fractions of Daily Traffic are as Follows:					
1–0	2–0	3–0	4–0	5–0	6–0
7–0.05	8–0.1	9–0.1	10–0.1	11–0.1	12–0.1
13–0.1	14–0.1	15–0.1	16–0.1	17–0.05	18–0
19–0	20–0	21–0	22–0	23–0	24–0

Additional saving can be achieved by computing the total data rate (in bps) of voice conversations from each site and adding the regular data traffic and constructing a new VHD file. One can achieve an optimum star-data topology consisting of two switches and 56Kbps lines. Its topology is identical to that for the optimum voice network (Exhibit 2) and its monthly cost is about the same as for the optimum voice network. The cost of the separate data network disappears completely. The new monthly saving of $33,392 savings represents 47.1 percent of the existing costs. These additional savings resulted from the fact that the 56K bps lines used in the inte-

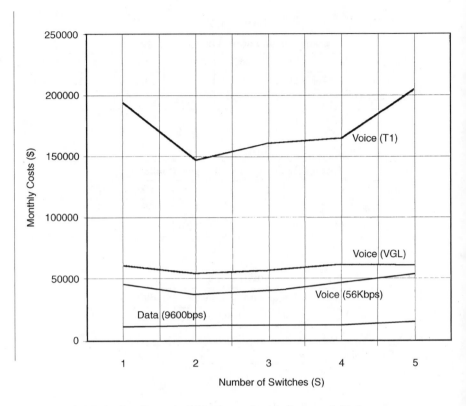

Exhibit 2.   Cost vs. number of switches and link types.

grated voice/data (IVD) network had enough excess capacity to handle the data traffic. Such a phenomenon is similar to the one experienced by network managers working with the larger T1 networks of the 1980s. Those enterprise voice networks had enough excess capacities (in the T1 trunks) to handle the data traffic. The broadband data networks of the future should have enough excess capacity to handle the voice and image traffic.

The preceding examples illustrate only small enterprise networks. Bigger savings can be expected through optimization of larger enterprise networks. Basically, savings result from two facts: 1. integrated networks make use of excess capacity, and 2. aggregation of many separate applications allows the deployment of transmission facilities with higher capacities that generally cost less on a per-transaction basis. Now every network manager has unlimited opportunities to provide a cost-effective integrated network to the enterprise. There is no excuse for not attempting to save big bucks for any strategically minded enterprise.

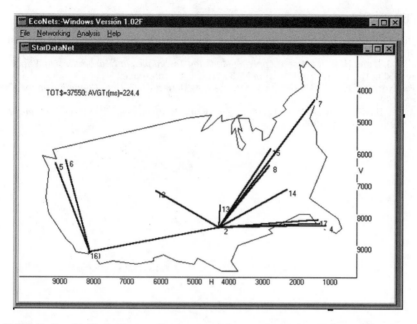

Exhibit 3. Optimum star-data network topology for IVD application.

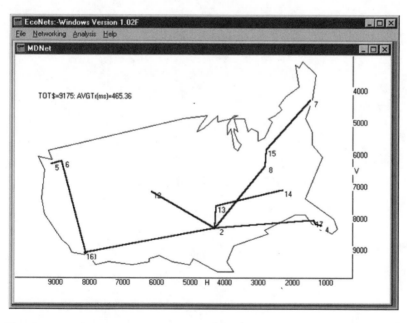

Exhibit 4. Optimum MD-data network topology with two switches.

NETWORKING

REFERENCES

1. Sharma, Roshan L. *Introduction to Network Design Using EcoNets Software*, International Thomson Computer Press, Boston, 1997.
2. Fike, J. L and H. D. Jacobsen. *Applying Modeling Techniques in Network Design*, Paper presented at the June 3, 1991 Session M13 at the ICA Conference.
3. Van Norman, H. J. "WAN Design Tools: the New Generation," *Data Communications*, October 1990.
4. Axner, David. "New Tools for Predicting Network Performance," *Business Communications Review*, November 1995.

Chapter 41

Enterprise Network Monitoring and Analysis

Colin Wynd

INTRODUCTION

Growing User Expectations:

Users are starting to expect error-free network connectivity with guaranteed uptime and response time. Users are also expecting that network services are delivered regardless of the underlying technology. Business end users also expect that data transmission will be secure. This increase in reliance on client/server applications as a fundamental part of conducting business means that end users need to rely on the network as much as the phone. Thus, whether the IT department is ready or not, the network is expected to be as reliable as the phone system.

The Changing Face of the Business Environment:

Corporations are more geographically dispersed, and entities that once were autonomous are working closely together. The network has become a critical method of communicating among these various groups. Applications are now client/server rather than on a central mainframe, meaning that the network must be operational for the end users to perform.

As the use of the network increases, more groups can be geographically dispersed. The increased focus on work/life balance has increased the number of work-at-home participants. The side-effect is that the amount of traffic on the network also increases.

This chapter discusses the role that network monitoring and analysis takes in administrating networks. We start by explaining network monitoring and where it fits into the IT management arena before showing the range of functionality that network monitoring brings to the IT manager's arsenal.

NETWORK MONITORING AND ANALYSIS DEFINED

Distributed network monitoring is the ability to view a remote network and perform monitoring and analysis on that remote network as if it were local. In the past, portable devices were carried out to remote sites and placed onto the network when problems were occurring on that segment. Having a network monitoring device on a segment only when there are problems means that the segment is not being monitored 99 percent of the time. Monitoring devices permanently placed on mission-critical segments can constantly monitor traffic. This means that analysis can be performed over and above fault management.

Exhibit 1 shows an example of remote monitoring agents installed on a large enterprise network with a variety of media types such as WANs, switches, FDDI, and ethernet.

The agents or "probes" reside on the remote segments and collect information of the traffic that it sees. The segments can be of any media type from various LAN media types such as ethernet, FDDI, Token Ring, or some WAN protocol such as Frame Relay. The segments can be geographically dispersed, but in general must be interconnected. The network

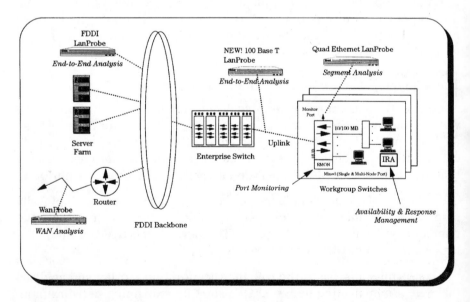

Exhibit 1. Remote monitoring agents installed on a large enterprise network.

management console contains a suite of applications that collect the network information from these remote agents and interpret it using power graphical user interfaces. Interestingly, the network management console communicates with agents using the same network that the agents are monitoring (out-of-band communication between the manager and agents is also possible).

With this configuration, network administrators can use monitoring tools to manage the whole network. Some functions that the network administrator can perform are:

Network Performance Management: The ability to continuously monitor certain network statistics to ensure adherence to the service level agreement; setting network thresholds to identify anomalies and the creation of baselines to aid in determining "normal" network performance.

Network Security Monitoring: Ensuring that only authorized users are accessing the network. This includes both monitoring the effectiveness of firewalls as well as internal security monitoring.

Fault Management and Availability: Being able to troubleshoot network problems in a timely fashion and monitor the availability of servers from the end users' perspective.

Capacity Planning: Traffic profile modeling allows the network manager to do a quick "what if" analysis before reconfiguring network resources. Having the appropriate data of past network trends determines what changes need to be made in the future to handle the ever-growing network.

NETWORK MONITORING AND ANALYSIS IN THE IT ENVIRONMENT

The IT management environment covers the whole scope of devices that reside on the network, as well as the network itself, that enable business end users to function. We can break this down into four components:

Systems Management is concerned with the performance of the computers on the network, and usually deals with issues like database performance and disk use on file servers.

Element Management is concerned with managing the various networking devices, like bridges, routers, and hubs. Typical management issues deal with configuration tables, throughput, link states, and port partitioning. A device management application usually shows a picture of the device on your screen, complete with installed cards and indicator lights.

Desktop Management is concerned with the end user workstations and PCs. The management issues are PC config files, disk use, application support, etc.

Network Monitoring and Analysis is primarily concerned with the activity on the wire itself. It is looking at the flow of data across the network in an effort to understand network performance and capacity, and to resolve problems related to networking protocols.

Service level management (SLM) is the strategy of defining, controlling, and maintaining the desired levels of IT service for the business end user. Business end users define with the IT department the level of service that is needed to support them. The level of service is turned into a set of objectives that the IT department can then monitor.

Network monitoring and analysis allows the IT department to manage one part of the end-to-end management picture. System, database, and application management issues are not discussed in this chapter.

STANDARDS OVERVIEW

Network monitoring has benefited from several standards. The main standard currently in use for network monitoring is the RMON standard which defines a method of monitoring traffic up to the DataLink layer (Layer 2) in the OSI stack. The RMON2 standard, which currently has not yet been ratified by the IETF, defines how to monitor traffic at the network layer (OSI Layer 3) and some portions of the application layer (Layer 7):.

Simple Network Management Protocol (SNMP)
Simple Network Management Protocol version 2 (SNMPv2)
Remote Monitoring (RMON) standard
Remote Monitoring version 2 (RMON2) standard

Why Perform Network Monitoring?

As part of an IT department's Service Level Agreement (SLA) with its business end users, IT must maintain a certain level of network service. To be able to do this, the network must be monitored to ensure error-free connectivity, responsiveness, and level of throughput. If the network is not monitored then it would be impossible for the IT department to guarantee any level of service.

In today's competitive environment, new client-server applications are quickly appearing in business environments, some examples are the WWW, Lotus Notes, andnetwork DOOM. If the network is not being monitored, then the effect of adding one of these network-intensive applications is unknown, and eventually one will bring the network to its knees. If the environment is being monitored, then network bandwidth can be monitored and traffic trends analyzed to ensure that network bandwidth will always exceed future growth.

The ability to monitor trends changes the IT from being reactive — waiting until something breaks before resolving the problem; to being proactive — resolving potential issues before they break. The IT department should now blend into the background allowing business end users to focus on their own functions.

Who Does Network Monitoring?

Since there are many areas to network monitoring, many people are involved. Here are some generic descriptions:

Network Manager Responsible for long-term strategic decisions regarding the network, involved in looking at new technologies such as 100Base-X or ATM, and deciding where and when to modify bandwidth, this person tends to look at network trends, performing forecasting and capacity planning.

Network Engineer Responsible for day-to-day operations of the network, upgrades network devices, adds capacity, and also acts as a second line of support for problems that the operations center engineer cannot resolve.

Operations Center Engineer Most large corporations have a centralized monitoring center staffed with "level 1" engineers who attempt basic troubleshooting of problems. These engineers monitor for events that are triggered by servers, workstations, or network devices that can alert the operations center on potential problems. These engineers are the first line of support and are constantly in reactive mode.

What Data Is Provided?

Monitoring the network means that information on every single packet on every single segment can be gathered. Network monitoring really means deciding which data are important and should be gathered, and which data are redundant. Corporations with a large number of segments need to decide on only a few critical pieces of information, otherwise they are inundated with data. The cost of analyzing the network would exceed the actual cost of the network! Some of the most critical measurements that should be gathered are:

1. Utilization: Segment utilization information should be gathered to generate trends for capacity planning purposes, baselining purposes, and performance information.
2. Error rates: Total error rate information can give performance indicators, baselining the error rate of the network, correlated with utilization it can give indicators of physical layer network problems.

3. Protocol distribution. This can generate trends for changing application mixes, monitoring the usage of new applications and the effect of new applications on the network.
4. Top talkers can also give indications on the performance of the network, performance of machines, and load of applications and services on the network. Top talkers can also indicate potential new applications that are unknown to the network department (new Internet applications such as PointCast have been discovered using this method).
5. Latency measurements (echo tests) lead to trends in performance.

How Does Network Monitoring Work?

Network monitoring is a large subject and there are many proprietary protocols that are involved. We will only cover standards-based protocols, plus the most widespread proprietary protocols.

The Simple Network Management Protocol (SNMP)

The Simple Network Management Protocol (SNMP) was a draft standard in 1988 and finally ratified in April 1989. SNMP is described by Request For Comments (RFC) 1098. SNMP has three basic components:

Agent   A software program that resides in a managed element of the network such as a hub, router, or specialized device.
Manager   Communicates with the agent using the SNMP commands
Management Information Base (MIB)   A database that resides with the agent and holds relevant management information.

The diagram in Exhibit 2 shows the relationship among the three components (agent, MIB, and manager).

There are five types of SNMP commands called protocol data units (PDU's):

1. *Get request:* A manager requests (from the agent) the value of a variable stored in the MIB.

2. *Get-Next request:* Used by the manager to request information on multiple variables. Used to reduce network traffic. If one variable is not available, no values are returned. Also used to retrieve unknown rows, if available.

3. *Set request:* The manager instructs the agent to set an MIB variable to the desired value.

4. *Get-Response:* Sent by the Agent as a response to a SET or Get-Next command as either an error or identical to the SET to show it was accepted, or to a Get-Next with the value portions of the request filled in. The Manager checks its list of previously sent requests to

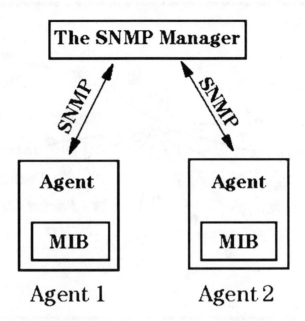

Exhibit 2. Relationship between agent, MIB, and manager.

locate the one that matches this response and, if none is found, the response is discarded, otherwise it is handled.

5. *Trap:* One of two unsolicited messages sent from the agent to the manager, often used for event notification.

THE MANAGEMENT INFORMATION BASE TREE

MIBs are hierarchical in nature (Exhibit 3); this allows unique identifiers for each MIB variable (or Object). Some MIBs of interest are:

RFC1213 — MIBII — basic system information and basic level statistics
RFC1757 — RMON (Remote Monitoring)
RFC1513 — RMON (Remote Monitoring) extension for Token Ring

There are several advantages that network management applications have with SNMP:

- The protocol is easy to implement
- The protocol requires few resources to operate
- The protocol is mature, stable, and well understood
- The protocol is widely available (on most computers) and most network devices have some form of agent/MIB embedded within them

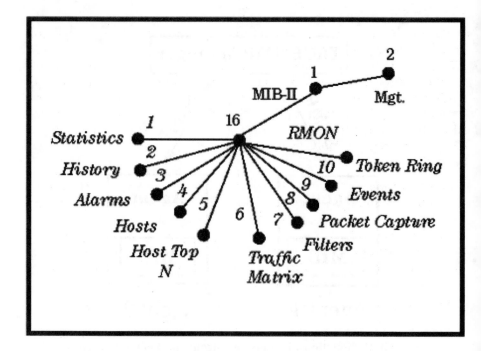

Exhibit 3. The hierarchical nature of MIBs.

However, as networks have grown and the need for network management has become more imperative, several disadvantages with SNMP have become apparent. Some of these disadvantages are:

- Limited security
- Lack of a block transfer
- Polling-based protocol
- Trap limitations

SNMPv2

SNMPv2 is a proposed standard that is attempting to address these issues. Some of the proposed extensions to the standard include:

- Manager-to-manager communication capability.
- Additional SNMP commands (PDU's):
  — Get BulkRequest for getting whole tables
  — InformRequest, Manager-to-Manager PDU
- Reliable traps

The last area of contention with SNMPv2 is security. Currently, there are two proposed drafts that are attempting to address the security issue.

The Remote Monitoring Protocol (RMON)

The RMON standard is a specific standard for performing remote monitoring on networks. The RMON standard is defined by two standards: RFC 1757 and RFC 1513. The standard defines a MIB that is broken down into ten groups; the first nine define monitoring of ethernet networks and the tenth defines extensions for Token Ring. There are currently no standards for monitoring FDDI, 100Base-X, or WAN networks. RMON vendors have added their own proprietary extensions for these additional media types. RMON is limited as it only gives visibility up to the DataLink Layer (Layer 2) in the OSI stack.

Statistics Group This group contains many segment statistics in 32-bit counters such as packets, dropped packets, broadcasts, and multicasts. These are just counters and not studies.

History Group This group contains segment history statistics for various counters such as broadcasts, errors, multicasts, packets, and octets. These numbers are for certain time periods. RMON defines two default time periods: — five seconds and 1800 seconds.

This means:

Alarms group This covers threshold monitoring and trap generation when that threshold has been reached. Allows alarms to be set of various counters and patch match. Traps can start and stop packet capture.

Host Group Contains host table and traffic statistic counters, plus a time table of discovery.

Host Top N Contains studies for X time and X hosts, listing top talker for the study group.

Traffic Matrix Group Contains matrix of MAC layer (Layer 2) conversations. Information such as error, packets, and octets sorted by MAC address.

Packet Capture/Filter Group These two groups are used together. Packet capture group contains the packets that have been captured. Multiple instances can be created.

Token Ring Group Contains specific information about Token Ring such as ring order, ring station table, and packet size distribution for history studies.

Remote Monitoring version 2 (RMON2) Protocol

The RMON standard brought many benefits to the network monitoring community, but also left out many features. The RMON2 standard is trying to address this. RMON2 attempts to address these issues by allowing the monitoring of Layer 3 (Network Layer) information as well as protocol distribution up to Layer 7 (Application Layer).

603

NETWORK PERFORMANCE MANAGEMENT

Performance management means being able to monitor segment activity as well as intrasegment traffic analysis. Network managers must be able to examine traffic patterns by source, destination, conversations, protocol/application type, and segment statistics such as utilization and error rates. Network managers must define the performance goals and how notification of performance problems should happen, and with what tolerances. Some objectives that network managers are faced with are:

- Baselining and network trending: How to determine the true operating envelope for the network by defining certain measurements (such as segment utilization, error rate, network latency) to check your service level objectives and out-of-norm conditions which, if left unchecked, may have drastic consequences on networked business users' productivity.
- Application usage and analysis: Helps managers answer questions such as, "What is the overall load of your WWW traffic?", and "What times of the day do certain applications load the network?" This allows network managers to discover important performance information (either realtime or historic) that will help define performance service level objectives for applications in the client/server environment.
- Internetwork perspective: Is traffic between remote sites and interconnect devices critical to your business? With Internetwork perspective capabilities you can discover traffic rates between subnets and find out which nodes are using WAN links to communicate. It can also help you define "typical" rates between interconnect devices. Internetwork perspective can show how certain applications use the critical interconnect paths and define "normal" WAN use for applications.
- Data correlation: Allows you to select peak network usage points throughout the day and discover which nodes were contributing to the network load at that peak point in time; which nodes they were sending traffic to; and which applications were running between them.

The diagram (Exhibit 4) shows an example of traffic flow between several segments. The thickness of the line (and the color) indicates the volume of traffic. With this information it is easy to identify potential WAN bottlenecks.

The second diagram (Exhibit 5) shows clients and servers correlated with a time graph. Being able to determine how much one particular server affects the network can help in the positioning of that server and again improve performance.

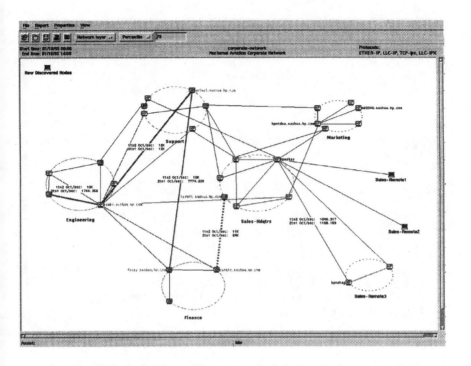

Exhibit 4. Traffic flow between several segments.

NETWORK SECURITY MONITORING

Security management encompasses a broad set of access control policies that span network hosts, network elements, and network access points (firewalls). Consistent policies are the key here; the objective is to support access and connectivity that is appropriate to the business need while restricting clearly inappropriate network-based access. As in other activities, constant monitoring for specific violations is critical, as is a notification mechanism. For certain conditions, immediate, automatic action may be required (i.e., "Shut down this connection," or "Shut down the firewall"). Monitoring should include both passive and active monitoring (probing).

Access level monitoring ensures that the controls and security that are in place are actually performing to expectations. Monitoring the traffic flow to a firewall, for instance, ensures that no intruders are accessing internally. Access level monitoring polices the "police" and ensures that nothing has been overlooked by the security.

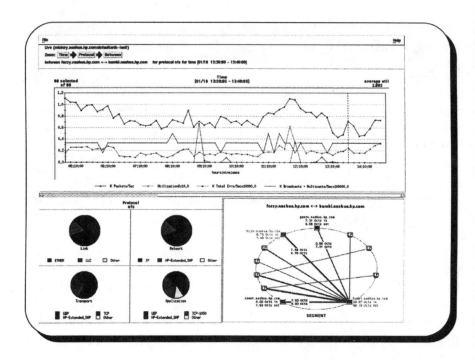

Exhibit 5. Clients and servers correlated with a time graph.

FAULT MANAGEMENT AND AVAILABILITY

Fault management is the continuous monitoring of the network and its elements, and the detection of failures within the network environment. When a failure is detected, then notification of the failure must occur in a timely fashion. The failure must be qualified with respect to other failures and prioritized.

Fault management systems include software bundles to detect and notify a centralized system of these failures. The centralized system normally includes some form of discover and mapping software that allows the network manager to have a graphical view of the network. These notifications must be correlated so that event storms are eliminated. A trouble ticketing system can also be incorporated so that a document trail is kept of the problem and allows a mechanism to communicate the status of the problem to the end users.

Another aspect to fault management is availability. This is the monitoring of servers from business end users' perspective to ensure that the machine is available to the end user. Tracking and notification of any interruption of client/server access is a critical part of the IT department's function.

CAPACITY PLANNING

Network demand is growing at unprecedented rates. New applications such as SAP and the World Wide Web (WWW) are encouraging extensive use of the network. Graphics are now sent regularly over the network (either through a corporation's Intranet or over the Internet). As network managers increase bandwidth, new applications for the network (such as Voice-over-IP or multimedia) become viable. This causes another spurt of demand for the network.

Capacity planning allows the network manager to look forward by looking at the past, and helps the manager to forecast what the demand will be. This means that the IT department can keep one step ahead of demand.

NETWORK REPORTING

Part of the IT department's function is to demonstrate that it is performing its function to the prescribed level. Being able to document that the network is running at the level agreed to in the service level agreement is an important justification tool.

It's critical that any reports are generated automatically, otherwise reports will not be generated or the effort to generate them will be too substantial to make it worthwhile.

LIMITATIONS OF NETWORK MONITORING AND ANALYSIS

Monitoring the network with the RMON standard means that only DataLink layer (Layer 2) information is collected. This is not high enough in the OSI stack to gather information about traffic trends of client-server applications.

The RMON2 standard defines a method of monitoring up to Layer 7 at certain times. RMON2 does not define continuous monitoring of all Layer 7 traffic, nor does RMON2 define any metrics for performance management.

SUMMARY

Enterprise network monitoring and analysis is a fast-changing environment. From the early days just a few years ago of monitoring the physical layer of the networks to the future of application layer service level management, the whole arena is helping IT management take control of the distributed environment that it spans.

Network monitoring and analysis will always have several aspects that have been described in this chapter, and the tools for implementing service level agreements between business end users and IT departments are quickly maturing.

However, network monitoring is only part of the total end-to-end solution that must include the whole environment that business end users operate. This means that systems, databases, and application monitoring tools must be deployed in conjunction with the network monitoring tools so that the whole environment can be viewed. Some tools, such as HP's PerfView product, that for the first time seamlessly integrate database, application, network, and system information on a single pane of glass for the end-to-end view that is necessary in this complex environment in which IT must now work, are just being released .

REFERENCES

Peter Phaal. *Lan Traffic Management*, Prentice Hall, ISBN: 0-13-124207-5
Dah Ming Chiu and Ram Sudama. *Network Monitoring Explained*, Ellis Horwood, ISBN 0-13-614-710-0
Nathan Muller. *Focus On OpenView*, CBM Books, ISBN 1-878956-48-5
Marshall T. Rose. *The Simple Book*, Prentice Hall, ISBN 0-13-812611-9

Chapter 42
Integrating Voice and LAN Infrastructures and Applications

David Curley

Integration of voice and LAN networks will be an essential IT strategy for many businesses in the next three to five years. Consolidating the long-separate voice and data networks has implications not only for the network infrastructure, but also for the PC, the telephone set, the PBX, and the IT organization itself. This chapter is a road map to guide organizations in making the right voiceLAN-related investment decisions.

PROBLEMS ADDRESSED

VoiceLAN is the transmission of voice traffic over a LAN infrastructure. VoiceLAN enables server-based telephony architecture for voice switches, terminals/phone sets, and applications.

Today, voice traffic is transmitted across a separate circuit-switched infrastructure with a PBX or key system (for smaller offices) serving as a centralized switch. Under a voiceLAN scheme, both data and voice traffic are interleaved and switched as frames or cells over the same data network.

Organizations should consider running their voice traffic over the LAN infrastructure for several reasons:

- **Single infrastructure.** VoiceLAN eliminates the need for a cabling plant dedicated to voice only. Converged voice/data traffic running over a single wire reduces the up-front cost of equipment procurement (e.g., cable, patch panels, racks, installation), cable plant management (i.e., dealing with moves, adds, and changes), and maintenance.
- **Single organization.** VoiceLAN allows enterprises to consolidate and streamline separate support organizations for data and voice networks. This convergence produces a more efficient, less costly management

structure that spends less time "coordinating" and more time delivering network services and applications to users.

- **Breaking PBX Lock-in.** For the most part, PBXs are proprietary, single-vendor systems, which usually means they are inflexible and expensive to maintain. VoiceLAN deployment paves the way for an open client/server model to be applied to telephony, creating a less rigid vendor-client relationship.
- **New level of CTI.** Current CTI systems allow data and voice application environments to "talk" to each other by means of computer-to-PBX links. CTI is included implicitly in the voiceLAN model. VoiceLAN also distinguishes itself from CTI because data and voice applications actually share the same set of standards and software interfaces. Thus voiceLAN leverages both media far beyond what is possible under present CTI systems, and has the potential to give organizations a distinct competitive advantage in the marketplace.

MIGRATING THE LAN INFRASTRUCTURE

Migration to voiceLAN is likely to encompass a number of smaller elements or activities. Migration cannot happen overnight, but is an evolutionary process that includes beneficial steps along the way. Over time, organizations can focus on improving elements of their network infrastructure, their desktop workstations, and their organizations in addition to their telephone systems.

A first step in deploying voiceLAN is to upgrade the present LAN infrastructure to support the demands of voice traffic without affecting the flow of existing data traffic. Infrastructure refers to the cabling plant and the local networking equipment used to carry traffic from end station to end station (i.e., hub, bridge, router, switches, and network adapters). The PBX is not considered part of the infrastructure in a voiceLAN environment; rather, the PBX will evolve into a call server that can be considered another type of end station on the LAN.

Solutions for Delay-Sensitive Applications

Voice bandwidth is not usually of much concern when using LANs for transmission. An uncompressed high-quality voice conversation needs only 64 Kbps, and compression or packetization reduces bandwidth requirements further. This represents only a small fraction of a dedicated 10 Mbps Ethernet LAN segment.

More important, voice is a delay-sensitive application that demands minimal latency (or minimal variations in latency, otherwise known as "jitter") in communications. The vast majority of LANs today are based on shared-bandwidth media. With Ethernet LANs, all users contend for bandwidth on a first-come, first-served basis. Token Ring LANs are somewhat more deterministic since each end station transmits only when that end station holds the token, which passes from end station to end station at more or less regular time intervals. However, under both of these shared-bandwidth schemes, significant transmission delays, as well as variations in transmission delay, occur — severely disrupting a real-time voice conversation between end stations.

Desktop Switching

Part of the solution to this problem is to provide dedicated bandwidth to each user end station through desktop LAN switching. In a fully switched network, end stations do not contend (as in Ethernet) or wait (as in Token Ring) for bandwidth with other users; instead, each user workstation gets its own dedicated LAN segment for connectivity into the network. Migrating to a fully switched network (i.e., a single workstation or server per dedicated switch port) entails replacing existing shared-media LAN hubs with LAN switches.

Dedicated LAN switching has become affordable. Commodity Ethernet switches currently sell for less than $200 per port ($US), and ATM25 switches can be obtained for less than $400 per port ($US).

Minimize Routing

LAN switching only addresses bandwidth contention to the desktop. Links between desktop switches, or from desktop switches to building/campus switches, must also provide predictable, minimal delays for voice communications.

In most enterprise networks, routers are used to calculate paths and forward packets between LAN segments at Layer 3 of the OSI model. These routing algorithms introduce significant delay and usually add noticeable latency to voice communications. By contrast, switching involves a much simpler and faster process. Segmenting the network at OSI Layer 2 through switching, rather than at Layer 3 through routing, increases the capacity of the network to support delay-sensitive applications such as voice.

Although routing will continue to be necessary, especially in larger enterprise environments, implementation of voiceLAN requires minimizing routing in favor of switching. If deployed properly, switching removes the delay-inducing routing process from the path of most network traffic.

In many cases, this migration step entails replacing a collapsed backbone router with a backbone switch. The routing function can either be centralized through a one-armed router (or route server model) or distributed in switches providing desktop or departmental connectivity. In either case, traffic is typically switched through the network and only passes through a routing function when absolutely necessary.

Controlling LAN Backbone Traffic

Migrating the network from shared-access LANs and routing to switching is a prerequisite to voiceLAN implementation. However, a major challenge remains in ensuring that voice can be properly supported on the backbone links (e.g., trunk) between LAN switches.

Supporting both data and voice over a common backbone LAN infrastructure is essentially a bandwidth-contention issue — determining how to make sure that delay-sensitive voice traffic is not preempted by other data traffic traversing the same links. Various techniques for prioritizing different traffic, reserving bandwidth, or guaranteeing network-delay characteristics may be applied. Two solutions to this problem are roughly categorized as the frame-switching/IP and ATM-centric approaches.

Frame Switching/IP-based Solution. Because of the rapid decline in price of Ethernet switches and the large installed base of Ethernet adapters, switched Ethernet has become the most popular solution for organizations deploying desktop switching. It is only natural for many organizations to consider Ethernet (especially Fast Ethernet) trunks for interconnecting desktop switches to each other or to LAN backbone segment switches.

However, as Ethernet frames are switched across the network, delay problems may still occur for voice. Ethernet frames are variable in length, and Ethernet has no mechanism for prioritizing one frame over another. Therefore, as network traffic increases, small frames carrying a voice payload may often have to wait in switch buffer queues behind large frames carrying data. Because voice has a delay tolerance of only 75 milliseconds, the lack of prioritization across a switched Ethernet network may degrade the quality of voice communications. Furthermore, this fundamental problem will not disappear with expanded bandwidth under Fast (or gigabit) Ethernet.

RSVP. Among the most promising solutions to Ethernet's lack of prioritization or guaranteed latency is to handle the problem at Layer 3 via the RSVP. RSVP, which is under development by the IETF and leading network product vendors, operates by reserving bandwidth and router/switch buffer space for certain high-priority IP packets such as those carrying voice traffic.

In effect, RSVP enables a packet switching network to mimic certain characteristics of a circuit-switching multiplexer network. However, RSVP is still only able to set up paths for high-priority traffic on a "best effort" basis; thus it cannot guarantee the delay characteristics of the network.

Furthermore, as an OSI level 3 protocol, RSVP support requires that routing functionality be added to switches.

RSVP's best-effort capability is sufficient for several delay-sensitive applications, such as non-realtime streaming video or audio. However, it is questionable whether RSVP can support real-time voice communications over the LAN to a level of quality and reliability that is acceptable in a business environment.

ATM-Based Backbone Solutions. An alternative solution for delivering voiceLAN over a common data infrastructure is ATM. ATM was designed specifically to support both voice and data traffic over a common infrastructure and provides multiple QoS levels.

ATM's CBR service guarantees a virtual circuit of fixed bandwidth for high-priority traffic such as voice. In addition, ATM uses a relatively small, fixed-length cell (53 bytes) rather than a variable-length frame to transport traffic, thereby limiting the maximum time any one cell must wait in a switch buffer queue. The use of ATM links/trunks between LAN switches neatly solves the problem of supporting both voice and data traffic for that portion of the network.

ATM to the desktop is more problematic, however. The most common standard for ATM LANs operates at 155 Mbps over Category 5 UTC cable or optical fiber. However, deploying 155 Mbps ATM to every desktop is currently too expensive for the vast majority of organizations (although it is beginning to be deployed as a LAN backbone technology).

In order to deploy a reliable voiceLAN solution cost-effectively using ATM, a lower-cost access technology must be deployed to the desktop. However, this access technology must also be able to extend the benefits of ATM's QoS from the ATM backbone all the way to the desktop.

An organization can choose from among several potential access solutions, including ATM25, Ethernet using IP/RSVP, or Ethernet/CIF.

ATM25 Access. ATM25, as its name implies, is a 25 Mbps version of ATM designed specifically for desktop connectivity to a 155 Mbps ATM backbone. ATM25 provides all of the QoS benefits of higher-speed ATM and can be used to build end-to-end ATM networks. ATM25 can also operate over category 3 UTC cable, whereas 155 Mbps ATM and Fast Ethernet require organizations to upgrade their UTP cabling to Category 5 UTP cable.

The downside of ATM25 is that it requires replacing all legacy network adapters where voiceLAN will be deployed. In addition, ATM25 adapters and switches are still considerably more expensive than 10BaseT Ethernet adapters and switches.

Yet, if deploying voiceLAN is a top priority for your company, installing a network featuring 155 Mbps ATM in the backbone and ATM25 to the desktop may be the most reliable and logical solution. Although ATM25 is a more expensive option than switched 10 Mbps Ethernet, the cost of an ATM25 connection (including adapter and switch port cost) fell substantially in 1996 to an average street price of $400 to $450 ($US).

Ethernet RSVP/IP Access. The most popular desktop connectivity option for data networking continues to be Ethernet, and the addition of desktop switching and Fast Ethernet technology only continues this trend. The challenge is combining IP over Ethernet network access links with ATM in the backbone in such a way that voiceLAN performance requirements can be satisfied.

One solution requires Ethernet-to-ATM desktop switches to include routing and RSVP support. The desktop end station sends voice in IP packets (further encapsulated inside Ethernet frames) to the switch, using RSVP to request bandwidth to be reserved for the voice conversation. The desktop switch then terminates the IP connection and converts the voice payload to ATM cells for transmission across the backbone (or the desktop switch may forward these IP datagrams across the ATM backbone without terminating the IP connection). The desktop switch is also responsible for mapping the RSVP bandwidth reservation request (at the IP level of the architecture) to an appropriate ATM QoS for the ATM connection.

Although this approach appears to provide the best of both worlds by combining an ATM backbone with the popularity of switched Ethernet to the desktop, it has not been demonstrated to be capable of guaranteeing the necessary quality of service needed for voice communications.

Ethernet CIF Access. CIF allows a desktop application to place voice traffic in ATM cells that are subsequently inserted into Ethernet frames by the network adapter driver for transport over the link from the adapter to switch. At the Ethernet switch, cells are extracted from the frames and sent across the ATM backbone.

CIF's primary advantage is that high-priority traffic, such as voice, can be given the necessary QoS from the desktop across the ATM network without having to actually install ATM end-to-end in the network. Furthermore, because voice does not utilize IP, the desktop Ethernet switch can be simpler and need not include more expensive and computer-intensive routing functionality. In this way, CIF may be a potential alternative to RSVP/IP for organizations migrating to switched Ethernet to the desktop but also interested in deploying voiceLAN.

CIF's ability to guarantee quality of service comes at a price. CIF requires installation of special software or NIC drivers in workstations to accomplish the framing of ATM cells. In addition, transporting traffic inside of ATM cells, which are in turn encapsulated by frames, entails significant overhead, reducing the usable bandwidth on an Ethernet segment to 6 Mbps to 7 Mbps.

CONSOLIDATION OF THE CABLING PLANT

A consolidated cabling plant that supports both voice and data is one of the primary benefits of implementing voiceLAN. With voiceLAN, the cabling plant supporting voice communications (e.g., cabling runs, patch panels, cross connects) becomes a redundant, backup infrastructure that can be removed when the voiceLAN network stabilizes.

No matter what technology is used for voice transport (i.e., ATM or IP), voiceLAN deployment requires optical fiber in the risers of buildings for backbone connectivity. Most large organizations have already installed fiber for their LAN backbone and therefore no upgrade to the cabling plant is necessary. Exhibits 1 and 2 depict a consolidation of cabling plants through voiceLAN technology for a typical organization.

MIGRATING THE DESKTOP

The deployment of voiceLAN also entails a migration of the desktop PC to become telephony-enabled. Exhibit 3 illustrates the voiceLAN-enabled desktop environment. This migration has two components: hardware and software.

Hardware Upgrades

In a pure voiceLAN architecture, all voice calls are received via a PC and its LAN adapter card rather than via a desktop telephone wired to a PBX or voice switch. There are two alternative human interfaces for people to interact with the PC to receive voice communications: the PC itself and the traditional desktop telephone.

By using the PC as the interface, voice traffic is processed by a PC sound card and the user employs a PC-attached microphone and headset. This solution is appropriate for users who are already using a microphone and headset to keep their hands free for typing (e.g., telemarketers, travel agents, help desk operators). Disadvantages of this setup include the fact that voice packets are processed by the PC's CPU, potentially hampering performance of other applications that might be running simultaneously. In addition, if the PC locks up, the user's conversation may be interrupted.

For most users the desktop telephone is still appropriate as their voice communications interface. However, in a voiceLAN solution, this phone set must be able to connect directly to the PC so that voice traffic can be received directly from the network adapter card without having to pass

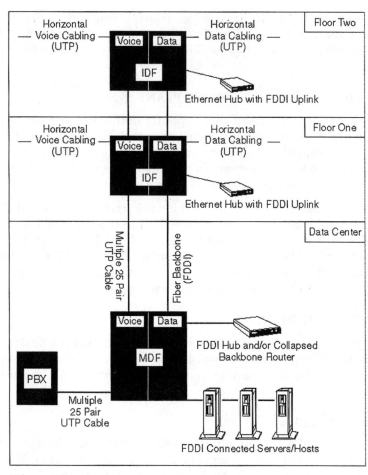

Key:
FDDI fiber distributed data interface
IDF   intermediate distribution frame
MDF   main distribution frame
PBX   private branch exchange
UTP   unshielded twisted pair

Exhibit 1. Legacy Voice and Data Cabling Infrastructures.

through the CPU. Today this can be accomplished through a third-party plug-in card.

Universal Serial Bus. A more elegant solution for accomplishing a direct connection is the USB interface, originally developed by Intel. Within the past year, the motherboards of most new PCs included USB interfaces as standard features.

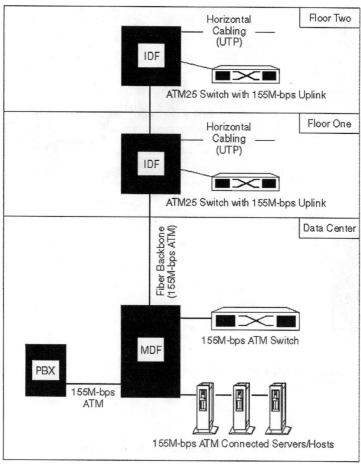

Key:
ATM asynchronous transfer mode
IDF intermediate distribution frame
MDF main distribution frame
PBX private branch exchange
UTP unshielded twisted pair

Exhibit 2. Consolidated Cabling Infrastructure.

The USB supports 12 Mbps of throughput and allows USB-compatible telephone sets to connect directly to the PC without the need for an additional plug-in card. This alternative greatly reduces the cost of deploying voiceLAN. Several vendors have released or will soon release telephones conforming to the USB standard.

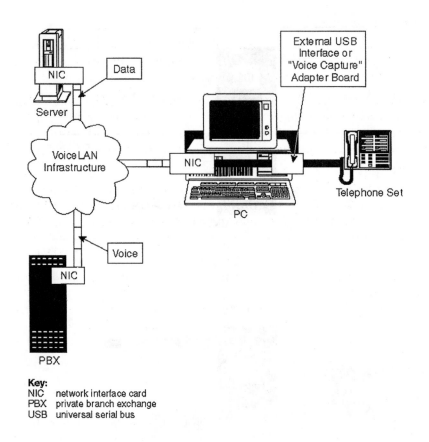

Exhibit 3. The VoiceLAN-enabled Desktop.

Firewire Bus. An alternative standard called Firewire — originally developed by Apple Corp., but currently being promoted by Sony and other consumer electronics companies — is also being introduced in new products.

The Firewire bus runs at speeds of up to 400 Mbps, which makes it appropriate for video traffic as well as voice. This high level of performance also may make Firewire too expensive for ubiquitous deployment, particularly if voiceLAN, not video, is the driving application. PC vendors may also be slower to develop Firewire-compatible telephones because of the Macintosh's declining share of the business market. Therefore, deploying USB-compatible phones is currently the most prudent choice for voiceLAN migration at the desktop.

Software Upgrades

To take maximum advantage of voiceLAN technology, PC-resident applications need to communicate with the PBX and PC-attached desktop phone sets. For this, a standardized software interface is required.

Most PBXs today support several such software APIs, though many of these interfaces provide translation of commands between the PBX and mainframe hosts for use in CTI applications such as call center applications. For Windows applications, most PBXs support Microsoft's TAPI. TAPI is available for Windows 95.

Microsoft Corp. is introducing a newer API, combining its Windows data transmission API (Winsock) with its voice communications API (TAPI). This consolidated API, known as Winsock 2, makes it even easier for developers to write integrated voice and data communications applications.

Clearly, the migration to a voiceLAN architecture is made much easier for organizations planning a substantial (Wintel) PC procurement in the next six months. These PCs are considered "voiceLAN ready" because they include both USB motherboards and systems software supporting TAPI/Winsock 2 APIs. Legacy PCs would need to have TAPI/Winsock 2 software and a third-party adapter board (for handset connectivity) installed.

MIGRATING THE PBX

Legacy Telephony

Today's PBX and telephony systems are analogous to the host and dumb terminal model of the mainframe era. PBXs are relatively inflexible, proprietary, and expensive to maintain and upgrade in the same way mainframes are. Phone sets are still the most ubiquitous desktop instrument for telephony communications, but the PC offers the most intuitive interface to advanced features. Moving from the traditional PBX model to a server-based telephony model represents the final stage in the migration to a fully integrated voice and data network.

Linking Distributed PBX Components

For organizations with large campus environments, an intermediate step between the legacy PBX and server-based telephony may be an architecture featuring multiple PBX components distributed throughout the campus.

This type of architecture has traditionally required a dedicated fiber backbone to connect multiple units. Under a voiceLAN solution, these units, outfitted with network adapter cards, can be connected over a LAN backbone infrastructure. This infrastructure is already in place in most larger campus network environments. In this case, the horizontal connection between the PBXs and the telephone sets at the desktop can continue to use the traditional voice network infrastructure.

There are two advantages to this architecture:

1. Distributed PBXs scale more cost-effectively than a single, large PBX.
2. The necessity for installing and maintaining dual backbones, one for voice and one for data, is eliminated.

Because this architecture does not implement voiceLAN to the desktop, it represents only a partial step toward a server-based telephony architecture. However, it also does not necessitate replacing old PCs with new ones outfitted with USB interfaces.

Server-Based Telephony

A server-based telephony architecture allows for the traditional functions of the PBX to be broken down into its components and distributed on the voiceLAN network. The switching function of the PBX can be handled by the frame or cell switches of the data network, whereas the call control function can be moved to a server. Specific telephony applications can also be moved to distributed application servers and integrated with other networked data applications.

Initial Implementation Tips. Implementing the ultimate voiceLAN architecture (depicted in Exhibit 4) cannot be accomplished through a wholesale changeover, except perhaps when an organization moves to a new building. Rather, this new architecture is typically deployed alongside the legacy PBX/dedicated voice network in the same way that organizations have deployed distributed servers running alongside centralized mainframes.

Server-based telephony should be implemented initially in specific workgroup environments. The best candidates are those workgroups that can best leverage server-based telephony applications that are available today.

Where a voiceLAN model is implemented, the user's port on the legacy PBX should be left unchanged until the voiceLAN deployment has stabilized and has been thoroughly tested. This is recommended because it provides, during the migration, redundancy and a backup system that can deliver phone service to the user.

The first phase of server-based telephony applications installed at the desktop is relatively basic. This configuration is similar to desktop PCs running terminal (i.e., phone handset) emulation and communicating with a

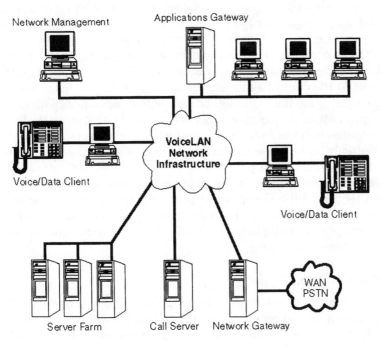

Key:
PSTN public switched telephone network
WAN   wide area network

Exhibit 4. VoiceLAN Architecture.

LAN-attached mainframe (i.e., the PBX). While the integration with networked data applications is limited compared to a full-scale, server-based telephony architecture, it does give users an intuitive GUI interface for voice communications and allows the users a certain level of integration with their desktop applications.

Desktop Telephony Applications. Following are some examples of desktop telephony applications that should be considered for implementation in this initial phase. In these examples, the applications are enhanced by voiceLAN in that they are melded with real-time voice communications:

- **GUI phone.** At its basic level, this application running on the desktop provides a phone handset interface on the PC. The GUI phone prompts users to take more advantage of advanced call features that they are reluctant to utilize today simply because of the nonintuitive interface of existing phone handsets.

621

- **Integration with PIM software.** Integrating the GUI phone with PIM software provides a seamless link between the user's PIM application (e.g., an advanced electronic Rolodex) and the user's actual communications interface (e.g., the GUI phone). This application offers functionality similar to call center applications to general users right at their desktops.
- **GUI voice mail.** Voice mail can easily benefit from a graphic representation. At the click of a mouse, users scroll through a list of voice mail messages — saving, deleting, or forwarding messages. With this type of application, voice messages are treated as objects that can be manipulated in the same way data files are. For users, this method is potentially far more user-friendly and time-efficient than using the keypad of a phone handset.
- **Integrated messaging.** When voice mail is decoupled from the PBX architecture, full integration with other types of messaging applications (i.e., e-mail) can more easily take place. VoiceLAN simplifies the process of combining message media and potentially reduces the cost of integrated messaging.

MIGRATING USERS

As the voiceLAN network is tested for its reliability as a dedicated voice network, the organization can begin to migrate the general population of users. Individual users or entire workgroups can be moved on a line-by-line basis by installing a USB PC and USB handset at the desktop, eventually eliminating the legacy phone set connected via the dedicated voice network. The order in which users/workgroups are moved depends on each user/workgroup's ability and willingness to take advantage of integrated voice/data applications.

While the general population of users is being migrated, the organization should also begin to deploy more advanced applications in the original test-bed workgroups. These applications can be tightly integrated with networked data applications (as opposed to desktop applications). The client/server applications that can be deployed in this final stage include:

- **Collaborative applications.** A server-based telephony architecture facilitates the integration of voice communications to collaborative software that allows multiple people to work on the same document while communicating.
- **Voice/database applications.** At present, computer telephony integration permits a certain level of integration between PBXs and databases; however, deploying such applications is expensive and generally reserved for telemarketing or customer service applications. A server-based telephony architecture allows high-end CTI functionality to be deployed on a much wider scale and to be made accessible to the general user population.

CONSOLIDATING THE VOICE AND DATA ORGANIZATIONS

One of the biggest advantages of deploying voiceLAN is the integration of voice and data network support teams and the eventual reduction in support costs. Many organizations have already begun consolidating their support organizations for voice and data without deployment of a voiceLAN architecture. Migrating to voiceLAN and to a server-based telephony architecture forces organizational consolidation among personnel from the voice and data environments.

Infrastructure Maintenance and Support Staff

The first operational element that needs to be integrated is the maintenance and support of the network infrastructure. In many organizations, these teams function separately. Initially, the voice team continues to maintain the legacy voice infrastructure, but that task should gradually disappear as users/workgroups move to the voiceLAN infrastructure.

The lighter burden for infrastructural maintenance allows personnel previously dedicated to supporting voice systems to be placed into applications development teams with members from both the data and voice environments. This blending of organizations mitigates some of the potential conflicts between groups of people from the voice and data environments. The consolidation of staff from the voice and data environments is also necessary to develop applications that tightly integrate voice and data. Furthermore, it may also reduce worries about job security on the part of voice-only staff, who may fear they have become expendable. Above all, a consolidated organization that supports all forms of network communications in the enterprise is better able to deliver increasingly sophisticated network services and applications to users.

RECOMMENDED COURSE OF ACTION

Achieving the end goal of voiceLAN implementation requires a series of logical steps. Individual organizations may start the migration at different points depending on their installed base of equipment, economic issues, or other decisions made to meet customer service demands and strategic business goals. The course of implementation may take three to five years. During that time, many technology hurdles will be overcome with standards development. Other issues, such as bandwidth congestion and the need for cost-efficiencies, are causing organizations to take a close look at convergent technologies that can solve problems today.

Various compelling events may precipitate these voiceLAN migration steps. Examples of such events, often designed to simplify management, satisfy growth, or save money, may include:

- Maintenance contract renewal
- Growth of new locations or branch offices
- Voice or data system upgrades
- Hiring of new personnel with new skills
- Reorganization (e.g., downsizing or substantial moves and changes)
- New bandwidth requirements (backbone and/or selected user work groups)
- Optimizing wide-area access
- Delivery of training (i.e., video) to the desktop
- Improvements in communications via voice-annotated text or other media

Exhibit 5 summarizes, in table format, the key decision points in the migration to a voiceLAN network. The table is a broad road map for organizations that wish to begin factoring voiceLAN into their network architecture planning today. Decisions about information technology or services investments and their implications, are grouped in four areas — IT strategy, enterprise requirements, workgroup requirements, and desktop applications.

VoiceLAN in the backbone is the first logical step that can be implemented now to satisfy immediate business goals — notably, cost-efficiency and network management — and lay the framework for a converged network in the future. Implementing voiceLAN in the workgroup and at the desktop are steps that will be taken in the medium- to longer-term.

When selecting a vendor to work with as a business partner in the development of a voiceLAN implementation, corporate network managers should evaluate the vendors':

- Published plans for voiceLAN implementation
- Actual delivery of products included in these plans
- Inclusion of voice as an integral component of an overall strategy rather than as a future possibility
- Commitment to emerging voice-enabling standards

Voice system vendors — or those vendors providing the call servers, telephony sets, and voice software components — must meet additional criteria, including:

- Migration to open, standards-based products
- Track record in investment potential
- Demonstrated experience in CTI
- Partnerships with IT leaders for "best in class" solutions
- Defined migration path to ATM (e.g., describing which telephony products can be leveraged and used in the new infrastructure and which products are no longer needed)

Decision Points / Migration Steps	Typical Situation	Recommendation	Impact
Strategy	• Voice not a part of IT strategy • Separate budgets • Separate planning • Separate organizations	• Ensure voice and voiceLAN are embedded in IT strategy • Voice must be considered integral component of overall plan	• As compelling events occur and decisions are made, organization continually moves closer to voiceLAN goal
Enterprise	• More bandwidth required for workgroup or user applications • Corporate pressure to reduce costs and provide productivity improvements • Cost savings or simplicity (elimination of duplicate infrastructures) sought	• Evaluate opportunity to converge voice/data on single backbone • Upgrade or replace existing backbone LAN • Converge voice/data functional organizations	• Bandwidth issue resolved • Simplified infrastructure • Organization positioned for voiceLAN
Workgroup	• Application-specific bandwidth requirements • Productivity improvements and competitive advantage sought • Remote offices demanding "head-office" type functionality and access	• Voice-enable applications • Evaluate server-based telephony solutions • Exploit opportunity to trial voiceLAN technology on workgroup basis • Extend voiceLAN-capable technology to workgroup via ATM or switched Ethernet access network	• Maximize productivity • Move another step closer to voiceLAN • Force a break from traditional voice model
Desktop	• Disparate voice and computing instruments and applications • Dual wiring infrastructure • Lost productivity	• Ensure strategy supports evolution to single wiring to the desktop • Opportunity to evaluate computer-attached telephones • Roll out in logical manner (starting with R&D organization, then general business groups, finally call centers)	• Final leg of voiceLAN convergence to the desktop • Achieve simplicity, cost savings through streamlined moves/changes • New applications deployment and enhanced productivity

Exhibit 5. Decision Points/Recommendations for VoiceLAN Migration.

Section IX
Electronic Messaging

Chapter 43
Introduction to Client/Server Messaging

Bill Kilcullen

The computer revolution is now reaching into homes across the world and making possible things that were dreams just a few, short years ago. If we look at human history and the progress curve, we see that as the advances in technology increased through the ages, the human experience improved at an equal rate. Going back to the days of the pony express, the railroad, and the telegraph, each advance in communications technology allowed further increases in the application of technology and the advancement of civilization. The advances in the past century have been remarkable but, in particular, the last 20 years has encompassed the most dramatic events in modern history.

The computer revolution has been the driving force behind providing us an unparalleled view of the world.

We have seen images of the moon and other planets in our solar system. The computer-aided warfare of the Desert Storm campaign gave us a view of the modern battlefield never before imagined. As history unfolds, we are on the scenes live and, in some cases, part of the action. The greatest single contributor to this communication explosion is the ability of electronic messaging to span the globe and deliver information 24 hours a day, 7 days a week.

WHY ELECTRONIC MESSAGING?

In today's business climate, electronic messaging plays an ever-growing part in the expansion of commerce around the globe. It has grown from a simple utility program into a complete system with a full set of resources to manage and maintain inter- and intra-company communications. Businesses view their electronic messaging system as any other strategic asset, to be used to gain a competitive advantage, and are spending large amounts of capital to build and maintain these systems.

Electronic messaging brings anytime and anywhere communications capabilities to business that transcends the time zone, the network boundary, and language barriers. By virtue of its store-and-forward nature, electronic messages can flow during weekends and holidays and carry important data day or night. While we are sleeping, messages are still winding across the network, working to provide us with timely information when we arrive at work and turn on the computer. Messages can cross organizational boundaries as well, shortening the link between the business and the customer.

WHAT IS ELECTRONIC MESSAGING?

Electronic messaging today consists of a multitude of information that can be required to conduct business. Messaging systems carry more than just simple e-mail messages that communicate a greeting or thought. They carry mission-critical data in the form of structured and unstructured data types and forms. An electronic message must support not only text but also multimedia such as voice and video, spreadsheets, compound documents, presentations, and other formats.

The source of the electronic message varies according to the type of applications being used. Where once it was assumed that e-mail would come from one or two predefined sources, a system today can ill afford to discriminate. For example, the concept of the universal inbox is inherent to electronic messaging systems in use today. This means that a single inbox can support information from such diverse sources as proprietary e-mail format, fax, voice, video feeds, Internet news feeds, and structured data from a database. All this information must be viewable in a standard way to the user, and the system gives the user the capability to arrange and manage the storage and retrieval of the information.

HISTORY OF ELECTRONIC MESSAGING

Electronic messaging began with the advent of the telegraph, which has all the elements of today's systems, although in very rudimentary form. The idea was to move information from point a to point b via electric impulses carried on a wire. These impulses were coded as either long or short, and the alphabet was translated by combining a series of longs and shorts. For example, one short and one long represent the letter A.

As technology advanced, this concept was expanded to include transmitting audio signals and video signals across the wire and via radio waves. The idea remained the same: to cross great distances in a short amount of time with a maximum of information. Soon the telegraph gave way to a five-level encoding method for sending telex messages that were decoded by teletype machines. Western Union telex is probably the first form of e-mail as we know it today. With telex, a message could be sent at anytime to anyone, anywhere in the world. With the divestiture of AT&T in the 1980s, the use of phone lines to carry data began to expand rapidly. New services appeared almost daily, and official electronic mail was born.

By the late 1980s and early 1990s the desktop computer began to make inroads into businesses, and with them came the first networks and file servers. Sneaker net gave way to these new file and print servers and users were able to share information between single PCs. The early e-mail systems were based upon this technology of file sharing. The first e-mail applications essentially put a fancy interface around the file-copy-and-store methodology of early local area network (LAN) servers. Hence, the term, shared file e-mail systems.

EVOLUTION OF ELECTRONIC MESSAGING

The limitations of the shared file e-mail systems became apparent as companies put more and more users on the systems and added line of business and mission-critical applications to them. Security, scalability, and reliability are required to support tens of thousands of users and each of these areas is a weakness in a shared file mail system where the client software does the lion's share of the work with the server really being a passive repository for files. These mail systems do have advantages in terms of ease of use and installation. They provide the user with most, if not all, of the capabilities required to boost productivity and augment communications. The administration and maintenance of these systems is lacking the tools required to keep up with a busy system.

As the PC LAN has evolved to include iron-clad security, client/server application processing and distributed computing has become the norm in organizations, so has the electronic messaging system evolved to take advantage of the newest technology. In a client/server system, the client software can focus upon providing the best possible user interface and request services from the server only when required. This enhances security, decreases the load on the network, and provides the user with a rich set of functionality tailored to the desktop. Support for remote connectivity, offline storage and access to information, and added capability such as calendaring and scheduling are a natural part of the desktop client.

The server now provides a complete set of messaging and management functions that allows for integrated account creation, security permissions, and administration of messaging attributes from a central console. The server provides storage capabilities, message handling and tracking, complex routing, multiprotocol support, and a complete range of services to the messaging clients. The server in this client/server model is an active component or set of components that acts as an integral part of the messaging system and shields the client software from the programming and networking complexities associated with providing a company-wide electronic messaging system.

Unhindered by the monolithic architecture common to shared file systems, the client/server model for messaging systems allows emerging technologies, such as Internet protocols, to be rapidly added to the system without requiring modifications to all parts of the system. This same architecture allows for developers to extend the system rapidly and with common programming interfaces and tools. Server-side scripting languages and visual development tools such as JavaScript and Microsoft Visual Basic simplify the process of building applications that take advantage of built-in server functionality for routing and replication.

THE ANATOMY OF A MESSAGING SYSTEM

A client/server electronic messaging system consists of the following functional components at a minimum:

- User interface
- Message store
- Message transfer agent
- Access unit or gateway
- Address books
- Directories

User Interface (UI)

The user interface (often referred to as the user agent) is the software that is installed on the desktop computer and is used to connect the user of the system to the system itself. In the past, this was most often a proprietary software program unique to each messaging system such as Microsoft Mail for PC networks or IBM/Lotus cc:Mail for Windows. In today's advanced systems, with standard interfaces such as Microsoft's Messaging Application Programming Interface (MAPI), it is common for a multiplicity of software to be able to interact with different servers from other vendors.

Most systems support connectivity to the server for purposes of electronic messaging from other clients, including web browsers such as Internet Explorer and Netscape Navigator. In general, this user interface provides the user with experience when interacting with the messaging system. It will display the messages, provide for addressing and message creation and editing messages, and often includes advanced functions such as forms creation and rules. The user interface is essentially the inbox from the end-user perspective.

Message Store (MS)

This is what is commonly referred to as the "Post Office." The message store is an active process that provides for the organization of data that is part of the messaging system. Long gone are the days when this data was only text e-mail messages. The message store of today's systems must support many different data types and, unlike a standard database, this data in the messaging world is generally unstructured. In order to support the universal inbox paradigm, the message store must be able to file, store, and retrieve such diverse data types as word processing documents, e-mail messages, graphics presentations, compound documents, video, and audio. It must accept data from a multitude of sources and provide for an ever-increasing storage capability.

The message store is self-maintaining, keeping and reporting statistics on usage and size while being able to recover from small and large failures alike in a timely fashion. The message store also must be able to replicate itself to different servers for maximum utilization of network bandwidth. In addition, today's electronic messaging system relies on the message store as a way to build forms and applications for distribution among all the system users.

Message Transfer Agent (MTA)

The heart of any messaging system is the process that is responsible for transferring messages across a wide range of messaging protocols. The MTA is a complex process that must be able to store and then forward messages using a number of different networking protocols as well. The MTA is critical to the reliability and scalability of the entire system since it must process all the messages that flow through the system.

The MTA establishes and manages connections with remote systems, dynamically updates routing information, takes ownership of messages while they are in transit, and is the key component in providing message tracking and tracing capabilities. The MTA is usually called upon to expand distribution lists as it is delivering mail messages, and also processes system control type messages that pass between servers using a messaging infrastructure in absence of network bandwidth.

Access Unit or Gateway

The standards bodies recognize the term *access unit* (AU), but most of the LAN world uses the term *gateway*. A gateway is a key component in a messaging system for a number of reasons. One reason is that seldom are two systems entirely alike in their support for a native protocol for messaging. In order to communicate between these systems, a gateway is required. What does a gateway do? It converts files and formats from one system to the other, and also handles the address mapping that is required. For example, in an X.400-based messaging system, an address may look like this:

[C = US;A = ATTMAIL;P = SATELLITE;PN = BILL KILCULLEN]

and an SMTP mail address may be represented as: [billki@TheRaceNet.com]. Both are valid within their native systems, but crossing from one to the other will require that each address be mapped into the format of the other.

In addition to the addressing, the file format and attachment handling capability of each system is different, and so the gateway must act to convert these as well. As servers become more powerful and more of the gateway functionality is built into systems like Microsoft Exchange, this handling of diverse systems becomes easier, faster, and more reliable. Systems such as Lotus Domino Server and Microsoft Exchange server offer a number of built-in or add-on components that run with the core services and provide gateway functionality.

Address Books

Address books are generally associated with user interface software since that is where they are viewed and often created and stored. There are a number of different address books in a messaging system. These are generally divided into a server-based address book often called a global address book (GAL), and a desktop version often called a private address book (PAB). Their names are also descriptions of their functions.

The GAL is available to all users of the system and is managed and maintained by the server, and specific administration tools and programs are focused on the GAL. It is usually distributed across multiple servers, depending upon the system being used, and can be copied/replicated to the local workstation for operation offline from the server. The GAL is used to ensure that the latest copy of addresses is available across the entire mail system.

The PAB is a private copy of addresses and, while it may include addresses that are globally available, usually contains private addresses that are not shared among other users except in special cases. The PAB is usually only updated when a user is notified of a change to an address that is stored there and not by any global functionality that is applied to the GAL.

Directories

Not to be confused with an address book, a directory is a requirement for the operation of a large electronic messaging system. An address book is a subset of the information that is contained in a directory in most client/server messaging systems in use today. The directory contains all the attributes used by the system for determining a multitude of things about the system and how it is used. The directory contains the user access levels, the routing information, extended attributes about a user (such as names, addresses, telephone numbers, department codes, ID numbers), and a host of other items not required for merely messaging.

A directory also contains the system-level objects such as the location of servers and the organization of the messaging system into domains or sites, and provides a mechanism for not only determining the location of a user but also the location of a process or connection. In Microsoft Exchange, for example, the directory is the way that the administration of the entire system can be managed from a single console anywhere in the network.

The directory service provides maintenance and management of the directory objects and handles updates and replication across the entire system. Portions of the directory can be replicated to other systems. A standards-based directory eases the difficulty when integrating with other directory systems. As in the gateway example above, the directories for most systems are not alike and, thus, a common denominator must be used when putting together different systems. The directory should have tools to export its contents and import contents from other sources.

THE NETWORK AND ELECTRONIC MESSAGING

No discussion of messaging fundamentals is complete without talking about the underlying network. We have already discussed how messaging systems have evolved from the shared file architecture to the client/server architecture. It is time to look at the network and its impact on the design and operation of a messaging system.

Right from the beginning, the network that transported the data for a telex message determined a great deal about the message itself. Due to the limitations of these early networks, only a restricted character set could be used to transmit information. As the capability of the network architecture grew, so did its ability to support more data at greater speeds. As the network bandwidth and protocols evolved into the LAN, computers could transfer more diverse data types via these expanded protocols. Suddenly, e-mail became a tool for transfer of files that included more than just message text.

ELECTRONIC MESSAGING

Audio files, video, graphics, and compound documents are common attachments to electronic messages. These require a tremendous amount of bandwidth and standardized protocols for transfer and recognition. The universal model for understanding how the network is closely related to the capabilities of the electronic messaging system is the seven-layer OSI model for interconnecting computers. Essentially, this model separated all the tasks required for two or more computer applications to communicate and divided these tasks into layers that could be more easily understood. Once understood, these layers also became the specification for building software that could be integrated into other systems.

OSI AND MESSAGING

The seven layers in the model are, from topmost to bottommost:

- Application
- Presentation
- Session
- Transport
- Network
- Data link (media access)
- Physical

The premise here is that for two systems to communicate across a network, each end system must be running the same stack. (**Note:** This may be an oversimplification, but for the purposes of this chapter it will suffice.) Each layer in the stack is defined to provide a set of services to the layer above it, so the application layer requests a service from the presentation layer which responds to the application layer. It is also defined that each layer will communicate with its corresponding layer on the end system. In this way, the messaging application on System a can prepare and transfer a message to the messaging application on System b without having to write code for each layer of service.

For messaging systems, the most important layers are the application layer, which provides service to the user interface; the transport/network layers, which provide the rules and protocols for connection/transfer of content; and the physical layer, which determines that a connection can exist. In practical terms, this means that in order for System a to send e-mail to System b, the user interface must be the same or converted, the transport and network must be the same or converted, and the physical connection must exist. This is easier said than done.

In a pure OSI world, each system would be running all seven layers and there would be no intermediate systems to contend with. However, not all systems are created equal and an X.400 mail system is probably the only example of a service that uses the OSI model from top to bottom. In this standards-based world, the ITU-TS, formerly CCITT, publish on a four-year cycle with committees meeting constantly to create, refine, and publish their recommendations for adoption. For example, X.400 Message Handling System was first published in 1984 and updated in 1988 and 1992. X.500 Directory System is another example of a standard introduced in 1988 and updated in 1992, although the trend is away from a four-year cycle which is deemed too long to be practical in today's fast-moving environment.

THE INTERNET AND MESSAGING

In contrast to X.400, Internet messaging systems use only four layers to accomplish the same functionality. These systems rely on TCP/IP to support all of the transport and network functions with applications directly interfaced to this stack through a variety of defined interfaces. The two lower layers are exactly the same as OSI layers one and two. Most TCP/IP protocol stack software contains utilities for file transfer (FTP), mail (SMTP), domain name service (DNS), and other applications that are completely compatible with that particular stack. This brings us to a point of difference between the OSI standards process and the Internet request for comment (RFC) mechanism.

Before any X.400 software was ever developed, the standard itself was put through a rigorous period of evaluation against compliance rules. Next came a period of software testing in CCITT certification labs, and then software being run through interoperability testing before being given final certification. This helped to ensure some level of interoperability. The Internet specifications are published and sample code is often included for evaluation and comment and, since the code is readily available in most cases, implementations begin almost immediately. The World Wide Web (W3) steering committee watches over this process as well as the Internet Task Force; however, it is usually some period of time before the interoperability of RFCs are verified.

The Internet has evolved from its beginnings as a network of government and academic institutions exchanging information to a worldwide web of systems that tie together industry, business, government, and education. The original intent of the Internet was a network dedicated to creating and distributing information as freely and as unencumbered as possible. Initially funded by government and public funding, the Internet is currently undergoing a major transformation as commercialization is driving the need to rebuild the infrastructure that provides the network.

Where it was once a given understanding that X.400 would be the interconnection for messaging between companies, the Internet has now assumed that mantle and is proving to be a common denominator for messaging that serves a best-effort delivery system. This is another departure from the X.400 MHS, where the system provides a service level that guarantees a certain level of quality for a given level of cost. It is assumed that as the Internet grows in acceptance and more and more service providers from the X.400 world cross over, the Internet will include a guaranteed delivery mechanism.

ELECTRONIC MESSAGING ARCHITECTURES

There are a number of architectures that led to the client/server model in use today. Each of the major computer system architectures has its own unique approach to providing basic electronic messaging services. We now examine a few of the more popular architectures and how they came about, as well as their strengths and weaknesses.

The Local Area Network and Messaging

The LAN provided a medium for easily exchanging data between PCs. It was natural for the developers of early e-mail systems to leverage this existing architecture for the delivery of mail. These early LAN systems such as Novell Netware and Microsoft LAN Manager provided services to clients for sharing files and printers, and transporting files from one locale to another.

As previously mentioned, Microsoft Mail for PC Networks and cc:Mail from IBM/Lotus capitalized on this network capability and developed applications that provided easy-to-use front ends for creating, storing, and sending these files using the underlying network transport. This allows client workstations to send mail messages to other users of the system and attach files such as desktop productivity applications like word processing documents, spreadsheets, and presentations.

This type of system is also known as the shared file system, since the operation relies upon the ability of the network operating system to share e-mail files. The store or Post Office is generally a passive file upon which client software must take action, using the memory and CPU of the workstation to act upon this data file. The server processor and memory are marginally impacted, even in large environments.

The strengths of these types of systems are that they are easy to install and set up, and they work well for small workgroups and enable rapid transport of information across the network. This is coupled with the fact that they take advantage of the underlying network and do not require extensive rework of the network. The weaknesses of this type of system are that it is difficult to manage and maintain, security is marginal, scalability is suspect, and the technology is outdated.

Mainframe-Based Systems

The mainframe mail system consists of a host computer system and workstations that are able to access the data on the mainframe. Multitudes of terminal users can share mail, schedule, and workflow information, as well as applications in a secure, easily managed system. The central host can communicate with other hosts but, most often, the users of the system have one host that acts as the provider of mail and other services. In this terminal-based model the messaging and file processing is handled by the central host computer.

This architecture simplifies providing access, storage, and security for the mail users, and provides a central processor for applications other than messaging such as calendar and scheduling, file, and printing services. The disadvantages of the mainframe system is that updating them is costly; making adds, changes, and deletes to the directory can be tedious and time consuming; and the cost of the resources is well above PC alternatives. Building custom applications and then keeping them updated is also problematic in these systems and can hinder change in business processes required to maintain a competitive edge due to long lead times.

Typically, a host system is outperformed on a total cost of ownership analysis since the hardware and software maintenance costs can be quite steep in this type of system when compared to a PC solution. Another disadvantage is the lack of tools for rapid application development and deployment in the mainframe world, again compared to the PC model.

Client/Server-Based Systems

A client/server mail system divides the processing between the client machine and the server or servers in the system. Typically, the data store is a set of active processes that maintain, organize, transfer, and back up information. This type of system usually includes a number of modular components that work together to create a synergistic system for electronic messaging.

In addition, these types of modular systems are easily expanded in order to add the latest and greatest technology that comes along. A good example of this modularity is Microsoft Exchange server. Each of the major elements of a mail system that we mention in this chapter is included as a separate set of processing within Exchange; they work together to create a better whole. One of the amazing paradigm shifts in modern business was Microsoft's amazing turnaround to embrace the Internet standards and technology when it became apparent that doing so would provide a competitive advantage.

Client/server electronic messaging systems offer the ability to rapidly install and deploy the system across the enterprise while easing the training and management burden. Most of these systems include a directory service that aids in the rapid deployment of the system itself, along with easing the tasks of management and ongoing maintenance. These systems do have certain disadvantages in areas of complexity of migration and connectivity operations, but generally fare well in a total cost of ownership (TCO) comparison.

Web-Based Messaging Systems

Web-based messaging systems are rapidly evolving from the file-based systems. The rapid development and deployment of servers that support Internet protocols and provide services to the user agents for message storage and transfer is becoming the norm. This is causing most of the existing client/server vendors to provide these web-based services along with their proprietary or X.400-based systems. For instance, Microsoft, IBM/Lotus, and Netscape all support a broad range of web services that ship with their server software.

It is important to note that these web systems are still in evolutionary phase and need to be combined with existing technology and components to provide a complete system. Currently, they are mandatory additions to the internal network for providing ease of access from the growing population of Internet browsers like MS Internet Explorer and Netscape Navigator, to mention two of the more popular. These protocols and the tools to use them, along with a messaging system, provide a relatively easy way to publish select information to a much wider audience.

Gateways

We mentioned the term *gateway* earlier in this chapter, and in this section we discuss them in some more detail. As previously defined, a gateway is a process that translates the format and the data between two or more systems. In the case of messaging systems, this really means either to/from a proprietary format such as Microsoft Mail for PC Networks to IBM/Lotus cc:Mail, or to/from a standards-based system such as X.400 to SMTP. In many cases, gateways also serve to map addresses and translate formats between a proprietary system and a standards-based one.

The other general characteristic regarding gateways is the complexity of going beyond a one-to-one relationship. In the case of a company that only has one messaging system that needs to be interfaced to a second messaging system of different format and protocol, this establishes a one-to-one relationship, which is fairly simple to understand, set up, and maintain. With companies that have multiple types of systems that must be interfaced, the complexity of this scenario is dramatically increased. With two systems, one has one pair of gateways; with three systems, one will have three pairs of gateways to contend with.

There are vendors that provide a multiprotocol messaging gateway system designed to meet the need for supporting connection with a number of different messaging systems. Typically, these systems work by taking in any of the standard messaging formats as well as the most popular proprietary ones, converting their elements into a single data structure, and storing the results. This common data can then be reformatted to meet the requirements of any of the other supported systems, addresses mapped, and the entire messages with attachments forwarded to the receiving systems.

Some sample systems are listed below:

- Examples of proprietary formats
  — Microsoft Mail
  — cc:Mail
  — Lotus Notes
  — PROFS
  — All in One
  — Others
- Examples of messaging standards
  — X.400
  — SMTP/MIME
  — POP3
  — IMAP4

SECURITY

Security in a messaging system consists of a number of different requirements. There is the user identification, access and authentication to the network, and the messaging system itself. There is the file system security that is provided by the network operating system, and then there is the encryption and message authenticity (digital signatures) within the messaging system to consider.

A well-constructed client/server messaging system integrates the network access control with the messaging system access control so that one id and password is all that is required to access the network and gain access to the services available. These systems also tie file system security to this same id in the form of granting privileges to system resources predicated upon the actual id that is being authenticated by the system.

Within the messaging system, the messages themselves can be encrypted and digitally signed so that if a message is intercepted while being transferred, it cannot be read or changed without detection. When a message is encrypted, the originator of the message typically applies the encryption using a private key, which can then only be decoded by the recipient with the originator's public key. There are, of course, other types of encryption, but this public/private key method is most common in messaging systems.

In addition to encryption, a message can be signed using this same key pair and the content of the message itself to come up with a signature. If the message is somehow changed during transmission, the signature will not match when decoded by the recipient, because the message is no longer the original version. These keys can be managed within the messaging system or by interfacing the system with a completely separate security system.

APPLICATIONS

Client/server electronic messaging systems serve as ideal platforms for developing applications that span the entire organization. In many cases, the only way to distribute data from one end of the organization to the other is to use the messaging infrastructure to do so. This trend started because the file-based systems for messaging discussed earlier in this chapter were such systems that went anywhere the underlying network went and, in some cases, transcended the network with connection capability through public networks.

The newer client/server electronic messaging systems have been designed from the ground up to incorporate the tools and services necessary to build and support a number of group computing applications. For example, many applications are built directly into the system, such as calendaring/scheduling, bulletin boards, discussion groups, and public forums and surveys. Messaging-aware applications, such as word processors that use the messaging system directory to create a mailing list, are being included with the server systems. Also included are the applications programming interfaces (APIs) that allow developers to rapidly build and deploy messaging-enabled applications that use the underlying messaging infrastructure to perform complicated routing and workflow decisions.

An entirely new wave of tools and interfaces for building and distributing web-based applications that can use the messaging system for directory or security and authentication are being included with the server suites, such as Microsoft's Backoffice. Visual development tools allow for the rapid design and distribution of data systems through the messaging system, and to the WWW for view by browsers across the Internet as well as by proprietary system clients. The web experience is growing strongly on a daily basis, and more and more of the infrastructure is created and updated to support the Internet protocols and provide the business class levels of service required.

THE FUTURE OF ELECTRONIC MESSAGING

The future in electronic messaging is held in submerging services into the lower levels of the operating system where they become less and less apparent to the end user, but more and more important to the overall system performance. Server suites are including more and more capability to link to the data farms built over the years and provide access to this data across the organization in a variety of useful ways.

In terms of the dedicated messaging systems, such as Microsoft Exchange servers, to survive in the Internet space, the services they provide are moving deeper and deeper into the operating system. This allows those services to take advantage of any shift in the supporting protocols for network, routing, and transport. There is also a growing trend to add middleware services to the messaging infrastructure and take advantage of its capabilities to replicate data and deliver messages across a variety of public and private networks.

The trend is also to build collaborative tools such as the management of tasks, documents, and contacts directly into the messaging system and expose the interfaces to them so that developers can extend those existing capabilities or build new applications that take advantage of what the infrastructure provides. This simplifies the application builder's task significantly since the complexities of message handling and routing are pre-handled by the server.

The future also holds much better news along the directory front. One of the common complaints in the electronic messaging area, even with the advent of client/server systems, is the lack of a common directory standard. That is changing with the addition of the Internet services such as the Lightweight Directory Access Protocol (LDAP) being added to the shipping messaging systems. With Windows NT 5.0 offering a stronger directory architecture, a set of directory access tools and interfaces, and a growing number of X.500 directory implementations, the future for integrating directories across systems is starting to look very possible in the near term.

Adding to this a greater level of support for X.509 certificates for security capabilities, with more systems recognizing multiple certificate authorities, means building a messaging system with greater capability to integrate with a security infrastructure is becoming easier to do. The convergence of security protocols for messaging such as PGP and S/MIME also make it easier for planners to begin building the next generation systems that will take advantage of these capabilities to make business-to-business messaging more efficient to deploy.

ELECTRONIC MESSAGING

Never before has there been as wide a range of protocols and formats being natively supported in the messaging world. All in all, it is an exciting time to be part of the messaging world as the Internet adds new and exciting capabilities to the new range of client/server messaging systems being developed and deployed in the world today.

Chapter 44
Messaging Gateways
Peter M. Beck

Gateways are a necessary evil in today's world of diverse electronic messaging systems and networks. They serve the important function of linking together users of different environments which, without a gateway, would not be able to exchange messages effectively.

This chapter explores the many facets of gateway technology. The topic is timely and vast, but also somewhat confusing as a result of a lack of standardization, unique jargon, and a moving-target quality.

ASSESSING THE MESSAGING ENVIRONMENT'S COMPLEXITY AND COSTS

At first glance, the concept of an electronic messaging gateway seems straightforward, particularly to the nontechnical observer. On closer examination, however, gateway issues can be quite complex, controversial, and even costly if mishandled.

The fact is that a very wide range of different messaging environments exist today inside and around the fringes of almost any large organization. These varieties of messaging can range from legacy mainframe systems to local area network (LAN)-based packages to extremely rich value-added networks (VANs) and the Internet. On the horizon in many organizations is new or increased use of groupware and a shift to client/server products for messaging. The protocols, addressing methods, data formats, and capabilities in each of these environments are very different.

In a perfect world, gateways would be unnecessary. Users would simply standardize on one messaging type and discontinue the use of everything else. Unfortunately, it is not quite that simple. An example helps illustrate the point (see Exhibit 1).

A large, multinational corporation uses several types of electronic messaging systems internally. The firm's U.S. headquarters is using IBM's Professional Office System (PROFS) product on a centralized mainframe. Alternatively, the corporation's engineering and production divisions recently deployed a large new network and began using Microsoft Mail. Because of an acquisition,

0-8493-9969-6/99/$0.00+$.50
© 1999 by CRC Press LLC

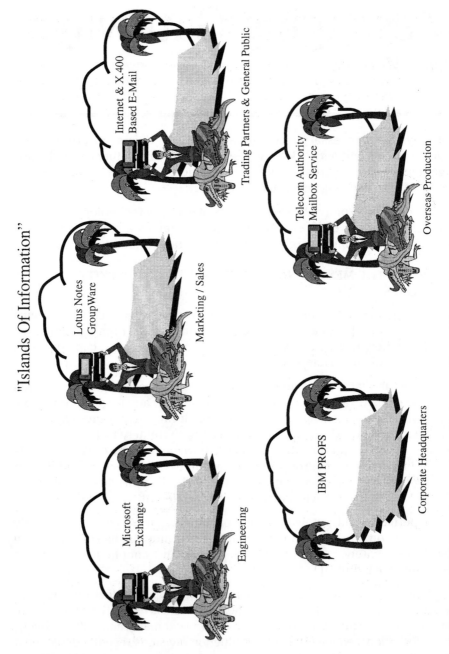

Exhibit 1.   Multinational Corporation with Many Different Messaging Environments.

many factories have been added overseas in a country where the local communications authority provides an e-mail service.

Each of the groups is fairly satisfied as long as they stay on their island of information. Users cannot easily exchange messages with users in other divisions, however, because the systems essentially speak different languages. To make matters more complicated, employees must exchange messages with external trading partners and the general public by way of several different types of public networks, including the Internet. Finally, senior management would like to see fax, groupware, and possibly electronic commerce considered in any long-term solution.

Although this scenario sounds like enough to perplex even the most savvy data communications experts, it is quite typical in today's fast-moving world. Several high-level questions come to mind immediately, including:

- How can gateway technology be used to link all of these messaging environments together?
- In what particular areas are careful analysis and planning especially important before starting a project?
- How much will this sort of connectivity cost to put in service, and how can these costs be recovered or justified?
- What level of expertise is required to put gateway technology to work successfully?
- What sorts of products, facilities or features, and services are available?
- What are some of the issues, pitfalls, and long-term hidden costs?

BASIC GATEWAY FUNCTIONS

Before embarking into the more detailed aspects of gateways, it is important to discuss functions in somewhat simple terms. In other words, what does a gateway system really do?

At the most basic level, a gateway must be able to act as a middle man, facilitating the exchange of messages between the two (or more) different environments it links together. As shown in Exhibit 2, each message received by the gateway from Environment A must be evaluated in terms of its sender, format, content, and intended destinations.

Next, the gateway must perform a translation. This essentially renders the message suitable for the destination, shown as Environment B. The degree to which the message remains intact as it traverses the gateway depends on many factors, most of which will be touched on later in this chapter.

Finally, the message must be sent by the gateway into Environment B for subsequent delivery to the intended recipients. During message handling, several additional functions are often performed by a gateway. These

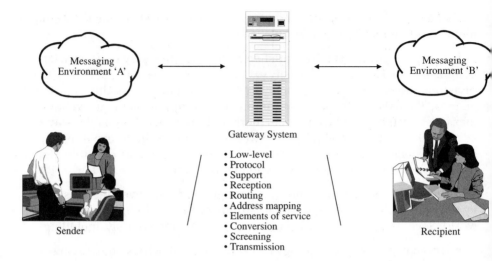

Exhibit 2. **Basic Gateway Functions Linking Messaging Type A to Type B.**

might include creating log entries for tracing purposes, archiving the message itself, and updating statistical-billing counts.

The process just described is, of course, oversimplified for the sake of illustration. Each electronic messaging environment has its own special characteristics that make it unique. Despite this, it is useful to break things down further into a set of generic functions that practically all gateway systems must provide to some degree. These functions include the following:

- Message reception processing
- Routing-address mapping
- Element of service handling
- Screening
- Message transmission processing

Message Reception Processing

As with any technical issue, it helps to divide things into steps. The first step to consider for a gateway is the initial transfer of a message into the gateway system for processing. This is referred to as *reception*.

Externally, message reception usually works as follows: First, the sender submits a message addressed to a recipient in another environment. One of the components of the recipient's address, typically the post office or domain name, results in the message being forwarded into the gateway system for handling.

The internal mechanisms actually required for reception might vary greatly depending on the situation at hand. It could range from relatively simple transfers of formatted ASCII text over a modem-telephone line connection to very complex communications protocol handshaking over a dedicated high-speed link.

When interfacing with a LAN-based messaging system, a gateway usually achieves *message exchange* by a combination of file server access and an applications programming interface (API). APIs are important for several reasons, which will be discussed later. In any case, as part of this step a gateway typically checks the message for errors, creates a log entry indicating the reception, and stores the message in preparation for the next step.

Routing and Address Mapping

Once a message has been successfully received, the next step is to determine where the message should be sent. This is referred to as *message routing*.

Routing can be accomplished in a variety of ways. Some low-cost gateway products do not really perform routing at all. They simply force all messages received from one environment into another environment serviced by the gateway. Other more flexible products use a combination of predefined routing rules or a directory to decide where to send a particular message.

The difference between routing and address mapping is subtle, and the two are often confused. Actually, they are two separate functions. Routing is the process of deciding where to send a message. Address mapping refers to the rendering of the recipient (and sender) addresses on transfer out of the gateway. Both are certainly among the most important functions a gateway provides.

In a simple example of address mapping in a gateway, to reach an external trading partner named John Smith (who works in the accounting department at a fictional company called ACME), a user of Lotus cc:Mail might send a message to the following address: JOHN SMITH at GATEWAY. When processing the message, the gateway system might need to render, or map, this address into the recipient's true Internet electronic mail address, which could be: SMITHJ@ACCOUNTING.ACME.COM.

Like message routing, address mapping functions can be accomplished in many different ways. These include the use of predefined rules, the use of a directory, or a combination of the two. When implemented correctly in a gateway product, the end results should always adhere to the following two basic rules: the sender should be able to easily address a message to a recipient in another environment using a familiar addressing method, and the recipient of a message should be able to easily identify and reply to the sender.

Element of Service Handling

The term *element of service* is electronic messaging jargon for a feature offered to users. For example, the sender's ability to designate a message for high-priority delivery is an element of service.

As might be expected, it is very important for a gateway to handle each element of service in a consistent, meaningful fashion when transferring a message from one environment into another. Sometimes this involves a rather straightforward conversion or mapping; such is usually the case when handling message priority.

Often, however, the element of service is trickier. For example, some modern messaging environments allow users to request return of content in case an error condition prevents delivery to the intended recipient. This amounts to something like requesting a package be returned by the postal service when the mailman cannot deliver it. Electronically performing a conversion of this element of service in a gateway can be fairly involved. To illustrate, the following are some of the steps a gateway might perform:

- Recognize the reception of a nondelivery type notification message containing returned content.
- Extract the returned content section from the notification.
- Perform a correlation to determine which recipient could not receive the message.
- Translate the often cryptic nondelivery reason code into a plain English text that the sender will hopefully understand (e.g., recipient's address incorrect).
- Render the returned content, recipient address, and the reason text into a notification message appropriate for the sender's environment.
- Transmit this notification back to the sender.

Element of service handling is where the bulk of all difficult message processing is performed in a gateway. It is therefore the one area where especially careful analysis and planning pay off, particularly when older legacy systems are involved.

Every important element of service offered in each environment linked by the gateway should be thought of in terms of how it will be handled. This is because there are often gaps or, even worse, subtle differences in the way elements of service work in one product or environment versus another. The return of content feature is a perfect example. Some products or environments support it wonderfully, but many do not.

Screening

What happens if a user in one environment unknowingly attempts to send a very long message by way of a gateway to a user in another environment that only supports very short messages? Ideally, the message should be gracefully discarded by the destination environment and the sender should be notified. At worst, the message might cause a serious problem in the destination network. In any case, gateways are usually required to screen messages for conditions like this and take corrective action. The action taken depends on the type of error condition. For example, when detecting an overlong message, a gateway might prevent transfer or perhaps perform a splitting operation.

Other conditions gateways usually check for to prevent problems include: invalid content or data, illegal file attachment, too many recipients, or a missing or invalid sender's address. How well a gateway performs this type of screening often dictates how successful an implementation will be over the course of time. A poorly designed gateway can cause problems if it allows "bad" messages to enter into an environment not expecting to have to deal with these sorts of error conditions.

Transmission Processing

The final step in handling any message is its transfer into the recipient's system or network, referred to as *message transmission processing*. Much like reception processing, the actual functions required can vary greatly. Most important is that the gateway adheres to the rules of the destination environment and provides for safe, reliable transfer of the message. On completion of this step, the gateway has fulfilled its main responsibility for the message.

GATEWAY COMPONENTS

Now that basic functions have been examined, it is appropriate to take a look at the main components that comprise a gateway system. Without focusing on a single product or scenario, this discussion must be left at a high level — but it is interesting nevertheless. The typical gateway system can be broken down into both hardware and software components. Hardware is more concrete, so it is an appropriate place to start.

Hardware Components

Generally, the minimum hardware needed for a gateway is a computer, generous amounts of main memory, and some sort of mass storage device (e.g., a hard disk). This might range from a PC with a small hard drive to a multiprocessor server with huge amounts of storage. The exact system required will depend on such factors as the operating system selected, throughput desired, fault tolerance needs, communications protocols used, and message archiving and logging requirements.

It is worth mentioning that many gateway products are what is termed *hardware model independent*. In other words, the vendor really supplies only software. If this is the case, the vendor usually indicates minimum hardware requirements and leaves it up to the person deploying the gateway to decide on details (e.g., what exact model of computer to buy). Beyond the basic computer and its storage device, hardware components are very specific to the situation. Perhaps the most frequently used is a network interface card (NIC). The two basic types of cards are Ethernet and Token Ring.

When a gateway must be connected to a public network (e.g., the Internet or a VAN), it is common to have a communications hardware device in the configuration. This might take the form of an X.25 adaptor card, a multiport asynchronous controller board, or modems. High-end gateway systems often use additional equipment (e.g., a CD unit or magnetic tape drive). A CD unit is essential for loading and installing software components. A tape drive is often useful for backing up the system hard drive, archiving messages, and saving billing and statistical information.

Software Components

Gateway software components fall into one of the following three categories: operating system software, gateway applications software, and third-party support software.

Operating System Software. The operating system is the fundamental, general-purpose software running on the computer. It allows reading and writing to a disk, allocating memory resources, and a user interface mechanism. Examples of operating systems software supported by gateway product suppliers include UNIX, Novell NetWare, Windows NT, and MS/DOS.

Applications Software. Applications software is the set of programs that perform the actual message handling in the gateway. This might be as simple as one single program/file or as complex as a whole directory structure filled with dozens of software modules, each performing a special function.

Third-Party Software. Typically a certain number of third-party software components are necessary in a gateway system. Examples of this are device drivers, communications protocol stack components, and tape archive and backup packages.

GATEWAY CONFIGURATION MODELS

Individual hardware and software components must be put together in a certain way to make things work. This is referred to as a *configuration*.

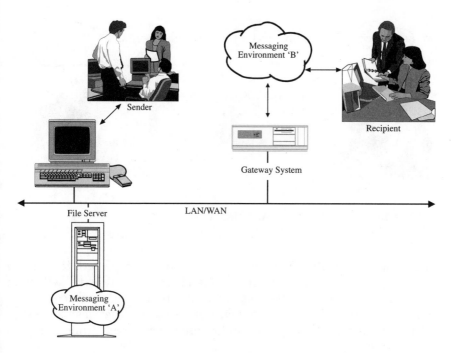

Exhibit 3.   Stand-alone (Dedicated Machine) Gateway Model.

Gateway configuration models fall into three categories: stand-alone or dedicated, colocated, and distributed processing.

Stand-Alone or Dedicated Model

The stand-alone configuration model (see Exhibit 3) is typical in today's environments. For this, a separate computer is dedicated to performing the gateway functions. All hardware and software components reside in this type of single box system. In some sense, this is the easiest gateway configuration to understand and explain because messages enter the box in one form and come out in another.

This model has several other advantages. First, all or most of the computer's resources can be allocated to the job at hand. Second, very little — if any — change is required in the environments being linked together by the gateway. When considering this model, one important question to ask is, how will the gateway system be managed? This is particularly true if a number of gateway systems will be deployed across a wide geographical area.

Colocated Model

Colocating the gateway components in the same main computer system where one or more of the electronic messaging environments to be linked

653

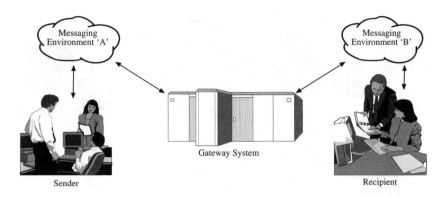

Exhibit 4.   Co-located Gateway Model.

---

resides is also possible (see Exhibit 4). The disadvantage with this model is that gateway functions, which are often resource-intensive, will steal power from the main computer system. In addition, it may be necessary to add hardware and software components into a system that has been in operation and running unchanged for quite some time — something generally frowned upon.

Sometimes management advantages are associated with using this model. Often an already familiar set of commands, reports, and alarms can be used to manage the gateway.

Distributed Processing Model

As shown in Exhibit 5, one of the newer and more interesting configurations now available from some product suppliers actually allows gateway functions to be distributed across multiple computers. In this model, clever software design allows for a high-speed exchange of information between dispersed gateway components. Typically, a file server acts as a central, common repository for information. This effectively forms one logical gateway system out of pieces running on several computers.

With the availability of hardware as a relatively cheap commodity (due to reduced hardware prices) today, this configuration model is worth examining. For large-scale gateways, it offers advantages in the area of scalability, load sharing, and fault tolerance.

GATEWAY SCENARIOS

This section offers a brief summary of three fictional but realistic scenarios in which gateway technology is used. Most actual situations will match, or at least have much in common with, one of these scenarios.

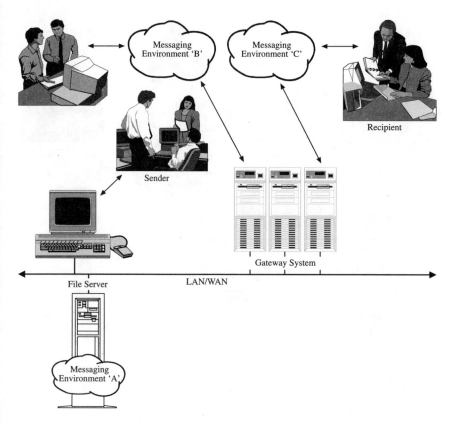

Exhibit 5.   Distributed Architecture Gateway Model.

Scenario One: Linking LAN Messaging to the Outside World through a Network Service Provider

This scenario is very typical today for a large organization that has deployed any one of the very popular and powerful LAN-based e-mail packages available (e.g., Lotus cc:Mail, Microsoft Exchange, or a Novell MHS-compliant product). Inevitably, users start to ask how they can exchange messages with external trading partners. Some discover on their own that if they use a somewhat crazed mix of packages, network access subscriptions, and a modem, they can communicate individually. But this gets messy, expensive, hard to control, and is a bad long-term solution for any organization of size.

The best answer for business-quality messaging is to deploy what is known as an X.400 gateway (see Exhibit 6). This essentially links the LAN-based e-mail environment to the outside world via a network service pro-

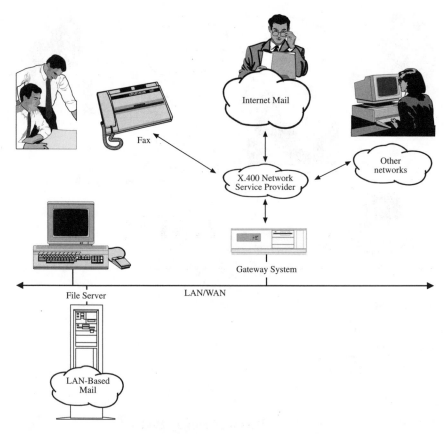

Exhibit 6.   Scenario One: X.400 Gateway Used to Communicate with the Outside World.

vider. In the U.S., the more well-known service providers include MCI, AT&T, Sprint, GE Information Services, and IBM Advantis.

X.400 Implementations. Gateways can exchange messages with the network service provider by way of X.400. This is a very flexible, rich, and open set of standards or protocols for messaging. Lower-level communication protocols (e.g., X.25, TCP/IP, and OSI transport/session) are used to ensure the reliable exchange of data.

Also important is that in this configuration the gateway forms what in X.400 terminology is referred to as a *private management domain* (PRMD) for the organization. To send a message to anyone in an organization, external trading partners must specify this PRMD by name in the address. Many network service providers offer enormous capabilities, including international access points, links to other carriers, Internet mail access, EDI capabilities, fax delivery, and detailed billing. In other words, they provide immediate connectivity and huge potential. Of course, this is not free. There is normally a charge for the communications link and for each message sent through or stored on the service.

Benefits to Users and Administrators. So what does having a setup like this mean to users in the organization? Now they can exchange messages with external trading partners by way of their normal desktop e-mail application. They only have one mailbox to deal with and do not have to be trained to use several packages or understand different addressing schemes. The payback in large organizations can be enormous.

What are some of the administrative advantages when using a gateway in this scenario? First, all messages exchanged with external trading partners can be logged and archived in one central point — the gateway. This is much neater, easier to manage, and more economical to the organization than allowing users to send, receive, and store correspondences in a chaotic fashion.

Second, the network service provider and gateway, to a certain degree, act as a security firewall between the outside world and the organization's private network.

Finally, it can be said that these companies are professionally staffed, 24-hour operations that will lend a hand with some of the issues pertaining to providing business-quality communications.

[*Author's Note:* An increasingly popular and in most cases more economical solution is to deploy an Internet mail gateway. Again, this can link one's local environment to the outside world via an Internet service provider (ISP) such as UUNET, AOL, or Sprint. Direct Internet gateways present additional issues such as security, reliability of the Internet as a transport network, and, as of this writing, the lack of certain value-added features such as delivery confirmation. For example, it is usually necessary to deploy a separate firewall system to protect one's local network from unauthorized access. However, because of the rapid growth of Internet e-mail as the *de facto* standard for messaging, a direct Internet mail gateway should be part of any large organization's strategy.]

Scenario Two: Tying Together Legacy and Modern Messaging Environments

This scenario is also quite common as an attempt is made to tie a legacy messaging environment together with one of the newer messaging environments by gateway technology. Often a very large investment in money, personnel, and political chips has been made in the legacy network. Examples include messaging running on older mainframe hosts, specialized networks for civil aviation and banking, and government or military systems.

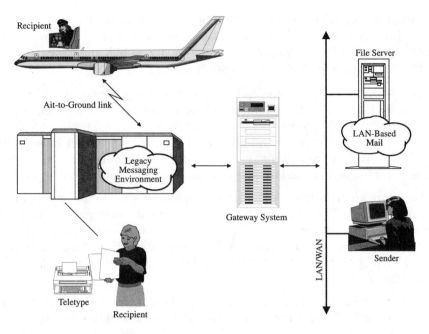

Exhibit 7. Scenario Two: Tying Legacy and Modern Messaging Environments Together.

Sometimes gateways are required for a very long transition period as the legacy environment is phased out. Other times, the investment in the legacy network is so large that there is no end in sight. The gateway becomes a permanent fixture, allowing for a modern user interface to an older or very specialized environment (see Exhibit 7). Gateway issues are sometimes difficult in this type of scenario and often require some degree of customization. This is because of the large difference in capabilities offered in the legacy environment versus the modern environment.

The legacy environment may have specialized features that do not convert unambiguously into an element of service used in the new environment. On occasion, it is even a challenge to determine enough about how a long-ago-deployed environment functions to effectively set up a gateway. Address space restrictions can also be an issue in this scenario.

For example, many older legacy networks use a simple seven- or eight-character addressing format. Given a fixed number of possible character combinations, it simply is not possible to allocate a separate address in the legacy network for each potential recipient when linking to a huge new environment (e.g., Internet mail). In cases like this, it is necessary to work with a gateway product provider to make special provisions.

Scenario Three: The Electronic Mail Hub

This scenario, in which several different noncompatible packages are being used inside a single large organization, exists frequently. It is usually the result of a merger or acquisition, a high degree of decentralization, business-unit autonomy, or just poor planning. In addition, during the past several years some organizations have stumbled into this scenario as a result of deploying groupware at the departmental or division level and beginning a slow shift toward using its built-in e-mail capabilities for forms, workflow, and electronic commerce.

Whatever the cause, multiple gateways are sometimes configured together into a master, hub-like system (see Exhibit 8) used to link all of the environments together. If this approach is used, gateway issues take on a new dimension of importance and complexity. The master system becomes mission-critical. For example, should this single central system break down entirely, all of the messaging environments are disconnected from each other. In many situations, a failure like this can be very costly to an organization.

A master, hub-like system can also be far more complex to run than a simple two-way gateway. It is not uncommon for administrators to request

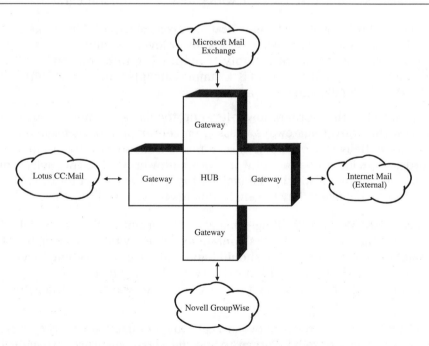

Exhibit 8.   Scenario Three: Multiple Gateways Configured as an E-Mail Hub.

ELECTRONIC MESSAGING

the use of an outside professional service organization to perform the initial design, installation, and testing of such a system.

GATEWAY FACILITIES AND FEATURES

This is where gateway products differentiate themselves. Low-end products typically offer a minimum set of facilities and features — just enough to get the job done. On the other hand, more expensive high-end products deployed by large organizations generally supply a comprehensive set of facilities and features. These usually allow for a much better level of service. The facilities and features can be broken down into the following two categories: message handling-related facilities and features, and management or administration facilities and features.

Message Handling Facilities and Features

Message handling-related facilities and features dictate how well a particular gateway performs its main job of reliably moving messages from one environment to another. Although usually not directly visible to users, they are the "meat and potatoes" of any gateway. What follows here is a short definition of some of the more important messaging handling facilities and features. Administrators should look for these in any products being considered and discuss them with gateway vendors/integrators.

Support for Lower-Level Communications Protocol Layers. Much like a river with barges floating downstream, a lower-level communications protocol provides a means of reliably transporting information, such as messages, from point A to point B. Examples include Ethernet, TCP/IP, X.25, IPX/SPX, Appletalk, and OSI Transport/Session.

Even today, the world of lower-level protocols can sometimes be complex. With regard to gateways, message reception and transmission functions essentially ride on top of these types of transport protocols. In other words, these functions cannot work without lower-level connectivity. This means a gateway product must include top-quality support for the particular flavors being used by the environments to be linked together.

Prioritized Message Handling. This is an important feature, especially in environments where messages contain extremely vital, time-sensitive information. Ideally, a gateway should handle messages according to a first-in, first-out (FIFO) order within priority grade. This means, for example, that a message marked as high priority will be forwarded by the gateway before a message marked as low priority.

There is a big difference between a gateway product that simply converts the priority field from one format to another versus one that actually handles messages internally based on priority. In the case of the former, an administrator might have to explain to the CEO why the junk e-mail got through the network before his or her urgent message to all vice-presidents.

Delivery Notifications. During the past decade, all sorts of mechanisms have sprung up in an effort to make electronic messaging more reliable and generally useful for commerce. One such mechanism is delivery notifications.

Essentially, this is an element of service that allows the sender to request a confirmation be returned by the destination system or network indicating successful delivery of a message. The delivery notification is the equivalent of requesting that the postal service return a receipt when a package is delivered by a mailman.

It is extremely important that a gateway be able to handle the delivery notification element of service. This usually refers to several capabilities, including: forwarding a sender's request for delivery notification into the destination network (typically as part of the message envelope or header), processing or translating any delivery notifications returned by the destination system or network and relaying information back to the sender, and issuing delivery notifications when appropriate.

A word of caution about notifications: Not all gateways handle this element of service correctly or consistently. Some gateways issue a delivery notification immediately on successful reception of a message. This is premature, and can be very misleading to the sender. Also, some gateways issue a delivery notification on transferring a message into a legacy or proprietary network, again, potentially misleading to the sender. Administrators should be aware of these issues and, at a minimum, alert users to the fact that there may be inconsistencies.

Directory Facility. It is fair to say that no two system or network managers ever agreed on the best way to handle electronic messaging directories. This holds especially true in the case of gateways. In any event, many gateway systems use some type of local directory facility. This directory is typically used for routing messages, mapping addresses, and sometimes even to define lower-level communications protocol-related information.

To save work for administrators and make things consistent, gateway product providers have come up with some ingenious ways to automatically populate and maintain a gateway's local directory. These include features known as directory synchronization and auto-registration.

Arguably, the best place to not have a local directory facility is within a gateway. This is because of management concerns. A large, enterprisewide messaging network with dozens of different gateways — each with its own local directory to populate, maintain, synchronize, and backup — is easy to imagine. Even with some degree of automation this can be a nightmare.

The use of a local directory facility can be one of the first difficult issues encountered during a gateway project. Methods and technologies are available to minimize the use of local directories in gateways; however, they require the right planning, product, and people factors.

Automatic Registration. Automatic registration is a useful feature in some situations. To avoid the administrative work of what otherwise might amount to the defining of thousands of entries in a gateway local directory, a clever technique is used. Users essentially define themselves in the directory by way of messaging.

When a user for the first time sends a message through a gateway, his or her address is automatically registered in the directory. On responding, the recipient's address is registered. Slowly but surely, the gateway's local directory is populated as needed, allowing users to communicate easily and take advantage of advanced messaging features (e.g., replying and forwarding).

Directory Synchronization. When tying different messaging environments together with gateway technology, the consistency of directories is almost always a challenge. Each time a user is added or deleted from one environment, the user should also be added or deleted in a gateway's local directory, and in the directory of the other environments as well. This process is called *directory synchronization.*

Most gateway product providers either include automatic directory synchronization as a feature or sell it as a separate add-on facility. Many organizations (including the U.S. Department of Defense) are looking to X.500 technology to help solve directory- and security-related issues. X.500 is actually a set of open standards that provide for defining, distributing, and accessing directory information. Many experts feel that using an X.500-based directory, in combination with synchronization tools, is an effective long-term strategy when linking diverse messaging environments.

Wild Addressing. Wild addressing is sometimes referred to as *in-line* or *native addressing.* It is a feature that allows users to easily send a message to an external trading partner using a public electronic mail address specified in its original format (e.g., taken right from a business card).

For wild addressing to work, the gateway must be capable of accepting and using a public electronic mail address encapsulated within a normal environment-specific recipient address. The intended recipient does not have to be registered in the gateway's directory, hence the name wild addressing.

Wild addressing is most valuable in situations where much ad hoc communications with external trading partners is required and it is impractical or cumbersome to register them in the gateway's directory. Because this is an increasingly important feature to look for in a gateway, an example is ap-

Exhibit 9.   **Sender Uses Public E-Mail Address Taken from Business Card (via Wild Addressing).**

propriate. Exhibit 9 represents a typical business card for Bob Jones, a manager of a toy store chain. Bob Jones's public e-mail address is shown as: BOB_JONES@TOYSRGOOD.COM.

The president of another company, Sally Roberts, wishes to send Bob a thank-you message for the order he placed for 30,000 model airplanes. For this example, it is assumed that Sally's firm uses Lotus cc:Mail on a LAN and has an Internet mail type gateway. At the cc:Mail TO: prompt, Sally might look at Bob's business card and set the address for him as follows: BOB_JONES@TOYSRGOOD.COM at IGATEWAY.

The gateway would receive the message from the cc:Mail network as a result of Sally specifying "at IGATEWAY." Next, the gateway would perform the necessary message translation into Internet format. It would include the recipient address exactly as entered by Sally, but with the "at IGATEWAY" stripped off. The gateway in this case would not require a directory entry be defined for Bob, nor would it perform any validation (other than perhaps basic syntax checks) on the address.

Error Handling and Message Repair. What happens when a message is received by a gateway system with an error? Perhaps the address of the recipient is misspelled or the message is not in the expected format.

For cases like this, it is quite important that the gateway recognize the error and handle it gracefully. Sometimes it is appropriate for the gateway to automatically issue a negative notification response back to the sender. In many circumstances, however, this is not possible or not desired. The message might be from a far-away international location and contain vital, time-sensitive information. For this, a repair-correction facility in the gateway is very useful. It allows the administrator to view the message, correct it, and resubmit it for delivery.

Transmission Retry. Every network administrator understands Murphy's law and plans accordingly. The administrator tries to shield users from equipment failure, communications line outages, and software bugs.

Transmission retry is a gateway feature network administrators will therefore appreciate. It provides for the automatic retry by the gateway of a failed transmission attempt into the destination network. An additional capability allows the administrator to adjust the maximum number of retries, and the wait period between retries should be included as part of this feature.

File Attachment Support. Most newer messaging environments allow users to attach a file (e.g., a word processing document) to a message being sent. Some of the more sophisticated packages even allow for the launching of a particular application (e.g., a word processor) to view or edit a file attachment. It is therefore quite reasonable for users to expect a gateway to allow for the transfer of a message containing a file attachment from one environment into another. In fact, most gateways do allow for this.

Unfortunately, however, a few interesting pitfalls must be considered when it comes to file attachments. For example, one of the environments being linked together by a gateway may not even support file attachments. In this case, the gateway should detect any message containing an attachment, prevent its transfer into the destination network, and inform the sender.

Another fact of life is that there is often a loss of functional ability when a message traverses a gateway. For example, the file name, creation date, and access privileges are usually dropped as the message passes through a gateway into another environment. This situation has attracted much attention in recent years and may be improved in next-generation standards and products. For now, the bottom line is to use caution when planning to mix file attachments and gateways.

Applications Programming Interface (API) Support. An API is actually a standardized mechanism gateway that software developers use to interface with a compliant messaging environment. Examples of well-known APIs include vendor-independent messaging (VIM), the messaging applications programming interface (MAPI), common messaging calls (CMCs), and the X.400 applications programming interface (XAPI).

What do all these names and acronyms really mean in the context of gateways? First, if a gateway software product uses one of these standard mechanisms to access a messaging environment it services (versus a homemade interface), it helps ensure future compatibility. If the environment changes (e.g., a version upgrade), the gateway itself will be minimally affected. This can be very important in today's world of constant new product releases.

For example, gateway software written to use VIM for interfacing with Lotus Notes Mail generally will not be affected when a new version of Notes is released. The second reason support for an API is desirable is that larger organizations with special needs sometimes must customize or enhance a gateway product themselves. This can be much easier if a standard API has been used versus another access method.

Management and Administration Facilities and Features

These facilities and features allow the administrator of a gateway system to ensure a high quality of service to users. Over the long haul they are invaluable, especially in high-traffic volume situations and when message accountability is of the utmost importance.

While on the topic of management, it should be noted that this is also an area of much activity in the messaging industry. As of this writing, product vendors, network service providers, and users are working together to formulate standards for better messaging management. These efforts promise to bring about increased compatibility across different hardware and software platforms, and are certainly worth watching in the context of gateways.

Alarms and Reports. Many gateway products have become sophisticated enough to automatically detect problems and alert an administrator before users are affected. This might take the form of a visual/audible alarm or perhaps a report printout. In any case, the ability to detect events such as an excessive backlog of messages awaiting transfer, a failed software component, or a communications link outage is very important.

Billing and Statistics. A billing or statistical facility is essential in most large-scale settings. Regardless of how well a gateway is functioning and how happy users are, the issue of cost justification and recovery usually arises. In some organizations, a so-called chargeback policy that allows the cost of a gateway service to be paid for by the specific departments most frequently using the service is put in place. For this, very detailed usage information (often in the form of counts) must be generated by the facility on a weekly or monthly basis.

Also, if the gateway is used as a link to a network provider, billing and statistical information can be used to prove that overcharging is not taking place. Finally, should there be a need to expand or enhance the gateway service, the information provided by a billing or statistical facility can help justify the cost. It is always easier to advocate something with the numbers to back it up in hand.

Message Tracing. Message tracing is a feature that offers the administrator the ability to determine exactly when a message was received and transmitted by a gateway. This feature is usually accomplished via the automatic generation of some sort of log entries (usually written to disk). Often, the log entries contain detailed information (e.g., the sender, the recipients, the time of reception, the time of transmission, and the message priority level).

This is a feature found in all better gateway products. It is certainly a requirement for any project involving business-quality communications.

Message Archiving. As its name indicates, archiving refers to the short- or long-term storage of messages handled by the gateway. Short-term storage is usually on disk; long-term storage is typically performed using tape.

Archiving can be considered a high-end facility, but not necessary in all gateway situations. This is because archiving often takes place outside the gateway in the environments being linked together.

Despite this, there are instances when this feature proves useful. For example, in a gateway used to link a private network to a public electronic messaging environment, archiving might be used to record all messages sent outside the organization.

Message Retrieval or Resend. This feature provides the retrieval and viewing of selected messages by the administrator from an archive. An administrator can typically pick a certain message or range of messages to be retrieved from the archive. This is done by specifying a date-time range, a particular sender, or a particular recipient.

Associated with retrieval is the ability of the administrator to actually resend a message. This is useful in environments where messages are sometimes garbled or lost on their way to an endpoint.

Alternate Routing. Once found only in very large-scale backbone message switching systems, alternate routing is a feature now finding its way into some gateway products. It allows the administrator to redirect messages from one destination to another during vacation periods, equipment outages, office closures, or temporary personnel shifts. Some very high-end gateway products even offer an automatic alternate routing feature, which is activated without any manual intervention when there is some sort of component failure.

Hold and Release. This feature is simply a way in which the administrator can instruct the gateway to temporarily stop sending messages to a particular destination environment. Messages queue up in the gateway until the administrator issues a release command.

Remote Management. This facility allows the administrator to manage a single gateway system or perhaps a whole network of gateway systems from a single location. In its simplest form, this feature is sometimes offered by a so-called remote control software package. This essentially allows an administrator to take control of a system from a remote location by a telephone line or a network connection. Video display, mouse, and keyboard information is exchanged across the connection, giving the effect that the administrator is actually on-site. Almost all of the features normally provided locally can then be used remotely.

More sophisticated (and expensive) management solutions are now becoming available for gateways. These go beyond simple remote control in that they provide a single console facility for monitoring, controlling, and troubleshooting multiple gateways dispersed across a network. Graphical displays, showing overall status as well as actual or potential trouble spots, are often included in such packages.

Security. One item sometimes overlooked by those tasked with putting an electronic messaging gateway in service is security. Perhaps this is because a messaging-only gateway, unlike a general-purpose access unit allowing file transfers and real-time login sessions, is viewed as somewhat less dangerous.

Many issues must be considered when deploying a gateway, particularly if one (or more) of the environments being linked together is considered secure. Should a particular sender be allowed to access the destination network by way of the gateway? Are messages containing file attachments screened for viruses as they transit the gateway? Is there password protection when connecting to a public network? These are all important questions that must be asked ahead of time.

QUALITIES TO LOOK FOR IN A GATEWAY PRODUCT

Everyone, from managers to administrators to users, desires quality, especially in something that is eventually used by the entire organization.

667

What should administrators look for when deciding on a gateway product? The answer, of course, varies depending on the type of organization, messaging environments to be linked together, and the budget available.

Certain points should be ensured before even beginning. The hardware and operating system platforms should be reliable, up-to-date, well-supported by vendors and third-party suppliers, and, if possible, fit the organization's overall information technology strategy. Beyond these basics, many additional gateway-specific qualities must be checked.

Ease of Installation and Configuration

Nothing is more frustrating than starting a project with a product that is difficult to install and configure. Gateways by their nature are not simple desktop applications — they are data communications systems, and often complex ones at that. Some vendors have done a better job than others at designing and documenting installation and configuration procedures. This is usually a positive sign when considering a product.

Documentation

Administration manuals, utilities reference guides, cookbook-type procedures, and even release notes fall into the category of documentation. Administrators should ask to see these ahead of time to avoid any unpleasant surprises during the first month of a project.

Reliability

Even if the installation goes well and the documentation is perfect, over the long term perhaps nothing matters as much as the reliability of the system. Design problems, not-ready-for-prime-time early product releases, and nasty software bugs can be the downfall of even a carefully planned endeavor.

Administrators should check with other users of the gateway product. If not many can be found or they will not discuss their experiences, it is a bad sign. Some product suppliers can be enticed to actually help set up an evaluation system at little or no cost to allow an organization to test drive a gateway.

Flexibility

Administrators should look for a gateway product that offers maximum flexibility in terms of its message handling and management facilities. After the gateway is in service, it should be possible to add an interface to another messaging environment, perform version upgrades, and perform maintenance easily. Is it possible to do these things while the system is running or is a complete shutdown required?

Throughput

Some gateway systems perform incredibly poorly in this category. Message throughput rates of one message per minute are not unheard of when complex translations, protocols, and routing decisions are necessary.

In low-end situations this may not be an issue worth spending much time and money on, but in many cases it is. Unfortunately, vendors are traditionally averse to handing out performance statistics because it involves them in a numbers game that is difficult to win. Even when they do, the numbers should be taken with a grain of salt and should be proven first-hand if possible.

Scalabilty and Ease of Expansion

It is rare for a single, standard issue gateway system to be deployed across an entire large organization. In one location only a small-capacity gateway might be needed. In another location a high-capacity gateway might be necessary. If the same basic gateway product can be used in both instances, perhaps by adding more powerful software or hardware components where they are needed, the gateway can be considered scalable and easy to expand.

Fault Tolerance

In some messaging environments any downtime is totally unacceptable. Such is the case when messaging is used to facilitate point-of-sale transactions, air transportation, or military operations. For networks like this, gateways must be just as bulletproof as all of the other components in the network. This is referred to as fault tolerance.

Solutions that provide hardware fault tolerance include specially designed casings, redundant storage devices, and even the use of a complete backup (hot-standby) system. On the software side, some gateways include a mechanism designed to restart components automatically in the event of a failure. Features like this are usually rather expensive, but can be vital.

Value

Getting the most for the organization's money is always important. In general, a low- to medium-end gateway software product used to link two commonly found environments (e.g., Microsoft Mail and Internet mail) can be obtained for $5000 to $10,000. This price can be deceiving, however. In larger organizations, the true cost of a project is usually in manpower (e.g., analysis, installation, configuration, testing, trial service, and support).

If the situation calling for a gateway requires customization, fault tolerance, high throughput, or special message accountability-archiving, deploying a gateway may amount to a much more significant investment. High-end products start at approximately $40,000 for the basic software license, with hardware and software options often increasing the cost well beyond this figure. The payback point in terms of increased productivity can be difficult to measure and prove. Most experts believe that in a large organization, where e-mail has become business-critical, it is reached quite quickly.

STEPS TO DEPLOYING A GATEWAY

The following sections detail the actual steps involved in selecting, deploying, and running an electronic messaging gateway.

Up-Front Analysis and Planning

During this step, which might last anywhere from several days to several months, the functional requirements for the gateway are considered, confirmed, and documented.

In a small-scale, low-budget scenario, the resulting document might amount to just a few pages of bulleted requirements. For a very large organization with complex issues, this document might be quite long. In this case, it usually serves as part of a request for proposal (RFP) sent to gateway product vendors.

The rule of thumb is that the more precise the functional specification document, the better a vendor will understand the organization's true needs and, hence, the less chance of any misunderstandings.

Picking a Vendor or Product

In today's business climate, giving advice on how to pick a vendor is difficult. Some household names in the computing industry seem to be doing poorly these days, while new, upstart firms blossom almost overnight (and sometimes disappear just as quickly).

It is important to know that most of the larger, more well-known messaging product vendors have in fact formed relationships with smaller firms to supply gateway technology. This is a win-win situation for the partnering firms, with the larger company rounding out its offerings and the smaller company receiving royalties. At least in theory, this makes it less risky for the buyer because the large company stands behind the gateway product.

One idea when trying to select a gateway vendor is to check the Electronic Messaging Association's (EMA) Products Service Guide. Published annually, it lists dozens of gateway providers. A few of the larger, more well-known names include Control Data Corp., Digital Equipment Corp., Infonet, Lotus, Microsoft, Novell, and Worldtalk Corp.

Many smaller, less-known companies have good products. When considering these vendors, regular attendance and participation in organizations (e.g., the EMA) usually indicate a healthy company with a commitment to the messaging industry, as well as a desire to listen to the needs of the user community.

Do-It-Yourself vs. Outsourcing

Installing, configuring, and putting in service a business-quality gateway system is often a task an organization can handle on its own. There are times to call in an expert, however, especially if the project involves customization, a legacy system no one on staff understands, links to a public network, unusual time constraints, or complicated lower-level protocol issues.

Often, even large organizations with big IS departments will rely on the product vendor, an expert consulting firm-integrator, or a network provider to supply at least a few months of planning, training, and support. Some large organizations have even gone the route of completely outsourcing the selection, deployment, administration, and maintenance of their entire messaging infrastructure, including gateways. For those wanting to focus on their core business, such companies as CSC, Control Data, Infonet, EDS, Lockheed Martin Federal Systems, and a host of smaller firms are more than willing to give birth to, rear, and even babysit an organization's messaging environment — for a hefty price.

Initial Testing

Once the gateway is installed and configured, a period of initial testing begins. During this period, the administrator checks to make sure that all the basics work well. Messages and notifications (if applicable) are exchanged, facilities and features are tried, and overall reliability is confirmed. This is an appropriate time to torture-test the gateway. Examples of "tests" to try include large messages, messages with multiple recipients, messages with file attachments, and high-priority messages. Not to be forgotten is a duration or high-load test.

Larger organizations will go so far as to write an acceptance test plan (ATP). Often a payment schedule milestone is associated with successful completion of this ATP. Then, if everything seems acceptable, it is time to begin trial operation.

Trial Service and User Feedback

No matter how much testing has been done, trial service is always interesting. This is a chance to see how well the gateway performs in a live environment with a small, select group of users exchanging messages by way of the gateway.

Before the trial service begins, administrators must make sure of a few things. First, users should be given some advance notice, explaining why the gateway is being put in place and how it will affect them. Second, all of the parties involved (technical and nontechnical) must be sure of the role they are to play. Gateways, because of their nature of tying together different messaging turfs, are often a "political hot potato" in an organization. One single person or group must clearly be in charge of administering the gateway during the trial operation.

Another thing to carefully consider is the selection of users. It is helpful to find a small group of users who meet the following criteria:

- Users who have an interest in seeing the gateway project succeed (perhaps the department needing to exchange messages with an important external trading partner)
- Users who are somewhat computer literate
- Users who seem willing (and have the time) to offer constructive feedback

A department under unusual workload pressure or a group of users who will in any way feel threatened by the new gateway capabilities should be avoided.

Live Service and Maintenance

Assuming that the trial service went well, the gateway is ready to be cutover into full-scale operation. During this step, message traffic levels will typically escalate steadily until all users are aware of the gateway and are actively using it to communicate. It is during this step that administrators must reckon with the cost of providing help to users and quickly troubleshoot any problems.

For example, one or two users might discover that the gateway allows them to transport huge amounts of information to a remote database system by way of messaging — something they always wanted to do but found difficult. This may be fine, and in fact help prove the gateway useful, but perhaps it will have to be restricted to off-peak hours.

Maintenance issues become very important at this point. These include regularly scheduled hardware housekeeping and careful backup of software, configuration information, and perhaps directory facility files. In some cases, messages must be archived to tape on a periodic basis.

SUMMARY

Gateways are complicated beasts. In the likely continued absence of widespread standardization, however, there is often no choice but to use them to link different messaging environments together. The important steps to go through during a gateway project include an analysis phase, product selection, installation and configuration, initial testing, trial operation, and live service.

During the analysis phase, many important issues must be considered. Depending on the particular situation, these might include hardware-software choices, configurations, message routing, address mapping, directory use, element of service handling, lower-level communications protocols, and systems management.

When examining different products, certain qualities are desirable. Reliability, high throughput rates, flexibility, fault tolerance, scalability, and ease of administration fall into this category.

Gateways come in various grades, from low-end products that just get the job done to high-end systems with advanced facilities and features. Keeping in mind that the initial cost of a product can range from a few thousand to a few hundred thousand dollars, administrators should strive for the best range of features and facilities possible within their budgets.

The key to success with gateways is a common-sense recipe. Ingredients include effective planning, selecting the right products, successfully dealing with integrators and network service providers, as well as a healthy dash of sheer hard work. When these are mixed together correctly, electronic messaging gateway technology can be useful and rewarding to an organization.

Chapter 45
Enterprise Directory Services

Martin Schleiff

Many consulting organizations, trade associations, and vendors are touting directory services as the center of the communications universe. They believe that enterprises will benefit as they put increasing efforts and resources into their directory services. Application directory services (e.g., the address books in today's e-mail packages) are devoted to enhancing the functional ability of a particular product, service, or application to its user community. Even though e-mail address books are capable of displaying and possibly administering some information about e-mail users, they are not geared to manage corporate-critical information and deliver it to other applications, users, and services. The predicted benefits are not realized until a company embraces the concept of an enterprise directory service.

APPLICATION VS. ENTERPRISE DIRECTORY SERVICES

Perhaps the simplest way to contrast application and enterprise directory services is to consider the community, or user base, being served. Application directory services typically have a well-defined user base. This may consist of the users of a particular calendaring or scheduling system, or an electronic messaging system. Where multiple, disparate e-mail systems are deployed, the community may consist of the users of all interconnected messaging systems, and the application directory service may include processes that synchronize directory information between each system.

Enterprise directory services focus on providing a core set of fundamental services that can be used by many environments and customer communities. The prime objective is to leverage the efforts of few to the benefit of many (see Exhibit 1).

The enterprise directory service provides an enabling infrastructure on which other technologies, applications, products, and services can build. It is wise to establish this infrastructure even before receiving hard require-

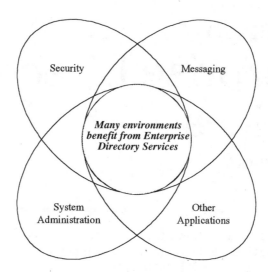

Exhibit 1. Enterprise Directory Services Environment.

---

ments from specific customer environments. Two symptoms of companies that lack enterprise directory services are hindered deployment of new technologies and applications, and redundant processes that have been built by each environment to meet its own needs.

Another way to contrast application and enterprise directory services is to consider how they evaluate the merit of a potential new service. Providers of enterprise directory services will consider the potential for their efforts to eventually be leveraged across multiple user communities. If only one community will ever use the new service, little advantage is associated with hosting that service at the enterprise level. It might be more appropriate to encourage that community to build its own service and offer to support its efforts with managed directory information. For example, if an organization wishes to track the activities of its employees on various projects, an enterprise directory service would likely decline the request to track activities, but offer to support the project by providing access to the appropriate employee information.

WHAT GOES ON IN AN ENTERPRISE DIRECTORY SERVICE?

In a nutshell, any directory service consists of activities and processes to collect and publish information. Many directory services also add value by integrating various types and sources of information into commonly usable formats.

Services that are likely candidates to be provided as part of an enterprise directory service include the following: information solicitation, registration, naming, authentication, directory synchronization, and coordination of publication infrastructure. Each of these services is briefly described in the following paragraphs. Consideration is given to some of the issues and challenges facing the providers of directory services.

Information Solicitation Services

Providers of enterprise directory services can be characterized as data hungry; they realize that empty directories are worthless. They continually seek new and better sources of information to include in their directories. Frequently, these information sources are less than enthralled about expending any efforts and resources that do not directly benefit their own causes.

For example, the human resources department of a subsidiary may not see the benefit of including subsidiary employee information in the directories of the parent company. Likewise, a payroll organization may not fully appreciate that the information they maintain about who is authorized to sign an employee's time card could also be used to approximate the company's management hierarchy. Presenting this information in a directory provides visibility of the company's dynamic organizational structure.

Enterprise directory service providers tend to accept information in any way they can get it. Data submitted by e-mail, file transfer protocol (FTP), floppies, facsimile, phone calls, and even yellow sticky notes are readily accepted in any format. A service provider would rather bend over backward than impose the service's conventions on a hesitant supplier and risk losing their willingness to provide information. In fact, the most critical task in providing enterprise directory services is to build and maintain relationships with data providers.

Service providers also realize that directories with misleading information are worse than worthless. They therefore fret continually about the condition of the data they receive and publish.

At the system level, service-level agreements normally provide some level of confidence about the availability of systems and the quality of hardware and software support. The challenge for enterprise directory service providers is to expand this concept to include information.

Agreements with information sources help identify the quality and availability of the information that will appear in the directory. Information does not need to be perfect to be meaningful and useful, as long as the quality characteristics of the information are made known to users so they can make value judgments about how to use the information appropriately.

Registration Services

Whenever possible, enterprise directory service providers attempt to acquire directory content from other sources — they prefer to be information publishers rather than information owners. Sometimes, however, no managed source for a particular type of information can be identified. In such cases, building a registration service to collect the desired information may be considered. The following list offers examples of registration activities that may be included in an enterprise directory service:

- *Collection of workstation e-mail addresses.* In most messaging environments, e-mail address information can be collected from a well-defined group of administrators. Unfortunately, where UNIX and other workstations are abundant, administration tends to be much less defined and coordinated. In such areas, each workstation may have its own messaging system, and each user may be responsible for administration of his or her own system. There is probably not a single source from which to obtain address information for a large company's workstation community.
- *Primary address designation.* Many people have more than one e-mail mailbox. For example, engineers may prefer to use their UNIX systems for messaging, yet their managers may require them to maintain an account on the same mainframe used by all the managers. Individuals may require the flexibility to work with binary attachments offered by a LAN messaging system and still maintain a mainframe account to use a calendaring system that scales to enterprise levels. With frequent migrations from one messaging system to another, large groups of people may have multiple mailboxes for several weeks while they gain familiarity with the new system and transfer information from the old system. All these cases breed confusion among senders when it is not apparent which system holds the intended recipient's preferred mailbox. Registration services may be established to let individuals designate their preferred mailbox (or preferred document type or preferred spreadsheet type).
- *Information about nonemployees.* The human resources department is an obvious source of employee information to be included in a directory. The HR department, however, probably does not track information about nonemployees who may require access to a company's computing resources, and who may have e-mail accounts on the company's systems. A service to register, maintain, and publish information about contractors, service personnel, and trading partners may be considered.
- *Information about nonpeople.* Other entities that may be appropriate to display in a directory include distribution lists, bulletin boards, helpdesks, list servers, applications, conference rooms, and other nonpeople entities.

Caution is advised when considering to offer registration services, because such services frequently require extensive manual effort and will significantly increase the labor required to run the enterprise directory service. Also, the enterprise directory service then becomes a data owner and can no longer defer data inconsistencies to some other responsible party. Even though resources are consumed in providing such services, the benefits can far outweigh the costs of uncoordinated, inconsistent, absent, or redundant registration activities.

Naming/Identification Services

A naming service simply provides alternate names, or identifiers, for such entities as people, network devices, and resources. A prime example is domain name service (DNS), which provides a user-friendly identifier (i.e., host.domain) for a networked resource and maps it to a very unfriendly network address (e.g., 130.42.14.165).

Another popular service is to provide identifiers for people in a format that can be used as login IDs or e-mail addresses, and which can be mapped back to the owners. LAN-based messaging systems frequently identify and track users by full name instead of by user ID, assuming that people's names are unique across that particular messaging system. This is one of the major hurdles in scaling LAN-based messaging systems beyond the workgroup level. A naming service could manage and provide distinct full names and alleviate a major scaling problem.

Naming services should adhere to the following principles when defining identifiers.

1. *Stable and meaningless.* Identifiers, or names, are like gossip; once they become known, they are difficult to change, recall, and correct. Inherent meanings (e.g., organizational affiliation or physical location) should not be embedded in an identifier because these values change frequently, rendering the identifier inaccurate or out of date.
2. *Uniqueness.* Identifiers must be unique within a naming context.
3. *Traceable back to an individual.* To effectively manage a system, knowledge about the system's users is required.
4. *Extensible to many environments.* Many companies are striving to minimize the number of user IDs an individual must remember to gain access to myriad accounts. Others hope to eventually implement a single logon by which their users can access any computing resource.
5. *User friendly.* Identifiers should be easy to convey, easy to type in, and easy to remember.
6. *Easy to maintain.* Algorithmically derived identifiers (e.g., surname followed by first initial) are easy to generate, but such algorithms may cause duplicate identifiers to be generated if they are not checked against some registry of previously assigned identifiers.

Some of the principles are in contention with each other, so enterprise directory service providers must identify a practical balance of desirable characteristics. A hybrid approach might incorporate some of the following rules:

- Algorithmically assign identifiers (ease of generation)
- Include a maximum of eight characters (extensible to many environments)
- Base identifiers on people's real names (semi-stable and user friendly)
- Use numbers as needed in the rightmost bytes to distinguish between similar names (uniqueness)
- Register the identifiers in a database (traceable back to owner and guaranteed uniqueness)
- Allow individuals to override the generated identifier with self-chosen vanity plate values (user friendly)

Naming an entity should occur as soon as that entity is known (e.g., on or before an employee's hire date), and the identifier should immediately be published by the enterprise directory service. Then, when system administrators establish user accounts for an entity, they can find the entity's identifier in the directory and use that identifier as the user ID. Thereafter, the identifier can be used to query the directory for a user's updated contact and status information. This approach enables system administrators to focus on managing user accounts instead of employee information.

Authentication/Confidentiality Services

The swelling interest in electronic commerce has brought much attention to the need for encryption and electronic signature capabilities. The most promising technologies are referred to as public-key cryptographic systems (PKCS), which provide two keys for an individual — one a private key and the other a public key (see Exhibit 2). A private key must remain known only to its owner. An individual's public key must be widely published and made easily available to the community with which that person does business.

Information encrypted with an individual's public key can only be decrypted with the associated private key. Therefore, information can be sent confidentially to its recipient. Information encrypted with an individual's private key can only be decrypted with the associated public key. Therefore, a recipient can authenticate the origin of the information.

Companies are now grappling with such PKCS deployment issues as which organization will manage keys, which algorithms will be used to generate keys, if private keys will be held in escrow, and whether employees will be allowed to use company-generated keysets for personal use. The one issue that seems clear is that public keys should be published in

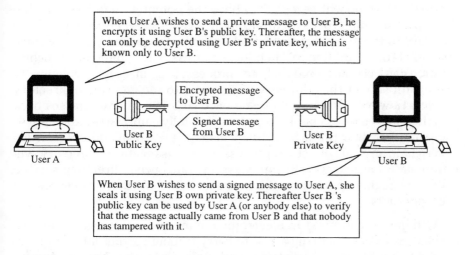

When User A wishes to send a private message to User B, he encrypts it using User B's public key. Thereafter, the message can only be decrypted using User B's private key, which is known only to User B.

Encrypted message to User B

Signed message from User B

User B Public Key

User B Private Key

User A

User B

When User B wishes to send a signed message to User A, she seals it using User B own private key. Thereafter User B 's public key can be used by User A (or anybody else) to verify that the message actually came from User B and that nobody has tampered with it.

Exhibit 2.   Public Key Encryption: How It Works.

a directory service. Soon, enterprise directory service providers will be grappling with their own issues (e.g., when the directory should actually begin to carry public keys, how to encourage vendors to build products that can query a directory for somebody's public key, how many keys should be carried for an individual, and how to make those keys accessible to trading partners and other areas beyond corporate boundaries).

Directory Synchronization Services

The press routinely represents cross-platform directory synchronization as the most difficult task in a directory service. Depending on the approach taken, this situation may be true. Several messaging system vendors provide products that can synchronize non-native address books into their own. If a company attempts to use such products to synchronize address books from more than two vendors, a true mess will result.

A much more effective method is to synchronize each address book with a central (probably vendor neutral), bidirectional synchronization service. The central synchronization service can pool the addresses from all participating messaging communities, translate between native and common address formats, and finally make the pooled addresses available to each community in its respective native format. The advantages of a central service over two-way address book synchronizers can be likened to the advantages of providing a messaging backbone service instead of two-way e-mail gateways. Large companies taking the centralized approach have been able to provide cross-platform synchronization services with minimal resources (e.g., one allocated headcount).

Directory standards (e.g., X.500) have the potential to further simplify cross-platform directory synchronization. If vendors ever half-embrace the standard to the point that their products actually query an X.500 service instead of (or in addition to) their local address books, directory synchronization can become a unidirectional process. Each messaging community would still submit the addresses of its users to the enterprise directory service. However, there would be no need to bring other addresses back into their local address book. If vendors ever fully embrace the standard to the point that their products actually manage their own address information right in an X.500 directory, processes for cross-platform directory synchronization are altogether unnecessary. Enterprise directory service providers ought to encourage their vendors to include these capabilities in their products.

With growing interest in electronic commerce, enterprise directory service providers are being asked to carry trading partner information in local directories. In response to such requests, and in the absence of better solutions, service providers commonly exchange files containing address information with trading partner companies and then incorporate the address information into their own processes.

A better approach would be to link the directories of the trading partner companies so that each company is responsible for its own information; there would be no need for a company to obtain a file of trading partner addresses and manage the information locally. This is yet another area where directory standards provide hope for a better future. The X.500 standards specify the technologies and protocols required for such an inter-enterprise directory. Before participating in an interenterprise X.500 directory, service providers will need to evaluate their company policies on external publication of directories, access control to sensitive information, and the readiness of trading partners to participate.

What Is X.500?

X.500 is a set of international standards, jointly developed by the International Telecommunications Union-Telecommunications Standards Sector (ITU-TSS) and the International Standards Organization (ISO), that specifies standards-based directory components and protocols. Some of the major components and protocols include the following:

- *Directory System Agent (DSA)*. This is where information resides. Multiple DSAs can replicate and distribute information among themselves. They can communicate among themselves to resolve directory queries.
- *Directory User Agent (DUA)*. This enables a user (or application) to access information stored in DSAs. DUAs may be stand-alone programs or incorporated into other applications (e.g., an e-mail user agent).

- *Directory System Protocol (DSP)*. This protocol is used by DSAs to communicate among themselves to resolve queries.
- *Directory Access Protocol (DAP)*. This protocol is used to communicate between DUAs and DSAs. A Lightweight Directory Access Protocol (LDAP) has been defined that is less bulky than DAP and that is appropriate for desktop devices.

X.500 Infrastructure Coordination Services

Various approaches can be taken for deployment of X.500 technology. Frequently, X.500 is included as a component of some other product the company wishes to deploy. For example, a company may purchase a new message transfer agent (MTA) that includes an X.500 DSA to manage message routing information; a company can also acquire a public-key crypto system product that includes X.500 to publish public keys, or a company may use X.500 as a distributed computing environment (DCE) global directory.

Another approach is for a company to first deploy a stand-alone X.500-based directory service, and then tie in messaging, security, and other products as they are acquired. In a large company, some combination of these approaches may occur simultaneously. Setting up X.500 for a particular application is much easier than setting up a general X.500 infrastructure, but it is not the preferred approach.

It is likely that various computing communities will acquire their own X.500 directory system agents to meet their own special needs. Unless the efforts of these groups are coordinated, conflicting definitions, incompatibilities, and redundant efforts and data will emerge — foiling the potential for the efforts of the few to be leveraged to the benefit of the many.

Even though the enterprise directory service may not own all the directory components, it is the best place to organize the activities of these components. Coordination activities include acting as the company's registration authority, managing the root DSA within the company, providing a map of the company's directory information tree, registration of new DSAs, schema management, registration of object classes and attribute types, controlling where new information is incorporated into the directory, and managing replication agreements.

A SERVICE PROVIDER'S PERSPECTIVE ON X.500

These days, technologists promote technologies as directory services, vendors market products as directory services, and standards bodies represent specifications as directory services. Enterprise directory service providers must remember that all these are just tools by which to provide a directory service, and it is their responsibility to select the appropriate tools to best deliver their services. They must discern between what works in theory, what works in principle, and what works in practice.

X.500 technology is sound, but until vendors actually deliver products that use the technology it will remain difficult to justify a serious investment in establishing X.500 infrastructure. Home-grown applications are driving X.500 deployment in some companies, but even in these companies a stronger vendor commitment would ease the burden of justification.

Information Management Issues

X.500 is frequently cast as a panacea for directory services. This is not true; the biggest challenges for enterprise directory service providers are information management issues.

X.500's strength is in information publication, not information management. In some companies, X.500 receives more attention from the security and systems administration communities than from messaging organizations. These communities have much more stringent requirements for timely and accurate data; service providers will need to revamp processes and clean up content to meet these requirements. Remembering that directories with bad information are worse than worthless, service providers will need to give as much attention to information processes and relationships with data providers as they do to X.500 technologies.

Database Issues

X.500 is often described as a type of distributed DBMS. This can be misleading, and some applications that began building on X.500 have had to back off and use conventional database products. X.500 is well suited for information that is structured, frequently accessed by a heterogeneous community, primarily read only, and latency tolerant. X.500, however, lacks database capabilities (e.g., referential integrity or the ability to update groups of information in a single operation). A common debate concerns whether data should be managed in X.500, or if it should be managed in a database and then published in X.500.

Directory Information Tree Structure

Most literature suggests that there are only two basic models to follow when designing the X.500 directory information tree (DIT): the DIT should reflect either a company's organizational structure or its geographical structure.

In fact, both the organizational and geographical approaches violate the first principle of naming (stable and meaningless identifiers). Frequent reorganizations and relocations will cause frequent changes to distinguished names (DNs) if either the organizational or the geographical model is followed. When designing a DIT, sources of information must be considered. For example, in companies where all employee data are managed by a central human resources organization, it may not make sense to artificially divide the information so that it fits a distributed model.

These observations are not intended to discourage use of X.500-based directory services; rather, they are intended to encourage cautious deployment. Reckless and inappropriate activities with X.500 will likely damage its chances for eventual success in a company, and this technology has far too much potential to be carelessly squandered. The previously lamented lack of vendor products that use X.500 can also be taken as a window of opportunity for companies to gain X.500 experience in a controlled manner before some critical application demands knee-jerk deployment. An ideal way to start (assuming that the information is already available) is to build an inexpensive and low-risk "White Pages" directory service using the following components:

- *A single DSA and LDAP server.* Inexpensive products are available today; a desktop system can provide good response for thousands of White Pages users. Worries about replication agreements and getting different vendors' directory system agents to interoperate can be postponed until the service grows beyond the capabilities of a single DSA.
- *A simple Windows DUA.* Vendor-provided directory user agents can be purchased. Unfortunately, many vendor products tend to be so full-featured that they risk becoming overly complex. An in-house-developed DUA can provide basic functions, can be easily enhanced, can be optimized for the company's directory information tree, and can be freely distributed. Freeware Macintosh DUAs are also available.
- *A Web-to-X.500 gateway.* Freeware software is available.
- *A White Pages Home Page that resolves queries through the Web-to-X.500 gateway.* This brings the service to a large heterogeneous user community.

A precautionary note about deploying such a service is that users will consider it a production service even if it is intended only as a pilot or prototype. Support and backup capabilities may be demanded earlier than expected.

ROLES AND RESPONSIBILITIES

As companies attempt to categorize enterprise directory services, especially those that include X.500, they begin to realize the difficulty in identifying a service provider organization. An enterprise directory service is as much a networking technology as it is an information management service, or a communications enabler, or a foundation for security services. One cannot definitely predict that messaging will be the biggest customer of the service or that HR information and e-mail addresses will be the most important information handled by the service. Possibly the best approach is to create a new organization to provide the enterprise directory service.

To build and provide effective directory services, service providers must be intimately familiar with the data so they can witness the changing characteristics of the information, recognize anomalies, and appropriately relate various types of data. Rather than assign an individual to a single role, it is preferable to assign each individual to multiple roles so that nobody is too far removed from the data, and so that no role is left without a backup.

Roles and responsibilities fall into the following categories: operations management, product management, project management, and service management.

Operations Management. Directory operations management focuses on quality and availability of directory data as specified in service-level agreements. Responsibilities include the following:

1. Operate day-to-day directory processes and provide on-time availability of deliverables.
2. Ensure that the directory service is accessible by supported user agents.
3. Register information that is not available from other sources.
4. Interface with existing data suppliers to resolve inaccurate information.
5. Validate data, report exceptions, and track trends.
6. Staff a user support helpdesk.

Product Management. Directory product management focuses on the type of products and services offered to directory customers, as well as tools and processes to best provide the services. Responsibilities include the following:

1. Acquire, build, and maintain tools that enable or improve day-to-day operation of directory processes. Appropriate skills include database development, programming in various environments, and familiarity with the company's heterogeneous computing environment.
2. Establish and administer service-level agreements with information providers and customers. Negotiate formats, schedules, and methods of information exchange between the directory service and its suppliers and customers.
3. Provide and maintain approved directory user agents to the user community.

4. Promote current capabilities of directory services to potential customers.
5. Build directory products to meet customer needs.

Project Management. Directory project management focuses on the near-term future of directory services. Responsibilities include the following:

1. Conduct proof-of-concept projects to explore new uses of directory services.
2. Coordinate activities to put new uses of directory services into production.
3. Conduct proof-of-concept projects to explore the use of new technologies in providing directory services.
4. Coordinate activities to deploy new directory technologies into production.
5. Consult and assist customer environments in incorporating directory services into their applications and services (e.g., assist with LDAP coding, assemble toolkits to ease coding against directories, train application developers in use of toolkits, and provide orientation to the enterprise directory service).
6. Ascertain which projects are most needed. Possible projects include interenterprise directories, participation in global directories, authentication and access control, public keys in directories, electronic Yellow Pages, combining disparate registration services, achieving DNS functional ability with X.500, explore the use of whois++ and finger as directory user agents, partner with other groups to achieve synergy with WWW and other technologies, and assist corporate communications organizations to optimize electronic distribution of information bulletins.
7. Participate with appropriate forums to define and establish international standards.

Service Management. Directory service management focuses on the soundness of current and future directory services. Responsibilities include the following:

1. Coordinate project management, product management, and operations management efforts.
2. Author and maintain service descriptions.
3. Run change boards and advisory boards.
4. Coordinate X.500 infrastructure (registration point for DSAs, object classes, and attributes).
5. Develop and gain consensus on position statements and direction statements.
6. Formulate business plans and justify required resources.

7. Act as focal point for major customer communities; collect requirements, assess customer satisfaction, and gain consensus on direction statements.
8. Represent the company's interests at external forums and to vendors.

SUMMARY

It is important to have realistic expectations of a directory service. Some who expect that a directory will provide huge payback as a single data repository and source of all corporate information may be disappointed. Others who consider directories to be of limited use beyond messaging will reap only a portion of directory benefits. It is difficult to predict which visionary ideas will become practical applications in the near future.

Probably the most vital point to consider when planning for an enterprise directory service is flexibility. In light of dynamic customer demands, new sources and types of information, increasingly stringent requirements for quality data, and emerging technologies, many service providers have elected to use a database to manage directory information (exploiting its data management capabilities) and a directory to publish managed data (capitalizing on its publication strengths).

As buzzwords proliferate, it is easy to get caught up in the glitter and pomp of new technologies. Wise service providers will realize that the important part of directory services is service, and that the role of new technologies is simply to better enable the providing of a service.

Chapter 46
Enterprise Messaging Migration

David Nelson

The goal of this chapter is to discuss large enterprise messaging migration projects and help the information technology professional avoid many of the common pitfalls associated with these types of projects. Messaging migration is the process of moving users from one or more source e-mail systems to one or more destination e-mail systems. Large enterprise projects are those involving anywhere from a few thousand users to over 100,000 users.

The checklists and methodology in this chapter can save frustration, time, and money. For example, what does it cost an organization if enterprise e-mail directories are corrupted and e-mail is down for hours or days due to a migration? What happens in the middle of a messaging migration project if the gateways cannot handle the traffic load and e-mail is terminally slow? What's the impact if stored messages are lost? How about personal address books? What's the benefit of completing the migration sooner than planned?

E-mail, or messaging, is necessary for people to do their jobs. It is no longer a "nice to have" form of communication — it is mission-critical. A recent Pitney-Bowes study found that the average office worker sends and receives more than 190 messages per day[1]. Even though much of this e-mail is superfluous, many messages concern important meetings, projects, and other information necessary to do one's job. Messaging is indeed a valuable resource and changing e-mail systems should be treated with care.

WHY MIGRATE?

There are many reasons why organizations are migrating to new messaging systems. New systems have more capabilities and attractive features. Older systems have become difficult to maintain. Some older systems will not be made Year 2000 compliant. An environment of 6, 12, or more different e-mail systems, which is common in large enterprises, is difficult and costly to manage. The basic idea behind messaging migration is to simplify, consolidate, and lay a foundation for future applications.

Current E-mail Systems

Over the years, large enterprises have "collected" many different e-mail systems. They may have started out using mainframe computers and implemented e-mail systems like IBM's PROFS, Fischer's TAO or EMC2, or H&W's SYSM. Engineering or manufacturing divisions may have used DEC VAX computers and implemented VMSmail or ALL-IN-1. Later on, sales and marketing groups may have implemented PC LANs with Microsoft Mail, Lotus cc:Mail, DaVinci, or a number of other PC-based e-mail systems.

Each different computing environment carries with it a proprietary e-mail system. Each e-mail system has its own method of addressing users and storing messages. Enterprises have overcome these differences with gateways, message switches, and directory synchronization products. Over time, many have discovered that a complex environment of many different messaging systems is not ideal.

Some of the problems associated with multiple e-mail systems include the following:

- Lost messages
- Long delivery times
- Complex addressing
- Corrupted e-mail attachments
- Inability to communicate with Internet mail users

Future Outlook

Which e-mail systems will enterprises migrate to? It's important to note that many enterprises will never be able to migrate to a single e-mail system. Mergers and acquisitions, different business division needs, and new technology will invariably introduce different e-mail systems over time. There is, however, a benefit in reducing the number of messaging systems and having the processes and technology in place to perform messaging migrations. In their report on messaging migration, Ferris Research stated, "Migration is a fact of life and is going to remain a fact of life."[2]

Internet mail has had a tremendous impact on today's messaging environment. The ability to communicate with millions of people on the Internet is of great benefit. The Internet mail standard of RFC-822 addressing and SMTP/MIME format (simple mail transport protocol/multipurpose Internet mail extensions) has also become the *de facto* corporate e-mail standard.

New client/server messaging systems support SMTP/MIME and also add new functionality like:

- Group scheduling and calendaring
- Public bulletin boards
- Shared documents and databases
- Collaborative groupware applications
- Application development environments

Some of the leading client/server messaging systems include the following:

- Microsoft Exchange
- Lotus Notes
- Novell GroupWise
- Netscape Messaging Server

PROJECT SPONSOR(S)

Politics play a very large role in the success of enterprise messaging migration projects. A successful project requires a sponsor that can ensure a timely decision on the company's new e-mail standard and the process that will be followed to get there.

The main concern is that the new e-mail system has to be agreed upon by all of the key decision makers in the organization and the migration process cannot disrupt the business. Each business unit will have its own unique requirements and seasonality. While the CEO may not have time to sponsor the messaging migration project, it's important that he or she provides leadership and support for the project. Business unit managers are also key members of the leadership team. Some organizations go the other direction, forming "grass-roots" committees that span all the different business units so that consensus can be formed. Whatever the approach, it's critical to gain buy-in from the entire organization.

Do not underestimate the time that will be required to gain consensus for your messaging migration project. In some large enterprises, this first step can take months. Look at other large IT projects that have touched all business units within your enterprise to gauge what the consensus forming stage will be like.

USE CONSULTANTS

There are many reasons to bring consultants in on your messaging migration project. First of all, they've been involved in enterprise messaging migration projects and you can benefit from their experience. Second, they can augment your resources so that your staff can stay focused on other critical projects. Finally, they are viewed as having an objective opinion and can help you gain consensus across different business units.

691

Each of the messaging vendors (Microsoft, Lotus, Novell, Netscape, etc.) has its own consulting services organization. Some of the independent consulting organizations that specialize in messaging migration include:

1. Wingra Technologies
   1-800-544-5465
   http://www.wingra.com
   info@wingra.com
2. Control Data Systems
   1-888-RIA-LTO4
   http://www.cdc.com
   info@cdc.com
3. Digital Equipment Corp.
   1-800-DIGITAL
   http://www.digital.com
   info@digital.com
4. Hewlett-Packard
   1-800-752-0900
   http://www.hp.com
   info@hp.com

DEVELOP A MIGRATION PLAN

A well thought-out migration plan is the cornerstone of a successful enterprise messaging migration project. If you've hired a consulting organization, migration planning will be one of their services. You will work closely with them to define what's important for your organization. The checklist in Exhibit 1 shows the basics that should be included in your messaging migration plan.

Define the Current Environment

The first step in the planning process is to define your current messaging environment. One of the best ways to start is to develop a network diagram. This diagram should show the e-mail systems in your enterprise and how they're connected. A simplistic diagram is given in Exhibit 2 to illustrate what a messaging network diagram should look like.

The description of your messaging environment should include:

- Names and vendors of existing messaging systems
- Number of users on each e-mail system
- Geographic locations of existing e-mail systems
- Names and vendors of existing gateways and/or message switch
- Current Internet address standard
- Message traffic volume within systems, between systems, and external to the Internet or other networks

692

Exhibit 1. Migration Plan Checklist.

- Executive Overview
- Project Goals
- Current Messaging Environment
- New Messaging Environment
- Migration Infrastructure
- Message Switch
- Directory Synchronization
- Migration Technology
- Migration Timing
- Migration Policies
- Date range of stored messages
- Message and attachment size restrictions
- Personal address books
- Messaging-enabled applications
- Distribution lists
- Bulletin boards
- Service levels
- Delivery times
- Functionality
- Risk Analysis
- Gantt Chart/Timeline
- Budget

- Average message size
- Average message store size — number of messages and size in megabytes
- Network bandwidth between systems and different geographic locations
- Names and contact information for the people who manage each of the current messaging systems, gateways or message switch, and networks.

Choose the Destination System

The choice of destination system will depend on a number of things. Sometimes it's simply a matter of sticking with a preferred vendor. Other times the decision is driven by a particular application or fit with existing standards. Some of the market-leading client/server messaging systems and their relative strengths are listed below:

- Microsoft Exchange
  - Good integration with Microsoft Office and Microsoft Outlook
  - Good solution where the main need is for e-mail
- Lotus Notes
  - Wealth of third-party applications
  - Strong groupware functionality

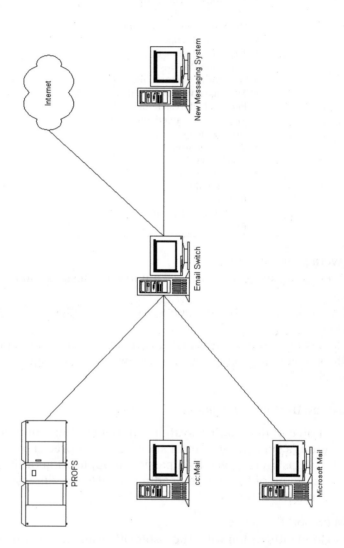

Enterprise Messaging Network Diagram

Exhibit 2. Simple Enterprise Messaging Network Diagram.

- Novell GroupWise
  — Strong integration with Novell network servers
- Netscape Messaging Server
  — Pure Internet standards

New System Requirements

Once you've decided on the destination system, you will need to define the requirements for that system. Some of the things you'll need to look at include the following:

- Standard messaging server configurations
- Standard desktop client configurations
- User training required
- Number of messaging servers required
- Geographic locations of messaging servers
- Network bandwidth requirements between servers

Migration Infrastructure

The messaging migration infrastructure includes technology to provide the following:

- E-mail gateway services
- Enterprise directory services, including directory synchronization
- Internet mail routing
- Message store migration

For enterprises with more than two different e-mail systems, an e-mail switch is required. The e-mail switch should be scalable so that it can handle the peak load when half the enterprise is on the old e-mail systems and half are on the new system. One large enterprise with more than 100,000 users found that they needed six to ten message switches to handle their peak loads. Several message switch vendors are listed below:

1. Wingra Technologies
   Product: *Missive*
   1-800-544-5465
   http://www.wingra.com
   info@wingra.com
2. Control Data Systems
   Product: *Mail*Hub*
   1-888-RIA-LTO4
   http://www.cdc.com
   info@cdc.com
3. Lotus Development Corp.
   Product: *LMS*
   1-800-343-5414
   http://www.lotus.com
   info@lotus.com

Migration technology should work with the message switch to ensure that addresses are translated correctly as message stores are migrated. Migration and integration, or coexistence, technology will also need to work together so that e-mail routing is updated as users switch to their new e-mail system. Migration technology should also make it easy to select a group of users to migrate, move their message stores and personal address books, create accounts on the new messaging system, and update the enterprise directory. It is also useful if message store migration can occur in a two-step process so that the bulk of stored messages can be moved two to three weeks ahead of the time and the remainder can be moved the weekend prior to the cutover date. This is an elegant way to deal with the large size of message stores, often measured in gigabytes.

Migration Timing

In this section of the migration plan, you will define which groups of users will be moved when. Usually it makes sense to approach migration on a business unit basis. Since 80 percent of e-mail is within a functional group, it makes sense to move each group at the same time. This approach will also allow you to take into account the seasonality of different business units. A retail operation, for example, will not want any system changes to occur during their peak selling season, often around Christmas time. Other business units may want to avoid changes around the time leading up to the end of their fiscal years. Migration timing will be negotiated with each business unit. Date ranges will need to be laid out for each business unit for installing new messaging servers and desktop hardware and software, training users, migrating message stores, and cutting over to the new system.

Migration Policies

There are several different philosophical approaches to messaging migration. One approach, often referred to as the "brute-force" method, advocates moving everyone at the same time and disregarding stored messages and personal address books. Another philosophy is to view messaging migration as a process and message stores as the knowledge of the enterprise.

Messaging migration technology is available to perform format and address translations between the old and new systems, preserve folder structures, and move personal address books and distribution lists. As mentioned earlier, it is critical that the migration technology you choose be integrated very tightly with your message switch and directory synchronization infrastructure. This integration will allow addresses to be translated properly so that stored messages can be replied to. Also, it's important that the migration technology feed into your directory synchronization and message routing processes so that e-mail will continue to flow properly as users are moved to the new messaging system.

Assuming your organization would like to retain the valuable information contained in stored messages and personal address books, the next step is to define your migration policies. Your migration policies will need to cover the following areas:

- Personal folders and stored messages — what will be migrated?
  — Restrictions on dates
  — Restrictions on message or attachment sizes
  — Preservation of status flags, i.e., read or unread
- International characters — for users in France, Quebec, Asia, or other parts of the world, will their folder names, message subjects, and e-mail addresses contain the same characters as they do in their current e-mail systems?
- Address translation as messages are migrated — will users be able to reply to stored messages from within the new e-mail system?
- Archives and laptops — will these message stores need to be moved to a server before they can be migrated?
- Internet mail addresses — will they change as users are migrated? What will the new standard be?
  — Personal address books
  — Distribution lists
  — Bulletin boards
- Personal calendars — is there a way to move appointments to the new system?
- Mail-enabled applications — often these have to be rewritten to work with the new messaging system
- Service-level agreements — what can users expect in terms of availability and e-mail delivery times during the migration?

Risk Analysis

The risk analysis section of your migration plan will define which elements of the migration process are reversible and what the backout plans are. If moving a group of users results in the corruption of all the e-mail directories in your enterprise, how will you back out those changes so that e-mail can continue to flow properly? Have current message stores and directories been backed up properly? What's the impact if the project timeline slips? These are some of the questions that need to be addressed in the risk analysis section of your migration plan.

Project Timeline

A project timeline is useful both as a means of communication and as a way to manage the overall project. The timeline should, at a glance, show the steps involved, their interdependencies, and the resources required to achieve your objectives. A high-level timeline is given in Exhibit 3 to illustrate the basic structure.

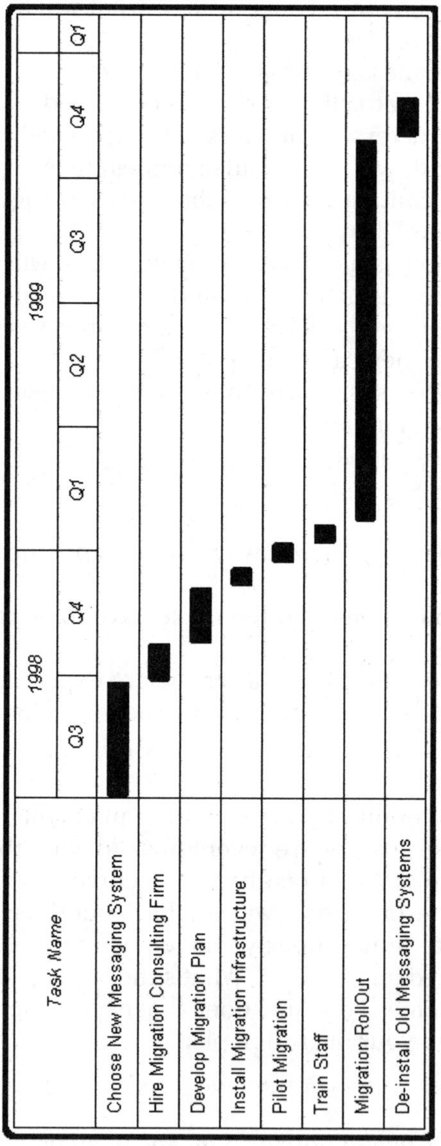

Exhibit 3. Sample Migration Timeline.

COMMUNICATE THE PLAN

Your migration plan will not have much meaning unless you communicate it within your organization and gain support for it. For your management, you should communicate the following:

- Why your enterprise is migrating
- What the new messaging standard will be
- When the migration will take place
- Benefits of migrating

Management in this case has a very broad meaning. Executive staff, business unit managers, and functional managers will all need to know about the messaging migration plan. Methods for communicating the plan include e-mail, formal meetings, or interoffice memos.

Of course, the rest of the organization will also need to know what's going to happen. E-mail users should receive information telling them:

- High-level view of the reasons the enterprise is migrating
- What the new e-mail standard will be
- When new hardware or software will be installed on their desktops
- Their new account name and initial password
- Training schedule
- What will happen to their stored e-mail, folders, and personal address books
- What their external Internet mail address will be
- When they should begin using their new e-mail system
- Who to contact with questions or issues

Because of the need to communicate individual account names and passwords, user communication will probably take the form of e-mail or interoffice memos with some form of mail-merge capability. For some of the more general information, you may consider developing a brochure or flyer describing the project and its benefits.

EXECUTE THE PLAN

You will need to decide who is going to perform messaging migration for your enterprise. Will it be internal IT staff, your migration consultant, or another third party? The key considerations are whether you have the resources and whether you want them devoted to messaging migration.

The first step in testing your migration plan is to perform a migration pilot. Set up a test lab that includes your primary e-mail systems, your messaging integration and migration technology, and your destination e-mail system. It's very important that this pilot be performed in a test lab environment. This is the stage where you will discover problems with your messaging migration plan. You will not want to introduce these problems into your production mail environment. Go through all of the steps of your migration plan and document your results. Change your plan as required.

The next step is to migrate the first business unit on the schedule. Communicate with the users what will be happening and how it will affect them. Again, document the results and adjust your migration plan as you go.

For the remainder of the project, which can often last 12 to 24 months, you will be repeating the migration process on a business unit basis. Standard project management practices should be followed to set milestones and make sure the process stays on track. Once complete, you can shut down and deinstall your old e-mail systems and wait for the next migration opportunity.

SUMMARY

The goal of this chapter was to describe enterprise messaging migrations and help the IT professional avoid many common pitfalls. The critical success factors for an enterprise messaging migration project include the following:

- Consensus and leadership
- Use of consultants
- Detailed planning
- Tightly integrated messaging migration and coexistence technology
- Communication with management and users
- Project management

Messaging migration is a complex process, but with careful planning an enterprise can deploy new e-mail systems on time and within budget.

References

1. *Pitney Bowes' Workplace Communications in the 21st Century*, May 18, 1998, Institute of the Future, 1 Elmcroft Road, 6309, Stamford, CT 06926-0700, http://www.pitneybowes.com/pbi/whatsnew/releases/messaging_1998.htm
2. *Migration of E-mail Systems*, February 1998, Jonathan Penn, Ferris Research, 408 Columbus Avenue No. 1, San Francisco, CA 94133, telephone 415-986-1414, http://www.ferris.com

Chapter 47
Preparing Organizations for Lotus Notes/Domino Solutions

Michael Simonyi

INTRODUCTION

Every once in a while, a product emerges in the information technology industry that captures the imagination of the community as a whole. Lotus Notes/Domino, a product that fits this description, is actually a set of products encased in a well-designed and integrated chassis. This chassis provides a wide array of functionality and opportunity for the Information Technology department to utilize in providing a service-oriented infrastructure for the entire organization. The Notes environment provides the following functionality:

- communications (e-mail and C&S)
- groupware
- workflow
- applications development (macro level, Lotus Script, and Java tools)
- World Wide Web wervices (SMTP and NNTP)
- document management
- security
- integration (for attaching to new or older legacy systems)

Each of the preceding functions provides the basis for the construction of a corporatewide knowledge center. Although it is possible to construct such a knowledge base with individual tools and products, the general consensus dictates that the time involved in integrating dissimilar products and tools can best be suited to customizing the Notes environment for one's business needs. Often, varied tools and products increase the overall

0-8493-9969-6/99/$0.00+$.50
© 1999 by CRC Press LLC

cost of ownership at all levels in an organization rather than lowering them.

Having multiple options of information delivery at one's disposal is paramount in today's ever-changing business environment, and Lotus Notes/Domino is a product that can deliver that information to every crevice of an organization with efficiency and security.

Although Lotus Notes/Domino is a very powerful product, there are areas for which it is not intended, for example, a transaction processing system. However, it can be utilized to complement an existing transaction processing system by emulating the workflow environment of an organization or performing reporting functions and delivering critical information to key stakeholders. This article presents a walk-through of the required steps that are necessary to plan for and implement a Lotus Notes/Domino solution, including the following activities: planning the knowledge-based architecture, organizational acceptance, rollout (including pilot phase), follow-up projects, and future projects. These form the basic framework for the solution.

Defining the Overall Framework for Lotus Notes

In approaching the overall project for a Lotus Notes/Domino-based solution, the following areas require detailed analysis:

- hardware platform and operating system platform
- load requirements (number of users and desired system intent)
- training requirements (users and systems)

PLANNING THE KNOWLEDGE-BASED INFRASTRUCTURE

Some of the key requirements for introducing Lotus Notes into an organization are the initial planning activities. The number of users to be supported by the system, offices and geographical layout of the organization, and corporate requirements and security will all be paramount in making decisions for building the Lotus Notes infrastructure. For example, although Lotus Notes/Domino is operating system-independent, the choice of operating system for deployment depends on the number of users supported by the system, overall growth of the system, system response, and availability. In general, a rule of thumb is to double or triple mass storage requirements up front in an effort to cap reconfiguration and maintenance issues in the future. This is primarily due to the fact that as Notes rolls out into the organization, more uses are found to capture data, knowledge, and business processes. An SMP platform should be considered wherever medium to heavy document search and retrieval functions are to be performed, heavy security and encryption will be required, or expected growth is projected to double within two years. Memory requirements

EXHIBIT 1 — **Operating System Requirements for a Notes-Based Solution**

Requirement	Operating System	Hardware
<100 users	Windows NT/UNIX	Midrange Intel server
<200 users	Windows NT/UNIX	High-end Intel server, entry level UNIX server
>200 users < 1000 users	UNIX, AS400, Windows NT*	Entry level UNIX server — low-end enterprise UNIX server, multiple high-end Intel server
>1000 users < 20,000 users	UNIX, AS400, S390, Windows NT*	Mid–high-end enterprise UNIX server, Multiple high-end Intel servers
>20,000 users	UNIX, AS400, S390	Clustered UNIX enterprise servers, High-end System 390

* This exhibit assumes single-server capacity unless otherwise noted.

should also be increased up front for future growth potential as well as for maintaining optimal performance when additional load is placed on the server. It is far better to grow into a system than to outgrow it during the rollout.

Exhibit 1 presents a table showing the operating system requirements for a Notes-based solution. The platform, as mentioned previously, depends on a large set of criteria. However, should the system require mission-critical status in a 24×7 environment, the choice of operating platform will become apparent. In addition, an organization's hardware standards will also affect the choice of platform. When deciding on the operating system and its configuration, plan for at least two to four weeks of configuration and testing time to make sure the system will perform as expected. Prior to performing any work, it is prudent to collect any and all materials regarding the hardware, operating system, and Notes configuration FAQs for the platform. This will let one gauge the amount of time and effort that will be required for this phase of the project.

DOCUMENTATION STRUCTURE

The outline for documentation of the system follows a hierarchical pattern (see Exhibit 2). At the top lies the overall high-level description of the environment. This layer is designed as an executive summary and master reference. Underneath are the highly technical guides for the environment's construction. There are three technical guides, one each for the hardware, the operating system, and Lotus Notes.

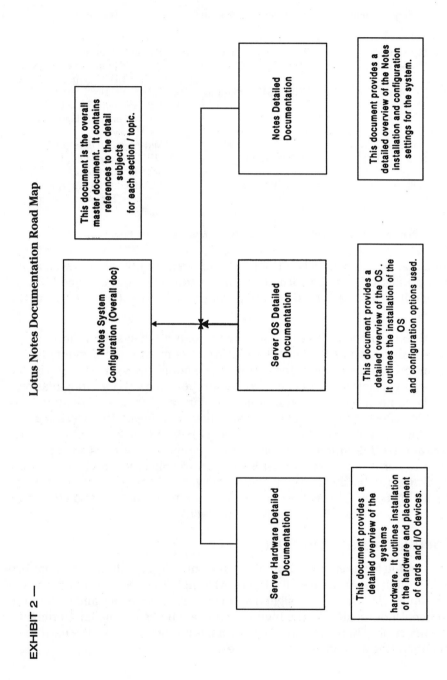

Lotus Notes Documentation Road Map

Notes System Configuration (Overall doc)

This document is the overall master document. It contains references to the detail subjects for each section / topic.

Notes Detailed Documentation

This document provides a detailed overview of the Notes installation and configuration settings for the system.

Server OS Detailed Documentation

This document provides a detailed overview of the OS. It outlines the installation of the OS and configuration options used.

Server Hardware Detailed Documentation

This document provides a detailed overview of the systems hardware. It outlines installation of the hardware and placement of cards and I/O devices.

EXHIBIT 2 —

The guides are laid out in step-by-step fashion. The style promotes the ability to capture all essential details for the construction of the hardware environment, operating system configuration, and Lotus Notes configuration. It is advisable that as the documentation undergoes revision, each member of the installation team be given the opportunity to install the system from scratch and verify the accuracy of the documentation. This technique allows the members of the team to gain a full understanding of the system and enhance their ability to support the system when moved into production. The added benefit of using this type of installation approach directly affects disaster recovery. The system documentation built during the installation process is, in effect, disaster recovery documentation that has been thoroughly compiled for accuracy. When completed, the documentation and copies of the software are sent to the recovery site where they can be utilized in disaster recovery testing. These materials, together with a regularly scheduled backup cycle, will provide the basis for a strong disaster recovery process.

Exhibit 3 presents a table showing a table of contents for the System Hardware Reference, System OS Reference, and the System Lotus Notes Reference guides. The specific contents will vary according to the hardware and OS requirements selected for the Lotus Notes installation.

SAMPLE PROJECT PLAN

Exhibit 4 shows a sample project plan that can be used as a starting point for a Lotus Notes/Domino-based initiative. The project plan includes activities for research, system management, configuration, installation, and training. The plan can be customized for specific projects

PLANNING FOR ORGANIZATIONAL ACCEPTANCE

Unlike the current file-based systems that have been available for over a decade, and the attachments that everyone has become accustomed to, the Lotus Notes/Domino operating environment utilizes no drives, drive letters, or file systems. Although these elements still exist underneath Notes, they are irrelevant to the Notes operating environment. With Lotus Notes, there are fields which are part of documents, and documents reside in databases. The paradigm shift can be extreme for some users who are accustomed to opening up their word processor, creating a file, saving it into a directory or a nested series of directories, and then sending the document for review (or whatever the case may be). With Lotus Notes, one would create a document within a document library, provide a title for the document and additional details, and then create the word processing document directly within the context of the Notes document. The document libraries

EXHIBIT 3 — Table of Contents for Sample Reference Guide

System Hardware Reference

1. General hardware overview
1.1 Hardware components
2. Hardware overview
2.1 I/O system setup
2.2 Memory setup
2.3 Network setup
2.4 Processor setup
3. Diagnostics information
3.1 System configuration revision
3.2 System diagnostics revision
4. Initial installation CMOS configuration
4.1 Preliminary setup
4.2 System hardware design diagram
4.3 System burn-in test results
Appendices system
Diagnostics output
System configuration
Output OS HCL OS HCL
Test results for system

System OS Reference

1. OS software installation overview
1.1. Initial software installation process
1.2. Interactive installation process
1.3. Package installation process
2. OS revision patch overview
3. OS Y2K-ready analysis
4. OS disk setup
5. Operating environment specifics
5.1. Profile and environment configuration
5.2. File systems configuration
5.3. Administration configuration
5.4 System logging configuration
5.5. User accounts and groups
5.6. Security configuration
5.7. Remote admin configuration
5.8. Pre Notes installation configuration requirements
5.9. Post Notes installation configuration requirements
6. Fault recovery testing process
6.1. Mirrored drive tests
6.2. Array drive tests
6.3. System power interruption test
6.4. Other tests

System Lotus Notes Reference

1. Software installation notes
1.1. Preparations checklist
2. Security standards
2.1. Corporate database security standards
2.2. Network security
2.3. Lotus Notes security
2.4. Encryption security
2.5. Maintaining security
3. Lotus Notes systems management
3.1. Notes directory structure
3.2. User/departmental group naming conventions
3.3. Name and address book configuration
3.4. Performance management
3.5. Server administration
3.6. Domino server administration
3.7. User administration
3.8. Client desktop/laptop configuration
3.9. Application distribution
3.10. Server partitioning
3.11. Notes cluster setup
4. Communications
4.1 Mail topology
4.2. Managing mail

4.3. External mail systems
  4.3.1. SMTP (Internet mail)
  4.3.2. x.25
  4.3.3. CC:Mail
  4.3.4. Microsoft Exchange
  4.3.5. Other
5. Systems support network
  5.1. The help desk
  5.2. Support roles
  5.3. Delegation of duties
6. Training
  6.1. Training priorities
  6.2. Training requirements
  6.3. Training outline
7. Database management
  7.1. Database development standards and guidelines
  7.2. Development methodology
  7.3. Database maintenance
8. Maintenance cycle
  8.1. Monitoring license usage and maintenance
  8.2. Server upgrade maintenance
  8.3. Client upgrade maintenance
  8.4. Maintenance of this document and supporting documents
9. Backup and recovery
  9.1. System backup devices and media
  9.2. Database backup options using replication
  9.3. Backup strategy
  9.4. Recovery strategy

7. OS maintenance requirements
  7.1. Daily OS task maintenance
  7.2. Weekly OS task maintenance
  7.3. Monthly OS task maintenance
  7.4. Yearly OS task maintenance
  7.5. Patch maintenance
  7.6. Upgrade maintenance
Appendices
OS-specific command set

EXHIBIT 4 — Sample Project Plan

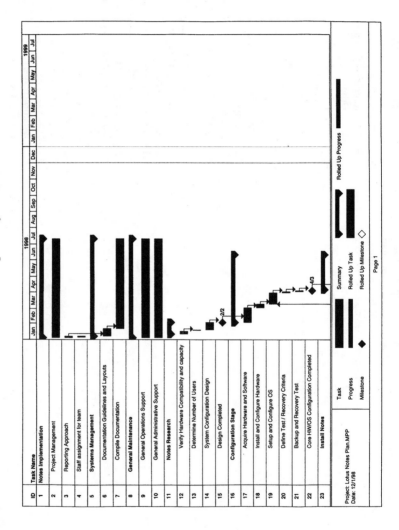

EXHIBIT 4 — Sample Project Plan (*continued*)

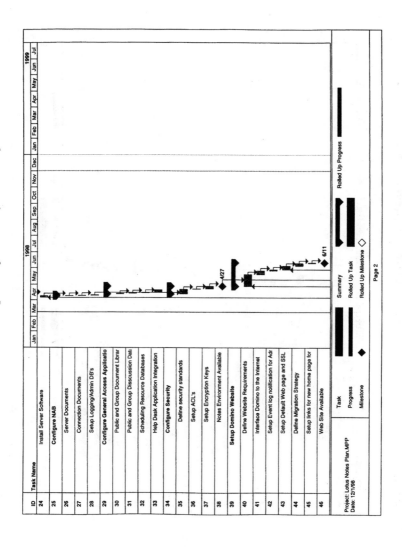

ID	Task Name
24	Install Server Software
25	**Configure NAB**
26	Server Documents
27	Connection Documents
28	Setup Logging/Admin DB's
29	**Configure General Access Applicatio**
30	Public and Group Document Librar
31	Public and Group Discussion Data
32	Scheduling Resource Databases
33	Help Desk Application Integration
34	**Configure Security**
35	Define security standards
36	Setup ACL's
37	Setup Encryption Keys
38	Notes Environment Available
39	**Setup Domino Website**
40	Define Website Requirements
41	Interface Domino to the Internet
42	Setup Event log notification for Adr
43	Setup Default Web page and SSL
44	Define Migration Strategy
45	Setup links for new home page for
46	Web Site Available

Project: Lotus Notes Plan.MPP
Date: 12/1/98

Task
Progress
Milestone ◆

Summary
Rolled Up Task
Rolled Up Milestone ◇

Rolled Up Progress

Page 2

709

EXHIBIT 4 — Sample Project Plan (continued)

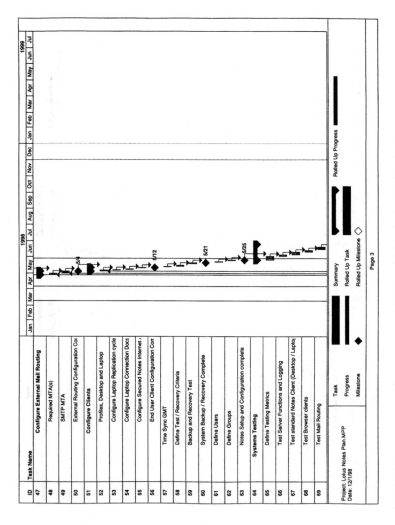

EXHIBIT 4 — Sample Project Plan *(continued)*

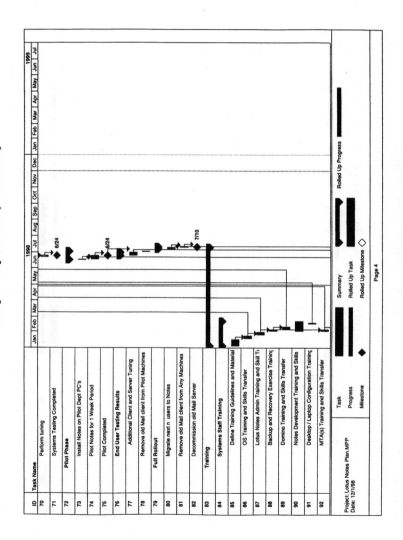

EXHIBIT 4 — Sample Project Plan (continued)

ID	Task Name
93	SMTP Training and Skills Transfer
94	End User Training Sessions
95	Define Training Guidelines and Material
96	Pilot Training Session (n users)
97	Revise Training Material
98	Session 1 (n users per session)
99	Session n
100	Completed User Training

1998
Jan | Feb | Mar | Apr | May | Jun | Jul | Aug | Sep | Oct | Nov | Dec

1999
Jan | Feb | Mar | Apr | May | Jun | Jul

7/10

Project: Lotus Notes Plan.MPP
Date: 12/1/98

Task
Progress
Milestone

Summary
Rolled Up Task
Rolled Up Milestone

Rolled Up Progress

Page 5

allow for review cycles and document distribution by utilizing the underlying e-mail architecture of the product. It is also possible to have full-text indexes to search these documents for words or phrases or create spanning indexes that search multiple databases of documents.

This is an extreme example; however, the point to understand here is that sufficient training must be provided for in making the transition to Lotus Notes/Domino. The training must span not only the user community but also the systems community. Lotus Notes/Domino is an effective tool in delivering information within and outside of an organization. Understanding the utility of the product and how it can be used effectively will directly relate to the product's acceptance by the organization at large. If more than a simple e-mail system is required, then Lotus Notes/Domino is the product of choice.

The training must effectively transmit the concepts of what Lotus Notes/Domino is and what it can do in relation to the organization. This will involve the cooperation of the IT areas, departmental heads, and the training team to assess the needs to achieve an effective course outline and useful accompanying materials. The most effective training plan constitutes an in-house approach for reasons of familiarity with the environment and practical exposure to the technology within the organizational boundaries. The key concept here is to make sure that all the key players are involved in the project from day one. This provides a stake in the project for each player, and a means for establishing benefits for them on an individual basis.

Selecting projects for the Lotus Notes/Domino environment will also provide a base for its introduction into the organization. Applications that can be deployed should include Help Desk, Human Resources, corporate directories, and daily bulletins. Some other applications, such as departmental or group level discussion and document libraries, will provide additional areas for collaboration of information. Discussion databases offer unique opportunities to document minutes of meetings and allow for authorized access to these minutes during and after their compilation.

Ideally, development scenarios for the development teams should begin by encompassing relatively small- or medium-sized projects that will utilize a broad range of Lotus Notes-rich development areas. This will, in turn, provide enough developmental exposure to varying streams and degrees of Lotus Notes/Domino development and instill core aspects of the overall development environment.

ROLLOUT INTO THE ORGANIZATION

Once the applications base has been determined for the Lotus Notes/Domino rollout, the selection of a pilot group or department will need to be determined. The key components for the pilot group should be (1) fairly unbiased to existing environment and the future environment, (2) a good mix of casual and power users, and (3) a reputable department or group. To set up a pilot within the systems area is not a good idea, although perhaps they would be the first group of individuals using the system. A user department or group will provide more constructive feedback during the pilot phase.

Once the pilot phase has been completed, any and all feedback from the experience should be acted upon. In any case, there may be action items that can be utilized by all areas of the organization that should be applied if possible. These should be prioritized in order of enhanced functionality, performance tuning, or specific departmental requirements. The departmental requirements should be collected and prioritized for development projects or subprojects after the initial rollout period has expired. These types of requests are usually more complex than they first appear and will require analysis to develop the solutions.

FOLLOW-UP PROJECTS

Once the rollout of Lotus Notes/Domino has been successfully carried out, it will be necessary to bring the management team back together to discuss the project's highlights and mistakes. These are learning experiences that will help identify areas that can be used to streamline future development projects, and offer insight into problem areas and how to handle them in the future.

FUTURE PROJECTS

Once the rollout of Lotus Notes/Domino has been completed and it is well established within the organization and operating optimally, additional development can begin. The primary areas of development should begin with information dissemination applications, workflow processes, and business process improvement functions.

Information dissemination applications are used to deliver data and knowledge to individuals who require up-to-the-minute information to perform their job functions or make decisions. These types of applications require careful analysis of the individual requirements and most likely will require the design of a security framework that allows only authorized individuals to gain access to this type of information. Information bases such as sales forecasting, corporate health, and corporate planning will fall into this category.

Workflow processes are business-specific functions that follow a defined path toward completion. Such processes as purchase orders, expense reporting, and change management fall into this category. These are applications specifically designed to follow a defined path in order to complete a process wherein proper signoff and approvals are required.

Business process improvement functions are those that can be designed to streamline otherwise manual-intensive reporting tasks, or information processing and delivery tasks. These are typically intensive functions that undergo a large degree of hand-holding to accomplish a given task and can be categorized under workflow if necessary. Other areas that fall under this category would include any business processes that have evolved over time and have become uncontrollable or unintelligible. These are usually processes that follow an ill-defined path to completion.

Other areas of development may focus around the World Wide Web or Internet in the pursuit of commerce applications that may become a priority within the organization to enter a different market place and continue to compete with rivals. The ability of Lotus Notes/Domino to perform dynamic information translation into HTML and present it on the Web in real time is unparalleled. To be in a position to save time and money in quick "get to" market situations is increasingly becoming the norm, and to be able to present product information or other data to the Web as it is required is a strong requirement these days.

Along with many other attributes, Lotus Notes/Domino provides the basis for the construction of a strong, reliable, and secure communications infrastructure for enterprise.

Michael Simonyi is an IT professional working for private sector enterprise organizations. He has over 12 years of practical and theoretical experience, from mainframe systems to PC networks. His areas of expertise center on practical systems management, networking, databases, and application architecture, with emphasis on getting a job done right once and very well.

Chapter 48
Integrating Electronic Messaging Systems and Infrastructures

Dale Cohen

As a company grows and changes computing systems, the job of implementing a messaging system turns from installing and maintaining software to integrating, fine-tuning, and measuring a series of systems — in other words, managing an ongoing project. For organizations integrating multiple e-mail systems, this chapter discusses the goals of a rollout and gives sample implementation scenarios.

PROBLEMS ADDRESSED

Implementing a messaging system infrastructure requires taking small steps while keeping the big picture in mind. The complexity of the endeavor is directly affected by the scope of the project.

If implementing messaging for a single department or a small single enterprise, a vendor solution can probably be used. All users will have the same desktop application with one message server or post office from that same application vendor.

By contrast, integrating multiple departments may require proprietary software routers for connecting similar systems. When building an infrastructure for a single enterprise, the IT department may incorporate the multiple-department approach for similar systems. Dissimilar systems can be connected using software and hardware gateways.

If the goal is to implement an integrated system for a larger enterprise, multiple departments may need to communicate with their external customers and suppliers. The solution could implement a messaging backbone or central messaging switch. This approach allows the implementers to deploy common points to sort, disperse, and measure the flow of messages.

0-8493-9969-6/99/$0.00+$.50
© 1999 by CRC Press LLC

If an organization already has an infrastructure but needs to distribute it across multiple systems connected by common protocols, the goal may be to make the aggregate system more manageable and gain economies of scale. Implementations can vary widely, from getting something up and running to reducing the effort and expense of running the current system.

HOW TO ACCOMPLISH ROLLOUT AND MANAGE CONSTRAINTS

Messaging is a unique application because it crosses all the networks, hardware platforms, network operating systems, and application environments in the organization. Plenty of cooperation will be necessary to accomplish a successful rollout. The traditional constraints are time, functionality, and resources, though implementers must also manage user perceptions.

Resource Constraints: Financial

In an international organization of 5000 or more users, it is not unreasonable to spend $200,000 to $500,000 on the backbone services necessary to achieve a solution. The total cost — including network components, new desktop devices, ongoing administration, maintenance, and end-user support — can easily exceed $2500 per user, with incremental costs for the e-mail add-on at $300 to $500 per year.

The initial appeal of offerings from Lotus Development Corp., Novell Inc., and Microsoft Corp. is that a component can be added at a low incremental cost. In reality, the aggregate incremental costs are huge, although most of the purchaser's costs are hidden. For a corporate PC to handle e-mail, the corporatewide and local area networks and support organizations must be industrial strength.

Although this investment may at first glance seem prohibitively high, it allows for add-ons such as web browsers or client/server applications at a much lower startup cost. Vendors argue that they make it possible for the buyer to start small and grow. It is more likely that an organization will start small, grow significantly, and grow its application base incrementally. In the long run, the investment pays for itself repeatedly, not only for the benefits e-mail provides, but for the opportunities the foray offers.

Resource Constraints: Expertise

It is easy to underestimate the expertise required to operate an efficient messaging infrastructure. Most IT departments are easily able to handle a single application in a single operating environment. Multiple applications in multiple operating environments are a different story.

Messaging systems must be able to deal with multiple network protocols, various operating systems, and different software applications — all from different vendors. Given these facts, it is difficult to understand why already overburdened LAN administrators would take on the significant systems integration responsibilities of a messaging system rollout.

When confronted with problems during a messaging system integration, the staff must be able to answer the following questions:

- Is it a network problem or an application issue?
- Is it an operating system-configured value or an application bug?
- Can the problem be handled by someone with general expertise, such as a front-line technician or a support desk staff member?

Skill Sets. Individuals performing the rollout must be technically adept, have strong diagnostic skills, and understand how to work in a team environment. They must be adept with multiple operating systems and understand the basics of multiple networks. Ideally, they understand the difference between a technical answer and one that solves the business issue at large.

Many organizations make the mistake of assigning first-tier support staff to an e-mail project when systems integrators are called for. The leanest integration team consists of individuals with an understanding of networks and their underlying protocols, operating systems, and two or more e-mail applications. Database knowledge is very useful when dealing with directories and directory synchronization. A knowledge of tool development helps automate manual processes. Application monitoring should occur alongside network monitoring because nothing signals a network error as well as an e-mail service interruption.

Cross-Functional Integration Teams. The most efficient way to coordinate a rollout is through cross-functional teams. It is important to incorporate e-mail implementation and support into the goals of the individuals and the teams from which they come. Many organizations do this informally, but this method is not always effective. A written goal or service level agreement is extremely helpful when conflicting priorities arise and management support is needed.

When creating the core messaging integration team, it is very helpful to include individuals from WAN and LAN networking, systems, operations, and support desk staff, in addition to the individual application experts from each e-mail environment.

Functionality and Scope

At any point in the project, network administrators may find themselves trying to implement an enterprisewide solution, a new departmental system, a corporatewide directory service, or a solution for mobile e-mail users. When building a house, it is commonly understood that the plumbing and waste systems must be installed before hooking up the bath fixtures. This is not the case with messaging.

A messaging system rollout should start with a basic infrastructure "plumbed" for future expansion, and be followed directly with reliable user functionality. Results should be monitored and measured, and original infrastructure issues should be revisited as appropriate. Project success comes with regular reports on what has been delivered, and discussions of incremental improvements in reliability and services.

Supporting Internal and External Customers

No matter how good the features of any product or set of products, if the system is not reliable, people cannot depend on it. If the system is perceived as unreliable, people will use alternative forms of communication.

To satisfy user needs, the IT department should separate internal customers from external customers. Internal customers are those who help provide a service. They may be IT management, support personnel, or networking staff — they could be considered internal suppliers.

Because of the nature of most organizations, internal customers are both customers and suppliers. They need to be provided with the means to supply a service. For example, IT management may need to create step-by-step procedures for the operations staff to carry out. If the information technology group cannot satisfy the requirements of internal customers, it probably will not be able to satisfy the needs of external customers.

External customers are the end users. If they are in sales, for example, external customers may include the enterprise's customers from other companies. It is the job of the IT staff to provide external customers with messaging features, functionality, and reliability so they can do their jobs.

IMPLEMENTATION MODELS AND ARCHITECTURES

It is helpful for network managers to know how other enterprises have implemented messaging systems. The next few sections describe the various components of the infrastructure, common deployment architectures, and how to plan future deployments.

Infrastructure vs. Interface

Often messaging systems are sold with the emphasis on what the end user sees. Experienced network managers know that this is the least of their problems. The behind-the-scenes components, which make the individual systems in an organization work as a near-seamless whole, include:

- Network services
- Message transfer services
- Directory services
- Management and administration services

Network Services. The network services required for a messaging rollout involve connectivity between:

- Desktop and server
- Server to server
- Server to gateway
- Gateway to foreign environment

It is not unusual to have one network protocol between a desktop device and its server and a second protocol within the backbone server/gateway/router environment. Servers may communicate via WAN protocols such as TCP/IP, OSI, DECnet, or SNA, and the desktops may communicate over a LAN protocol such as IPX or NetBIOS. WAN connections may occur over continuous connections or over asynchronous dialup methods.

The network administrator's greatest concern is loss of network connectivity. It is important to understand how it happens, why it happens, how it is discovered, and what needs to be done on an application level once connectivity is restored.

If the network goes down, e-mail will be faulted. Weekly incident reports should be issued that cite direct incidents (i.e., an e-mail component failure) and indirect incidents (i.e., a network failure) as well as remote site issues(i.e., a remote site lost power). Such information can help to clarify the real problem.

Message Transfer Services. The message transfer service (also termed the message transport system) is the most visible part of the messaging infrastructure. The message transfer service is responsible for moving a message from point A to point B. This service consists of one or more message transport agents and may be extended to include gateways and routers. The most popular services are X.400 and SMTP international standards, and IBM's SNA Distributed Services (SNADS) and Novell's Message Handling Service (MHS) proprietary industry standards.

X.400. More widely used in Europe than in North America, X.400 is popular because it:

- Provides universal connectivity
- Has a standard way of mapping features
- Is usually run over commercial WANs so it does not have the security problems associated with the Internet

SMTP. Simple Mail Transfer Protocol's allure is its simplicity. Addressing is easier and access to the Internet is relatively simple compared with establishing an X.400 connection. Because it is simple, there is not much that can go wrong. However, when something does go wrong, it is usually monumental.

Directory Services. The directory service is critical to a company's e-mail systems, but it is also problematic. The problems are a result of the difficulty in keeping directories up-to-date, resolving redundant or obsolete auto-registered entries, and failures of directory synchronization.

The directory serves both users and applications. End users choose potential recipients from a directory. The directory should list enough information for a user to distinguish between the George Smith in accounting and the George Smith in engineering. Some companies include in their directory individuals who are customers and suppliers. The ability to distinguish between internal users and external users is even more important in these cases.

Management and Administration Services. Management refers to scheduled maintenance and automated housekeeping procedures that involve system-related tasks such as reconfiguration and file maintenance. The constant I/O on messaging components leads to disk and sometimes memory fragmentation. Regular defragmentation procedures, including repro/reorg, tidy procedures, and checkstat and reclaim, are required. Whatever the environment, such procedures should be done more often than is recommended to prevent problems from occurring.

Alerts and Alarms. Alerts and alarms are extremely helpful because the system can tell the user if there is a potential problem. Alerts generally refer to warnings such as "too many messages in queue awaiting delivery." Alarms are a sign of a more serious problem, such as a "disk full" condition.

Mail Monitoring. Mail monitoring is typically an administrative function. One way of monitoring a system is to send a probe addressed to an invalid user on a target system. On many systems, the target system will reject the message with a "no such addressee" nondelivery message. When the initiating system receives this message, it indicates that mail flow is active.

Timing the round trip provides a window to overall system performance. A message that does not return in a pre-established timeframe is considered overdue and is cause for further investigation.

Reporting. Reporting is used for capacity planning, measuring throughput and performance, chargeback, and statistical gathering. At initial implementation, network administrators will generally want to report

Exhibit 1. Implementation Scenarios

	Enterprise	
	Single	**Multiple**
Single Department	One-Tier Single System	Two-Tier Similar Systems
Multiple Departments	Two-Tier Dissimilar Systems	Three-Tier Cross-Enterprise Systems

breadth of coverage to demonstrate the reach of the infrastructure. Breadth can be measured by counting users and the number of messaging systems within each messaging environment.

Performance can be measured by reporting the volume — the average number of messages delivered per hour, or messages in each hour over a 24-hour period. This measure can be divided further by indicating the type of message (i.e., text only, single/double attachments, read receipts). This information gives network managers a measurable indication of the kind of features the user community requires.

For network planning purposes, it may be useful to measure volume or "system pressure," ignoring the number of messages sent and focusing on the number of total gigabytes sent per day.

IMPLEMENTATION SCENARIOS: A TIERED APPROACH

Manufacturing environments have long used a tiered approach to messaging for distributing the workload of factory floor applications. As environments become more complex, the tiered approach offers additional flexibility.

An entire enterprise can be considered a single department, indicating the need for a one-tier system where clients are tied into a single server or post office. Multiple departments in a single enterprise or a single department communicating with multiple enterprises require routers and gateways to communicate with the world outside. When multiple departments need to communicate with each other and with multiple enterprises, a messaging backbone or messaging switch is called for.

Exhibit 1 summarizes the implementation scenarios discussed in this chapter.

One-Tier Messaging Model

A single department in a single enterprise will most likely deploy a one-tier messaging model. This model consists of a single messaging server or post office that provides all services. It may be as large as an OfficeVision system on a mainframe or a Higgins PostOffice on a Compaq file server running NetWare. The department need only concern itself with following corporate guidelines for networking and any naming standards.

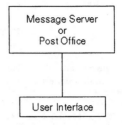

Exhibit 2. One-tier Model.

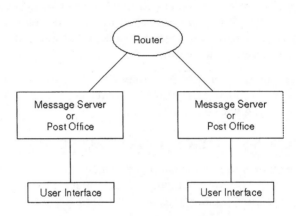

Exhibit 3. Two-tier Model.

Caution should be observed when using corporate guidelines. It is often simple to apply mainframe conventions when standardizing PC LAN-based applications. Many large organizations tend to forget that the whole reason for deploying desktop computers is to move away from mainframe conventions (e.g., 8-character user IDs) that are nonintuitive for users. Exhibit 2 shows a typical one-tier model within a single department of an enterprise.

Two-Tier Model: Multiple Servers

As the number of e-mail users grows, or multiple departments need to be connected, an organization will probably deploy multiple servers. This two-tier model can consist of integrating similar messaging systems from the same vendor or from different vendors. Exhibit 3 illustrates a connection between two departments using the same vendor software connected via application routers.

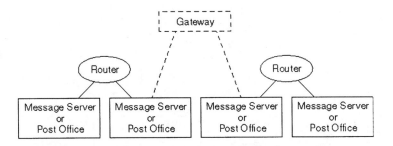

Exhibit 4. Using Application Gateways.

In a typical PC LAN environment using a shared-file system such as cc:Mail or Microsoft Mail, the router acts the same way as the PC. The post office is completely passive. When users send messages, their workstations simply copy the message to the file server as an individual file or as an insertion into a file server database. In either case the PC workstation actually does the work — the post office simply serves as a shared disk drive. The router is also an active component, but has no user-moving messages. It periodically moves messages from one post office to another without user interaction.

Application Gateways for Integrating Dissimilar Systems

Many enterprises have different departments that have chosen their own e-mail systems without a common corporate standard. To integrate dissimilar systems, application gateways can bridge the technical incompatibilities between the various messaging servers (see Exhibit 4).

A simple gateway can translate cc:Mail messages to GroupWise. A more complex gateway can bridge networks (e.g., Ethernet to Token Ring), network protocols(i.e., NetWare to TCP/IP), and the e-mail applications.

Converting one e-mail message to the format of another requires a lot of translation. Document formats (i.e., DCA RFT to ASCII), addressing formats(i.e., user@workgroup@domain to system:user), and message options (i.e., acknowledgments to read or deliver receipts) must all be translated.

Gateways can emulate routers native to each environment. They perform message translations internally. The alternative to this approach is to place the gateway between the routers as opposed to between the post office and the routers — this is not an end-user design, it is merely a function of the vendor software (see Exhibit 5).

If an enterprise is large, network administrators may want to make use of economies of scale to handle common administration, common gateways to X.400, and Internet networks. The network administration staff

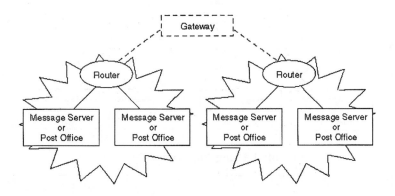

Exhibit 5. Placing a Gateway between Routers.

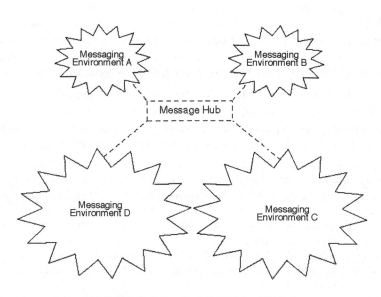

Exhibit 6. A Central Switching Hub.

may simply need points in its network where it can measure progress. Gateways from each environment to every other environment can be provided, but this solution becomes costly and difficult to maintain. A better approach would be to use a central switching hub or a distributed backbone, as shown in Exhibit 6.

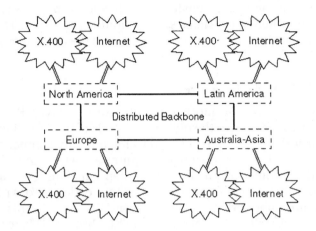

Exhibit 7. Worldwide Distributed Hubs.

Distributed Hubs

The central switch or hub allows for a single path for each messaging environment to communicate with all other messaging environments. The central hub, if it is relatively inexpensive, can be expanded into the distributed model. This is often done as the aggregate system grows and requires additional performance and capacity.

However, this implementation can be taken to an extreme, as seen by the number of companies that have grown PC LAN/shared file systems beyond their original designs. It is inexpensive to grow these systems incrementally, but difficult to provide end-to-end reliability. Most organizations plug the technical gaps in these products with the additional permanent and contract personnel to keep the multitude of routers and shared-file system post offices up and running.

Some organizations have taken this distributed hub approach to the point where they have multiple connections to the Internet and the X.400 world (see Exhibit 7). Some organizations offer the single message switch for their global environment, and their messages are more well-traveled than their administrators. A message sent from Brussels to Paris may stop in Los Angeles on the way because of the central switching mechanism. In addition to local switching, the distributed hub allows for redundancy.

THREE DEPLOYMENT ARCHITECTURES AND OPTIONS

Most companies deploy e-mail systems using variations of three architectures: a common platform, where all e-mail systems are identical; a multiple backbone where each e-mail environment has its own gateway; or a common backbone where all systems share common resources. The following sections describe these architectures along with the advantages and disadvantages of each.

Common Platform Architecture

For years, a major automotive manufacturer delayed PC LAN e-mail deployment in deference to the purported needs of the traveling executive. Senior managers wanted to be able to walk up to any company computer terminal, workstation, or personal computer anywhere in the world and know that they would be able to access their e-mail in the same manner. This implies a common look and feel to the application across platforms as well as common network access to the e-mail server. In this company's case, PROFS (OfficeVision/VM) was accessible through 3270 terminal emulators on various platforms. As long as SNA network access remained available, e-mail appeared the same worldwide. This IBM mainframe shop had few problems implementing this model.

The common platform model is not unique to IBM mainframe environments. Another manufacturer used the same technique with its DEC ALL-IN-1 environment distributed across multiple VAX hosts. As long as a DECnet network or dialup access was available, users could reach their home systems. The upside of this approach is that an individual's e-mail files are stored centrally, allowing for a single retrieval point. The downside was that the user had to be connected to process e-mail and was unable to work offline.

This strategy is not limited to mainframe and minicomputer models. A number of companies have standardized on Lotus Notes, Microsoft Mail, or Novell's GroupWise. None of these products are truly ready for large-scale deployment without IT and network staffs having to plug the technical gaps.

Multiple Backbone Model

The multiple backbone model assumes that an organization integrates its e-mail systems as though it were multiple smaller companies. The OfficeVision/VM system may connect via Advantis to reach the Internet and X.400 world. The cc:Mail WAN may have an SMTP gateway for access to the Internet and an ISOCOR MTA for access to the Message Router/X.400 gateway. All the various e-mail environments may have a proprietary Soft*Switch gateway for access to the IBM/MVS host so that everyone who needs to can access their OfficeVision/400systems (see Exhibit 8).

On the surface, this hodgepodge of point-to-point connections may seem a bit unwieldy, but it does have advantages. Users of cc:Mail can

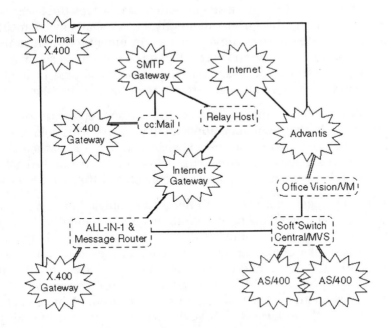

Exhibit 8. The Multiple Backbone Model.

---

address Internet e-mail users by filling out an SMTP template rather than waiting until the cc:Mail administrator adds recipients to the cc:Mail directory. OfficeVision/VM users can fill out a simple address block within the text of their message to reach an Internet user. AS/400 users can send mail to an application that forwards the message on their behalf. The trouble occurs when the recipients of the AS/400 users try to reply — they end up replying to the application that forwarded the message rather than the original sender, or originator, of the message.

This architecture may still work. If each e-mail environment had its own gateway, network administration could offer multiple connections to the Internet.

Common Backbone

The common backbone takes two forms:

1. A central e-mail hub or message switch on a single system that serves as the common denominator among all e-mail environments
2. A distributed model where all backbone components run a common software protocol

The common hub involves a single switch that serves the users' applications, thus serving their needs indirectly. Each e-mail environment has an application gateway that converts its environmental format to that of the common hub. Other systems are attached to this hub in a similar manner. Messages destined for dissimilar environments all pass through this central point to be sorted and delivered to their final destinations.

The distributed backbone takes the central hub and replaces it with two or more systems sharing a common application protocol. This solution offers the ability to deploy two or more less expensive systems rather than a single, more expensive system. Any system connected to any point in the backbone can use any other service (e.g., gateway) connected to that same backbone.

Network managers may decide to purchase a single hub and gradually add systems to form a distributed backbone. Should you decide to use a common backbone protocol like X.400 or SMTP, there is an advantage. Because these protocols are available from a number of vendors, the cc:Mail/X.400 gateway could connect to an X.400 system running in an HP9000, DEC/Alpha, or Intel/Pentium system — all running the same protocols. It is possible to change distributed servers without having to change the gateways to these servers. Exhibit 9 illustrates three-tier flexibility.

A third approach is to use one central server or a distributed backbone of similar systems. In the central server/central hub approach, all e-mail environments use application gateways to connect to the central switch. There they are routed to their target environment.

Two-tier models may seem most convenient because they can use the offerings of a single vendor. One problem is that the system must use that vendor's protocols for a long time. Three tiers allow the layers in the model to be changed, which allows for ease of transition.

Under most application scenarios, changing one component of the messaging environment entails changing all the pieces and parts with which it is associated. It may be necessary to provide adequate support staff and end-user training, or hire consultants to handle the need for temporary staff during the transition — a significant business disruption.

For example, in one environment, users have Microsoft Mail on their desktops and a traditional MSmail post office is used, as well as message transfer agents (MTAs), to route mail between post offices. The engineering department uses OpenMail. The IT group would like to begin consolidating systems. With minor changes to the desktop, IT can retain the Microsoft Mail user interface, remove the back-end infrastructure, and use the same OpenMail system as the OpenMail desktop users by consolidating the second tier and simplifying the support environment. The client

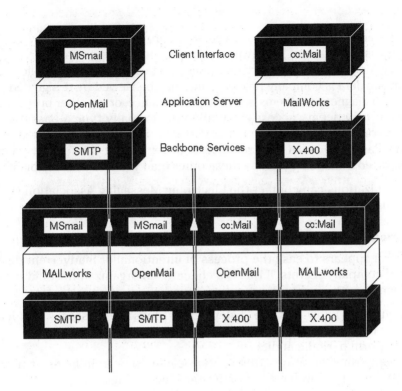

Exhibit 9. Three-tier Flexibility.

---

changes somewhat because it is using a different directory server and message store, but it appears as a minor upgrade to the users — no significant training is necessary.

Likewise, IT can change the back end and still allow the OpenMail systems to communicate with the MAILworks and ALL-IN-1 systems without locking into a single vendor solution. This is a feasible option. Today, users can plug an MSmail client into a MAILworks or OpenMail server. Novell recently announced the ability to plug a cc:Mail or MSmail client into its GroupWise XTD server. A Microsoft Exchange client plugs into various servers, and Lotus's cc:Mail can plug into anything.

ESTABLISHING MESSAGING POLICIES AND PROCEDURES

An organization can prevent misunderstandings, conflicts, and even litigation if it publishes its policies and procedures for messaging applications at the outset. Most important are privacy and confidentiality.

ELECTRONIC MESSAGING

Privacy

A privacy policy serves two purposes: to properly inform employees that their messages may not be private, and to protect the organization from legal liability. Most organizations create a policy that cautions users as follows: All electronic data is company property and may be viewed by designated personnel to diagnose problems, monitor performance, or for other purposes as the company deems necessary. While you normally type a password to access your e-mail and you may feel that your messages are private, this is not the case. The e-mail you create, read, or send is not your property nor is it protected from being seen by those other than you and your recipients.

Organizations can contact the Electronic Messaging Association (EMA) in Arlington, VA, for a kit to aid in developing a privacy policy.

Proprietary and Confidential Information

E-mail appears to ease the process of intentional or inadvertent disclosure of company secrets. If this is a concern, an organization could try the following:

- Let users know that the IT department logs the messages that leave the company.
- Perform periodic audits.
- Apply rules or scripts that capture e-mail to or from fields, making it possible to search on competitor address strings.

Some systems insert a header on incoming e-mail that says: "WARNING: This message arrived from outside the company's e-mail system. Take care when replying so as not to divulge proprietary or confidential information."

A company may also specify that proprietary information should not be sent to Internet addresses if security measures on the Internet are inadequate for the company's needs. Users may be asked to confirm that only X.400 addresses are used. It is helpful to incorporate any such e-mail ground rules — for example, that the transmission of proprietary information without a proper disclosure agreement is grounds for dismissal — as part of the new employee orientation process.

RECOMMENDED COURSE OF ACTION

One of the most important elements of a successful messaging system rollout is a staff that is well-versed in the workings of the network, operating system, backup procedures, and applications.

Network Connections

An implementation needs individuals who can set up network connections efficiently. A messaging system needs procedures in place to notify users when a network link is unavailable. If the network goes down, often one of the first applications blamed is e-mail. It is the job of the network staff to diagnose the problem quickly and have the right people remedying the problem.

Operating Systems

Many e-mail groups have their own systems and servers and operate them as their own. Consequently, many successful organizations pair systems programmers or senior software specialists with systems engineers who can provide installation services and upgrade support.

Backup

Most messaging support organizations are not set up to provide 24-hour support. It is important to borrow methodologies from the mainframe support environment and staff an operations center that can answer phone calls, fix problems, and backup and archive applications regularly.

Applications Support

This function demands staff members with:

- Excellent diagnostic skills
- Excellent communication skills
- Database and business graphics experience
- Cross-platform network experience
- A basic understanding of the operating environment of each of the platforms

E-mail integration by its nature involves cross-platform expertise. Most applications are fairly straightforward. In the case of an integrated infrastructure, an organization may need people familiar with NetWare, SNA, TCP/IP, and LAN Manager. They may also need to understand Mac/OS, UNIX, OS/2, and VMS.

When staffing an implementation, the key is to match expertise across the various groups within the company. The team should be application-centric with contributors from across the enterprise. If an implementation is properly staffed, and the implementers keep in mind the big picture as well as the daily objectives, the messaging system rollout is far more likely to be a success.

Section X
Internet and the World Wide Web

Chapter 49
Integrating the Web and Enterprisewide Business Systems

Chang-Yang Lin

This chapter examines the various issues related to enterprisewide business applications in the context of the Web. Managers need to be aware of Web capabilities and limitations, including standards of security, performance, backup, and user management, as well as the processes for integrating the Web and corporate applications. Intranet solutions are also discussed.

INTRODUCTION

The growth of the World Wide Web, or the Web for short, has been phenomenal since the popular multimedia web browsers Mosaic and Netscape became available in 1994. Some 1996 figures show that 50 percent of the web sites are used by commercial corporations, as compared with 13.5 percent in the previous year, and that percentage is increasing monthly as more corporations discover the advantages of maintaining an online presence. Commercial web sites are still mainly used as marketing tools to provide information about company history, locations, and products, as very few Web sites can respond to information inquiries on enterprise or legacy data that is mostly stored on mainframe computers. As for mission-critical applications (e.g., customer order entry, customer invoicing, billing, and accounts receivable), they are almost nonexistent on web sites. This is partially because current web technology is not mature enough to facilitate effective and risk-free transaction processing over the Internet.

With the remarkable growth of the Web, users, both customers and employees, will inevitably request the ability to access enterprise data via the Web as well as to run web-based enterprisewide applications. Managers have many issues to consider before setting a plan in motion to satisfy these users' needs. In addition to providing background information on the

0-8493-9969-6/99/$0.00+$.50
© 1999 by CRC Press LLC

Web and its capabilities, this chapter describes the four primary components of the Web. Key terms are examined, including HyperText Transfer Protocol (HTTP), HyperText Markup Language (HTML), and Uniform Resource Locator (URL). The chapter also discusses Web limitations and the "unanswered" business questions; the limitations of current technology are identified. Intranets and their use in corporate settings are examined. The chapter introduces approaches for tying the Web and enterprise systems into a coherent system. The development tools and products for the integration are also identified. Finally, the chapter presents planning issues useful in preparing for web-based enterprisewide business applications.

THE WEB AND ITS CAPABILITIES

The World Wide Web is a way of organizing the Internet that allows users to search for and retrieve information quickly and easily in a nonlinear way. This information is structured into small chunks, called pages, and it can be displayed page-by-page through electronic links. Pages may store information in a variety of formats including numbers, text, graphic images, video, audio, and programs. Essentially, the Web is a collection of independent, yet interrelated, pages wired together by hypermedia links.

Technically, the Web is a kind of client/server networking technology for the purpose of requesting and providing services. The Web is composed of four components: clients, servers, publishing tools, and communication protocols.

Web Clients

A web client acts as a front-end browser for requesting service from the servers. Popular web browsers include Netscape Navigator, Mosaic, and Microsoft's Internet Explorer. These browsers are generally equipped with graphical user interfaces (GUIs), which make Internet navigation relatively easy.

Web Servers

A web server is the back-end distributing system that processes and manages requests for service from the clients. Popular web servers include Netscape's Commerce Server, Microsoft's Internet Information Server, Process Software's Purveyor, and O'Reilly and Associates' WebSite. These web servers can be evaluated in terms of such factors as performance, security, and manageability.

Publishing Tools

The HyperText Markup Language (HTML) is an open platform language used to define web pages. This language includes a set of tags that must be embedded in the text to make up a hypertext document. Thus, creating an HTML page involves primarily the process of tagging documents; HTML encoding can be done by inserting the code in a standard ASCII text file, inserting tags in a word processing program, or using special software programs that build the code for the user. Such programs allow the user to select, through menus and interactive commands, the desired effects; the program then builds the appropriate HTML code.

Although word processors and other text editors can be used to create web pages from scratch, tools specifically designed to publish web pages are available to make working with HTML easier. Examples of these publishing products include Interleaf's Cyberleaf, SoftQuad's HotMetal Pro, InContext Systems' Spider, HTML Assistant Pro, HTMLed, and HotDog. All these products automate at least the tagging process by supporting intuitive what-you-see-is-what-you-get (WYSIWYG) screens, menu, toolbar, and drag-and-drop interfaces. In addition, some products such as Cyberleaf are equipped with utility programs able to convert Microsoft Word or WordPerfect documents into HTML pages. The capabilities of these web publishing tools can be classified loosely into four groups:

- **HTML Editing.** These features are used to enforce HTML syntax rules and to manage the HTML tags for formatting text, designing forms, inserting Universal Resource Links (URLs), and calling up photos, video clips, or sound files.
- **Fundamental Word Processing.** These features are used to create and edit the text.
- **Previewing and Testing.** These features invoke any web browser to preview or test HTML pages in WYSIWYG form.
- **Document Conversion.** These features convert documents from plain ASCII text files or specific software-dependent files into HTML formats.

Whereas creating simple pages using these publishing tools requires no specific skills, rich and interactive online pages will require extensive knowledge and skills to integrate hyperlinks, multimedia, and embedded objects.

Communication Protocols and URLs

The Web depends on three protocols to facilitate communications. The Internet protocols include TCP/IP, HyperText Transfer Protocol (HTTP), and Universal Resource Locators (URLs) to communicate over the multiple networks. HTTP is the method that web servers and web clients use to exchange HTML pages. This method is built on the concept of hypertext/hypermedia that permits the nonlinear accessing of the pages.

URLs define the unique location where a page or service can be found. An example of URL would be http://home.netscape.com/comprod/index.html.

This URL begins with the letters http as the transfer format, which indicates that the last portion of the address (i.e., index.html) is an HTML page. The section after ":// ," in this case, home.netscape.com, represents the host computer where the information is stored. This is also referred to as the "home" page or the web site of the Netscape Communications Corporation because it can be used as the starting point to explore other pages in detail. Anyone can publish a home page or start at someone's home page. The rest of this URL is a path name to the file.

URLs do not always begin with the letters http. Other formats are also available, including ftp and News. Together, URLs and Internet protocols enable users to reach, in addition to the Web, other Internet resources such as e-mail, FTP, Gopher, Telnet, and discussion groups via web browsers.

Search Engines

In addition to the above four components, search engines are constantly being created that help users find the web sites that store desirable information. WAIS (http://www.wais.com), InfoSeek (http://www.infoseek.com), Yahoo (http://www.yahoo.com), WebCrawler (http://www.webcrawler.com), Lycos (http://lycos.cs.cmu.edu), and SavvySearch (http://guaraldi.cs.colostate.edu:2000) are often used for web searches. These search engines organize their own databases, start their own search mechanisms to support queries ranging from simple query statements to complex formations and even natural-language queries, and they return a list of URLs. Without these searching machines, finding a list of desirable URLs from the vast, unstructured, uncoordinated Web resources is time-consuming and could take the users months of point-and-click navigation to assemble.

WEB LIMITATIONS: UNANSWERED BUSINESS QUESTIONS

With its capabilities, the Web has been able to facilitate electronic business transactions. Product promotion, customer support, and electronic publishing are a few examples of functions in which web technology has been successful. Nevertheless, from a business perspective, four fundamental questions, described below, remain unanswered. These questions have prevented many corporations from carrying out business on the Web.

- **Is the web navigation mechanism effective?** The Web employs the hypertext mechanism for navigation. For a typical query, the user is often required to do some clicking on the mouse to reach a desirable web site. Once arrived at a web site, more clicking is required before information may be obtained. Although searching engines have alleviated some of the difficulty in reaching web sites, users are still required to do a lot of clicking and bouncing around from page to page following pre-designed links. Such a simple navigation mechanism is not flexible enough to give users more specific information and quicker responses to business queries.

- **Is the web data structure adequate to support information reporting and query responses?** The Web employs a hypermedia data structure in which information is stored in small chunks, called pages. Text documents and other object-oriented data are fitted into these pages. However, traditional record-based business data and numerical data are not suitable for storage in pages, partially because business data, if stored in pages, cannot be easily accessible on a record-by-record basis. In addition, HTML is just not powerful enough to handle record-oriented business data, nor does it allow user-controlled queries to be easily formulated. Consequently, key information cannot be provided under present web-based data structure.

- **Can enterprise data or legacy data be available on the Web?** To date, enterprise data — mostly transaction oriented — is stored mainly in mainframe computers. Security and performance concerns are two major reasons why enterprise data is mostly inaccessible from the Web. Methods and techniques are being developed to bring mainframe-based data into the Web. At present, these methods and techniques are not feasible and therefore transaction-related information on order status, invoice, bill of lading, and payment will mostly remain unanswered.

- **Is the Web suitable for mission-critical business applications?** The Web is not set up for on-line transaction processing and has failed to meet the standards of security, performance, backup, and user management. For example, web technology is inadequate to perform the five security-related tasks (i.e., authentication, certification, confirmation, nonrepudiation, and encryption); therefore, an interactive transaction between trading partners is not reliable. Besides the security concern, other key factors have also contributed to a lack of web-based mission-critical business applications. These factors include stateless conditions during transaction processing, questionable bandwidth to handle real interactive transactions, and lack of user preparedness for electronic commerce.

INTRANETS

Despite a lack of legacy data on the Web and immature web technology for effective transaction processing, an increasing number of corporations are now turning to the Web as their IS solution for addressing business problems within corporations. It is predicted that internal web or intranet usage will surpass external Internet usage by the year 2000. The key factors for adopting intranets are open platform standards (e.g., HTTP and HTML), ease of installing web servers and using web clients, and multimedia capabilities.

The range of intranet applications that can be developed is virtually unlimited. Currently, corporations are deploying intranets as a way to organize their internal communications. Examples of these intranets are:

- Web-based internal e-mail systems
- Project planning, monitoring, and reporting
- Forums for brainstorming, collaborations, or problem solving
- Delivering marketing materials, training materials, or software products
- Online customer information queries
- Online human resource queries on employee benefits, company policies, personnel information, employee and telephone directories, job listings, and training and education workshops

One main concern of deploying intranet applications on the Web is security. Currently, several measures are being installed, including firewalls. Most firewall products focus on keeping external Internet users from getting into intranet applications. Others ensure that users are authorized to access the information they seek.

INTEGRATING THE WEB AND ENTERPRISE SYSTEMS

The process of integrating the Web and enterprisewide systems or building some intranet applications can be approached from two directions. One involves converting enterprise data into hypermedia pages. The other involves building a link between these two systems. Regardless of which approach is used, the goal remains the same; that is, making enterprise data and the various business applications accessible through web browsers. The use of web browsers eliminates concerns about heterogeneous hardware and various operating systems over the Internet and intranets as well.

Building links to tie the Web and enterprise systems into a coherent system is much more feasible than converting to hypermedia pages. This is partially because the linkage programs will not interfere with the normal operations of enterprise systems for supporting day-to-day business activities and management decisions. Both researchers and vendors have been placing their emphasis on developing architectures and tools to support the construction of the linkage programs.

Converting to Hypermedia Pages

Enterprise systems are characterized by a variety of data structures, including traditional flat files, relational databases, IMS databases, object-oriented databases, and special package-related files (e.g., spreadsheet files, song clips, and photo images). Theoretically, this data can all be converted into hypermedia pages to support applications ranging from information inquiry to transaction processing over the Web.

Although current technology is not mature enough to support certain tasks effectively over the Web (e.g., complex interactive transaction processing), migrating key enterprise data to the Web will certainly give customers speedy query responses for such applications as marketing and electronic cataloging.

Building Linkage Programs

Building the linkage programs to tie the Web and enterprise systems into a coherent system involves two similar approaches: augmenting HTML programs and augmenting enterprise programs.

Augmenting HTML Programs. The augmented HTML programs include a data-access subprogram. In addition to the data-access function, many augmented programs may include programs to facilitate interactive input and to merge the enterprise data into pages for presentation. These subprograms may contain SQL statements or procedure codes, called scripts. Examples of these tools or products include DECOUX, SWOOP, OpenUI and OpenWeb, WebDBC, and Open Horizon's Connection for Java.

DECOUX supports an augmented form of HTML that includes embedded SQL statements. SWOOP supports the generation and maintenance of web systems that store information in an ORACLE relational database. The development tools OpenUI and OpenWeb, WebDBC, and Open Horizon's Connection for Java are based on the function-call models that let developers integrate prebuilt, vendor-driven key components together using C++ or other nonprogramming tools. These tools are now being investigated for applications such as hotel reservations, payroll, and human resources.

Augmenting Enterprise Programs with Embedded HTML Statements. Advanced features of HTML, such as forms, are embedded into enterprise programs and used to capture input transaction data from web clients. The input data are then fed into enterprise programs for processing. For example, Visual Object COBOL 1.0 by Micro Focus uses CGI to link HTML forms to COBOL programs and therefore let COBOL programs take input from HTML forms.

Besides using the above tools, Java, Sun's object-based open-system language, can be used to create the linkage programs to tie key components together. Furthermore, Java is said to be able to create web-enabling interactive applications from scratch.

CHALLENGES AND STRATEGY ISSUES

As commercial web sites and users continue to grow at an incredible rate, corporations are faced with an opportunity: incorporating web technology into enterprisewide applications to improve their competitiveness in the global market. The following is a list of questions and suggested solutions that address this opportunity:

- **How do corporations attract potential customers via the Internet and the Web?** They can build a presence on the Web, and then expand and enhance their web pages.
- **How do corporations make enterprise data accessible via the Web to enhance service effectiveness for both employees and customers?** They can move enterprise data into a HTML format, use web technology to connect legacy data, build search and index mechanisms to enterprise data, or develop intranet applications.
- **How do corporations deal with the barriers slowing down the implementation of enterprisewide systems, such as multiplatforms, security, bandwidth, and multiple development tools?** Organizations can plan both external and internal webs as an ideal solution for multiplatforms, or make intranets a solution for addressing the internal communication concerns. They can also install security tools or firewalls to prevent unauthorized users from reaching vital legacy data or applications, and implement systems to track appropriate technologies, such as web development tools, web servers, and security tools.
- **What strategies will corporations need to develop to remain competitive?** They can recognize the Web as one part of an IS solution and integrate traditional systems and web-based systems. Managers can support a new intranet development environment. Organizations can prepare for electronic commerce and provide staffing and training for web technology.

Regardless of web technology's effectiveness for certain tasks, the rapid growth of the Web and its impact in the global market should not be viewed lightly. Facing these challenges and thus effectively deploying the Web to empower users requires planning. The following sections expand on the previous suggestions for better planning.

BUILDING A PRESENCE ON THE WEB

Corporations should position themselves on the Internet's Web by building home pages without any delay. As competitors' presences on the Web increase, one way to guarantee the failure of the above challenges is to adopt a "wait on it" approach.

EXPANDING AND ENHANCING THE PAGES

Simply migrating paper-based product catalogs to the pages and recording CEO's welcome messages is insufficient to attract potential customers to visit the organization's web site repeatedly. Corporations need to think of new ways to both enhance and expand the pages. These may include:

- **Making key enterprise data accessible via web browsers** Enterprise data always serves as a foundation from which information can be derived. Both predesigned and *ad hoc* queries on key enterprise data must be considered to reflect friendliness and flexibility.

- **Providing additional services and facilities from the pages** Examples of these services include customer and technical support; downloading reports, forms, policies and procedures, or software products; and online documentation. Examples of facilities may include a registration form to collect users' information and interests, a special form to allow the users to comment on products, and a platform to facilitate interactive communications.

PLAN INTRANET APPLICATIONS

How the Web is used within a corporation must be planned. Although many applications may be developed based on web technology, those that involve communication, information sharing, and information distribution should be planned and built first.

PREPARE FOR ELECTRONIC COMMERCE

As web technologies continue to mature, the solutions designed to prevent security breaches, stateless transactions, and performance concerns will be gradually available. Thus, corporations must prepare for electronic commerce by making enterprisewide applications — including mission-critical applications — web-capable. This may include building web-capable applications from scratch, linking the enterprise data to the Web, and building the linkages between existing enterprise applications and the Web.

Corporations should identify and plan the projects for electronic commerce. Information reporting or inquiry projects may be built first, because linking SQL databases to the Web will be easier to do. Designing special searching mechanisms on enterprise data will also be necessary for fast inquiry response.

Building the linkages between existing enterprise applications and the Web can be performed next. The proven tools and techniques necessary for building such linkages should be evaluated and selected. Depending on the specific needs of the individual corporations, applications to be linked are ranked.

EDUCATION AND TRAINING

Both developers and users must accept proper training for the emerging web technology. Overall, developers and users should understand how the Internet and the Web can be accessed, used to gather information, and implemented to create business opportunities. The users who are responsible for publishing must learn HTML tools to create pages. Developers must learn the development tools to reengineer applications on the Web. Developers mastering the tools, including such programming languages as C++ and Java, will be essential for successful web-enabled transformation.

CONCLUSION

Web capabilities are extensive and growing more complex and sophisticated at a rapid rate. To keep abreast of such changes, systems developers must consider such factors as security, transfer protocols and languages, and development tools and environments. All capabilities must be evaluated in context of the enterprise — its goals as well as its propensity for risk-taking. Only with a careful weighing of the advantages and disadvantages can an organization move into the technology of the World Wide Web.

Chapter 50
Business-to-Business Integration Using E-Commerce

Ido Gileadi

Now that many of the Fortune 1000 manufacturing companies have implemented ERP systems to streamline their planning and resource allocation as well as integrate their business processes across the enterprise, there is still a need to be integrated with the supply chain.

To reduce inventory levels and lead times, companies must optimize the process of procurement of raw materials and finished goods. Optimization of business processes across multiple organizations includes redefining the way business is conducted, as well as putting in place the systems that will support communication between multiple organizations that have their own separate systems, infrastructure, and requirements.

This type of business-to-business electronic integration has been around for some time, in the form of EDI (Electronic Document Interchange). EDI allows organizations to exchange documents (e.g. purchase orders, sales orders, etc.) using standards such as X.12 or EDIFACT, and VANs (Value Added Networks), for communication. The standards are used to achieve a universal agreement on the content and format of documents and messages being exchanged. EDI standards allow software vendors to include functionality in their software that will support EDI and communicate with other applications. The VAN is used as a medium for transferring messages from one organization to the other; it is a global proprietary network that is designed to carry and monitor EDI messages.

The EDI solution has caught on in several market segments, but has never presented a complete solution for the following reasons:

0-8493-9969-6/99/$0.00+$.50

- High cost for setup and transactions meant that smaller organizations could not afford the cost associated with setup and maintenance of an EDI solution using a VAN.
- EDI messages are a subset of all the types of data that organizations may want to exchange.
- EDI does not facilitate online access to information, which may be required for applications such as self-service.

With the advance of the Internet, both in reliability and security, and the proliferation of Internet-based e-commerce applications, e-commerce has become an obvious place to look for solutions to a better and more flexible way of integrating business-to-business processes.

The remainder of this article will discuss a real life example of how internet and e-commerce technologies were implemented to address the business-to-business integration challenge.

BUSINESS REQUIREMENTS

The business requirements presented to the e-commerce development team can be divided into three general functional area categories:

- General requirements
- Communicating demand to the supply chain
- Providing self-service application to suppliers

General requirements included:

- 100 percent participation by suppliers—The current EDI system was adapted by only 10 percent of suppliers
- Minimized cost of operation to suppliers and self
- Maintainance of high security level both for enterprise systems and for data communicated to external organizations
- Utilization of industry standards and off the shelf applications wherever possible. Minimized custom development
- Supplier access to all systems through a browser interface

Demand requirements included:

- The sending of EDI standard messages to suppliers
  830—Purchase Schedule
  850—Purchase Order
  860—Purchase Order Change
- Advance notice of exceptions to demand through exception reports.

Exhibit 50.1 describes the flow of demand messages (830,850,860, exceptions) between the manufacturer and supplier organization. The demand is generated from the manufacturer ERP system (Baan, SAP, etc.); it is then delivered to the supplier through one of several methods we will discuss

Exhibit 1. Demand Flow

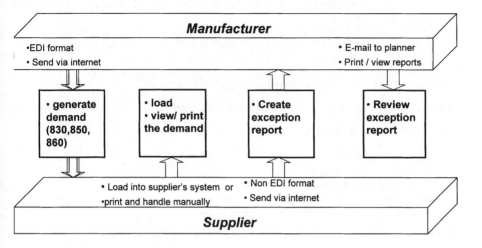

Exhibit 50.1

later. The supplier can load the demand directly into their system or use the supplied software to view and print the demand on a PC. The supplier can then produce a report indicating any exception to the expected delivery of goods. The exception report is sent back to the manufacturer and routed to the appropriate planner, who can view the report and make the necessary adjustments later. The supplier can load the demand directly into their system or use the supplied software to view and print the demand on a PC. The supplier can then produce a report indicating any exception to the expected delivery of goods. The exception report is sent back to the manufacturer and routed to the appropriate planner, who can view the report and make the necessary adjustments. Self-service application requirements included:

- The means for suppliers to update product pricing electronically thereby ensuring price consistency between manufacturer and supplier
- The provision of online access with drill-down capabilities for suppliers to view the following information:
  Payment details
  Registered invoices
  Receipt of goods details
  Product quality information

TECHNICAL REQUIREMENTS

The technical solution had to address the following:

- Transportation of EDI messages to suppliers of various levels of computerization
- Complete solutions for suppliers that have no scheduling application
- Seamless support for small and large supplier organizations
- Batch message processing and online access to data
- Security for enterprise systems as well as data transmission.
- Utilization of industry standards and off the shelf products

Once again we can divide the technical requirements into three categories:

- General requirements
  Low cost
  Low maintenance
  High level of security
  Industry standards
- Batch message management
- online access to enterprise information

A review of the three main categories of technical requirements reveals the need for a product to support message management (EDI and non-EDI); and for the same or a different product to provide online access. The selected products will have to possess all the characteristics listed under general requirements.

E-COMMERCE PRODUCT SELECTION

Selection of e-commerce products for the purpose of developing a complete solution should take the following into consideration:

- What type of functionality does the product cover (online, batch, etc.)?
- Is the product based on industry standards or is it proprietary?
- Does the product provide a stable and flexible platform for the development of future applications?
- How does the product integrate with other product selections?
- What security is available as part of the product?
- What are the skills required to develop use of the product, and are these skills readily available?
- Product cost (Server, user licenses, maintenance)
- Product innovation and further development
- Product base of installation
- Product architecture

The E-Commerce team selected the following products:

- WebSuite and Gentran Server from Sterling Commerce—This product was selected for handling EDI messages, communication EDI, and non-EDI messages through various communication mediums. This product provides the following features:
  Secure and encrypted file transfer mechanism

Support for EDI through VANs, Internet and FTP

Browser operation platform using ActiveX technology

Simple integration and extendibility through ActiveX forms integration

Simple and open architecture

Easy integration with other products

EDI translation engine

Baan Data Navigator Plus (BDNP) from TopTier was selected for online access to the ERP and other enterprise applications. The product has the following main features:

Direct online access to the Baan ERP database through the application layer

Direct online access to other enterprise applications

Integration of data from various applications into one integrated view. Hyper Relational data technology, allowing the user to drag and relate each item data onto a component, thereby creating a new, more detailed query that provides drill-down capabilitie.

Access to applications through a browser interface

Easy to use development environment

Both products had been recently released at the time we started using them (Summer of 1998). This is typically not a desirable situation as it can cause the extension of a project due to unexpected bugs and gaps in functionality. We have chosen to select the products above for their features, the reputation of the companies that developed them, and the level of integration the products provided with the ERP system we had in place.

E-COMMERCE SOLUTION

Taking business and technical requirements into account, we put together a systems architecture that provided appropiate solutions.

On the left side of Exhibit 2 are the client PCs located at the supplier's environment. These are standard Win NT/95/98, with a browser capable of running ActiveX components. Both the applications (WebSuite and Top-Tier) are accessed through a browser using HTML and ActiveX technologies. As can be seen in the diagram, some suppliers (typically the larger organizations) have integrated the messages sent by the application into their scheduling system. Their system loads the data and presents it within their integrated environment. Other suppliers (typically smaller organizations) are using the browser-based interface to view and print the data, as well as manipulate and create exception reports to be sent back to the server.

Communication is achieved using the following protocols on the internet:

751

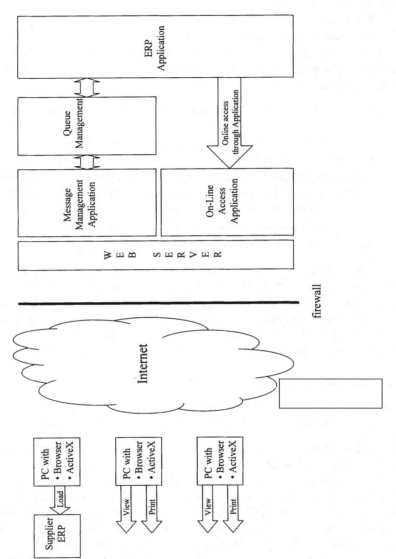

Figure 2. Technical Architecture

Exhibit 50.2

- http, https—for delivery of online data
- Sockets (SL), Secure Sockets (SSL)—for message transfer

All traffic enters the enterprise systems through a firewall, for security. Security will be discussed in the following section.

On the Enterprise side, the client applications first access a web server. The Web Server handles the http/https communication and invokes the server-side controls through an ASP page.

The online application (TopTier) intercepts the http/https communication address to it and interprets the query. It then provides a result set, which it integrates through an HTML template, to be sent back to the client PC as an HTML page. The online access application communicates with the ERP application through the application API, or through ODBC.

The message management application, WebSuite, communicates to the message queue using server-side ActiveX controls and ftp to send and receive files between systems. The message management application communicates with the ERP and other enterprise applications, using a set of processes that can read and write messages, to a shared mounted disk area.

This system architecture supports a mechanism for transferring messages in a secure and reliable fashion, as well as providing online access to data residing in the enterprise systems; this is accomplished through a browser interface with minimal requirements from the supplier and minimal support requirements.

SECURITY

The are two categories of security that must be handled:

- Enterprise systems security from outside intrusion
- Data security for data communicated over the web

Security for the enterprise is intended to prevent unauthorized users from accessing data, and thus potentially damaging enterprise systems and data. This is handled by various methods that are far too many to have a meaningful discussion in this article. The following is a review of the steps taken to secure the system on this project; these are by no means the only, or the complete set of, measures that can be taken. In addition, each organization may have different security requirements. On this project we have

- implemented a firewall that provided the following:
  limited IP and PORT addresses
  limited protocols allowed (http, https, IP)
  required User Authentication at the firewall level
  abstracted Server IP address

- •provided for authentication at
  front office application layer
  back office application layer
  operating system layer
  firewall layer
- •provided domain settings
  the web server machine is not part of the enterprise domain
  the web server machine has IP access to other servers

Data security is required to protect the information that is transferred between supplier and manufacturer over the public domain of the Internet. The intent is to secure the data from unauthorized eavesdroppers. There are many methods to protect data; these methods can be grouped into two main categories:

- •Transferring data through a secure communication channel (SSL, https), a method that utilizes
  authentication
  certificates
  encryption
- •Encryption of data. This method is typically used in conjunction with the previous method, but can be used on its own. There are various encryption algorithms available. The encryption strength, or cipher strength, defined as how difficult it would be to decrypt data without the keys, can vary and is designated in terms of number of bits (i.e. 40bit, 128bit, etc.). For our project, we have selected Microsoft Crypto API, which is supported both by the web Server (IIS 4) and by the client browser (IE 4). The cipher strength selected was 40bits, to allow access to the application from outside theU.S. and Canada, where 128bit cipher strength for browsers is not available.

CONCLUSION

Manufacturing organizations striving to reduce inventory levels and lead times must integrate business processes and systems with their supply chain organization. E-commerce applications utilizing the Internet can be used to achieve integration across the supply chain with minimal cost and standard interfaces.

When implementing e-commerce applications, it is recommended to select those that can be used as infrastructures in the development of future business solutions that address new requirements. Selecting applications that provide technology solutions with a development platform, rather than those that provide an integrated business solution, will provide a platform for the development of future business applications, as the use of e-commerce proliferates through organizations.

Chapter 51
Developing a Trusted Infrastructure for Electronic Commerce Services

David Litwack

For businesses to embrace open systems such as the Internet as a means of conducting commercial transactions, methods of ensuring security must be more fully developed. This chapter proposes ways of confirming sender and recipient identities, protecting confidentiality, and date and time stamping in an effort to develop a trusted network infrastructure for electronic commerce.

INTRODUCTION

The use of internetworking applications for electronic commerce has been limited by issues of security and trust, and by the lack of universality of products and services supporting robust and trustworthy electronic commerce services. Specific service attributes must be addressed to overcome the hesitation of users and business owners to exploit open systems such as the Internet for commercial exchanges. These service attributes include:

- **Confirmation of identity (nonrepudiation).** This indicates proof that only intended participants (i.e., creators and recipients) are party to communications.
- **Confidentiality and content security.** Documents can be neither read nor modified by an uninvited third party.
- **Time certainty.** Proof of date and time of communication is provided through time stamps and return receipts.

•**Legal protection.** Electronic documents should be legally binding and protected by tort law and fraud statutes.

SERVICE ATTRIBUTE AUTHORITY

To support these service attributes, an organization or entity would need to provide:

- •Certificate authority services, including the registration and issuance of certificates for public keys as well as the distribution of certificate revocation and compromised key lists to participating individuals and organizations
- •A repository for public key certificates that can provide such keys and certificates to authorized requesters on demand
- •Electronic postmarking for date and time stamps, and for providing the digital signature of the issuer for added assurance
- •Return receipts that provide service confirmation
- •Storage and retrieval services, including a transaction archive log and an archive of bonded documents

These service attributes could be offered singly or in various combinations. The service attribute provider would have to be recognized as a certificate and postmark authority. The following sections describe how a service attribute provider should work.

Certificate Authority

Although public key encryption technology provides confidentiality and confirmation of identity, a true trusted infrastructure requires that a trusted authority certify a person or organization as the owner of the key pair. Certificates are special data structures used to register and protectively encapsulate the public key users and prevent forgery. A certificate contains the name of a user and its public key. An electronic certificate binds the identity of the person or organization to the key pair.

Certificates also contain the name of the issuer — a certificate authority (CA) — that vouches that the public key in a certificate belongs to the named user. This data, along with a time interval specifying the certificate's validity, is cryptography signed by the issuer using the issuer's private key. The subject and issuer names in certificates are distinguished names (DNs) as defined in the International Telecommunications Union-Telecommunications Standards Sector (ITU-TSS) recommendation X.500 directory services. Such certificates are also called X.509 certificates after the ITU-TSS recommendation in which they were defined.

The key certificate acts like a kind of electronic identity card. When a recipient uses a sender's public key to authenticate the sender's signature

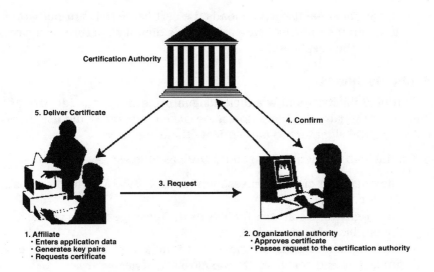

Exhibit 1. The Registration Process.

(or when the originator uses the recipient's PKS to encrypt a message or document), the recipient wants to be sure that the sender is who he or she claims to be. The certificate provides that assurance.

A certificate could be tied to one individual or represent an organizational authority that in turn represents the entire organization. Also, certificates could represent various levels of assurance — from those dispensed by a machine to those registered with a personally signed application. Additional assurance could be provided by the personal presentation of a signed application along with proof of identity, or by the verification of a biometric test (e.g., fingerprint or retina scan) for each use of the private key.

Exhibit 1 shows a possible scenario for obtaining a certificate. The registration process might work as follows:

- The affiliate (i.e., candidate for certificate) fills out the application, generates private-public key pairs, and sends for the certificate, enclosing his or her public key.
- The organizational authority approves the application.
- The organizational authority passes the certificate application to the certification authority.
- The certification authority sends back a message confirming receipt of the application.
- After proper proofing, the certification authority sends the certificate to the applicant-affiliate.

- The applicant-affiliate then loads the certificate to his or her workstation, verifies the certificate authority's digital signature, and saves a copy of the certificate.

Digital Signatures

Exhibit 2 illustrates how a digital signature ensures the identity of the message originator. It shows how a message recipient would use an originator's digital signature to authenticate that originator.

On the Web, authentication could work as follows:

- The originator creates a message and the software performs a hash on the document.
- The originator's software then signs the message by encrypting it with the originator's private key.
- The originator sends the message to the server attaching his or her public key and certificate to the message, if necessary.
- The server either requests the originator's public key from a certificate/key repository or extracts the certification from the originator's message.

With this service, the authentication authority could either attach an authentication message verifying the digital signature's authenticity to the originator's message, or provide that authentication to the recipient via a publicly accessible database. Upon receipt, the recipient would either acknowledge the originator's authenticity via the attached authentication message or access the public key and certificate from the publicly accessible database to read the signature.

To provide such levels of assurance, the certification authority must establish proofing stations where individuals and organizations can present themselves with appropriate identification and apply for certificates. The authority must also maintain or be part of a legal framework of protection and be in a position to mount an enforcement process to protect customers against fraud.

Certificate Repository

The certificate authority also provides the vehicle for the distribution of public keys. Thus the certificate authority would have to maintain the public key certificates in a directory server that can be accessed by authorized persons and computers.

Exhibit 3 shows how subscribers might use such a repository. Certificates could be retrieved on demand along with their current status. Additional information, such as e-mail addresses or fax numbers, could also be available on demand.

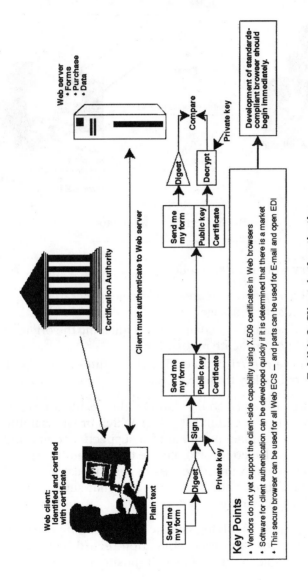

Web server
- Forms
- Purchase
- Data

Compare

Digest

Decrypt

Private key

Certification Authority

Client must authenticate to Web server

Send me my form

Public key Certificate

Send me my form

Public key Certificate

Web client: Identified and certified with certificate

Plain text

Digest

Sign

Private key

Send me my form

Key Points
- Vendors do not yet support the client-side capability using X.509 certificates in Web browsers
- Software for client authentication can be developed quickly if it is determined that there is a market
- This secure browser can be used for all Web ECS — and parts can be used for E-mail and open EDI

Development of standards-compliant browser should begin immediately.

Exhibit 2. Client Authentication.

759

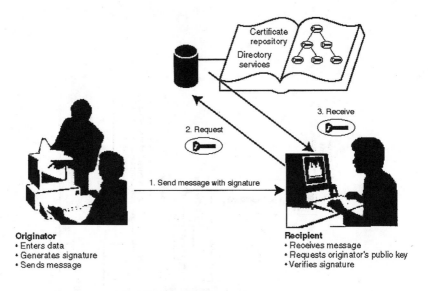

Originator
* Enters data
* Generates signature
* Sends message

Recipient
* Receives message
* Requests originator's public key
* Verifies signature

Exhibit 3. Certificate Repository.

The repository would work as follows:

- The message originator creates a message, generates a digital signature, and sends the message.
- The recipient sends a signed message requesting the originator's public key from the certificate repository.
- The certificate repository verifies the requester's signature and returns the public key to the recipient.

The certificate authority could also use the certificate repository to maintain a certificate revocation list (CRL), which provides notification of certificates that are revoked pursuant to a suspected compromise of the private key. This service could also require that the authority report such compromises via a compromised key list to special customers — possibly those enrolled in a subscribed service — and that such notifications be made available to all customers.

Finally, transactions involving certificates issued by other certificate authorities require that a cross-certification record be maintained and made publicly available in the certificate repository.

Electronic Postmark

A service providing an electronic date and time postmark establishes the existence of a message at a specific point in time. By digitally signing the postmark, the postmarking authority assures the communicating parties that the message was sent, was in transit, or received at the indicated time.

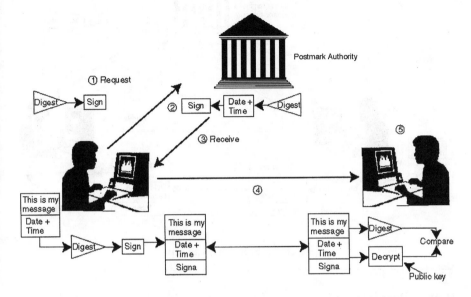

Exhibit 4. Electronic Postmark.

This service is most useful when the recipient requires the originator to send a message by a specified deadline. The originator would request the postmark authority to postmark the message. The authority would receive a digest of the message, add a date and time token to it, digitally sign the package, and send it back to the originator, who would forward the complete package (i.e., signed digest, time stamp, and original message) to the recipient as shown in Exhibit 4.

Electronic postmarking functions as follows:

- The originator sends a request to the postmark authority to postmark a message or document (i.e., a digital digest of the message or document).
- The postmark authority adds date and time to the message received and affixes its digital signature to the entire package.
- The postmark authority sends the package back to the originator.
- The originator sends the original message or document plus the postmarked package to the recipient.
- The recipient verifies the postmark authority signature with the authority's public key and reads the message or document.

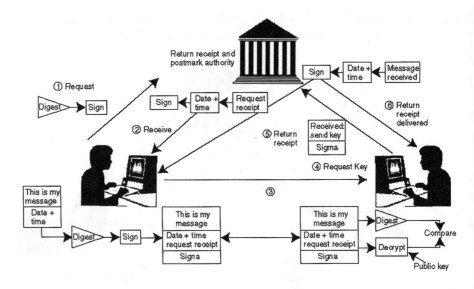

Exhibit 5. Return Receipt.

Return Receipts

This service reports one of three events: that a message has transited the network, that it has been received at the recipient's mailbox, or that the recipient has actually decoded and opened the message at a specific date and time. In the latter instance, the transaction delivered to the recipient that has been encrypted might be set up only to be decrypted with a special one-time key, as shown in Exhibit 5. This one-time key could be provided by the postmark authority upon receipt of an acknowledgment from the recipient accompanied by the recipient's digital signature.

Here is how return receipt might work:

- The originator sends a message digest to the return receipt and postmark authority (the authority) with a request for a postmark and return receipt.
- The authority receives the message digest, adds date and time, encrypts the result, attaches a message to the recipient to request the decryption key from the authority upon receipt of the message, and affixes its digital signature to the package.
- The authority returns the postmarked, receipted package to the originator, who sends it to the recipient.
- The recipient receives the message package and makes a signed request for the decryption key from the authority.

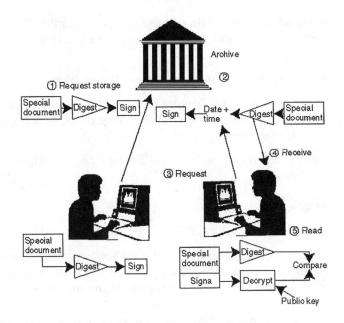

Exhibit 6. Storage and Retrieval.

- The authority receives the recipient's request, verifies the recipient's digital signature, and sends the decryption key to the recipient, who then decrypts and reads the message.
- The authority simultaneously forwards the return receipt to the originator.

Storage and Retrieval Services

These services include transaction archiving where copies of transactions are held for specified periods of time, as illustrated in Exhibit 6. The service might also include information (i.e., documents, videos, or business transactions) that can be sealed, postmarked, and held in public storage to be retrieved via any authorized access. Likewise, encrypted information (i.e., documents, videos, or business transactions) can be sealed, postmarked, and further encrypted and held in sealed storage for indefinite periods of time. Each of these storage and retrieval capabilities must carry legal standing and the stamp of authenticity required for electronic correspondents.

Storage and retrieval works as follows:

- The originator sends a request to the archive to archive a document or message for a specified period of time and designates this information as publicly retrievable.

- The archive adds date and time to the message, verifies the identity of the originator, affixes a digital signature to the package, and archives the package.

- A customer requests the document from the archive.

- The archive retrieves the document, adds a date and time stamp to the package, affixes another digital signature to the new package, and sends it to the recipient.

- The recipient verifies the first and second archive signatures and reads the message.

USE OF COMMERCIAL EXCHANGE SERVICES

Electronic Commerce Services (ECS) may be used in one of three ways:

- The originator sends a message to the authority with a request for service, the authority provides the service and returns the message to the originator, and the originator forwards the message to the recipient.
- The originator sends a message to a value added network (VAN), which then forwards the message to the authority with a request for services. The authority provides the service and returns the message to the value added network, which then forwards the message to the recipient.

- The originator sends a message to the authority with a request for service and the address of the recipient. The authority then forwards the message directly to the recipient.

All of these services could be provided by a single authority, by a hierarchy of authorities, or by a network of authorities, each specializing in one or more of these services.

AVAILABLE TECHNOLOGIES FOR ELECTRONIC COMMERCE

Currently, three major technologies are capable of providing electronic commerce services — e-mail, the World Wide Web, and open EDI. Typical of advanced technologies, security elements are the last to be developed and yet are essential if these technologies are to be deemed trustworthy for electronic commerce.

The issues of confidentiality, confirmation of identity, time certainty, and legal protection apply to all these technologies. The solutions — certification, key repositories, postmarking, return receipts, and storage and retrieval — are equally applicable to each of these technologies. Although the state of universality and interoperability varies among these technologies, they are all in a relative state of immaturity.

Secure E-mail

Electronic messaging's most classic manifestation is e-mail. Because of its capacity for handling attachments, e-mail can be used to transfer official business, financial, technical, and a variety of multimedia forms.

DMS and PEM.

Both the Department of Defense standard for e-mail, which is based on the ITU's X.400 standard for e-mail (called the Defense Message System or DMS), and the Internet e-mail standard, the simple mail transfer protocol (SMTP), have made provisions for security. The DMS uses encapsulation techniques at several security levels to encrypt and sign e-mail messages. The security standard for the Internet is called Privacy Enhanced Mail (PEM). Both methods rely on a certificate hierarchy and known and trusted infrastructure. Neither method is fully developed.

Secure World Wide Web

The phenomenal growth of the Web makes it a prime candidate for the dissemination of forms and documents. Organizations see the Web as a prime tool for services such as delivery of applications and requests for information. However, web technology has two competing types of security: one at the application layer that secures hypertext transfer protocol (HTTP) formatted data (known as SHTTP), and one at the socket layer that encrypts data in the format in which it is transported across the network.

In addition, vendors do not yet support either client-side authentication or the use of X.509 certificates. Although software for such activities as client authentication can be developed relatively quickly, vendors have to be convinced that there is a real market for such products. This technology is about to emerge and, although it will emerge first to support web applications, it will also speed the development of e-mail and EDI security services.

Secure Open EDI

Until now, EDI has been used in closed, value-added networks where security and integrity can be closely controlled. Signing and encryption have been proprietary to the EDI product in use or to the value-added EDI network provider.

By contrast, open EDI running across open networks requires adherence to the standards that are still being developed, and a yet-to-be-developed infrastructure that can ensure trusted keys. To date, the various schemes to accelerate the use of open systems for EDI have not captured the imagination of EDI users and providers.

THE OVERRIDING ISSUE: A PUBLIC KEY CERTIFICATE INFRASTRUCTURE

The suite of services and technologies described in this chapter depend on trusted public keys and their bindings to users. Users could be completely assured of the integrity of keys and their bindings if they were exchanged manually. Because business is conducted on a national and international scale, users have to be assured of the integrity of the registration authority and the key repository in an inevitably complex, electronic way.

One as-yet-unresolved issue is whether such an authority or authorities should be centralized and hierarchical or distributed. The centralized, hierarchical scheme would mean that certification authorities (and purveyors of the accompanying services) would be certified by a higher authority that, in turn, might be certified by yet a higher authority — and so on to the root authority. This kind certification would create a known chain of trust from the highest to the closest certification authority. This scheme is often referred to as the Public Key Infrastructure (PKI).

The alternative assumes that the market will foster the creation of a variety of specialized certification authorities to serve communities of interest. A complicated method of cross-referencing and maintaining those cross references in the certificate repository for each community of interest would then develop.

The outcome of this debate is likely to result in a combination of both methods, such as several hierarchies with some kind of managed cross-referencing to enable public key exchanges between disparate communities of interest when required. Following are some of the issues yet to be resolved:

- Agreement on the exact contents of certificates
- Definition of the size of prime numbers used in key generation
- Establishment of the qualifications required for obtaining a certificate
- Definition of the identification and authentication requirements for certificate registration
- Ruling on the frequency with which certificates are renewed
- Agreement on the legal standing and precedence for such technology

CONCLUSION

Groups such as the Internet Engineering Task Force (IETF), the Federal Government Public Key Infrastructure (PKI) users group, and even the American Bar Association are tackling these knotty issues.

In fact, with toolkits now available that allow the user to become his or her own certificate authority, everyone can get into the act. Private companies such as VeriSign are establishing themselves as certification authorities so that users will give their public keys and certificates credence. The National Security Agency wants to become the certificate authority for the U.S. federal government. The U.S. Postal Service is intent on offering electronic commerce services to businesses and residences by acting as the certificate authority and provider.

An infrastructure will emerge, and it will probably work for users very similar to the way that it has been described in this chapter.

Chapter 52
Knowledge Management on the Internet: The Web/Business Intelligence Solution

Jason Weir

In the 21st century, you won't be able to tell where your enterprise ends and the World Wide Web begins. What's more, you won't really *care*—any more than you care now about which tabular scheme your computer's operating system uses to store and retrieve data on your hard drive. That's because the web promises to transform the enterprise so that concepts like *local storage* and *remote access* will be so obsolete as to seem quaint. The web will be so tightly integrated with the methods people use to access, analyze, and present corporate information that it'll become increasingly inaccurate to talk about business intelligence *applications*. Rather, people will manipulate enterprise data in a rich business intelligence environment.

Like a natural ecological system, a business intelligence environment will feature a variety of processes working in harmony to ensure the growth and enrichment of the system as a whole. In more concrete terms, business intelligence will evolve away from a model in which functionality is dumped on every desktop whether the user needs it or not, and where widely used data is needlessly duplicated across several personal hard drives, when it could be shared and updated centrally. Users will gain access to server-based business intelligence services according to their needs. And crucial data in the environment—from full-fledged reports to simple executive buttons—will be stored and shared out centrally.

The web will not be just another networking pipeline; it'll be an actual application platform on a par with—indeed, seamlessly integrated within—major operating systems. Applications that run over the web in this way are called *thin clients*. Microsoft's next-generation operating system already incorporates the web look and feel into its desktop interface so that everything—locally stored files, programs, and external web sites—appear as links do in web pages, and the globe-sprawling web itself appears as an extension of the desktop.

And what we now call *fat* business intelligence applications—feature-rich, flexible, muscular programs that require at least some logic to reside on the desktop—will nevertheless use web technology (like Java *applets*) and access web-based resources as just another part of the enterprise *view*.

That's what's coming in the 21st century. The question now facing the enterprise is simple: How do we build a business intelligence environment for the web that will get us there?

THE ENTERPRISE AND BUSINESS INTELLIGENCE

To understand just what the web means for business intelligence, you have to first look at how enterprises access, analyze, publish, and distribute corporate information. The complex task of extracting meaningful information from relational databases, multidimensional databases, and Relational Online Analytical Processing (ROLAP) servers into a point-and-click affair has been greatly simplified by modern technologies from a variety of vendors. For many Fortune 1000 companies, these business-oriented, high-performance repositories—deployed as *data warehouses* or, more recently, *data marts*, in the case of departmental repositories—have become the standard method of organizing data from an enterprise's operations. They rely on these business intelligence systems to help cut costs, find new revenue opportunities, or change the enterprise and its processes to meet new challenges.

CHALLENGES OF THE WEB

While the web's promise for revolutionizing the enterprise is now well recognized, so, too, are some of its challenges. From a business intelligence perspective, web technology is still evolving. Unaided, it can't deliver the kind of functionality or performance required by the enterprise. From the standpoint of Information Technology (IT) professionals, the web is a new frontier very different from the client/server landscape they know so well. web technologies are still in flux, yet the onus is on IT to choose a web/business intelligence solution that employs technology most likely to be relevant years down the road. In short, IT has to pick a winner when the picking is tough. Research has shown that concerns about business intelligence over the web break down into roughly three key themes:

- The **security** of mission-critical (and expensive) corporate information systems
- The **scalability** of web-based systems when large volumes of information are exchanged between databases and web clients
- The burden of **administration** that may come with adopting web systems that operate separately from existing business intelligence environments and that create a separate "stream" of web-specific materials (reports and so on) that duplicates work done in the fat-client environment

SECURITY

When it comes to security, the web suffers from a largely unjustified image problem. Because it was developed around open standards, the web is thought to be wide open to all manner of electronic larceny—wiretapping, hacking, spoofing, and other security-compromising activities. Although such vulnerabilities may apply to poorly managed web sites, a robust web security toolkit exists nevertheless, consisting of public-key encryption, digital certificates, user-specific security "cookies", secure sockets, and so on.

However, these security measures were developed largely for uses of the web—electronic commerce, for instance—that have nothing to do with business intelligence. In a typical, secure electronic-commerce transaction (the online purchase of a book using a credit card, for example), the security measures applied are short-term and session-bound; once the customer sends an encrypted message containing his credit card number and the order is logged, the relationship between buyer and seller is over as far as the web server is concerned.

But in business intelligence environments, users aren't customers who encounter corporate information on a one-time basis. Rather, they have an ongoing relationship with the enterprise's data sources; they're individual *users* of data as well as members of one or more *user groups*, and they may fulfill organizational *roles* that cut across these groups. In a business intelligence environment, a marketing strategist is a single user, but is also a member of the Marketing group with full access to Marketing-specific reports, data tables, and data models. She may also be a manager with access to financial data appropriate for this organizational role. In other words, she has a *user, group*, and *role* security profile that reflects her various responsibilities within the organization. With its emphasis on encryption, web-specific security cannot account for such continuous roles and relationships to enterprise data.

SCALABILITY

This is one concern about the web that's justified, at least where data-intensive, high-volume business intelligence requirements are concerned. Enterprise web servers were really designed only to dole out web pages—and when there are too many users knocking at their doors, even this simple task proves too much for most of them. Asking a web server to handle a complex query with a results set of 5000 records is like pumping data through a pinhole.

What's more, a web server alone doesn't have the smarts to handle something like a simple SQL query; it can hand off data processing to secondary processes using the Common Gateway Interface (CGI), but it then promptly forgets about the job until that secondary process returns results. This *occasionally connected session* is at odds with the needs of a business intelligence environment, which requires a *persistent* connection among client applications, processing services, and data sources.

Persistence is key for any business intelligence session because the user needs an unbroken connection to services handling connectivity, query processing, security, and the like. A persistent session means faster performance of business intelligence tasks and much less chance of losing data. Conversely, data in an occasionally connected session is slowed, and may even be lost, as it's passed from secondary processes through the web server to the client. It's rather like being served by absent-minded waitstaff who have to be constantly reminded who you are, where you're sitting, and what you ordered.

ADMINISTRATION

From the point of view of many IT professionals, it looks like deploying business intelligence capabilities over the web means reinventing the wheel. They've invested a lot of time and resources making the client/server model work for a sizable community of users. Now they have to use different technology—some of it pretty new and risky—to reach an even larger audience. Worries over administration break down into three categories:

• *Managing two environments*—Just because the enterprise is serving a wider audience of users over the web doesn't mean it's going to dump its fat-business intelligence clients. Many users will continue to need the expanded range of functionality that only resident client applications can provide. So if the web/business intelligence solution isn't compatible with the fat clients, IT now has *two* environments to manage, each with its own particular challenges, foibles, and infrastructure requirements. And if a fat-client user wants to use the web as well, IT has to set up and maintain a second security profile.

•*Managing two streams of content*—If the environments are separate, so, too, are the materials created and stored in those environments—different report formats, different semantic layers, different query formats, and so on. This perpetuates the gap between fat-client users and the rest of the enterprise, because it precludes sharing content among users with differing business intelligence needs and access privileges. From the point of view of the enterprise, a report is a report, and web and fat-client users alike must view, interact with, and share the same content if the environment itself is to be enriched.

•*Installing and maintaining plugins*—One way a vendor can really woo a crowd at trade shows is to build browser-specific plugins. These plugins look and feel like fat desktop applications because they *are* fat desktop applications, only they're running inside a web browser instead of within a normal desktop window. While such products make great parlor tricks, they suffer from some fatal flaws:

They're big—in thin-client terms, 1.8 Megabytes is the size of an aircraft carrier.

They're platform-specific, meaning that you have to buy different plugins for different operating systems and even different versions of those systems.

They're web browser-specific, meaning the plug-in you buy for Netscape Navigator doesn't work on Microsoft Internet Explorer.

Finally, and what's most important, these plugins *must be installed individually on each desktop*. Theoretically, you could ask your enterprise's 2000 users to install the plugins themselves. However, most IT professionals know that their user audience has different levels of technical sophistication—and they also know to whom the job of installing the plugins will fall. It'll fall squarely on themselves. This type of desktop-centric deployment is a fat-client requirement: what's gained by making it a web client requirement too?

WHAT DOES THE ENTERPRISE NEED IN A WEB/BUSINESS INTELLIGENCE SOLUTION?

Clearly, it needs a web solution that addresses the three crucial concerns discussed above. Such a web solution must use a security model that promotes users' ongoing relationships with corporate data, as well as with other users, other teams, and other departments within the organization. It must be scalable, circumventing as much as possible the bottlenecks inherent in web server technology. It must be seamlessly integrated with its fat-client counterpart and must serve users—regardless of platform—the same business intelligence content. Finally, such a web solution must be able to balance these concerns about security, scalability, and ease of administration with web users' needs for powerful, meaningful access to the organization's business intelligence resources. In short, what is needed is a well-managed web/business intelligence solution.

So exactly what is needed to bring about such a solution? A discussion of some basic principles and emerging technologies that will enable a robust and effective web-based business intelligence solution will help outline this.

FIRST PRINCIPLES

If it's going to succeed, a complex endeavor like a web/business intelligence environment must start from first principles. These should be few in number but be applied without wavering. So before we get into all the technology, here are some first principles:

- No gaps or stovepipes—The enterprise is an unbroken continuum of needs. A business intelligence environment should reflect this, leaving no gaps among user communities. In fact, web functionality and fat-client functionality should overlap, so that learning and experience are applicable when users gain new levels of access.
- Tight integration—Many organizations have spent the last five years reengineering their business processes, eliminating organizational stovepipes in favor of tightly integrated ones. Why should business intelligence vendors set back the clock by delivering technologies that separate users arbitrarily?
- Common services, common data—The business intelligence systems that service this spectrum of needs must be holistic; web (or thin) clients and fat clients should merely be different outlets for the same data. And, as much as possible, thin and fat clients should be administered by the same logic and processing services.
- Standard technologies—Budgets aren't bottomless, and resources aren't infinite. Technologies that become obsolete within two years are useless to the enterprise. So any web-enabled business intelligence solution should employ technologies that are most likely to become industry standards with lasting value.

With these first principles defined, a brief discussion of the technologies that enable web business intelligence is necessary.

THE BASIC ELEMENTS OF A WEB/BUSINESS INTELLIGENCE SOLUTION

First, what elements are involved in a web/business intelligence solution? In other words, what is the architecture of the environment? While vendors in the business intelligence space offer a variety of different packages comprised of various components, most share the following services as part of their solution.

Web/Business Intelligence Server. This is a server dedicated to housing the business intelligence solution for the enterprise. It may be completely dedicated to remote or occasionally connected users accessing the system via the Internet, or "balanced" with in-house activities. It houses the database and related applications required for the web/business intelligence solution.

Session Management Services. These services control a web client's access to the server, track the use of various other services, detect whether the session has been discontinued, and clean up after the web client has moved on. These services also monitor the performance of the session.

File Management Services. These include directory management, file naming, and file transfer services used by web clients. For example, the directory management service maintains a list of materials (for example, reports and data models) that a web user sees in their business intelligence "portfolio".

Scheduling, Distribution, and Notification Services. These services allow a web user to schedule reports, queries, and information refreshes at a given time. Some tools enable event-based triggers, such as reports generated when inventory levels of a particular product drop below a certain level, or when sales of a specific product line increase to a given value. Notification can be sent via e-mai; by "push", or channel, technologies; or by way of a proprietary solution.

Load Balancing Services. Depending on the number of users, organizations may find it necessary to offload activity to alternate servers. That is, as more users share the same resource pool on a single server, the need to create duplicate, or mirrored, systems arises. Load balancing services manage the entire resource pool in a manner similar to what is called a "clustered" environment. A cluster is two or more systems that essentially act as a single unit. Clusters are transparent to both end users and, for the most part, even administrators.

Application Services. These services are the brains of the operation. They enable simple web browsers to become powerful front-end query and analysis tools. Some business intelligence vendors offer complete web-enabled solutions that include browser plugins for end-user query, analysis, and reporting while others rely on proprietary applications to perform these tasks.

SUPPORTING TECHNOLOGIES

Now that the basic elements of the web business intelligence solution have been discussed, a brief introduction to some of the technologies used to enable robust and effective solutions is useful.

The Plumbing—CORBA, IIOP, and the Business Repository

Consider all the different "audiences" to which the web/business intelligence solution has to "play." A typical enterprise has a mixture of Windows platforms (Windows 3.1, Windows 95, Windows NT) and perhaps some AS/400 and UNIX systems as well. To complicate matters, there are popular web browsers offered by Netscape and Microsoft, with several different versions of each.

Obviously, there cannot be a separate copy of information formatted for the different versions of end-user tools on each platform. Somehow, the server has to be able to talk to all of these clients and give them what they need in a format they can use. It's rather like asking an interpreter at the United Nations to translate for several delegations at once—a daunting task even for the most accomplished linguist. What would make that beleaguered interpreter's life a lot easier would be a universal translator. In essence, this is what CORBA does.

CORBA. The Common Object Request Broker Architecture (CORBA) is a specification that allows applications to:

- •Communicate with one another even though they're running on different platforms. For instance, a UNIX version of the business intelligence server can service a Windows 95 desktop.
- •Move commonly used services, or objects, from the desktop to another location on a network—in this case, onto the business intelligence server. This is the heart of the distributed computing systems model that's fast becoming adopted in enterprise software.

Overseeing CORBA is the mandate of the Object Management Group (OMG), a coordinating body with a membership of over 750 companies. Established in 1989, the OMG promotes "the theory and practice of object technology for the development of distributed computing systems." The group's CORBA specification (now at 2.0) forms the standards by which Object Request Broker (ORB) vendors create their products. More specifically, the OMG defines the Interface Definition Language (IDL) and the Application Programming Interfaces (APIs) used to keep ORBs talking to one another.

Think of the ORB as middleware; but instead of mediating a connection between, say, a desktop client and a database, it sets up connections between the client and the application objects it needs located on a network. Thanks to the ORB, the client does not actually have to have that application object running on the desktop, nor does it need to know where the object actually is on the network. All the client needs to know is where the ORB is; the ORB in turn takes care of finding the object, passing on the client's request, and returning the results of the object's work to the client. All of this is transparent to the user.

IIOP. In a distributed object environment, ORBs need a robust, persistent pipeline through which to communicate. The Internet Inter-ORB Protocol (IIOP) is that pipeline. Adopted in 1994 as part of the OMG's CORBA 2.0 specification, IIOP is designed for interoperability among objects. This means that if an object meets CORBA 2.0 specifications, it can by definition speak to any other CORBA 2.0-specified objects, even if they're made by different vendors.

What's more important to web-enabled business intelligence, IIOP is a persistent communications protocol, a stark contrast to the HyperText Transfer Protocol (HTTP), the impersistent method web servers use to take in and serve out data. Throughout a web query session, the ORBs keep in constant touch with one another, exchanging user requests, returning results, and handling other background processes. Unlike a web server, ORBs never hang up on one another as long as there's a job to be done. In other words (going back to our plumbing metaphor), IIOP provides a robust pipeline in an environment where a user needs continuous access to services like database access or query processing.

Java and XML. Originally developed by Sun Microsystems as a platform-independent programming language for consumer electronics devices, Java has quickly become the de facto standard for extending the capabilities of the web beyond the confines of HyperText Markup Language (HTML). Based loosely on C++ (the object-oriented programming language in which most desktop programs are coded), Java programs—called applets—are designed to run in any environment that supports a Java Virtual Machine (JVM). Microsoft and Netscape have fully integrated JVMs into their web browser products.

For web/business intelligence purposes, Java provides:

- A method of deploying application interfaces (data models, for instance) that are identical to the ones used by in-house applications
- The means to render data (results sets from queries, reports, and so forth) in much more flexible ways than is possible using HTML
- A way to circumvent the impersistence of the web server; Java applets can be "carriers" for ORBs, thus helping establish the IIOP pipeline between the web client and the business intelligence server

This use of Java and XML means that web business intelligence solutions can be freed from the limited presentation abilities of HTML. For instance, HTML cannot deliver the WYSIWYG control required for reports because it cannot handle X-Y positioning, that is, the ability to put a particular object (a graphic, chart, or block of text) in one precise spot on the page. Java and XML handle X-Y positioning perfectly so that reports look exactly the same whether viewed over the Web or in a fat client.

CONCLUSION

In summary, by combining emerging technologies like CORBA, IIOP, Java, and XML with robust web-enabled business intelligence tools, web/business intelligence solutions offer organizations a superior weapon in today's competitive global economy. Companies can gain real competitive advantage by transporting the proven effectiveness of in-house decision support systems to the web.

Section XI
Project and Systems Management

Chapter 53
A Model for Project Management

Michael A. Mische

Effective technical and project management is neither trivial nor simple. Systems integration implicates far more than legacy systems and new "go-to" technologies and affects more than the traditional information management and technology (IM&T) organization. Reengineering and systems integration efforts extend into the very culture and structure of the enterprise and must be managed formally.

The complexities of systems integration and reengineering projects require an effective project management methodology that addresses not only the technical aspects of the project but also organizational and cultural changes. Unfortunately, many integration and reengineering efforts do not meet their targets, and the methods used to manage those projects are in part a contributing factor to their failure. This chapter discusses the strengths and weaknesses of traditional project management methods and provides a new framework for managing the systems integration project.

THE NEED FOR A NEW APPROACH TO PROJECT MANAGEMENT

To avoid the pitfalls that plague many integration efforts, IM&T organizations are sending legions of analysts and programmers to project management and quality improvement training courses. Although these steps are appropriate and, in many cases, necessary, the typical two- or three-day project management seminar is inadequate in providing any meaningful assurance that the integration project will be completed in an efficient and cost-effective manner. Recognizing the benefits of external resources, IM&T organizations are turning to third-party systems integrators and management consultants. Engaging a systems integrator to facilitate the integration process helps avoid many of the common problems associated with systems integration; however, external consultants and systems integrators are hired to do a specific task for a limited time and are quickly gone from the scene after the project is over. They do not have to live with the consequences of the process. Internally, many IM&T organizations lack

0-8493-9968-8/99/$0.00+$.50
© 1999 by CRC Press LLC

the global perspective, political empowerment, and broad-based business knowledge necessary to manage the multidisciplinary approach to systems integration. Thus, it is common to see some combination of resources dedicated to the systems integration project.

The experiences of many organizations in the systems integration and reengineering arena emphasize the need for a more effective method for managing these highly complex and inherently risky projects. Mounting evidence indicates that 70 to 80 percent of systems integration and reengineering efforts end in failure, at least in the sense that projects fall short of expected goals and results.

The traditional project management methods that were so effective in managing classic systems development and operational improvement efforts are simply not up to the rigors of cross-platform and cross-functional systems integration. The project management needs of a systems integration and reengineering project are very different today, and the classic project management methods were not designed to be used in projects that involve cross-functional processes, rapid migration paths to new technologies, and the inevitable flattening of the organization. Organizations can no longer rely solely on Gantt charts and dozens of MIS personnel huddled in cubicles around terminals to manage multimillion-dollar efforts.

With systems integration projects spanning several years and running into the tens and hundreds of millions of dollars, senior leadership is well justified to ask, "Why integrate?" In many cases, the wholesale replacement of systems and outsourcing of the entire IM&T function could be less expensive and far more effective in supporting the organization.

Responsive project management considers the integration process systematically and anticipates the project's effects on the entire organization rather than on just the individual applications, IM&T department, hardware, and software. Where traditional project management processes have focused on individual elements of project management, such as work plans, PERT charts, and project team reporting relationships, managing systems integration endeavors requires the management of systemic change. The pace at which most systems integration projects move mandates that resources, new "go-to" technologies, project problems, and issues be identified in an accelerated, preemptive manner, as opposed to a reactionary manner. Project management for systems integration must be both opportunistic and preventive. Managing these megadollar efforts requires a framework that melds the best of the tried-and-true, traditional project management practices with new measurements, and a process that provides for the constant examination of the functional relationships and technical dependencies among key project variables and processes. The project management practices for systems integration must address not only the typical IM&T technical issues but also the rate of organizational change that is related to systems integration. Thus, there is a preemptive dimension to the systems integration management process that must be provided.

A MODEL FRAMEWORK FOR MANAGING THE SYSTEMS INTEGRATION PROJECT

A starting point for managing systems integration projects requires a definition for project management. Defined as a process, project management is a coordinated set of processes that provides for:

- The effective management of project resources
- Optimized application of project resources
- Correct, consistent, and timely measurement and communication of project status

The model framework for managing the systems integration project has five components:

1. A Comprehensive Project Work Plan (CWP)
2. A Project Management and Tracking System (PMT)
3. Project Team Organization (PTO)
4. Quality Assurance Process (QAP)
5. Employee Training and Process Simulation (ETS)

Collectively, the five components are important because they provide:

- Empowered work groups
- A uniform discipline and structure to follow and manage resources.
- A structure that emphasizes quality in the project management process
- A balance between traditional practices, which concentrate on control and reporting, and the modern need to be anticipatory in the project management process
- A process to measure and manage the rate of project progress and technological and organizational change effectively

Project Team Organization

An effective and functional project team is paramount to the success of any integration effort. It makes little difference how encompassing and refined the project work plan is if the tasks are assigned to a team with mediocre abilities or insufficient time.

Conversely, it is tremendously demoralizing to a potentially effective team to be harnessed by an ineffective work plan or inept project leadership. The project teams should be staffed by cross-functional and multidisciplinary individuals who are technically competent and proficient in their knowledge of the business.

Effective project management requires that a multidisciplinary and cross-functional team structure be used to integrate key technology requirements, organizational responsibilities, and business processes. Process integration requires an empowered team structure for the governance and management of the project. The organization structure for integration is composed of specialty teams, each dedicated to a specific purpose and need. The specialty teams include key leadership, management, and knowledge workers. Sponsorship, accountability, and responsibility for the results of the project and its process are shared across disciplines. Not all the project teams work simultaneously throughout the process of integration. The project plan, team specializations, project phases, and individual work schedules drive the timing and sequencing of the teams. Certain teams, such as those with a highly specialized focus and finite purpose, disband once their work has been completed. Other teams have a constant role through project completion. The structure also lends itself to the inclusion of customers, trading partners, suppliers, and business alliance members to function as team members.

Because each integration and reengineering effort is unique, there are no set rules either for the number and types of teams required to support and manage the integration process effectively or for the number of individuals assigned to a team. In general, it is best to limit the number of individuals assigned to any one team to no more than ten. Ideally, teams should be composed of three to seven people, with one core team responsible for the entire effort. The teams are integrated into the overall working structure through the management practices and tools incorporated in the CWP and PMT, including direct reporting by individual team leaders; oversight by the project steering committee; structured weekly, biweekly, monthly, and quarterly briefing sessions; and a consistent training program for all project team members in the practices and processes of project management.

The organization structure for the integration and reengineering effort should be diamond-shaped rather than hierarchical. This structure is flatter and more conducive to the simultaneous coordination of many specialty teams, and helps to create a more seamless communication flow among teams and individual team members. It also supports the integration of skill sets, responsibilities, and knowledge, and helps ensure the proper balance of these factors as well as organizational levels throughout the systems integration project.

THE COMPREHENSIVE PROJECT WORK PLAN (CWP)

The nucleus of systems integration project management is the CWP. As discussed in the next chapter, the CWP contains all of the tasks, staffing assignments, deliverables, dependencies, prerequisites, milestones, and estimated effort necessary to complete the integration process. The CWP is organized into six components.

Project Overview

The initial component of the CWP provides for a narrative description of the project. Providing a broad conceptual overview is important because it establishes the formal rationale, expectations, and parameters in which the project is performed. It also provides for a common basis from which to assess the project and serves as an effective reference point when communicating about the project. The major items included in the overview include:

- Objectives, scope, and intended results of the integration effort
- Organization of the project's phases and life cycle
- Estimated level of effort and types of resources required
- Interdependencies among tasks and work products
- Description of project teams and responsibilities
- Expectations and anticipated benefits
- Timing and calendar for the effort

Project Phases

The second level of the CWP provides a high-level description and representation of the integration project's life cycle. Organizing the effort into discrete life cycle phases such as those described in Chapter 54 creates an effective and convenient working structure. For each phase of the integration project, narrative and supporting representations are developed describing:

- Objectives, purpose, and scope of the integration effort, with linkages to business objectives and organizational benefits
- Specific activities to be accomplished
- Timing and relationships among phases, activities, and tasks
- Estimated level of professional effort for each phase and the distribution of that effort
- Major deliverables and work products to be developed
- Staffing assignments at the project team level
- Measurements and standards for evaluating the effectiveness of the phase and quality of work performed

Developing a clear representation of the phases and work plan for the integration project is important to understanding the structure of the project and measuring results and progress.

Detailed Project Work Plan

The third element of the CWP provides a detailed description of how the systems integration work is to be performed. This involves the development of detailed work plans, activity lists, tasks, work steps, and staffing assignments for the integration project. The detailed project work plan includes:

- •Descriptions of the detailed activities, tasks, and work steps to be performed
- •Detailed descriptions of the individual work products and project deliverables to be developed
- •Timing requirements and key assumptions about the tasks and the development and presentation of deliverables and work products
- •Identification of dependencies and critical path issues related to the work plan
- •Identification of individual responsibilities, task assignments, budgets, and labor estimates
- •Assessment of critical path items and the interdependencies between tasks, deliverables, and project team assignments

Project Team Organization

The fourth part of the CWP provides the identification and description of the project teams assigned to perform the integration project. The description includes:

- •A definition of the project team and its role, purpose, and charter in the integration effort
- •The activities, tasks, and work steps assigned to each team and their respective dependencies and timing
- •The assignment of the work products to be produced by each team
- •An estimate of the number of days of commitment to the project for each team and the dependencies among the teams

Individual Team and Task Assignments

The fifth component of the CWP provides for the assignment of individual team members to a particular project team, tasks, and project deliverables. Specific topics addressed in the individual team and task assignments include:

- • Individual tasks and work product assignments
- • Days or estimated hours of commitment to complete each task and work product

• Timing and schedule for completing tasks and work products assigned and their dependencies on other products and activities

Daily To-Dos

The sixth and final level of the CWP is the daily to-do list, which summarizes all the activities that are assigned to team members to be worked at or completed on a daily basis. It is, in a sense, a production schedule for the integration process. Because of the fluidity of the systems integration process, the daily to-do lists are subject to changes. As such, they not only consider major changes in the work plan and immediate needs and opportunities, but also anticipate the availability of personnel and factor them into the individual schedules of each member of the project team.

An important but almost always overlooked measure is the rate at which the project team works compared to the planned activities. Developing this measure requires capturing data on the time spent by the individual project team member directly on the assignment as compared to time spent on other activities and total available time. This measure is called the effectivity rate.

THE PROJECT MANAGEMENT AND TRACKING SYSTEM (PMT)

The second component of the systems integration project management structure is the PMT, which facilitates the tracking and management of the CWP and individual work plan tasks. A project management process composed of uniform procedures and forms designed to capture information about the individual activities and results of the project, the PMT can be automated and used with any third-party project management software. The PMT requires training and discipline if it is to be used effectively to manage and measure the progress, status, and quality of the integration effort. The PMT helps ensure the continuous calibration of actual results achieved to the original project plan through the use of consistent progress tracking metrics.

Managing the systems integration process requires a combination of individual status reporting and detailed work plan updating procedures. Systems integration projects require the constant assessment of the following items:

1. *Consistent application.* The practices, procedures, and methods used to enable project management must be consistently applied, with no exceptions or deviations from schedules.
2. *Procedures and practices.* Project management involves the constant application of procedures and recurring practices that are designed to capture, normalize, and assess data about the project and individual project team member performance.

3. *Multiple inputs.* Systems integration projects have a multitude of activities and processes under way at any one point. As such, project management must provide for multiple sources of information and evaluation points.
4. *Measurements.* An effective project management process must not only report on progress but measure and assess it against established baselines. The measurements must be valid, meaningful, and, most importantly, consistently applied.
5. *Constant calibration.* Once measured, the project must be constantly evaluated and calibrated to its intended goals, expectations, objectives, and original and revised schedules for completion and financial requirements.

Communicating the progress and disposition of the systems integration process is key to managing the activities of those assigned to the project and the expectations of the organization. Systems integration projects necessitate that communications be meaningful, frequent, and in a standard format that is easy to comprehend, use, and reference. Exhibit 1 provides an illustration of the PMT process.

The major elements of the PMT process include:

- PMT practices and procedures
- PMT project management structure and reporting framework
- PMT management reports
- Team leader reporting procedures and forms
- Team member reporting procedures and forms
- CWP updating procedures
- CWP tracking procedures
- Change management processes
- Standard metrics and measures

Exhibit 2 shows the various forms and procedures that are used in the management of the project and their frequency of use.

The project management and tracking system (PMTS) is a coordinated process of procedures, forms, and practices for managing the systems integration project. The PMTS can be used to support a variety of projects and is especially effective for those which are large and complex and have a number of resources assigned to them. The PMT is composed of six forms (see Exhibit 3). The forms are used throughout the life of the project to collect and organize a variety of data related to actual performance of the systems integration. The major requirement for use of this project management process is discipline. That is, the project team must constantly use the forms and procedures to collect, organize, and present data about the integration process to accurately reflect the progress and quality of the effort. Exhibit 3 provides a summary of frequency of use for the var-

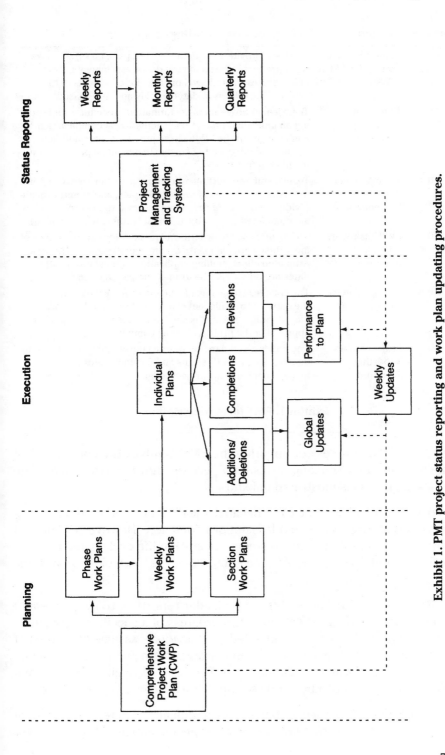

Exhibit 1. PMT project status reporting and work plan updating procedures.

PROJECT AND SYSTEMS MANAGEMENT

Number	Form	Description
1.0	Comprehensive Project Work Plan (CWP)	The CWP provides the detailed work plan, tasks, subtasks, work products, start and stop dates, assignments, deliverables, and estimated level of effort for all aspects of the project. The CWP is updated weekly and is PC-based.
2.0	Team Leader Reporting Procedures	Team leader procedures are formatted procedures for reporting on individual project team activities, accomplishments, and changes to the CWP. These procedures are updated weekly and are used to coordinate individual project team member activities.
3.0	Team Member Reporting Procedures	Team member reporting procedures are formatted forms and procedures used to communicate, track, and monitor the individual activities of personnel assigned to the project. They are completed weekly by individual project team members.
4.0	CWP Task/Work Product Additions	The form is used to describe minor additions and deletions of individual work plan tasks on the overall project. The task, estimated effort, staffing implications, and start and stop dates are provided. The form is completed weekly.
5.0	Change Management Control	The change management form is used to describe and assess the impact of a significant change in the project's scope, work plan, or staffing plan. It is used as necessary and requires the approval of the project steering committee.
6.0	Project Status Reporting Structure/ Formats (PSR)	The PSR is a standard set of procedures and forms that summarizes the project's status and communicates progress to management and the project team.

Exhibit 2. PMT forms description.

ious forms. The process of updating the PMT involves the completion of time logs and task-tracking forms on a periodic and recurring basis. The updating process is illustrated in Exhibit 4.

Form 1 of the PMT is the CWP. Because the CWP is different for each systems integration effort, a sample is not provided here. However, Chapter 54 provides a discussion of the systems integration life cycle, which can be used as a model for developing the comprehensive work plan for systems integration.

Form 2 of the PMT is used for team leader reporting, to aggregate and summarize the individual activities and progress of a specific project team (see Exhibit 5). The form is completed by individuals assigned to a project team, submitted to the team leader, and aggregated to provide a representation of work performed and completed. The form reconciles work accomplished to the work planned and assigned for a specified period of time.

Form 3 is used to collect detailed information and updates for individual tasks and work steps that are assigned to specific individuals (see Exhibit

Frequency of Use

PMT Component	Form	Weekly	Biweekly	Monthly	Quarterly	As Needed
Project Management Tracking System (PMTS)	—	•	•	•	•	
Comprehensive Project Work Plan (CWP)	1.0	•	•	•	•	•
Team Leader Reporting	2.0	•				
Team Member Reporting	3.0	•				
CWP Updating Procedures	4.0	•				
CWP Additions/Deletions Procedures	4.0	•				•
Change Management Procedures	5.0					•
Project Status Reporting	6.0	•		•	•	
Presentations to Project Steering Committee (PSC)	—					

Exhibit 3. PMT forms and frequency of use.

6). The form also collects information about how an individual team member is performing to the preplanned budget, the status of individual productivity, and additions and deletions to the individual's workload. One of the most important data elements captured by this form is the summarization of unplanned activities and interruptions, which can adversely affect individual productivity and the status of tasks and work steps.

Form 4 is used to collect information that will update the CWP. The form summarizes additions, deletions, and extensions to the work plan including estimated effort, new start and completion dates, and project team assignments (see Exhibit 7).

Form 5 is used to facilitate change management. Change management is integral to any successful integration effort. Form 5 is designed to collect, describe, and assess the impact of changes to the work plan. The form summarizes important information such as economic impact and the effect of the change on the critical path of the effort (see Exhibit 8).

Form 6 provides a standard structure for summarizing the key criteria and information about the systems integration effort. The standard format ensures consistency and continuity are achieved in assessing the status of the project and in communicating the results of the project (see Exhibit 9).

Examples and instructions for each of the forms that comprise the PMT are provided below.

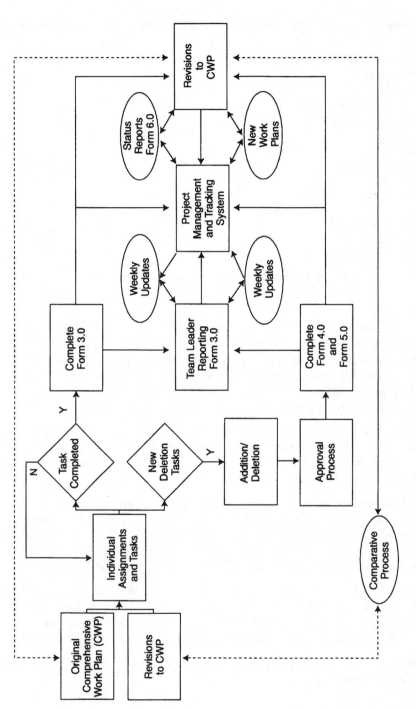

Exhibit 4. PMT: updating the comprehensive project work plan.

Project Name:	Form 2.0 Team Leader Reporting

Reporting Period:	From	(1)	To	(End)

Your Name: (2) Self-Explanatory   **Extension:**

Project Team Leader: (3) Self-Explanatory   **Extension:**

Project Status Report

Activities Accomplished This Period			Activities Accomplished to Date		
	Tasks	Hours		Tasks	Hours
Activities Completed	(10)	_____	Original Plan	(4)	_____
Additions	(11)	_____	Completed to Date	(5)	_____
Deletions	(12)	_____	Additions to Date	(6)	_____
			Deletions to Date	(7)	_____
			Net Tasks Not Completed	(8)	_____
			Tasks in Process	(9)	_____

Exhibit 5. Team leader reporting.

Forms Description

Form Title: **Team Leader Reporting**
Form Number: 2.0

Form Description

Purpose
To Summarize Individual Activity and Progress by Project Team and Leader

Used By	Reference Contacts
Project Team Leaders Project Management Group	

Format Description

Reference Number	Description
1. For Week Ending	Time Reporting Period
2. Your Name	Your Name
3. Project Leader	Project Team Leader's Name
Project-to-Date Totals	
4. Original Plan	Number of Tasks and Hours in the Original Plan
5. Completed to Date	Number of Tasks Completed Project to Date
6. Additions to Date	Number of Tasks and Hours Added Project to Date
7. Deletions to Date	Number of Tasks and Hours Deleted Project to Date
8. Net Tasks Not Completed	Net Number of Tasks to Be Completed Project to Date
9. Tasks in Process	Number of Tasks Currently in Process
Current Period Totals	
10. Completed	Tasks Completed During the Current Reporting Period
11. Additions	Tasks and Hours Added to the Plan During the Current Reporting Period
12. Deletions	Tasks and Hours Deleted from the Plan During the Current Reporting Period

---

Exhibit 5. (Continued)

Effective Date:_____

Procedure

Procedure for

Project Leader Reporting and Individual Time Sheet Collection
Facilitates Individual Project Team Leaders in the Completion of Weekly Project
Team Leader Reports and in Collecting Weekly Reports from Team Members

Procedure Supports	Frequency
Forms Used: 3.0, 4.0 Forms Completed or Submitted by This Procedure: 2.0.	Weekly

Responsibility	Reference Contacts
Individual Project Team Leaders	

Procedure Steps

Example Procedures for Collecting Team Member Reports:

1. Collect all time sheets from project team members (Forms 3.0 and 4.0) by 2:00 pm every week.
2. Verify that all team member time sheets have been collected.
3. Review all time sheets for hours worked, estimates to complete, revised start or end dates, status of activities, unplanned activities, and comments.
4. If necessary, identify any new tasks or projects (see Form 4.0) that develop. The new tasks or projects should be documented using the procedures provided on Form 4.0.
5. Resolve any questions or issues that arise from entries on the time sheets with respective team members before submitting to project controller.
6. Approve all time sheets for use by initialing the upper right-hand corner.
7. Submit to the project controller no later than Monday at 10:00 am.

Example Procedures for Completing the Summary Sheet:

1. Enter the time reporting period in Field Number 1 for week ending. Reporting periods begin at 7:00 am on Monday and end at 5:00 pm the following Sunday.
2. Enter the total number of tasks that have been completed for this project in Field Number 5, Completed to Date. This number can be obtained from the Activity Status, Time, and Usage. Report by counting the number of tasks that have a status of "Complete."
3. Enter the total number of tasks and total hours that have been added to this project in Field Number 6, Additions to Date. This number must be accumulated each week, for the duration of the project.

Exhibit 5. (Continued)

4. Enter the total number of tasks and total hours that have been deleted from this project in Field Number 7, Deletions to Date. This number must be accumulated each week, for the duration of the project.

5. Calculate the net tasks not completed, Field Number 8, for this project. This total is derived by adding additions to date, Field Number 6, To Original Plan, Field Number 4, and then subtracting from that sum Completed to Date, Field Number 5, and Deletions to Date, Field Number 7.

6. Enter the number of tasks that are currently in process in Field Number 9, Tasks in Process. This number can be obtained from the Activity Status, Time, and Usage report, by counting the number of tasks that have either a status of start or a percent complete number in the status column.

7. In Field Number 10, Completed, enter the number of tasks that were completed during the current reporting period. This number must be obtained by comparing the total number of completed tasks from the Activity Status, Time, and Usage reports from the current and previous period.

8. Addition for the Current Period, Field Number 11, must be derived from the Task Maintenance forms received from the team members for the current reporting period.

9. Deletions for the Current Period, Field Number 12, must also be derived from the Task Maintenance Form 4.0, received from the team members for the current reporting period.

Exhibit 5. (Continued)

Using the PMT to Update the Plan

Implicit in using the PMT successfully is the updating of the CWP and the production of status reports. Specific PMT procedures include:

1. *Team leader reporting procedures.* Team leader procedures are formatted procedures for reporting on individual project team activities, accomplishments, and changes to the CWP. These procedures are updated weekly and are used to coordinate individual project team member activities.

2. *Team member reporting procedures.* Team member reporting procedures are formatted forms and procedures used to track and monitor the individual activities of personnel assigned to the project. They are completed weekly by individual project team members.

3. *CWP task/work product additions.* This weekly form is used to describe minor additions and deletions of individual work plan tasks in the overall project. The task, estimated effort, staffing implications, and start and stop dates are provided.

Project Name:	Form 3.0 Team Member Reporting

Reporting Period: From (1) To (End)
Your Name: (2) Self-Explanatory Telephone:
Project Phase or Section: (3)

**Using the Individual Work Plan from the Comprehensive Work Plan,
Complete the Following:**

							This Period				
Status as of: _____							**New Accounts/Estimates**				
(4) Task #	(5) Plan	(6) Account	(7) Estimate to Completion	(8) Start Date	(9) End Date	(10) Status	(11) Account Use	(12) Estimate to Completion	(13) Start	(14) End	(15) Status
3.2.1.10 Database (Example)	40	32	12	1/1/95	1/10/95	A	8	4	1/10	1/10	A
(16) Unplanned Activities -Mtgs.				—	—		32				
(17) Total Actual Usage This Period: 40											
(18) Comments or Outstanding/Anticipated Problems											

Exhibit 6. Team member reporting.

Form Title: **Project Team Member Reporting**
Form Number: **3.0**

Form Description

Purpose
Used Weekly by Each Member of the Project Team, IM&T, and Functional, to Report on Tasks, Effort, Activities and Accomplishments.

Used By	Reference Contacts
Individual Project Team Members	

Format Description

Reference Number	Description
1.	Time Reporting Period: Monday, 7:00 am, Through Sunday, 5:00 pm
3.	Project Description
4.	Task Number and Task Description
Project-to-Date Totals	
5. Planned	Number of Hours Planned to Work on the Task
6. Actual	Actual Hours Incurred on the Task Project to Date
7. Estimate to Complete	The Latest Estimate, in Hours, to Complete the Task, as of 5:00 pm of the Previous Week
8. Start Plan/Revision	Planned Start Date of the Task
9. End Plan/Revision	Planned End Date of the Task
10. Status	Status of the Task (Blank = Not Started, Compl = Complete, Strt = Started)
11. Actual Usage	Actual Hours Incurred on the Task for the Reporting Period
12. Estimate to Complete	New Estimate to Complete in Hours
13. New Start	New Start Date for the Task
14. New End	New End Date for the Task
15. Status	Status for the Task
16.	Unplanned Activities Description Section
17.	Total Hours Worked During the Reporting Period
18.	Comments or Anticipated Problem Description Section

Exhibit 6. (Continued)

Effective Date:_____

Procedure

Procedure For
Project Team Member Reporting

Procedure Supports	**Frequency**
Forms Used: 3.0 Forms Generated: 2.0	Weekly
Responsibility All Project Team Members	**Reference Contacts**

Procedure Steps

Procedures for Completing the Time Sheet:

1. For each task worked during the reporting period, enter the actual hours in Field Number 11, Actual Usage. Enter whole hours only.
2. In Field Number 12, Estimate to Complete, enter the number of hours remaining to complete the tasks. Enter whole numbers only.
3. If the actual start date of the task will be different from the planned start date, enter the new start date in Field Number 12, New Start.
4. If the end date of the task will be different from the planned end date, enter the new end date in Field Number 14, New End.
5. If the task is completed during the reporting period, enter a C or Comp in Field Number 15, Status.
6. Describe any unplanned activities in Section 16, Unplanned Activities, not related to the project that were worked on during the reporting period. These unplanned activities categories are vacation, sick days, holiday, training not related to the project, or tasks not related to the project. Include hours worked on each unplanned activity and a brief description, if necessary.
   The time worked on new tasks that has been approved to be added to the plan should not be entered in this section, but entered on the time sheet provided for this purpose (see Form 4.0).
7. Total the hours incurred on the project-related tasks listed on the time sheet and the hours from unplanned activities and enter in Field 17, Total Usage for Period. This total should equal the total work hours for the week.
8. Enter any comments or problems in Section 18, Comments/Outstanding or Anticipated Problems.
9. Each project team member receives a time sheet for each week that includes tasks that have been assigned to work on. The time sheets are to be completed and turned in to the appropriate team leader for each project by 2:00 pm Friday.
   Time sheets are distributed on Tuesday morning of the current reporting period. Reporting periods begin on Monday at 7:00 pm and end on the following Sunday at 5:00 pm.

Exhibit 6. (Continued)

Project Name:		Form 4.0 CWP Maintenance New/Deleted Tasks									
Reporting Period: From (1) To (End)											
Your Name: (2) Self-Explanatory **Extension:**											
Project Team Leader: (3) Self-Explanatory **Extension:**											
Project Status Report											
Activity Number (If Known)	**Task Description**	**Original Budget**				**Revised**					
		Actual	Est. to Comp	Start	End	Status	Est. to Comp	New Start	New End	Assign To	
(4)	(5)	(6)	(7)	(8)	(9)	(10)	(11)	(12)	(13)	(14)	

Comments: For additions to the project plan, indicate predecessor and successor activities.

(15)

Exhibit 7. CWP maintenance.

Form Title:	**CWP Maintenance**
Form Number:	**4.0**

Form Description

Purpose
To update the CWP

Used By All Project Team Members	**Reference Contacts**

Format Description

Reference Number	**Description**
1. Reporting Period	Dates Covered by Form
2. Your Name	Person Completing Form
3. Team Leader	Team Leader's Name
4. Activity Number	Task Number
5. Task Description	Title of Task
6. Actual	Actual Hours Expended to Date
7. Estimate to Complete	Estimated Hours to Complete Task
8. Start	Original Start Date
9. End	Original End Date
10. Status	C = Complete, D = Delete, N = New Task, R = Revision to Existing Task
11. Estimate to Complete	Estimate to Complete Task, Revised
12. New Start	New Start Date
13. New End	New End Date
14. Assigned To	Project Team Member's Initials
15. Comments	

Exhibit 7. (Continued)

PROJECT AND SYSTEMS MANAGEMENT

Effective Date:

Procedure
Procedure for

To update existing tasks in the CWP, revise existing estimates, designate tasks as complete, designate precedessor/succesor activities, provide additions and deletions, revise work schedules, change work step/task responsibilities and assignments, and revise start and stop dates.

Procedure Supports Forms used: N/A Forms generated: 4.0	**Frequency** Weekly or as Needed
Responsibility All Project Team Members	**Reference Contacts**

Procedure Steps

Procedures

1. Item 1 – Complete reporting date
2. Item 2 – Complete your name
3. Item 3 – Complete project team leader's name
4. Enter 4 – (activity number) and 5 (project description) for the project to perform task maintenance.
5. Item 10 – Enter the code for the type of change/project maintenance to be performed:

   – Enter an N to add a task to the project.
   – Enter a C to show the completion of a task.
   – Enter an R to change or revise an existing project task.
   – Enter a D to delete an existing project task.
6. Enter 5 (task description) as indicated on the form. The task description is required for all task maintenance.
7. Indicate 7 (start date) and 8 (end date) for the task. This information is required only for adding new tasks or changing the dates for revised tasks.
8. If a new task, enter the new task number.
9. Provide information about the resources assigned to the task in Section 14 (Resource Assignments). Resource information is required only for adding new tasks or for changing the resource assignments for revised tasks.
   – Indicate the number of 11 (hours) planned for each individual assigned to the task.

Exhibit 7. (Continued)

Procedure Steps (Continued)

Procedures

10. Use Section 15, Comment, for any explanatory information about the changes being performed. For added tasks, indicate the existing predecessor task that the added task must follow.

11. Submit the completed form to the team leader.

12. The team leader reviews the task maintenance form and must approve it before it can be entered into the project plan.

13. Task maintenance is entered into the CWP before the entry of time sheet information.

Exhibit 7. (Continued)

---

4. *Change management control.* The change management form is used to describe and assess the impact of a significant change in the project's scope, work plan, or staffing plan.

5. *Project status reporting structure and formats (PSR).* The PSR is a standard set of procedures and metrics that summarize the project's status and communicate progress to management and the project team.

Translating updates into an effective project is almost always a problem because of the high level of discipline that is required; however, updating the plan can become routine, indeed mechanical, if the correct practices, procedures, and discipline are in place.

Using the PMT to Measure Progress and Status

Using a consistent and valid measurement system is important because it supports trend analysis, isolates problems, indicates progress, and helps to manage expectations. There are 16 critical measurements of progress and status for the systems integration project:

1. Number of tasks actually accomplished this reporting period and to date as compared with those planned in the original and revised CWP

2. Hours or days actually expended this reporting period and to date as compared with those planned in the original and revised CWP

3. Percentage of actual completion of tasks, effort, and work products as compared with what was planned in the original and revised CWP

4. Number of work products actually completed as compared with those planned in the original and revised CWP

Number	Form	Description
1.0	Comprehensive Project Work Plan (CWP)	The CWP provides the detailed work plan, tasks, subtasks, work products, start and stop dates, assignments, deliverables, and estimated level of effort for all aspects of the project. The CWP is updated weekly and is PC based.
2.0	Team Leader Reporting Procedures	Team leader procedures are formatted procedures for reporting on individual project team activities, accomplishments, and changes to the CWP. These procedures are updated weekly and are used to coordinate individual project team member activities.
3.0	Team Member Reporting Procedures	Team member reporting procedures are formatted forms and procedures used to communicate, track, and monitor the individual activities of personnel assigned to the project. It is completed weekly by individual project team members.
4.0	CWP Task/Work Product Additions	The form is used to describe minor additions and deletions of individual work plan tasks on the overall project. The task, estimated effort, staffing implications, and start and stop dates are provided. The form is completed weekly.
5.0	Change Management Control	The change management form is used to describe and assess the impact of a significant change in the project's scope, work plan, or staffing plan. It is used as necessary and requires the approval of the project steering committee.
6.0	Project Status Reporting Structure/Formats (PSR)	The PSR is a standard set of procedures and forms that summarizes the project's status and communicates progress to management and the project team.

Exhibit 7. (Continued)

5. Project milestones and phases actually completed as compared with those planned in the original and revised CWP
6. Tasks added to the CWP this reporting period and to date as compared with those planned in the original and revised CWP
7. Tasks deleted from the CWP this reporting period and to date as compared with those planned in the original and revised CWP
8. Hours per days of effort added to the CWP this reporting period and to date as compared with those planned in the original and revised CWP

	Date: (1)
Project Name:	**Form 5.0** **Change Management**

Reporting Period: From:_____ (2)_____
To:_____(2.1)_____

Your Name:_____ (3)_____
Project Leader:_____(3.1)_____

Description and Sponsorship:_____ (4)_____

Rationale and Benefits:_____ (5)_____

Economic Impact:

Estimated Hours:[_____ (6) _____]   Estimated Earliest Start:____ (13) ____
Estimated Resources:$____ (7) ____   Estimated Latest Start:____ (14) ____
Estimated Costs:_____ (8) _____   Estimated Earliest End:____ (15) ____
New H/W Costs:_____ (9) _____   Estimated Latest End:____ (16) ____
New S/W Costs:_____ (10) _____
Other Costs: [_____ (11) _____]
Total: $_____ (12) _____

Sensitivity Analysis:

Overall Impact on Project:____ (17) _____
Overall Economic Impact:____ (18) _____
Business Risk:____ (19) _____

Approvals: (20)

_____ _____ _____
_____ _____ _____
_____ _____ _____

Exhibit 8. Change management.

Effective Date:

Procedure

Procedure for

Documenting changes to the project, software, scope, and team. It should be completed when any material change to scope or requirements is contemplated.

Procedure Supports Forms Used: Forms Generated: 5.0	Frequency As Needed
Responsibility Project Management Team	Reference Contacts

Procedure Steps

Procedures

1. Complete items 1 through 5, as specified.

2. Complete items 6 through 16, stressing economic impact and impact on human resources.

3. Complete items 17 through 19, with particular emphasis on business risk.

4. Complete item 20. All changes to the project's scope, timing, budget, and resources must be formally approved.

Note: All changes to the project scope, requirements, design, timing, and budget must be reviewed and approved before performing any changes or establishing commitments and new dates.

Exhibit 8. (Continued)

Forms Description

Form Title: Change Management   **Approved:** _____

Form Number: 5.0   **Not Approved:** _____

Form Description

Purpose

To document the potential impact and decisions regarding changes to the project's scope, timing, and resources.

Used By	Reference Contacts
Project Management Team Forms Generated: 5.0	

Format Description

Reference Number   **Description**

1. Date   Date Completed

2. Reporting Period   Period of Reporting

3. Your Name   Your Name

4. Project Leader   Project Leader's Name

5. Rationale Benefits   Description of Benefits and Rationale for Change

6-16   The impact on the project's budget and timing are described here.

17-19. Sensitivity   Description of the Business Risk and Risk to the Project

20. Approvals

Exhibit 8. (Continued)

PROJECT AND SYSTEMS MANAGEMENT

Project Name:	Form 6.0 Status Report Format

Project Name: From: _____(1)_____   To:_____

Prepared by: _____(2)_____   Submitted to: _____(3)_____

Summary of Status: (4)

Accomplishments This Reporting Period			Comments
	Number	Hours	
Tasks Completed	(5)	(5)	
Products Completed	(6)	(6)	
Tasks Added	(7)	(7)	(11)
Tasks Deleted	(8)	(8)	
Tasks Active	(9)	(9)	
Tasks Started	(10)	(10)	

Accomplishments To Date			Planned Activities
	Number	Hours	1. 2. 3. 4.
Total Tasks Assigned	(12)	(12)	
Total Tasks Completed	(13)	(13)	5. (17)
Total Tasks Added	(14)	(14)	6.
Total Tasks Deleted	(15)	(15)	7.
Total Tasks Active	(16)	(16)	8. 9.
Tasks Started	(17)	(17)	10. 11.

Issues Requiring Management Attention:

(18)

Signature:_____

Exhibit 9. Status report format.

808

Form Title:	Status Report Format	Form Number:	6.0

Form Description

Purpose
This form is used to provide a high-level activity summary and status report on weekly progress. The form also serves as a template for monthly and quarterly reporting.

Used By	Reference Contacts
Project Management Team Project Leaders (Selectively)	

Format Description

Reference Number	Description
1. Reporting Period	Reporting Date (Usually Weekly)
2. Prepared by	Your Name
3. Submitted to	Reporting Relationship
4. Summary of Tasks	Narrative Description of the Status of the Project
5. Tasks Completed	Number of Tasks Completed This Reporting Period
6. Product Completed	Number of Work Products or Milestones Completed This Reporting Period
7. Tasks or Hours Added	Number of New Tasks and Hours Added to the CWP This Period
8. Tasks/Hours Deleted	Number of Tasks and Hours Deleted from the CWP This Period
9. Tasks/Hours Active	Number of Tasks and Hours That Are Underway, in Process and Active During This Reporting Period
10. Tasks/Hours Started	Number of Tasks Initiated This Period
11. Comments	Any Pertinent Comments Related to This Reporting Period
12. Total Tasks/Hours Assigned	The Number of Total Tasks Assigned for the Entire Project
13. Total Tasks/Hours Completed	The Number of Total Tasks Completed, Inclusive of This Reporting Period, for the Entire Project
14. Total Tasks Added	The Total Number of New Tasks Added to the CWP from Project Inception Through This Reporting Period
15. Total Tasks Deleted	The Total Number of Tasks and Hours Deleted for the Project
16. Total Tasks Active	The Total Number of Tasks Active for the Entire Project
17. Planned Activities	Activities Planned
18. Issues	Any Issues
19. Signature	—

Exhibit 9. (Continued)

9. Hours per days of effort deleted from the CWP this reporting period and to date as compared with those planned in the original and revised CWP

10. Work products added to the CWP this reporting period and to date as compared with those planned in the original and revised CWP

11. Work products deleted from the CWP this reporting period and to date as compared with those planned in the original and revised CWP

12. Tasks actually initiated and in process this reporting period as compared with those planned in the original and revised CWP

13. Financial reconciliation of capital and expense outlays and commitments as compared with those planned in the original budget and project description

14. Revised CWP as of the update date based on items 6, 7, 8, 9, 10, and 11

15. Distribution of labor by resource type (i.e., programmer, analyst, manager, or user) and use as compared with those planned in the original and revised CWP

16. Forecasted labor needs as compared with those planned in the original and revised CWP

Using the PMT for Reporting and Communication

The final component of the PMT is status reporting and communication. To be useful in tracking progress and meaningful in communicating that progress, status reports must be produced in a periodic and timely manner and must be consistent in style, format, and content. The status reports for the systems integration project must address six topics:

1. Project summary
2. Accomplishments this reporting period
3. Planned activities next period
4. Issues requiring management attention
5. Financial summary
6. Other items

Developing the status report in this format helps to consolidate the project into a meaningful framework and can isolate the issues and major accomplishments. The report should be supported by exhibits and an analysis of the 16 measurements of progress.

QUALITY ASSURANCE PROCESS (QAP)

The QAP component is the fourth component of project management for systems integration. Creating a quality assurance standard and measurement process for the integration project is difficult. There is, of course, an extensive list of statistical measures available to determine the quality of software design and performance. However, measuring quality and ensuring quality are two very different activities. Measuring the quality of the process in the integration effort generally involves the evaluation of ten major project attributes:

1. Quality of communications
2. Quality of process management and project tracking
3. Quality of training and end-user ability to use the system fully
4. Quality of individual performance, attitudes, and relationships
5. Quality of management reporting
6. Consistency with or compliance to internal, American Institute of CPAs (AICPA), and other management or regulatory agency standards, requirements, and guidelines
7. Consistency with the organization's TQM initiatives
8. Continuous refinement and improvement of the work plan, staffing plan, and milestones
9. Quality of team performance
10. Quality and usefulness of metrics

As a component of project management, quality assurance must be embedded into daily project management practices. Quality is the responsibility of the project steering committee, EDP auditing and independent advisors, project manager and project team leaders, and individual project team members. Assessing the quality of the integration process can be supported partially through the use of the terminally ill integration project (TIIP) score described in Chapter 55, which is designed to assess the key components and project management practices of the integration effort to provide both a prospective and perspective view of the process.

If an external systems integrator is used, the quality assurance process may be outsourced to the integrator by adopting the quality standards and practices of the integrator. Expanding the role of the EDP auditor in the systems integration project can also help improve quality and the overall effectiveness of the project management process. Some of the major activities that the EDP auditor can perform include:

•Providing perspective on AICPA, regulatory, and control issues as related to the implementation effort
•Ensuring that project management standards are maintained as appropriate
•Providing independent perspective on the quality of the process used to manage resources and implement the project
•Serving as a consultant to the project team for the interpretation of regulatory requirements, assessing alternatives, providing perspective on enterprisewide issues, and evaluating the applicability of pro-

fessional standards as related to the design, execution, and implementation of the project
- Conducting specific tests of validation and documentation for the work that was performed and the benefits derived
- Performing periodic reviews of the project management practices, standards of work produced, documentation generated, and compliance to work plans
- Confirming project status for the project steering committee
- Participating with IM&T and end users in "sign-offs" of work process results, work products, deliverables, and acceptance tests
- Participating in comprehensive unit and integrated testing of the software, databases, and conversion processes
- Participating in comprehensive, integrated load testing of software in a full-stress transactions testing environment
- Performing special audit tests for data integrity, conversion accuracy, and system security, including logical and physical access controls
- Contributing to work plan development, monitoring, and weekly status reporting

EMPLOYEE TRAINING AND PROCESS SIMULATION (ETS)

The fifth and final element of the project management model involves employee training together with system testing and process simulation. A major deficiency in the management of many integration projects is the transition from the state of working on the integration to one of actual integration, implementation, and sustained production. Often, deficiencies and many postimplementation problems can be traced to the training and education of the work force in the use of the new systems and changes in business processes. Despite the millions of dollars spent on employee development, most organizations remain ill-equipped to train employees in large and complex integration projects. In systems integration projects, the reeducation and redirection of employees are important to the success of the project and use of integrated systems.

To help accomplish the transition to an integrated systems environment, employees should participate in education and training programs specifically tailored for the integration effort and the introduction and use of new business processes and technologies. This education must extend beyond the usual user class about new software and hardware and into areas related to process change. Training for the implementation and use of integrated technologies and reengineered organizations must be accomplished at three levels:

1. General project orientation
2. Project team training
3. Specialized team training

General Project Orientation

The general orientation level should provide an overall perspective on the background, history, approach, resources, expected benefits, milestones, processes, etc. associated with the integration effort. Emphasis is directed to presenting the metrics used to measure both quality and progress.

This initial level is designed for a general audience of employees, including executives. Fundamental to the overall success of the project and project management process are the application and use of the project management standards and practices as well as the effective use of the CWP and PMT project management methods.

Project Team Training

The second level of training is directed toward employees and individuals assigned to the systems integration team who are responsible for performing according to the work plan. The second level of the education program is related to the practices of project management and the effective application of those practices to the integration and reengineering project. PMT education concentrates on providing the essential information and knowledge on how to use PMT to its fullest advantage.

Specialized Team Training

Finally, comprehensive training occurs in the third level. This training is highly specialized and is intended for those employees who are actually going to use the integrated systems and new processes. As such, it is concentrated and focused on individual topics, such as use of the new software, database design and accessibility, implementation and use of new processes, and computer and network operations.

SUMMARY

Managing systems integration is a full-time and specialized endeavor. These projects are very large, extremely complex, and demand a high level of management attention. The process described in this chapter takes a very fundamental approach to project management. It requires a structured work plan, formal staffing assignments, and the constant discipline to capture information and update and report on the effort. The key performance metrics described in this chapter will help ensure that any systems integration project is effectively measured and that its progress is accurately assessed.

Chapter 54
The Systems Integration Life Cycle

Michael A. Mische

With process reengineering and organizational transformation becoming mainstays for many organizations, the major performance issue for information management and technology (IM&T) executives and professionals is speed — that is, speed defined as the rapid delivery of enabling solutions and responsive and cost-effective IM&T services to an increasingly sophisticated and demanding user community. Providing cost-effective computing solutions has always been a major goal for the IM&T professional; however, with reengineering and systems integration projects taking on increasing importance and megadollar proportions, the issue of rapid development and deployment of integrated solutions and enabling technologies is elevated to a new level of prominence and visibility in the enterprise.

The realities of systems integration, as discussed by several authors in this book, are that these projects are large, complex, and often mission critical to any operational reengineering effort. The advances in technologies combined with the needs created by a less hierarchical organization create a new set of urgencies and priorities for the delivery of systems that bear little resemblance to historical precedents.

Several key factors drive the need for the accelerated delivery of enabling solutions. At one time, technology created competitive advantage; today, however, systems are easily replicated. Therefore, competitive advantage through technology is short-lived and lessening. Organizations cannot wait three, four, and five years for traditional systems development and integration methods to deliver enabling solutions. By the time solutions are fully implemented and available for users, their needs, management sponsors, and technologies have all changed.

Another factor is that technology is advanced and adaptable. At one time, large mainframes, special rooms and environments, and many people were required to support complex programs and interfaces; today, the computing environment has evolved and contains smaller, easier to support, and far friendlier technologies that are rapidly deployable.

Also driving the need for accelerated delivery is improvements in the quality of technology. Historically, some of the more fundamental measures of IM&T success included such criteria as technically correct programs, rapid response times, and 99 percent systems availability. Today, processing accuracy, technically correct applications, and system availability are fundamental "givens": they are prerequisites and no longer the predominant measures of an IM&T organization's effectiveness. Therefore, users and executives have a different set of expectations for IM&T performance that are beyond the traditional technical performance measures.

In addition, organizational transformation and operational reengineering are redefining entirely new applications and data needs. In the process, they are creating new opportunities for using technology and leveraging human resources.

End users are also simply smarter and more comfortable with technology. They understand technology and what is and is not possible. As a consequence, users are far more demanding of the systems provided, and more discriminating of the services, resources, and costs of the IM&T organization. They are holding the IM&T organization and the quality of systems and services delivered to much higher standards.

As a consequence of these changes, there is a need for a more flexible and accelerated approach to systems integration and the deployment of technology-enabling solutions. This chapter explores some of the issues associated with integrating systems in the context of reengineering, and offers an overview of a new life cycle methodology for the systems integration and development processes. This model is called the process-driven integration model (PDIM).

THE PROCESS DRIVEN INTEGRATION MODEL

For the most part, the historical systems development life cycles (SDLCs) were restricted to use by the IM&T department for the development of new systems. In a sense, systems integration projects have relied on the traditional SDLC methodologies, or some derivative of the traditional SDLC, as a guide for developing systems integration work plans and managing the integration process. The classic SDLC provided a formal structure for developing mainframe and mid-range systems, a structure that included a number of phases and work steps. Some methodologies had as few as 4 phases, and some had 12 or more.

Over the course of time, variants to the traditional models were introduced and evolved to include computer-aided systems engineering (CASE) tools and joint user designs to support the systems integration process. Without question, the traditional SDLC methods were relatively effective in aiding the development of classic mainframe-based systems and facilitating the integration of function-specific systems. However, systems integration projects in support of reengineering are proving to be an entirely different matter. Whereas the classical methods benefited from a limited number of mainframe and proprietary technologies and methods, systems integration in support of operational reengineering and organization transformation involves the complete spectrum of technology, applications, data structures, and significant organizational and operational changes to the IM&T organization. Whereas the development process and integration of systems were once restricted to a finite set of applications and related data, integration in the reengineered enterprise requires cross-functionality and portability of technology and applications in support of leaner and more agile operations and organizational structures.

For most organizations attempting to reengineer, the traditional methods for systems development and the development project life cycle are no longer effective models for the management of the system integration processes that are required to support new cross-functional and leaner organizations. They are too slow, rigid, mechanical, and bureaucratic. The needs of reengineering and organizational transformation mandate a more accelerated approach to systems integration and providing enabling technologies to support the systemic changes related to reengineering. Hence, in systems integration and reengineering there is a need to bridge the gap between traditional SDLCs and contemporary demands for the rapid delivery of integrated solutions.

Readdressing the concepts and principles of the traditional SDLC model in the context of reengineering is fundamental to effective project management and successful integration. A new model must provide for a fast-track integration process that successfully leverages technology to realize and support process reengineering and organizational transformation. To be effective in supporting reengineering, the new systems integration methodology (SIM) must provide for the successful melding of reengineering and systems development.

The following characteristics help to define the SIM for reengineering. This chapter presents a new template for managing and performing the systems integration project in the context of reengineering. The model is composed of a five-phase life cycle. The manager must:

1. Establish the integration environment.
2. Assess integration requirements and applications design.
3. Assess data requirements and design integrated data warehouses.

4. Develop and prototype integrated systems.
5. Implement integrated systems. Exhibit 1 provides an illustration of the PDIM's five phases. This approach provides for the management of activities, practices, and progress reporting in a process-driven methodology. The model can be applied to the most complex as well as the simplest of integration efforts. Each of the five phases has a specific purpose, objective, work plan, work products, and level of complexity and risk associated with it. The main objective is to create speed and integration to support reengineering. The model comprises over 125 primary work steps and 35 major work products.

The five-phase model for systems integration provides a number of advantages for the organization performing integration and reengineering. First, it is a convenient method for framing the process and scope. Second, the model can be used to organize the activities and resources assigned. Third, the model provides for easy tracking and reporting of activities and progress. It is designed to be performed concurrently with reengineering and supports a concept called continuous integration.

Integration process acceleration is accomplished through the combination of several techniques that are implicit in the process-driven methodology. The process-driven approach to systems integration achieves the rapid deployment and delivery of integrated systems by using many of the reengineering concepts that are applied to business processes and the principles of concurrent engineering. The major principle is to view the systems integration project as a continuous and harmonious process rather than distinct or separate pieces that somehow must fit together. In this regard, the PDIM has the following key attributes:

- Use of concurrent engineering practices and techniques
- Adoption and adaptation of business process reengineering principles
- Front-loading of critical human resources into the design and assessment stages of the integration process
- Use of quality function deployment (QFD) techniques to ensure that design changes are recognized early in the integration process and are minimized later in the effort to help ensure efficiency

The need for front-end loading of critical customers and resources is important to the PDIM. In the traditional model, resources are gradually increased or ramped-up: resources are at a peak near project completion. In contrast, the PDIM assigns and applies the necessary user, external, and internal resources early in the process. This allows a number of activities to be performed concurrently and facilitates the exchange of knowledge and information that support the design process. Acceleration in the inte-

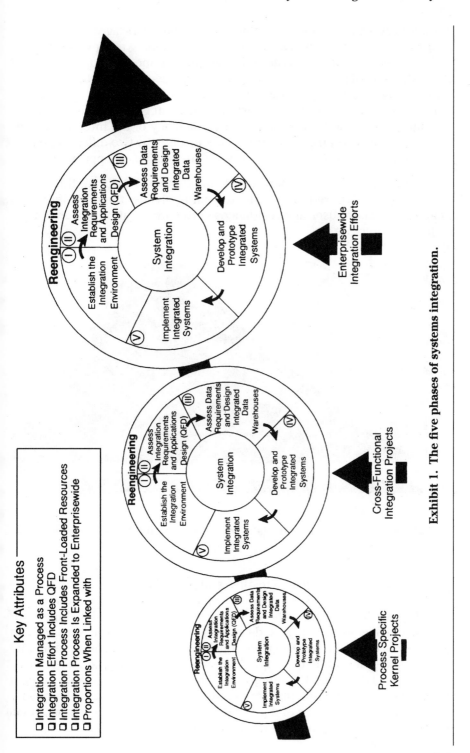

Exhibit 1. The five phases of systems integration.

819

gration process is supported in a number of ways. First, greater emphasis is placed, during the first two phases, on developing a knowledge of the technical aspects of the integrated environment and developing a robust understanding of the analytical and functional needs of the integration process. A fluent knowledge of the target technical environment and the new to-be processes (i.e., to be supported by the integrated environment) is absolutely essential to the success and efficiency of the integration time line. These phases can be performed concurrently by two different components of the project team with the results converging, as appropriate.

Second, Phase 3 can be performed simultaneously. During this phase, databases and data requirements are commonly identified, defined, and assigned to warehouses and residences in the organization's overall information architecture.

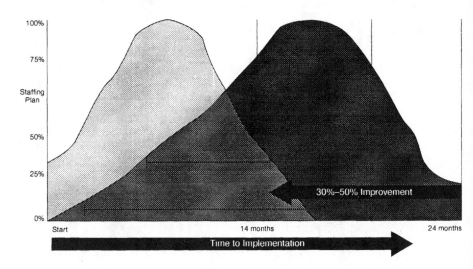

Exhibit 2. The potential effects of front-end-loaded integration projects.

Third, user training, system testing, and performance tuning are all done concurrently in Phase 4. The processes are performed in the context of prototyping, which allows the convergence of users and developers for testing and fine-tuning integrated systems and business processes. Exhibit 2 compares the PDIM and the traditional life cycle methodology in light of the resources and time to completion each requires. In general, the PDIM should help accelerate the integration project by as much as 40 percent when used with effective project management practices and the proper CASE tools. The resources under PDIM are also applied much earlier and in greater numbers than in the traditional methods

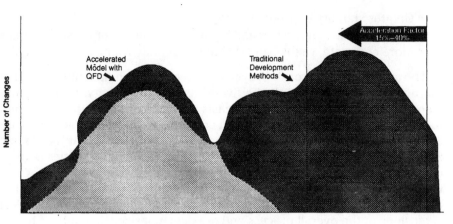

Time to Implementation

Exhibit 3. The potential effect of QFD on systems integration.

The other major characteristic of this approach is the use of QFD. QFD is integral to any efficient product and process design and can be adapted to the systems integration process. Thus, QFD is primarily a process designed to integrate the "voice of the customer" into the design process. This is critical to accelerating the implementation of systems integration efforts because it can identify changes to the base design of the target environment early in the process. The earlier changes are identified, the better, as early detection limits leapfrogging and scope creep, which can both be fatal to the systems integration process. Exhibit 3 provides an example of QFD's potential impact on the changes and change management process of systems integration as compared to typical methods.

Essential to the QFD process is the creation of cross-functional teams and the front loading of the appropriate resources to the project. The creation of cross-functional teams in QFD, as in business process reengineering and organizational transformation, is fundamental to ensuring that all salient issues and target attributes are visible to the design team. The process ensures that data requirements have been interpreted properly and that relative data is factored into the design. The process also provides for the incorporation of definable measurements and results into the integration process early in the effort. These are important attributes in managing the integration project and ascertaining the project's progress and quality. The combination of these attributes makes QFD an integral component of the accelerated systems integration effort. Some of the other benefits of the QFD process in systems integration include:

• Accelerated design and development times
• Lower project development costs

821

- Greater stability of product design
- Improved use of resources and higher contribution for those resources
- More complete, visible, and defined target environment and results

The accelerated approach to systems integration requires the melding of the above techniques with the five-phase methodology. In deploying resources and budgeting time, emphasis is placed on techniques designed to ensure that changes are minimized and that long-lead-time activities are identified as early as possible. These activities help ensure that the staffing is adequately applied and that outsourcing long-lead-time activities is given consideration. As a result of using the accelerated approach, the actual implementation of the integrated system becomes a routine activity rather than an event. Implementation and deployment become natural and logical extensions of the overall process and are deemphasized, in contrast to historical approaches. The following distribution of effort is suggested for the five phases of systems integration. The manager must:

1. Establish the integration environment — percent of effort: 10 to 15.
2. Assess integration requirements and applications design — percent of effort: 25 to 30.
3. Assess data requirements and design integrated data warehouses — percent of effort: 25.
4. Develop and prototype integrated systems — percent of effort: 25 to 30.
5. Implement integrated systems — percent of effort: 5 to 10.

The total distribution of the manager's time should equal 100 percent.

PHASE 1: ESTABLISHING THE INTEGRATION ENVIRONMENT

The purpose of this phase is to create the technical environment for systems integration and establish that environment's support and operating structure. The technical environment includes processors, servers, routers, operating systems, personal computers, workstations, memory, controllers and peripheral equipment, database environments, and networks. The technical environment typically involves a three-tier computing architecture and distributed computing environment, which include mainframes or mid-range consolidating processors, local and wide area networks, and workstations in the form of personal computers.

Key Processes

The following key processes are performed in this phase. The staff:

- Conducts initial technical environment orientation and training
- Develops the physical technical environment plan
- Creates the physical technical environment

- Develops the technical environment connectivity and networking plan
- Acquires the technical environment
- Installs the CPU technical environment
- Installs all system software related to the technical environment
- Installs the peripherals
- Conducts the technical environment tests
- Conducts the technical environment connectivity tests
- Conducts all the peripheral tests
- Validates the tests
- Establishes all working areas and partitions as appropriate
- Refines the instruction sets as necessary
- Establishes final configuration of all peripherals
- Readies the production environment
- Certifies the production environment for application readiness

Key Work Products/Results

This phase, upon completion, should produce or demonstrate the following:

- An integration-ready production environment
- A certified operational environment
- Trained operations and support personnel
- Trained applications personnel
- An enabled applications environment

PHASE 2: ASSESSING REQUIREMENTS AND APPLICATION DESIGN AND CAPABILITIES

This phase is designed to develop formal functional requirements and technical specifications for the integration of systems and data. It usually involves the acquisition, design, and installation of software to support reengineered business processes and an integrated systems and data environment. During this phase, a comprehensive assessment is performed to formally document user requirements that enable reengineering. These are linked to immediate needs and new to-be operations and processes.

Once the requirements are documented and new to-be processes defined, a search is performed for enabling software that supports the new processes and end-user requirements. The process usually includes an assessment of both internal software that currently supports a process and external sources that are available from third-party vendors. In performing the assessment, the gaps between the functionality of existing software and the needs of reengineered processes are identified and evaluated in the context of technological feasibility, need, cost-performance, and return on investment. The functional requirements for process reengineering and systems integration are compared and mapped to the specific capabilities of the existing systems that are targets subject to the integration effort. Once mapped, the gaps are assessed and ranked according to priority for severity, and plans are developed to address them.

In performing this phase, the integrator must develop estimates for several key areas, including the number of concurrent users who will be performing functions on the integrated systems, estimates of transaction volumes to be supported by the integrated environment, and data volumes. These are used to direct where, within the overall information technology architecture, the applications and data should reside. This sizing is especially important when considering the use of a client/server integration strategy.

Key Processes

The following key processes are performed in this phase. The staff:

- Develops functional test cases and flows based on to-be process and integration needs
- Develops transaction tests
- Develops flow tests
- Identifies functional linkages
- Develops detailed assessment procedures
- Develops assessment criteria and expected results
- Develops documentation procedures
- Identifies and acquires application software systems and products
- Confirms application software systems and products
- Loads application software products, as needed
- Develops final application software production assessment procedures
- Establishes an application software production testing schedule
- Performs an application software assessment
- Documents performance characteristics
- Assesses the performance compared to standard benchmarks and reengineering targets
- Documents performance results
- Performs comparative assessment:
  —By function
  —By module
  —By existing system
- Documents assessment results
- Determines interface requirements:
  —To and from flows
  —Timing and frequency

—Files and data
- Determines enhancement requirements
- Identifies key changes to existing systems and acquired packages
- Evaluates the impact of discrepancies and changes on the project and budget
- Performs retests, as necessary
- Readies the application software environment for integration

Key Work Products/Results

This phase, upon completion, should produce or demonstrate the following:

- Application software products reconciled to contract
- A readied application software system environment
- An initial application software testing and validation
- An integrated application software testing and training environment
- An integrated application software production performance profile
- A comprehensive report on comparative assessment
- Integration and interface requirements
- An application and database enhancement list
- Database requirements
- An economic assessment of changes

PHASE 3: ASSESSING DATA REQUIREMENTS AND DESIGNING INTEGRATED DATA WAREHOUSE ENVIRONMENT

Phase 3 of the SIM is designed to identify, define, redefine, and rationalize data elements necessary for the realization of systems integration. This is perhaps one of the more rigorous processes. It directly involves end users in creating consensus definitions through the comprehensive mapping of existing and to-be data elements to the required and to-be logical and physical structures. The process also requires a normalization of all data definitions and a rationalization of all data elements.

Key Processes

The following key processes are performed in this phase. The staff:

- Establishes data dictionary standards, including:
  —Developing dictionary and definitions
  —Determining logical structures
  —Determining physical structures
  —Identifying logical and physical relationships and dependencies
  —Documenting any unique or unusual data structures, dependencies, uses, and sources
- Identifies all pertinent existing data elements, including

—Populating data dictionary with definitions
—Determining logical data structures
—Determining physical data structures
—Identifying logical and physical relationships and dependencies
—Documenting any unique or unusual data structures, dependencies, uses, variants, and sources
• Performs data mapping, including
—Identifying common data and equivalents
—Identifying data discrepancies
—Determining rationalization data requirements
—Determining normalization data requirements
—Developing discrepancy resolution plan
—Developing rationalization and normalization plan
• Performs rationalization and normalization, including:
—Determining data normalization rules
—Determining data rationalization rules
—Developing data rationalizations and normalizations
• Develops an integrated data dictionary
• Develops an initial integration data conversion and population plan

Key Work Products/Results

This phase, upon completion, should produce or demonstrate the following:

• A data map
• Rationalized data
• Normalized data
• A data dictionary
• A database conversion and population plan

PHASE 4: DEVELOPING PROTOTYPE AND INTEGRATED SYSTEMS

Phase 4 of the SIM is designed to develop, test, install, and document integrated systems that support reengineering and new business processes. Systems are developed for the integrated environment and are tested through a prototyping process that links them with new business practices. The prototyping process tests overall systems performance by simulating transaction volumes and the environment that the systems will support.

During Phase 4, a series of comprehensive unit and full-system integration tests are performed on the communications network, applications, and databases.

In developing new applications, the integration process is facilitated by the use of CASE tools, such as PowerBuilder. These tools have capabilities that support systems development through the use of templates, formal rules, and standard presentation techniques. The integration effort also benefits from the use of project management software and database definition and development tools.

Key Processes

The following key processes are performed in this phase. The staff:

- Develops overall integration, programming, and interface specifications
- Develops integration work plans, including:
  —A conceptual overview
  —A program structure
  —Input/output shells
  —Files accessed/generated
  —Frequency/timing
  —Control programs
  —Data structures
- Develops programs, performs integration, and develops:
  —Presentation standards
  —Logic standards
  —Programming specifications
  —Programs and applications
- Documents programs for:
  —System/program
  —User/development
- Performs tests, including
  —Developing test procedures
  —Developing test criteria
  —Performing tests
  —Documenting results
- Resolves all discrepancies
- Validates all programs for production use
- Places validated interfaces in preproduction library
- Finalizes all documentation

Key Work Products/Results

This phase, upon completion, should produce or demonstrate the following:

- Integration and programming specifications
- Final programs
- Production programs and interfaces
- A secure preproduction library
- Formal test plans

827

- Established criteria
- A formal acceptance
- Substantiated documentation
- Audit trails
- Documented procedures
- A preproduction fine-tuning list

PHASE 5: IMPLEMENTING INTEGRATED SYSTEMS

The objective of this phase of the project is to prepare, convert, and migrate to the integrated application and database environment. The integrated systems environment represents the culmination of the systems integration process. During this phase, enabling solutions are delivered, and users are trained to exploit fully the capabilities of integrated technology and applications.

Key Processes

The following key processes are performed in this phase. The staff:

- Develops formal testing procedures and scenarios, including:
  —Functionality tests
  —Transaction tests
  —Compliance tests
  —Substantive tests
  —Data relationships and validity
  —Access control
  —Interfaces, linkages, and feeds
  —Special tests
- Develops specific transaction loads (i.e., volumes) for performance testing
- Develops testing plan
- Develops documentation procedures, including:
  —Error recording
  —Error resolution
- Establishes performance documentation
- Develops sign-off procedures from:
  —Testing team
  —Project managers
  —Project steering committee
  —End users
  —Quality assurance
- Develops the preproduction fine-tuning list
- Establishes the data conversion schedule
- Develops the data conversion standards and documentation
- Develops a detailed data conversion plan

- Develops the data conversion and testing plan
- Performs data conversion and populates the database structures
- Performs the following tests and validates test results:
  —Transactions tests
  —Validation tests
  —Accuracy tests
  —Read/translation tests
  —Population tests
- Documents test results
- Isolates validated databases for preproduction
- Documents databases
- Develops data administration and management standards

Key Work Products/Results

This phase, upon completion, should produce or demonstrate the following:

- Populated databases
- Validated data
- A documentation trail
- An updated data dictionary
- Populated data repositories
- Completed programs and integrated systems
- A completed multitiered computing environment

SUMMARY

The systems integration process is essential to the reengineering efforts of any process and organization. The approach described above represents an outline for accelerating the systems integration process. The major objective of any integration is the effective melding of technology, applications, and data into a framework that supports cross-functional business processes, accessibility to data, and leaner organizational structures.

However, as in reengineering, speed of delivery is of the essence. The rapid delivery of systems is necessary to support reengineering and to fully exploit the investment in technology. In this regard, the methodology presented must be supported through the use of rapid development techniques and tools and CASE products.

Chapter 55
Symptoms of the Terminally Ill Systems Integration Project

Michael A. Mische

Building responsive systems in today's demanding business environment creates many challenges, even for the most seasoned and sophisticated information management and technology (IM&T) organization. The challenges and risks become far greater when the integration of applications, data, and technologies is combined with the reengineering of business processes and organizations. Although much investment has been made in project management and automated development tools, the risk of failure in systems integration remains extraordinarily high. Nonetheless, the need to integrate systems is compelling, and the systems integration industry continues to grow at a tremendous pace.

Problem projects have been a part of the technology industry since its inception. In some instances, the projects are absolute bottomless pits: the purpose, plan, process, or technology was wrong or inappropriate from the outset. In others, project leadership and commitment were at fault. The technology was fine; the implementation was not. Regardless, the propensity for failure remains high. This chapter discusses the warning signs and symptoms of a high-risk systems integration project that goes awry and dubs these problem systems "terminally ill integration projects" (TIIP).

IMPLICATIONS OF THE TERMINALLY ILL INTEGRATION PROJECT

The effect of these terminally ill integration efforts can be devastating to the organization and its IM&T group. Some of the consequences of a TIIP include diminished shareholder value, diluted asset value, reduced return on investment, loss of earnings, reduced consumer confidence, outright interruption of business, and the potential for noncompliance with regulatory requirements and contractual obligations. Finally, there is the effect on people. All too often, a TIIP results in employee terminations or the emotional decision by management to stop projects or outsource IM&T.

SYMPTOMS OF THE TERMINALLY ILL INTEGRATION PROJECT

After decades of experience and hundreds of millions of dollars invested in technology, virtually every major organization continues to experience difficulties in the delivery of integrated systems and reengineered business processes. Companies may be reluctant to acknowledge them, but the problems are there.

There are three essential issues related to the management and performance of business systems integration projects:

- Why are the traditional project management methods seemingly so ineffective in predicting and correcting problem integration projects?
- How can the risks of systems integration projects be minimized?
- How can systems integration and reengineering projects be better managed to achieve superior results?

An understanding of some of the influences on the integration process provides a framework for addressing these issues. First, systems integration projects usually involve large and complex technologies and applications, including legacy systems that have been in the company for years, if not decades. For example, one financial institution's demand-deposit system that was subject to an integration process had executable code structures, data structures, and language dating back to 1967. The existence of these obsolete structures increased the level of effort as well as the risk of the integration project. Second, traditional project management methods and practices tend to concentrate on what has been accomplished, not necessarily on how it was accomplished and its relationship to formal work plans and measures. Third, systems integration requires not only changes in technology but some combination of process, cultural, operational, and organizational change, and these types of changes are difficult for many organizations.

Complex Technologies and Applications

The first major influence on the systems integration process relates to the diverse technologies and application systems that are the targets of the integration effort. Found in virtually every enterprise, these applications include stand-alone, specialty applications that are shared in a network or work group environment, and legacy systems that were built for a single purpose and user. The legacy systems represent the core of applications for many organizations as they support common business processes. Developed over a period of years, the legacy systems have become part of the organization's culture and fiber, and users commonly exercise a high level of ownership over them. By today's standards, legacy systems are cumbersome and usually involve highly fragmented applications and databases built over the years to satisfy specific transaction and information needs of the owners. These systems are fragile and are inherently risky to integrate because of their extensive interfaces, fragile code structures, and numerous processing dependencies. Further complicating the issue of legacy systems and systems integration is that many are processed on mainframe computers with proprietary operating system software requirements. In certain instances, application and system software support may no longer be available from the source vendor. Thus, the older applications and legacy systems are, by their very nature and composition, complex, large, and difficult to integrate. They represent high-risk endeavors.

The target "go-to" technologies for integration also provide new challenges for the systems integrator. The migration paths from traditional mainframes, aged applications, and rigid data structures to new client/server technologies and distributed mid-range computing environments are, for the most part, uncharted or only partially mapped. Still others are unproven, both technically and functionally. Regardless, there are no truly convenient or fail-safe methods. As many organizations are learning, migration and integration costs are quite high. In many instances, organizations attempting to migrate do not have sufficient resources to assign to or support the integration process adequately. Therefore, they must place a greater dependency on external systems integrators and contractors.

Traditional Project Management Techniques

The second major influence on the integration process centers on the basic assumptions and characteristics of traditional project management methods. IM&T professionals have relied on a variety of project management techniques and automated tools to track the effort of a project. Some of these methods have been helpful in the management of traditional systems development and implementation projects, but few have been successful in significantly reducing the risk of integration project failure. They are not designed to withstand the systemic changes associated with systems integration, nor are they designed to improve the quality of results delivered. Traditional project management methods concentrate on a predetermined work plan and do an excellent job of explaining what has happened; however, they provide very little insight into what will happen. In this respect, traditional project management techniques are neither diagnostic nor preventive. They are largely reactionary in design and use.

Organizational Change

The third influence involves both organizational and operational changes. As integrated systems are implemented, the organization must also change to best optimize its use of technology and integration. Many organizations have duplicate procedures and deeply entrenched management practices that the systems integration changes. Acceptance of the integration process and the related operational changes can be slow and, in many cases, management openly opposes the changes. Very often, the systems integrator hears, "This is how the system does it, and this is how I want it." The process can almost be self-defeating. Thus, the systems integration project can be compromised by the very operational processes and organization that it is designed to support. Successful systems integration almost always requires the management of the design of new processes, new strategies, and organizational change, and therein lies one of the main reasons for the failure of many integration projects.

IDENTIFYING THE TIIP

TIIPs have very distinct qualities and many early warning signals. Unfortunately, many of these signals are subtle; if viewed individually, each on its own may not necessarily set off any alarms. However, when viewed collectively and with confirming indicators, the collective qualities of the TIIP can be quite revealing. There are ten qualities that distinguish and differentiate the TIIP as a problem integration effort:

1. The project exceeds its financial budget, estimated work effort, and forecasted completion schedule by at least 25 percent.
2. The project is poorly documented in terms of changes in project objectives, scope, requirements, assumptions, work plan, and staff.
3. The project is not linked to any meaningful and measurable strategy, business objective, or organizational need.
4. The project is failing, will fail, or has failed to meet its intended objectives, stated benefits, and established scope.
5. The project and project team are in a constant state of turmoil marked by date slippages, inconsistent plans, and numerous changes in team composition, requirements, and users.
6. The project and its work products are considered by independent parties to be inadequate for the purposes of the project, or to be of poor or inferior quality.
7. The project is not structured with the appropriate skills, project management techniques, time commitments, project sponsorship, and leadership.

8. The project appears to lack sufficient organizational commitment and support.
9. The project objectives are not clearly aligned with tangible goals and value derivation targets.
10. Human implications of the effort, as related to changes in performance measures, cultures, organizational alignments, and behaviors, have not been addressed.

The majority of terminally ill systems integration and reengineering projects can be avoided. As defined earlier, a TIIP has distinguishing characteristics that relate to personnel, processes, technologies, and project management practices. The 11 most prevalent warning signs of a TIIP include:

1. Improper or inadequate project leadership
2. Inappropriate or inadequate project sponsorship and commitment
3. Inappropriate or inadequate project partnering and shared responsibility
4. Unclear strategy and vision and ineffective project planning that is linked to the vision
5. Unrealistic or mismanaged user, sponsor, or senior management expectations
6. Inadequate or ineffective project management practices
7. Inappropriate target go-to technology and applications
8. Ineffective or inadequate project measurements, communications, and status reporting
9. Inappropriate or inadequate project team staffing, organization, and management structure
10. Unidentified or underestimated project risk and operational exposure
11. Unclear linkage to new business processes and related organizations

Each of these symptoms influences the dynamics of the systems integration and reengineering process differently. The level of influence that any symptom can exert on a project depends on the culture of the organization and the type and complexity of the integration. The symptoms can occur and reappear at any time throughout the life of the integration and reengineering effort. Although there are many more factors that can influence the process and outcome of the integration process, these symptoms are pervasive as signals of the status and pending outcome of the project.

Improper or Inappropriate Project Leadership

The proper type and level of project leadership are essential to any integration and reengineering effort. Integration projects must have leadership that provides for the effective management and coordination of resources and activities within the enterprise. Effective project leadership ensures that responsible personnel demonstrate management over the entire spectrum of integration and reengineering activities while facilitating process changes and the removal of organizational barriers. Effective project leadership and ownership extend beyond the traditional boundaries of title, organizational lines, and budgets to encompass a personal commitment to the success of systems integration and the reengineering process. Some of the key indicators of improper or ineffective project leadership and management are listed here. The project leader:

- Lacks a thorough understanding of the project and its objectives, issues, processes, and team dynamics
- Demonstrates apathy toward the project or off-loads the responsibility for project leadership to the project team or users
- Fails to provide a sufficient amount of quality time and attention to the project and members of the project team
- Fails to understand or practice sound project management standards, such as time reporting, quality reviews, and team-building sessions
- Lacks the organizational credibility or support for the project, fails to influence other departments, or fails to remove organizational and operational barriers
- Fails to provide the project team with effective direction in team assignments, quality reviews, and morale building and fails to serve as a protector for the team in the organization
- Fails to communicate the project effectively to the appropriate areas of the organization
- Fails to forge synergistic relationships with key users, external contractors, and organizational peers regarding the integration effort
- Underestimates the difficulty of change or barriers to change

Inappropriate and ineffective project leadership and management occur when the wrong people are trying to manage the integration process. In the context of a TIIP, project leadership is inappropriate when the leaders do not possess the necessary knowledge, empowerment, or technical and business skills to manage the integration process and resources assigned successfully. An all-too-familiar example of inappropriate organizational sponsorship occurs when the IM&T organization becomes the proponent for process and organizational change. In these situations, the integration process is driven by IM&T and new technology that may be superimposed on an unwilling user community. It may also be unnecessary. This type of leadership virtually guarantees an unsuccessful effort and does not result in any significant systemic changes. Usually, this approach results in the complete organizational rejection of the project.

Inappropriate or Inadequate Project Sponsorship

Inappropriate or inadequate project sponsorship is similar to ineffective project leadership. However, project sponsorship usually occurs at a higher level in the organization and often involves cross- departmental processes and managers. Inappropriate sponsorship occurs when the wrong person or group of people attempts to sponsor and support the integration effort. In these instances, the sponsor is usually beyond the managerial purview and organizational empowerment necessary to effect the process, cultural, and organizational changes related to successful business and systems integration. When this occurs, the integration project sponsor simply does not have the authority for effecting change external to his or her immediate area of influence. Key indicators of inappropriate sponsorship include:

- Lack of organizational acceptance for the project
- Increased organizational resistance and tensions surrounding the project
- Diminishing political support for the project sponsor and for the project in general
- Failing to align the integration project with the organization's strategies, goals, priorities, and business initiatives

Quite simply, for any systems integration effort to be successful, it must be sponsored by the appropriate senior executive and aligned with the organization's requirements and priorities. For example, in the early 1980s, a major financial institution was funding a $5 million project designed to provide a new worldwide financial reporting system. The project was about one-third complete when a senior-level officer thought to conduct a briefing for the executives in charge of that portion of the business. The project team prepared and delivered a spectacular status report. The most senior executive complimented the project manager and then informed him of the organization's decision to deemphasize its international operations! The major question is why the project was allowed to move forward in the first place.

Inappropriate or Inadequate Project Partnering and Shared Responsibility

In integrating systems and business processes, it is imperative to have a constructive and active partnership with all organizational elements involved. The likelihood of a failed integration effort significantly increases when owners, sponsors, users, and those empowered with the integration effort fail to forge synergistic and constructive working relationships. In managing and executing the integration project, cultivation and continuous evaluation of the interaction between project partners and their shared responsibilities are essential. Warning signs of inappropriate partnering include:

- Failure of project sponsors, partners, and leaders to adhere to formal strategies, goals, and objectives
- Failure of project sponsors, partners, and leaders to participate actively in project meetings, working sessions, and team development sessions
- Reluctance of project participants to assume equal responsibility for the outcome of the project and collective responsibility for the results achieved
- Reluctance of partners to contribute the necessary time, resources, and skills to the project or to express a personal interest in the success of the project
- Failure to facilitate organizational and operational change on the part of project sponsors, partners, and leaders, who may exhibit a reluctance to abandon proprietary systems and processes

Unclear Vision and Ineffective Project Planning

The creation and sharing of a common vision for the integration project are absolutely essential to the success of any integration and reengineering effort. A vision is important to establishing expectations for the effort's success and for implementing effective quality and progress measures. The vision helps to establish the parameters, scope, objectives, and expectations for the project. The vision is also necessary for understanding the interrelationships among reengineering, integration, and the deployment of enabling technology. Key indicators of a poorly defined vision and disconnection between the vision and integration effort are when the vision is:

- Unstated, underdeveloped, or unclear
- Not shared among participants and those who have a stake in the project
- Not linked to any meaningful business strategy, goal, or need
- Inconsistent or is subjected to many changes
- Not understood by the project team or organization
- Not clearly and consistently communicated

Effective project planning is fundamental to the success of any systems integration effort. A project with poorly developed work plans, task lists, milestones, activity dependencies, staffing assignments, timing, requirements, and project management standards is destined to become a TIIP. A responsive systems integration project plan provides for the description of the project, its intended approach, the assumptions used, major benefits and risks, contingency plans, project team(s) and staffing assumptions, and the relationship to key prerequisites and requirements. Some of the more important warning signs of poor project planning exhibit themselves when the project work plan:

- Is not fully developed at the outset of the effort or is being developed on the go
- Does not integrate the corresponding process and organizational changes within an overall effort
- Does not adequately address the timing requirements of the project and is not linked to any significant objective or schedule
- Does not stipulate the project's staffing requirements, assignments, and management responsibilities
- Does not stipulate the milestones for the effort
- Does not define the deliverables and work products to be produced or does not link them to specific tasks and assignments
- Does not identify the essential activities, their sensitivities to change, and the project's critical path items and their potential level of importance to the overall integration process
- Does not consider or provide a contingency plan for recalibrating the project
- Is not fully communicated to and understood by the project team or organization attempting to perform integration
- Is not linked to tangible business goals and objectives

Another consideration that affects the outcome of the integration process is the duration of the effort. Projects that have a long completion horizon are extremely vulnerable to disruption and represent a far greater risk for failure than those that have a short and tightly defined completion schedule. Protracted systems integration efforts are susceptible to any number of threats, including management, personnel, and organizational changes; changes in vendor product offerings; economic downturns; and user impatience. In general, systems integration and reengineering projects that require more than 12 to 14 months to complete are at significant risk for failure or major financial and schedule overruns. Some of the key warning signs of inordinately long or delayed projects are when:

- The project milestone dates and relationships among milestones are constantly changing
- The project schedule is protracted because of personnel shortage, insufficient time dedicated to the process, organizational inertia, and changing business priorities or to accommodate other priorities
- The project goes more than two months without any meaningful results
- The project is subject to delays caused by vendors, suppliers, internal organizational changes, or contractors

- The project is delayed because of changing sponsorship, scope, or objectives; unstable user requirements; or inappropriate technical design

Unrealistic or Mismanaged User, Sponsor, or Senior Management Expectations

Establishing the proper level of organizational expectations is critical to the project management process for systems integration. Expectations that are distorted or miscommunicated adversely affect the systems integration project and the efforts of the project team. Some of the more common examples of mismanaged expectations include:

- Commitment to unrealistic objectives, deliverables, and completion dates
- Oversimplification of the complexity of the project and its requirements, issues, and organizational implications
- Failure to understand fully the risks associated with the effort
- Reliance on technical solutions to cure fundamental operational problems or organizational and managerial inadequacies
- Failure to establish the essential criteria for measuring both success and progress

Inadequate or Ineffective Project Management Practices

There is a direct correlation between the quality of the project management processes and the results of the systems integration process. Systems integration mandates that the project is completed on time and within budget, satisfies sponsor expectations and objectives, minimizes the risks of and possibilities for failure, and, most importantly, delivers value. Effective systems integration project management requires the constant tracking and monitoring of results, quality, and effort. Specific warning signals of ineffective project management and progress tracking include:

- The project managers and project team members are not adequately trained in the concepts, principles, and practices of project management.
- The project has inadequate or inappropriate change management procedures.
- The project undergoes constant reshuffling of priorities and leapfrogging of design and requirements.
- The project team does not fully comprehend the project work plan, schedule, design constraints, or staffing assignments.
- Project management is inconsistent in updating the project work plan, staffing assignments, and status of project deliverables.

- The project team members are not tracking, evaluating, and explaining variances in the project budget, labor, tasks, staffing assignments, milestones, schedules, and time estimates.
- The project team is not practicing or does not have the ability to perform dynamic task and responsibility allocation for resources, work products, and personnel.
- The project team is not documenting its work results.
- Project management practices and the individual capabilities of the project managers are of paramount importance to the system integration effort and the avoidance of terminally ill projects. Effective project management must anticipate the direction, issues, and potential pitfalls of the effort. Failure to create a forward-looking project management process leads to a terminally ill systems integration project.
- Adherence to a realistic time and milestone schedule is also fundamental to the success of the integration process. Significant slippages in time lines, labor estimates, task assignments, work products, and deliverables are all indicative of a more severe problem with the overall project and its management structure. As a rule, any unplanned variance greater than 25 percent has an adverse effect on the project and its budget.

Inappropriate Target Go-To Technology and Applications

The selection of the target go-to technology and the originating technologies for the integration process influence project success. The use of new or unproven go-to technologies creates additional risks and complications for the integration effort. The new go-to technologies for integration often involve additional labor, incremental training, and higher learning curves for those involved — all of which contribute to a higher propensity for failure. Many organizations that are attempting integration, for example, through the use of client/server technologies, are learning that they lack a full understanding of that environment's technical requirements; therefore, their effort is greater than anticipated. Some of the more common signals of using inappropriate technology to integrate include:

- Using technology to treat, but not cure, an organizational problem or fundamentally deficient business and management process
- Selecting the wrong go-to technology
- Using go-to technology that cannot support user requirements, processing loads, and required response times
- Using go-to technology that is unproven in performance, vendor support, and acceptance in the marketplace
- Choosing go-to hardware or software that is not mainstream technology or that is difficult to support

- Custom developing essential applications using unproven methods or unproven external integrators
- Failing to link the integration effort with an overall organizational architecture and strategic and reengineering plan

Ineffective or Inadequate Project Measurements, Communications, and Reporting

Failure to measure and communicate adequately the project status contributes to the demise of many integration projects. The project status, direction, needs, issues, and results need to be constantly and consistently communicated to the appropriate elements of the organization. Key signs of dysfunctional measurements and communications include:

- Lack of standard project management practices, tools, and reporting formats
- Lack of predetermined measurements for quality, consistency, progress, and milestones
- Lack of periodic reporting intervals
- An absence of milestone variance tracking for individual team members
- Absence of monitoring the quality of project work products and deliverables
- Lack of substantive participation and feedback from users, project sponsors, and leadership
- Lack of tracking and managing against the appropriate criteria

In systems integration projects, effective project communications possess four essential qualities:

1. Communications and presentations are consistently formatted.
2. Communications occur at regular and frequent intervals and are delivered to the same audience.
3. Communications are unfiltered, realistic, and based on published metrics, work plans, schedules, and milestones.
4. Communications and status reports are distributed to and reviewed by the proper audiences.

Each of these must be present to ensure proper and responsive communications.

Inappropriate or Inadequate Project Team Staffing, Organization, and Management Structure

The proper mix and use of staff, together with the correct distribution of management responsibilities, are significant determinants of the systems integration process and the quality of results achieved. Clues to a poorly organized or managed project team include:

- The project team has insufficient time commitments to perform the project and has conflicts in assignments, performance measurements, and time.
- The project team is composed of an inappropriate mix of staff skills, experiences, and organizational levels.
- Project team members are inadequately trained or technically deficient in the areas assigned, or are placing too much reliance on on-the-job training and outside consultants.
- The project team members do not understand their roles and responsibilities or are not personally committed to those roles.
- Individual project team members and project managers lack the discipline and structure to support the necessary project management practices.
- The project team receives inconsistent direction or incorrect leadership signals.
- The project team does not have adequate cross-process representation or organizational participation, or is perceived by users and management as an IM&T project only.
- The project team has undergone constant changes and turnover in its composition, management, membership, and structure.
- The project team and integration effort lack a protector who functions as an organizational insulator from distractions, disruptions, and adverse managers.
- The project team has poor rapport and morale among its members.
- Project team members are not documenting their work and reporting their efforts and accomplishments in a structured and consistent manner.

In assembling the staff for the systems integration effort, the project team members should be selected and assigned to the effort based on the project's technical, functional, and organizational requirements, and on the members' individual abilities to contribute to the effort. Some of the key factors to be considered in assigning personnel to the integration team include:

- The professional qualifications and personal attributes of individual team members
- The level of working rapport, relationships, and camaraderie among team members
- The leadership qualities of individual team members
- The individual morale and enthusiasm of team members
- The specific project knowledge, awareness, and cross-functional business perspectives of the individual team members

Unidentified or Underestimated Project Risk and Operational Exposure

Understanding, estimating, and managing risks are all crucial to the success of any integration and reengineering process. Often these risks are overlooked or improperly evaluated. Risk is a relative measure and concept for any organization. Evaluating the risk of the integration effort requires the identification of three types of risk: technical, financial, and business.

Technical risk includes factors that are related to the technologies and applications that are the target of the integration process. Technical risk includes assessing:

- The level of technical integration risk of hardware, communications, software, and databases
- The degree of risk surrounding compatibility issues
- The communication network risk
- The risk of vendor stability and ongoing maintenance support
- The risk of not developing the technical competencies for sustaining the integration process

Financial risk refers to the sensitivity of the project budget to variances in hardware, software, personnel, and training. It also includes a measurement for return on investment in the project and the ability of the integration effort to achieve its financial goals. Financial risk involves the assessment of:

- The total project budget
- The cost of hardware, software, and contractors
- Ongoing support and maintenance
- The total cost of process and organizational changes
- The probability of success in generating the anticipated direct and intrinsic value

Business risk involves the measurement of the impact of the project on current and future operations. The key measure and concern of business risk is determining the organization's sensitivity to any missed time lines or shortfalls in the integration effort. In its most severe sense, a late integration project can completely disrupt an organization and cause a cessation of operations. Business risk requires the assessment of:

- The impact of the project on the operations and organization
- The organization's sensitivity to delays in the project and the potential impact on customers and business partners
- The risk associated with using internal and external resources on the project

THE TIIP ASSESSMENT METHODOLOGY

There are a number of statistical methods available to assist in profiling the behavior of a systems integration and reengineering project and its potential outcome. The ten symptoms described in this chapter can be applied to virtually any systems integration and reengineering effort using the TIIP assessment methodology. The methodology includes a simple intuitive algorithm that gives the ten symptoms subjective weightings and evaluation criteria. The methodology facilitates the identification of potential problems and helps in developing corrective action steps for projects that represent a risk of becoming TIIPs. The specific weighting criteria are:

- Improper or inadequate project leadership and management: .15
- Inappropriate or inadequate project sponsorship: .05
- Inappropriate or inadequate project partnering and shared responsibility: .10
- Unclear vision and ineffective project planning: .10
- Unrealistic or mismanaged user, sponsor, or senior management expectations: .05
- Inadequate or ineffective project management practices: .20
- Inappropriate target go-to technology and applications: .10
- Ineffective project measurements, communications, and status reporting: .05
- Inappropriate or ineffective project team staffing, organization, and management structure: .15
- Unidentified or underestimated project risk and operational exposure: .05

The total TIIP score weightings equal 1.00. The result, or TIIP score, of each symptom is based on a scale of 10 points. Application of the methodology requires the review of each of the ten symptoms and the subjective rating of the key indicators of each symptom, as well as experienced judgment and high business acumen. The indicators are rated using a scale of 1 to 5. A score of 1.0 indicates the worst possible case; a score of 5.0 represents the best possible case. For example, in evaluating the leadership and sponsorship symptom, a score of 20 is derived as the sum of the indicators. This score is multiplied by the symptoms weighting factor of .15 to obtain a TIIP score of 3.0. A similar review and computation are performed for the remaining nine symptoms. Once the TIIP score for each of the ten symptoms has been calculated, the individual scores are summed to a grand total. Projects with a total TIIP score between 1 and 40 can represent significant risk with the potential for failure. In contrast, those projects that have a high numerical TIIP score (i.e., 75 to 100) could have a high potential for success. Projects with TIIP scores of 40 to 74 are in the gray area and should be carefully evaluated as these projects can quickly become terminally ill.

PROJECT AND SYSTEMS MANAGEMENT

The use of the TIIP score methodology is by no means foolproof or fail-safe. It can, however, provide a simple and potentially effective means of evaluating the quality and tendencies of any systems integration and reengineering project. The ten symptoms provide pragmatic insight into those items that can exert significant influence on a systems integration and reengineering project. They are tangible, measurable, and effective indicators to monitor. Exhibit 1 provides an example of the TIIP assessment methodology.

SUMMARY

Systems integration remains a major area of activity for virtually every organization. Integration is necessary for many organizations, and the ability to effectively manage the integration effort is essential to the process. The use of the ten symptoms and the TIIP assessment methodology can be of potential value to any organization in managing and reducing the risks of these complex and important projects.

There are a number of statistical methods available to assist in profiling the behavior of a systems integration project and its potential outcome. The 10 symptoms can be applied to virtually any systems integration and reengineering effort using the Terminally Ill Integration Project (TIIP) Assessment Methodology. The methodology includes a simple, intuitive algorithm that provides the 10 symptoms with subjective weightings and evaluation criteria. The methodology facilitates the identification of potential problems and helps in developing corrective action steps for projects that represent a risk of becoming or are a TIIP. The specific weighting criteria are:

Symptom	Weighting Factor
1. Improper or Inadequate Project Leadership and Management	.15
2. Inappropriate or Inadequate Project Sponsorship	.05
3. Inappropriate or Inadequate Project Partnering and Shared Responsibility	.10
4. Unclear Vision and Ineffective Project Planning	.10
5. Unrealistic or Mismanaged User, Sponsor, or Senior Management Expectations	.05
6. Inadequate or Ineffective Project Management Practices	.20
7. Inappropriate Target Go-To Technology and Applications	.10
8. Ineffective Project Communications and Status Reporting	.05
9. Inappropriate or Ineffective Project Team Organization and Management Structure	.15
10. Unidentified or Underestimated Project Risk and Operational Exposure	.05
Total TIIP Score Weightings	**1.00**

Question 1

Symptom	Evaluation Poor			Excellent		Weighting Factor	Total Score
	1	2	3	4	5		
Improper or Inappropriate Project Leadership and Management (Weighting Factor = 15%)							
The proper type and level of project leadership and management are essential to any integration and reengineering effort. Integration projects must have leadership that provides for the effective management and coordination of resources and activities within the enterprise. The key indicators of improper or ineffective project leadership and management include:							
• Project leadership lacks thorough understanding of the project, its objectives, issues, processes, and team dynamics.							
• The project leader demonstrates apathy for the project or off-loads the responsibility for project leadership to the project team or users.							

Exhibit 1. The terminally ill integration project assessment methodology.

847

Question 1 *(Continued)*

	Evaluation						
	Poor				Excellent	Weighting	Total
Symptom	1	2	3	4	5	Factor	Score
• The project leader fails to provide a sufficient amount of quality time and attention to the project and members of the project team.							
• The project leaders and managers fail to understand or practice project management standards, such as time reporting, quality reviews, and team-building sessions.							
• The project leaders and managers lack the organizational credibility or support for the project and fail to influence other departments or remove organizational and operational barriers.							
• The project leader and manager fail to provide effective direction for the project team with regard to team assignments, quality reviews, morale building, and serving as protectors for the team in the organization.							
• The project leader and manager fail to communicate the project effectively to the appropriate areas of the organization.							
• The project leader and manager fail to forge synergistic relationships with key users, external contractors, and organizational peers regarding the integration effort.							
Total TIIP Score Multiplied by Weighting Factor:						.15	

Question 2

	Evaluation						
	Poor				Excellent	Weighting	Total
Symptom	1	2	3	4	5	Factor	Score
Inappropriate or Inadequate Project Sponsorship and Alignment (Weighting Factor = 5%) Inappropriate or inadequate project sponsorship is similar to ineffective project leadership. However, project sponsorship usually occurs at a higher level in the organization and often involves cross-departmental managers. Inappropriate sponsorship occurs when the wrong person or group of people attempt to sponsor and support the integration effort. Key indicators of inappropriate sponsorship include:							

Exhibit 1. (Continued)

Question 2 *(Continued)*

Symptom	Poor 1	2	3	Excellent 4	5	Weighting Factor	Total Score
• There is a lack of organizational acceptance for the project.							
• Organizational resistance and tensions surrounding the project and efforts of the systems integration project team are increasing.							
• Political support for the project sponsor and project in general is diminishing.							
• Managers fail to align the integration project with the organization's goals, priorities, and business initiatives.							
Total TIIP Score Multiplied by Weighting Factor:						.05	

Question 3

Symptom	Poor 1	2	3	Excellent 4	5	Weighting Factor	Total Score
Inappropriate or Inadequate Project Partnering and Shared Responsibility (Weighting Factor = 10%) In integrating systems and business processes, it is imperative to have a constructive and active partnership with all organizational elements involved. The likelihood of a failed integration effort significantly increases when owners, sponsors, users, and those empowered with the integration effort fail to forge synergistic and constructive working relationships.							
• Project sponsors, partners, and leaders fail to adhere to formal project management standards and practices, schedules, time lines, and responsibilities.							
• Project sponsors, partners, and leaders fail to actively participate in project meetings, working sessions, and team development sessions.							
• Project participants are reluctant to assume equal responsibility for the outcome of the project and collective responsibilities for the results achieved.							
• Partners are reluctant to contribute the necessary time, resources, and skills to the project or to express a personal interest in the success of the project.							

Exhibit 1. (Continued)

Question 3 *(Continued)*

Symptom	Evaluation Poor 1	2	3	4	Excellent 5	Weighting Factor	Total Score
• Project sponsors, partners, and leaders fail to facilitate change and exhibit a reluctance to abandon proprietary systems and processes.							
Total TIIP Score Multiplied by Weighting Factor:						.10	

Question 4

Symptom	Evaluation Poor 1	2	3	4	Excellent 5	Weighting Factor	Total Score
Unclear Vision and Ineffective Project Planning (Weighting Factor = 10%) The creation and sharing of a common vision for the integration project is absolutely essential to the success of any integration and reengineering effort. The vision also helps to establish the parameters, scope, objectives, and expectations for the project. Effective project planning is fundamental to the success of any systems integration effort. Projects with poorly developed work plans, task lists, milestones, activity dependencies, staffing assignments, timing, requirements, and project management standards will become a TIIP. Key indicators of a poorly defined vision and disconnection between the vision and integration effort include:							
• The vision is unstated, underdeveloped, or unclear.							
• The vision is not shared among participants and project stakeholders.							
• The vision is not linked to any meaningful business goal or need.							
• The vision is inconsistent or is subjected to many changes.							
• The vision is not understood by the project team or organization.							
• The project work plan is not fully developed at the outset of the effort or is being developed on the go.							
• The project work plan does not adequately address the timing requirements of the project and is not linked to any significant objective or schedule.							

Exhibit 1. (Continued)

Question 4 *(Continued)*

Symptom	Poor 1	2	3	4	Excellent 5	Weighting Factor	Total Score
• The project work plan does not stipulate the staffing requirements, assignments, and management responsibilities for the project.							
• The project work plan does not stipulate the milestones for the effort.							
• The project work plan does not define the deliverables and work products to be produced or does not link them to specific tasks and assignments.							
• The project work plan does not identify the essential activities, sensitivities to change, and critical path items of the project and their potential level of importance to the overall integration process.							
• The project work plan does not consider or provide a contingency plan for staffing and task completion based on changing project assumptions.							
• The project work plan is not fully communicated to and understood by the project team or organization attempting to perform integration.							
• The project plan is not linked to tangible business goals and objectives.							
• The key measurements for progress and quality are not defined in the project plan.							
• The project milestone dates and relationships among milestones are constantly changing.							
• The project schedule is protracted because of lack of personnel, insufficient time, organizational inertia, changing business priorities, or to accommodate other priorities.							
• The project goes more that two months without any meaningful results being produced.							
• The project is subjected to delays caused by vendors, suppliers, internal organizational changes, or contractors.							
• The project is delayed because of changing sponsorship, unstable user requirements, or inappropriate technical design.							
Total TIIP Score Multiplied by Weighting Factor:						.10	

Exhibit 1. (Continued)

PROJECT AND SYSTEMS MANAGEMENT

Question 5

Symptom	Evaluation Poor 1	2	3	4	Excellent 5	Weighting Factor	Total Score
Unrealistic or Mismanaged User, Sponsor, or Senior Management Expectations (Weighting Factor = 5%) Establishing the proper level of organizational expectations is critical to the project management process for systems integration. The more common examples of mismanaged expectations include:							
• Project members commit to unrealistic objectives, deliverables, and completion dates.							
• Project members oversimplify the complexity of the project and its requirements, issues, and organizational implications.							
• Oversimplifying the complexity of the project, its requirements, issues, and organizational implications.							
• Project members do not fully understand or evaluate the project risks.							
• Project members rely on technical solutions to cure fundamental operational problems or organizational and managerial inadequacies.							
Total TIIP Score Multiplied by Weighting Factor:						.05	

Question 6

Symptom	Evaluation Poor 1	2	3	4	Excellent 5	Weighting Factor	Total Score
Inadequate or Ineffective Project Management Practices (Weighting Factor = 20%) There is a direct correlation between the quality of the project management processes and the results of the systems integration process. Systems integration mandates that the project is completed on time and within budget, satisfies the expectation and objectives of the sponsors, and minimizes the risks and possibilities for failure. Specific warning signals of ineffective project management and progress tracking include:							
• The project managers and project team members are not adequately trained in the concepts, principles, and practices of project management.							

Exhibit 1. (Continued)

Question 6 *(Continued)*

	Evaluation					Weighting	Total
	Poor				Excellent		
Symptom	1	2	3	4	5	Factor	Score
• The project has inadequate or inappropriate change management procedures.							
• The project is experiencing constant reshuffling of priorities and leapfrogging of systems design and functional requirements.							
• The project team does not fully comprehend the project's work plan, schedule, design constraints, or staffing assignments.							
• Project management does not update or is incapable of updating the project work plan, staffing assignments, and status of project deliverables.							
• The project team members do not have the ability to track or are not tracking, evaluating, and explaining variances for the project's budget, labor, tasks, staffing assignments, milestones, schedules, and time estimates.							
• The project team is not practicing or does not have the ability to perform dynamic task and responsibility allocation for resources, work products, and personnel.							
• The project team does not have the ability to document or is not documenting the results of their work.							
Total TIIP Score Multiplied by Weighting Factor:						.20	

Question 7

	Evaluation					Weighting	Total
	Poor				Excellent		
Symptom	1	2	3	4	5	Factor	Score
Inappropriate Target "Go-To" Technology and Applications (Weighting Factor = 10%)							
The selection of the target "go-to" technology and originating technologies for the integration process will influence the success of the project. The use of new or unproven "go-to" technologies creates additional risks and complications for the integration effort. Some of the more common signals of using inappropriate technology to integrate include:							
• Technology is used to treat, but not cure, an organizational problem or fundamentally deficient business and management process.							

Exhibit 1. (Continued)

Question 7 *(Continued)*

Symptom	Evaluation					Weighting Factor	Total Score
	Poor			**Excellent**			
	1	2	3	4	5		
• The wrong "go-to" technology was used.							
• "Go-to" technology is used that cannot support user requirements, processing loads, and required response times.							
• "Go-to" technology is used that is unproven with respect to its performance, vendor support, and acceptance in the marketplace.							
• "Go-to" hardware or software is chosen that is not mainstream technology, proven, or easily supported.							
• Essential applications are custom developed using unproven methods or external integrators.							
• The integration effort has not been linked with an IT architecture and strategic plan.							
Total TIIP Score Multiplied by Weighting Factor:						.10	

Question 8

Symptom	Evaluation					Weighting Factor	Total Score
	Poor			**Excellent**			
	1	2	3	4	5		
Ineffective or Inadequate Project Measurements, Communications, and Reporting (Weighting Factor = 5%) Failing to measure and communicate adequately the status of the project contributes to the demise of many integration projects. Key signs of dysfunctional measurements and communications include:							
• A lack of standard project management practices, tools, and reporting formats.							
• A lack of predetermined measurements for quality, progress, and milestones.							
• A lack of periodic reporting intervals.							
• An absence of milestone variance tracking for individual project team members.							
• An absence of monitoring the quality of project work products and deliverables.							
• A lack of substantive participation and feedback from users, project sponsors, and leadership.							

Exhibit 1. (Continued)

Question 8 *(Continued)*

Symptom	Evaluation Poor				Excellent	Weighting Factor	Total Score
	1	2	3	4	5		
• A lack of tracking and managing against the appropriate criteria.							
Total TIIP Score Multiplied by Weighting Factor:						.05	

Question 9

Symptom	Evaluation Poor				Excellent	Weighting Factor	Total Score
	1	2	3	4	5		
Inappropriate or Inadequate Project Team Staffing, Organization, and Management Structure (Weighting Factor = 15%) The proper mix and use of staff together with the correct distribution of management responsibilities are significant determinants to the systems integration process and the quality of results achieved. Attributes of a poorly organized or managed project team include:							
• The project team has insufficient time commitments to perform the project and has conflicts in assignments and time.							
• The project team is composed of an inappropriate mix of staff skills, experience, and organizational levels.							
• The project team members are not adequately trained or technically competent in the areas assigned or are placing too much reliance on on-the-job training and outside consultants.							
• The project team does not understand its roles and responsibilities or is not personally committed to those roles.							
• Individual project team members and project managers lack the discipline and structure to support the necessary project management practices.							
• The project team receives inconsistent direction or incorrect leadership signals.							
• The project team does not have adequate cross-process representation or organizational participation or is perceived by users and management as an IT project only.							

Exhibit 1. (Continued)

PROJECT AND SYSTEMS MANAGEMENT

Question 9 (Continued)

Symptom	Evaluation Poor 1	2	3	4	Excellent 5	Weighting Factor	Total Score
• The project team has experienced constant changes and turnover in its composition, management, membership, and structure.							
• The project team and integration effort lack a protector who functions as an organizational insulator from distractions, disruptions, and adverse managers.							
• The project team has poor rapport and morale among its members.							
• Project team members are not documenting their work and reporting their time and accomplishments in a structured and consistent manner.							
• The level of working rapport, relationships, and camaraderie among team members is low.							
• Leadership qualities of individual team members are poor.							
• Individual morale and enthusiasm of team members are poor.							
• The project team has specific project knowledge, awareness, and cross-functional business perspective.							
Total TIIP Score Multiplied by Weighting Factor:						.15	

Question 10

Symptom	Evaluation Poor 1	2	3	4	Excellent 5	Weighting Factor	Total Score
Unidentified or Underestimated Project Risk and Operational Exposure (Weighting Factor = 5%) Understanding, estimating, and managing risks are all crucial to the success of any integration and reengineering process. Often these risks are overlooked or improperly evaluated. Risk is a relative measure and concept for any organization.							
• Technical risk includes factors related to the technologies and applications that are the target of the integration process. Technical risk occurs when:							

Exhibit 1. (Continued)

Question 10 *(Continued)*

Symptom	Evaluation Poor 1	2	3	Excellent 4	5	Weighting Factor	Total Score
—The level of technical integration risk of hardware, communications, software, and databases is low.							
—The degree of risk surrounding compatibility issues is low.							
—The communication network risk is low.							
—The risk of vendor stability and ongoing maintenance support is high.							
• Financial risk refers to the sensitivity of the project's budget to variances for hardware, software, personnel, and training. It also includes a measurement for return on investment in the project and the ability of the integration effort to achieve its financial goals. Financial risk involves the assessment of the systems integration effort and occurs when:							
—The total project is high relative to other projects.							
—The cost of hardware, software, and contractors is proportionately high relative to other projects.							
—Ongoing support and maintenance is predicted to be high.							
• Business risk involves the measurement of the project's impact on current and future operations. The key measure and concern regarding business risk is determining the sensitivity of the organization to any missed time lines or shortfalls in the integration effort. In its most severe form, a late integration project can completely disrupt an organization and cause a cessation of operations. Business risk occurs when:							
—The impact of the project on the operations and organization has not been addressed.							
—The sensitivity of the organization to delays in the project and potential impact on customers and business partners have not been addressed.							
—Risk associated with using internal or external resources have not been addressed.							
Total TIIP Score Multiplied by Weighting Factor:						.05	
Total of All TIIP Scores: (Higher TIIP Scores = Safer Projects)						100	

Exhibit 1. (Continued)

Chapter 56
Contracting for Systems Integration

Jagdish R. Dalal

Contracting for systems integration is no different than contracting for any other service. Many information technology (IT) managers, however, are fearful of contracts and the contracting process, which is in fact no different from any systems analysis and problem-solving process. Contracts are a necessary part of business transactions, and all managers are expected to understand contract implications, even though corporate lawyers are usually available to help them through the maze of contractual and legal jargon. Systems integration projects require that the IT manager be well versed in the contracting process and able to provide the leadership to the team engaged in purchasing services.

THE PURPOSE OF THE CONTRACT

Although today's business climate promotes such terms as *business partnership* and *shared objective procurement,* contracting for service does not necessarily imply an adversarial relationship between the IT function and the service provider. The terms of the contract are written to formalize the relationship and establish the basis for a definitive plan of action throughout the life of the agreement. The contract enables the two parties to fulfill the requirements of the business relationship on a formal basis rather than an implied one. It also helps the parties to settle any differences if the business relationship does not work out as envisioned. This may not necessarily come about because of a lack of performance on the part of either party, but possibly because of changed business conditions. Either way, the contract becomes important in times of disagreement or dispute.

Clearly, the emphasis is on settling any issues while the business relationship is in a formative stage, rather than at a later stage when one or both parties are in a noncooperative position. Thus, the maxim "a contract is best defined while the relationship is solid" should be kept in mind and should drive the contracting process. A corollary to this maxim is "the hard-line terms should be negotiated at the beginning of the relationship, not at the end." If a dispute causes the end of the business relationship, neither party will be willing to acquiesce to the other's requirements.

CONTRACTING AND SYSTEMS INTEGRATION

Systems integration depends on procuring parts of systems and integrating them as a purchased service to solve a business problem. The field of systems integration is not new. The defense industry has used systems integration techniques for decades rather successfully. Because systems integration by nature requires procurement of services, contracting for it successfully is a key metric for the IT manager. Even though many aspects of this procurement are similar to purchasing other IT products and services, enough differences exist so that an inexperienced or underestimating IT manager can create a short- and long-term business problem. Therefore, a rigorous contracting process is a key factor of success for the IT manager.

Most managers also find that there is pressure to conduct the business on a laissez-faire basis, euphemistically referred to as a "handshake deal," where the IT manager and the systems integrator generally define the business relationship and mutual expectations and immediately proceed to conduct business. There are also documented conflicts where an unsuspecting IT manager contracted for systems integration by accepting the integrator's terms and conditions and then regretted it during times of conflict. There are also stories of failed systems integrators that accepted the standard form purchase order from the purchasing company, were not able to live up to the terms, and went out of business.

THE KEYS TO SUCCESSFUL CONTRACTING

This section identifies keys to success when contracting for systems integration activities.

A Clearly Predefined Process for Service Acquisition. As in systems development, systems integration involves the pressure to expedite delivery and an erroneous perception that the use of a predefined process will only slow down accomplishing it.

To the contrary, a predefined process allows the manager to ensure that all aspects of acquisition and contracting are thought of ahead of time, along with their consequences and alternatives to the desired results. This eliminates a last-minute scramble or, worse, having to live with a contract that may be detrimental to business over the longer term.

Metrics for Measuring the Success of the Contracting Process. The tendency is to ignore metrics for managing results. In contracting for systems integration, a clear set of metrics should be identified and constantly revisited during the negotiations to ensure that the end results can be achieved. These metrics should include both in-process measures for the contracting process, such as interim mileposts of accomplishments, and cost of contracting. They should also have some end result measures, such as final contract terms (e.g., value and terms). These measures allow the manager to oversee the contracting process and ensure that the end results meet the expectations.

Clear Understanding of the Integration Business, Requirements, Players, and Their Methods of Operation. Thorough research must be conducted before commencing the contracting process. This provides the IT manager with the knowledge about the systems integration business, how various contracts have been created and managed in other companies, who the major players are in the industry, and how they conduct their business. This knowledge allows the systems integration contractor to ensure that the vendors do not, knowingly or unknowingly, lead the project manager in a direction that is not appropriate for the business or application. An example of this would be to understand various business affiliations, including ownership or a joint venture, of a potential vendor, and to evaluate its business proposal or technical proposal in light of the project manager's discovery. In today's business, where many alliances and partnerships are being formed to compete in the marketplace, a vendor may propose a set of products more from its business affiliations than the individual merit those products may represent. This may not be in the organization's best interests.

Benchmarking. Benchmarking is a process used by many project managers to learn about the best practices and experiences in the industry and then use that knowledge to guide the acquisition process. There are many books and articles on the subject of benchmarking and they are highly recommended.

Learning from the Marketplace. Another useful practice used by many companies that are in the process of acquiring these types of services is learning from the marketplace, by issuing what is commonly referred to as a request for information (RFI) before engaging vendors in bidding for business. This is a useful step when the state of the industry or the vendor capabilities are not well understood or technically complex. Through the RFI process, a manager can learn a lot about what is available before having to make any commitments to potential vendors. This step does, however, add time to the acquisition process, but the benefit of a better understanding of the marketplace offsets the added time.

Detailed, But Realistic, Project Plans. The project manager should never rush into the contracting phase — and should never begin the performance of the systems integration activities before the contract is completed.

A detailed project plan, including understanding the interim mileposts and the output, is essential to achieving a sound systems integration contract. Absence of such a plan leads to being pressured into an arrangement that may be detrimental to the business. Examples exist of failed systems integration projects that have created major public relations problems for both the contracting and vendor parties, which could have been avoided if the contracting parties had devoted the time and diligence to understand the deliverables and ensure through the contract remedies for untoward actions.

There are also examples of companies entering into the performance part of the agreement before "inking" the deal with the vendor. This creates a situation in which the entire leverage has shifted from the buyer to the seller, thereby creating difficulties in managing the relationship objectively. No responsible businessperson should either endorse or tolerate such a situation.

Enrolling Qualified Team Members to Help the IT Manager in Contracting

When setting out to develop and negotiate a systems integration contract, a team of qualified individuals must be formed to assist in the process. Such a team would generally include:

- *A lawyer.* Despite all the jokes about their being an impediment to progress, lawyers serve an essential function in ensuring long-term success of the agreement.
- *A staff member from finance.* This person should be able to consult on the financial aspects of the deal. Generally, most people understand the accounting aspects of such a deal, but there are other critical disciplines of finance that are just as, if not more, critical to the overall success of a systems integration contract. For example, any substantial contract should consider the treasury aspects of the deal (payment terms and conditions and, in some instances, currency translation).
- *A tax law expert.* As an increasing number of U.S. states begin to tax services, there will be a requirement to engineer the tax aspect of the systems integration deal. There are some legitimate options that a tax lawyer can propose for the contract that would minimize the tax exposure over the duration of the contract.

- *A human resources (HR) representative.* This is especially helpful if the systems integration involves combining company and integrator resources to work on the project. HR staff can provide guidance as to what cultural aspects should be considered when contracting in such an environment, and also provide contracting terms such as *noncompete or notification for recruiting*, if allowed. They could also explain other countries' labor laws in the case of a multinational contract that would be subject to the national labor laws of other countries.
- *Technical consultants.* Technical consultants, preferably from the systems integration architecture and design team, ensure that there are no technical "gotchas" in the contract.
- *A show-me attitude.* Developing and maintaining a healthy dose of skepticism throughout the entire contracting process ensures that nothing is left to chance. Skepticism allows managers to document everything and ensures that they are following the process with discipline.

CONTRACTING FOR SUCCESS

Exhibit 1 depicts a contracting process that can be used in procuring a systems integration business. The five stages are

1. *Project definition and planning stage.* This stage defines the project dimensions for systems integration contracting. Specifically, managers:
   — Define the scope.
   — Define the contracting process and a preliminary timetable, including deliverables.
   — Establish in-process measures and result measures for the contracting process.
   — Develop preliminary cost and schedule estimates.
   — Collect data from the industry and other sources.
   — Prepare the RFI and potential bidder list.
   — Establish the contracting process team, recruit members, and establish the processes and roles for the team members.
2. *Request for information, or preliminary data-gathering, stage.* In this stage, an RFI is prepared to send to the vendor, and the preliminary data gathering takes place. Specifically, managers:
   — Issue RFIs and collect information from the RFI responses.
   — Evaluate the RFI responses and modify the process, objectives, and end result expectations based on facts gathered.
   — Conduct benchmarking exercises to learn from other companies' experiences and include them in the project principles.

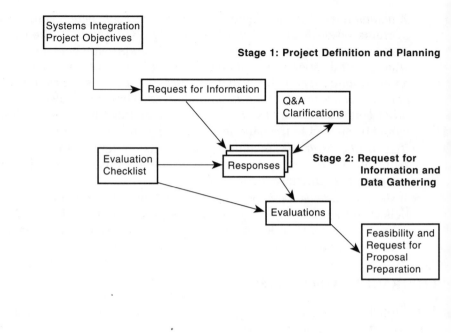

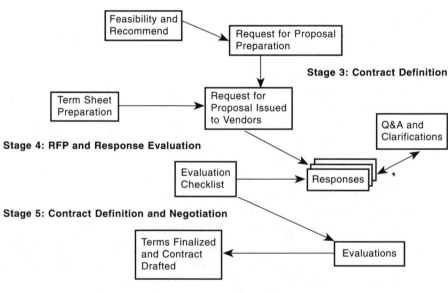

Exhibit 1. The contracting process.

—Conduct the final go/no-go analysis and obtain management approval for proceeding with the systems integration project acquisition.

— Finalize the team members and ensure that the confidentiality, conflict of interest, and other ethical matters and codes of conduct are developed, communicated, and accepted.

3. *Contract definition stage.* In this stage, all the contract details are finalized, and the team is fully prepared to engage vendors. Specifically, managers:
    — Complete final RFP instructions.
    — Develop contractual terms and fallback positions.
    — Develop detailed project definition and vendor expectations (i.e., specifications, resources, costs, and schedules) and include them as part of the RFP to the vendors.
    — Define and agree to the RFP response evaluation process.

4. *RFP and response evaluation stage.* In this stage, the RFP is issued to the vendors and their responses are received. Specifically, managers:
    — Issue RFPs to the vendors, with clarifications and format instructions to ensure that their responses will be according to the managers' criteria for evaluation.
    — Collect RFP responses and evaluate them using the predefined evaluation criteria and scoring method.
    — Identify the leading vendor who can at least meet the minimum requirements, rather than just identifying who has the highest score among the bidders.
    — Identify for the leading vendor the issues and concerns, including clarification of its response, that must be resolved as part of the contracting process and that must be dealt with in the contract.
    — Inform the vendors of the final selection decision and ensure that for all respondents no issues have been left unaddressed as a result of the process or misinterpretation of the responses. Managers can best deal with this up front rather than letting it become the last stumbling block before finalizing a contract with one vendor.

5. *Contract finalization and negotiation stage.* In this stage, the contract negotiations and the crafting of the agreement take place leading to the contract, specifically:
    — The contracting officer and the bidder agree to contractual terms.
    — These contracting terms should be the same as the terms the manager developed in the earlier phase, including the definition of the fallback positions.
    — The manager develops the contractual language and finalizes it.
    — The manager finalizes all the deliverables and terms for the deliverables.
    — The manager obtains management and project team approvals.
    — The manager awards the contract.

THE CONCEPT OF THE TERM SHEET PROCESS

One of the approaches that may lead to developing a contract and negotiating the contract with vendors in a rather painless fashion and in a short period is the "term sheet" process. Xerox has used this concept rather successfully in developing a landmark outsourcing contract in near record time.

A term sheet is a list of desired contractual terms, and various negotiating postures to take around each of the terms. Developed in the first stage of the contracting process, the term sheet would include all of the contractual terms that the project manager would like in the contract and, in that respect, it can be viewed as a contract mock-up. The terms would define the most desirable position that the manager would like to see in the final contract.

The term sheet is then sent to the bidders as part of the RFP process, and each bidder is asked to respond to each of the terms directly. Bidders are asked to provide their level of compliance to each of the terms or identify alternate terms that may be acceptable to them. For example, an organization may want to use a specific U.S. state as a venue for all dispute jurisdiction. The bidder may prefer a different state and thus would be obliged to identify its desire in its RFP response; this should help avert longer negotiations during a later stage.

Another benefit of this approach is that it forces the organization to think through its requirements and desired contractual terms at an earlier stage of the procurement process, when there is less pressure to finalize the contract. Exhibit 2 shows a mock-up of such a term sheet that can be included as part of the RFP.

UNDERSTANDING THE CONTRACT

Although courts of law can ensure that the contractual terms agreed to by the parties are generally legal (e.g., one party cannot require the other to do something illegal just because that party agreed to it in the contract), the terms that are agreed on by the parties govern the settlement of differences. Therefore, it is important for contracting parties to include all agreements in the contract rather than imply them during negotiations. For example, many contracts include in their warranty section a statement that "The written warranty supersedes all other warranties expressed or implied." In the following section, a brief overview is provided of the standard contract terms that one would generally find in a systems integration contract.

Article	Term	Yes	No	Vendor Comment
1.1	The contractual agreement shall be between the "buyer" and "vendor" and is the sole basis for doing business.			
2.2	All disputes shall be resolved first by using the arbitration process described in schedule 2.2 and shall be governed by the laws of the State of New York.			
4.1	Vendor shall comply with the project management process defined by the buyer from time to time and shown in schedule 4.1.			
4.2	Vendor shall comply with all standards and architectural requirements for the systems as defined by the buyer from time to time and shown in schedule 4.2.			
5.1	Schedule 5.1 is the specifications for the systems integration project, which the vendor agrees to accept for the delivery of the final product.			

Exhibit 2. A sample term sheet as part of a request for proposal.

Identification of the Parties and Framework of the Contract

This is the preamble to the contract. It identifies the parties and their legal entities that would be involved in purchasing or providing systems integration services. This section is critical if the systems integration service requires the use of a specific organization or a partnership in providing the service.

This article would also identify the state, country, or even world court whose laws would govern the terms of the agreement. It is not necessary to file in the state where one or both parties generally do business. For example, many lawyers believe that New York laws are much better than most states when addressing software agreements. The choice of governing law becomes important if litigation occurs later. One party could also gain a home field advantage over the other if jurisdiction is not located in a common, acceptable court of law.

Another section of this article can also define the process for litigation. For example, the two parties may agree to follow a certain process, including arbitration, before filing any lawsuit. For example, binding arbitration instead of litigation is a way to speed up the results and reduce legal expenses.

Contractual Relationships

This article identifies the relationship between the purchaser and service provider. This may later determine the limits of liability or fiscal consequences for the two parties.

Another aspect of the contractual relationship is that it may or may not allow the assignment of the contract by the service provider under certain conditions. These conditions may be predefined in the contract or may simply be identified as requiring specific approval beforehand. This is a very common clause in systems integration contracts in which the buyer has contracted with the systems integrator based on its expertise in the field rather than its ability to manage other suppliers.

The Glossary

This is an important article for a systems integration contract, as it defines the terms as they are used in the body of the contract or if they are not mentioned but are materially important to the execution and fulfillment of the contract. For example, in a systems integration contract for software services, the word software should be clearly defined, whether it means object code or object and source code.

Scope of Deliverables and Considerations

This is the most important article of the contract. In this article, the scope of deliverables, such as delivery of services and products, is defined with their value, called considerations. This article, therefore, describes in detail the services performed, the prices for those services, and the terms governing those prices, such as payment methods. This article also describes in sufficient detail the acceptance process and criteria for the services received.

Contract Modification Process and Terms

This article provides the process for modifying the contract. Some contract modifications, such as change of address, are rather routine and can be provided for easily; others, such as a change in the scope of delivery, require a detailed process and a set of predetermined terms. Both types of modifications should be thought through and provided for in the contract.

Contract Conclusion and Termination Provisions

This article defines the normal contract conclusion, typically the end of the delivery of the systems integration project deliverables. The contract identifies the normal transfer of various rights and obligations, such as intellectual property rights, in cases when the relationship ends in a normal fashion. The two parties may either agree on a follow-up to the contract, such as maintenance services, or termination of the relationship as the deliverables are completed and accepted. If appropriate, renewal of the contract terms can be defined in such an article.

This section of the article defines how one or both parties may find a justifiable cause for terminating the agreement before its normal conclusion. This may result from nonfulfillment of contract terms, or may even allow termination by convenience of the two parties involved. If the termination is due to nonfulfillment of the contract terms, an elaborate notification process is usually required and defined in this article. The terms of this process are usually referred to as default provisions. Usually, a set of terms is defined to cure this default condition which allows the party to prevent the contract from being terminated for cause. This part of the contract is generally one of the most difficult to negotiate because of the potential to create adversarial positions. Therefore, if these terms and anticipated positions are predefined, the two parties can reach acceptable common ground much less painfully.

Another critical clause within this article prevents the systems integrator from bringing any type of court-sanctioned injunction in the event of a dispute. This clause is important to the organizer who may want to procure these same services from any other sources, if necessary, to support the business needs.

Patent/Copyright Indemnification and Rights

In a systems integration contract, it is important to know the exact rights of the two parties with reference to the patent or copyright rights regarding the product or services delivered. The contract should also provide for a specific methodology and consequences for patent/copyright infringement should one be discovered later on.

Force Majeure

Webster's New Collegiate Dictionary defines the term *force majeure* as "an event or effect that cannot be reasonably anticipated or controlled." This clause states that some or all contractual terms associated with nonperformance by one or both parties are not affected by such events as natural calamities (e.g., flood or earthquake) or other agreed to, unforeseen events (e.g., war or local disturbances).

Damages and Limits of Liability

This article defines how damages for actions other than indemnified ones are calculated and assessed against the contracting parties. It can include liquidated damages, such as additional staffing or out-of-pocket expenses. This clause generally conflicts with standard, vendor-provided terms of limitations of liability. It can also include definition of consequential damages for problems. However, this clause is fairly difficult to define and even more difficult to reach agreement on with the systems integrator. Consequential damages would provide for claiming expenses as an indirect result (e.g., lost revenue and expense reduction not achieved) of fault, and parties find it therefore more difficult to agree on the scope of such damages.

The limitation of liability generally provides protection for the systems integrator by ensuring that the liability damages do not exceed some agreed-to amount. This is critical in situations in which the product of the systems integrator is, in turn, included in the product sold by the company.

Acceptance and Suitability of Use

In a systems integration product involving software, these terms are crucial. As a purchaser of the systems integration product/service, the IS manager must clearly define the acceptance criteria, including testing scenarios and acceptable levels of defects, as well as define the terms regarding the specifics of such deliverables as training and documentation in addition to the product. These terms must be agreed on with the systems integrator before the contract negotiations.

On the other hand, the inclusion of a suitability-of-use term for software products is relatively rare. Most contracts do not provide for any warranty from defect for software-based products, and therefore suitability of use also becomes an issue that must be understood and agreed upon by the two parties before contract finalization.

Warranty and Maintenance Provisions

Terms within this article provide for the warranty and associated process and actions for correcting faults in the delivered software or hardware or both. On the other hand, the maintenance terms provided in the agreement require the systems integrator to provide ongoing maintenance, for a fee. This section defines terms governing upgrades and software updates to fix bugs from previous revisions. This is a critical element of the contract for a systems integration acquisition because of the very nature of the procurement.

Access to Source Code, Title Rights, and Support of Product

Many, if not most, of the purchased software products give the purchaser rights to the executable object code but not the source code. An important clause pertains to the purchaser's ability and right to access source code under certain conditions. Under normal circumstances, if the source code is not available and if there is a maintenance agreement with the vendor, the customer's access to the source code is unimportant. However, if the integrator is no longer able to maintain the product, as a result of either a business or technical difficulty, there must be a solid provision for access to the source code. This is sometimes accomplished through an agreement to place the source code in escrow with a third party, such as an attorney, bank, or disaster recovery firm.

COMMON MISTAKES

There are some common mistakes that must be avoided through proper planning and diligent adherence to the process and details. Some of the more common mistakes include:

- The contract may be only a general, rather than definitive, framework of understanding between the two parties.
- Not all aspects of contractual understanding are agreed upon before execution of the contract or the agreement is not put in writing.
- Not all the required disciplines in the organization are involved in reviewing the contract.
- More specifically for the systems integration contract, the contract does not define in sufficient detail and clarity the following:
  - —Specifications for the final deliverable
  - —Definition of various deliverables, such as content and form
  - —Definition of various standards and architecture requirements and the process for their acceptance/modification
  - —Budget and schedule for the deliverables
  - —Acceptance and approval processes for various deliverables
  - —Specific responsibilities of the integrator regarding implementation, such as training and warranty
  - —Ongoing responsibilities and their specific terms, such as maintenance and enhancements

SUMMARY

Purchasing for systems integration products is not any more complicated or difficult than procuring a technical product/service. The IS manager who invests in thorough planning, adherence to a disciplined process, and a solid understanding of contractual requirements will come out ahead with a successful agreement that protects the company's interests.

Chapter 57
Choosing a Systems Integrator

Michael A. Mische

Selecting a systems integrator can be a perplexing, emotional, and time-consuming process. Not only is the competition among integrators increasing, but the proliferation and rate of change of technology have created countless options and choices. In less than a decade, technology has changed from a field dominated by mainframe computers, rigid applications, and highly complex and intricate interfaces to one that is defined by end-user computing, client/server components, workstations, enterprise-wide networks, and data sharing. There is very little agreement as to what actually constitutes a systems integration project and systems integration services. Integrators themselves disagree about what constitutes systems integration, and few can define it in contractual terms rather than as a substantive service. Whereas once organizations seeking integration consultants had only the Big Six accounting firms, hardware and software vendors, and a few regional and boutique contract programming firms from which to select, today's choices are varied and constantly growing. Thus, the industry has a real need for an effective method to help guide the organization through the choices and options in the systems integration and service provider marketplace.

This chapter provides a perspective on how to evaluate and select a systems integrator. The seven principles discussed here provide a simple and convenient method for the selection process, and have been developed as a result of experience on both sides of the systems integration table.

THE NEED FOR A SYSTEMS INTEGRATOR

Confronted by never-ending technical and business challenges, end users and information management and technology (IM&T) organizations are finding themselves under enormous pressures to improve performance and accelerate the delivery of enabling systems. No longer is it sufficient for the IM&T organization to simply react to users and supply systems and technologies to satisfy yesterday's needs. In the decade of organizational

0-8493-9968-8/99/$0.00+$.50
© 1999 by CRC Press LLC

transformation, IM&T organizations must anticipate their users and function as enablers of process and organizational change. To address their needs, many organizations rushed into situational management and development programs, such as total quality management, computer-aided systems engineering, joint application designs, client/server technologies, and a host of others, only to be disappointed by results that fell far short of oversold benefits and inflated expectations. Many found that the costs involved greatly exceeded the benefits derived; still others learned of the "hidden" costs.

Uncertain, understaffed, or lacking the resources necessary to support an integration effort successfully, many organizations are turning to external consultants that provide systems integration and reengineering services. With daily per-person billing rates ranging from several hundred dollars to over $10,000, selecting an integrator can be a confusing and difficult challenge. Systems integrators can contribute much to the process and the organization. Used properly, the systems integrator can assume the majority of the project risk, supplement or supersede internal resources, and deliver turnkey results. Systems integrators can also contribute perspective to their clients' business processes and internal management capabilities. The organization can engage the appropriate integrator and find its money well spent; the organization that chooses the wrong integrator not only wastes its money but finds that its vision and project may never be realized. Thus, there are risks and advantages to using a systems integrator. Some of the more significant benefits are that integrators:

- Bring a fresh perspective and energy to any systems integration project, which can be invigorating and extremely beneficial to the organization and overall integration process
- Have stamina and a clearly defined role; they are not distracted by the everyday business needs or organizational politics
- Have tools and methods that can be brought to the organization in various forms and as the need requires
- Can be held accountable for their performance on a legal, moral, financial, and professional bases. Unlike internal resources, organizations have a legal recourse with integrators.

THE PRINCIPLES OF SELECTING A SYSTEMS INTEGRATOR

In light of the variety and diversity of systems integrators, selecting and effectively using an integrator's services are challenges, even for the most experienced organization. A natural starting point is with any existing relationships that the organization may have with integrators. The buyers of services (i.e., the clients) and providers (i.e., integrators) know one another, their cultures, and their capabilities. Presumably, they have an established rapport and a track record of working together. Nevertheless, each integration situation is different, and the needs for an integrator may be different. The following 12 principles provide a basic framework for evaluating the capabilities of the prospective integrator.

PRINCIPLE NUMBER 1: THERE ARE FIVE TYPES OF SYSTEMS INTEGRATORS

Although the market is undeniably large and varied, one could easily group systems integrators into one of five basic types of systems integration firms:

1. Blue Chip management consulting firms
2. Big Six public accounting firms, many of which have now become limited liability partnerships for their consulting services
3. Global integrators
4. Proprietary vendors
5. Contractors

Briefly, the Blue Chip firms, which include such pedigree names as A.T. Kearney; McKinsey, Bain & Co.; and Booz, Allen & Hamilton, are known as breeding grounds for extensive intellectual talent and strategic management savvy rather than as technical service providers of information technology. Although the Blue Chip firms are a source for systems integration talent, that is not their major area of internal investment and personnel development. In this regard, Blue Chip firms may not necessarily be the best resource for systems integration services.

The once Big Eight and now the Big Six accounting/consulting firms represent a large pool of systems integration talent. These firms include such stalwarts as Andersen Consulting, Ernst & Young, and Price Waterhouse. Although Big Six firms are predominantly known for their accounting and tax services, they are also known for their extensive consulting capabilities. With revenues in excess of $1.5 billion, Andersen Consulting is one of the largest providers of integration services, and is the dominant force in the Big Six arena. Big Six clients typically include middle- and upper-level managers in both the private sector and government. Billing rates per person for systems integration projects generally range from $1000 per day per person to more than $6000 for certain senior partners. However, Big Six firms have a reputation for discounting their rates, as competition within the peer group is fierce. Discounts of 25 to 50 percent of their standard hourly rates are not unusual, especially for long-duration projects and audit clients. The Big Six represent a tried-and-true source for integration services.

Global integrators are a new breed of firms that are quickly establishing themselves as dominant forces in the marketplace. In a sense, global integrators are a hybrid of the Blue Chip and traditional Big Six firms in that they can bring both highly skilled management consulting services and technical IM&T service providers to their clients. These firms include such organizations as IBM Consulting, CSC, TSC, SHL Systemhouse, and EDS. Many global integrators, such as EDS and TSC, began as technical service providers and evolved into firms that meld technology with business processes. Their rate structures are competitive with the Big Six and Blue Chip firms. Global integrators are quickly becoming some of the best sources for systems integration assistance and general management consulting in the marketplace today.

Proprietary vendors include hardware and software manufacturers and value-added resellers that provide integration and management consulting services. However, their capabilities tend to be restricted to their own product offerings or specialized product line and are usually less extensive with respect to general management consulting issues and services. As captive service providers, proprietary vendor integrators have a distinct orientation toward making their products work and do not necessarily concentrate on making sweeping changes to the organization through reengineering and reinvention. Therefore, the organization runs the risk that vendor integrators can be less dimensional in their approach to integration, which may lead them to miss broader opportunities for radical improvement and competitive advantage through integration and reengineering business processes. Professional management consulting services, at least in the classical context of the Blue Chip, global integrator, and Big Six firms, are not necessarily their main stream of business or source of revenue. Hardware and software vendors make the majority of their money from the sale of software, new releases, and annual maintenance fees, not from hourly rates for systems integration and project management professionals. The rates span the spectrum from several hundred dollars per day per person to over $2000 per day per person. In all but a few situations, the use of vendor integrators may not be as desirable as the alternative sources for systems integration talent.

Finally, the fifth group of systems integrators is composed of the sole practitioner and contract programming firm. Contractors include a growing group of individuals who have a particular industry orientation and specialized technical or application system skill set. Contractors can sell their talents either directly to the organization or to a contract programming firm that brokers them to a needful organization. Contractors are generally used in a specific role and work under the client's direction. The billing rates for the contractor firms are quite low compared with the other types of systems integrators. Some rates range from a low of $35 per hour for a programmer to as much as $125 per hour for an experienced project manager. Contractors can be most effective when the engaging organization is supplementing its own resources and has an extremely strong project management and quality assurance function in place.

PRINCIPLE NUMBER 2: SYSTEMS INTEGRATORS ARE COMMODITY SERVICE PROVIDERS

The services, capabilities, and qualifications among systems integrators are all similar. Core services, which relate to the technical aspects of integration and project management, are fairly uniform among integrators. Virtually all types of systems integrators can provide the same technical resources, similar types of references, and experienced project managers. The issue is understanding what combination of skills and talents is needed by the project and matching them with integrators.

As a starting point for evaluating and selecting a systems integrator, the organization should understand that system integrators have four very important qualities:

1. They possess a number of specialized skills and capabilities.
2. Their marketable products include time and people — and they charge for them.
3. They possess tools, techniques, and information that organizations may lack or can only partially assemble.
4. They can deliver turnkey results while usually assuming the risk of the project.

This is where the subtle differences among integrators can be found, which can help differentiate integrators in a relatively homogeneous marketplace. These differences are primarily the result of structure, management, development of personnel and methodologies, and the transference of project risk to the integrator.

The Big Six, Blue Chip, and global integrators are primarily professional consulting firms. These firms have established standards of work and a well-defined structure of responsibility and accountability. They have the capability to manage, assume the risk of, and perform multimillion-dollar and multiyear projects. They can manage, supply personnel, and deliver completed projects to their clients anywhere at any time. These firms are in the full-time business of providing professional services and are constantly seeking, training, cultivating, and employing highly talented and well-compensated individuals to provide consulting and integration services to their clients. They have extensive infrastructures and organizational arrangements that provide not only a high level of client service but also the structure and management to develop personnel, manage resources, develop intellectual capital, evaluate project status and progress, and assess the quality of work performed. They offer their professionals well-defined career paths, and the internal competition among the employees and partners/officers helps ensure a steady stream of competent and responsive resources.

Most importantly, these firms have two other major operational elements. They measure their consulting performance not only based on client feedback but according to their own standards, which are often more rigorous than those of the client. Also, they have internal methods for managing risk, assuring quality, measuring progress, and generating value for the client. Clients that hire this type of firm generally transfer all or a significant portion of project risk to the integrator.

In contrast, vendor and contractor integrators tend to be less formal in their organizational structure and their work performance. They normally have partial, not complete or significant, responsibility for the project. Similarly, they rarely assume the majority of risk for the entire project. Contract integrators are usually assigned to an internal team and function under the management of the client rather than their sourcing firm. Typically, their standards of work, performance, and quality are those of the client, and their performance is based on client acceptance of their skills.

PRINCIPLE NUMBER 3: THE CLIENT MUST UNDERSTAND THE INTEGRATOR'S FEE STRUCTURE AND BILLING PRACTICES

Systems integrators generate their revenues and earnings based on hourly or daily rates and the mix of staff assigned to a project. In general, the more experienced and advanced in the organization the person is, the higher the billing rate. Typically, the Big Six, Blue Chip, and systems integration firms try to achieve at least a 3.0 multiple between their cost of service for an employee and the employee's billing rate to the client. For example, if a project manager at a Big Six accounting firm were compensated at $100,000 per year, plus benefits and burdens of an additional 35 percent, his or her total cost of service would be $135,000, or $64.65 per hour, based on a standard of 2088 hours per year. For client billing purposes, the project manager's minimum standard hourly rate would be at least $195 per hour, plus administrative recovery and add-on charges of $10 to $50 or more per hour. Thus, the hourly rate to the client would be anywhere from $205 to $250. Again, discounts should be available for large projects and long-term client commitments. In general, the greater the duration, the greater the discount, especially when Big Six audit clients are involved.

The systems integrator measures project profitability by using a concept called realization, which is computed by multiplying the number of hours or days the person worked by the person's standard billing rate to derive the theoretical total standard revenue generated by that person.

This amount plus total expenses serves as the denominator of a profitability equation. The total fee at standard plus expenses is divided into the total amount of cash collections in addition to expenses reimbursed on the project and received from the client. Another method of computing realization is to consider net fees collected divided by total fees at standard. Either method provides a profitability picture of the vendors' economics. For example, if a $250-per-hour Big Six manager worked 100 hours on a project, his or her total chargeable time would generate a revenue of $25,000, at standard rates. If the Big Six firm billed and collected the entire amount of fees, net of expenses, the realization percentage would be 100 percent, and the firm's profitability would be enormous.

Conversely, if there were a fixed-fee contract, a set budget with not-to-exceed limits, or a dispute about the hours worked or quality produced, profitability could be lower. For example, if $25,000 of chargeable time revenue were generated, but only $12,000, net of expenses, was collected, the realization on the project by the systems integrator would only be a dismal 48 percent — a generally unprofitable figure by the time fully-loaded costs were applied.

In negotiating rates with a systems integration vendor, the concept of realization must be understood and used to negotiate discounts. A client should never pay the standard rates of the systems integrator, as there are numerous alternatives in the marketplace. In negotiating with a potential integrator, the client always should ask the integrator for its standard rates as a basis to negotiate lower rates. As noted, Big Six accounting firms can be aggressive discounters and have significant room to negotiate. As a rule, the more resources supplied by the integrator and the longer the duration of the project, the greater the discount. In general, if the project is extensive, the integrator has higher chargeability per person assigned to the project and can afford to give greater discounts.

Chargeability, the second major element in the integrator's profitability equation, is the lifeblood of any professional services firm, as it represents the percent of time that an employee, partner, or officer actually bills to clients. For example, if a Big Six project manager billed 1535 hours to clients during his or her firm's fiscal year, his or her chargeability would be 75.3 percent, based on a 2088-hour year. Considering a standard billing rate of $250 per hour, the firm would expect to generate $633,750 in service revenues from the project manager — measured against a cost of service of $135,000. In general, integrators, especially the Big Six, try to achieve a minimum of 60 percent chargeability per person, depending on the organizational level and the individual's responsibilities.

PRINCIPLE NUMBER 4: THE CLIENT MUST KNOW ITS REQUIREMENTS AND HOW TO USE AN INTEGRATOR

No guidelines, rules, or criteria guide the decision as to when to use a systems integrator. The classic method of using the systems integrator involves securing an integrator's services on a well-defined assignment or project. Generally, organizations that use this traditional approach outsource their integration requirements and risk to the integrator in the form of a stand-alone project. The client must have a well-defined project with tightly defined schedules, deliverables, and performance measurements or it leaves itself open to the discretion of the integrator.

Many organizations agonize over what type of systems integration firm to hire. The larger firms certainly have more assets, bigger payrolls, established practices, and greater overhead than the smaller firms. However, as many organizations learned through their own downsizing efforts, bigger is not necessarily better, quantity does not translate into quality, and having an office in every city does not guarantee a service advantage to the client. For example, many of the Blue Chip and Big Six firms have downsized and closed offices. The pervasive considerations and guiding criteria in selecting a systems integrator are the credentials, capabilities, and commitment of the individuals assigned directly to the project.

The capabilities and personal qualities of the individual consultants combined with the philosophy and operating structure of the firm are the determining factors in rendering exceptional services. Smaller systems integration and contractor firms can provide the same services and the appropriate depth of resources as those of the Big Six, global integrators, or Blue Chip firms. In certain situations, smaller firms may be better positioned to provide higher quality service, more experienced consultants, and lower rates because the pressures of profitability (i.e., realization) and keeping masses of junior and less experienced people busy (i.e., chargeability) are not present. The contractor firms have an ability to staff client needs selectively with the "best of the best" rather than just relying on internally available resources. Because of their operating structures, the large firms rely on personnel leverage; the greater the leverage of junior to senior resources, the more advantageous it is to the larger firm. This relationship, combined with internal performance pressures to maintain high levels of chargeability — which is common to all of the large, professional service firms — may not represent the best situation for the client. Alternatively, the larger firms have instant access to resources. Also, depending on the unique circumstances of the client, using a big-name firm may be desirable when the organization is seeking insurance, expects to be or is in litigation, believes it is advantageous to extend such an existing business relationship to an audit, or needs masses of people to accomplish very controllable and homogeneous tasks.

PRINCIPLE NUMBER 5: THE CLIENT MUST UNDERSTAND WHO WILL DO THE WORK

The relationship of selling integration services to the actual performance of the services is a key concern for many organizations considering the use of a systems integrator. Typically, in the large Blue Chip and Big Six firms, selling is the responsibility of the partners, officers, and a select group of senior managers. A few firms have even tried using professional salespeople. Because of their orientation and emphasis on personnel leverage, the majority of client work is usually performed by less experienced staff and mid-level management personnel rather than the partners or officers. Contractors and sole practitioners generally service their clients with professionals who have extensive industry and consulting experience. Therefore, it is always important to know exactly who will work on the project, when they will work on it, and how much time they will spend on it.

PRINCIPLE NUMBER 6: PROSPECTIVE CUSTOMERS, SHAREHOLDERS, AND CLIENTS DO NOT KNOW OR CARE WHO THE SYSTEMS INTEGRATOR IS

Some clients are sensitive to the stature and name of the systems integrator. Others may look for public relations and advertising value in using a well-known name. However, the use of a systems integrator's name in marketing and advertising provides little, if any, advantage in attracting prospective customers or clients. Most people have no or, at best, only limited knowledge of systems integrators. In the final analysis, customers and clients judge the organization and firm by its performance and services rather than by the name of the consultant used to integrate technology. Customers and clients only care if the system works, and shareholders are only concerned if the integration process failed or was significantly over budget or past due. In the case of failure, they may find greater legal recourse if a larger firm was used.

PRINCIPLE NUMBER 7: THE CLIENT MUST UNDERSTAND VALUE AND GET A GUARANTEE

Judging the quality of an integration firm is difficult, as all firms have positive and negative client experiences and successful and unsuccessful projects. The client must evaluate an integration firm by its consultants and their personal commitment to the organization and its values, not just by its name or technical prowess. All system integrators have experience, methodologies, and credentials, and all claim quality service. All have positive and negative client references. Usually, they have been successful, at least from a technical perspective, in the process of integration, or they simply would not be in business. However, technical competency is not the issue; the process used by the integrator is the most important aspect of the experience. Systems integration firms almost always tout the value of their services and the results of their efforts. However, very few, if any, offer any tangible proof of value or guarantees.

Warranties and guarantees are difficult to craft in professional service industries. Generally, Blue Chip firms do not warrant or guarantee work, the results of their work, or client satisfaction. American Institute of CPA rules prohibit Big Six accounting firms from offering guarantees. Very few contractors can afford the financial implications of a warranty if something goes wrong, and software vendors usually invoke their products' disclaimers. However, most integrators stand behind their work and usually seek to enhance their value to their clients.

Performing a thorough check of the vendor's references is another method of performing due diligence on a prospective systems integrator. However, references can be deceiving, as they are often based on subjective criteria, impressions, and hearsay. When checking an integrator's references, the client should develop a complete perspective of the experience curve, both positive and negative, and develop an understanding of what the integrator did well and where it may have fallen short. When exploring negative experiences, more important than learning what went wrong is understanding how the integrator reacted and responded. References are opinions and should be used only to calibrate thoughts and impressions — not as the basis for the decision.

Even for the most experienced and discriminating of clients, asking the correct questions can greatly improve the prospects of engaging a responsive integrator. Using the following simple but revealing 12 rules to ask the right questions will facilitate the effort and enhance the process.

Ask Specific, Direct, and Detailed Questions. A major portion of the integrator's role and test of competency is communication style and the ability to listen, interpret, and spontaneously respond to changing client demands, attitudes, and concerns. The client should beware of integrators that appear to have strong biases, as their independence and objectivity could be compromised when evaluating needs, direction, and available alternatives.

Understand the Integrator's Background, Experience, and Familiarity with the Issues. A major portion of the integrator's job is to bring perspective to the client's organization. The client should strive to engage integrators that have a broad perspective and demonstrate empathy. The client should avoid integrators that have a narrow perspective or rely on a limited knowledge base, and should be careful of integrators that have "canned" answers for everything or have to do an inordinate level of research.

Understand the Integrator's Approach, Work Plan, Work Products, and Deliverables. The client should relate the consultant's people, process, and work products to the organization's needs and expectations and verify that the integrator is not providing generic methods, standard products, "warmed-over" reports, or a cookbook approach. If senior resources are needed, the client must ensure that the integrator provides them and does not attempt to "bait and switch" the project with less experienced junior people. The client must normalize the integrator's responsibilities and the engaging organization's expectations in a contract and stipulate the work plan, deliverables, time schedules, and all costs in the contract. The client should always reduce the scope, deliverables, and timing to written form.

Assess the Individual Personality and Chemistry of Those Assigned to the Project. The client should evaluate whether the integrator is open and honest and whether it is trying to establish a personal rapport. The client should check for whether the integrator has a personal interest in the success of the project and evaluate the integrator's ability to listen, interpret, restate, and provide feedback. References for both successful and unsuccessful projects are important, as is an understanding of how the integrator responded to clients. The client should seek integrators that will make a personal commitment to the organization.

Match the Integrator's Technical and Managerial Abilities to the Organization's Needs. The organization engaging the systems integrator must be absolutely realistic about and confident of its needs, objectives, and scope of the integration effort and technical requirements. The organization must be honest in the assessment of the need for an integrator, what role the integrator will play, and what type of integrator is needed. Being the world's foremost integrator of mainframe technology probably will not help when the organization is trying to implement client/server components if the mainframe is not the issue. Similarly, engaging a technical integration firm to solve fundamental business and organizational issues will not achieve much either.

Understand the Integrator's Internal Performance Measures and Quality Measures. When selecting a systems integrator, the client should determine how the integrator, in turn, selects and assigns personnel to the project. Determining the average number of years of experience as a consultant and systems integrator and billing rates is also important. The client should determine the basis and criteria used to match consultants to the needs of the project; the client should also address such issues as whether the integration firm stresses chargeable time, pressuring consultants to force more work and additional fees.

The client should challenge the integrator's objectivity on all issues. If the integrator represents or has business relationships with other vendors, the client should find out what those relationships are and how integrity and independence are maintained. Clients should avoid systems integrators that are self-centered or driven by their internal performance measures for personal billing targets, the next sale, or client profitability (i.e., realization), as they may compromise their commitment to the client's best interests.

Develop a Comprehensive Understanding of the Project. The client must stipulate the following in a contract:

- How the work is to be performed, the work plan, and when the work is to be performed
- What deliverables will be produced, what they will be composed of, and what tangible results will be produced
- Who will do the work, staff responsibilities, experience, organization level, and billing rate
- How many personnel days or hours are estimated to complete the project and the basis of the estimate
- Who in the integrator's organization is personally accountable for the quality of work, performance of the people assigned, and budget
- How much the total fees are and what the rates are by hour or day for each person assigned to the project

Determine Whether the Integrator Is Considered an Expert or Just Highly Experienced. The client should determine whether the integrator has rendered expert testimony in litigation cases, has been litigated against as a direct result of its performance, or has appeared as an expert before legislative bodies, such as state legislatures or the U.S. Congress.

Determine Whether the Integrator Is a Leader or an Accomplished Journeyman. Several questions should be posed. Does the integrator publish? Does the integrator actively research and develop ideas, concepts, and approaches? What intellectual capital does the integrator contribute that is important, new, or different? What intangible contributions can the integrator make to the project and the engaging organization?

Understand How the Integrator Establishes the Fees and Rates for Its Professionals. Questions that help determine this include: Are fees based on hourly or daily rates? What is the integrator's rationale and justification for the rates? Why does the integrator believe that it is worth the rate charged? What are the integrator's multiples for cost of service and billing rates? What are the chargeability goals of the integrator? What component of the rate is overhead? Are expenses truly out-of-pocket or are there blanket add-on charges for administration?

Develop a Knowledge of the Integrator's Quality Commitment and Client Satisfaction Processes. The client should determine how the integrator measures quality and client satisfaction. If surveys are used, who reviews them and how quickly? Surveys take weeks, and sometimes months, and are usually performed, evaluated, and responded to far too late in the process. What does the integrator believe the client's role to be in the project, quality, and satisfaction?

Determine How Many Other Clients the Integrator Has. The integrator may have many clients that may be doing well; however, its attention to detail and individual situations may be compromised. A key measure of an integrator's success is not growth, number of people, profits, or how many clients a firm has, but how many potential clients the integrator turns away and why.

SUMMARY

There is little doubt that systems integrators can provide valuable service and resources to the organization. However, they must be selected and managed carefully. Above all, the client organization must be realistic and honest in its self-assessment. It must also have a clear and stable understanding of its project, the scope, and major deliverables to be received. In selecting a systems integrator, the decision should be based on value to be received, not prices charged. In the final analysis, the client has choices and controls not only the process but the results.

Index

A

Access control services, 135

Access services

  for databases, 66, 94–95

  for documents, 67, 97

Active help services, 75

ActiveX

  Allegris and, 277

  in component-based models, 303

  component standards, 313–314, 315–316

  controls, 82

  in relational database design, 362

Address books, 634

Addressing

  allocation services, 73, 148

  for enterprise networks, 567–568

Address Resolution Protocol (ARP), 153

AES (Application Environment Specification), 280

Alerts/alarms

  e-mail services, 722

  messaging gateways, 665

Allegris

  Constructor, 277

  DataDesigner, 272

  object-oriented framework, 275–278

  Object Repository, 277–272

  Workshop, 275–277

Analytic browser, 486, 490, 494–495

AOR (Allegris Object Repository), 277–278

APIs, *see* Application programming interfaces

Apollo reservations network, 192–193

Application Developer's Kit, 283

Application development, *see also* Applications

  considerations for, 265–266

  cross-platform

    C and C++ constructs, 266–267

    4GL tools used, 273–274

    GUI development, 270–271

    Java used, 279

    proprietary APIs used, 267–270

    Win32 on UNIX used, 271–272

  distributed computing

    accessing databases, 286–287

    core DCE services, 280–281

    digital DCE services, 281–284

    distributed objects, 288

    message-oriented middleware, 285–286

    PC-DCE and DFS, 284

  electronic messaging, 642–643

  heterogeneous database access, 296–298

  integration over multiple applications

    applications differences, 256, 257

    approach and architecture considerations, 256, 258

    background, 253–254

    business layer logic, 259–260

implementation approaches, 258–259

needs example, 254–255

mainframe interfacing

  BackOffice, 288–289

  Novell NetWare, 295–296

  SNA gateways, 289–290

  SNA Server, 290–292

  SQL Server, 293–294

  Transaction Server, 294–295

  UNIX, 292–293

object-oriented framework

  Allegris, 275–278

  DSC++, 274–275

  Systems Toolkit, 279

  zApp, 278–279

Application Environment Specification (AES), 280

Application programming interfaces (APIs)

  CORBA vs. DCOM, 205

  interoperability and, 191, 193, 202

  JavaBeans, 226–229

  messaging support, 664–665

  proprietary, for cross-platform development

    advantages to use, 267–268

    disadvantages to use, 268

    emulated, 269–270

    layering and subset support, 268–270

    layering plus extensions, 269

Applications

  architectures, 49

  layers, using DCOM, 363–364

  mulitiered, 354–356

  RDBMS example, 356–357

  development, *see* Applications development

  integration interface services, 75

interoperability, 190–191

logic, 81

programming interfaces, *see* Application programming interfaces

services, 75

Architectures

  applications

    layers, using DCOM, 363–364

    mulitiered, 354–356

    RDBMS example, 356–357

  business, 15, 48–49

  characteristics of, 45

  client/server

    benefits of, 46–47

    characteristics of, 45

    EIA, 47–50, 80–82

    need for, 43–45

  communication, *see* Communications architectures

  component-based development, 301–302

  CORBA, *see* Common Object Request Broker Architecture

  database management system, 368–369

  data warehousing

    data considerations, 461–462

    granularity, 459

    history involved, 460

    information management, 462–463

    metadata management, 463–464

    methodology, 464

    subject area determination, 458–459

    time element, 460–461

  distributed database design, 348–350

  EIA

    architectural categories, 48–50

    business logic, 80

    layers of, 47–48

technical architecture, *see* Technical architecture

electronic messaging

client/server-based, 639–640

gateways, 640–641

LANs, 638–639

mainframe-based, 639

web-based, 640

federated environment

characteristics of, 415–417

functional requirements, 417–420

information-sharing techniques, 413–415

IT systems integration, 14, 15

JavaBeans API

customization, 227

event handling, 227

introspection, 228

persistence mechanism, 227

property control, 226–227

run-time vs. design-time, 228–229

security, 228

RDBMS

layer design using DCOM, 203–204

mulitiered, 354–356, 363–364

routers, 570–571

server-based computing

client-based disadvantages, 173–174

components of, 174–175

features and benefits, 177–178

ICA, 175–176

solution scenarios, 178–181

Windows-Based Terminal, 176–177

Web-enabled data warehouses, 477–478

ARP (Address Resolution Protocol), 153

Asynchronous messaging, 119

Asynchronous Transfer Mode (ATM), 149, 613–614

ATM25 access, 613–614

Attribute search, 98

Audio/video services, 71, 142

Authentication services, 70, 680–681

Authorization services, 70

B

Baan Data Navigator Plus (BDNP), 751

BackOffice (Microsoft), 288–289

Base services, 77–80

Batch services, 79

BDK (JavaBeans Development Kit), 217

BDNP (Baan Data Navigator Plus), 751

BEA Jolt, 298

BeanBox, 218

BeanInfo class, 221–222

Benefits audit after systems integration, 16–17

Binary large objects (BLOBs), 106

Boeing Corp. and system integration, 5–6

Bolt-on applications, 547

Boolean search, 98

Business/IT alignment framework

benefits of, 23, 38–39

implementation of

breakthrough objectives and processes, 24–25

business models, 25–26

functional mapping, 29–30

information models, 26–27

solution mapping and selection, 27–29

technology enablers and models, 27

technology standards, 27

industrial applications

existing business, 35–38

greenfield operation, 31–34

overview, 21–22

strategy for, 22–23

Business logic

concepts involved, 80

distribution considerations, 82

packing considerations, 81–82

purpose of, 80

TP monitor used to manage, 312

Business process reengineering and systems integration, 9, 539

Business solutions architecture, 15, 48–49

Business-to-business electronic integration

business requirements, 748–750

e-commerce product selection, 750–751

e-commerce solution, 751–753

EDI and, 747–748

security, 753–754

technical requirements, 750

C

C++

Allegris Constructor and, 277

cross-platform application development, 266–267

object-oriented framework with DSC++, 274–275

Systems Toolkit, 279

Canonical model, 421

Capacity planning tools, 57–58

CASE tools, 384–385

Cell Directory Server, 283

Cell of a server, 411

Certificate authority, 756–758

Certificate repository, 758, 760

CGI (common gateway interface), 478, 479

Chargeability, 881

Chrysler Corp. and system integration, 5–6

CI (Communications Integrator), 192–193

Circuit switching services, 73, 147

Citrix, 175

Client/server netcentric environments

architectures

benefits of, 46–47

characteristics of, 45

EIA, 47–50, 80–82

need for, 43–45

characteristics of information, 86–88

database services

access, 66, 94–95

described, 93–94

indexing, 65, 95–96

replication/synchronization, 66, 94

security, 66, 95

storage, 64, 96

DBMS and, 372

DDBMS framework

disk mirroring, 107–108

information gateways, 107

information replication, 106–107

matching functions and features, 108

multimedia information storage, 106

nontextual information storage, 106

referential integrity, 102–103

stored procedures, 100–102

triggers, 102

two-phase commit, 104–106

described, 112

distributed database strategy

design rules, 91–92

potential benefits, 88–89

potential challenges, 89–91

reasons for considering, 88

document services

  access, 67, 97

  described, 96

  indexing, 67, 97–98

  replication/synchronization, 67, 96

  security, 67, 98–99

  storage, 66, 99

  versioning, 67, 99

electronic messaging

  applications, 642–643

  architectures, 638–640

  described, 630

  evolution of, 631–632

  history of, 630–631

  Internet and, 637–638

  OSI network model, 636–637

  security, 641–642

  system components, 632–634

  trends in, 643–644

information distribution example, 85–86

information services framework, 92–93

interoperability of, *see* Interoperability of
    client/server environments

in legacy systems, 439–440

programming components, 311–312

vs. server-based role, 173–174, 176

Codes table services, 75

COM, *see* Common Object Model

Commercial off-the-shelf (COTS) software,
    see Enterprise resource planning

Common gateway interface (CGI), 478, 479

Common Object Model (COM)

  COM+, 211–212

  component standards, 75, 313–314

  DCOM architecture and, 130, 202–203,
      211–212

  described, 129–130

Common Object Request Broker
    Architecture (CORBA), 129

  architecture elements, 198–200

  DBMS and, 368–372

  vs. DCOM

    architectures, 204–205

    industry support, 209

    interoperability with, 211

    language support, 209

    maturity, 210

    performance, 210

    platform support, 208–209

    programming, 206–207

    protocols supported, 211

    scalability, 207–208

    security, 207

    World Wide Web support, 210–211

  described, 197–198

  distributed objects environment and

    DCE compared to, 249–250

    described, 244–245

    significance of standard, 246–247

    specifications and implementation,
        245–246

    structure and, 200–202

  history, 198

  interoperability issues, 191, 193, 202, 211

  Java links using, 335

  programming components, 314–315

  for Web-enabled business intelligence,
      776–777

Common user interface tools, 53

Communication fabric services, 72–73

Communications architectures

  communication services

    core messaging, 68–69, 118–126

    directory, 135–137

functions, 117

security, 70, 132–135

specialized messaging, 69–70, 126–132

summary, 143

virtual resource, 70–71, 137–143

described, 111–112

network media services

capabilities, 151

functions, 117–118

media access, 151–153

physical media, 153–154

summary, 154

physical environment overview, 115–117

principles, 112–115

transport services, 72–73

circuit switching, 147

functions, 117

message, 144–145

network address allocation, 148

packet forwarding/internetworking, 145–147

QoS, 73, 148–150

security, 73, 147–148

summary, 150

Communication services

core messaging, 68–69

described, 118–119

implementation of, 119–120

streaming, 69, 124–126

styles, 119

types of, 120–124

directory, 135–137

functions, 117

security, 70

access control, 135

encryption, 133

identification/authentication, 133–135

specialized messaging, 69–70

CTI, 130–132

database, 128

described, 126

EDI, 132

e-mail, 127–128

legacy integration, 132

ORB, 128–130

summary, 143

virtual resource, 137–143

Communications Integrator (CI), 192–193

Communications services

virtual resource, 70–71

Competitive advantage of systems integration, 4

Component-based development, *see also* Relational DBMS

basic architecture, 301–302

benefits of, 300, 305

component models, 303

component types, 302–303

component uses, 304

definition, 299

implementation challenges, 305–306

programming components

client/server, 311–313

component definition, 309–310

DCOM vs. CORBA, 206–207

design and use, 316–317

functional classifications, 310

granularity classifications, 310–311

life cycle process, 317–319

standards, 313–316

weaknesses, 300–301

Component framework services, 75

Comprehensive project work plan (CWP)

daily tasks, 787

detailed description of work, 786

individual assignments, 786–787

overview, 785

phases, 785–786

team organization, 786

Computer-Telephone Integration (CTI), 69–70, 130–132

Configuration and asset management tools, 56–57

Constraint heterogeneity, 369

Context search, 98

Contracting for systems integration

common mistakes, 873

contract sections, 868–873

elements of success, 862–865

process stages, 865–867

purpose of contracts, 861–862

term sheet, 868

Convergent integration in systems integration, 7–8

Cooperative processing applications, 186

CORBA, *see* Common Object Request Broker Architecture

Core messaging

described, 118–119

implementation of, 119–120

services, 68–69

streaming, 69, 124–126

styles, 119

types of services

file transfer, 69, 120–121

message-oriented, 69, 122–124

remote procedure calls, 69, 121–122

streaming, 69, 124–126

Corporate antenna critical issues, 552, 558

CIOs role, 557

data collection, 555–556

organizational implications, 557

processing and distribution, 556–557

Costs of systems integration

EcoNets savings, 589–593

ERP, 514–515, 516

Java corporate applications development, 332–333

WAN transmission facilities, 583

COTS (commercial off-the-shelf) software, *see* Enterprise resource planning

Creeping commitment, 14

Cross-platform development

APIs and

advantages to use, 267–268

disadvantages to use, 268

emulated, 269–270

layering and subset support, 268–270

layering plus extensions, 269

for applications

C and C++ constructs, 266–267

4GL tools used, 273–274

GUI development, 270–271

Java used, 279

proprietary APIs used, 267–270

Win32 on UNIX used, 271–272

directory synchronization, 681–682

server-based computing architectures, 179

CTI (Computer-Telephone Integration), 69–70, 130–132

CWP, *see* Comprehensive project work plan

D

Data abstraction, 81

Database Access Middleware (DBAM), 70, 128

Database interoperability, 189

Database management system (DBMS), 64

  CORBA and, 369–370

  distributed, *see* Distributed DBMS

  heterogeneous architectures, 368–369

  heterogeneous database system integration

    client/server communications, 372

    CORBA approach, 370–372

    transformations, 373–374

  IDL and, 370

  interoperability issues, 367–368

Database services, client/server

  access, 66, 94–95

  described, 93–94

  indexing, 65, 95–96

  messaging, 70, 128

  replication/synchronization, 66, 94

  security, 66, 95

  storage, 96

Data marts, 471, 489, *see also* Data warehousing

Data migration, *see* Migrating data

Data mining, 365, 486

Data prioritization for QoS, 150

Data warehousing

  alternatives to, *see* Distributed integration

  architecture/data strategy

    data considerations, 461–462

    granularity, 459

    history involved, 460

    information management, 462–463

    metadata management, 463–464

    methodology, 464

    subject area determination, 458–459

    time element, 460–461

  challenges of

    competitive analysis, 467–468

    executive commitment, 467

    failure risk, 466

  definition of, 449–451

  design requirements for PDIM, 825–826

  history of, 486–487

  options for

    middleware, 489

    number of interfaces, 488

    replication, 488–489

  reasons for considering, 465–466

  stages of development

    access tool selection, 471–472

    administration, 472–473

    business requirement identification, 468–469

    data sourcing, 469

    target architecture, 469–471

  strategy

    development, 451–453

    framework for, 454–458

  Web-enabled

    architectures for, 477–478

    implementation, 481–482

    infrastructure, 478–481

    security issues, 475, 476–477, 480–481

    strategies for, 476–477

DBAM (Database Access Middleware), 70, 128

DCE, *see* Distributed Computing Environment

DCOM, *see* Distributed COM

Decision support data warehouse, 470–471

DECmessageQ (DmQ), 286

Defense Message System (DMS), 765

Desktop manager services, 62

Development architecture

components of, 53–56

productivity improvements from, 52–53

purpose of, 52

Development Solution for C++ (DSC++), 274–275

Digital DCE Services, Windows NT, 298

Application Developer's Kit, 283

Cell Directory Server, 283

Runtime, 282

Security Server, 283–284

Digital signatures, 758

Direct manipulation services, 62

Directories, 635

Directory services

applications vs., 675–676

communication architectures for, 135–137

e-mail systems and, 722

functions of

authentication/confidentiality, 680–681

directory synchronization, 662, 681–682

information solicitation, 677

naming/identification, 679–680

registration, 677–679

roles and responsibilities, 686–688

X.500 standards

adoption issues, 683–684

components and protocols, 682–683

directory information tree, 684–685

infrastructure, 683

Directory synchronization for messaging, 662, 681–682

Discovery requests, 423–424

Disk mirroring in DDBMS framework, 107–108

Distance vector protocols, 146

Distributed COM (DCOM)

architecture, 203–204

COM/COM+ architecture and, 130, 202–203, 211–212

vs. CORBA

architectures, 204–205

industry support, 209

interoperability with, 211

language support, 209

maturity, 210

performance, 210

platform support, 208–209

programming, 206–207

protocols supported, 211

scalability, 207–208

security, 207

World Wide Web support, 210–211

programming components, 313–315

relational database design using

ActiveX components, 362

architecture layers, 363–364

effective change management, 364

Distributed Computing Environment (DCE)

component standards, 313–315

core services, 280–281

digital services

Application Developer's Kit, 283

Cell Directory Server, 283

Runtime, 282

Security Server, 283–284

object request brokers

CORBA compared to, 249–250

end user benefits, 249

network administrator benefits, 247–248

programmer benefits, 248–249

remote procedure calls and, 238–239, 248

Distributed DBMS (DDBMS)

database design

corporate strategy planning, 344–345

current DBMS technology, 341–343

development phases, 343–344

distributed environment architecture, 348–350

limitations of commercial products, 342–343

management and, 345–347

standards considerations, 350–351

strategy, 345

database strategy

design rules, 91–92

potential benefits, 88–89

potential challenges, 89–91

reasons for considering, 88

framework

disk mirroring, 107–108

information gateways, 107

information replication, 106–107

matching functions and features, 108

multimedia information storage, 106

nontextual information storage, 106

referential integrity, 102–103

stored procedures, 100–102

triggers, 102

two-phase commit, 104–106

integrated systems

data analysis stages, 429–430

data model construction, 431

EDMS and, 434–436

entity-relationship mapping, 430–431

functional decomposition, 430, 431

Distributed integration, *see also* Distributed DBMS

data marts, 471, 489

data warehousing history, 486–487

data warehousing options

middleware, 487

number of interfaces, 488

replication, 488–489

described, 490–491

gateways, 494–495

internet/intranet technology use, 491–493

long-term implications, 495–496

servers, 490, 493–494

Distributed object technology

distributed objects

application development, 288

compound document applications, 240–241

described, 239–240

multipoint connectivity and, 238–239

object-oriented programming

described, 241–242

vs. object-oriented databases, 355

object wrapping, 242–244

object request brokers

CORBA, 129, 200–202, 244–247

DCE and CORBA contrasted, 249–250

DCE description and uses, 247–249

DmQ (DECmessageQ), 286

DMS (Defense Message System), 765

Documents, electronic, *see also* Database management systems; Electronic messaging

business-to-business integration using, 747–748

document description, 432–434

management systems, 434–436

security and, 765

Document services

access, 67, 97

described, 96

indexing, 67, 97–98

replication/synchronization, 67, 96

security, 67, 98–99

storage, 66, 99

versioning, 67, 99

Domains

definition and application design, 316–317

services, 137

Domino, *see* Lotus Notes/Domino

Driver services, 79

DSC++ (Development Solution for C++), 274–275

E

E-commerce trusted infrastructure

business-to-business integration using, 751

commercial exchange services, 765

public key certificate infrastructure, 766

service attribute authority

certificate authority, 755–757

certificate repository, 758, 760

digital signatures, 758

electronic postmark, 760–761

return receipts, 762–763

storage and retrieval services, 763–764

service attributes, 755–756

technologies for, 764–765

EcoNets

capabilities, 587–589

example of use, 589–593

ECS (Electronic Commerce Services), 764

EDA (Electronic Data Access), 296

EDI, *see* Electronic Document Interchange

EIA, *see* Enterprise Information Architecture

EJBs (Enterprise JavaBeans)

architecture description, 229–232

services, 232–234

Electronic Commerce Services (ECS), 764

Electronic Data Access (EDA), 296

Electronic Document Interchange (EDI)

business-to-business integration using, 747–748

messaging services, 70, 132

security and, 765

Electronic document management system (EDMS), 434–436, *see also* Database management systems

Electronic messaging, *see also* E-mail systems integration; Messaging migration

applications, 642–643

architectures

client/server-based, 639–640

gateways, 640–641

LANs, 638–639

mainframe-based, 639

web-based, 640

described, 630

evolution of, 631–632

history of, 630–631

Internet and, 637–638

OSI network model, 636–637

security, 641–642

system components

address book, 634

directories, 635

gateway, 633–634

message store, 633

message transfer agent, 633

user interface, 632

trends in, 643–644

Electronic postmark, 760–761

Element of service, 650

E-mail systems integration, *see also* Electronic messaging; Messaging migration

considerations for, 717–718

deployment architectures

common backbone, 729–731

common platform, 728

multiple backbone, 728–729

functionality and scope, 718–719

implementation scenarios

application gateways, 725–726

distributed hubs, 727

one-tier messaging model, 723–724

two-tier multiple server model, 724–725

infrastructure vs. interface

alerts/alarms, 722

directory services, 722

mail monitoring, 722

management/administration services, 722

message transfer services, 721–722

network services, 721

reporting, 722–723

internal/external customer support, 720

messaging services, 69, 127–128

privacy policy establishment, 732

proprietary/confidential information policy establishment, 732

resource constraints, 718–719

specialized messaging, 127–128

staff knowledge requirements, 733

Employee training and process simulation (ETS), 812–813

Empress Heterogeneous Database Server, 296

Encryption

media access service and, 152–153

services, 70, 133

transport-layer, 147–148

Enterprise directory services, *see* Directory services

Enterprise Information Architecture (EIA)

architectural categories

overview, 48–50

technical architecture, *see* Technical architecture

business logic

concepts involved, 80

distribution considerations, 82

packing considerations, 81–82

purpose of, 80

layers of, 47–48

Enterprise JavaBeans (EJBs)

architecture description, 229–232

services, 232–234

Enterprise networks, *see* Networks

Enterprise resource planning (ERP)

background, 254, 551–552

benefits of company-wide integration, 508–510

external focus

critical data issues, 555–557

information access assessment, 554–555

need for, 552–553

types of external data, 553–554

implementation concerns

company-wide integration, 512–514

consultant selection, 512–515

costs, 516

employee selection, 517

employee training, 517–518

morale, 518

reengineering, 511–512

strategic implications, 511

time involved, 515–516

top management commitment, 510–511

vendor selection, 516

knowledge transfer implications, 534–536

lifecycle of applications, 546–547

market size, 507

packaged software risk management

   business reasons for using, 522

   disadvantages, 523

   recommendations for buying, 529–530

   requirements definition, 524–525

   risks associated with, 523

   software license negotiations, 525–527

   software maintenance considerations, 527–528

   vendor evaluation, 529

post-implementation situations, 547

risks involved, 507–508

ROI disappointments, 545, 547

SAP knowledge transfer phases

   background, 533–534

   continuous learning, 544

   deployment, 542–544

   design and development phase, 539–542

   opportunity evaluation, 536–539

second wave initiative, 548–549

strategy focus

   budgeting, 504–505

   business fit of package, 502–503

   components of, 501–502

   existing resources, 503

   implementation logistics and scheduling, 504

   overview, 499

   project drivers, 500

   resourcing of workers, 500–501

   users, 503–504

   visibility and profile, 501

Environment management tools, 54–55

Environment services

   application, 75

   component framework, 75

   operating system, 76

   runtime, 73–74

   system, 74–75

Environment verification services, 75

ERP, *see* Enterprise resource planning (ERP)

Error handling/logging services, 75

Error recovery, 152

Ethernet, 612, 614–615

ETL (extraction, transformation, and loading) tools, 461–462

ETS (Employee training and process simulation), 812–813

Event management tools, 58

Execution architecture

   base services, 77–80

   communication fabric services, 71–73

   communication services, 67–71

   environment services, 73–76

   information services, 64–67

   overview, 59–61

   presentation services, 61–64

   transaction services, 76–77

Executives

   commitment to data warehousing, 467

   commitment to ERP, 510–511

   roles and responsibilities in IS departments, 17

Extraction, transformation, and loading (ETL) tools, 461–462

F

Fast Ethernet, 612

Faulty management tools, 57

Fax services, 71, 141

FDM (frequency division multiplexing), 152

Federated environment architecture

characteristics of

autonomy types, 416–417

heterogeneity, 415–416

functional requirements

information discovery, 418

information exportation, 418

information importation, 418–420

information-sharing techniques, 413–415

5270 and Java, 337

File services, 75

File sharing services, 71, 139–140

File transfer and access management (FTAM), 121

File transfer protocol (FTP), 121

File transfer services, 69, 120–121

Filtering

in routers, 573

in transport-layer, 148

Firewire bus, 618

Form services, 62

4GL products, 266, 273–274

Frameworks for components, 310–311

Frequency division multiplexing (FDM), 152

FTAM (file transfer and access management), 122

FTP (file transfer protocol), 121

Full-text search, 98

Functional data warehouse, 471

Functional decomposition, 430, 431, 434

G

GAL (global address book), 634

Gateways, *see also* Middleware

database messaging services, 128

in DDBMS framework, 107

described, 381–382

to distributed integration, 494–495

in electronic messaging, 633–634

in e-mail systems integration, 725–726

in enterprise networking, 573–574

messaging

basic functions, 640–641, 647–651

business scenario for, 645–647

components, 651–652

configuration models, 653–654

deployment steps, 670–672

management and administration capabilities, 665–667

message handling capabilities, 660–664

qualities to look for, 667–670

use scenarios, 655–660

Gentran Server, 751

Global address book (GAL), 634

Graphical user interfaces (GUIs), 43

development in cross-platforms, 269–270

/MUI interoperability, 190

object-oriented framework with DSC++, 274–275

Groupware interoperability, 190

GUIs, *see* Graphical user interfaces

H

Healthcare Data Exchange (HDX), 193–194

Help desk tools, 59

Hewlett-Packard (HP) business/IT alignment

benefits of, 23

breakthrough objectives and processes, 24–25

business models, 25–27

existing business example, 35–38

functional mapping, 29–30

greenfield operation example, 31–34

solution mapping and selection, 27–29

technology enablers and models, 27

technology standards, 27

HyperStar Fast Path Server, 297

HyperText Markup Language (HTML), 329–330, 735–739

HyperText Transfer Protocol (HTTP), 121, 739–740

I

ICA (Independent Computing Architecture), 175–176

Identification/authentication services, 133–135

IDL (interface definition language)

  CORBA and, 200, 245–246

  in DBMS, 370

  Java and, 232

IMAP4 (internet message access protocol), 128

IMM (Internet Management Model), 496

Independent Computing Architecture (ICA), 175–176

Indexing services

  for databases, 65, 95–96

  for documents, 67, 97–98

Information gateways, *see* Gateways

Information management tools, 56

Information replication in DDBMS framework, 106–107

Information solicitation and directory services, 677

Information systems (IS)

  for manufacturing

    improvement steps, 168–171

    information delivery teams, 168

    organizational models, 164, 166–168

    role in, 158–159

  new management process

executive roles and responsibilities, 17

global demands, 11–12

objectives and deliverables, 15–17

principles, 12–14

Information technology (IT)

  business/IT alignment framework

    benefits of, 23, 38–39

    implementation of, 24–30

    industrial applications, 31–38

    overview, 21–22

    strategy for, 22–23

  management process

    executive roles and responsibilities, 17

    global demands, 11–12

    objectives and deliverables, 15–17

    principles, 12–14

In-process components, 362

Input services, 62

Integrated data server design

  bottom-up approach, 390

    data modeling, 392–393

      source data element identification, 392

      target schema definition steps, 393–397

  reasons for using, 389–390

  recommendations, 399

  top-down approach, 390, 397

Integrated DBMSs

  data analysis stages, 429–430

  data distillation, 434

  data model construction, 431

  EDMS and, 434–436

  electronic documents, 432–434

  entity-relationship mapping, 430–431

  functional decomposition, 430, 431, 434

Integrating package processes, *see* Processware for package integration

Interconcept dissimilarity, 424

Interconnectivity in systems integration, 7

Interface definition language (IDL)

    CORBA and, 200, 245–246

    DBMS and, 370

    Java and, 232

Interface logic, 81

International Telecommunications Union-Telecommunications Standards Sector (ITU-TSS), 756

Internet Inter-ORB Protocol (IIOP)

    CORBA and, 211

    Java links using, 335

    for Web-enabled business intelligence, 777

Internet/intranet technology and distributed integration, 491–493

Internet Management Model (IMM), 496

Internet message access protocol (IMAP4), 128

Internet resources

    Allegris, 275

    BackOffice (Microsoft), 288

    BDK download, 217

    Digital DCE Services, 281

    EDA, 296

    Empress, 296

    JavaBeans Guidelines, 222

    Java tools, 216

    JDK download, 217

    message switch vendors, 695

    messaging migration consultants, 692

    Novell, 295

    Open Software Foundation, 280

    PC-DCE and DFS, 284

    search engines, 740

    SNA Server and, 292

    Systems toolkit, 279

    zApp, 278

Interoperability of client/server environments

    business issues

        IT infrastructure management, 186–187

        physically distributed environment, 187

    CORBA and, 191, 193, 202

    CORBA and DCOM, 211

    database management system, 367–368

    distributed applications definition, 186

    middleware solutions

        description and types, 191–192

        example of use, 193–194

        message-oriented, 192–193

        strategies for, 196

        trends in development, 194–195

    mobile database

        database sharing techniques, 421–428

        federated environment architecture, 413–420

        mobile federation example, 412–413

        terminology, 411

    network routers, 572

    in systems integration, 7

    technical challenges

        applications, 190–191

        databases, 189

        groupware, 190

        GUI/MUI, 190

        networks, 188–189

        network variety, 188

        object/software components, 189–190

        platforms, 189

Intraconcept similarity indicator, 424

Intranets, 741–742

IP Stream Switching, 149

IP Switching, 150

IPv6 addresses, 568

IS, *see* Information systems

IT, *see* Information technology

ITU-TSS (International Telecommunications
Union-Telecommunications
Standards Sector), 756

J

Java

applets, 330

corporate applications development with

development costs, 332–333

effectiveness and efficiency, 331–332

program and programmer portability,
332

speed considerations, 331

support and maintenance, 333

technical training, 333–334

cross-platform application development
using, 279

database integration, 334–335

described, 329

enterprise server platform

architecture description, 229–232

services, 232–234

JavaBeans, *see* JavaBeans

operating system integration, 335–336

security, 228, 233–234, 336

shortcomings, 338

technology review, 225–226

visual authoring tools, 334

for Web-enabled business intelligence,
777–778

Web protocol support, 337

JavaBeans

API architecture

customization, 227

event handling, 227

introspection, 228

persistence mechanism, 227

property control, 226–227

run-time vs. design-time, 228–229

security, 228

background, 215–216

bean-building illustration, 216–219

BeanInfo class, 221–222

in component-based models, 303

component standards, 315–316

guidelines, 222

old code into Beans, 219–221

JavaBeans Development Kit (BDK), 217

Java Data Base Connectivity (JDBC), 232,
334–335

Java Development Kit (JDK), 333

Java Interface Definition Language (IDL), 232

Java Management API (JMAPI), 234

Java Message Service (JMS), 232

Java Naming and Directory Interface (JNDI),
232

JavaScript, 329

Java Transaction Services (JTS), 234

JDBC (Java Database Connectivity), 232,
334–335

JDK (Java Development Kit), 333

JMAPI (Java Management API), 234

JMS (Java Message Service), 232

JNDI (Java Naming and Directory Interface),
232

JTS (Java Transaction Services), 234

L

LANs (local area networks)

messaging and, 638–639

voice integration, *see* VoiceLAN

Legacy systems

application interfacing, 298

described, 439–440

distributed data processing

   message-oriented middleware, 443–445

   RDBMS, 441–442

   remote procedure calls, 442–443

integration messaging, 70, 132

mainframe interfacing

   BackOffice, 288–289

   Novell NetWare, 295–296

   SNA gateways, 289–290

   SNA Server, 290–292

   SQL Server, 293–294

   Transaction Server, 294–295

   UNIX, 292–293

migration steps, 446

Libraries, object, *see* Object library management

License management tools, 58

Link-state protocols in transport services, 147

Local area networks (LANs)

   messaging and, 638–639

   voice integration, see VoiceLAN

Location transparency, 90, 91

Lotus Notes/Domino

   development areas, 714–715

   documentation structure, 703–705, 706–707

   functions, 701

   infrastructure planning, 702–703

   organizational acceptance plan, 705, 713

   pilot group selection, 713–714

   sample project plan, 708–712

M

Mailboxes, 128

Management Information Base Tree (MIBs), 601–602

Manufacturing, global

   categories of data in, 160–162

   data-driven application framework, 162

   horizontal business integration strategy, 158

   information systems

      delivery teams, 168

      improvement steps, 168–171

      organizational models, 164, 166–168

      role of, 158–159, 164

      quantity of IS data involved, 159–160

Media services, networks

   access, 73, 151–153

   capabilities, 151

   functions, 117–118

   physical media, 153–154

   summary, 154

Memory management with Java, 331–332

Message-oriented middleware (MOM)

   application development, 285–286

   described, 443

   interoperability solutions, 192–193

   message versioning, 443–444

   self-describing data, 444–445

   services, 69

      capabilities, 122–123

      streaming, 124–126

      types of, 123–124

Message transfer agent (MTA), 633

Message transport services, 72, 144–145

Messaging

   core

      described, 118–119

      implementation of, 119–120

      services, 68–69

      streaming, 69, 124–126

styles, 119

types of, 122–124

electronic, see Electronic messaging

LANs and, 638–639

migration, see Messaging migration

multi-system integration, see E-mail systems integration

specialized

CTI, 69–70, 130–132

database, 70, 128

EDI, 70, 132

e-mail, 127–128

legacy integration, 70, 132

ORB, 128–130

services, 69–70

Messaging gateways

basic functions

address mapping, 649–650

element of service, 650

message reception processing, 648–649

purpose of, 640–641, 647–648

routing, 649–650

screening, 651

transmission processing, 651

business scenario for, 645–647

components

hardware, 651–652

software, 652

configuration models

colocated, 653–654

distributed processing, 654

stand-alone, 653

deployment steps, 670–672

management and administration capabilities

alarms and reports, 665

alternate routing, 666–667

billing and statistics, 665–666

hold and release, 667

message archiving, 666

message retrieval, 666

message tracing, 666

remote management, 667

security, 667

message handling capabilities

API support, 664–665

automatic registration, 662

delivery notifications, 661

directory facility, 661–662

directory synchronization, 662

error handling, 664

file attachment support, 664

lower-level communications protocol support, 660

message repair, 664

prioritization, 660–661

transmission retry, 664

wild addressing, 662–663

qualities to look for, 667–670

use scenarios

electronic mail hub, 659–660

LAN linked to outside, 655–657

legacy tied to modern, 657–658

Messaging migration, see also E-mail systems integration; Electronic messaging

communicating the plan, 699

consultants role, 691–692

new functionalities, 691

plan development

current environment defined, 692–693

destination system choice, 693, 695

infrastructure, 695–696

policies, 696–697

project timeline, 697–698

risk analysis, 697

system requirements, 695

timing, 696

plan execution, 699–700

project sponsorship, 691

reasons for considering, 689–690

MIBs (Management Information Base Tree), 601–602

Middleware, see also Gateways

applications development and, 285

data access using

described, 443

message versioning, 443–444

self-describing data, 444–445

data warehousing implementation using, 489

for distributed applications, 285

interoperability solutions

description and types, 191–192

example of use, 193–194

message-oriented, 192–193

strategies for, 196

trends in development, 194–195

mechanism selection and evaluation, 382–384

object, see CORBA; DCOM

in relational databases, 380–382

Migrating data

in relational database design, 384–385

structural inconsistencies, 401–403

tools and services, 408–409

value inconsistencies, 406–408

voiceLAN

backbone traffic control, 612–615

delay-sensitive applications, 610–611

desktop migration, 615–619

desktop switching, 611

PBX migration, 619–622

router minimization, 611–612

user migration, 619–622

MIME (multi-purpose internet mail extensions), 127

Mobile database interoperability

database sharing techniques

discovery, 422–424

exportation, 421–422

importation, 424–427

querying and transaction processing, 427–428

federated environment

characteristics of, 415–417

functional requirements, 417–420

information-sharing techniques, 413–415

mobile federation example, 412–413

terminology, 411

MOM, see Message-oriented middleware

Monitoring and tuning tools, 58

MTA (message transfer agent), 633

Multicasting, 146

Multimedia information storage, 106

Multiplexing, 152

Multi-purpose internet mail extensions (MIME), 127

MultiWin, 175

N

Name services, 137, 679–680

Native database messaging services, 128

Netcentric computing, see Client/server netcentric environments

Netscape Communications, 329

Networks

address allocation services, 73, 148

applications, 573–574

background, 595

e-mail system services, 721

global considerations

  addressing, 567–568

  hierarchical schemas, 568–569

  routing protocols, 569–570

  WAN transit delays, 566–567

interoperability, 188–189

media services, 73

  capabilities, 151

  functions, 117–118

  media access, 151–153

  physical media, 153–154

  summary, 154

monitoring and analysis

  capacity planning, 607

  critical data measurements, 599–600

  definition, 596–597

  fault management, 606

  IT environment, 597–598

  limitations of, 607

  network reporting, 607

  people involved, 599

  performance management objectives, 604

  reasons for, 598–599

  RMON/RMON2, 603

  security management, 605

  SNMP, 600–602

  SNMPv2, 602

networking steps, 562

planning and design tasks

  database creation, 578–579

  performance issues, 582–584

  traffic engineering, 579–582

planning and design tool

  design issues, 585

  EcoNets capabilities, 587–589

  EcoNets example, 589–593

  new technology, 587

  old technology, 586–587

routers

  capacity and architecture, 570–571

  filtering, 573

  internetwork protocol support, 571–572

  interoperability, 572

  network management, 572–573

  network technology support, 572

  technology integration, 562–564

  vendor solutions selection, 564–566

Network Service Access Point (NSAP), 568

Nontextual information storage, 106

Novell NetWare, 295–296

NSAP (Network Service Access Point), 568

O

Object library management

  configuration management

    principal tasks, 324

    release planning, 326

    tool selection considerations, 325–326

  design authority, 323–324

  quality control and testing, 326–327

  successful implementation elements, 322–323

  task assignment, 327–328

Object Management Group (OMG), 129, 197

Object-oriented databases

  vs. object-oriented programming, 355

  vs. relational databases, 353

Object-oriented data server, 382

Object-oriented DBMS (OODBMS), 64, 96

Object-oriented framework for application development

Allegris, 275–278

DSC++, 274–275

Systems Toolkit, 279

zApp, 278–279

Object-oriented programming

described, 241–242

vs. object-oriented databases, 355

object wrapping, 242–244

Object Request Brokers (ORBs)

client/server components and, 312, 313

COM, 129–130

CORBA, 129, 200–202, 244–247

DCE and CORBA contrasted, 249–250

DCE description and uses, 247–249

described, 128–129, 369

interoperability and, 189–190

messaging, 70

Object Transaction Services (OTS), 208, 246

Object wrapping

bridging function, 243–244

described, 242–243

wrapping techniques, 244

ODBC (Open Data Base Connectivity), 334–335

OMG (Object Management Group), 129, 197

Omni SQL Gateway, 297

OODBMS (object-oriented DBMS), 64, 96

Open Data Base Connectivity (ODBC), 334–335

Open database messaging services, 128

Open Software Foundation (OSF), 280

Operating system services, 76

Operational data store, 470

Operations architecture tool categories, 56–59

ORBs, see Object Request Brokers

Organizational change and systems integration, 9

OSF (Open Software Foundation), 280

OSI model

DCE and CORBA support, 249–250

messaging and, 636–637

OTS (Object Transaction Services), 208, 246

Out-of-process components, 362

P

PAB (private address book), 634

Packaged software, see also Enterprise resource planning

business reasons for using, 522

disadvantages of, 523

recommendations for buying, 529–530

requirements definition, 524–525

risks associated with, 523

software license negotiations

licensing background, 525–526

strategies for, 526–527

software maintenance considerations, 527–528

vendor evaluation, 529

Package integration processes, see Processware for package integration

Packet forwarding/internetworking services, 72–73, 145–147

Paging services, 71, 142–143

PBX migration

distributed component linkage, 619–620

legacy telephony, 619

server-based telephony, 620–622

PC-DCE and DFS and applications development, 284

Performance management tools, 58

Personal productivity tools, 54

Phone services, 71, 140–141

Physical media services, 73, 153–154

PKCS (public-key cryptographic systems), 680–681

PKI (Public Key Infrastructure), 766

Platform architecture for EIA, 49–50

Platform interoperability, 189

PMID, see Process driven integration model

PMT (project management and tracking)

assessment items, 787–788

elements of, 788

form examples and instructions, 792–796

forms and description, 788, 790–791

plan updates using, 796–803, 804–809

progress and status measurements, 803–804, 810

status reports, 810

team organization, 783–784

Policy routing protocols for transport services, 147

POP (post office protocol), 127

Portable Operating System Interface for Unix (POSIX), 332

Porting and Java, 332

Post office protocol (POP), 127

Presentation services, 61–64

Print services, 71, 139

Privacy policy establishment, 732

Private address book (PAB), 634

Private management domain (PRMD), 656

Privilege levels, 422

Process driven integration model (PDIM)

acceleration of integration, 818–820

attributes, 818

distribution of manager's time, 822

life cycle phases

data and warehouse design requirements, 825–826

environment establishment, 822–823

overview, 817–818

prototype development, 826–827

requirements and capabilities assessment, 823–825

system implementation, 827–829

QFD uses, 818–819

SDLC background, 816–817

Process management tools, 54

Processware for package integration

application integration needs example, 254–255

applications differences, 256, 257

background, 253–254

business layer logic, 259–260

implementation approaches, 258–259

integration approach and architecture considerations, 256, 258

Production control tools, 59

Profile management services, 74

Program and project management tools, 55

Programming components

client/server, 311–313

component definition, 309–310

DCOM vs. CORBA, 206–207

design and use, 316–317

functional classifications, 310

granularity classifications, 310–311

life cycle process, 317–319

standards

ActiveX, 313–314, 315–316

CORBA, 314–315

DCOM, 314–315

JavaBeans, 315–316

Project management

comprehensive project work plan

daily tasks, 787

detailed description of work, 786

individual assignments, 786–787

overview, 785

phases, 785–786

team organization, 786

employee training and process simulation, 812–813

framework for systems integration, 783

need for new approach, 781–783

quality assurance process

attributes evaluation, 811

auditor activities, 811–812

tracking and

assessment items, 787–788

elements of, 788

form examples and instructions, 792–796

forms and description, 788, 790–791

plan updates, 796–803, 804–809

progress and status measurements, 803–804, 810

status reports, 810

team organization, 783–784

Proprietary/confidential information policy establishment, 732

Protocols

communication, web-based, 738–739

described, 68–69, 119

in enterprise networking, 564, 566

Java and Web support, 337

lower-level communications support, 660

message transfer agent and, 633

POP, 127

RMON, 603

routing, 569–570

SNMP, 600–602

TCP/IP, 69, 119, 637

transport services, 146–147

Public-key cryptographic systems (PKCS), 680–681

Public Key Infrastructure (PKI), 766

Push/pull services, 78

Q

QFD (quality function deployment), 816, 820–821

QoS, see Quality of Service

Quality assurance process (QAP)

attributes evaluation, 811

auditor activities, 811–812

Quality function deployment (QFD), 818, 820–821

Quality management tools, 54

Quality of Service (QoS)

data prioritization for, 150

transport services, 73, 148–150

Query language heterogeneity, 368

Query processing heterogeneity, 368

Queue management services, 80

Quickstrike initiatives, 13

R

RARP (Reverse Address Resolution Protocol), 153

Rdb Distributed Product Suite (Oracle), 287

RDBMS, see Relational DBMS

Realization, 880–881

Real-time control protocol (RTCP), 125

Real-time streaming protocol (RTSP), 125

Real-time transport protocol (RTP), 125

Recovery management tools, 57

Reengineering

of business processes, 9, 539

ERP implementation, 511–512

for SIMs, see Process driven integration model (PDIM)

Referential integrity in DDBMS framework, 102–103

Registration and directory services, 677–679

Relational DBMS (RDBMS)

application architecture example, 356–357

complex data support

data extraction, 380

example of, 378–379

middleware, 380–382

servers, 382

component-based design and, 354

data access using, 441–442

database storage, 64, 96

data-component approach

advantages/features, 358–359

disadvantages/limitations, 359–360

granularity considerations, 360–361

mining, 365

design using DCOM

ActiveX components, 362

architecture layers, 363–364

effective change management, 364

mechanism selection and evaluation, 382–384

migrating schema and data, 384–385

structural inconsistencies, 401–405

tools and services, 408–409

value inconsistencies, 406–408

multi-tiered architectures, 354–356

vs. object-oriented format, 353

Remote control, 139

Remote management tools, 58

Remote Monitoring Protocol (RMON/RMON2), 603

Remote procedure calls (RPC)

data access using, 442–443

in DCE, 238–239, 248

multipoint connectivity and, 238–239

services, 69, 121–122

Replication/synchronization services

for databases, 66, 94

for documents, 67, 96

Report and print services, 62, 79

Resource management services, 77

Resource Reservation Protocol (RSVP)

enterprise networks and, 612–613, 614–615

QoS and, 149

Restart/recovery services, 79

Return receipts, 762–763

Reusable software, 321

Reverse Address Resolution Protocol (RARP), 153

Risk management

data warehousing, 466

ERP, 507–508

packaged software

business reasons for using, 522

disadvantages, 523

recommendations for buying, 529–530

requirements definition, 524–525

risks associated with, 523

software license negotiations, 525–527

software maintenance considerations, 527–528

vendor evaluation, 529

Rlogin, 139

RMON/RMON2 (Remote Monitoring Protocol), 603

ROI disappointments in ERP, 545, 547

Role management services, 80

Route management services, 80

Routers

    capacity and architecture, 570–571

    filtering, 573

    internetwork protocol support, 571–572

    minimizing routing with voiceLAN, 611–612

    network management, 572–573

    network technology support, 572

    protocols, 569–570

RPC, see Remote procedure calls

RTCP (real-time control protocol), 125

RTP (real-time transport protocol), 125

RTSP (real-time streaming protocol), 125

Rule management services, 80

Runtime services, 73–74, 282

S

SAP R/3 knowledge transfer phases

    background, 533–534

    continuous learning, 5442

    deployment and training environment, 542–544

    design and development

        business process analysis, 539

        end-user training development, 541

        script development, 540

        skills training, 540–541

        technology-assisted learning, 541–542

    opportunity evaluation

        elements of, 536–537

        executive learning, 538

        team member learning, 538–539

        team member selection, 537–538

Scalability

    of DCOM and CORBA, 207–208

    of the Web, 772

Schema heterogeneity, 368

SDLCs (systems development life cycles), see Process driven integration model (PDIM)

Search engines, 740

Second wave initiative, ERP, 548–5497

Secure hypertext transfer protocol (S-HTTP), 121, 765

Security

    business intelligence concerns, 771–772

    business-to-business integration, web-based, 753–754

    certificate authority, 756–758

    certificate repository, 758, 760

    concerns for the Web, 741

    CORBA and DCOM, 207

    digital signatures, 758

    e-commerce and, 765

    electronic messaging, 641–642

    in enterprise directory services, 680–681

    in messaging systems, 641–642, 667

    network management, 605

    services

        access control, 135

        applications, 75

        for communication, 70, 133–135

        CORBA vs. DCOM, 207

        for databases, 66, 95

        for documents, 67, 98–99

        encryption, 133

        identification/authentication, 133–135

        from Java, 233–234, 336

        JavaBeans, 228

        privilege levels, 422

        system, 74

    web-enabled data warehouses and, 475, 476–477, 480–481

    tools, 58

transport, 73, 147–148

Security Server, 282–284

Semantic consistency in systems integration, 7

Semantic heterogeneity, 369

Server-based computing architectures

client-based disadvantages, 173–174

components of, 174–175

features and benefits, 177–178

ICA, 175–176

solution scenarios

branch office, 178–179

cross-platform, 179

remote, 180

thin client, 180–181

web-based, 179–180

Windows-Based Terminal, 176–177

Servers

data, 382

distributed integration, 490, 493–494

S-HTTP (secure hypertext transfer protocol), 121, 765

Simple mail transfer protocol (SMTP), 127, 722, 765

Simple Network Management Protocol (SNMP), 600–601

SIM (systems integration methodology), see Process driven integration model (PDIM)

SMTP (simple mail transfer protocol), 127, 722, 765

SNA Client for UNIX, 292–293

SNA Server (Microsoft), 290–292

SNA (Systems Network Architecture), 289–290, 337

SNMP (Simple Network Management Protocol), 600–602

SNMPv2, 600

Software distribution tools, 56

Software license and maintenance negotiations

considerations for, 527–528

licensing background, 525–526

strategies for, 526–527

Software reuse, 321

Specialized messaging services

CTI, 130–132

database, 128

described, 126

EDI, 132

e-mail, 127–128

legacy integration, 132

ORB, 128–130

services, 69–70

SQL

for database services, 64, 66

gateways, 95

stored procedures and, 100–102

SQL Server (Microsoft), 293–294

State management services, 75

Storage services

for databases, 64, 96

in DDBMS framework, 100–102

for documents, 66, 99

message forwarding and, 119

and retrieval, 763–764

Streaming services, 69, 124–126

Summary services, 154

Sun Microsystems, 329

Synchronization services, see Replication/synchronization services

Synchronous messaging, 119

System building tools, 54

Systems development life cycles (SDLCs), see Process driven integration model (PDIM)

System services, 74–75

Systems integration

benefits of, 4

characteristics of, 8

contracting for

common mistakes, 873

contract sections, 868–873

elements of success, 862–865

process stages, 865–867

purpose of contracts, 861–862

term sheet, 868

design and engineering of, 15–16

development life cycle, see Process driven integration model

integrator selection, see Systems integrator selection

motivations for, 3

problems with projects, see Terminally ill integration projects

realities vs. myths, 8–10

states of, 6–8

strategies for, 12–13, 22–23

technological definition, 5–6

Systems integrator selection

need for, 875–876

principles of

evaluate as commodity service providers, 879–880

get a guarantee, 884

know your requirements, 882

research types available, 877–879

understand fee structure and billing practices, 880–881

understand integrator name is unimportant, 883

understand value, 883–884

understand who will do the work, 883

rules for, 884–887

Systems Network Architecture (SNA), 289–290, 337

Systems Toolkit, 279

T

Tag Switching, 150

TAPI, 619

TASI (time asynchronous speech interpolator), 579

Task and memory management services, 74–75

TCP/IP protocol, 69, 119, 637

TDM (time division multiplexing), 152

Team productivity tools, 55

Technical architecture

business logic

concepts involved, 80

distribution considerations, 82

packing considerations, 81–82

purpose of, 80

TP monitor used to manage, 312

development architecture

components, 53–56

productivity improvements from, 52–53

purpose, 52

execution architecture

base services, 77–80

communication fabric services, 71–73

communication services, 67–71

environment services, 73–76

information services, 64–67

overview, 59–61

presentation services, 61–64

transaction services, 76–77

operations tool categories, 56–59

overview, 50–51

Telnet, 138

Terminal emulation, 337

Terminally ill integration projects (TIIP)

assessment methodology, 845–846, 847–859

implications of, 831–832

qualities of, 834–835

symptoms of

complexity of technologies, 832–833

organizational change reluctance, 834

reliance on traditional management techniques, 833–834

warning signs

dysfunctional measurements and communications, 842

inadequate risk identification, 844

inadequate sponsorship, 836

inappropriate technology, 841–842

ineffective planning, 838–839

lack of partnering/shared responsibility, 837–838

long/delayed projects, 839–840

poorly managed team, 842–843

poor management practices, 840–841

poor project leadership, 835–836

unclear vision, 838

unrealistic organizational expectations, 840

Terminal services, 71, 137–138

3270 and Java, 337

3270 Emulation, 138

TIIP, see Terminally ill integration projects

Time asynchronous speech interpolator (TASI), 579

Time division multiplexing (TDM), 152

TIS (Total Information Solutions), 552, 553, 555

Tn3270, 138

Total Information Solutions (TIS), 552, 553, 555

TP monitor services, 77, 312

TP (Transaction Processing), 207–208

Traffic engineering in networks

basic concepts, 579–580

flow models

existing networks, 581

life cycle growths, 582

new networks, 580–581

time-consistent averages, 581–582

Transaction Processing (TP), 207–208

Transaction Server (Microsoft), 294–295

Transaction services, 76–77, 368

Transmission Control Protocol/Internet Protocol (TCP/IP), 69, 119, 637

Transparency, 90–91, 349

Transport service interfaces, 574

Transport services, 72–73

circuit switching, 147

functions, 117

message, 144–145

network address allocation, 148

packet forwarding/internetworking, 145–147

QoS, 73, 148–150

security, 73, 147–148

summary, 150

Triggers in DDBMS framework, 102

Trusted infrastructure, see E-commerce trusted infrastructure

Tunneling in enterprise networking, 566, 574

Two-phase commit (2PC) in DDBMS framework, 104–106

U

Unified Modeling Language (UML), 323

Universal data server, 382

Universal Resource Locators (URLs), 739–740

Universal serial bus (USB), 616–617

UniVerse, 297

UNIX

cross-platform application development and, 266, 271–272

SNA client for, 292–293

WISE used with, 271–272

URLs (Universal Resource Locators), 739–740

USB (universal serial bus), 616–617

User administration tools, 59

User navigation services, 63

V

Value Added Networks (VANs), 747–748, 764

Versioning services for documents, 67, 99

Virtual data warehouse, 470

Virtual resource services, 70–71

audio/video, 71, 142

fax, 71, 141

file sharing, 71, 139–140

paging, 71, 142–143

phone, 140–141

print, 71, 139

terminal, 137–138

Visual Basics, 355

VoiceLAN

benefits of, 609–610

cabling plant consolidation, 615

desktop migration

hardware upgrades, 615–618

software upgrades, 619

migration to

backbone traffic control, 612–615

delay-sensitive applications, 610–611

desktop switching, 611

router minimization, 611–612

PBX migration

distributed component linkage, 617–618

legacy telephony, 617

server-based telephony, 618–620

recommendations, 621–622

user migration, 620

voice and data consolidation, 621

W

WAN

transit delays, 566–567

transmission facilities, 583

Warehousing, see Data warehousing; Web-enabled data warehouses

WBT (Windows-Based Terminal), 176–177

Web browser services, 63–64

Web-enabled data warehouses

architectures for, 477–478

implementation, 481–482

infrastructure

application query engine, 479–480

data warehouse, 480

security, 480–481

Web masters, 478–479

Web site, 479

security issues, 475, 476–477, 480–481

strategies for

access control and security, 476–477

business relationships considerations, 476

new component support, 477

Web services, 77–80

Web site addresses

Allegris, 275

BackOffice (Microsoft), 288

BDK download, 217

Digital DCE Services, 281

EDA, 296

Empress, 296

JavaBeans Guidelines, 222

Java tools, 216

JDK download, 217

message switch vendors, 695

messaging migration consultants, 692

Novell, 295

Open Software Foundation, 280

PC-DCE and DFS, 284

search engines, 740

SNA Server and, 292

Systems toolkit, 279

zApp, 278

WebSuite, 751

Wild addressing for messaging, 662–663

Win32 and WISE, 271–272

Windows-Based Terminal (WBT), 176–177

Windows Interface Source Environment
    (WISE)

emulators, 272

SDKs, 271–272

Windows NT

BackOffice, 288–289

cross-platform application development
    and, 266

Digital DCE Services, 298

Application Developer's Kit, 283

Cell Directory Server, 283

Runtime, 282

Security Server, 283–284

SNA Server and, 290

Winsock 2, 619

WISE (Windows Interface Source
    Environment)

emulators, 272

SDKs, 271–272

Workflow services, 79–80

Workgroup/workflow/E-mail
    interoperability, 190

World Wide Web

business intelligence concerns

administration, 772–773

scalability, 772

security, 771–772

business intelligence solutions

elements of, 774–775

first principles, 772–773

supporting technologies, 776–778

capabilities, 738

components

communication protocols, 739–740

publishing tools, 738–739

search engines, 740

URLs, 739–740

web clients, 738

web servers, 738

CORBA and DCOM support of, 210–211

integrating enterprise systems

building a presence, 744–745

building linkage programs, 743

challenges of, 744

conversion to hypermedia pages,
    742–743

education and training, 746

intranets, 741–742

limitations for businesses, 740–741

X

X.400

features of, 127, 721

gateway, 655–657

mail systems, 636–637

X.500 standards

adoption issues, 683–684

components and protocols, 682–683

directory information tree, 684–685

infrastructure, 683

XML for Web-enabled business intelligence, 777–778

X Window system, 138

zApp Developer's Suite 3, 278–279